SYSTEMS, STRATEGIES, AND SKILLS OF COUNSELING AND PSYCHOTHERAPY

LINDA SELIGMAN
George Mason University

Merrill
Prentice Hall

Upper Saddle River, New Jersey
Columbus, Ohio

Library of Congress Cataloging-in-Publication Data

Seligman, Linda
   Systems, strategies, and skills of counseling and psychotherapy / by Linda Seligman.—
1st ed.
     p. cm.
   Includes bibliographical references and index.
   ISBN 0-13-020060-3
   1. Counseling. 2. Psychotherapy. I. Title.

BF637.C6 S445 2001
158'.3—dc21

00-056100

Vice President and Publisher: Jeffery W. Johnston
Executive Editor: Kevin M. Davis
Editorial Assistant: Christina M. Kalisch
Developmental Editor: Heather Doyle Fraser
Production Editor: Linda Hillis Bayma
Production Coordination: Carlisle Publishers Services
Copyeditor: Dawn Potter
Design Coordinator: Diane C. Lorenzo
Cover Designer: Ceri Fitzgerald
Cover art: ©Super Stock
Production Manager: Laura Messerly
Director of Marketing: Kevin Flanagan
Marketing Manager: Amy June
Marketing Services Manager: Krista Groshong

This book was set in New Baskerville by Carlisle Communications, Ltd. It was printed and bound by
R.R. Donnelley and Sons, Inc. The cover was printed by Phoenix Color Corp.

10 9 8 7 6 5 4 3 2
ISBN: 0-13-020060-3

To all my clients and students who have taught me so much

ABOUT THE AUTHOR

Linda Seligman is a full professor at George Mason University in Fairfax, Virginia, where she is co-director of the doctoral program in education. Previously, she served as coordinator of the university's counseling and development program. A licensed psychologist and licensed professional counselor with a private practice in Fairfax, she has worked in a variety of clinical settings, including psychiatric hospitals, mental health centers, substance abuse treatment programs, foster care, and corrections.

Dr. Seligman received a Ph.D. in counseling psychology from Columbia University. Her research interests include diagnosis and treatment planning, counseling people with cancer, and career counseling. She has written eight books, including *Selecting Effective Treatments, Diagnosis and Treatment Planning in Counseling,* and *Promoting a Fighting Spirit: Psychotherapy for Cancer Patients, Survivors, and Their Families,* as well as more than 50 professional articles and book chapters. In addition, she has lectured throughout the United States and Canada on diagnosis and treatment planning and is a nationally recognized expert on the subject.

Dr. Seligman has served as editor of the *Journal of Mental Health Counseling* and president of the Virginia Association of Mental Health Counselors. In 1986, her colleagues at George Mason University selected her as a Distinguished Professor; and in 1990, the American Mental Health Counselors Association designated her as Researcher of the Year.

PREFACE

PURPOSES OF THIS BOOK

I have been a counselor educator for more than 20 years, have taught many courses on systems and strategies of counseling and psychotherapy, and have supervised hundreds of women and men seeking to become counselors or psychologists or to be licensed or certified in those professions. Many of the students and professionals I have taught and supervised have complained that their years of training had left them ill-prepared for clinical work. To some extent, their concerns reflected the understandable self-doubts of beginning clinicians who recognize the importance of their work and want to help their clients as much as possible. However, I have also heard them worry about how to integrate theory and practice, when to use the treatment approaches they have learned, and what they should actually do when facing clients.

I have designed this book to address some of those concerns. My objectives include providing a clear, concise, meaningful, coherent, and useful overview of both well-established and emerging approaches to counseling and psychotherapy. In addition, I have worked to bridge the gap between theory and practice and to teach the salient skills associated with each treatment system. For example, rather than present each treatment approach in isolation and separate theory and practice, I group treatment systems according to whether their primary focus is on background and context, emotions and sensations, thoughts, or actions. These four areas of focus can be represented by the acronym BETA (background, emotions, thoughts, actions). Introductory chapters on each of these areas help readers to understand the commonalities among theories in each of these groups and determine which approach is best suited for them and their clients.

Each chapter includes a skill development section that teaches one or more key skills associated with the treatment system under review. For example, Chapter 3, which introduces theories emphasizing background, teaches readers how to conduct an intake interview; Chapter 22, on brief solution-based therapy, teaches goal setting; Chapter 7, on the developmental/psychodynamic theorists, introduces interpretation; and Chapter 15, on theories emphasizing thoughts, teaches ways of eliciting and disputing dysfunctional cognitions. By Chapter 25, which presents the last section on skill development and teaches the process of termination, readers should have developed the basic clinical skills they will need as counselors or psychotherapists.

This book focuses primarily on systems of counseling and psychotherapy that are designed for treatment of individuals. Many of these approaches, of course, are also useful in the treatment of groups and families, as we discuss throughout the book. However, treatment approaches that are used almost exclusively in group or family counseling are beyond our scope and should be covered in separate courses and texts on couples and family treatment and group therapy.

ORGANIZATION OF THIS BOOK

This book consists of 7 parts and 26 chapters. Later in the preface, I will discuss ways to use this book in courses on theories and techniques of counseling and psychotherapy.

Part One, which includes Chapters 1 and 2, presents the BETA acronym (background, emotions, thoughts, actions) around which this book is organized. These chapters introduce client and clinician characteristics associated with successful counseling and psychotherapy regardless of the clinician's theoretical approach. Ethical considerations essential to effective treatment are also reviewed. In addition, I introduce the Diaz family—Edie, her husband Roberto, and their daughter Ava—who appear throughout the book to illustrate treatment systems and strategies. Skill development sections in Part One focus on role induction, self-assessment, and development of a sound therapeutic alliance.

Part Two focuses on systems of counseling and psychotherapy that emphasize background and context. Such systems maintain that, to promote insight and change, practitioners must address people's histories and early experiences. Chapter 3 examines the importance of background in understanding and helping people and teaches how to use questions and how to conduct an intake interview to obtain background information. Chapter 4 provides an overview of psychoanalysis as developed by Sigmund Freud. Skill development here focuses on using a lifeline to gather background information. Chapter 5 considers Individual Psychology, the approach developed by Alfred Adler, and teaches how to use early recollections to gather information and promote client self-awareness. Chapter 6 introduces Analytical Psychology as developed by Carl Jung and considers the skill of Jungian dreamwork. Chapter 7 discusses the developmental/psychodynamic theorists whose work has built and expanded on Freud's landmark work, including Anna Freud, Karen Horney, Harry Stack Sullivan, Melanie Klein, Helene Deutsch, Heinz Kohut, and others. Although many training programs give little attention to these theorists, some understanding of their contributions gives clinicians both depth and breadth in their knowledge of well-established treatment systems and emerging approaches. This chapter also considers the skill of interpretation. Chapter 8 discusses transactional analysis, developed by Eric Berne, and reviews the skill of using strokes and injunctions to facilitate change. Chapter 9 provides information on brief psychodynamic psychotherapy and reviews the skill of identifying people's focal concerns.

Part Three focuses on systems of counseling and psychotherapy that emphasize the importance of identifying and changing emotions and sensations. Chapter 10 considers the importance of emotions in people's lives and teaches the skill of reflecting meaning and emotions. Chapter 11 discusses person-centered counseling as developed by Carl Rogers and examines the skill of clinician self-disclosure. Chapter 12 focuses on existential therapy and reviews the skill of values clarification. Chapter 13 introduces Gestalt therapy, developed primarily by Fritz Perls. The skill development section offers information on the Gestalt approach to exploring dreams. Chapter 14 reviews emerging approaches that emphasize emotions and sensation, including narrative therapy, feminist therapy, constructivist therapy, transpersonal therapy, and focusing, and considers the skill of using visualization in treatment.

Part Four focuses on treatment systems that emphasize identification and modification of dysfunctional thoughts. Chapter 15 reviews the importance of cognitions in people's lives and discusses ways of eliciting and disputing self-destructive cognitions. Chapter 16 focuses on cognitive therapy, developed primarily by Aaron Beck, and considers the use of homework in treatment, an essential skill of cognitive therapists. Chapter 17 focuses on rational emotive behavior therapy as developed by Albert Ellis and teaches the use of rational-emotive imagery. Chapter 18 reviews emerging approaches emphasizing thoughts, including neurolinguistic programming, eye movement desensitization and reprocessing, and thought-field therapy, and considers the skill of anchoring.

Part Five discusses treatment systems emphasizing assessment of actions and strategies designed to change behavior. Chapter 19 presents an overview of the research on the importance of actions and behavior in people's lives and considers the skill of assessing behaviors. Chapter 20 focuses on both behavioral and cognitive behavioral approaches to treatment and reviews systematic desensitization, a powerful tool for effecting behavioral change. Chapter 21 describes reality therapy, developed primarily by William Glasser, and examines the skill of caring confrontation. Chapter 22 reviews solution-based brief treatment approaches along with the skill of goal setting, which is essential in successful treatment.

Part Six discusses eclectic and integrated treatment systems, which draw on a range of theoretical approaches to develop an individualized treatment plan. Chapter 23 presents an overview of integrated and eclectic treatment approaches along with the skill of treatment planning. Chapter 24 provides information about specific integrated and eclectic approaches, focusing particularly on multimodal therapy (developed by Arnold Lazarus) and dialectical counseling and therapy (developed primarily by Allen Ivey and Sandra Rigazio-DiGilio). The chapter also considers ways of developing a BASIC I.D. profile as it is used in multimodal therapy.

Part Seven concludes the book. Chapter 25 presents detailed information on clinician and client characteristics associated with successful treatment and discusses commonalities of effective treatment. It also considers the skill of terminating the treatment process. Chapter 26 synthesizes material by reviewing the major treatment systems according to a structured format. It also provides a questionnaire to help readers identify which type of clinical approach seems most appropriate for them to use.

Special Features

Each chapter that presents a treatment system follows the same organization to facilitate comparison and ease of use. The chapter begins with a brief overview of the system and a biographical sketch of its developer, highlighting any clear connections between the person's background and the theory. The next two sections present the treatment approach, describing its theoretical concepts as well as its goals, the therapeutic alliance, and specific related strategies. Subsequent sections discuss the approach's application to diverse populations, its current use, research substantiating its value, its strengths and limitations, and its contributions to counseling and psychotherapy. A summary highlights important aspects of the approach, and the chapter ends with a list of recommended readings.

Accompanying each chapter is a series of exercises divided into three categories: those for large groups, for small groups, and for individuals. The exercises are designed both to promote understanding of each system of counseling and psychotherapy and to encourage development and practice of the skills reviewed in the chapter. These exercises will be useful in the classroom and will also help individual readers develop self-awareness, knowledge, and skills.

Case studies are another useful feature. As I have mentioned, members of the Diaz family illustrate the treatment approaches, thus allowing readers to see how theories apply to people of both genders, different ages, and different cultural backgrounds. Although each case study is complete in itself, reading all of them provides an overview of treatment for these family members.

Like most books on theories and techniques of counseling and psychotherapy, this one considers the application of each treatment system to people from diverse backgrounds. In addition, it considers the application of each approach to the treatment of various mental disorders as described in the American Psychological Association's *Diagnostic and Statistical Manual of Mental Disorders*. Because diagnosis has become an essential tool for mental health professionals, a discussion of which system is most likely to effectively treat which mental disorders should help clinicians develop successful treatment plans for their clients.

USES OF THIS BOOK

This book has been designed for flexibility and ease of use. Although each college and university has its own curriculum and required courses, this book can be adapted to almost any curriculum in counseling and psychology. Following are a few suggestions for using the book:

1. The structure is ideally suited for use in a two-semester course on theories and techniques of counseling and psychotherapy. The first three parts (the 14 chapters covering introductory material, treatment systems emphasizing backgrounds, and emotions and sensations) could be covered in the first semester, with the remaining four parts (focusing on cognitive, behavioral, and eclectic treatment approaches) covered in the second semester. If each class session covers one chapter, then any remaining classes can be used for role playing and exams.

2. The skill development sections in each chapter are designed to accompany the treatment system taught in that particular chapter. However, these sections can be used independently of the theoretical portions, perhaps taught in a third semester following a two-semester course on treatment systems or used as part of a practicum or internship to facilitate skill development.

3. Like the skill development sections, the exercises are intended to accompany review of the treatment system in each chapter. However, they are designed to be used flexibly. Large-group exercises are appropriate for classroom discussion. Small-group ones allow clusters of approximately four students to practice and improve clinical skills. Individual exercises ask students to work alone, with responses being written in their journals.

Faculty members, of course, can choose to use any or all of the exercises that accompany each chapter. Ideally, time should be allocated, either during or outside of class, for at least some of the large- and small-group exercises in each chapter. However, if time is limited, the individual exercises allow students to continue their learning and skill development outside of class. Although instructors may choose to review students' journals at the end of the semester to determine whether they have completed the individual exercises, I encourage them not to grade or evaluate these journals so that students feel free to express themselves, try out new skills, and gain learning and self-awareness. Students should be told at the beginning of the course if they will be required to share their journals in any way.

4. Groups of chapters can be combined to create a course. For example, the following selected chapters encompass the four types of clinical approaches and could be used in a one-semester course on established theories of counseling:

Chapter 1: Overview of the Book
Chapter 2: Overview of Contexts of Effective Treatment
Chapter 3: Overview of Background and Context
Chapter 4: Sigmund Freud and Psychoanalysis
Chapter 5: Alfred Adler and Individual Psychology
Chapter 10: Overview of Emotions and Sensations
Chapter 11: Carl Rogers and Person-Centered Counseling
Chapter 13: Gestalt Therapy
Chapter 15: Overview of Thoughts

5. A variety of mini-courses can be created from the contents of this book. For example, Part 2 could be used for a course on psychodynamic and psychoanalytic approaches to treatment; Part 4 for a course on eclectic and integrated approaches to treatment; and Chapters 9, 14, 18, 22, and 24 for a course on emerging approaches in counseling and psychotherapy.

Feel free to be creative and innovative in using this book—and if you come up with some good ideas, please share them with me at LindaSeligman@aol.com.

ACKNOWLEDGMENTS

I received a great deal of personal and professional support in writing this book. I am especially thankful to Lynn Field, M.A., L.P.C., psychotherapist at the Women's Center in Vienna, Virginia, and doctoral student in counseling at George Mason University. As my graduate assistant, she made an invaluable contribution to this book through her research and editing skills as well as her good judgment, clear feedback, and encouragement. (Her chocolate-chip cookies also helped.) Thanks also to Carol J. Kaffenberger, M.Ed., Ph.D., an educator and elementary school counselor for 25 years, and currently an associate professor in the Counseling and Development Program at George Mason University. Her encouragement and help with research on this book as well as her contributions to my other professional projects have meant a great deal to me.

Rosanne Shepler, L.P.C., analyst-in-training at the C. G. Jung Institute of New York, with a private practice in Vienna, Virginia, offered helpful suggestions and additions to the chapter on Jungian analytical psychology. Janice Miner Holden, Ed.D., professor in the College of Education at the University of North Texas at Denton, carefully reviewed and made knowledgeable additions to the section on transpersonal therapy. Nancy Newport, L.P.C., L.M.F.T., a psychotherapist in private practice in Fairfax, Virginia, and a trainer in brief therapy approaches, reviewed and made valuable suggestions for the chapter on solution-based brief therapy. Francine Shapiro, Ph.D., who developed eye movement desensitization and reprocessing (EMDR), read and discussed with me the section on EMDR. Robert E. Wubbolding, Ed.D., director of the Center for Reality Therapy in Cincinnati, Ohio, training director at the William Glasser Institute, and faculty member at Xavier University in Cincinnati, reviewed and offered useful suggestions for the chapter on reality therapy.

The faculty, administrators, and staff of the Graduate School of Education at George Mason University, particularly Dean Gary Galluzzo, Associate Dean Martin Ford, Dr. Gerald Wallace, and Janet Holmes provided time and support that facilitated my work on this book. Thanks also to Kevin Davis, executive editor at Merrill/Prentice Hall, who invited me to write the book and provided much assistance along the way. I am also grateful to the many students and clients I have met over the years and from whom I have learned so much.

I would like to thank the colleagues who reviewed this edition: Deborah Barlieb, Kutztown University; Michael Duffy, Texas A&M University; Harold Engen, University of Iowa; Bette Katsekas, University of Southern Maine; and Michael Scheel, University of Utah.

Finally, special thanks to my husband, Robert M. Zeskind, who is always there to help me find balance and joy in my life.

DISCOVER THE COMPANION WEBSITE ACCOMPANYING THIS BOOK

Technology is a constantly growing and changing aspect of our field that is creating a need for content and resources. To address this emerging need, Prentice Hall has developed an online learning environment for students and professors alike—Companion Websites—to support our textbooks.

In creating a Companion Website, our goal is to build on and enhance what the textbook already offers. For this reason, the content for each user-friendly website is organized by topic and provides the professor and student with a variety of meaningful resources. Common features of a Companion Website include:

For the Professor—

Every Companion Website integrates **Syllabus Manager**™, an online syllabus creation and management utility.

- **Syllabus Manager**™ provides you, the instructor, with an easy, step-by-step process to create and revise syllabi, with direct links into Companion Website and other online content without having to learn HTML.
- Students may logon to your syllabus during any study session. All they need to know is the web address for the Companion Website and the password you've assigned to your syllabus.

- After you have created a syllabus using **Syllabus Manager**™, students may enter the syllabus for their course section from any point in the Companion Website.
- Clicking on a date, the student is shown the list of activities for the assignment. The activities for each assignment are linked directly to actual content, saving time for students.
- Adding assignments consists of clicking on the desired due date, then filling in the details of the assignment—name of the assignment, instructions, and whether or not it is a one-time or repeating assignment.
- In addition, links to other activities can be created easily. If the activity is online, a URL can be entered in the space provided, and it will be linked automatically in the final syllabus.
- Your completed syllabus is hosted on our servers, allowing convenient updates from any computer on the Internet. Changes you make to your syllabus are immediately available to your students at their next logon.

For the Student—

- **Topic Overviews**—outline key concepts in topic areas
- **Electronic Bluebook**—send homework or essays directly to your instructor's email with this paperless form
- **Message Board**—serves as a virtual bulletin board to post—or respond to—questions or comments to/from a national audience
- **Chat**—real-time chat with anyone who is using the text anywhere in the country—ideal for discussion and study groups, class projects, etc.
- **Web Destinations**—links to www sites that relate to each topic area
- **Professional Organizations**—links to organizations that relate to topic areas
- **Additional Resources**—access to topic-specific content that enhances material found in the text

To take advantage of these and other resources, please visit the *Systems, Strategies, and Skills of Counseling and Psychotherapy* Companion Website at

www.prenhall.com/seligman

BRIEF CONTENTS

CONTENTS

PART TWO: TREATMENT SYSTEMS EMPHASIZING BACKGROUND AND CONTEXT

Chapter 9:
Brief Psychodynamic Therapy   **177**

PART THREE: TREATMENT SYSTEMS EMPHASIZING EMOTIONS AND SENSATIONS

Chapter 10:
Overview of Emotions and Sensations   **197**

Chapter 11:
Carl Rogers and Person-Centered Counseling   **210**

NOTE: Every effort has been made to provide accurate and current Internet information in this book. However, the Internet and information posted on it are constantly changing, so it is inevitable that some of the Internet addresses listed in this textbook will change.

PART ONE

PROVIDING EFFECTIVE COUNSELING AND PSYCHOTHERAPY

Chapter 1
Overview of the Book

Chapter 2
Overview of Contexts of Effective Treatment

Chapter 1

OVERVIEW OF THE BOOK

TREATMENT IS EFFECTIVE

Psychotherapy and counseling are effective! Study after study has conclusively demonstrated the healing power of therapy. In his 1995 research, described as "the most extensive study of psychotherapy on record," (p. 969), Martin Seligman found that 87% of people who reported feeling "very poor" and 92% of those who said they felt "fairly poor" before therapy showed clear improvement by the end of treatment. Lambert and Cattani-Thompson's (1996, p. 601) review of the literature yields similar findings: "Counseling is effective. . . . The effects of counseling seem to be relatively lasting. These effects are attained in relatively brief time periods, with the percentage of clients who show substantial improvement increasing as the number of counseling sessions increases" (p. 601).

In this postmodern era of counseling and psychotherapy, clinicians and researchers no longer ask about the worth of treatment but have moved on to ask more challenging and complex questions. What are the important ingredients of a successful therapeutic relationship? When is psychotherapy most likely to work? What are the characteristics of successful clinicians? What client traits, attitudes, and behaviors contribute to successful treatment? How can these characteristics be fostered? What systems of psychotherapy and treatment strategies are effective and under what circumstances? What skills are integral to effective counseling? These are only a few of the questions that today's clinicians are asking and that will be addressed in this book.

RATIONALE FOR THIS BOOK

Some years ago, I overheard a conversation between two graduate students who were completing a course in theories and techniques of counseling. "Well," said the first one, "I know all about the theories of Freud and Adler and Rogers and Glasser, and I got an *A* on the exam, but I don't really know what to say or do when I sit down with a client."

"I guess I feel the same," said the second student. "Maybe we'll learn what to do in the next class."

Systems of counseling and psychotherapy are not very meaningful if they are taught only from a theoretical viewpoint. Because this is an essential body of knowledge, teaching should be designed so it is meaningful and useful to students and enhances their overall development as clinicians. That is the goal of this book.

We focus in this book on systems, strategies, and skills of counseling and psychotherapy in ways that reflect current knowledge about effective treatment and in a format that both promotes intellectual understanding of theories and interventions and contributes to readers' professional growth, skill development, and confidence. By developing their clinical skills along with their cognitive grasp of treatment approaches, graduate students as well as practicing counselors and psychotherapists will be better prepared to help and collaborate with their clients.

OVERVIEW

This book is divided into seven parts designed to teach systems and strategies of counseling and psychotherapy as well as important skills associated with them.

Part 1 presents an overview of the elements of successful treatment. In addition to the practitioner's theoretical model and intervention strategies, such elements include characteristics of the client, the clinician, and their relationship; client diversity; and standards for ethical practice. By mentioning these factors in the introductory part of the book, I hope readers will gain an appreciation for the number of determinants that can affect treatment outcome. Nevertheless, because this information is even more meaningful after readers acquired knowledge of treatment systems and strategies, I offer additional information about the association between treatment outcome and characteristics of clients, clinicians, and their alliance in the last part of the book. The key skills taught in Part 1 are self-assessment, role induction, and the development of a therapeutic alliance.

Parts 2 through 6 cover the important systems, strategies, and skills of psychotherapy and counseling. These parts are organized to clarify and emphasize underlying similarities and differences among approaches.

Four broad systems of change are identified:

1. Theories that emphasize the importance of *background* in treatment
2. Theories that emphasize the importance of *emotions* in treatment
3. Theories that emphasize the importance of *thoughts* in treatment
4. Theories that emphasize the importance of *actions* in treatment

Remembering the acronym BETA (background, emotions, thoughts, actions) will make it easier for you to recall these systems.

The structure for organizing this book departs from the traditional way in which most books on systems of counseling and psychotherapy are organized. Some present theories in chronological order, while others have no clear framework. The grouping of treatment systems according to similarity of emphasis (background, emotions, actions, and thoughts) was developed to promote understanding of the various treatment approaches and their similarities and differences. This framework will also facilitate the teaching of treatment systems because it emphasizes underlying commonalities.

Part 2 focuses on treatment systems that emphasize the importance of people's history and background in the development of their current concerns. These theories of psychotherapy include

- Freudian psychoanalysis
- Adlerian individual psychology
- Jungian analytical psychology
- Other developmental/psychodynamic (neo- and post-Freudian) approaches to treatment, including object relations therapy as well as the theories of

Karen Horney, Melanie Klein, Anna Freud, Helene Deutsch, Harry Stack Sullivan, and others
- Transactional analysis
- Brief psychodynamic psychotherapy

The key skills taught include identifying a focal concern, gathering background information, and making good use of questions and interpretations.

Part 3 emphasizes treatment systems that focus on emotions and sensations. This part reviews Carl Rogers's person-centered therapy, existential psychotherapy, and Fritz Perls's Gestalt psychotherapy and briefly discusses narrative therapy, transpersonal psychotherapy, Eugene Gendlin's focusing, feminist therapy, and constructivist therapy. Key skills covered include reflection of meaning and emotions, self-disclosure, use of dreams and imagery in treatment, and values clarification.

Part 4 focuses on treatment systems that emphasize the importance of thoughts in determining both emotions and behavior. These include Aaron Beck's cognitive therapy and Albert Ellis's rational emotive behavior therapy. We also consider neuro-linguistic programming, Francine Shapiro's eye movement desensitization and reprocessing, and thought field therapy. Key skills include identification and modification of dysfunctional thoughts, use of homework, and anchoring.

Part 5 addresses theories that emphasize the importance of actions and behavioral change strategies. These include behavior therapy, cognitive behavior therapy, William Glasser's reality therapy, and brief solution-based therapy. Key skills include goal setting, assessment and modification of behavior, systematic desensitization, and use of caring confrontation.

Parts 2 through 5 all begin with an introductory chapter providing an overview of the common focus (background, emotions, thoughts, or actions) shared by the theorists discussed in that section. Individual chapters then follow, focusing on each of the treatment systems sharing that common focus. Discussion of each system is organized according to the following outline:

- Introduction to the theory
- Information on the primary person who developed the theory
- Overview of the development and evolution of the theory
- Basic theoretical concepts
- The treatment process, including goals, therapeutic alliance, and strategies
- Application of the theoretical approach, including the multicultural, diagnostic, or other groups for which its use is indicated and information on current research and status
- Evaluation of the system, including strengths, limitations, and contributions
- Presentation of one or two specialized techniques associated with the system
- Illustration of the theory with a case example involving a member of the Diaz family (introduced later in this chapter)
- Exercises designed to promote learning and application of the treatment system, including large-group (in-class), small-group, and individual activities
- Summary of the system
- Recommended readings

Part 6 reviews integrated and eclectic approaches to counseling and psychotherapy, including Arnold Lazarus's multimodal therapy, Allen Ivey and Sandra Rigazio-Digilio's developmental counseling and therapy, and other integrated and eclectic treatment systems. Skill development focuses on treatment planning and use of the BASIC I.D. assessment format of multimodal therapy.

Finally, Part 7 provides additional information on relevant contexts of treatment, including characteristics of the client, the clinician, and their alliance; the problem or diagnosis; the treatment setting; and third-party payers. It also provides a structured comparison of the major treatment systems that have been discussed in this book as well as information on important commonalities of successful treatment. A questionnaire is provided to help you select your preferred style of counseling. The key skill covered is termination of the treatment process.

EXERCISES TO PROMOTE LEARNING

At the end of each chapter, I include exercises to help you learn more about treatment systems and strategies as well as associated skills. There are three categories of exercises: those for large groups or the class as a whole, those for small groups (approximately four participants), and those for individuals. The following instructions will help you use these exercises.

Large-Group Exercises: General Instructions

The large-group exercises have been designed for use in a classroom or with a group of at least five people. They have been crafted to help you process new material, share ideas, and discuss clinical problems and thought-provoking questions. Although these exercises are generally self-explanatory, you will benefit from the involvement of a teacher or a leader who structures and oversees them.

Small-Group Exercises: General Instructions

Small-group exercises appear in most chapters. These are designed for groups of four students or participants, usually divided into two dyads. Because group members need to develop rapport with one another and feel comfortable about giving and receiving feedback, the composition of the small groups should change no more than once, if at all, during a semester. Although each small-group exercise is presented only once in a chapter, time should be allowed, if possible, for each member to take both client and clinician roles in the exercise.

To facilitate learning, group members should tape-record all small-group exercises, including role plays in which they participate as well as feedback from other members. Because people sometimes have difficulty absorbing immediate feedback, taping allows them to review the exercises later and think about how to use feedback to improve their skills.

While two members of the group are engaged in a simulated counseling session, the other two should observe and take notes so that they can provide clear and specific feedback. One observer should also make sure that the exercise is completed in the allotted time. Once the role play has finished, the person in the clinician role should initiate the feedback process by assessing his or her own performance, focusing on strengths as well as areas for improvement. Feedback from the person in the client role should come next. Finally, the two observers should provide their feedback.

Feedback is most helpful if it is specific and constructive. Strengths should be emphasized first and then suggestions made for ways to address weaknesses. People receiving feedback should have an opportunity to share their reactions and obtain clarification if needed. The process should be helpful and promote growth and learning; it should never make people feel attacked or humiliated.

Individual Exercises: General Instructions

The individual exercises are designed to promote introspection and self-awareness. Because they require considerable disclosure, I discourage their use in a group format. However, if instructors decide to have people share their responses or want to review written replies, they should make their intentions clear before students complete the exercises so that participants can decide how much they want to share about themselves.

Readers will probably benefit most from the individual exercises if they keep their responses in a journal or a notebook. In this way, they will have a record of their ideas and can review them throughout their training. Looking back at these journal entries in future years is likely to be interesting, giving readers the opportunity to see how their thoughts and perceptions have evolved over time.

PRESENTATION OF CLIENTS IN CASE ILLUSTRATIONS

All the case studies in this book center on the Diaz family. Because not all theoretical models are appropriate for all people, I have chosen to discuss three people rather than one, applying each of the major treatment systems to a member of this family: Edie Diaz; her husband, Roberto; and their daughter, Ava. Although they present with a wide range of difficulties, there are many avenues open for helping them improve the quality of their lives, as the case examples will illustrate. By studying these examples, readers will learn to apply the systems, strategies, and skills presented in the chapters.

Edie

Edie has initiated the request for treatment. Now age 38, she is a white Jewish woman. She was born in Brooklyn, New York, and lived with her biological parents and older sister until Edie was four years old. Her father was an accountant, and initially her mother stayed at home with the children. When Edie was four, her mother discovered that Edie's father was having an affair and insisted on a divorce. At that point, the father, who had been very close to Edie, withdrew from the family. Her mother found employment as a sales clerk in a department store to support her family.

The children were cared for by Edie's maternal grandparents. The grandmother resented her caretaker role and was very critical of the children, especially Edie. The grandfather sexually abused both Edie and her sister. Both grandparents are now deceased, but Edie has clear memories of the mistreatment she received and continues to experience strong feelings of resentment toward them.

When Edie was 10 years old, she was diagnosed with cancer. She had to undergo chemotherapy, which caused her to lose her hair. Teasing from her classmates contributed to her already low self-esteem. However, a positive aspect of her illness was the return of her biological father to her life. He visited her regularly in the hospital, brought her gifts, and gave her a sense of family once again. Her father has continued to have contact with her, and at present they see each other at least once a month.

Although Edie's prognosis for recovery was not good, she has been in good health since her treatment for cancer. However, her treatment raised questions about whether she could become pregnant.

When Edie was 14, her mother remarried. Edie described her stepfather as physically and emotionally abusive. He yelled at the children, told them they were worthless, and frequently hit them. Edie dealt with this by avoiding her stepfather as much as possible and becoming very close to her older sister. She was afraid to complain to her mother about the stepfather's behavior, thinking that her mother would be angry and would punish her.

Edie continued to live with her mother and stepfather until she was 18. She had always been a good student and was able to earn a scholarship. After college, she received a master's degree in library science and worked as a librarian until Ava was born.

Edie never dated much before she met Roberto. He had installed a computer system in the library and then asked Edie out for lunch. After dating for six months, Roberto proposed marriage, and Edie accepted. They were married when Edie was 24 and Roberto 28. Although their relationship was initially very close, with many shared interests and activities, their unsuccessful efforts to conceive a child had an adverse effect on the marriage. After a year of infertility treatments, Edie finally got pregnant and gave birth to Ava. Despite subsequent treatments, she was not able to conceive a second time, a source of great sadness to her.

Edie has reported marital difficulties since her difficulty in becoming pregnant. She stated that she felt the cancer had cursed her whole life and she could never be normal. When Ava was born, Edie left her job to care for her child. She very much missed her rewarding career but felt that she had to do everything in her power to safeguard her only child. She has reported longstanding and increasing symptoms of sadness, loneliness, and discouragement. Since her marriage, she has gained more than 50 pounds and finds little joy or intimacy in her relationship with Roberto. Finally, last year, she resumed work as a librarian. However, she is now experiencing strong feelings of self-doubt, guilt, and worry about Ava.

Edie has maintained contact with her mother and sister as well as with her father. Her mother is still married to the stepfather who abused Edie, and she finds it painful to be in his presence. She also has never been willing to let Ava visit them without her because of concern that the stepfather might abuse Ava. Edie and her sister communicate frequently by e-mail but see little of each other because of geographic distance. Her sister has had a series of unrewarding relationships with men and now has an intimate relationship with a woman—her best relationship so far, according to Edie.

Roberto

Roberto's background is very different from Edie's. He was born in New York City, the fifth of eight children. Although he had contact with both his mother and his father, his parents separated when he was young. Nevertheless, he describes his family as warm and loving, always ready to help. Roberto's grandparents had come to the United States from Puerto Rico and had never been financially successful; but they, too, maintained close family ties.

Roberto's neighborhood was rough, and he had been involved with street gangs since early childhood. His father taught him to defend himself with both fists and weapons. Because he was tall and stocky and had few fears, Roberto became a leader among his peers.

Roberto had little interest in school, preferring to teach himself. When he was 17, he decided to leave school and study computers. He received a GED as well as some specialized training in computers and now has a job he enjoys, installing Internet systems. He takes great pride in his abilities and his success in earning a good income for his family.

Roberto had two brief marriages and many relationships before he met Edie. He was impressed by her intelligence, stability, and caring and hoped that by marrying her he would find the committed relationship he was seeking. He stated that, although he was very attached to his family, he was disheartened by Edie's long period of unhappiness. He reported that they were rarely intimate and no longer had a rewarding relationship. He told the therapist that he was almost at the end of his rope and that Edie had better make some changes fast if this marriage were to continue. At age 42, he was eager to get his life back on track.

Ava

Ava, age 10, is a tall girl who resembles her father both physically and temperamentally. She has recently been misbehaving at school, and her teacher describes her as a bully. A good student, Ava has excelled in English and history but seems to be losing interest in school. She has one close friend in the neighborhood but otherwise socializes with a wide variety of children.

DEVELOPMENT OF SYSTEMS OF COUNSELING AND PSYCHOTHERAPY

Before the late 19th century, people had little understanding of emotional difficulties and mental disorders. Until then, some people with severe disorders were forcibly confined in institutions and exposed to largely ineffective treatments while those with mild or moderate difficulties typically received no help.

The development of psychodynamic approaches to psychotherapy, spearheaded by the work of Sigmund Freud, led to the emergence of what has been called the first force of psychotherapy (Ivey, Ivey, & Simek-Morgan, 1997). Viewing the past as the source of present difficulties and emphasizing unconscious processes and long-term treatment, psychodynamic approaches provided a solid foundation for the field of psychotherapy but had clear limitations.

The research and practice of B. F. Skinner as well as more modern theorists such as Albert Ellis, Aaron Beck, William Glasser, and Donald Meichenbaum led to the emergence of the second force: emphasizing cognitive and behavioral theories and interventions. Behavioral approaches, widely used in the 1970s, have been integrated with cognitive approaches that were developed primarily in the 1980s, leading to the cognitive behavioral approaches that received considerable attention in the 1990s. Cognitive and behavioral treatment systems emphasize the influence of thoughts and actions on emotions. They use interventions that focus on the present and seek to minimize dysfunctional cognitions and behaviors while replacing them with more helpful and positive thoughts and actions.

Carl Rogers's innovative work emerged in the 1960s and provided an important therapeutic perspective that has led to the development of the third force, existential-humanistic psychotherapy. The work of Fritz Perls, Viktor Frankl, and others have contributed to this force, which emphasizes the importance of emotions and sensations and of people directing and finding meaning in their own lives.

Now, at the beginning of the 21st century, clinicians are entering the era of the fourth force. Elements of first-, second-, and third-force systems of treatment are integrated as part of a comprehensive and holistic effort to understand clients as fully as possible. Awareness of gender, cultural, and other aspects of the person's identity must be attended to and comprehended for clinicians to maximize their ability to develop a positive therapeutic relationship and help their clients. Joining with clients and grasping their multiple perspectives of themselves and their world is essential. Networking and collaboration with other professionals, providers of community resources, and important people in clients' lives are now viewed as integral to treatment. New approaches such as eye movement desensitization and reprocessing and narrative therapy are providing powerful ways to understand people's experiences more fully and help them play an active and powerful role in changing their emotions and perceptions.

INGREDIENTS IN POSITIVE CHANGE

Although more than 350 forms of counseling and psychotherapy have been identified and described (Corsini & Wedding, 1995), successful treatments have common ingredients that promote change:

- A therapeutic relationship characterized by collaboration, trust, mutual investment in the therapeutic process, shared respect, genuineness, positive emotional feelings, and a holistic understanding of clients and their cultural and social backgrounds and environments
- A safe, supportive, and healing environment
- Goals and a sense of direction, preferably explicit but sometimes implicit
- A shared understanding between clinicians and clients about the nature of the problems and concerns to be addressed in treatment and the change processes that will be used to resolve them
- Therapeutic learning, typically including feedback and corrective experiences
- Encouragement of self-awareness and insight
- Improvement in clients' ability to identify, express constructively, and modify their emotions
- Improvement in clients' ability to identify, assess the validity of, and modify their thoughts
- Improvement in clients' ability to assess and change dysfunctional behaviors as well as acquire new and more effective behaviors that promote coping, impulse control, sound relationships, and good health

Successful treatment is reflected in attitudinal shifts. According to Weissmark and Giacomo (1998), these include "significant changes from beginning to end of treatment in the patients' assessments from external to internal, from reactive to selective, and from unconditional to conditional" (p. 107). In the context of sound conceptions of reality, successful treatment promotes hope and optimism as well as feelings of mastery and self-efficacy (Kleinke, 1994). You will find more information on the common ingredients of effective treatment in Chapter 26.

Despite the plethora of systems of psychotherapy and counseling that have evolved over time and the many commonalities among them, some theories emerge as particularly powerful sources of knowledge for clinicians. These theories provide the foundations for understanding how people develop and change as well as the tools needed to help people move forward with their lives. According to Stuart (1998), those systems that have proven their value over time are theoretically "robust, . . . reasonably well validated . . . and have clearly defined pragmatic roles in intervention practice" (p. 7). According to Hansen, Stevic, and Warner (1986), an effective theory is also "clear, easily understood, and communicable . . . coherent and not contradictory . . . comprehensive, encompassing explanations for a wide variety of phenomena . . . explicit, generating research" (p. 356). Effective theories are grounded in an understanding of human development; they provide a framework for gathering and organizing information and exploring individual personality; they present a theory of development and change that helps us understand people and their concerns; they provide steps and interventions that encourage learning and growth and that allow for evaluation of progress and modification of treatment plans if needed; they provide reassurance and direction; and they promote further study and improvement of the treatment process.

This book reviews those systems of counseling and psychotherapy that should be part of the repertoire of today's clinicians. Whether clinicians describe themselves as eclectic, as do more than 75% of current therapists (Walborn, 1996), or affiliate with a particular theoretical model, these systems and strategies all shed light on people's challenges and change processes and provide skills that facilitate positive change. Clinicians are no longer seeking the one right theory but the concepts and skills they need to form a sound therapeutic alliance with clients and develop treatment plans that are likely to ameliorate difficulties and improve growth and development.

But systems and strategies of counseling and psychotherapy are only part of the treatment process. Current research suggests that the theoretical systems and interventions used in psychotherapy are just one factor in producing change. In a survey of clients, Miller, Duncan, and Hubble (1997) found that people attributed 40% of the change they experienced in treatment to *extratherapeutic factors* (including the internal resources of the person and events in their lives), 30% to the *therapist-client relationship*, 15% to particular *techniques and interventions*, and 15% percent to the person's *hope and expectation of positive change.*

Several important points emerge from this finding. First, clinicians may not be as powerful as one might think; clients' lives and inner resources seem to be the most powerful factor in change. Consequently, clinicians must take the time to know and understand their clients, to grasp their perspectives on the world, to hear their stories, and to learn about their lives so that the clinicians can help them to make the most of those extratherapeutic factors. Second, the therapeutic alliance is of great importance. Promoting a positive relationship characterized by conditions and interactions that encourage desired changes can make a significant difference in the success of the treatment process. Chapter 2 provides more information on the importance of the client, the clinician, and their alliance in the success of the treatment process.

Observing that interventions influence change directly by only 15% of the difference, readers may be tempted to ask, "Why, then, pay so much attention to learning treatment systems and strategies?" In reality, 60% or more of client change can be attributed to treatment systems and strategies. In addition to their direct influence (15%), the skills and strategies of the clinician are largely responsible for the development of the therapeutic alliance (30%) and for engendering hope and positive expectations in clients (15%). Furthermore, counseling and psychotherapy can also make a difference in people's ability to make positive use of extratherapeutic factors such as support systems, community resources, and educational programs. Thus, treatment systems and strategies are important for not only their direct impact on symptoms and problems but their indirect impact on the development of client attitudes and behaviors associated with successful treatment.

ASPECTS OF MENTAL HEALTH

Just as it is important for clinicians to be aware of the breadth of factors in positive change as a backdrop to studying systems and strategies of treatment, so is it useful for them to have a concept of mental health. Witmer and Sweeney (1992) have advanced a holistic model for optimal health and functioning that delineates five important aspects of people's lives:

- Spirituality (values, beliefs, ethics, sense of purpose and direction, optimism, inner peace)
- Self-regulation (sense of worth, mastery over one's own life, spontaneity and emotional responsiveness, sense of humor and creativity, awareness of reality, physical fitness and health)
- Work (psychological, social and economic benefits of paid work, volunteer work, child rearing, homemaking, education)
- Friendship (positive interpersonal relationships and social support, activities, interactions)
- Love (intimate, trusting, sharing, cooperative, long-term relationships)

These five areas are helpful in providing a map of healthy functioning. More important, for purposes of this book, they delineate areas for assessment. Deficits in any of the five areas are likely to impair functioning, to require help, and to be an appropriate focus for treatment. Knowledge of the systems, strategies, and skills of therapeutic intervention will enable clinicians to help their clients make changes that will move them toward healthy functioning.

SUMMARY

This chapter has provided an overview of the book, including information on the BETA framework, the structure of each chapter, ways to use the exercises for greatest benefit, and a description of the three clients who will be used for the case illustrations. In addition, we briefly considered the development of systems of counseling and psychotherapy, reviewed some of the ingredients that facilitate positive change, and provided a model for mental health.

Chapter 2

OVERVIEW OF CONTEXTS OF EFFECTIVE TREATMENT

As you learned in Chapter 1, skillful application of appropriate systems and strategies of intervention are essential to effective treatment. However, a broad range of other factors also have a strong relationship to treatment outcome. This chapter focuses on those other factors, which include the following:

- Characteristics of the client
- The therapeutic alliance
- Core conditions in effective therapeutic relationships
- The training and skills of an effective clinician
- Characteristics of the clinician
- Ethical guidelines

The final section, "Skill Development," focuses on self-assessment and the skills of role induction and the development of a positive therapeutic alliance.

CLIENT CHARACTERISTICS

Both the personal qualities and the backgrounds of clients help determine the success of their treatment. Clinicians can maximize the positive influence of these factors in three ways. First, they need to be aware of factors that are likely to correlate with therapeutic outcome. Second, they need to get to know the client as an individual, paying attention to culture, religion and spirituality, relationships, socioeconomic status, physical health, family background, history, and abilities. This understanding will help clinicians view the world through their clients' eyes and determine interventions that are likely to be well received and effective. Finally, clinicians can take steps to instill or develop in clients those qualities that are typically associated with a positive therapeutic outcome—in a sense, socializing the person to treatment (Walborn, 1996). This process, called role induction, will be discussed later in the chapter.

Clients who succeed in treatment are motivated to present their concerns, collaborate with the clinician in a mutual endeavor, and take steps to improve their lives. They are able to develop a problem-solving attitude and maintain positive expectations of change (Sexton & Whiston, 1991). Some research has found a positive correlation of client intelligence, education, socioeconomic level, and initial symptoms of depression or anxiety with likelihood of positive outcome. Client gender and age seem unrelated to outcome.

People who are most likely to benefit from the therapeutic process are those who have a realistic idea of what counseling or psychotherapy is and what it can do and who harbor no misconceptions about the process. They recognize that at least some of their difficulties come from within themselves and that they have the power to improve their situation. They are willing to experience some anxiety or discomfort and are motivated to expend effort to effect positive change. They view the need for personal change as significant and can identify a specific problem (Lambert &

Cattani-Thompson, 1996). They are psychologically minded and have reasonably good ego strength. They have a history of some positive interpersonal relationships. Kivlighan, Patton, and Foote (1998) suggest that "the client's ability to form relationships (attachment style) moderates the relationship between counseling experience and working alliance." They describe those clients who can form positive relationships as having a "need for intimacy, trust in others, freedom from the fear of abandonment" (p. 274).

THE THERAPEUTIC ALLIANCE

The formation of a positive therapeutic alliance is, of course, determined by both the talents of the clinician and the relationship style and perceptions of the client. Clients who perceive their clinicians as empathic, caring, and credible and who feel understood by them are likely to progress in treatment, while those who have a negative perception of their clinician, whether or not that perception is grounded in reality, are less likely to make progress. In addition, clients who can use role models, support, and the caring of others to help themselves are likely to benefit from the counseling relationship.

Mutuality can enhance the therapeutic relationship. A feeling of shared warmth, affection, affirmation, and respect has been found to contribute to a positive therapeutic outcome (Waterhouse & Strupp, 1984). Clients who identify with their clinicians also are more likely to have positive outcomes. Research is indicating, with increasing clarity, "that therapist relationship skills and strength of the therapeutic alliance are the most powerful predictors of client outcome across many therapeutic orientations" (Green & Herget, 1991, p. 321).

The interaction of client and clinician factors can make a difference in clients' feelings of mutuality and their ability to identify with their clinician. For example, Dorothy Beck (1988) found that most people prefer clinicians who are relatively close to them in age; and Coleman, Wampold, and Casali (1995) stated that people who had not been well assimilated into the culture in which they were living preferred clinicians whose cultural background was similar to their own. These findings suggest that clients should be asked about any qualities or characteristic they might prefer in a clinician. If possible, they should be matched with a clinician who fits that profile.

Although the client-clinician relationship evolves over time and can continue to improve throughout the treatment process, clients' perceptions of the quality of the therapeutic alliance form early and tend to be stable. Walborn (1996) concluded that a positive therapeutic alliance must develop by the fifth session if treatment is to be successful. The treatment systems discussed throughout this book will provide clinicians with many skills and strategies that they can use to develop and enhance the all-important clinician-client relationship and thereby maximize the likelihood of a successful treatment outcome.

Clarkson (1990) delineated five types of psychotherapeutic alliances:

1. *Working alliances,* focusing on shared goals and an agreement to engage in certain tasks to achieve those goals

2. *Transferential/countertransferential relationships,* with clinicians communicating little of their own lives and personality but seeking to foster and analyze transference relationships
3. *Reparative/developmentally needed relationships,* most often used with severely damaged clients and offering reparenting and nurturing in an effort to compensate for deprivation in early relationships
4. *I-you relationships,* emphasizing immediacy and mutuality in the therapeutic relationship, with the clinician serving as a role model and an instrument for healing
5. *Transpersonal relationships,* characterized by the healing presence of the clinician, who communicates the sense of therapy as a shared journey leading to personal growth and increased spirituality

This classification system seems useful in enabling clinicians to examine the nature of their therapeutic relationships. Few clinician-client relationships represent a pure version of any one of these five types; most incorporate elements of two or more. Being conscious of the nature of their therapeutic alliances can help clinicians be more intentional and thoughtful in their interventions to form therapeutic relationships that are most likely to be helpful.

ESSENTIAL CONDITIONS OF EFFECTIVE THERAPEUTIC RELATIONSHIPS

Carl Rogers's person-centered counseling, discussed in Part 3 of this book, emphasizes the importance of some essential therapist characteristics that he believed would promote client self-esteem and self-efficacy. In recent years, most other systems of counseling and psychotherapy have come to recognize the importance of these growth-facilitating qualities in all therapeutic relationships, regardless of the clinician's theoretical orientation. The ability of the counselor or psychotherapist to communicate these qualities can have a major impact on the process and outcome that may exceed the impact made by any one technique or approach. As Neukrug and Williams (1993) have stated, "We all seem to want a therapist who is viewed as competent, caring, warm, and trustworthy and who has a good amount of clinical orientation" (p. 60). Although specific interventions can effect change in specific problem areas, the essential conditions of the therapeutic relationship make it likely that those interventions will succeed.

Empathy is the clinician's ability to see the world through the client's eyes and to communicate that understanding so that the client feels heard and validated. In such cases, clients feel their clinicians can relate to their experiences and are with them emotionally. According to Lambert and Cattani-Thompson (1996), empathy, or the feeling of being understood by one's therapist, is strongly associated with positive change and seems to be an even better predictor of outcome than technique is.

Trustworthiness communicates to clients that the clinician can be relied on to behave in ethical ways, to have the knowledge and skills needed to provide a productive direction to the session, to protect the client from harm and humiliation during treatment, to show respect for the client, and to be an advocate for what is best for the client. Clinicians foster trust when they honor commitments to clients, including being on time and keeping scheduled appointments; are clear about fees and payment schedules; help clients obtain third-party payments; return clients' telephone calls; remember information that clients have shared with them; and follow up on homework and unfinished discussions from a previous session. Stability and reliability are essential ingredients in most therapeutic relationships and can offset some of the confusion and chaos that many clients experience in their lives.

Caring gives clients the message that they matter to the clinician and that the clinician is concerned about them and their lives. Caring is transmitted through emotional warmth, appropriate reassurance, interventions that communicate positive regard for and confidence in the client, an interest in and focus on what is important to the client, and therapeutic activities that empower the client. Caring clinicians do not use clients to satisfy their own emotional needs or want clients to think, feel, or behave in certain ways. Clinicians who are confrontational and aggressive rather than warm and caring have a higher likelihood of a negative outcome than do those who transmit caring (Lambert & Cattani-Thompson, 1996).

Genuineness and congruence have not received clear support in the research literature but continue to be viewed as important to the establishment of a positive therapeutic relationship. Clinicians with these qualities give clients clear, accurate, unambiguous, and honest yet sensitive messages. The clinician is not verbalizing great concern while counting the minutes until lunch. If clinicians believe the client is making a harmful or self-destructive choice or is behaving in ways that are likely to alienate others, they address these issues in treatment. They provide feedback and clarification and show the client possible ways to change but never coerce, attack, or humiliate the client.

Persuasiveness (social influence) is the process of encouraging clients to take reasonable and growth-promoting risks, to make thoughtful decisions and healthy choices, to disclose and process feelings and experiences that may reawaken pain, and to move forward toward their goals. Clinicians whom clients perceive as credible and admirable seem more likely to have a positive persuasive influence and to become role models for their clients.

As with other essential conditions of treatment, clinicians must be careful that they do not move beyond encouraging positive change into an authoritarian role in which they tell clients how they should be and make value judgments of the clients' thoughts, feelings, and actions. Occasionally, clients present a danger to themselves or others, and clinicians must intervene forcefully to prevent a suicide or physical injury. However, under most circumstances, they must protect clients' rights to decide what is best for themselves. Persuasiveness is a positive force that provides people with the information, tools, models, and sense of empowerment they need to make good choices for themselves.

Hope is the final essential condition of psychotherapy that we will consider. Therapy and counseling are hard work for both clients and clinicians. For people to persist in that process and tolerate the increased anxiety it often causes as well as the commitment of time and finances, they must believe that their treatment has something positive to offer them and that, at the end of therapy, they will be better off than they were before treatment. The essential conditions of psychotherapy are intertwined and build on each other. Consequently, empathy, trustworthiness, caring, congruence, and persuasiveness all facilitate the development of hope in our clients. In addition, clear and mutually agreed-on goals and procedures, the clinician's communication of direction and optimism, emphasis on the client's strengths, and a collaborative relationship between client and clinician all can build the client's positive expectation of change (Green & Herget, 1991).

IMPORTANT CLINICIAN SKILLS, TRAINING, AND EXPERIENCE

Training and experience make a difference in clinician effectiveness. Martin Seligman (1995) found that psychologists, psychiatrists, and social workers all had a similar overall level of effectiveness and were more effective than "long-term family doctoring" was (p. 965). Crits-Cristoph et al. (1991) found that inexperienced therapists had more varied and often less successful outcomes than experienced therapists did. However, research has not always given clear support to either the importance of advanced training in counseling and psychotherapy or the value of experience (Beck, 1988). In part, that may be because the helping professions have not reached a consensus on which skills and training experiences are most important in developing effective clinicians and because clinicians do not all benefit equally from their training and experience. Recent research has been moving toward a consensus on necessary skills and experiences (Sexton, 1995a).

A review of the literature suggests that clinician training should include the following areas of preparation and competency (Seligman, 1996a, pp. 22–28):[1]

A. Helping Relationship
   1. Knows the developmental stages of the helping relationship.
   2. Knows the desirable and recognized therapeutic conditions most likely to facilitate development and positive change.
   3. Is able to build a collaborative working relationship with clients.
   4. Is familiar with common reactions to a helping relationship (e.g., defense mechanisms, transference, modeling and identification, culturally related responses, change, and verbal and nonverbal responses).
B. Communication Skills
   1. Possesses and can model good oral and interpersonal communication skills.
   2. Can write clearly and correctly and can prepare well-written reports, letters, and other communications.
   3. Can generally hear and respond appropriately to both overt and covert, verbal and nonverbal client messages.
   4. Can communicate empathy, positive regard, genuineness, and acceptance and use constructive confrontation and other essential listening behaviors needed in intervention.
   5. Can teach communication skills to individuals or groups and promote improved interpersonal relations.

[1]Adapted from Seligman, L. (1996). *Diagnosis and treatment planning*. New York: Plenum. Used by permission.

   6. Can communicate to people the nature of the treatment process and help them to understand both its value and its limitations.
   7. Can effectively conduct an interview or discussion with people from various educational, cultural, and socioeconomic backgrounds.
C. Human Growth and Development
   1. Understands the processes and principles of normal human development and the typical concerns of various age groups including neonatal, childhood, adolescent, and adult development as well as concepts of aging and dying.
   2. Can discriminate between healthy and disturbed development and has knowledge of abnormal psychology.
   3. Is familiar with the common personality types and patterns.
   4. Understands cognitive development.
   5. Understands sexual development and behavior.
   6. Can take a holistic view of clients.
   7. Can enable others to gain understanding of their own development.
D. Assessment and Appraisal Procedures
   1. Knows the indications and contraindications for an assessment or appraisal procedure.
   2. Can conduct psychosocial histories, assessments, intake interviews, and mental status examinations.
   3. Knows when to refer people for physical and neurological examinations.
   4. Is familiar with the appropriate use, interpretation, strengths, and limitations of instruments that are widely used in assessing development, intelligence, abilities, interests, values, and personality.
   5. Can use assessment to facilitate diagnosis, treatment planning, and provision of mental health treatment.
E. Techniques and Theories of Counseling and Psychotherapy
   1. Knows the general principles and practices for the promotion of optimal mental health.
   2. Is familiar with and able to use a broad range of cognitive, behavioral, and affective treatment systems and strategies.
   3. Is skilled in crisis intervention, problem solving, and other brief, action-based methods of intervention.
   4. Is familiar with social models of intervention including therapeutic use of self, milieu therapy, and therapeutic communities.
   5. Can teach coping and interpersonal skills including decision-making, assertiveness, and nonjudgmental listening.
   6. Knows the kinds of situations for which the various systems and strategies of intervention are especially useful.
   7. Can provide a theoretical rationale for approaches to treatment.
   8. Is able to engage effectively in many levels of counseling and psychotherapy (e.g., individual, family, group, organization, community).
   9. Can assess people's needs and can develop both preventive and remedial treatment plans which effectively meet those needs.
  10. Can help people to set viable long- and short-range goals.
  11. Can promote client motivation and deal effectively with resistance.

F. Clinical Skills and Services

  1. Knows the principles and practices of diagnosis, treatment, and prevention of mental and emotional disorders and dysfunctional behavior.
  2. Is familiar with the specific models and methods for assessing mental status and identifying abnormal, deviant, or dysfunctional behavior, affect, or cognition.
  3. Is knowledgeable about the nature and use of the *Diagnostic and Statistical Manual of Mental Disorders.*
  4. Knows the indications and contraindications for mental health intervention.
  5. Can develop sound and comprehensive treatment plans.

G. Group Counseling and Psychotherapy

  1. Possesses understanding of group development, process, and dynamics.
  2. Can help others to understand and modify group process.
  3. Can work effectively with both small and large groups, homogeneous and heterogeneous groups.
  4. Knows the strengths and limitations of group counseling and can determine when and how it is likely to be helpful.
  5. Has competence in systems and strategies of group counseling and psychotherapy and can assist groups in overcoming obstacles.
  6. Understands the goals and procedures of different types of small groups (e.g., growth, problem solving, support, education).
  7. Is knowledgeable about member selection and member and leadership roles in groups.
  8. Is familiar with intervention strategies to be used in groups for special populations (e.g., children, parents, physically ill, chronically mentally ill).

H. Career Counseling

  1. Understands the changing patterns and meaning of work in modern society.
  2. Understands the lifelong process of career development and the broad scope of career counseling.
  3. Is familiar with sources of career information and knows how to help people acquire and use that information.
  4. Is familiar with a broad range of inventories designed to assess interests, abilities, and values and can use those instruments effectively as a part of career counseling.
  5. Can promote improved life/work planning via client self-exploration, values clarification, development of alternatives, decision-making, reality testing, pre-retirement planning, leisure counseling, and other appropriate techniques.
  6. Can help people develop the skills needed for effective job seeking (e.g., interview skills, résumé writing).

I. Family (Couples) Counseling and Psychotherapy

  1. Has understanding of patterns of family dynamics and of the family life cycle.

        2. Can determine when family/couples therapy would be an effective treatment modality.

        3. Is familiar with and able to use the major systems and strategies of family and couples treatment.

        4. Can use methods to promote positive parent/child interaction.

J. Behavioral Medicine

        1. Has a basic understanding of neurophysiology.

        2. Has knowledge of theories and techniques of relaxation, exercise, nutrition, stress management, holistic health, and their appropriate uses.

        3. Understands the application of behavioral approaches to such problems as smoking, eating disorders, and drug/alcohol misuse.

K. Therapeutic and Mood Altering Chemicals

        1. Is aware of the most frequently abused chemical agents, their classification, and physical effects.

        2. Understands the signs and stages of chemical dependence and abuse.

        3. Knows what to do in the event of undesired effects of chemical agents.

        4. Is familiar with commonly used psychotropic medications.

        5. Knows when and how to make a referral for a medication evaluation.

L. Consultation

        1. Understands the roles and responsibilities of the consultant.

        2. Understands organizational development.

        3. Can function independently and define own goals and those of clientele with little structure or supervision.

        4. Can attend to and balance organizational and individual needs.

        5. Can promote problem-solving and conflict resolution.

        6. Can facilitate communication and change in schools, businesses, and other organizations in a way that fosters self-help and increased competence.

M. Training, Supervision and Program Development

        1. Can develop programs that reach large numbers of people and promote mastery and shared learning.

        2. Is comfortable in a teaching role and can integrate teaching and counseling skills.

        3. Can conduct in-service training programs.

        4. Is aware of a variety of models of and approaches to supervision.

        5. Can supervise, train, and work effectively with indigenous, professional and paraprofessional workers.

        6. Possesses administrative skills.

        7. Can coordinate and collaborate effectively with other human service workers.

        8. Can plan and execute outreach programs and approaches to bring services to communities.

N. Social Systems and Community Organization

        1. Understands the place of mental health treatment in the larger context of society including human services, politics, and economics.

2. Understands and can use the principles of social change, social systems analysis, community intervention, public education, community planning and organization.
3. Can understand issues as well as individual and community needs.
4. Can identify and work effectively with both community strengths and growth-inhibiting and stressful aspects of the community and can assess the need for community change.
5. Can take a multifaceted approach to helping others.
6. Can assume the roles of advocate, change agent, and political activist when appropriate.
7. Can build coalitions and collaborate with others to help people.
8. Is familiar with and can make effective use of educational, community, and other resources via referral, linkage, advocacy, and consultation in order to provide a comprehensive and continuous system of services.
9. Can facilitate the strengthening of socially devalued groups.
10. Can involve the community in program planning and develop and draw on community leadership.
11. Has knowledge of causes and dynamics of major social problems (e.g., substance misuse, child abuse, rape, delinquency), their legal ramifications, and ways to prevent and treat them.
12. Has a broad range of approaches to help others develop their life skills and their abilities to help themselves (e.g., parent effectiveness training, assertiveness training, sex education).
13. Is familiar with the concepts of outreach and prevention in mental health.

O. Diverse Populations
1. Is aware of and appreciates individual, life style, and cultural differences.
2. Can interact well with people of all ages and backgrounds, functioning at various intellectual and emotional levels, and can understand their points of view.
3. Can take account of the effect that a cultural and environmental background has had on a person's development.
4. Can help people who represent diverse populations to become aware of their needs and set their own priorities and goals and can accept the validity of their wants.
5. Can help people develop and make use of appropriate support systems.

P. Research
1. Understands the principles of assessment and evaluation.
2. Is conversant with important research in the fields of counseling and psychology.
3. Can understand, plan, and conduct research studies.
4. Appreciates the importance of evaluating the impact of one's efforts and the need for accountability.
5. Can develop and execute valid evaluation procedures.

Q. Self-Growth and Awareness
1. Has the conviction that individuals, families, groups, and communities can change and improve.

2. Is open-minded and emotionally stable.
3. Has tolerance and respect for all people and their values.
4. Is aware of and can deal with own prejudices and stereotypes as well as those of clients.
5. Is flexible and able to cope with constant change.
6. Can function effectively as leader, team member, and autonomous helper.
7. Has good overall awareness of own strengths and weaknesses, likes and dislikes.
8. Is committed to lifelong learning and professional development.
9. Understands the ethical standards of counselors and psychotherapists and behaves in a way that is consistent with those standards.

A study by Sexton (1995b) indicated that, when clinicians rated the importance of their skills, two of the most important were knowledge of theories of counseling and psychotherapy and an understanding of models of intervention used with individuals. These two competencies reflect the primary focus of this book. The skill rated as the most important, understanding abnormal behavior, certainly also has considerable relevance to using systems and strategies of counseling and psychotherapy successfully and will also be discussed in this book. Although many of the other competencies just listed do not seem to relate directly to knowledge and application of treatment systems and strategies, all of them do play a real part in helping clinicians function effectively in their profession and become sensitive to and able to address the wide variety of needs and concerns that clients present.

This broad and extensive array of skills and competencies may seem daunting. However, novice clinicians already possess some of these abilities when they begin training in a mental health profession. Many are taught in graduate school, while others are developed when clinicians embark on their internships and postgraduate work experience. These are competencies that develop and improve over time and characterize outstanding clinicians. At the end of this chapter, you will have the opportunity to assess some of your own skills.

PERSONAL CHARACTERISTICS OF THE EFFECTIVE CLINICIAN

As we have discussed, empathy, trustworthiness, caring, genuineness, persuasiveness, and the ability to instill hope in the therapeutic relationship are important qualities for a clinician. The literature also suggests personal and professional qualities in clinicians that can help establish effective therapeutic relationships. Many are the same qualities that most of us value in friends and colleagues. Najavits and Weiss (1994) found a significant association between *strong interpersonal skills* and clinician effectiveness. Clinicians who were friendly and likable, patient and flexible tended to be more successful than those who were angry, judgmental, rigid, or anxious. People who have a sense of humor; are willing to take reasonable risks; can acknowledge their mistakes and limitations; have realistic self-confidence, self-esteem, and fulfillment in their own lives; affirm rather than diminish others; and are motivated toward personal and professional growth also tend to be successful clinicians (Corey, Corey, & Callanan, 1998). These exemplary clinicians are responsible and ethical and have a sense of direction and initiative in their own lives. Awareness of self and others is another asset, particularly sensitivity to and respect for individual differences and ethnic and cultural experiences. Other important characteristics are objectivity and the ability to view the world through the eyes of another.

Clinicians' values also seem linked to outcome. Lafferty, Beutler, and Crago (1989) found that more effective therapists placed significantly less importance on having prosperous and exciting lives and more importance on being intelligent and reflective than did less effective clinicians. In general, clinicians who are emotionally stable, well-adjusted, and optimistic are more likely to be effective (Sexton & Whiston, 1991). These characteristics seem to be much more important than are factors such as a clinician's age, gender, or cultural background.

Walborn (1996) has suggested that many people seek to become clinicians because they know what it is like to feel lonely and to experience emotional pain. On the other hand, effective clinicians are most likely to manifest emotional health and well-being as well as the ability to put their own needs aside at least temporarily so they can understand, support, and help others. Apparently, having personal difficulties in the past does not prohibit people from later becoming effective clinicians. In fact, the process of honestly looking at and bravely tackling their own issues and concerns may help people develop the positive traits that are likely to be found in successful clinicians.

DEMOGRAPHIC CHARACTERISTICS OF THE EFFECTIVE CLINICIAN

Research does not provide much information about the relationship of clinician background to effectiveness. Factors such as clinicians' professional discipline (e.g., psychology, counseling, social work), their age, and their gender do not bear a clear relationship to outcome. One interesting variable that has shown a correlation with outcome is clinicians' perception of having difficulties during their own childhood (Poal & Weisz, 1989; Watts, Trusty, Canada, & Harvill, 1995). Whether this finding is due to clinicians' increased sensitivity to family issues or to genuine difficulties while growing up is unclear.

ETHICS

Each professional association for clinicians, including the American Counseling Association and the American Psychological Association, has its own set of ethical standards. Familiarizing oneself with and abiding by those ethical standards is an essential part of sound clinical practice. Although a detailed discussion of the ethical standards for each of the mental health professions is beyond the scope of this book, I review selected standards here because of their importance and relevance to the systems, strategies, and skills presented in this book.

Maintain Clients' Well-Being (Do No Harm)

Clinicians should always keep in mind the importance of maintaining the well-being of their clients. Implicit in this guideline is the message that clinicians need to be aware of the boundaries of their competence and avoid using strategies that present a high risk to the client or that are outside of the scope of the clinician's training and expertise. They should be sure to do no harm to their clients.

Another aspect of doing no harm is respecting clients' rights, taking time to understand them as individuals, appreciating the importance and impact of their cultural background, and emphasizing their strength and growth. Clients should never be demeaned or attacked; rather, they should be empowered.

Confidentiality

Confidentiality is an important aspect of the therapeutic relationship. It helps clients feel safe in treatment and encourages them to share with clinicians material that might be painful or embarrassing. At the same time, confidentiality has limitations, particularly for clients who are minors, who present a danger to themselves or others, or who have abused a child or an elderly or disabled person. Clients need to be informed of the guidelines that determine when clinicians can and cannot maintain confidentiality so that the clients can make informed decisions as to what information they want to share in treatment.

Duty to Warn

Clinicians have a duty to protect clients who threaten suicide or other forms of physical harm to themselves. In addition, clinicians have a duty to protect others who are endangered by a client. In fulfilling these duties, clinicians sometimes have to break confidentiality, perhaps to tell a spouse that his wife is actively suicidal and or report to child protective services a man who has sexually abused his daughter. The decision to break confidentiality is usually an extremely difficult one, and clinicians are encouraged to seek consultation from a colleague or supervisor when faced with such an issue.

Dual Relationships

To protect the nature of the therapeutic relationship, it is generally considered unethical for clinicians to have other concurrent relationships with their clients. For example, clinicians certainly should not initiate intimate relationships with their clients nor share social activities, business dealings, or most other nontherapeutic interactions. The converse also holds true. People who are already students, family members, business colleagues, or good friends of a clinician generally should not be accepted as clients of that clinician at the same time. Ethical standards differ in terms of when, if ever, a clinician can appropriately develop a personal relationship with a former client. However, all standards agree that while someone is a client, the clinician should avoid other types of relationships with that person.

Other Important Ethical Standards

Many other ethical standards, of course, have relevance to the substance of this book, including guidelines on documentation, assessment, and supervision. Again, readers are strongly encouraged to familiarize themselves with the ethical standards for their professional association as well as for licensed mental health professionals practicing in their state to ensure that their practice meets the highest ethical standards.

SKILL DEVELOPMENT AND EXERCISES

This chapter has emphasized the importance of the personal characteristics of the clinician and the therapeutic alliance in determining treatment outcome. The following sections include information to help you develop and explore three skills that are relevant to both the contents of this chapter and your development as effective clinicians:

1. Role induction
2. Self-assessment
3. Building a positive therapeutic alliance

Role Induction

The process of role induction has received increasing attention as an integral part of treatment. Familiarizing clients with the nature of counseling and psychotherapy, with their responsibilities in this collaborative process, and with the kinds of changes that can realistically be expected from treatment can help both client and clinician view themselves as engaged in a common endeavor that is likely to succeed. This can contribute greatly to the efficiency and success of the process. Acosta, Yamamoto, Evans, and Skilbeck (1983) found that clients who received pretreatment preparation were more motivated, had a better understanding of treatment and their role in the process, seemed more motivated and optimistic about improvement via treatment, and demonstrated greater willingness to self-disclose and discuss their concerns.

Role induction is the process of orienting people to treatment so they are more likely to become successful clients who understand and can make good use of the therapeutic process. Role induction typically entails discussing the following topics with clients early in the therapeutic relationship and ensuring that clients understand and are comfortable with the information that has been discussed:

- How treatment promotes positive change
- The kinds of issues and concerns that usually respond well to counseling or psychotherapy
- The collaborative nature of the client-clinician relationship
- The role and responsibilities of the clinician
- The role and responsibilities of the client
- The importance of honesty and self-disclosure on the part of the client
- Ethical aspects of the therapeutic relationship, especially guidelines for maintaining and breaking confidentiality
- Information on contacting the clinician and handling client emergencies
- Clinician's fees and appointment schedule
- Use of forms to obtain third-party payments

Exercises in Role Induction   *Classroom/large-group exercise:* Discuss the meaning and importance of each of the items on the list you have just read. Decide if any items should be added to or omitted from the list. Examine positive and negative ways to communicate information about each item to clients.

Small-group exercise: General instructions on conducting small-group exercises appear in Chapter 1. Review that explanation before beginning this exercise.

Form into groups of four people. One participant should role-play one of the three clients introduced in Chapter 1: Edie, Roberto, or Ava. A second participant should assume the clinician role and conduct a role induction with this client. The other participants should observe the role play and provide feedback on the following items. Remember that feedback should be specific and constructive; therefore, observers should take notes during the role play so that they can remember specific statements to be discussed. Suggesting alternative statements or procedures will make your feedback especially useful. Keep the focus on the content and the process, not on the person, and be sure to pay attention to strengths in the role play as well as areas needing improvement.

1. Consider whether the important items in the role induction were presented clearly. Were some items omitted? What items were described particularly well? What changes would you suggest?
2. Discuss the clinician's nonverbal communications, including tone of voice, rate of speech, eye contact, and posture. How did these affect the role induction process?
3. How did the client seem to react to the role induction? Should the process have been modified in any way to fit this person's needs?

Self-Assessment

Exercises in Self-Assessment   *Individual exercises:* General instructions on individual exercises appear in Chapter 1. Review that explanation before beginning these exercises.

1. Previously in this chapter, we identified six essential characteristics of effective therapeutic relationships: empathy, trustworthiness, caring, congruence/genuineness, persuasiveness, and hope. List each of these characteristics on a piece of paper. Then select at least one (but no more than three) in which you believe you already have some skill. For each, write out your rationale for believing you would be successful in transmitting that quality to a client. For example, you might perceive yourself as strong in persuasiveness because you can easily engage people in conversations, are articulate and well spoken, and have extensive knowledge of mental disorders and their treatment. You might believe clients are likely to view you as trustworthy because you almost always remember your commitments and are well organized.

For each of the items you did not select, write down one change you might make to maximize your ability to transmit that characteristic to clients. For example, you might try to communicate more caring to others by deliberately acknowledging positive statements they have made about themselves. To improve your ability to communicate hope, you might focus on making fewer judgmental statements and instead look for new possibilities.

2. Clinicians typically present clients with a self-disclosure statement during their first meeting. That statement gives clients information about the clinician, usually including his or her beliefs about the purposes of treatment and how it helps people to change. Write a brief paragraph to share later with your class or small group about your conception of counseling or psychotherapy and how it facilitates change. If you already have some familiarity with theories of counseling and psychotherapy, include some information about your preferred treatment system and why you view that approach as especially powerful.

Building a Positive Therapeutic Alliance

Building rapport and a positive therapeutic alliance are gradual processes that evolve throughout treatment. However, the first few sessions form the foundation for that alliance. If the therapeutic relationship does not begin well, clients may terminate treatment prematurely, obviously precluding future efforts to form a sound working alliance. Consequently, counselors and therapists must actively engender rapport and collaboration from the first moment of contact with the client.

Following are some procedures and interventions that can promote rapport and development of a positive therapeutic alliance:

- Facilitate the client's efforts to begin treatment by providing a role induction (described previously), including clear information on policies, use of third-party payments, the roles of client and clinician, and other details. Be sure that clinician and client have a shared understanding of how treatment will proceed.

- Support the client's decision to seek treatment by discussing the importance of taking a first step and the courage that is involved in seeking help.
- Establish and consistently follow the session guidelines, including starting and ending times; follow up on homework tasks; promote active client participation; ensure that sessions have a productive structure; and clarify fee collection.
- Discuss the person's expectations for treatment, encouraging realistic hope for positive change. This can be accomplished by acknowledging the person's difficulties and discussing ways in which treatment can usually help with such concerns.
- Develop with the client shared and specific goals that reflect those hopes and expectations and are meaningful to the client.
- Understand and value the client's perspectives on the world.
- Communicate warmth and concern in a professional manner, showing empathy for the client's feelings and experiences.
- Demonstrate congruence and genuineness in verbal and nonverbal messages. Sometimes sharing a small piece of information about yourself, especially if it establishes a commonality between you and the client, can convey genuineness. Examples would be a brief mention of a visit you made to the client's hometown or your shared enjoyment of the client's favorite hobby. Be careful not to focus too much on yourself or share very personal material.
- Engage the client actively in the therapeutic process and begin to engender both a sense of empowerment in the client and confidence in the treatment. This can be accomplished by suggesting small, manageable, helpful steps or activities that the person can do between sessions.
- Be sure to acknowledge and build on successes and support networks that the person has already established.

Exercise in Building a Positive Therapeutic Alliance   *Classroom or small-group exercise:* Assume that you have an individual counseling session with each of the members of the Diaz family (introduced in Chapter 1). Here are their opening statements to you:

> **Edie:**   This is going to be very hard for me. I'm not used to talking about myself and don't feel ready to tell you some of the things that have happened to me.
>
> **Roberto:**   I can't take this much longer. If things don't go back to the way they used to be, I'm walking. How long do you think it will take you to fix Edie's problems?
>
> **Ava:**   I'm not sure why my mom wanted me to talk to you.

Each statement reflects some possible barriers to the establishment of a positive therapeutic alliance. Discuss the statements individually, drawing on what you already know about Edie, Roberto, and Ava from Chapter 1. Consider the possible

barriers to successful treatment and what strategies and skills you might use to facilitate the establishment of a positive therapeutic relationship with each person.

SUMMARY

This chapter has presented important information about the systems, strategies, and skills of counseling and psychotherapy, including the nature of a positive therapeutic alliance, client and clinician characteristics and abilities associated with successful treatment, and important ethical standards. Exercises and skill development sections discussed role induction, self-assessment, and the development of a sound therapeutic alliance.

PART TWO

TREATMENT SYSTEMS EMPHASIZING BACKGROUND AND CONTEXT

Chapter 3

OVERVIEW OF BACKGROUND AND CONTEXT

We are our histories, our families, the events in our lives, our joys and losses, our dreams, and more. All our experiences have shaped and continue to shape us. Most clinicians will probably agree that we cannot really understand our clients and the concerns they present in treatment unless we learn something about their backgrounds.

However, clinicians disagree considerably on the amount of time they spend in discussion of the past, on the importance they place on past experiences, and on the ways in which they address and make use of past experiences in ameliorating present concerns. This chapter focuses on systems of counseling and psychotherapy that emphasize understanding and working through unresolved problems and issues in the client's past. Clinicians advocating these approaches believe that unless treatment facilitates healing of past wounds and relieves developmental blocks, people will continue to repeat dysfunctional patterns.

According to treatment approaches that emphasize the past, a young man who had a seductive and unreliable mother probably will mistrust women and will have difficulty in not only forming healthy intimate relationships but also in viewing himself as worthy and capable of love and closeness. The woman who, as a child, saw the blood, pain, and grief associated with her mother's sudden miscarriage may be afraid of becoming pregnant herself, whether or not she can link her fears to her mother's loss. These examples reflect the potential impact of the past on the present. No matter if clinicians place considerable emphasis on the past or focus almost entirely on the present, they should have some understanding of their clients' backgrounds to make accurate diagnoses and plan treatments that are likely to succeed.

Chapter 4 begins the discussion of treatment systems that emphasize background with a consideration of Sigmund Freud's psychoanalysis. Although many other theories of human development and psychotherapy have been advanced since Freud's work began more than 100 years ago, he is generally regarded as the father of psychotherapy. His ideas and strategies continue to inform and contribute to modern treatment approaches. Alfred Adler and Carl Jung were Freud's colleagues early in their careers but ultimately broke with him and developed their own theories, which are discussed in Chapters 5 and 6. The ideas of neo- and post-Freudians, including Anna Freud, Melanie Klein, Karen Horney, Helene Deutsch, Harry Stack Sullivan, and the object relations theorists whose work was inspired and influenced by Freud's, are considered in Chapter 7. Finally, modern psychodynamic approaches, Eric Berne's transactional analysis, and brief psychodynamic psychotherapy, (developed by Malan, Sifneos, and others,) are presented in Chapters 8 and 9.

USE OF PAST EXPERIENCES

Incorporating the discussion and processing of past experiences into treatment can greatly enhance its impact. Following are some of the important functions of exploring a client's history.

Nearly everyone views their pasts as important to making them who they are. Most people who come to treatment expect to be asked about and to talk about their histories. Showing interest in their families, school experiences, and other aspects of their lives can communicate the clinician's wish to really know and understand clients. This effort to view clients as unique individuals who merit time and attention conveys caring and can help develop rapport.

Many people find it easier to talk about the past than the present, especially if they are currently experiencing considerable pain. Allowing people to spend some of their time talking about the past can give them a respite from the sadness and anxiety associated with their present concerns. Focusing on past successes, in particular, can engender hope, optimism, and self-confidence.

Psychodynamic theorists believe that the roots of current problems lie in the past and that exploration and interpretation of past experiences are essential to alleviating current concerns. Whether or not readers share that point of view, some understanding of the past can shed light on the nature and dynamics of people's current concerns and provide a context for understanding them more fully. Repetitive patterns can be identified, as can possible precipitants of current and future difficulties. For example, the adolescent cursing his teacher can be better understood by knowing whether he has had longstanding difficulty with authority figures or whether this is an isolated and uncharacteristic incident.

Diagnosis, using the *Diagnostic and Statistical Manual of Mental Disorders* (American Psychiatric Association, 1994) is becoming an increasingly important aspect of the clinician's role. Making an accurate diagnosis often depends on knowing the duration of a person's symptoms and whether and how often that person has experienced the same or other symptoms in the past. Taking a careful history is essential when making a diagnosis.

Similarly, the likelihood of developing an effective treatment plan can be greatly enhanced if clinicians have knowledge of their clients' histories. For example, a person's symptoms of severe depression, beginning a few months ago after a relocation, may be diagnosed as a major depressive disorder and treated with cognitive behavioral therapy. However, if the history reveals a pattern of not only recurrent depressive episodes but also episodes of extremely elevated mood (mania) and a background of abuse, the diagnosis would be a bipolar disorder; and some supportive therapy as well as medication may also be indicated, perhaps along with subsequent psychodynamic interventions.

In the current era of counseling and psychotherapy, sometimes referred to as the post-modern era, considerable emphasis is generally placed on understanding people from a holistic point of view. This involves learning about people's development, their cultural and socioeconomic backgrounds, their families, and other important aspects of their lives so that their perspectives on themselves and their world can be understood. Each person has a story to tell, and by listening to these stories and learning about people's lives, clinicians can see the world through their clients' eyes as much as possible. In this way, clinicians can minimize their biases and preconceptions and can truly know and respond to each person as a special individual.

Skill Development: Questions and Intake Interviews

This chapter introduces two fundamental skills: asking questions and conducting an intake interview. Questions are, of course, used throughout the treatment process to elicit information and to promote client self-exploration, self-awareness, and self-expression. However, they are especially important in eliciting background information.

Questions are the primary intervention used in conducting an intake interview. Many mental health agencies use a structured intake interview as a way to gather information on clients systematically and comprehensively. This keeps the kind of information obtained from clients consistent and increases the likelihood of obtaining information that is essential to understanding each client. Although counselors and psychotherapists in schools, private practices, and career counseling centers may not conduct formal intake interviews, those clinicians, too, can benefit from bearing in mind the topics that are usually covered in these interviews and eliciting that information from their clients in less structured ways.

Asking Helpful Questions

Questions are a powerful intervention. They can focus the treatment on core issues, elicit information, and deepen awareness and understanding. Questions can also exaggerate the power imbalance between clinician and client; make people feel judged, attacked, and demeaned; and turn a therapy session into an inquisition. Consider the following example:

Client: I got a speeding ticket on my way to our session today.

Response 1:   What happened?

Response 2:   How did you feel about that?

Response 3:   Why did you do *that?*

Response 4:   How fast were you going?

Each of the four clinician interventions will move the session in a different direction, some more positive than others. The first two responses are likely to be helpful. Response 1 gives the client an opportunity to describe and process the details of the incident, perhaps leading to information on behavior and impulse control; while Response 2 encourages exploration of feelings, perhaps leading to a discussion of emotions related to coming to the session. Neither response is judgmental, and both give the client many possible ways in which to respond. Responses 3 and 4, however, are not likely to have a positive impact on the therapeutic process. The third response may be interpreted by the client as suggesting that he or she made poor choices and perhaps deserves to be punished. The fourth response focuses the client on a specific piece of information. While this information may be relevant later in the discussion, asking for the speed immediately may suggest that it is the most important aspect of the incident. If, indeed, the person was going at a high speed, having to disclose that information to the clinician may be embarrassing and may even lead the client to withhold accurate information. Clearly, the nature and timing of a question are instrumental in both building rapport and achieving treatment goals.

When clinicians make an intervention or respond to clients, they should have considered the direction in which they want to move the session and the impact they want their words to have on the client. To beginning clinicians, having such a high level of awareness and direction may seem almost impossible. However, with training and experience, that sort of clinical thinking becomes rapid and almost automatic. Even beginning clinicians, however, should be able to look at a script of a treatment session and discuss the probable intention and impact of an intervention.

When formulating questions, clinicians should consider

- What information they want to elicit
- How they believe that information will advance the therapeutic process
- What they want to focus on or emphasize with their question
- What tone they want to establish in the session

The following information and guidelines should also be helpful.

Types of Questions   Questions can be open or closed. An open question is usually designed to elicit some narration, perhaps about the client's feelings, thoughts, behaviors, or experiences. Open questions encourage people to talk at greater length or depth. The open question is a broad one that gives clients responsibility and flexibility in how they might respond. Open questions often begin with "how," "could," "what," and "why" but may have other openers. Responses 1, 2, and 3 in the speeding ticket example are open questions, encouraging the person to respond with at least a sentence or two. Clinicians rely much more heavily on open rather than closed questions because they are more likely to promote client self-awareness and exploration.

Closed questions ask for a specific piece of information, often a fact, and invite a limited response of only a few words. Closed questions often begin with "who," "when," "where," "are," "do," and "is." Depending on the nature of the question, closed questions can make a person feel like he or she is on the spot. Response 4 in the speeding ticket example is a closed question.

Closed questions certainly have a place in counseling and psychotherapy. Questions such as, "Do you have siblings?" "Would you like to schedule an appointment for next week?" and "Where were you born?" certainly yield important pieces of information. In addition, closed questions can help narrow the focus of a session that seems to be drifting or help a confused client present clearer information. For example, the clinician might say, "It sounds like your experience of being robbed was terrifying and overwhelming. I'd like to get a clearer idea of what happened. When did you first realize you were being followed? . . . What did the thief say to you? . . . When did you decide to give him your money? . . . Who was the first person you told about the robbery?" Such questions can help people manage their emotions by focusing initially on facts rather than feelings.

Phrasing Questions   As with most interventions, questions should be phrased to be clear, concise, and easily understood. They should encourage and empower and move treatment toward its goals. In general, questions that begin with "what" and "how" promote exploration and are well received by clients, while questions that begin with "why" can sound negative and accusatory (as in Response 3).

Questions may end in a question mark or may be a statement that suggests a question, such as, "Tell me more about the robbery." These implied or indirect questions should follow the same guidelines as standard questions do.

Pacing of Questions   An uninterrupted series of questions can have a negative impact on the treatment process. Like questions beginning with "why," this pattern can increase a person's defensiveness and exaggerate the clinician's power. Even in an initial or intake session, clinicians should avoid a barrage of questions. Instead, other interventions, such as reflections of feeling and meaning, should be interspersed among the questions so that the session has the flow of a dialogue rather than an inquisition, preserving the collaborative nature of the therapeutic process.

Subject Matter of Questions   Of course, just as the format and the pacing of questions can have an impact on the development of the therapeutic relationship, so can the content of the questions. Although no topics are unacceptable in counseling and psychotherapy, clinicians should introduce topics when they believe clients will be fairly comfortable discussing them. For example, taking the initiative to ask about a history of abuse during the first 10 minutes of an initial treatment session seems unwise under most circumstances; however, that information is probably important to the eventual development of an effective treatment plan.

Questions usually should be presented so that they do not cause great discomfort. Asking questions about areas that the client is reluctant to discuss as well as about repressed memories or other highly charged subjects should be done with extreme caution.

Questions are likely to yield more useful information when they focus on the client rather than on people who are not involved in the treatment process. For example, asking, "What thoughts did you have when your father told you that your mother had left him?" is likely to be more productive than, "What was your mother's reason for leaving your father?" The first question keeps the focus on the client and encourages self-exploration, while the second takes the focus away from the client and asks for mind reading. At the end of this chapter you will find exercises designed to improve questioning skills, which will give you an opportunity to apply some of the concepts covered in this section.

Conducting an Intake Interview

An intake interview may be a formal process that precedes the referral of a client to another clinician, a structured interview that occurs during the first session or two of treatment, or simply the informal get-acquainted process that occurs during the early sessions of counseling. The primary purpose of the intake process is for clinicians to obtain enough information on clients' history, current life situation, presenting concerns, and characteristics to formulate an accurate diagnosis and develop a treatment plan that is likely to succeed. Clinicians also need to assess whether clients are at risk of harming themselves or others. Because the intake interview occurs during the first few sessions of the therapeutic relationship, clinicians must also orient clients to treatment (role induction, discussed in Chapter 2) and interact with them to foster development of rapport and a collaborative therapeutic alliance.

Although clients may be asked to complete forms to provide some information, the intake process is primarily a dialogue between client and clinician. Questions are the major vehicle for eliciting information; but as we have discussed, a barrage of questions is not likely to be productive in either eliciting important personal material or developing rapport. Clinicians should follow the guidelines for formulating questions (presented in the previous section) when conducting an intake interview.

Content of the Intake Interview An intake interview generally covers the following topics, with questions, sequence of subjects, and depth of interview adapted to the client's age, concerns, motivation for help, and level of self-disclosure (Seligman, 1996a):

- Demographic information, including age, marital status, family composition, educational background, occupation, and living situation
- Presenting problems, including reasons for seeking help, symptoms, onset and duration of difficulties, previous efforts to obtain help, and the impact of concerns on the person's lifestyle
- Prior psychological or emotional difficulties
- Current life situation, including important relationships, occupational and educational activities, and social and leisure activities
- Cultural, religious, and socioeconomic information
- Family background, including information on the composition of nuclear and current families, structure of and relationships within the families, parenting styles, parental role models and messages, and family values
- Developmental history
- Career and educational history
- Medical history, including significant past and current illnesses, medical treatments, and medication
- Health-related behaviors, including use of drugs and alcohol, exercise, diet, and overall self-care

In addition, clients should have the opportunity to provide information that may not have been covered in the intake interview but that they view as important to them and to anyone who is seeking to understand them.

EXAMPLE OF AN INTAKE INTERVIEW

The following intake interview is with Edie Diaz. Edie sought counseling from a community mental health center close to her home. Her therapist is a woman, about 10 years older than she is. Assume that Edie has already been provided with information about the nature of treatment and her role as a client.

When reading this transcript, pay particular attention to how questions are used in the interview. Look at whether they are open or closed and how they are integrated with other kinds of interventions. Think about what the therapist's intent might have been in asking each question. Also, compare the content of this interview with the list of topics usually covered in an intake interview. Often, an initial interview does not cover all parts of an intake interview. Are there important aspects of this client's life that were not discussed? Should these areas have been discussed in this session, or are they better left for exploration after Edie and her therapist build some rapport? Consider whether some topics or questions were particularly fruitful, while others may have had a negative impact on the session. Overall, how would you have improved this intake interview?

Therapist: Edie, we've gone over the consent-to-treatment forms and talked about the counseling process. Do you have any further questions about that information?

Edie: No, it all seems pretty clear.

Therapist: Well, feel free to ask any questions that come up during counseling.

Edie: Thank you. I will.

Therapist: I can see from the forms you completed that you are 37 years old and live with your husband, Roberto, and your daughter, Ava.

Edie: Yes, that's right.

Therapist: What prompted you to seek counseling at this time?

Edie: A lot of things. It's hard to know where to begin.

Therapist: We can start almost anywhere, and probably one issue will lead us to talk about another. But often people have a specific concern in mind when they actually pick up the phone to make an appointment. I wonder if that happened for you?

Edie: Well, yes, I guess it did. Ava will be 10 in about 6 weeks, and she and I were planning her birthday party. After she went to bed, I started to think about when I was 10. That was such a hard time for me.

Therapist: I can see even thinking about it brings up strong feelings. What made that such a hard time for you?

Edie: I was diagnosed with cancer when I was 10. It was awful. I had chemotherapy, lost all my hair, even my eyebrows, and gained lots of weight. Can you imagine what that's like for a child? I felt like such a freak. And everybody was acting like I was going to die. Almost everybody. . . .

Therapist: That must have been a terrible experience for you. Very frightening.

Edie: Yes, it was. And I'm so afraid it's going to happen to Ava. She just means the world to me. I couldn't stand it if she had to go through what I went through. And I still worry about my health too. The doctors told me years ago that I was cured, but it's hard for me to believe that.

Therapist: So not only are you worrying about Ava, who means so much to you, but also about yourself. . . . When you were talking about having had cancer, it sounded like someone came into your mind who had been optimistic about your prognosis. Who was that?

Edie: My father.

Therapist: How did that affect your experience with cancer?

Edie: It made an enormous difference. It was the one good thing that came out of that whole mess. You see, my parents divorced when I was about four. My mother told me my father had been involved with another woman, so she divorced him and tried to keep me and my sister away from him as much as possible. So I didn't see much of him for about six years. Then, when I was diagnosed with cancer, he insisted on seeing me. We really formed a relationship for the first time. He would take me out for ice cream and talk with me about what was happening to me. No one else would. Somehow he made things a little easier for me. And we've continued to be close ever since. He's really there for me.

Therapist: Sounds like you really value your relationship with him.

Edie: I do. I wish Roberto and Ava could have that kind of bond.

Therapist: We'll certainly talk more about your experience with cancer and your fears about Ava developing cancer, but maybe this is a good time to talk about your family situation. How do you perceive the relationship between Roberto and Ava?

Edie: It's interesting because they look a lot alike, both tall and big boned, have similar personalities, but they conflict quite a bit. Both of them are pretty headstrong. Roberto is really a workaholic. If he's not actually at work, he's glued to the computer, trying out some new piece of software or surfing the Internet. He's really good at his work and seems to thrive on new challenges, but he almost feels like a visitor in our home.

Therapist: How does that affect you?

Edie: I feel a real sense of loss. Roberto and I were so happy when we first married.

It felt like we couldn't be together enough. We would take walks and go dancing and go to the beach. Anything we did together was wonderful. And then gradually things changed. . . .

Therapist: Changed?

Edie: Yes, I guess it started when we decided to have a baby. That cursed cancer came into the picture again. The doctors thought it was unlikely that I could become pregnant because of all the medical treatments I had. But I was determined. We saw every specialist I could find, and after many months of trying I did become pregnant with Ava. That really took a toll on our marriage. Even sex went on a time schedule, just trying to do everything we could to conceive. It was worth it to have Ava, but things have been difficult ever since.

Therapist: So having Ava was a great joy for you, but it sounds like you had to pay quite a price.

Edie: Yes, and then when we tried to have a second child, things got even worse. Years of trying. I guess we have given up on that now, at least Roberto has. Ava is wonderful, but I still wish I had a second child.

Therapist: This sounds like a real loss for you.

Edie: Yes, it is.

Therapist: This, too, is something we want to talk more about. But I'd like to broaden the picture and talk about some other parts of your life. What would a typical day be like for you?

Edie: Not very exciting. I get up early, get dressed, wake Ava and Roberto, make breakfast, and help Ava get ready for school. After they both have left, if it's a day I don't have to go to work, I might clean the house, do some shopping, plan dinner, and then I make sure to be home when Ava gets back from school. If I have any extra time, I read or watch television. Last year I went back to work part time. I'm employed as a librarian, working two days a week.

Therapist: How do you feel about the way you spend your time?

Edie: It's all right. We have a beautiful home, and I want to be there for Ava. Lately I've started to think about working more hours, though. I loved being home with Ava, but I really missed having a job and being in more contact with the world. I was out of work so long that I was worried about learning the new computer systems that the libraries use, but I've managed so far.

Therapist: So for now, your time is focused on caring for your family and working part time. Let's look at some other aspects of your current life. In addition to your father, what contact do you have with other family members?

Edie: I see my mother fairly often. She comes over at least once a week, usually after Ava comes home from school, so they can have some time together.

Therapist: What is your time with your mother like?

Edie: We get along all right most of the time.

Therapist: I hear some mixed feelings there.

Edie: I just can't respect the choices my mother made, and it makes me angry. My mother remarried when I was about 14. I don't like to say this about anyone, but I really hate my stepfather. I lived with him and my mother for four years, and I don't think he ever said a kind word to me. Any little thing I would do wrong, like leave my school books on the table, he would scream at me and hit me. And he treated my mother that way too. Still does. I don't know why she stayed with him.

Therapist: Sounds like you have a lot of anger at your stepfather. How do you handle those feelings?

Edie: I try not to think about him much. I rarely see him; and of course, I won't let Ava be alone with him. But things still happen that make me angry. Like last week, my mother was visiting, and we were going to take Ava shopping to get a dress for her birthday party. We were practically out the door when he calls, saying he doesn't have to work late after all, and my mother should come home and make dinner. And off she goes without a second thought.

Therapist: So that was an example of a time when you had some bad feelings about your relationship with your mother as well as anger at your stepfather. How do those feelings affect your relationship with her?

Edie: I used to tell her how I felt. And when I was a teenager, I let her know how unhappy I was. But it didn't seem to make any difference to her, so I just gave up. She knows how I feel, but she won't change. It's a real barrier between us.

Therapist: It sounds like you have found a way to maintain a relationship with your mother but that you wish it could be better.

Edie: Yes, I do.

Therapist: That might be another aspect of your life that we could work on in counseling.

Edie: Yes, I'd like that.

Therapist: Besides your mother and father, I know you have an older sister. What is your relationship with her like?

Edie: That's another relationship that has had problems over the years. We used to be very close when we were children. She's four years older than I am, and she would try to protect me from . . . things.

Therapist: Protect you?

Edie: We had some problems with my grandparents, but I don't want to talk about that.

Therapist: That's fine. Perhaps as we continue to work together, you will want to talk about that, but that is up to you. How do you and your sister get along now?

Edie: We don't see each other much. She lives in Las Vegas, likes the fast track. Beth's had lots of problems with drugs and men. I tried to talk to her and helped her out with money a couple of times, but it never really made a difference. Actually, though, she seems to have settled down some. She's living with a woman. . . . I guess she's a lesbian. At first I was real uncomfortable with that, but whenever I call her, she seems okay. This sounds like her best relationship yet.

Therapist: So there has been a sort of reversal in your relationship with your sister. When you were younger, she tried to protect you from some difficult situations, but as adults, you have tried to protect her.

Edie: True, but neither of us was really able to protect the other one.

Therapist: You wish it had been different?

Edie: Yes, I do. But Beth is doing better.

Therapist: And that must be a relief for you. I wonder what your own use of drugs and alcohol is like?

Edie: No problems there for me. I had all the drugs I wanted when I had cancer. I never drank much, but I had to stop drinking for so long when I was trying to become pregnant that I just never started again.

Therapist: You've told me about your history of cancer, but what is your current medical condition like?

Edie: The doctors say I'm doing well, though they think I might go into menopause early because of the chemotherapy. I have gained a lot of weight though, nearly 50 pounds since before I was pregnant. I feel tired a lot . . . maybe because of the extra weight.

Therapist: Tell me about your sleeping and eating.

Edie: I have trouble falling asleep most nights, and then I'm tired for the rest of the day because I have to get up early. My eating isn't very good either. I try to make nutritious meals for my family, but I snack during the day . . . peanut butter, cookies, whatever is around. I know I should do something about my weight and get some exercise, but I've been saying that for years and haven't done anything. Maybe you can help me with that too.

Therapist: We can certainly talk about ways to address those concerns. There are a few more areas I want to cover before we finish our session today. I know you are employed as a librarian, but I'd like to hear more about your education and work.

Edie: I was always a good student and enjoyed school. I guess it was an escape for me from all the problems at home. The only time when school got bad was during my cancer treatments; all the kids would tease me, and I hated to go to school. I was never very social or popular, and I guess I withdrew even more after that. But I still got good grades. My goal was to get a scholarship so I could go away to college. And I did! So I left home when I finished high school and went to the state university, majored in English. I liked to read, so that major made sense to me. But after I graduated, I really didn't know what to do. I worked in sales for a while, but that was definitely not right for me. After a year or so, I decided to get my master's in library science. I borrowed some money from my dad and went to graduate school. I was able to get a good job with the New York Public Library right after I got my degree, paid my father back for the loan, and was moving up in the system when Roberto and I got married. I guess my priorities shifted then. I really focused more on my marriage and trying to become pregnant, but work was still really rewarding for me. I felt like I had found my niche there.

Therapist: So your academic work and your job as a librarian have been great sources of success and pride to you.

Edie: Well, you're putting it more strongly than I would, but I guess you're right. In some ways, I feel more comfortable in the library than anywhere else I've ever been.

Therapist: So it also is a source of comfort for you. There is almost a spiritual quality to your talk about the library, and that makes me wonder about the place of religion and spirituality in your life.

Edie: Formal religion doesn't mean much to me anymore. Both of my parents are Jewish, but we hardly ever went to synagogue, just on the high holidays. I never had any religious education either. Somehow my parents believed that Judaism would magically become important to me, but when I asked my mother if I could go to Hebrew school like some of my friends, she said it cost too much. I still put down Jewish on forms that ask about your religion, but I don't really practice the religion. And of course, Roberto isn't Jewish. His family was Catholic and they used to go to church, but he hasn't gone in years. I worry about Ava's lack of religious education, but she doesn't seem to miss it. I do talk to her about God, though. I think believing in God comforted me as a child, and I want her to have that feeling too. When she was little, I taught her prayers to say at bedtime, but I don't think she prays anymore. I gave you a long answer to your question, but I guess this is a part of my life that confuses me. I have always felt a connection to God, to a spiritual side of myself, but then I wonder if I'm being a hypocrite because I don't follow any organized religion. Maybe that's something we can talk about, too, but it's pretty far down on the list.

Therapist: We can get back to that, though. I'd like to hear some more about your childhood years. We've talked about your parents' divorce, your relationships with your sister and your parents, your stepfather, your treatment for cancer, and your enjoyment of most of your school years. What else stands out as important during those years?

Edie: Not too much. My mother says I was precocious as a baby, walking and talking early. I had a few friends in the neighborhood, but I've always been kind of shy and was never very popular. I only dated three or four guys very briefly before I met Roberto. I guess I haven't told you about my grandparents, my mother's parents. . . .

Therapist: What do you want to tell me about them?

Edie: They took care of us when my mother went back to work after the divorce. I don't want to talk about them any more right now.

Therapist: All right. Let's put that topic on the shelf until you want to take it down. What other parts of your life might be important to talk about?

Edie: I do want to mention my friend Sandi. She lived near me and had her first child when I was pregnant with Ava. Our children played together, and we became good friends. She had breast cancer about six years ago and I tried to help her with that. We got to be very close. She's doing great now. Three years ago she moved to California. I really miss her, but we're still in touch; e-mail is great for that.

Therapist: So Sandi is another important person in your life, but here's another relationship that has involved loss. What else do you want to be sure to mention before we finish our session?

Edie: I think that's about it. I didn't think I would have so much to say!

Therapist: Yes, you did cover a lot of ground. I can see that trying to get some help through counseling is really important to you and that you are already involved in that process. Even though we have covered a great deal, I'm sure we'll get back to most of these topics again and probably also find some important areas we overlooked, but it's time to stop for today. How did you feel about your first counseling session?

Edie: I liked talking to you; I wasn't sure I would. Where do we go from here?

Therapist: Let's schedule another appointment and try to hone in on some goals.

EXERCISES

The following exercises are designed to help you learn more about both asking questions and conducting an intake interview. In addition to working on these specific exercises, try to be more conscious of the questions you ask in your everyday activities, particularly when you meet a new person. Do you tend to ask open or closed questions? Are your questions just part of making conversation, or are you consciously trying to get to know the person you have met? Are you getting the responses you had hoped for? If not, what might you do differently?

Exercises in Questioning

Large-Group Exercise Read the following statements from a client, a 42-year-old woman whose husband has died recently, and then review the four clinician responses to each client statement. For each response, consider

- Whether the question is open or closed
- The impact each question is likely to have on the client
- The information you expect will be elicited by each question
- The direction in which each question moves the session
- Which question seems most likely to advance counseling in a positive way

Scenario 1

Client: It's been three months since my husband died and two months since I began treatment, but I miss him even more than I did right after his death.

Counselor A: Why do you think that is?

Counselor B: Do you think I am doing something wrong in counseling you?

Counselor C: What prevents you from getting over his death?

Counselor D: What feelings come up for you as you think about missing him?

Scenario 2

Client: Even though I miss George, I have gone back to work, and I'm concentrating fairly well.

Counselor A: How are you managing to do that?

Counselor B: How do you feel about that?

Counselor C: Do you think you are ready to stop counseling now?

Counselor D: Is your work still as demanding as it was?

Scenario 3

Client: I know I should get out and meet new people, but I just feel stuck.

Counselor A: Where are you stuck?

Counselor B: Did you sign up for the art class as we agreed?

Counselor C: What has helped you when you have felt stuck before?

Counselor D: Do you think you could be sabotaging your efforts to change?

Small-Group Exercise   Your client is a 12-year-old boy who is having difficulties related to socialization and self-esteem. For each client statement, write a question that you think will have a positive impact on the treatment process. Then share your questions with your group. For each of your questions, consider

- Whether the question is open or closed
- The impact the question is likely to have on the client
- The information you expect will be elicited by each question
- The direction in which each question moves the session

1. No matter how hard I try to make friends, it just doesn't work. There must really be something wrong with me.
2. I tried to talk to my dad about this problem. He said, "You just need to develop an interest in sports, and then you'll fit in fine with the other boys."
3. Roger asked me to sit with him at lunch. I really wanted to, but I felt so scared. I just said, "No, thanks," and walked away.

Exercise in Conducting an Intake Interview

Small-Group Exercise   General directions for the small-group exercises are included in Chapter 1. Refer to those directions before beginning this exercise.

Now that you have the ability to make good use of questions, try out that skill by practicing an intake interview. Divide into your groups of four people, and then break each of those groups into two dyads. Each pair should take a turn conducting an interview; one person should assume the role of the clinician, while the other becomes the client. Tape-record this interview to facilitate analysis and feedback.

The people who are being interviewed should think about a comfortable way to approach the intake process. They can assume a persona, making believe they are someone they know well and presenting information as that person might. Details can be changed to protect the person they are role playing. Interviewees might also choose to talk about themselves if that feels comfortable. As with any client, keep in mind that you do not need to answer all the clinician's questions, and it is your right to disclose as much or as little as you choose. However, because this is a learning experience, try to approach this exercise in a way that allows you to be a cooperative and collaborative client who will not present the clinician with too great a challenge. Allow approximately 20 minutes for the interview and 10 minutes for feedback.

While one pair is engaged in an intake interview, the other pair should observe and take notes, preparing to provide feedback. Remember to emphasize strengths when giving feedback. When identifying weaknesses in the role play, be sure to suggest alternatives that might have been more successful. Feedback should cover the following topics:

- The overall tone of the interview
- How well important areas of information were covered in the interview
- The nature of the questions that were asked
- The impact the questions seemed to have on the client
- Whether the questions elicited the desired information
- The direction in which questions moved the session
- The pacing of the questions and their integration with other types of interventions
- The strengths of the interview
- Ways in which the interview might have been improved

SUMMARY

This chapter has reviewed the importance of background in understanding clients. It has also provided guidelines, examples, and exercises to teach readers how to ask helpful questions and to conduct an intake interview that will successfully obtain background information while building rapport. Chapter 4 will present the ideas and approaches to treatment developed by Sigmund Freud, a master at using past history to help people change in positive ways.

Chapter 4

SIGMUND FREUD AND PSYCHOANALYSIS

In 1993, *Time Magazine* asked, "Is Freud dead?" The question of whether psychoanalysis, which reflects the ideas of Sigmund Freud, is obsolete has often been raised and explored. However, even the frequent revisiting of this question testifies to the strength and influence of Freud's theories. In 1998–1999, for example, the Library of Congress in Washington, DC, hosted a large exhibit titled, *Sigmund Freud: Conflict and Culture*. In 1999, Prochaska and Norcross reported that, among American psychotherapists, 18 percent of clinical psychologists, 12 percent of counseling psychologists, 35 percent of psychiatrists, 33 percent of social workers, and 11 percent of counselors viewed their primary theoretical orientation as psychanalytic or psychodynamic. An even greater testimony to Freud's impact lies in the foundation that his work has laid for today's counseling and psychotherapy. Freud succeeded in bringing our knowledge of personality, human development, and symptoms of psychological problems into the modern age. His efforts required great courage: he disagreed radically with the thinking of his peers, withstood years of verbal and written attacks, and worked prodigiously to advance his ideas. Because of Freud's contributions, clinicians' efforts to advance people's psychological growth and help them deal with emotional difficulties have become much more successful.

THE PERSON WHO DEVELOPED PSYCHOANALYSIS

Sigmund Freud was born in Freiberg, Moravia, on May 6, 1856. His father was 40 years old, a widower, with two sons, when he married his second wife, who was only 19 years old at the time. Freud was the couple's first child, born two years after his parents' marriage. As the first born and reportedly his mother's favorite (Jones, 1953), Freud always had a special place in his family, although his mother gave birth to 7 more children in the next 10 ten years. His father, a busy merchant with a commanding but gentle disposition, seems to have been a role model for his son. When Freud was 19 months old, his 8-month-old brother Julius died. Freud recalled feeling jealous and resentful of his brother and later reproached himself when his brother died. Early memories such as these seem likely to have contributed to Freud's later emphasis on the formative power of early childhood experiences.

Freud's family was Jewish, and this cultural and religious background affected Freud in many ways throughout his life. His Jewish heritage, with its emphasis on learning and family, contributed to Freud's appreciation for study, history, and in-depth analysis. It also influenced his place of residence and his career choice, probably colored the reception his work received, and eventually meant that he had to flee from Austria when Hitler came into power.

When Freud was a child, the ill-treatment of Jews in many parts of Europe led his family to move to Vienna, Austria (at that time a relatively safe place for Jews), where he spent most of his life. Freud was a diligent student, studying at the University of Vienna between 1873 and 1881, when he completed medical school. Jones (1953) has reported that career choices open to Jews in Vienna at that time included business, law, and medicine. Although Freud felt drawn to politics or social work, he chose medicine as the best option available to him. He was always interested in learning about the mind and did his residency in neurology, beginning his medical career in theoretical rather than applied medical work.

In 1884, Freud began studying and experimenting with cocaine as a tool to heighten mental powers (Mahoney, 1998). However, evidence of the negative impact of this substance on his colleagues dampened his enthusiasm for the drug.

Love was an important influence on his career. He became engaged to Martha Bernays, daughter of the chief rabbi of Hamburg, in 1882. To earn enough money to marry and support a family, Freud took a position at a psychiatric clinic. Over their four-year engagement, Freud wrote more than 900 letters to his wife-to-be, providing her with the details of his daily life.

He married Martha Bernays in 1886 and, about the same time, opened a private practice in neuropathology in Vienna. Growing up in a large family probably influenced him to have a large family himself and to value and feel comfortable with family around him. The couple had 6 children during the first 10 years of their marriage. Martha's sister Minna also was a part of the family, living with them from 1896 until her death in 1941, helping Martha and offering emotional support to Freud.

Freud's work and his family were the most important parts of his life. Jones (1955, p. 386) speaks of the "unshakable devotion and a perfect harmony of understanding" between Freud and his wife and of Freud's efforts to raise his children in an atmosphere that would keep anxiety low, minimize limitations and criticism, and allow personalities to develop freely. Although he often saw 10 patients a day, he found time for his hobbies, especially collecting antiquities, reading biographies and other literature, studying mushrooms and rare wildflowers, and traveling. He was much affected by family joys and sorrows, and his letters reflect the profound impact of the military involvement of his three sons and the capture of one during World War I, the death of his daughter Sophie in 1920, and the death of a grandson in 1923.

In that same year, Freud was diagnosed with cancer, probably related to the approximately 20 cigars he smoked each day. During his remaining years, he had 33 operations on his jaw and palate, which prolonged his life but caused him considerable pain. In his later years, he wore a prosthesis in his mouth and wrote frequently of the severe discomfort caused by this apparatus and his many surgeries. Despite this, he continued to see patients and to write until the year of his death. We will consider his works in the next section of this chapter.

In March 1938, the Nazis invaded Austria. Although he was 82 years old and was seriously ill, Freud decided that he must leave Austria. His daughter Anna and his son Martin had already been questioned by the Nazis, and the family members felt that they would not survive long in Vienna. Freud, his wife, and his daughter Anna left Vienna in June 1938 and went to England, where he was welcomed by friends. He tried to bring his four sisters with him. Unfortunately, they were not permitted to leave the country, and Freud was only allowed to leave money for their welfare. All four sisters died in concentration camps during the next five years.

Despite additional surgery in England, Freud's cancer was deemed incurable. Because he wanted to continue writing and seeing patients as long as possible, he put off taking the pain killers that might cloud his mind until four months before his death. He died on September 23, 1939, leaving a legacy that many of his followers have shaped into modern psychotherapy.

Freud's early work focused on the study of neurology. His research on the brain and spinal cord were his first notable contributions to the field. During the 1880s, he became interested in the work of Josef Breuer, a well-known physician in Vienna. Breuer was using hypnosis and verbal expression to treat emotional disorders. His famous case of Anna O., a woman who experienced conversion symptoms (paralysis of limbs; disturbances of sight, eating, and speech) as well as dissociative symptoms in relation to the death of her father, captured Freud's attention; and he became increasingly interested in psychological disorders (Freud, 1938). He began learning about neurotic disorders and ways to treat them. He learned hypnosis from Charcot and investigated the use of electrotherapy, baths, and massage treatments for people with psychological disorders. Although Freud sometimes used hypnosis, none of these other strategies seemed effective to him. Experimentation led him to initiate what he called the concentration technique, in which patients lay down with their eyes closed while Freud placed his hand on their foreheads and urged them to say whatever thoughts arose. He used questions to elicit material and promote self-exploration. This technique clearly is an early version of modern psychotherapy. Although Freud later stopped touching his patients in this way because of its erotic possibilities, he continued to emphasize the importance of patient self-expression and free association.

Freud first used the term *psychoanalysis* in a 1896 paper. His writings during the 1890s reflected growing awareness of the importance of sexuality in people's lives. He initially believed that symptoms of hysteria or neurosis were due to a childhood sexual experience, perhaps traumatic sexual abuse such as seduction of the child by the father. A combination of difficulty in substantiating this idea and the negative reactions it elicited led Freud to change his ideas. He subsequently focused more on infantile sexuality and fantasies rather than actual sexual experiences as instrumental in determining emotional difficulties. In retrospect, Freud probably was wiser than even he knew. More than 100 years later, clinicians are now well aware of the high incidence of child sexual abuse. Probably at least some of the patients who described to Freud early sexual experiences did indeed have them.

The combination of Freud's interest in understanding the human psyche and an effort to address some difficulties he was experiencing in his own life led him to explore the meaning of his own dreams and fantasies as well as his childhood sexual feelings toward his mother and anger toward his father. His major work, *Interpretation of Dreams* (Freud, 1938), was written between 1895 and 1899 and advanced the powerful concepts that dreams reflect repressed wishes and that mental and physical processes are intertwined. Freud's ideas were largely ignored or rejected when the book was published. However, again he expressed ideas that have only recently gained widespread acceptance: the close connection between the mind and the body.

Despite the mixed reactions to his work, Freud moved forward to collaborate with those colleagues who did share his viewpoints. In 1902, he suggested to Alfred Adler and several others that they meet to discuss Freud's work. This became the Vienna Psycho-Analytical Society, which met weekly at Freud's home. In 1910, Freud designated Carl Jung as president of the International Psycho-Analytical Association.

Adler and Jung eventually broke with Freud over theoretical differences, and both went on to make their own important contributions to psychotherapy. Chapters 5 and 6 of this book will discuss their work.

Growing international recognition of his work led to Freud's first visit to the United States in 1909, where he lectured at Clark University at the invitation of its president, Stanley Hall. Hall was a pioneer in experimental psychology and viewed Freud's work as a major contribution. Published as *Five Lectures on Psycho-Analysis*, these writings presented Freud's ideas in a simple, comprehensible way. They were widely read and broadened awareness of his work.

By this time, Freud had replaced hypnosis with free association in his work and was emphasizing that analysts should experience their own analysis, a requirement still maintained by programs that train psychoanalysts. He also believed that patients needed to lie on a couch during treatment in order to relax them, facilitate self-expression, allow transference reactions to develop, and enable analysts to think freely without worrying about their nonverbal messages. Patients were told never to withhold any thoughts so that Freud could understand the unconscious, typically sexually related fantasies, stemming from early childhood experiences, that had produced symptoms.

Freud's writings during these years included not only his theoretical works but also lengthy case studies that reflected the details of his ideas. *Dora* (Decker, 1998) was the report of an 11-week analysis that Freud performed on an 18-year-old woman whose father was having an affair. Her father's lover befriended Dora, while the woman's husband made sexual advances toward her, creating a situation that would cause most people to have emotional difficulties. *Little Hans* (Freud, 1936) was Freud's analysis of a five-year-old boy who would not leave his house because of a fear that he would be bitten by a horse. Freud conducted the analysis secondhand, meeting only with the boy's father, and enabled the father to help his son by using Freud's insights into the boy's displacement of his fear of his father onto horses. Fourteen years later, the boy visited Freud to report that Freud had cured him of his phobia of horses. Other important cases include the so-called Man with Rats, who had what Freud called an obsessional neurosis characterized by doubts and compulsions as well as terrifying dreams involving rats. This 11 month analysis was also very successful. Another patient, Wolf Man, sought help from Freud when the patient was 23 years old and almost totally incapacitated by his severe compulsions. Freud believed this man may have witnessed parental intercourse when he was a child, exacerbating his ambivalent feelings toward his father. After four years of treatment, this patient, too, was free of serious symptoms.

By World War I, Freud was seeing 12 to 13 patients a day, each for 55 minutes with 5 minutes in between. His services were sought by the rich and famous. He reportedly cured the conductor Bruno Walter of partial paralysis of his right arm in six sessions and required only four sessions to relieve composer Gustav Mahler of a problem with impotence by exploring its psychodynamic origins (Jones, 1957).

Freud's interests broadened during the war years. He became interested in what was then called shell shock or traumatic neurosis, symptoms that developed after exposure to war experiences. The primary treatment for this disorder had been electrical stimulation of the skin and muscles. According to Freud, psychoanalysis, not electricity, was the proper treatment for this disorder, which he believed reflected an emotional conflict between the desire to escape and to honor one's sense of duty. Freud's thinking paved the way for our modern understanding of posttraumatic stress disorder.

Freud also became interested in understanding homosexuality, writing, "Homosexuality is assuredly no advantage, but it is nothing to be ashamed of, no vice, no degradation, it cannot be classified as an illness" (Jones, 1957, p. 195). Here, too, Freud's ideas were very advanced; not until 1980 did the American Psychiatric Association officially determine that homosexuality is not a mental disorder.

Freud was less astute in his understanding of women and has been criticized for this, particularly during the 1960s, when women's groups denounced his work as antifeminist. Initially, he viewed women's psychological development as a variation of male psychological development (Stafford-Clark, 1965). However, he eventually came to realize his lack of understanding in this area. Jones (1955) quoted Freud as asking, "What does a woman want?" Jones concluded, "There is little doubt that Freud found the psychology of women more enigmatic than that of men." (p. 421). At the same time, Freud always valued women, including his wife; his daughter Anna, who will be discussed later in this book; and his women patients, colleagues, and supporters. His later work advanced a more contemporary view of women, perceiving them as more personal and emotional in their decisions than men are and as having a more flexible superego. These ideas are remarkably similar to those of Carol Gilligan (1993), which examine differences in girls' and boys' emotional development.

Freud continued to broaden his interests in his later writings, which addressed not only the human psyche but also art, religion, anthropology, sociology, biology, and literature. He began to place greater emphasis on context and society and acknowledged the important ways in which they both reflected and shaped human development. He expanded his definition of the unconscious, viewing it as containing more than simply repressed material, and also broadened his definition of sexuality, viewing it as a great source of energy. In addition, he expressed his approval of "lay analysts"—people such as his daughter Anna Freud, who had been trained in analysis, had themselves been analyzed, but had not received an M.D. degree. We may think of these lay analysts as the forerunners of today's non-medical clinicians: the psychologists, counselors, social workers, and psychiatric nurses who are our primary providers of psychotherapy.

IMPORTANT THEORETICAL CONCEPTS

Freud began his work as a theoretician, and it is through his comprehensive theory of personality that he has made his major contributions. This section reviews the most important aspects of his theory, including his concepts of human nature, the three structures of the personality, how personality develops, levels of consciousness, and the meaning of symptoms. Freud's ideas, like those of many of the theorists discussed in this book, have great depth and complexity; and this book can only provide an overview of those ideas. Readers are strongly encouraged to read more about all of these theorists.

View of Human Nature

Freud placed great emphasis on the influence of biology and of early childhood experiences. He believed that, because of biology, people go through predictable stages of psychosocial development and must struggle to find a balance between their strong sexual drives and their need to behave in socially acceptable ways. He also recognized the importance of context. For example, he viewed people as seeking to win love and approval by acting in ways that reflected the dictates of their families and societies.

Freud has been criticized for taking a deterministic stance, placing great emphasis on irrational and instinctual forces in shaping the person. Certainly, he does view those forces as very important, but perhaps the essential message in his work is that people need not be the victims of biology. Rather, we can use psychotherapy and other sources of help and personal growth to gain insight, lessen the power of the unconscious, and free ourselves to make conscious and healthy choices. Understanding early development as well as the pressures of the libido and the superego and strengthening our egos can enable us to lead the sorts of lives and have the sorts of relationships that we desire. Certainly, Freud himself achieved much both personally and professionally, apparently reflecting his own success in balancing the competing pressures inside him.

Personality Structure

According to Freud, the personality is comprised of three systems: the id, the superego, and the ego. These structures often overlap and intertwine and are not discrete entities, although each has distinctive properties. As a whole, they operate the personality.

The Id   The *id* is the first system of the personality. Present at birth, it encompasses all the inherited systems, including the instincts, and is largely unconscious. The id derives its energy from the bodily processes and is in close touch with the needs and messages of the body, seeking to meet them when possible. The id is subjective and emotional and, in its pure form, not moderated by the external world. Simply put, the id wants what it wants when it wants it. The id, like the infant in which it originates, is intolerant of tension, pain, and discomfort and seeks to avoid them by pursuing pleasure and gratification (the pleasure principle). It is demanding; and its needs, rather than logic, morality, or the constraints of society, determine the direction of its wants.

The id has two important strategies for obtaining pleasure: reflex actions and primary process. Reflex actions include automatic processes such as coughing and blinking, which reduce tensions, especially those of a biological nature such as a tickle in the throat or a speck in the eye. Primary process is more complex; it allows people to form a mental image of a remedy for their discomfort, a wish fulfillment. Freud believed that dreams served this function, offering a wish-fulfillment image. Although the image may assuage some of the discomfort, it also can cause frustration in failing to really resolve the problem. It is the ego, discussed later in this section, that takes form to help people truly find wish fulfillment and reduce discomfort in realistic ways.

Freud believed that people have both life instincts and death or destructive instincts. Although his concept of a death instinct has not received much support over the years, recognizing the possible presence of these forces can help us to gain insight into human development. Life instincts, reflecting the needs of the id, lead us to pursue pleasure and avoid pain. The *libido*, present at birth, is an important aspect of the life instinct. This was originally defined by Freud as sexual desire, but its meaning has been broadened over the years to refer to energy and vitality, a zest for life. A desire for sexual fulfillment is only one facet of the life instinct, but it is an essential one, the one that leads people to procreate and continue the human race.

The Superego   The *superego* can be thought of as the opposite of the id. The superego is a sort of rigid conscience that internalizes the rules and guidelines of a person's world. Messages from parents, teachers, and society as well as racial, cultural, and national traditions are important contributors to the development of an individual's superego. The moral code of the superego is a perfectionist one, diligently determining the difference between good and bad, right and wrong. The formation of the superego allows self-control to take the place of parental control. When people follow the idealistic dictates of their superego, they typically feel proud and righteous but may sacrifice experiences of pleasure and gratification. On the other hand, when they fail to listen to the superego, feelings of shame, guilt, and anxiety may result. The superego serves an essential function in curtailing the drives of the id; but like the id, the superego is too controlling and extreme in its directives. The id impels the person toward full gratification of all instinctual needs, while the superego seeks to block fulfillment of those same needs.

The Ego   The *ego*, like the superego, becomes differentiated from the id as the child develops, although it is energy from the id that provides the power for both the ego and the superego. The ego is not present at birth but evolves as the baby realizes its separateness from the mother.

The ego has been described as "the mental agent of rational and self-conscious selfhood" (Brunner, 1998, p. 83). It can be thought of as a mediator and organizer. The ego is aware of both the pressures of the id and the constraints of the superego. Using logic, intelligence, objectivity, and awareness of external reality, it seeks to integrate all those sources into choices and behaviors that promote self-preservation.

The ego is guided by the reality principle or reality testing and has considerable power; it can effect changes in the environment, postpone or suppress instinctual demands, and encourage sound moral judgment and flexibility. The ego seeks to moderate the primary process of the id while promoting fulfillment of its needs. A healthy ego can consider the internal and external demands and pressures on a person, modify and integrate those demands, decide when and how it is best for the person to respond to those demands, and formulate plans that will lead to wise choices and behaviors.

Keep in mind that Freud's concept of the id (the biological component), the ego (the psychological component), and the superego (the social component) is simply a sort of map designed to clarify the nature of the personality. Just as states and countries are separated by artificial boundaries, so are these structures of the personality separated as artificial constructs. In reality, they operate together as the internal forces that form our personalities. However, using this theoretical structure can facilitate understanding of strengths and areas of difficulties in a personality.

Stages of Development

Freud believed that people developed according to predictable stages, with the stages during the first five years of life being the most important. The nature of development during those early years is a major factor in determining the later emotional health of the person.

The Oral Stage   The *oral stage* makes up the first year or so of a child's life. The mouth is the most important zone of the body for the infant, with sucking and eating providing the nurturance that will sustain the child's life during the oral-incorporative phase. Biting is a way for the child to express aggression during the subsequent oral-aggressive period. The mouth also becomes the child's first erotic zone (Stafford-Clark, 1965). Issues of dependency and trust are particularly important during this initial stage (Erikson, 1963). In addition, Freud believed that developmental problems at this point could later manifest themselves in symbolic and sublimated forms through such symptoms such as gullibility (swallowing anything), overeating, and argumentativeness (oral aggressiveness).

The Anal Stage   Freud termed the second stage of development the *anal stage* because of the importance of toilet training and the process of elimination between the ages of one and three. Pleasure during the first stage was associated with the oral functions. In this second stage, the focus of gratification shifts to the social pleasure of impressing the parents and the physical pleasure of emptying the bowels. Issues of autonomy versus shame and doubt typically arise during this period (Erikson, 1963) as children test limits, make mistakes, and try out new behaviors while learning skills that will give them more independence and control over their lives. Feelings about the body and its functions also are shaped during these years.

Psychoanalytic theory associates the development of several important character traits with the anal stage. Parents who encourage bowel and bladder control using means that are punitive and restrictive are believed to promote stingy, compulsive, controlling, and withholding characteristics in their children; those who reward and praise their children lavishly for appropriate elimination are likely to foster creativity. Understanding the relationships between children's bodily functions and their subsequent personality development can help define healthy parenting as well as provide insight into emotional difficulties that may stem from developmental problems during the early years.

The Phallic Stage   The third stage, between ages three and five, is known as the *phallic stage*. According to Freud, this complex stage is strongly related to our adult sexual relationships. During these years, feelings of pleasure become associated with the genitals, and masturbation and sexual fantasies develop. Freud believed that at this age children harbor unconscious sexual desires for the parent of the other gender along with an unconscious wish to eliminate the parent of the same gender, who is perceived as standing in the way of the child's desires. In boys, this is termed the *Oedipus complex*, referring to a man who, according to the literature of ancient Greece, unknowingly married his mother. Fear of retribution from the father causes boys to develop castration anxiety, which, in turn, allows them to repress these feelings and resolve the Oedipus complex appropriately through identification with the father. In girls, the parallel situation is referred to as the *Electra complex*, named after a woman in Greek literature who had strong feelings of love and devotion toward her father. Freud hypothesized that the female equivalent of castration anxiety is penis envy, in which girls become jealous and resentful because of their lack of a penis. Girls, like boys, typically resolve this phase by identifying with their same-gender parent.

Freud has been much criticized for his concept of penis envy, but keep in mind his own acknowledgement that he did not have a good understanding of female psychology. Modern psychoanalysts acknowledge the possibility that a girl may experience penis envy but also believe that a boy may have womb or breast envy. However, they downplay the importance of both patterns, viewing them as only one of many internal and external experiences that may be important in children's development.

In addition, although Freud saw many parallels between the ways in which both boys and girls passed through this stage, many modern theorists have emphasized the difference inherent in the fact that for both genders, the mother is typically the first love and source of nurturance. Mothers are, of course, the same gender as their daughters but not as their sons. Most girls, then, must shift the primary source of their attachment from women to men while boys do not need to make this shift, probably an important difference in their development of love and attachments.

Many aspects of emotional development evolve during the phallic years, including self-esteem and self-image, sexuality, need for love and approval, feelings toward authority figures, and sense of initiative. Those who do not resolve this stage successfully may be troubled by guilt, difficulty in intimate relationships, and a negative or confused sense of self.

The Latency Stage   Freud viewed the time between ages 5 and 11 as a relatively quiet period in a child's sexual development; therefore, he called these years the *latency stage*. Sexual drives become less important, while social interests increase. Children turn outward, form relationships, progress through school, and develop rewarding hobbies and activities. Emotional development focuses on their ability to take on and succeed in new challenges and endeavors and to set and achieve realistic goals. Children who negotiate this stage successfully typically develop feelings of empowerment and have initiative, while those who cannot deal with the demands of this developmental stage may develop feelings of low self-esteem.

The Genital Stage   The final stage is the *genital stage,* which follows the latency stage and continues throughout the life span. During this stage, adolescents and adults solidify their personal identities, develop caring and altruistic feelings toward others, establish positive loving and sexual relationships, and progress in successful careers. Each stage builds on and integrates the growth and learning of the previous stage and ideally results in the development of an emotionally healthy adult.

Levels of Consciousness

Most people have few, if any, memories of times before the age of three or four. In addition, we all have had experiences we either cannot recall at all or that only come into awareness when something reminds us of them, triggering their recall. What has happened to those memories?

According to Freud, we have three levels of consciousness: the conscious, the preconscious, and the unconscious. The *conscious* is material in awareness, always available to us. The *preconscious* holds information that may not be part of current awareness but which can be readily accessed. This material may be benign, such as the memory of a person we knew years ago but do not think of until we see her again in the grocery store; or it may be aversive, such as the memory of a car accident that returns to us each time we hear the screech of car brakes applied in a hurry. The *unconscious* holds memories that are highly charged, including repressed drives and impulses (such as a child's sexual feelings toward a parent), and recollections of experiences that may be too painful or unacceptable to be allowed into the conscious or preconscious. Freud believed that the unconscious held many times more memories than were in the preconscious or the conscious. Psychoanalysis can bring memories from the unconscious into the conscious. However, without benefit of therapy, those memories are likely either to remain in the unconscious or to emerge into consciousness in symbolic or distorted ways, perhaps via dreams or symptoms.

One of the major issues in mental health today focuses on repressed memories of traumatic experiences. Many theorists and clinicians believe that experiences such as sexual or physical abuse of a child can be repressed by that child, sometimes emerging later in an altered form as a result of some reminder or trigger. Others, however, do not believe that this process happens and deny the reality of repressed memories. Freud certainly would support the concept that very painful memories can be buried in the unconscious.

Dreams and Other Reflections of the Unconscious

Freud believed that dreams, symptoms, and errors all reflected the unconscious and its fantasies. His books, *Psychopathology of Everyday Life* (1938) and *The Interpretation of Dreams* (1938) discuss, in depth, the process by which the unconscious is revealed. Freud believed that all dreams are meaningful and that dream analysis is perhaps the most important way to understand people. He viewed dreams as fulfilling wishes or impulses that could not be allowed into awareness, providing a vehicle for working through disturbing thoughts and feelings. Although people may recall the manifest content of dreams, the defenses of the ego displace and condense the underlying significance of a dream so that it is disguised. Repressed events and emotions may be represented in dreams by items or events that seem unimportant but may nevertheless cause anxiety because of their latent meaning.

For example, a young woman had a dream of herself frolicking in the park with a dog. Earlier that day, she had taken a walk and had come upon a couple making love. Analysis revealed that the dog represented a married co-worker of her father's whom she found attractive and indirectly may have also suggested an attraction to her father. The park was a place where she had seen sexual behavior taking place. The dream, then, reflected the fulfillment of her repressed wish to have a sexual relationship with her father's friend and perhaps reflected her childhood desire for her father.

For Freud, errors, omissions, slips, and poorly performed tasks also had latent meaning, and the term *Freudian slip* has now come to mean a misstatement that reveals an underlying wish or feeling that may not even have been in the person's conscious awareness. For example, a man who was attracted to his next-door neighbor, a woman called Lou, left her a note about a package that had been delivered to him by mistake. However, he addressed the note to "Dear Love" rather than "Dear Lou."

Defense Mechanisms

The ego uses defense mechanisms to protect people from anxiety, particularly anxiety arising from unacceptable wishes and impulses. Everyone has defenses. Some are healthy, mature defenses that promote adjustment and enable people to transform undesirable wishes into ones that can be fulfilled. For example, sublimation is a defense mechanism that can change a self-destructive sexual desire into the drive to create a work of art. On the other hand, some defenses distort reality and interfere with efforts to build relationships. An example is splitting, in which people view themselves and others as being either all good or all bad and vacillate from idealization to devaluation of themselves and others. Which defense mechanism people use at a particular time depends on their level of development and the degree of anxiety they are experiencing at the time.

The study of people's use of defense mechanisms is a fruitful line of inquiry today and provides insight into ways in which clinicians can help people cope with anxiety and other emotional difficulties. For example, a study by Snarey, Son, Kuehne, Hauser, and Vaillant (1987) focused on how men in early adulthood coped with infertility. The study found that men who were able to redirect their parenting needs into substitute parentlike activities such as mentoring a child or leading a youth group were most likely to eventually adopt a child and remain married. However, those men whose defense mechanisms did not enable them to redirect their needs in this way and instead used self-centered substitution styles such as focusing on themselves, their pets, or their possessions were more likely to divorce and least likely to achieve fulfillment of their generativity needs in middle adulthood.

Defense mechanisms can be categorized into the following four groups (Kaplan, Sadock, & Grebb, 1994; Seligman, 1996a):

1. Narcissistic or psychotic defenses are evident in children and people with psychotic disorders and in dreams. These defense mechanisms include distortion, denial, and delusional projection.
2. Immature defenses are common in adolescents as well as in people with mood, personality, and impulse control disorders. Included in this group are such defenses such as projection, regression, splitting, devaluation, and acting out.
3. Neurotic defenses are common in most people, although they can lead to or reflect problem areas. Included in this group are such defenses such as rationalization, intellectualization, and displacement.
4. Finally, prominent defenses found in healthy adults include humor, sublimation, conscious or semiconscious suppression, and compensation, among others.

TREATMENT USING PSYCHOANALYSIS

Extensive supervision and training is required to master the rich array of treatment strategies associated with psychoanalysis. As with the theory of psychoanalysis, this book presents an overview of these strategies, but readers should bear in mind that additional training will be needed before they can be used skillfully.

Goals of Psychoanalysis

The overall goal of psychoanalysis is "the best possible psychological equilibrium for the functioning of the ego" (Stafford-Clark, 1965, p. 213). Specific treatment objectives include the following (Baker, 1985):

- Improving the ego's conscious and mature control over irrational impulses and instincts
- Enriching the nature and variety of the ego defense mechanisms so that they are more effective, mature, and adaptable
- Encouraging development of perspectives that are grounded in an accurate and clear assessment of reality and that promote adjustment.
- Developing a capacity for healthy and rewarding intimate relationships along with the ability to express oneself in rewarding ways
- Reducing the perfectionism, rigidity, and punitiveness of the superego

Freud's writings offer a rich array of approaches to achieving these goals.

Therapeutic Alliance

Psychoanalysis as performed by Freud as well as by modern therapists is a long-term, intensive process. People are typically seen for treatment from two to five times a week for three to five years. Freud used 55-minute sessions with a 5-five minute break between sessions. He advocated having the patient lie on a couch while the therapist sat in a chair positioned behind the patient's head so the therapist could not be observed during the session. This was designed to both relax and reduce distractions for the patient and to allow the therapist to remain as anonymous as possible. Therapist neutrality was important in fostering the development of transference.

Although the patients do most of the talking in psychoanalysis, therapists are active in guiding the session in meaningful directions and promoting the uncovering of repressed material. They can be described as listening with a third ear attuned to underlying meanings, symbols, contradictions, and important omissions that may point the way to unlocking the unconscious. Questions, interpretations, free association, and encouragement of abreaction are common interventions that psychoanalysts use in their work.

Transference and Countertransference

In transference the patient projects onto the therapist characteristics of another person, usually a parent, and reacts to the therapist as though he or she really does possess those characteristics. Transference involves a distortion or misperception of the therapist and is not a direct response to the way the therapist actually is. Clearly, the unobserved and neutral psychoanalyst is more likely to elicit transference reactions than is a therapist who engages in self-disclosure and interacts more actively with clients.

Transference can be positive, negative, or mixed. For example, a client may project onto the therapist the seductive but loving traits of his mother (mixed), the angry and rejecting attitude of his father (negative), or the warm and nurturing characteristics of his grandmother (positive). Freud saw the establishment of transference as a key component of successful treatment. Some degree of emotional health and a capacity to form relationships is necessary for people to establish a transference. That is one reason why Freud's approach works best for people with neurotic rather than psychotic disorders who maintain contact with reality.

Three stages are involved in the lengthy process of working through a transference. Once the transference develops, it is further established and explored in order to elicit repressed material. Gradually, the original dysfunctional pattern reemerges, now in terms of the transference to the therapist. Finally, the origins of the transference are understood and resolved, freeing the client to relate to others in healthier ways and strengthening the ego.

Although countertransference was not a salient part of Freud's work, many therapists today from both psychoanalytic and other theoretical orientations pay attention to it. In countertransference, a clinician projects onto a client characteristics of important people in the clinicians's past. A therapist with a mother who often exhibited passive-aggressive behaviors might berate a client who was delayed by a traffic jam, projecting feelings toward the mother onto the delayed client. Clinicians should not assume that they are too skilled or insightful to develop countertransference reactions but should carefully monitor any strong emotional reactions they have to clients for the possibility of countertransference.

Free Association

Freud used many approaches to access repressed material, including analysis of dreams and transference as well as free association. The process of free association reflects the most important rule of psychoanalysis: people should say whatever comes into their mind without censoring or judging. Free association is the automatic linking of one thought to another, which we all experience. We may hear a song that reminds us of the dance we attended when we first heard it, reminding us of our date for the dance, reminding us of the rage a parent expressed when we returned home after curfew, reminding us of the beatings we received from that parent, reminding us of our repressed impulse to attack the parent. A song, then, through a chain of association, can bring up strong feelings of anxiety because of its link to emotions that we have been unable to accept and process successfully. Freud encouraged free association in his patients to facilitate their recall of past material and release intense feelings. Blocks in the chain of association are another source of information about repressed material.

Abreaction

Although Freud placed primary emphasis on uncovering repressed material, he also recognized the importance of emotions, discussed in depth in the next section of this book. He believed that affect needs to accompany the recall of past material in order for people to successfully understand and work through the importance that material has for them. To facilitate this link between emotions and the recall of repressed information, Freud employed a technique called abreaction in which, by reliving in the imagination the original experience, the emotions were also relived. This technique is used today not only in psychoanalytic treatment but also in other theoretical systems that seek to help people cope with strong emotional reactions to past events.

Interpretation and Analysis

The overriding techniques in all of Freud's psychotherapy are analysis and interpretation designed to promote awareness and insight. Whether his focus was on dreams, slips, transference, free association, or symptoms, the tools of analysis and interpretation allowed him to bring repressed material into consciousness. Once this had occurred, people could gain insight into and work through that previously repressed material and make connections between that material and their present difficulties, resulting in positive change.

Analysis is the process of thoroughly exploring and understanding the unconscious representations in the material people present in treatment. For example, in analyzing the dream of the young woman in the park (presented earlier in this chapter), Freud would explore with her the meaning of each item in the dream, including the park, the dog, and the woman herself. She would be encouraged to free-associate to the dream, to talk about both the emotions reflected in the dream and those she experienced upon awakening and recalling the dream, and to discuss events in the recent past that might have triggered the dream. Emphasis would be on the wish fulfillment represented by the dream and on suggestions of repressed, unacceptable sexual or other urges.

Interpretation is the process of elucidating the repressed meaning of the symbols in material that clients present and of linking those new insights to their present concerns and blocks. Working through previously repressed material, both emotionally and cognitively, enables people to understand the influence the past has had on them and to use the defenses and strategies of the ego to make choices that are wiser and freer of the negative impact of material repressed during the early childhood years.

APPLICATION OF FREUDIAN PSYCHOANALYSIS

Freud himself recognized that his approach was only suitable for a limited group of people. In light of the length and depth of the psychoanalytic process, readers might be tempted to conclude that it is designed for only those people with severe mental disorders. In fact, the opposite is true.

Application to Diagnostic Groups

During Freud's time, mental disorders were categorized into two broad groups: psychoses and neuroses. *Psychoses* involve a loss of contact with reality, a significant disturbance in a person's ability to accurately perceive and interpret both internal and external experiences. Because they are likely to be experiencing delusions, hallucinations, and other perceptual distortions, people with psychoses cannot engage in the sort of self-examination that is required in psychoanalysis. They are unlikely to benefit from this mode of treatment.

People with *neuroses,* on the other hand, experience disorders of thoughts, emotions, and behaviors that interfere with their capacity for healthy functioning. Although their defenses and difficulties may lead them to have some confusion and misunderstanding about the meaning of their experiences, they have a capacity to form relationships, can engage in productive analysis, and can distinguish dreams and fantasies from reality. In Freud's time, six major neuroses had been identified (Stafford-Clark, 1965):

1. Hysteria, (now known as conversion disorder), involving a loss or disturbance of the senses or motor ability such as blindness or paralysis without medical cause
2. Anxiety states, including what are now called phobias as well as generalized anxiety disorders, both involving unreasonable fears
3. Obsessional disorders, now called obsessive-compulsive disorders, involving preoccupation with cleanliness and ritualized behaviors, usually leading to feelings of hopelessness
4. Depression, especially the melancholic (nonreactive) type
5. Paranoid attitudes, comparable to today's paranoid personality disorder, involving pervasive suspiciousness, hypersensitivity, and sometimes jealousy
6. Sexual perversions, now called paraphilias

Freud divided the neuroses into two categories: transference neuroses, which involved a conflict between the id and the ego; and the narcissistic neuroses, involving a conflict between the superego and the ego. He believed that only transference neuroses, (the first four in the list) were treatable by psychoanalysis, although today most psychoanalysts view all nonpsychotic disorders as potentially treatable by psychoanalysis.

Application to Other Groups

Despite the broad applicability of Freudian psychoanalysis from a diagnostic point of view, other constraints limit the use and appropriateness of this approach. Few people have the time, financial resources, and inclination to engage in such intensive treatment. In addition, the slowly paced nature of the process; the relatively passive role of the client on the couch; and the emphasis on sexuality, early childhood, and the unconscious make the approach a poor choice for many people. Those in crisis, those who want to play a more active and equal role in their treatment, and those who are uncomfortable with or do not believe in Freud's focus on infantile sexuality are not likely to respond well to psychoanalysis. With its emphasis on talk, analysis, and uncovering, psychoanalysis is also a very western or Eurocentric approach and therefore may not be well received by people from different cultural backgrounds.

Current Use

Despite the limited application of psychoanalysis, schools to train psychoanalysts flourish in New York City, Washington, DC, and other large cities. Not only do people seek training in this approach, but clients seek psychoanalysis from both these training facilities and psychoanalysts in independent practice. Few modern psychoanalysts, however, draw exclusively on the ideas of Freud. Rather, they use his ideas as the basis for their work but incorporate into their therapy the ideas of his follow-ers as well as more recent theorists in psychoanalysis and psychodynamic psy-chotherapy. For additional information on training in psychoanalysis, contact the following organization:

American Psychoanalytic Association
309 East 49th Street
New York, NY 10017

Evaluation of Freudian Psychoanalysis

The continued attention to Freud's ideas reflects the important and enduring con-tributions of his work. Freud provided a solid foundation for future theorists who elaborated and expanded on his work. Their contributions will be discussed in the remaining chapters in Part 2.

Limitations

Psychoanalysis certainly has many limitations, many of which stem from its lengthy and costly format. In addition, the approach is not designed to help people with ur-gent concerns, pays little attention to the influence of people's cultural back-grounds, and says little about developing healthy adult lifestyles. Furthermore, it does not provide specific tools to help clinicians address substance misuse, relation-ship difficulties, and many other concerns presented by clients.

The research substantiating the value of this approach has been limited, partly because the lengthy and intense nature of the treatment means that each analyst works with only a small number of people and that each treatment process is unique. However, the Psychotherapy Research Project of the Menninger Foundation col-lected data between 1954 and 1984 on the use of psychoanalysis and psychoanalytic psychotherapy with 42 clients (Wallerstein, 1986). Approximately 60% experienced good or moderate outcomes, with most continuing to improve after treatment. Al-though these results are encouraging, they do not demonstrate that lengthy psy-choanalysis is superior to other treatment approaches at ameliorating difficulties. As with most systems of psychotherapy and counseling, additional research, particularly of a comparative nature, is needed, although the nature of psychoanalysis makes it difficult to conduct such research.

Strengths and Contributions

Probably Freud's most important contribution is the profound impact his think-ing had on our understanding of human development. Most of us acknowledge the importance of childhood experiences, understand the major role that sexual-ity plays in development, recognize the powerful influence of parent figures in our lives, assume that dreams and slips are often meaningful, accept the existence of the unconscious, and acknowledge that internal conflicts commonly occur within our personalities. We also recognize the healing power of the therapeutic relationship, believe that talk therapy can be a powerful vehicle for promoting positive change, and are optimistic that with treatment most people can be helped to lead more productive and rewarding lives. Whether or not we agree with the psychoanalytic model of treatment or with the emphasis on infantile sexuality, Freud's profound contribution to our understanding of psychological development and knowledge of psychotherapy is undeniable. Although few readers will go on to become psychoanalysts, all will find that their conceptions of mental health and mental illness and their approaches to treatment are affected by their knowledge of Freudian psychoanalysis.

SKILL DEVELOPMENT: THE LIFELINE

Freud's writings call attention to the predictable developmental stages of the early years and the profound impact that negotiation of these stages has on a person's subsequent development. In *Childhood and Society* (1963), Erik Erikson also defined stages of development and identified the central issue of each. His early stages parallel Freud's but continue through the life span. Erikson's model is used for this skill development exercise rather than Freud's because its consideration of the entire life span and its attention to positive growth experiences allow it to be used productively without extensive training in psychoanalytic methods. In addition, it is more appropriate for group discussion because it addresses overall development rather than emphasizing the role of sexuality and the early childhood years in development.

Erikson's model includes the following eight stages:

Stage 1: Basic trust versus basic mistrust (Freud's oral stage), the first year of life. *Positive development:* Developing trust in caregivers and learning that basic needs will be met fosters a person's trust in others.

Stage 2: Autonomy versus shame and doubt (Freud's anal stage), ages 1–3. *Positive development:* Mastering appropriate control over elimination functions can help children to learn independence and self-confidence.

Stage 3: Initiative versus guilt (Freud's phallic stage), ages 3–5. *Positive development:* Children form healthy attachments to parents of both genders and can identify with their same-sex parent. This enables them to develop feelings of competence, become able to make and trust their own decisions, and have the initiative to move forward with their lives.

Stage 4: Industry versus inferiority (Freud's latency stage), ages 6–12. *Positive development:* Development focuses on the importance of social and academic success. Children learn good work habits and become productive and able to meet new challenges.

Stage 5: Identity versus role confusion (Freud's genital stage), ages 12–18. *Positive development:* During the adolescent years, young people seek to develop their identities and formulate self-images that will greatly influence their abilities to love and work. These, according to Freud, are the two essential aspects of our lives.

Stage 6: Intimacy versus isolation, ages 18–35. *Positive development:* The goals of young adulthood include forming meaningful relationships and becoming part of a community.

Stage 7: Generativity versus stagnation, ages 35–60, the middle adult years. *Positive development:* Successful passage through these years is marked by feeling productive through rearing children, career accomplishments, or achievements in other areas of one's life.

Stage 8: Integrity versus despair, the later years. *Positive development:* People take stock of their lives, feel worthwhile, and have a sense of fulfillment and ego integrity.

Using developmental-stage perspectives to examine both our own lives and those of our clients can be very productive, and the systematic exploration of each stage can promote awareness of patterns and insight into milestones or turning points. The specialized skill in this chapter, the lifeline, is a tool that you can use for self-exploration as well as with clients. Before you actually complete the exercise that will help you to learn the skill of analyzing life patterns, read all the instructions in this section. Then read the case illustration, which presents a lifeline prepared by Roberto Diaz. This will guide you in developing and analyzing your own lifeline.

Draw a long line that reflects your life. Divide the line into eight parts, reflecting Erikson's eight stages, and mark out the corresponding ages on the line. For the first five stages, list each year individually. Beyond that, you may list years in groups of five years if you prefer. Think back over your life and think ahead to the years to come. Complete the lifeline so that it reflects your life in the following ways:

1. For each stage you have completed or are completing, list important events at the age at which they occurred. You may need to talk with family members to gather information about your early milestones. You might list events such as a death or divorce in your family, a family relocation, an illness in you or a family member, the birth of a younger sibling, or events that may seem less important but that made a great difference in your life such as bringing home a lost kitten, making a special friend, or learning to ride a bicycle.

2. For those stages that still lie ahead, list in parentheses events that you are hoping for and looking forward to next to the age at which you would like the event to occur. Such events might include marriage, having another child, traveling to Europe, buying a home, finishing graduate school and obtaining a job, or retiring to a tropical island.

3. Go through the lifeline a second time. This time draw in peaks and valleys to reflect the highs and lows that you have had or expect to have. They should be linked to the events you have listed.

4. Go through the lifeline a third time. For each of the eight stages, write down a positive word or phrase and a negative word or phrase to describe your actual or

anticipated passage through that stage. For example, for the industry versus inferiority (latency) stage, you might write, "Loved school, especially reading," and "Few friends, felt different."

5. Go through the lifeline a fourth time. This time, for each of the eight stages, write a statement indicating your assessment of your negotiation of that stage. For example, for the identity versus role confusion (genital) stage, you might write, "Developing a good personal sense of myself but still confused about who I am as a worker."

6. Take a final tour through your lifeline, reviewing all the information you have gathered about yourself and your life. Look for patterns or recurrent themes that might point to continuing areas of concern or problems that may arise in the future. For example, you might observe that all your successes are in the academic and occupational area, while most of your important disappointments are in the personal realm. Make a list of the patterns you observe. If you had done this exercise while in counseling, the information would probably provide direction for the treatment process as well as considerable insight into the way in which the past has influenced the present in your life. You might think about that for yourself.

CASE ILLUSTRATION

Roberto prepared the following lifeline as part of his treatment (see Figure 4-1).

STAGE 1: BASIC TRUST VERSUS BASIC MISTRUST (FREUD'S ORAL STAGE)

Important events: Just survived; a lot of kids in my neighborhood didn't. Told I was a big baby; always wanted to be fed.

Positive and negative descriptors: Maybe I needed a lot of attention because I always wanted to be fed. I wonder if I got much attention with all those other kids around; but knowing me, I yelled the loudest and got what I needed.

Assessment: I always knew my parents and grandparents loved me, and I have a lot of trust in my family, but I sure don't trust other people much.

STAGE 2: AUTONOMY VERSUS SHAME AND DOUBT (FREUD'S ANAL STAGE)

Important events: My younger sister was born. My older brother was hit by a car. I don't remember this stuff, but my parents told me about it. When we were toilet training Ava, I wondered about my own toilet training. I asked my mom, but she didn't really remember. I guess it wasn't much of a problem.

Positive and negative descriptors: I think I became self-sufficient really fast with so much going on in my family, but sometimes I feel angry without really knowing why. I used to feel ashamed of how I looked, always tall and big. I wonder if some of those bad feelings go back to that time period.

Assessment: Well, I got toilet trained! Seriously, I bet I just toilet trained myself; that's how things usually went in my family. I wonder if the

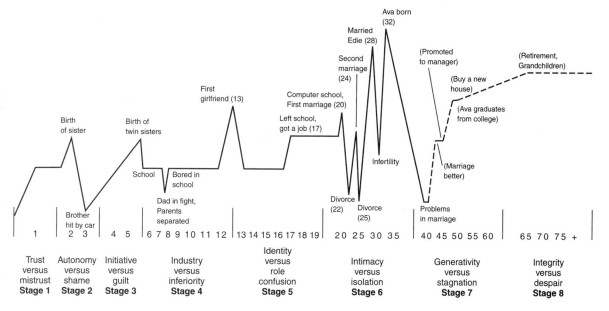

FIGURE 4–1   Roberto Diaz's lifeline

anger has to do with that. And I'm not very neat; that's a conflict between me and Edie.

STAGE 3: INITIATIVE VERSUS GUILT (FREUD'S PHALLIC STAGE)

Important events: Twin sisters were born. I can remember my parents bringing them home. No big deal though; they were numbers seven and eight. I started school at that time, some kind of special program. You know, my parents spoke Spanish at home and my English wasn't very good, so I got put in something like the Head Start programs they have now. I remember my dad really well from those years. He used to watch sports on TV-boxing, I think. I thought he was tough, just like those guys.

Positive and negative descriptors: Time with Dad was great, but I didn't like school.

Assessment: I can see myself maturing, using my father as a role model. He didn't think much of school.

STAGE 4: INDUSTRY VERSUS INFERIORITY (FREUD'S LATENCY STAGE)

Important events: Started public school. Dad got into a fight and came home all bloody; . . . that scared me. The major thing, of course, was that my parents separated.

Positive and negative descriptors: Needed to be real self-sufficient, and I was. I still didn't like school.

Assessment: I learned to take care of myself, started fixing cars with my brothers, and I was good at it. I couldn't get that school stuff though; . . . acted like I didn't care, but I did.

STAGE 5: IDENTITY VERSUS ROLE CONFUSION (FREUD'S GENITAL STAGE)

Important events: Had my first girlfriend and my first sexual relationship. Dropped out of high school and went to work fixing cars.

Positive and negative descriptors: I really felt important; sex and money did it. Work was harder than I thought; maybe leaving school wasn't such a great idea.

Assessment: I had a sense of identity, but I was full of myself; didn't really see I was going nowhere.

STAGE 6: INTIMACY VERSUS ISOLATION

Important events: Lots of things here. Got my GED and went to computer school, smartest thing I ever did. Got married, got divorced, got married, got divorced, met Edie, got married again. The big event: Ava was born. Started to make some real money; bought a house.

Positive and negative descriptors: Lots of mistakes, but at 35 I was on top of the world at home and at work.

Assessment: Really turned my life around and figured out who I was and what I wanted.

STAGE 7: GENERATIVITY VERSUS STAGNATION

Important events: I guess this is where I am now. Big problems in the marriage. Started therapy. (Hopefully, marriage gets better; I move into management at work; Ava goes to college. Probably bad stuff too; . . . parents getting sick, dying.)

Positive and negative descriptors: I'm doing my best to keep my family together; but that anger keeps coming up for me, especially when I feel trapped. If my third marriage doesn't make it, I guess I just can't do this marriage thing.

Assessment: A real crossroads. I've come so far, but it could all fall apart.

STAGE 8: INTEGRITY VERSUS DESPAIR

Important events: (I retire with a good pension. Edie and I retire to the beach. Ava gets married, and I become a grandpa. That's what I hope for.)

Positive and negative descriptors: (I feel great about what I've done, rebuilt my marriage, turned out a terrific kid, left work at the top. I guess the down side is getting sick, losing people I love. If Edie and I don't make it, I could just be a lonely old man.)

Assessment: (I can see the possibilities here, and I'm going to make the good ones happen.)

PATTERNS

1. I always had a great appetite: food, women, money. Sometimes I get too hungry and don't really think about things.
2. My anger gets me in trouble just like it did my dad. I have his toughness and I'm good with my hands like him, but we both fly off the handle.
3. Kids mean a lot to my parents and to me. Too bad we only had the one, but she's great.
4. I made lots of mistakes but never let them get me down. Knock me down, and I get up fighting. I guess that's really helped me.

ANALYSIS

Clearly, Roberto has shared a great deal of himself in this lifeline. In-depth analysis in treatment might focus on the following areas:

1. Patterns of impulsivity and impulse control: does his ego have difficulty controlling the demands of the id?
2. His difficult relationships with women, perhaps stemming from early issues with his mother.
3. His identification with the aggressive side of his father and his expression of his own aggressive impulses.

Insight and change in these areas, as well as others that might arise during the course of treatment, seem likely to help Roberto improve his capacity for intimacy.

EXERCISES

Large-Group Exercises

1. As a class, develop a hypothetical lifeline for Edie based on the information provided in Chapters 1 and 3. You may add additional information to enrich your knowledge of her as long as it is consistent with information you already have.
2. Discuss your predictions for the future of psychoanalysis. Be sure to provide a rationale for all your points.

Small-Group Exercise

Form into your groups of two dyads. Each dyad should take a turn conducting an interview on early childhood experiences, with one person in the dyad being the interviewer, the other the interviewee. Using the interview skills you learned in Chapter 3, spend 10–15 minutes asking your partner about his or her recollections of the following:

- Being fed by a caregiver
- Being toilet trained
- Developing an identification with the same-sex parent or caregiver

After each role play, observers should give the interviewer some feedback, using the guidelines in Chapter 1. Feedback should include (but not be limited) to (1) use of questions, (2) ability to elicit information, (3) client-clinician rapport, and (4) eye contact and other nonverbal behaviors.

Be sure to take care of yourself during this exercise and during all exercises in this book. You can choose what you do or do not want to reveal about your early childhood experiences. If you find strong emotions or troubling memories coming up for you, be cautious about sharing them. Remember that this is an exercise, not a counseling relationship. If any exercises are very troubling for you, consider the possibility that counseling might help you better understand and handle those feelings.

Individual Exercises

1. Now that you have an understanding of the id, the superego, and the ego, the three structures of the personality, you can be more aware of the dynamics of some of your inner conflicts. Write briefly about a time when you experienced a conflict between your id and your superego and how you resolved that conflict.

2. We all make mistakes, make slips, and forget commitments. Try to be more conscious of these processes in your own life for the next week. Each time you notice one of these errors, think about whether it is a random occurrence or whether it might reflect a wish or another psychological process.
3. Create and analyze your own lifeline, following the directions in the "Skill Development" section.

SUMMARY

This chapter has reviewed psychoanalytic theory and strategies as developed by Sigmund Freud. It also provided considerable information about Freud's background and on the development of his concepts, which are an important foundation of modern ideas of mental health and the treatment of mental disorders. His theory emphasizes the three structures of the personality (id, superego, and ego), the five stages of psychosexual development (oral, anal, phallic, latency, and genital), defense mechanisms, and levels of consciousness (unconscious, preconscious, and conscious). Treatment focuses on promoting insight by analysis of dreams and other clues to the unconscious, interpretation, and the development of transference.

RECOMMENDED READINGS

Freud, S. (1938). *The basic writings of Sigmund Freud* (A. A. Brill, Trans.) New York: Modern Library.
Jones, E. (1953, 1955, 1957). *The life and works of Sigmund Freud.* (3 vols.). New York: Basic Books.
Roth, M. S. (Ed.) (1998). *Freud: Conflict and culture.* New York: Alfred A. Knopf.
Stafford-Clark, D. (1965). *What Freud really said.* New York: Schocken.

Chapter 5

ALFRED ADLER AND INDIVIDUAL PSYCHOLOGY

For many years, Alfred Adler shared Freud's perspectives on human development and psychotherapy. However, as Adler's own thinking evolved, he began to disagree with the great emphasis Freud placed on biological and physiological determinants of psychological development. Although Adler believed that early childhood experiences played an integral part in future development, he came to view Freud's concepts as too deterministic and limited. He eventually broke with Freud and established his own theories of human development and psychotherapy, which he called *Individual Psychology.*

Compared with Freud's, Adler's ideas are much more compatible with current thinking about mental health. For example, he paid considerable attention to social context, family dynamics, and child rearing. As a result, his ideas have experienced a resurgence of popularity during the past 25 years or so and are now viewed as an important system of human development and psychotherapy, especially for clinicians working with children and their families.

THE PERSON WHO DEVELOPED INDIVIDUAL PSYCHOLOGY

Alfred Adler was born on February 7, 1870, in Vienna, Austria, the third of seven children. His father, Leopold Adler, was a merchant. Alfred Adler had a difficult childhood in many ways. When he was three years old, a brother died in the bed the two children shared (Orgler, 1963). Adler himself was prone to accidents and illnesses. Twice he was run over in the streets; he had pneumonia, suffered from rickets, and was generally sickly and delicate. This history left him with both a fear of death and an interest in becoming a physician. Another important consequence of his childhood medical problems was the considerable pampering he received, especially from his mother. However, when his younger brother was born, Adler felt dethroned as his mother shifted her attention from him to her new baby. This led him to transfer his attention to his father and to his peers, from whom he learned "courage, comradeliness, and social interest" (Orgler, 1963, p. 3). The impact of these early childhood events on Adler's subsequent ideas will become evident later in this chapter.

Although he was not generally a good student, he was very interested in psychology and social problems from childhood on. Even in his first professional position after he completed medical school, when he worked as an eye specialist, Adler was interested in the total person and sought to understand the connection between mental and physical processes. He found his subsequent work as a general physician more rewarding because it was a better fit with his beliefs. However, he was troubled by strong feelings of helplessness when treating patients with terminal illnesses. This led him to another career change; he entered the field of neurology while continuing to study psychology and social science in an effort to understand people more fully.

Adler's insights into personality development brought him recognition in his field and probably helped capture Freud's attention. In 1902, Freud wrote to Adler and several other leaders in the fields of neurology and psychology suggesting they meet at his home to discuss his work. This led to Adler's involvement in the formation of the Vienna Psycho-Analytical Society.

Descriptions of Adler's personal style at this time are mixed. Orgler's (1963) research suggests that Adler was warm and friendly, while Jones, Freud's biographer, describes Adler as "morose, cantankerous, contentious, and sulky" (1955, p. 130). Perhaps both descriptions reflected aspects of Adler's personality as well as his growing displeasure with Freud's emphasis on sexual impulses as the basic determinant of psychological development. Adler insisted that sexual impulses were only one of a number of important factors in development.

This rift finally led him to separate himself from the Psycho-Analytical Society, where he had reached a point of power and leadership, to form the Society for Free Psychoanalysis. In 1912, he renamed this organization the Society for Individual Psychology. His work for the rest of his life had the goals of deepening his understanding of people and finding better ways to help them. Adler's strong social interest prompted him to write and speak on child rearing and educational practices; establish child guidance clinics in the Viennese public schools; and initiate programs to train teachers, social workers, physicians, and other professionals in ways to promote children's mental health. Using live demonstrations and writing books for the general public, he made his ideas and techniques accessible to a wide audience, which was important to him. Beginning in the 1920s, he traveled frequently to the United States, where he generated considerable interest in his work.

Adler's tireless involvement in his work continued until his death. On May 28, 1937, while preparing for a lecture in Aberdeen, Scotland, he died of a heart attack.

THE DEVELOPMENT OF INDIVIDUAL PSYCHOLOGY

Adler's professional development falls roughly into four time periods. The first stage of his career followed his completion of medical school, when he seemed to be searching for a way to make a contribution through his work. Neither his initial work as a physician nor his subsequent work in neurological research seemed right for him, although he made contributions in both areas. His great interest was the mind rather than the body.

When he joined forces with Freud to further the field of psychoanalysis, Adler seemed, at least temporarily, to have found his place. Finally, in his second period, his focus was on promoting healthy emotional development. However, before long, he must have felt stifled by the apparent rigidity of some of Freud's beliefs and his limited interest in the whole person, including the person's social background and interest.

Adler's break with Freud signaled the third period in his professional development. This separation freed Adler to move forward with his own ideas. According to Ansbacher and Ansbacher (1956), Adler replaced "biological, external, objective causal explanation with psychological, internal, subjective causal explanation." (p. 9). He replaced the concept of the sexual drive and the libido with the drive to gain power and to become a fully functioning adult. The goal of Adler's theory of Individual Psychology was to comprehend the unique individual, a departure from what he perceived as Freud's overgeneralized ideas.

A final stage in Adler's career came after his service as a psychiatrist in World War I. Seeing the bond that developed among soldiers during the stressful war years showed him that the drive toward social interest was even stronger than the drive for superiority and power. He proposed that people's basic motivation is "an innate predisposition for social interest" (Grey, 1998, p. 8) and viewed people as driven primarily by needs for significance, self-worth, and social involvement. Clearly, his thinking moved in directions that are compatible with what many view as the fundamental purpose of psychotherapy: to help people feel empowered and self-actualized and build rewarding social involvement and relationships.

IMPORTANT THEORETICAL CONCEPTS

Adler's theories, like Freud's, have considerable depth and richness. Adler's concepts emphasized the unity and uniqueness of each individual. He believed that understanding people grew from knowledge of their goals and drives, their family constellation, and their style of life. Sweeney (1998) described Adler's theories as socio-teleo-analytic:

- *Socio.* This reflects Adler's emphasis on social interest, (his belief that people have a basic need to belong to a larger social whole) and his concern with the betterment of humankind.
- *Teleo.* This denotes his belief in the goal-striving nature of people, with behavior being purposeful and intended to help people achieve their goals. According to Sweeney (1998, p. 10), "the teleological aspects of Adler's theory reveal the optimistic, encouraging nature of his position." People are not victims of biology or circumstance but can choose to change both their goals and their behaviors.
- *Analytic.* Adler shared Freud's belief that much of what determines the direction of people's lives is unconscious and needs to be analyzed to bring their goals and lifestyle into conscious awareness.

View of Human Nature

Adler, like Freud, acknowledged the importance of the first five years of life in influencing people's future development. However, his view was less deterministic than Freud's. He believed that biological and physiological factors provided probabilities for future growth but that, "the self, with creative power as part of its inner nature, is the important intervening variable" (Ansbacher & Ansbacher, 1956, p. 179).

For Adler, those characteristics of the person that were determined by heredity and early upbringing were less important than what the person made of them. He believed that all behavior was purposeful and goal-directed, and that we can channel our behavior in ways that promote growth. For Adler, what matters to people is finding success, fulfillment, and meaning in life. Their actions reflect their efforts to achieve those goals, and the goals they value and how they seek to reach them are major factors in their development (Adler, 1963a).

The Importance of Feelings of Inferiority

Inferiority is a dimension of the early childhood years that Adler (1963b) believed has a great impact on development. Nearly all young children experience feelings of inferiority, perceiving themselves as small and powerless in relation to their parents and older siblings. How a small child is treated and how he or she deals with those feelings of inferiority are important factors in the child's development. Children who are motivated to reduce their feelings of difference and low self-esteem by social involvement with others, building up their strengths and abilities, making wise and creative choices, and striving in healthy ways toward growth and power are likely to develop in positive ways. On the other hand, children who are pampered or neglected and whose efforts toward empowerment are thwarted are far less likely to experience positive growth and development. Pampered children often grow up expecting others to care for them and so do not develop their own resources, while neglected children may become discouraged and hopeless when their efforts to overcome an inferior role are ignored or rejected.

Family Constellation and Birth Order

Another early source of influence on development is a person's family constellation and birth order. Adler placed considerable emphasis on the social nature of human problems. He believed that, through an examination of the family constellation, we can understand people's lifestyles. Conversely, by understanding their outlooks on life, we can understand the roles they have in their families (Dreikurs, 1973).

A person's family constellation includes the composition of the family, each person's roles, and the reciprocal transactions that a person has with siblings and parents during the formative years of early childhood. The child is not a passive recipient of these transactions; rather, the child influences the way in which parents and siblings respond as much as he or she is influenced by those interactions. Each child comes to play a role in the family that is determined by the interactions and transactions within that family (Adler, 1963b).

Children are shaped and affected by both their similarities to and differences from their families. According to Adler, we are particularly influenced by siblings who are most different from the way we are. That difference gives us the opportunity to compare and contrast ourselves with others, see new possibilities, and rethink the choices and roles we have taken on in our own lives.

Birth order is another aspect of families that, according to Adler (1963b), has a profound impact on development. He identified five psychological positions in the family:

1. *Oldest children,* of course, are temporarily only children until their first sibling is born. While they are the only child in the family, they tend to be the center of attention and often are spoiled. However, when siblings are born, oldest children usually feel dethroned and may feel threatened, angry, and jealous in response to losing their special role as only child. First borns, who initially grow up in a family of

Oldest child   Second child   Middle child   Youngest   Only
                                                                    child   child

adults, <u>tend to be dependable, responsible, and achievement oriented</u>. They generally continue to be well behaved to hold onto the parents' favor after the birth of the second child, but they also may become difficult if this effort is not successful.

2. The *second child* feels constant pressure to catch up and compete with the oldest child. Because second-born children realize they cannot really outdo the successes the first born has already achieved, they gravitate toward endeavors in which the older sibling is either unskilled or uninterested. A common pattern is for a first born to excel in a traditional area such as English or mathematics and for the second born to seek success in a more creative and less conventional area such as singing or drawing or to emphasize social rather than academic success. The more successful the first born, the more likely it is that the second born will experience self-doubts and move in directions opposite to those of the typically well-behaved and achievement-oriented first born.

3. The *middle child* feels squeezed between older children who have already found their place and younger children who may seem to receive more love and attention. Middle children often have difficulty finding a way to become special and can become difficult and discouraged, viewing themselves as unloved and neglected. This pattern is usually less evident in large families where two or more children share the role of middle child but is particularly likely in families with only three children.

4. *Youngest children* encounter two common pitfalls: they may feel a need to go at top speed at all times just to keep up with their older siblings, or they may become discouraged at the hopelessness of outdistancing their brothers and sisters and so may give up and remain the baby of the family. The youngest is spoiled in many families by both parents and older siblings. Decisions may be made for them, and they may not need to take on much responsibility for themselves or others. They may not be taken seriously but instead become a sort of charming pet in the family. However, they can also take on considerable power and become the family boss or tyrant. If they do seek to become independent, they usually will pursue interests that are all their own to avoid competition with others in the family. Their most likely ally is the oldest, who also has feelings of being different.

5. *Only children* have much in common with both first- and last-born children. They seek achievement like first borns and usually enjoy being the center of attention like the youngest. They may become pampered and spoiled, focusing only on

their own needs. On the other hand, if their parents are insecure, only children may adopt parental worries and insecurities. Because the other family members are all adults, these children typically mature early and learn to cooperate and deal well with adults.

Although research has validated many of Adler's assumptions about the impact of birth order on personality (Grey, 1998; Lombardi, 1996), variables within families can have a complex impact on these patterns. For example, when twins are born, families tend to treat one child as older than the other, artificially determining their birth order. When the first born is a girl or is impaired in some way, families may inadvertently promote the second child into the position of first born. High expectations will be held for that child, while the first born will be treated more like a second born. Very large families may operate as though they have more than one group of children, with each group having a child who functions as the oldest, one who functions as the youngest, and children in the middle. This is especially likely in families in which many years separate groups of children. In addition, Adler has pointed out that it is the way in which children respond to their positions rather than the actual positions that has an impact on their personalities and behaviors. Consequently, clinicians should not stereotype people according to their birth order. At the same time, exploring birth order and the influence it has played on the development of an individual's personality can facilitate understanding of that person.

Lifestyle

The composition and interactions of people's families exert the major influence on the development of their lifestyle, another important concept in Adler's theory (Sperry, 1996). According to Starr, (1973), "Adler concluded that each child in the family, out of his own inner capacities and his appraisal of the outer environment, experiences a different situation. He joined these attitudes into a characteristic pattern of behavior" (p. 95). Grey (1998) views lifestyle as the most fundamental of all of Adler's concepts, describing it as "the sum total of all the individual's attitudes and aspirations, a striving which leads him in the direction toward his goal of believing he has significance in the eyes of others." (p. 37).

Lifestyle, then, is the unique way in which each of us seeks to overcome feelings of inferiority and to achieve our goals. Although these goals nearly always involve attainment of significance, superiority, competence, and mastery, each person has an image, usually unconscious, of what his or her goals are. Adler used the term *fictional finalism* to describe the imagined central goal that guides our behavior. He believed that this goal is firmly established between the ages of six and eight and remains constant throughout a person's life. Our *private logic* is the route that takes us from our feelings of inferiority to the development of a lifestyle that we believe will enable us to reach our fictional goals. Dreikurs (1973), a follower of Adler who contributed greatly to the advancement of his work, described private logic as consisting of our immediate goals, our long-range goals, and the inner rationale we use for justifying our lifestyle as the way to achieve these goals.

Social Interest

Dreikurs distinguished between well-adjusted and maladjusted people on the basis of their goals and their lifestyles. Those people who are well adjusted have a private logic that reflects common sense as well as social interest, while those who are maladjusted focus only on their own needs and fail to recognize the importance of their social context and the needs of others.

This idea reflects Adler's (1963a) belief that development can be explained primarily by psychosocial rather than psychosexual dynamics. He believed that people are, by nature, social beings interested in belonging to a group and desiring to solve the problems of their society. Through our awareness that we are part of the human community and the development of our social interest, our feelings of inferiority, alienation, and anxiety diminish; and we develop feelings of belonging and happiness. We no longer view ourselves as alone and in a struggle to diminish others to advance ourselves. Instead, we recognize that the goods and ills in our society all have an impact on us and that we can best achieve our own goals of significance and competence by contributing to the greater good of our society. Adler's emphasis on social connectedness seems very up-to-date.

People's social interest is best reflected in their accomplishment of what Adler viewed as the three life tasks: occupation, love, and friendship. Social interest can be assessed by how successfully people are able to negotiate social relationships and the degree of closeness they maintain in those relationships. Although Freud wrote about the importance of love and work, Adler's addition of friendship to the important areas of our lives clearly reflects his emphasis on human connectedness. Although Adler emphasized the important role of early childhood experiences in determining the nature of our social interest, he also believed that social interest can be taught and developed in later life, conveying optimism not only for the individual but for our society.

Phenomenological Perspective

Another viewpoint compatible with current thinking on human development and psychotherapy is Adler's emphasis on the importance of a person's perception of reality, not what actually is or what others perceive. For Adler, the internal and subjective were more important than the external and objective. His theory can be thought of as *phenomenological,* meaning that he was concerned with the inner reality of a person, the way that person perceives the world. Adler saw each person as a unique individual and believed that only by understanding the person's perceptions of the world and his or her private logic, lifestyle, and goals can we really make sense of and know that person. This is the essence of Adler's Individual Psychology.

TREATMENT USING INDIVIDUAL PSYCHOLOGY

Although Adler emphasized the importance of the early childhood years, his theory is a growth-oriented model, reflecting the belief that people can reorient their thinking, leading to happier and more fulfilled lives. Adler's ideas have endured because they both are grounded in Freudian psychoanalysis and incorporate many elements of modern cognitive, behavioral, and humanistic treatment approaches.

Goals

Adler had a clear vision of what it meant to be a healthy, well-functioning adult. It meant being independent, emotionally and physically self-reliant, useful and productive, and able to cooperate with others for both personal and social benefit. The "inadequate responses of envy, greed, competition and sabotage" arise in people who have not developed these characteristics. (Beecher & Beecher, 1973, p. 2).

Through psychotherapy and education, Adler sought to help people realize that feelings of pain and inadequacy are caused not by others but by their own faulty logic and the behaviors and attitudes that stem from that logic. By enabling people to become aware of their faulty logic and to change both their thinking and their conditioned responses, a therapist can help them overcome their feelings of inferiority, dependency, and inordinate fears of failure and develop the self-confidence and social interest they need to achieve a healthier adjustment and a more rewarding lifestyle.

Therapeutic Alliance

One of the many ways in which Adler departed from the ideas of Freud was in his conception of the clinician-client relationship. Adler emphasized the importance of a cooperative relationship that involved establishment of shared goals as well as mutual trust and respect. This view was consistent with the aims of his treatment; he sought to foster responsibility and social interest and saw the establishment of a therapeutic relationship in which client and clinician collaborated to achieve goals they had formulated together as an important way to promote client growth.

Clinicians following Adler's model of treatment have a complex role that calls for the application of a broad range of skills. They should be supportive and encouraging, urging clients to take risks and helping them accept their own mistakes and imperfections. These clinicians are educators, fostering social interest and teaching clients ways to modify their lifestyles, behaviors, and goals. They are analysts who identify faulty logic and assumptions. They explore and interpret the meaning and impact of clients' birth order, dreams, early recollections, and drives. They are role models, demonstrating ways to think clearly, search for meaning, collaborate with another person, and establish and reach meaningful goals.

Both thinking and background are primary targets of the Adlerian therapists' efforts. Because private logic, lifestyle, and fictional goals are all concepts or cognitions stemming from heredity and early experiences, helping people understand these issues can clarify both feelings and behaviors. Then, helping people challenge and modify these fundamental beliefs can promote development of constructive and positive social interest and behaviors.

Stages of Treatment

Although they often merge and overlap, four stages in treatment can be identified in Adler's model: establishment of a collaborative therapeutic relationship, exploration and analysis, development of insight, and reorientation and change.

Establishing the Therapeutic Relationship Adler was ahead of his time in emphasizing the importance of building a positive therapeutic relationship. He advocated many of the approaches later described by Carl Rogers to build that relationship (see Chapter 11). Adler believed in the importance of true caring and involvement, the use of empathy, and both verbal and nonverbal techniques of listening to overcome the feelings of inferiority and fear that many clients bring with them into treatment. Initial questions explore clients' expectations for treatment, their views of their problems, how they have tried to improve their lives, and what has led them to seek treatment at the present time.

Encouragement is an essential component of this initial phase of treatment and is used throughout the therapy process to counter clients' discouragement. Sweeney (1998) has described seven actions that can be used in counseling as well as in other relationships to provide encouragement:

1. Focus on what people are doing rather than evaluate their performance. Asking, "What did you do to pass all your courses?" is more encouraging than "Did you get the best grades in your class?"
2. Focus on the present more than the past or the future.
3. Focus on behavior rather than the person. "Your careful driving really helped you deal with the sudden snowstorm" is more encouraging than "You're a great driver."
4. Focus on the effort rather than the outcome. "Sounds like you really feel good about developing your skating skills" is more encouraging than "Sounds like you are hoping your skills are good enough to make the team."
5. Focus on motivation from within (intrinsic) rather than without (extrinsic). "You must have felt a great sense of satisfaction, knowing that all your studying resulted in success on the bar exam" is more encouraging than "You finally passed the bar. Now you'll get that raise."
6. Focus on what is being learned rather than the lack of learning. "What did you learn from this challenging relationship?" is more encouraging than "You really need to make better choices in your friends."
7. Focus on what is positive rather than what is negative. "So the odds are on your side" is more encouraging than "So the physician said there is a 40 percent chance that your disease will recur."

Counseling and psychotherapy offer clinicians many opportunities to encourage clients and to show them genuine caring and concern. A telephone call to a client in crisis, a note to a client in the hospital, sharing an article on home buying with a client who is buying a first home are all appropriate ways for clinicians to form partnerships with clients and provide support and encouragement.

Exploration and Analysis   The goals of this phase of treatment are understanding clients' lifestyles, private logic, and fictional goals and identifying self-destructive behaviors and faulty logic. To accomplish this, Adler led clients on an in-depth exploration of their lives. He paid particular attention to the family constellation, clients' birth order, their dreams, their earliest recollections, and their motives or priorities.

Lifestyle assessment. Acting as what Mozdzierz, Lisiecki, Bitter, and Williams (1984) referred to as psychological explorers or lifestyle investigators, clinicians conduct a systematic exploration of clients' lifestyles. Focusing primarily on how people have addressed the tasks of love, work, and friendship, clinicians seek to gain a holistic understanding of their clients and comprehend their goals and private logic. Particularly important are assessing people's levels of satisfaction with themselves, their relationships, and their lives and looking for examples of faulty logic. Structured guidelines are available to help clinicians conduct comprehensive and informative lifestyle assessments. These can be found in *Understanding Life-Style: The Psycho-Clarity Process* (Powers & Griffith, 1987), *The Individual Psychology Client Workbook* (Powers & Griffith, 1986), and *Manual for Life Style Assessment* (Shulman & Mosak, 1988).

Family constellation and birth order. An understanding of the impact of the family constellation on a person comes from both objective and subjective sources. Objective information includes people's birth order, the number of children in the family, the gender of each child, the number of years between the births of each child, and any special circumstances such as the death of a child or the presence of a physical or intellectual disability in any of the children. Subjective information includes people's perceptions of themselves as children, how their parents felt about and treated each child, clients' relationships with their parents and siblings, ways in which they were similar to and different from their siblings, and patterns of rivalry and cooperation within the family.

Dreams. Although Adler did not place as much emphasis on the importance of understanding dreams as Freud did, he, too, used them as a vehicle for promoting self-awareness. De-emphasizing the role of symbolism, Adler viewed dreams as providing important information on lifestyle and current concerns. Recurrent dreams and recurrent themes within dreams were of particular interest to him, but he believed that both past and current dreams were useful sources of information.

Earliest recollections. What people perceive as their earliest recollections seemed to Adler to reflect their current lifestyle. It was unimportant if these memories were recalled accurately or even actually were the person's earliest memories. Adler (1931) believed that people only retained early memories that were consistent with their views of themselves. Consequently, what mattered were people's reports of their memories.

Adlerian therapists usually elicit at least three earliest memories to provide enough information to identify central themes that reflect the person's lifestyle. Once the memories have been elicited and written down, each memory is explored with the client. The clinician usually asks about the age when the person believes the recalled events occurred and the thoughts and emotions associated with the recollections. Exploration of the client's role in the memories as well as his or her relationships and interactions with other people in the memories are believed to reflect the person's lifestyle.

Priorities and ways of behaving. People's overall behavior also provides a rich and endless source of information about their lifestyles. Inquiring in detail about a person's behavior over a period of time or looking at a series of choices and actions can reveal consistent and repetitive behavioral patterns that reflect lifestyle. Adler and his associates (Adler, 1956; Mosak, 1971) have identified common ways in which people orient themselves toward the world:

- Ruling and dominating others
- Avoiding people and challenges
- Pleasing and seeking approval from others
- Controlling and managing
- Depending on others and needing to be cared for
- Pursuing superiority and perfection
- Seeking achievement
- Being the martyr or victim
- Seeking comfort
- Promoting social welfare and progress

Determining consistent patterns in people's relationships and behaviors is a useful route to identifying their goals and lifestyles.

Summarizing findings. After an extensive process of exploration, assessment, and analysis, clinicians formulate some hypotheses about the nature of clients' lifestyles, logic, and goals as well as the faulty assumptions and self-destructive thoughts that seem to be controlling their behavior. This information is presented to clients for discussion and revision, paving the way for the third phase of treatment.

Promoting Insight   This phase can be especially difficult for clinicians because they need to be both encouraging and challenging. While remaining supportive, they use interpretation and confrontation to help people gain awareness of their lifestyles, recognize the covert reasons behind their behaviors, appreciate the negative consequences of those behaviors, and move toward positive change. Several strategies help clinicians remain caring through this phase of treatment:

- They focus on the present rather than the past.
- They are more concerned with consequences than with unconscious motivation.
- They present their interpretations in ways that are likely to be accepted by clients.

Rather than being dogmatic or authoritarian, clinicians present their interpretations as guesses or hunches. They might say, "I have a hunch that you threw your little brother's hat in the sewer because you wanted more attention from your parents," or "I wonder if you have refused to lower the sale price on your house because the house represents part of your goal for the future." Clinicians are seeking to promote exploration and discussion rather than to have clients agree with them.

Change and Reorientation This final phase of treatment enables people to put their insights into action, make changes, and solve problems. Clients are helped to look at their lives from different perspectives and encouraged to make different choices. Clinicians continue to play an active role, presenting alternate possibilities, providing education and information, and helping people weigh their options and make decisions. Emphasis is on beliefs, attitudes, and perceptions because, according to Adler, if these are changed, then behavioral change will follow (Dinkmeyer, Dinkmeyer, & Sperry, 1987).

The reorientation phase can be divided into four parts (Sweeney, 1998):

1. Clients clarify their goals and determine whether they are realistic.
2. Common sense and clear thinking are applied to clients' feelings, beliefs, and goals. Although clients are reminded that their choices are their own, clinicians help people use common sense as a way of evaluating and, if necessary, modifying their thinking.
3. New learning is applied to the clients' lives.
4. Any barriers to progress are addressed and removed.

Interventions

Adler's Individual Psychology presents a wide range of creative and useful interventions. Many have already been discussed in this chapter, such as the use of earliest recollections and analysis of family constellation and birth order. Additional interventions include the following:

- *Acting as if* is a technique in which clinicians suggest to clients that they act as if they could accomplish something they do not believe they can do. A woman who is intimidated by her verbally abusive husband, for example, might be encouraged to act as if she had the courage to stand up to him and to leave the situation if he continues to berate and belittle her.
- *Avoiding the tar baby* is an intervention designed to help people avoid those traps and places where they frequently get stuck. Rather than participating in repetitive patterns, clinicians respond in unexpected ways to change the client's persistent self-destructive behaviors. For example, a client spent many fruitless evenings poring over his bills and feeling sorry for himself. Rather than encouraging him to work harder at this task, the clinician suggested that the client spend an evening with friends and plan to pay no more than one bill a day.
- *Catching oneself* encourages people to be more conscious of their repetitive faulty goals and thoughts. Clinicians facilitate this by identifying warning signs of difficulties and encouraging clients to view them as stop signs that allow

them to pause and redirect themselves. This concrete approach helps clients develop self-awareness and monitor themselves without being self-critical. For example, a man who often lost his temper and became inappropriately angry recognized that his whole body became tense before he exploded. He was taught to identify signs of physical tension, view them as stop signs, and use deep breathing as a quick and effective way to diffuse his anger.

- *Pushing the button* is designed to help people become more aware of the control they can have over their emotions rather than believe that their emotions control them. This technique involves encouraging people to alternately imagine pleasant and unpleasant experiences, observe the emotions that accompany each image, and recognize that they can determine which button to push. A young woman who frequently consumed too much alcohol at social events was encouraged to imagine the pride she took in remaining sober (pleasant experience) and the embarrassment and physical discomfort she felt after becoming intoxicated (unpleasant experience). Vivid images of these two contrasting experiences helped her abstain from alcohol.
- *Spitting in the client's soup* describes the clinician's identification of the underlying motivations behind clients' self-defeating behaviors and then spoiling their imagined payoff by making it unappealing. For example:

Client: I feel so awful that my girlfriend broke up with me. I've even thought about killing myself.

Clinician: I guess you want to make her feel guilty. But if you kill yourself, you won't be around to see how she's feeling . . . or go to college or buy that car you were talking about. You'll just be lying in the ground.

In addition to these specific techniques, which have grown out of the Adlerian model, clinicians who follow this theoretical model also use many other techniques. Some of these, including encouragement, interpretation, and use of questions, have been discussed previously in this book. Others include the following:

- *Immediacy* focuses the session on the interaction between the client and the clinician, often because it is a mirror of the client's transactions outside of the session. For example, a client accused the clinician of not liking him when she provided information on parenting that differed from the client's parenting style. The clinician helped the client see that whenever people disagreed with him, he viewed it as evidence that he was disliked.
- *Confrontation* involves pointing out discrepancies in the material that clients are presenting. For example, a counselor said, "Help me understand your decision to spend $1,000 on a wedding gown when you've told me that you're very concerned about being able to make the down payment on the house you want to buy."
- *Task assignments* are used throughout the treatment process. Client and clinician agree that the client will engage in a planned activity such as observing and listing times when he feels angry or exercising three times a week. Not only do the specific tasks advance the treatment, but the process of com-

ing to an agreement on tasks, making a commitment to complete them, and planning and executing the tasks can promote feelings of competence and responsibility.

- *Humor, silence, advice, and reflection of feeling* are other techniques in the repertoire of the Adlerian psychotherapist. This broad range of interventions offers clinicians many avenues to build rapport with their clients, promote insight and self-awareness, and encourage positive change.

APPLICATION OF INDIVIDUAL PSYCHOLOGY

Adler's model of Individual Psychology continues to be used with a broad range of clients. Particularly well suited for use with children, it has been adopted by many school counselors as well as clinicians who treat children. In addition, the approach has been used in couples counseling, career counseling, general counseling, and parent education.

Application to Children

Two men are primarily responsible for bringing Adler's ideas into American schools. Rudolf Dreikurs, a therapist and writer, drew on these ideas to teach effective parenting. *Children: The Challenge* (Dreikurs & Stoltz, 1964) has become a classic and is still used in parenting classes. Don Dinkmeyer (1982) designed a program called Developing Understanding of Self and Others (DUSO) that has been used in elementary schools to promote self-awareness, positive socialization, and feelings of competence and to advance the importance of encouragement in children's development.

Nicoll (1994) also developed classroom guidance programs based on Adler's theories. Nicoll proposed the following five-stage model for classroom use:

1. Increase awareness and appreciation of individual differences
2. Teach about the range of human emotions, promote awareness of our own feelings, clarify the impact our actions have on other people's feelings, and encourage the development of empathy
3. Foster good communication skills
4. Promote cooperation and collaboration skills
5. Encourage responsibility and use natural consequences

Dreikurs suggested that children's misbehavior is a reflection of their goals and lifestyle. He identified four possible motives behind such misbehavior (Dreikurs & Cassel, 1972):

- Attention getting
- Power

- Revenge
- Display of inadequacy

Teachers and parents both typically have negative responses to these behaviors. However, often their automatic reactions reinforce an undesirable behavior. For example, they may engage in a power struggle with the child who wants to be in charge or may frequently reprimand an attention-seeking child, inadvertently providing the desired attention. Dreikurs has suggested that, by understanding the goal of the misbehavior, people can address it more successfully. For example, teachers and parents should attend to and reinforce only the positive behaviors of an attention-seeking child and recognize the power of a child who wants to be in charge, encouraging cooperation and responsibility as part of his or her leadership role.

Adlerian play therapy is yet another extension of Adler's work. According to Kottman and Johnson (1993), its purpose is to "build relationships with children; to explore the ways children view themselves, others, and the world; to help children understand the ways they gain significance in their families and in school; and to help them explore new ways of gaining significance in interacting with others." (p. 42). Interventions used by Adlerian play therapists to effect positive change in children include:

- Encouragement
- Play and stories viewed as therapeutic metaphors
- Limit setting
- Analysis of early recollections and lifestyle
- Discussion of family constellation and atmosphere
- Verbal tracking
- Sharing of hypotheses to promote self-awareness
- Teaching new behaviors

Application to Parenting

Dreikurs had a vision of families that emphasized communication, respect, encouragement, teaching, the use of natural and logical consequences, and the expectation that children should assume age-appropriate responsibilities. He also recognized the importance of families having fun together, an aspect of family life that often is forgotten in our busy society. Dreikurs advocated the use of a weekly family council in which all family members convene at the same time each week to talk about their family and address any concerns or difficulties. Even young children should be involved in these meetings and should have the opportunity to express themselves. Not only can this process improve family functioning and empower each family member, but it instills early the importance of the social group (Zuckerman, Zuckerman, Costa, & Yura, 1978).

The Systematic Training for Effective Parenting (STEP) program is another important outgrowth of Adler's ideas. Developed by Dinkmeyer and McKay (1997), the program has been widely presented to parents and offers guidelines on motivating, disciplining, understanding, and encouraging children.

Programs that provide training in Adler's Individual Psychology typically emphasize education and offer community presentations to teach parenting and other interpersonal skills. A popular format involves a clinician interviewing members of one family while other families observe and then have the opportunity to provide feedback and discuss ways in which they could apply the information that emerged in the interview to their own families.

Application to Couples

Counseling with couples is another of the many applications of Adler's work. Dinkmeyer and Carlson (1985) have designed a program called Time for a Better Marriage that uses Adler's ideas to help couples improve their relationships. Designed as either a self-help manual or an adjunct to conventional therapy, this program emphasizes that partners need to understand each other's goals, provide encouragement, assume responsibility, and communicate effectively. Worksheets and skill cards help couples put learning into action. Dinkmeyer's view of marital happiness as a combination of self-esteem, social interest, and sense of humor is a concise reflection of Adler's concepts.

Application to Assessment

Adlerian theory, with its emphasis on understanding lifestyle and private logic, lends itself to the development of inventories that facilitate the assessment process. Many useful inventories have been developed that can aid the clinician in implementing this theory. Wickers (1988) and Manly (1986) developed the Misbehavior Reaction Checklist to help teachers and parents understand the purpose of a child's misbehavior. Several tools have been developed for use in lifestyle assessment. For example, Kern (1990) developed the Kern Lifestyle Scale, a self-scoring instrument designed to obtain lifestyle information for use in career, personal, and marriage counseling and in business settings as well as for promoting self-awareness. This inventory, as well as many other inventories, audiotapes, booklets, and other materials developed according to Adler's model, are published by CMTI Press ([800] 584-1733). All enhance the work of the Adlerian clinician.

Application to Other Client Groups

Adler's Individual Psychology has great breadth of application as evidenced by the many offshoots and extensions of his work. Most of the common problems and mental disorders seen in counseling and psychotherapy are amenable to treatment via this approach (Sperry & Carlson, 1996). Certainly, people with depressive, anxiety, or personality disorders typically are engaged in thoughts and behaviors that are ineffectual and unrewarding and that reflect an excessive focus on their own needs rather than their place in society and their family. Most of these clients are capable of engaging in the self-examination, self-awareness, and learning that are integral to the Adlerian approach. Children with behavioral problems are, of course, especially well suited to treatment via this approach. Even people with drug and alcohol problems, criminal behavior, and other impulse control disorders can be better understood and helped through Adler's model; they are certainly failing to meet their needs for power and belonging in positive ways (Adler, 1979; Dinkmeyer, Dinkmeyer, & Sperry, 1987). Although people with psychotic disorders may not be able to engage in the kind of self-examination that this approach requires, they may well be better understood through Adler's ideas. Mosak and Goldman (1995), for example, wrote about the unrealistic superiority goals of people with psychotic disorders, reflected in their irrational and nonconstructive thinking. This perspective seeks to make sense of the loss of contact with reality experienced by these clients and to use that understanding to help them.

Individual Psychology has much that would appeal to a diverse and multicultural population. The emphasis on culture (broadly defined to include ethnicity, class, religion, community, gender, age, and lifestyle), social interest and the family constellation, the importance of collaboration, as well as the limited attention to sexuality and unconscious determinants have wide appeal. On the other hand, Adler's approach in its traditional form is an in-depth, lengthy one that is not well suited to people in crisis or those who have little patience or motivation for treatment. His emphasis on individual responsibility and power as well as his exploration of early recollections also may be incompatible with the thinking of some people from nonwestern cultures. Consequently, the approach may need to be adapted to such clients.

Adler's approach does have particular relevance to people coping with disabilities. He wrote of the feelings of discouragement and inferiority and the efforts toward compensation that often emerge in people with disabilities. His understanding of this dynamic as well as his emphasis on understanding maladjustment and promoting healthy empowerment, responsibility, and realistic self-esteem should be very helpful in treatment of people who are having difficulty coping with disabilities (Livneh & Sherwood, 1991). At the same time, clinicians should be cautious not to overgeneralize and assume that all people with disabilities experience feelings of inferiority.

A logical extension of Adler's insights into people with disabilities is to people with other potential deficits in their lives, such as recent immigrants, people who grow up in one-parent homes, those who have experienced poverty or abuse, and those who feel disenfranchised for any reason. Adler's understanding of the connection between early experiences and the development of lifestyles and goals can provide considerable insight into the ways in which people with difficult backgrounds cope with their lives.

EVALUATION OF INDIVIDUAL PSYCHOLOGY

The strengths in Adler's treatment system far outnumber its shortcomings and weaknesses. Although developed about 75 years ago, his ideas seem remarkably timely and relevant today.

Strengths and Contributions

Adler's contributions, not only to the current practice of psychotherapy, but also to the thinking of some of the other leaders in our field, is enormous. Rollo May, Viktor Frankl, Carl Rogers, and Abraham Maslow all have acknowledged their debt to Adler (Hoffman, 1994). The development of existentialism, cognitive therapy, reality therapy, person-centered counseling, and Gestalt approaches to treatment all have been influenced by Adler's ideas. His work contradicted Freud's biological emphasis and drew attention to the human spirit and people's need to be special. Whether or not clinicians describe themselves as followers of Adler's approach, nearly all counseling and psychotherapy now reflects some of his concepts, including (1) the impact of early experiences and family constellation on current functioning; (2) the recognition that thinking influences emotions and behavior; (3) the emphasis on encouragement and support; (4) the relevance of lifestyle and goals; (5) the need to identify, understand the purpose of, and modify repetitive self-defeating behaviors; (6) the importance of a collaborative therapeutic alliance; and (7) the benefits of having a therapist and client with realistic and mutually agreed-on goals.

In addition, many of Adler's ideas have become more important than they ever were in light of some of the pervasive problems in our society today (Hoffman, 1994). Our growing awareness of the widespread abuse of children and the enduring harm that can result has focused attention on the adult significance of early childhood memories. Adler's call for changes in the "debilitating gender roles within the family and the workplace" (Hoffman, 1994, p. 329) has only been partially addressed in our society and still needs attention. His emphasis on responsibility, character building, and social interest seems especially relevant considering the many incidents of violence in schools. His emphasis on the importance of the father in the family and of sibling relationships are other areas of current attention.

Limitations

Although some empirical validation of Adler's ideas on the impact of birth order has been done (Lombardi, 1996), research on his theory and approaches to treatment is limited. Of course, this continues to be true for most of the treatment systems that are in use. However, to fully support the growing importance of this system, more research is needed. In addition, many of Adler's concepts such as common sense, fictional goals, and superiority are not well defined and risk oversimplification.

SKILL DEVELOPMENT: ANALYZING EARLIEST RECOLLECTIONS

Eliciting and analyzing people's earliest recollections can provide considerable understanding of their lifestyles and how they view the world. The following procedures and examples will help you learn to use early recollections in treatment. Exercises later in this chapter give you the opportunity to practice these skills.

1. *Eliciting the recollections.* Begin by inviting people to think back to their childhood, as early as they can remember, and describe at least three incidents that they recall. They should try to think about experiences when they were present that they actually remember clearly rather than retell family stories or events. The clinician should write down each recollection as it is described.

2. *Processing the memory.* Ask about the person's feelings during the memory; discuss any actions or movements in the memory, especially transactions between the client and others; ask about what part of the memory seems most vivid or important; and ask what meaning the memory has for the teller.

3. *Analyzing the memories.* Looking particularly for commonalities among the three or more recollections, consider the role of the client in the memories, the emotions associated with the memories, what other people are present and how they are interacting with the client, the nature of the situations recalled, and the way in which the client responds to the events and interactions in the memories.

4. *Interpretation and application.* Develop a hypothesis or hunch, based on the common themes and patterns in the recollections, as to what these memories disclose about the person's goals and lifestyle. Present this hypothesis to the client for discussion and clarification.

Consider the following three recollections provided by a 27-year-old single woman:

Recollection 1: I remember being in my crib. It was very dark and I felt afraid. I was crying. Then my father came into the room. He picked me up and held me. He said something like, "What's the matter? Everything is all right now."
Recollection 2: I was in a department store. Somehow I got separated from my mother. I looked around, and I couldn't see her. I didn't know what to do, and I started to scream. This man came over; I guess he was a salesperson or a manager in the store. He took me into a little room—an office, I guess— and he said he would help me find my mommy. He asked my name and then I heard something about a lost child over the loudspeaker. The man gave me some candy and kept talking to me. It seemed like a long time, but finally my mother came. She was crying too. I was so happy to see her.
Recollection 3: I was riding a tricycle, and I fell down. Nobody was around to help me. My knee was bleeding. I was crying and hurt, but nobody came. Finally, a neighbor heard me. He came out to see what the problem was, and then he called my mother. I felt better as soon as there was somebody to help me.

Analysis: In all three recollections, the woman is scared and perceives herself as needing help. Through crying, she is able to let others know that she needs help but is not able to otherwise help herself. In all three instances, she is rescued by a caring man. They reassure her and provide the help she needs. Although her mother subsequently provides help in two of the memories, it is the men who are there when the woman really needs help.

Discussion revealed that this woman often felt fearful and doubted her own ability to move ahead in her career and cope with her life. She had been engaged twice and was eager to marry, but both times her fiancés had broken the engagement, telling her that she was too needy and dependent. The woman became aware that, although she was a successful teacher, she expected to get into trouble in some way and was hoping to be rescued from the demands of her career by marriage. At the same time, she indicated that she didn't trust people very much, especially women, and that she often felt overwhelmed by the day-to-day demands of her life. By assuming a needy and helpless role, she was actually undermining her relationships but was acting as if the way to find a man to rescue her was to become as needy as possible: the child crying loudly for help. This useful information played an important part in her treatment.

CASE ILLUSTRATION

Ava, age 10, is Edie and Roberto's daughter. The family's counselor decided to have some individual sessions with Ava for several reasons. This was a way to get to know her and her role in the family better and to develop a positive relationship with her. In addition, both Edie and Roberto have expressed concerns about Ava's behavior. They describe her as always being willful and independent, but these problems have worsened in recent months. They report that she is disobedient, both at home and at school, and that her teacher has reported that some of the children do not want to play with her because she is "bossy." In addition, her grades have been declining.

Ava had met the counselor before and was willing to meet for an individual session. Ava was quite open and started off the session by describing how much she enjoyed seeing the cartoon version of the movie *Tarzan*. She had been particularly impressed by Tarzan's ability to swing through the trees, overcome the "bad guys," and help all the animals.

Ava also was willing to talk about some of her concerns related to her family. She described her mother as "crying a lot and moping around" while her father worked long hours and "just yells about everything." She also reported a dream that she compared to *Alice's Adventures in Wonderland* in which her mother seemed to be getting smaller while Ava was getting larger. As Ava talked, the counselor began to formulate hypotheses about the reasons for Ava's misbehavior, her lifestyle, and her goals.

Toward the end of the session, the counselor asked Ava to describe three early recollections:

Recollection 1: Ava recalled that when she was about four years old she became afraid of spiders. Once, while taking a walk with her father, she noticed a spider on her shoe and became upset. Her father brushed the spider off and squashed it. Ava was so impressed by this that she began squashing every bug she saw until her mother discouraged this.

Recollection 2: Another memory from a year or so later involved an incident when the mother of her friend Lori took Ava and Lori swimming. When Ava got out of the car, she swung her car door into another car and chipped the paint. The person sitting in the car complained to Lori's mother, but she just told him "not to make a big deal out of nothing" and took the children into the pool.

Recollection 3: The last memory involved a fight between her parents when Ava was in kindergarten. Her mother had burned the meatloaf that was to be served for dinner. When Roberto arrived home, he yelled at her mother for being careless. Edie began to cry, but Roberto just went into the other room and ordered pizza. Ava remembered thinking that the pizza was much better than the meatloaf would have been.

In all three memories, Ava's initial role is observer. Although her own behavior is a factor in the first two memories, what she recalled most sharply was the actions of the adults who used strength and anger to gain power and control. In the last two memories, other people's feelings are disregarded. Roberto and the friend's mother seem admirable to Ava while her own mother is viewed as weak.

These memories confirmed many of the counselor's hypotheses. Ava's misbehavior seemed to be a misguided attempt to gain power. She wanted to be in charge and wanted other people to stop telling her what to do. Her recollec-

tions suggest that she believed the way to obtain power was to become dominating, telling other people what to do as she has observed her father and others do. Her mother, who has a very different style, is devalued in Ava's mind because she seems to lack power. This has carried over to Ava's loss of interest in school, which her mother highly values. Unfortunately, however, Ava's behavior is harming her relationships with both her peers and her parents. Future sessions will involve both play therapy and talking to help Ava recognize her self-destructive efforts to obtain power and to change both her private logic and her repertoire of behaviors so that she finds more rewarding ways to gain power. This information also will be used in sessions with Roberto and Edie to help them deal more effectively with Ava.

EXERCISES

Large-Group Exercises

1. Ask for two or three volunteers from the class who are willing to share their earliest recollections. Taking one person at a time, list the memories on the board and then process and analyze them according to the guidelines in the "Skill Development" section. Encourage the person with the memories to play an active part in the analysis. Discuss the relationship of the patterns that emerge from the recollections to the person's lifestyle.

2. Refer to the history of Roberto as presented in previous chapters. Ask for two volunteers—one to role-play Roberto, one to role-play the interviewer. The person assuming the role of Roberto should feel free to be creative and add information as long as it is consistent with what is already known about Roberto. Engage in a role-played interview that will shed light on his lifestyle. The interviewer might ask about family constellation and birth order, earliest recollections, successes and disappointments both in childhood and as an adult, goals and values, and social involvement and relationships. After the role play, have a class discussion of the interview, with the goal of identifying Roberto's private logic, fictional goals, priorities, and lifestyle. Allow at least 45 minutes for this exercise.

3. In the classroom, divide the students into four groups based on their birth order. Groups will be needed for oldest, youngest, middle, and only children. Have each group meet for 15–20 minutes and discuss the following questions:

- What are the common characteristics of people with your birth order?
- What important differences emerged in your group?
- What are common misconceptions or stereotypes about people in your particular birth order?
- What impressions do you have about people in the other three birth order positions?

Each group should select a spokesperson who will present the group's conclusions to the class as a whole.

Small-Group Exercises

1. In previous chapters, you gained experience in conducting interviews and using open questions. You will be building on those skills in this exercise. Form into your groups of four people, but this time change partners so you are interviewing a different person. Spend about 15 minutes conducting an interview with that person, focusing particularly on the following four areas:

- Childhood behavior and misbehavior
- Family constellation
- Important values and goals
- Ways in which the person has sought to achieve those goals

Next the interviewer should lead the interviewee in a discussion of the patterns that emerged. Remember to be encouraging and not to make your partner feel embarrassed or uncomfortable.

At the conclusion of each role play, spend 5–10 minutes providing feedback on the following aspects of the exercise:

- Therapeutic alliance
- Use of open questions
- Ability to elicit relevant information on the four topics
- Use of encouragement

2. In your groups of four, discuss memories of times when you misbehaved as a child. Help each other determine whether the motive of the misbehavior was power, attention, revenge, or display of inadequacy. Then discuss helpful responses that your teachers or parents might have made to your misbehavior.

Individual Exercises

1. List at least three of your earliest memories. Process and analyze them according to the guidelines in the "Skill Development" section. What patterns emerge? What sorts of goals and lifestyle do they suggest? How does this information relate to your image of yourself? Write your memories and responses in your journal (described in Chapter 1).

2. Identify a challenge you are facing that you are not sure you can handle. Imagine yourself capable of dealing with that challenge successfully. Be sure the image of yourself is very clear and vivid in your mind. Now think about how this image of yourself would handle the challenge. As you address this issue in your life, act as if you are that image of yourself and keep reminding yourself that you can handle the situation. After you have made some progress, monitor your success. Think about how well this technique is working, and how you might improve on this intervention. Write a summary of this experience in your journal.

SUMMARY

Adler's ideas have made an important contribution to counseling and psychology and continue to be widely used. His model is useful with a broad range of people. His emphasis on encouragement and logic rather than pathology, power and importance rather than sexuality, and family and society rather than the unconscious are very appealing and contribute to clients' empowerment. Many of Adler's concepts, including goals, private logic, priorities, and lifestyle, provide a useful framework for understanding people. In addition, the interventions and tools that have grown out of his model help clinicians make use of his ideas to assess, educate, and encourage change in their clients.

Many opportunities exist for further education on Adler's work. The North American Society of Adlerian Psychology, the International Association for Individual Psychology, and the Rudolf Dreikurs Institute all hold annual conventions. Ongoing training can be obtained at Bowie State University in Bowie, Maryland, as well as the Alfred Adler Institutes in many cities, including Boca Raton, Florida; Chicago; and New York City. Information on these programs can be obtained from the North American Society of Adlerian Psychology ([312] 629-8801).

RECOMMENDED READINGS

Adler, A. (1963). *The practice and theory of individual psychology*. Paterson, NJ: Littlefield, Adams.
Dinkmeyer, D. C., Dinkmeyer, D. C., Jr., & Sperry, L. (1987). *Adlerian counseling and psychotherapy* (2nd ed.). Upper Saddle River, NJ: Merrill/Prentice Hall.
Dreikurs, R., & Stoltz, V. (1964). *Children: The challenge*. New York: Meredith.

Grey, L. (1998). *Alfred Adler, the forgotten prophet: A vision for the 21st century.* Westport, CT: Praeger.

Hoffman, E. (1994). *The drive for self: Alfred Adler and the founding of individual psychology.* Reading, MA: Addison-Wesley.

Individual Psychology: Journal of Adlerian Theory, Research, and Practice.

Chapter 6

CARL JUNG AND JUNGIAN ANALYTICAL PSYCHOLOGY

Carl Jung is another leader in the field of psychotherapy who, for part of his career, was affiliated with Freud and strongly influenced by the concepts of Freudian psychoanalysis. However, like Adler, Jung eventually broke with Freud because of their strong theoretical differences and went on to develop his own innovative ideas.

Although Jung's work continues through training institutes, current publications, and the practice of Jungian analysts, its complex and esoteric nature has prevented it from achieving the widespread acceptance that Adler's work has received. Nevertheless, Jung's interest in the ancestral roots of our psyche, dreams and symbols, and the development of wholeness through the integration of the conscious and the unconscious have captured the imagination and loyalty of many clinicians who thrive on the depth and challenge of his ideas. In addition, those ideas have served as the basis for the Myers-Briggs Type Indicator, a widely used personality inventory (discussed later in this chapter), and have influenced both art therapy and the incorporation of spirituality into clinical work.

THE PERSON WHO DEVELOPED JUNGIAN ANALYTICAL PSYCHOLOGY

Carl Gustav Jung was born on July 26, 1875, in Kesswyl, Switzerland. His father was a minister descended from a long line of clergy associated with the Swiss Reformed Church. Although Jung had two siblings, one died in infancy before Jung was born, and the other, a sister, was born nine years after him (Ellenberger, 1970). He was apparently a lonely and introverted child who began experiencing terrifying dreams at an early age (Ewen, 1993; Jung, 1963).

Jung's impressions of his parents had a great impact on his thinking, as his later work reflects. His father disappointed Jung because of the father's inability to fully experience his faith; Jung placed great emphasis on the experience of spirituality and viewed that as an important part of our inner world (Schwartz, 1995). Just as his father seemed to reflect polarization (the minister who was a disbeliever), so did his mother, a woman who followed socially accepted and often repressive standards in her outward behavior but seemed to have a different and almost clairvoyant inner self. The divergent personalities of his parents offered yet another polarity. The concepts of polarities and the persona (the parts of ourselves we show to the world) in Jung's theory may have originated in his family environment.

From adolescence, Jung was an avid reader who studied philosophy, anthropology, the occult, and parapsychology on his own. However, his formal education was more traditional; he attended medical school at the University of Basel. There he initially specialized in internal medicine, but his independent and original ideas made this a poor fit. He subsequently shifted his focus to psychiatry and obtained a position at a psychiatric hospital in Zurich, working under the supervision of Eugen Bleuler, a pioneer in the study of schizophrenia. Jung became involved in studying and administering word association tests, one of the first experimental efforts to learn more about the unconscious origins of mental illness.

When he was in his 20s, Jung completed his military service and married Emma Rauschenbach, daughter of a wealthy industrialist. Their marriage gave him some financial freedom and a full family life; the couple had four daughters and a son.

An important turning point occurred in 1907. Jung had defended Freud against an attack by a professor at the University of Heidelberg (Kelly, 1990). This led Freud to welcome Jung as his disciple and eventually as his successor, not recognizing the important differences in their ideas that had been present from the outset (Jones, 1955). The two worked closely for six years. During that time, Jung even accompanied Freud to lecture at Clark University in the United States. However, in 1913, Jung resigned as both president and member of the International Psychoanalytic Association because of his conviction that delusions and hallucinations frequently reflected universal archetypes rather than repressed memories from early childhood.

Jung continued to be a prolific theorist and writer throughout his life, with his work filling 18 volumes. Nevertheless, throughout his career, he had many periods in which he questioned himself and sought to resolve his doubts by immersing himself in his unconscious, using vehicles such as sand play, dialogues with figures in his dreams, and art to develop his understanding of the unconscious. Jung (1964) viewed his psyche as his greatest instrument: "My life is what I have done, my scientific work; the one is inseparable from the other. The work is the expression of inner development" (1963, p. 211).

Despite a heart attack and a near-death experience in 1944 and the unjust accusation of being pro-Nazi and anti-Semitic, Jung worked productively in his later years (Ewen, 1993). His work reflects his belief that the years from midlife on are the time when creativity and personality integration are at their height. Jung died on June 6, 1961, at the age of 85, having lived long enough to witness the considerable impact of his work.

THE DEVELOPMENT OF JUNG'S THEORIES

Jung's ideas, like those of most important theoreticians, went through many phases during the 60 years of his professional life. He gained renown early in his career because of his writings on mental disorders, especially *The Psychology of Dementia Praecox* (Jung, 1907). During the early years of his collaboration with Freud, Jung's writings focused primarily on his experimental studies of word association, memory, and physiological responses to emotional changes. The publication of *Symbols of Transformation* (Jung, 1912) led to the end of his association with Freud and marked a shift in his writings.

During the 20 years after his break with Freud, Jung's work continued to address many of the concepts that had grown out of psychoanalysis, notably analytical psychology, the ego, the conscious, and the unconscious. However, his view of these concepts was quite different from Freud's. Jung also wrote about art, literature, and culture during these years.

The focus of his writing shifted again during the last 25 years of his life. His work became increasingly spiritual, and he developed many of the constructs that make his work unique, including archetypes, the collective unconscious, anima and animus, the shadow, and the symbol of the mandala. (All will be discussed later in the chapter.) One of the most provocative works of this period was *Aion: Researches into the Phenomenology of the Self* (Jung, 1959) in which he drew connections among

Christ, the ego, the shadow, the anima-animus relationship, the historical and alchemical significance of the fish symbol, gnostic symbols, and the structure and dynamics of the self.

During his later years, Jung not only continued his writing but maintained a psychotherapy practice and lectured throughout the world. He received many honors and considerable professional recognition. His work has been continued by others. Particularly important is the International Association for Analytical Psychology, founded in Zurich in 1966 as a training and accreditation center for people interested in learning and practicing according to Jung's model of treatment (Kirsch, 1996). Interestingly, many of the early Jungian analysts in the United States were women.

IMPORTANT THEORETICAL CONCEPTS

Jung's theory, known as analytical psychology, rests on his concept of the psyche. His concept of psychotherapy, in turn, focuses on helping people integrate and make conscious aspects of the psyche or personality.

The Components of the Psyche

Figure 6-1 offers a simplified picture of Jung's conception of the psyche.

The Conscious Mind According to Jung, psychic functioning includes three levels: the conscious mind, the collective unconscious, and the personal unconscious. Jung believed as did Freud that the conscious mind was only a small fraction of the psyche, including two attitudes and four functions. The two attitudes are extraversion and introversion. The four functions include thinking and its opposite, feeling; sensation

FIGURE 6–1 Jung's conception of the psyche

extraversion
introversion

Conscious Mind
Ego
Persona
= 2 Attitudes and functions

— thinking feeling
sensation intuition

Unconscious Mind

Collective Unconscious	**Personal Unconscious**
Self	Repressed or forgotten memories
Archetypes	Complexes
Anima/animus	Archetypes
Shadow	Shadow
Images, myths, and symbols	

and its opposite, intuition. People tend to interact with the world through the dominance of one of the four functions. This is their primary or superior function. Its opposite function is the least developed, inferior function and is most problematic. Opposites in the personality provide psychic energy and, in the well-functioning person, are in balance. The attitudes and functions form the basis for the Myers-Briggs Type Indicator (discussed in the case illustration).

Ego. The ego is the center of the conscious mind. It is formed of perceptions, memories, thoughts, and feelings that are within our awareness and give us a sense of identity (Strean, 1994). The development of the ego, along with our bodily sensations, allows us to differentiate ourselves from others. Although the ego is relatively weak in relation to other parts of the psyche, it can protect itself by consigning threatening material to the personal unconscious through the process of repression. In this way, it connects and integrates the conscious and unconscious levels of personality.

Jung's concept of the ego is fairly similar to Freud's. The ego gives us our sense of the world and our reality. It therefore exerts considerable influence over our transactions with our environment.

Persona. The persona is the side of ourselves that we show to the outside world, the face of the collective psyche. This mask or protective facade enables us to function well in society, deal with other people, and pursue our daily needs and activities. Our persona may change in an effort to adapt to social situations and is affected by our relationships with and the demands of the group or person we are with at a particular time. The persona is a sort of compromise. It often does not reflect our true thoughts and emotions, which might not be socially acceptable. At the same time, it usually captures enough of who we are and what we need to make us comfortable with it.

The Unconscious Mind   Both Freud and Jung agreed on the nature of the unconscious up to a point. Both believed that it was a large and powerful part of the psyche and contained repressed material. However, Jung presented a more complex and potentially positive view of the unconscious, viewing it as a source of creativity and spiritual and emotional growth as well as of confusion and symptoms. The unconscious includes both the personal unconscious and the collective unconscious.

The Collective Unconscious   The collective unconscious has been described as the storehouse of latent memory traces inherited from the past that predispose people to react to the world in certain ways. The collective unconscious transcends individual experience and includes primordial motives or images passed on from our ancestors (Kelly, 1990; Strean, 1994). Fear of the dark and fear of snakes are examples of reactions that Jung believed originated in the collective unconscious, reflecting archaic remains.

The Self. The Self is the regulating center of the personality, integrating and balancing the needs and messages of the conscious, the personal unconscious, and the collective unconscious. It is in charge of the psychic totality of the person. Primarily located in the collective unconscious, the Self can emerge through dreams, symbols, perceptions, and images. It rarely emerges before the second half of our lives and is reflected in our more spiritual and philosophical attitudes. The Self gives the personality unity, equilibrium, and stability (Jung, 1953, 1960). It is the goal of personality development, approached but rarely reached.

Archetypes. The collective unconscious also includes a wealth of myths, images, and symbols of which archetypes are especially important examples. Archetypes are unconscious universal energies that have resulted from repeated human experience and predispose people to view the world in particular ways. They are innate and have been transmitted through cultures and generations; they do not develop anew for each person but exist in and of themselves (Herman, 1975). Archetypes reflect endless repetition of typical situations that have engraved forms and images in our psyches. They might be thought of as stereotypes or prototypes. Examples include the wise old man, the mother, the father, the child, the wife, the husband, the hero, the trickster, the prophet, the disciple, rebirth or reincarnation, and the Self (the ultimate goal of the individuation process) (Ewen, 1993). Archetypes appear in dreams and fantasies, often through archetypal symbols, and influence how we think, feel, and behave throughout our lives. Jung wrote extensively about certain well-developed archetypes.

The _anima_ is the psychological feminine component in a man, while the _animus_ is the psychological masculine component in a woman (Schwartz, 1995). The anima and animus are archetypes that have evolved from generations of experience with the other gender. They have two functions: they are a part of the self and are also projected onto others. Although Jung believed that people have great difficulty relating to the anima or animus in themselves, these archetypes influence the way we feel about and present the masculine and feminine sides of ourselves. The anima and animus also shape our relationships, especially with the other gender. For example, a man with feminine archetypes of the evil seductress, the self-sacrificing mother, and the dutiful daughter may project these images onto a woman with whom he is forming a romantic relationship, making it difficult for him to see clearly who this woman really is. The anima also allows the man to incorporate typically feminine attributes such as tenderness and devotion into his own personality to balance his typically masculine attributes.

Similarly, the woman projects the animus onto men with whom she has relationships. This process, in its negative form, may lead her to view men as overbearing and dominating while in its positive form it casts men in the role of knights in shining armor.

Awareness of the anima and animus can help them have a positive impact on our development and relationships. However, people who are overly identified with their persona—that is, too concerned about the impressions they make on others— are likely to be unaware of their anima or animus and to project it onto others in ways that misrepresent people and relationships (Jung, 1953).

The _shadow_ originates in ancestral archetypes but can be manifested in both the collective and the personal unconscious. It is our dark side that we do not wish to acknowledge, so we attempt to hide it from ourselves and others. The shadow includes morally objectionable traits and instincts and has the potential to create thoughts, feelings, and actions that are socially unacceptable, shameful, and evil. At the same time, the shadow's unrestrained and primitive nature is a wellspring of energy, creativity, and vitality. The shadow is, in a sense, the opposite of the persona.

The persona seeks social acceptance and approval, while the shadow embraces the socially reprehensible.

The shadow includes a person's unlived and unexperienced aspects. It generally reflects negative qualities and attributes, although it may also encompass the golden shadow—positive qualities that were not affirmed or allowed to come into existence while the person was growing up.

Determining the nature of the shadow is difficult, especially for ourselves. However, we have several places to look for information on our shadows. It is more likely to be evident in the manifestations of the personal unconscious rather than in archetypes of the collective unconscious, where its negative side may be too troubling for us to apprehend. Because the characteristics of our shadows are so unacceptable to us, they are the characteristics we are most likely to find objectionable in others and even to project onto people who do not possess them. Our own areas of moral weakness, difficulties in adaptation, and evidences of our own socially unacceptable behavior provide other clues to the nature of our shadows. Great efforts at self-knowledge are needed to comprehend our shadows, but the reward can be the ability to channel the obsessive and powerful attributes of the shadow into greater creativity and power.

The Personal Unconscious   The personal unconscious is unique to each person and formed over that person's lifetime. It adjoins the ego and includes memories of thoughts, feelings, and experiences that were forgotten or repressed; have lost their intensity and importance over time; or never had enough energic charge to enter consciousness. Jung agreed with Freud that the unconscious exerted considerable influence over our current thoughts, emotions, and behaviors. He also believed that bringing unconscious material into consciousness was an important part of both individuation and psychotherapy. However, he had a more positive view of the personal unconscious than Freud did, viewing it as holding negative and unacceptable memories but also providing a source of creativity and guidance.

Images from the personal unconscious can be triggered by daily stimuli. For example, a view of a child riding on a pony can bring back a long forgotten image of oneself as a young child being led around a ring on a pony. Memories that have merely been forgotten or deposited in the personal unconscious because of their lack of importance may be recalled clearly or in fragments when something triggers their entry into consciousness. Repressed material, however, will generally emerge from the personal unconscious in incomplete or disguised forms, via dreams or symbols.

Complexes. Complexes are located in the personal unconscious. They have an archetype at their core that has attracted a related and emotionally charged collection of feelings, thoughts, perceptions, and memories. Complexes are emotionally toned conglomerations that have an impact on our daily lives but, because they are located in the unconscious, are generally out of our awareness.

Complexes that have been discussed extensively in the literature include the Oedipus complex and the mother complex. The mother complex has as its nucleus an archetype of the mother. Through psychic energy, this complex emerges in and is reflected by life experiences and images related to the maternal archetype. In this way, it exerts considerable influence over a person, perhaps leading a man to search for his repressed ideal of the mother figure in all his relationships with women, thus preventing his establishment of a healthy adult sexual relationship.

Jung discovered complexes through his experimentation with word association tests. He found that key words triggered chains of thoughts and associations that reflected the complexes.

Concept of Human Development

Jung envisioned people's lives as divided into two periods (Strean, 1994). During the first half of life, we find our place and accomplish the basic tasks of developing values and interests, finding a partner, and making career choices. During the second half of life, with our foundation in place, we progress toward individuation. This begins with a transition period, a sort of second puberty, during the mid- to late 30s (Ewen, 1993). The search for individuation is a lifelong process in which a person becomes "a psychological individual, that is, a separate indivisibility or whole" (Jung, 1953, p. 383). As part of the process, the whole personality develops: we gain greater access to the unconscious and our latent potentials; we move toward a state of greater balance, harmony, and equilibrium; and clarify who we are in relation to the people in our lives and our society. We become more our own person and less a reflection of the ways in which we have been programmed throughout our lives. During the second half of life, the persona is weakened, the shadow is better integrated and understood, and archetypes emerge that empower us. Our values shift from a focus on materialism, sexuality, and procreation to an emphasis on spiritual, social, and cultural values. Our visions of our purpose and the meaning of our lives become clearer.

Jung's theory of development is an optimistic one, emphasizing growth that can accelerate throughout the life span. Part of the appeal of his ideas rests in his optimistic view of human development in the second half of life, contradicting Freud's emphasis on the early childhood years. The link between Jung's theories and existentialism (discussed later in this book) is evident in his emphasis on finding meaning in our lives.

Balance and Polarities

To Jung, life consists of opposites—polarities—with the nature of their balance determining the psychological health and development of the person. He viewed extremes as harmful because they prevent the opposite tendency from being realized and gaining satisfactory expression. A consequence of this imbalance is the tendency of any extreme emotion to turn into its opposite over time. For example, idealizing, unrealistic love can be transformed into hatred if the love object fails to live up to the ideal image.

The body has inborn self-regulating systems that govern energy flow and help maintain balance. These include the *principle of equivalence*, which states that energy lost in one system will reappear in another system, with the sum total of energy remaining constant; and the *principle of entropy,* in which the libido (defined broadly by Jung as total psychic energy) tends to flow from a more intense to a less intense component to prevent the overload of energy in any one area. Self-regulation is also facilitated by *transcendent functions,* which allow us to make the transition from one dimension of our personalities to another (Kelly, 1990).

Dimensions of Personality   Jung attributed individual differences in personality to two dimensions: the typical ways in which people apprehend internal and external stimuli, and the characteristic directions of their libidos (Jung, 1921).

The first dimension. This dimension includes the four functions that determine how we process internal and external stimuli:

1. *Thinking.* People whose thinking function is dominant react cognitively and intellectually, seeking to interpret and understand a stimulus.
2. *Feeling.* The feeling function is the opposite of the thinking function. People whose feeling function is primary react emotionally, focusing on pleasure, dislike, anger, and other feelings raised by a stimulus. Feelings reflect our valuation of every conscious activity and the importance or lack of importance those experiences have for us.
3. *Sensation.* Sensation involves receiving and identifying physical stimuli through the senses and relaying them to perceptual consciousness. People who have sensation as their dominant function look at the facts and the substance of a stimulus, seeking concrete evidence of its meaning and value.
4. *Intuition.* Intuition is the opposite of sensation. People whose intuition is their dominant function rely on hunches about where a stimulus has come from, where it is going, and what the possibilities are to determine their reactions and decisions related to the stimulus.

Each person has a dominant or superior function that serves as a primary way to organize experiences and perceptions and an inferior function that is closest to the unconscious. We have the least control over the inferior function, which causes us the most discomfort. Having balance or access to all functions is important in enabling people to operate fully in a range of situations.

One role of the unconscious is to compensate for the dominance of the superior function by encouraging the opposite tendencies. A personality that remains overly one-sided despite the efforts of the unconscious benefits from psychotherapy to restore balance.

The second dimension. This dimension describes the libido's (or energy's) direction of movement:

1. *Extraversion.* People in whom this attitude dominates direct their energy toward the outside world; they tend to be outgoing and adapt easily to external change. They are energized by social and interpersonal situations.

2. *Introversion.* This is the opposite of extraversion. People in whom this attitude dominates are most comfortable channelling their libido inward. Although they may have good social skills, they tend to be introspective and replenish their energy by being alone. Being with crowds of people can exhaust them.

Each of the four functions of the first dimension can be paired with each of the two attitudes of the second dimension, making eight possible personality types (e.g., Thinking and Introversion, Thinking and Extraversion, Feeling and Extraversion). The functions and attitudes may sound familiar because they form the basis for the Myers-Briggs Type Indicator (discussed later in the chapter).

TREATMENT USING JUNGIAN ANALYTICAL PSYCHOLOGY

Like Freudian psychoanalysts, Jungian analysts view treatment as a lengthy and intensive process. Ideally, people are seen two or more times a week, almost always with client and clinician facing one other rather than imitating Freud's positioning of client on the couch and clinician out of view (Schwartz, 1995).

Goals of Psychotherapy

Jungian analysis is deep and intensive, encouraging the emergence and understanding of material from both the personal and the collective unconscious. Regression allows access to the unconscious and is followed by progression as the painful and unacceptable elements of the unconscious are made conscious, acceptable, and meaningful. This ultimately leads to resolution of inner conflicts, greater balance and integration in the person, individuation, growth in creativity and energy, and the expansion of spiritual feelings.

Jungian treatment typically has four stages (Ewen, 1993):

1. *Catharsis and emotional cleansing.* This involves the discharge of strong emotions and the development of a therapeutic alliance.
2. *Elucidation.* The meaning of symptoms, the anima and animus, the shadow, and the person's current life situation and difficulties are clarified. In addition, childhood origins of emotional difficulties as well as immature and unrealistic thoughts and fantasies are worked through. Transference and countertransference are explored and analyzed during this stage; Jung believed that both provide information to guide the therapeutic process.
3. *Education.* Education is intended to remedy any gaps in development or maturation that have resulted from maladjustment or imbalances. During this stage, the clinician is supportive and encouraging, helping people take risks to improve their lives. Many people stop treatment at this point, but some continue to the fourth stage.

4. *Transformation.* This occurs when the person has greater access to the collective unconscious and the archetypes. It allows for an ego-Self dialogue, leading to further emergence of the Self and greater balance. This in turn promotes further individuation and self-realization (Dehing, 1992).

Therapeutic Alliance

Jungian analysts take an active part in the treatment process. They are not only analysts but also educators and collaborators in the therapeutic endeavor. Through interventions (discussed in the next section), clinicians promote the awareness and analysis of the unconscious, usually beginning with the recognition of the anima and the animus as well as the personal unconscious and the shadow. With awareness, these elements of the personality can become integrated and their impact on the person better understood and modified, leading to greater social awareness and personal transformation.

Jung placed great emphasis on the person of the clinician in the therapeutic process, not only as a transference object but as an individual. He believed that both client and clinician have an unconscious influence on each other that can facilitate treatment. So that the emotional growth of the clinician does not create a barrier to treatment, Jung insisted that every clinician following his approach to treatment undergo a personal analysis.

Jung saw transference as inevitable. In addition, he believed that although transference could promote self-healing, it also could promote undue dependence on the clinician (Allan & Lawton-Speert, 1993). Thus, objectivity on the parts of both clinician and client are important. While the past needs to be understood, Jung saw the reliving of past traumas as undesirable; rather, catharsis and an understanding of both past and present allow people to ameliorate their present difficulties without increasing their pain.

Interventions

Jungian psychotherapy begins by focusing on the conscious, building a therapeutic relationship, and laying the groundwork for safe and productive exploration of the unconscious. Once that groundwork has been established, Jungian analysts use a range of techniques to provide access to the contents of the unconscious. Initially, the threshold of consciousness is lowered, permitting unconscious material to emerge through derivatives in the client's material, including dreams, images, fantasies, and symbols. When the contents of the unconscious are brought into consciousness, they are explored, clarified, interpreted, and ultimately understood. Then the material can be integrated into the overall psyche of the person and further meaning found until the integration feels complete and natural and the person can instinctively use the knowledge from the unconscious.

Other than the following interventions and an exploration of the person's personality in terms of the four functions and two attitudes, Jung's theory does not devote much attention to techniques. In this approach, the material for analysis (dreams, visions, fantasies, and perceptions) is broad rather than the range of tools used to explore the material.

Dream Interpretation   Jung (1964) saw dreams as the phenomenon that provides the easiest access to the unconscious. Interpretation involves retelling the recalled dream; describing its impact on consciousness; exploring preceding events that may have triggered the dream; investigating the dream's objective and subjective content to look for archaic images and symbols of the unconscious; and assimilating the dream into consciousness, having made sense of it.

Use of Symbols   Jung's model of the psyche rests on his concepts of the Self and the archetypes. Therefore, Jungian work stresses the capacity to think symbolically and see the underlying dynamics and patterns driving clients' thoughts, feelings, and actions. These patterns may appear in symbolic and indirect forms in people's dreams, symptoms, fantasies, and other material. Clinicians' ability to understand this psychological subtext can be enhanced by their becoming familiar and conversant with the wide range of symbols found in myths, fairy tales, art, literature, and religions, which are our cultural storehouses.

For example, Diana, a female client, had a dream about Athena, the virgin goddess of wisdom, war and peace, and the arts, and acknowledged that she related to Athena. According to Greek mythology, Athena came into the world by leaping from her father, Zeus's head. Athena has the capacity to aim and concentrate and can be a torch bearer for those in the dark. Diana had little sense of her own feminine nature and overidentified with her father's thoughts and ideas. Like Athena, she had, in a sense, emerged from the head of her father and was now caught in her own father complex. Awareness of this pattern allowed the analyst to identify the imbalance in Diana and determine a helpful way to focus treatment. By working on her shadow (the inexperienced aspects of herself), Diana was able to experience herself differently and to interact with the world in a more embodied, genuine, and feeling manner.

Amplification is a tool used to explore the meaning of dreams and includes both subjective and objective processes. With the help of the clinician, the dreamer first engages in subjective amplification, exploring the personal meaning of each element of the dream. Then objective amplification is used to elucidate the collective or universal meaning of the dream by connecting the elements of the dream to universal and symbolic images from such sources as fairy tales and myths (Jacobi, 1973).

Word Association Tests   Here the clinician reads single words, one at a time, to the client, who replies with the first word that comes into mind. Unusual responses, repeated responses, hesitations, and physiological changes (flushing, visible tension) all provide clues to the presence of related complexes and other unconscious material. Associations also are used to explore the meaning of dreams.

APPLICATION OF JUNGIAN ANALYTICAL PSYCHOLOGY

Jung conceptualized his work as having broad application. Because he viewed hallucinations as related to the collective unconscious, he believed that his approach could be successful in treating people diagnosed with neuroses as well as those with psychoses. During most of his career, he focused on individual analysis. However, in his later years, he also acknowledged the benefits of both play therapy, (focused on children's acting out) and group therapy. Modern Jungian analysts have extended his theories to group therapy, viewing it as an adjunct to individual treatment that can teach people to operate more successfully as social beings (Allan & Lawton-Speert, 1993; Day & Mathes, 1992).

At present, the use of Jungian analysis is rather limited although a relatively small but growing number of people are studying and practicing this approach to treatment (Schwartz, 1995). Although Jung's attention to spirituality and universal symbols is likely to have some appeal and relevance to people from a broad range of cultures, the long-term, esoteric, and in-depth nature of his work makes it generally unsuitable for treatment of problems that have any urgency. Jungian analytical psychology seems more appropriately thought of as a method for achieving personal growth and self-awareness for people who believe that they have not achieved self-fulfillment and self-realization. This approach, then, seems best suited for people who already are fairly healthy but who believe that greater access to their spiritual dimension as well as greater understanding of their unconscious can bring them more integrated, balanced, and fulfilling lives. Although Jungian analysts also perceive their approach as helpful to people who are dealing with day-to-day problems (R. Shepler, personal communication, November 15, 1999), it is the growth-promoting aspects of this approach that are particularly compelling.

EVALUATION OF JUNGIAN ANALYTICAL PSYCHOLOGY

Perceptions of Jung's work vary widely. According to Ewen (1993),

> Jung's emphasis on our spiritual and religious longings has provoked considerable controversy. Proponents claim that Jung has justifiably extended the scope of psychology by calling attention to a vital area of human functioning. Critics argue that a scientific psychology cannot deal with such arcane issues as the nature of God and the existence of the supernatural, or that Jung's synthesis is shallow and unsuccessful. (p. 14)

Despite the esoteric nature of his theory, Jung's approach has left its mark. Clearly, his work has contributed to the thinking of the existentialists, the humanists, the Gestalt therapists, and other groups of psychological theorists. His emphasis on spirituality in a broader sense and the universality of people's images and experiences are very much in keeping with modern psychological thought.

Several current applications are evident. The Myers-Briggs Type Indicator, a widely used personality inventory, is based on Jung's work. His belief in synchronicity, the idea that nothing happens without having meaning and purpose, is reflected in the thinking of many transpersonal clinicians (see Chapter 14). His awareness that people have a strong need for meaning in their lives and his belief that people have an inherent teleological (purposive) tendency toward individuation and self-realization (Ewen, 1993) are reflected in existential thought. In addition, his concept of the collective unconscious places our lives in a broad context and further contributes to the meaning and historical continuity of our lives. Some regard Jung as among the first to recognize the importance of both play therapy and group therapy, both important modalities of treatment (Allan & Lawton-Speert, 1993; Day & Mathes, 1992). Some see his view of symptoms as messages about emotional needs or difficulties from the unconscious as useful in counteracting an overemphasis on pathology.

Several recent writers and theorists have drawn on Jung's ideas in their work. Their popularity attests to the continuing influence and importance of Jung's work. Marion Woodman, a controversial psychologist, has taken Jung's concept of symbols further and suggests that the body also carries the messages of the psyche. Without proper attention and release of bodily energies, the psychic promptings can manifest themselves as illnesses and addictions (McDonald, 1996). Woodman's (1982) writings focus particularly on women's issues. She applies Jungian thought to topics such as perfectionism, eating disorders, and creativity in women and has collaborated with Robert Bly, poet and leader of the men's movement.

Joseph Campbell's works are also derived from Jungian thought. Campbell focused his attention on myths, stating that myths embody the eternal essence of life and are about identity and the unrealized parts of the self (Ellwood, 1999). The influence of Campbell's writings about the mythological hero are reportedly evident in the *Star Wars* films. Another important and timely concept advanced by Campbell is the spiritual unity of culture and myths. Although Campbell's work, like Woodman's, is controversial, his writings have received considerable attention.

As further evidence of the relevance of Jung's work, consider the recent bestseller *Women Who Run with the Wolves: Myths and Stories of the Wild Woman Archetype* by Clarissa Pinkola Estes (1992), a Jungian analyst. Like Woodman, Estes used Jungian concepts to promote empowerment of women.

Despite growing attention to his ideas, Jung's work has not been well researched. His writing is dense and challenging, complicated by specialized terminology. His treatment approach is a lengthy one that de-emphasizes attention to crises. Many clinicians have difficulty understanding his work as well as appreciating its value to their clients.

Consequently, although Jung has a relatively small group of devoted followers, his work has not been embraced by most clinicians except in their use of the Myers-Briggs Type Indicator. However, interest in his concepts of symbols and archetypes have received considerable interest as people increasingly recognize the importance of spirituality in their lives. Jung does not offer much in the way of readily accessible tools and techniques, and the practice of Jungian analysis requires extensive training and supervision. Nevertheless, the thought-provoking nature of his work and the originality and depth of his concepts continue to lead people to become Jungian analysts and to read his works.

SKILL DEVELOPMENT: JUNGIAN DREAMWORK AND THE MBTI

Jung viewed dreams as a way to view current situations from otherwise unknown perspectives. He believed that in this way dreams compensated for the blind spots of consciousness. Through analyzing dreams, clinicians can link symbolic images and patterns to the dreamer's personal experiences and situations.

Whitmont and Perera (1989), Jungian analysts, have presented an approach to dream analysis using the Jungian model:

1. *Obtain an overview* of the dream, clarifying the action in the dream ego (central character) as well as that of the other characters. Look for any polarizations, dissonances, or repetitions.

2. *Examine the dramatic structure.* Dreams, like ancient Greek plays, have a sequence of unfolding elements, including the exposition (setting), the development of the action, the crisis, and the lysis (resolution).

The exposition (setting). Every dream is set in a particular time and place with particular people. The setting is key to understanding the motif of the dream. Does it take place in the client's childhood home because a dynamic from the past is occurring in the present? Who are the people in the dream? Unknown people in the dream who are the same gender as the dreamer are usually shadow figures (representing unacceptable and unexpressed aspects of the Self). Opposite gender figures can be representations of the anima or animus or can be related to parental complexes as well as images of the Self. Through associations, clinicians can explore the meaning of these figures with the dreamer.

Development of the action. The plot begins to thicken, and the story unfolds. Look at discrepancies if they occur. For example, if the dream ego is not afraid in a terrifying situation, ask the dreamer how he or she would react if this event occurred in real life. Clinicians may want to look for situations in the dreamer's waking life that reflect a similar sort of dynamic—in which the client is not in touch with fear when he or she should be.

While a dream may be related to an external situation involving other people, it is also an image of what is going on in the inner landscape of the dreamer. For example, a woman dreams that her supervisor, a male, is being harsh and demanding. That may well be an accurate reflection of her work environment; but more important, it reflects an inner dynamic as well—the woman's tendency to be harsh to and demanding of herself. Considering the dream's connection to both inner and outer experience allows clients to explore hidden aspects of their own psyche.

Crisis and lysis (resolution). The crisis of the dream occurs when the conflict comes to a head and something good or ill happens to resolve the deadlock (lysis). Often, a dream will end with no resolution, which means that the issue is still unfinished. Jung used the technique of active imagination with his clients. He had them imagine themselves going back into the dream and allowing the action to develop to see how the situation might resolve itself. He might also suggest that the client have a dialogue with a character in the dream to obtain more information. Such approaches usually bring up unconscious material and offer other avenues to exploring dreams.

3. *Identify the images* that need elucidation. Eliciting the dreamer's emotionally charged associations, explanations, and amplifications of aspects of the dream are the key to linking the conscious and unconscious and provide meaning and understanding. Meanings and implications of dream motifs are never fixed. Therefore, the only reliable criterion is the client's own recognition of what aspects of the dream mean to him or her. Analysts are careful not to impose their own associations, explanations, or amplifications on the client or the dream material. Jung once stated that clinicians should discard book learning and assume a stance of curiosity and ignorance when working with dreams.

Associations. Examine any ideas, feelings, reactions, or memories that come into the dreamer's mind when exploring images in a dream. By finding the emotional core of the associations, clinician and dreamer can then ground the dream in the dreamer's current reality.

Explanations. Explanations provide a rational meaning for the images in the dream and state what they stand for in terms of their function or significance. Explanations can be objective as well as subjective. The image of a desk in a dream, for example, might have the objective explanation of a place to study and work. The desk might also have a subjective explanation if it were the desk given to the dreamer by a loving and caring grandparent. Associations to that person would be pertinent as well.

Amplifications. The personal content of a dream often has a corresponding motif in fairy tales, myths, or other sources (e.g., the dream about Athena described previously). The analyst may recognize these motifs. However, unless the dreamer brings up a myth or fairy tale related to the dream, the analyst should not rush the client toward discovery of the connection. Giving the client the analyst's amplifications may impose and interfere with the client's own process of discovery and lead to intellectualizing and avoidance of the emotional core. On the other hand, if the client spontaneously connects the motifs in the dream with stories or images, exploration of that connection can be a fruitful source of information for the client.

4. Formulate a *psychological understanding* of the dream, knowing that it will be tentative until the dreamer identifies and accepts the meaning of the dream.

The following example provides a brief illustration of a Jungian dream analysis. A 35-year-old man presents a dream: "The dream starts with my car beginning to go down some steep embankment, and it rolls over and over and over. I am terrified. Then, I am outside and above the car looking down at my dead body."

In his associations to the images in the dream, the client connected his sports car to aspects of his personality. He liked the sense of power the car gave him and stated that it enhanced his feelings of importance at work. In looking at the car rolling, the client said that he felt like his life was going around and around. He felt out of control and confused about his relationship to his wife. He didn't know why he felt so distant from her. (Note the absence of females in the dream.) To his dead body, the client associated the feelings "eerie and upsetting." In the dream, he didn't know what to do and felt helpless and scared.

The client had separated from his wife and had invested his energy in his work. However, the dream suggested that he was not in control and that some aspect of himself that had been in power too long had to "die." This led to many sessions spent in discussing his confusion, fear, and lack of relatedness in his life until he was able to understand his situation more clearly and identify steps he could take to regain a sense of control.

Readers should keep in mind that although Jungian dream analysis may seem to be an intriguing and relatively straightforward intervention, in reality it requires considerable training and expertise. Keep the strategies discussed here in mind but use them with great caution. Another and somewhat less complex strategy for dream analysis, reflecting Gestalt approaches to using dreams productively in treatment, will be presented in Chapter 13. Dreams are a powerful source of information and insight and are frequently presented by people in counseling and psychotherapy. Both of these approaches should provide some avenues for productive exploration of dreams.

CASE ILLUSTRATION

Because of the extensive training required to successfully understand and practice Jung's approach and because it does not offer many tools to the typical clinician, I have chosen to illustrate what is probably the best known contribution of his work to modern therapy: the Myers-Briggs Type Indicator (MBTI) (Myers, McCaulley, Quenk, & Hammer, 1994). Based on Jung's concept of psychological functions and attitudes, the MBTI was initially developed by Katharine Briggs and her daughter Isabel Briggs Myers. One of the most widely used inventories, it has an extensive range of uses and is especially appropriate for people who are emotionally healthy or have only mild difficulties. The MBTI "is useful in promoting personal growth, self-awareness, leadership skills, team building, and career development, and in enhancing interpersonal skills" (Seligman, 1994). It is used with individuals, in couples counseling, and in work settings.

The inventory yields scores on four bipolar dimensions: introversion-extraversion, sensing-intuition, thinking-feeling, and judging-perceiving. Combinations of these scores yield 16 personality types. A children's version of the MBTI, the Murphy-Meisgeier Type

Indicator for Children, is available for children in grades 2–8. All preferences on these inventories are considered equally desirable; the inventory is not designed to diagnose pathology but to promote self-awareness. The definitions of the first six types have been discussed previously in this chapter. The remaining two, judging-perceiving, can be defined as follows:

- *Judging.* People whose personal profile reflects a strong judging component value planning, organization, order, and security. They may have a high need for achievement and generally are viewed as responsible and hard-working.
- *Perceiving.* People with high perceiving scores prefer to be open-ended, spontaneous, and flexible so that they can take advantage of opportunities when they present themselves. They tend to be casual and resourceful and typically choose last-minute pressure over long-range planning.

Roberto and Edie both completed the MBTI as a way of increasing their self-awareness and their understanding of their interactions and the strengths and weaknesses in their marriage. Edie's MBTI type was ISFJ (introversion, sensing, feeling, and judging), while Roberto's was ESTJ (extraversion, sensing, thinking, and judging). His thinking score was especially strong, while Edie's feeling score was quite strong. Similarly, a large gap was evident between Edie's introversion score and Roberto's extraversion score.

Each of the MBTI types reflects potential strengths as well as potential weaknesses. People with an MBTI type of ISFJ (like Edie) tend to be caring, sensitive, quiet, practical, and conscientious (Myers, 1998). If they feel unappreciated, they can become resentful and complain. They may have difficulty asserting themselves appropriately and maintaining objectivity.

On the other hand, people with an MBTI type of ESTJ (like Roberto) tend to be decisive and self-confident, outgoing, and concerned with outcome rather than process. They can be impatient, overbearing, and insensitive to the feelings of others.

An examination of Edie's and Roberto's MBTI types sheds light on some of their difficulties. Roberto tends to devalue Edie's feelings, particularly because, with her strong introversion, she has difficulty articulating her feelings directly. On the other hand, Edie tends to devalue Roberto's need for socialization and results and accuses him of being shallow and uncaring. Because both share sensing and judging preferences, they tend to have difficulty with spontaneity and flexibility, are uncomfortable with change, and are likely to spend too much time on work and chores, neglecting the pleasurable side of their lives.

Exploration of some of their similarities and differences helped the couple gain the understanding they needed to identify ways to make positive changes. For example, Roberto agreed to work on his tendency to be too critical of Edie and Ava, while Edie agreed to work on articulating her feelings and needs more clearly. Both recognized the importance of having more fun as a couple and as a family.

EXERCISES

Large-Group Exercise

Understanding Jungian concepts such as the following can be challenging:

- Animus/anima
- Shadow
- Collective unconscious/personal unconscious
- Self
- Persona
- Archetype

Discuss these concepts in class, exploring the meaning of each, how the concepts can be used in counseling and psychotherapy, and whether you believe they have validity.

Small-Group Exercise

Complete the Myers-Briggs Type Indicator. Have your group partner score your inventory and explain your results to you, while the other group members observe this process. Discuss with that person your understanding of your inventoried MBTI type and how it reflects or is inconsistent with what you already know about yourself.

After each interpretation, both participants and observers should provide feedback to the interviewer and the interviewee. Feedback should focus on but not be limited to the following areas:

- Use of open questions
- Clarity of information presented
- Adequacy of opportunity for the interviewee to react to the information

Individual Exercises

1. Write in your journal about the expression of the six Jungian concepts (listed in the large-group exercise) in your own life. Consider how each concept has manifested itself. For example, think about how your persona affects your social behavior and how your anima or animus has affected your relationships with the other gender.
2. Identify a fairy tale or a myth that seems meaningful to you. Do you relate to Beauty and the Beast, the Ugly Duckling, Bacchus, Robin Hood, or another well-known story or legendary figure? Write about how it reflects your own psyche and your view of yourself.

SUMMARY

Jung's analytical psychotherapy is solidly grounded in Freudian psychoanalytic thinking. However, Jung's many innovative ideas have called attention to the innate and inherent patterns that recur from one generation to the next and that influence psychological development, the importance of spirituality in our lives, our need for wholeness and balance, and the levels of the unconscious. As a clinician and educator on the personality, Jung sought to help people find knowledge, meaning, and fulfillment, as well as individuation and realization by developing and accessing awareness of their psyches.

Specialized training in Jung's analytical psychology can be obtained from institutes and societies throughout the world. Jungian training facilities in the United States include the C. G. Jung Institutes in New York City, Los Angeles, and Chicago. Jungian seminars are conducted by the CGJ Foundation, which can be reached at (800) 258-3533 or <http://www.jungianseminars.org>.

RECOMMENDED READINGS

The Journal of Analytic Psychology

Jung, C. G. (1961). *Memories, dreams, reflections.* New York: Pantheon.

Jung, C. G. (1964). *Man and his symbols.* Garden City, NY: Doubleday.

Kelly, W. L. (1990). *Psychology of the unconscious: Mesmer, Janet, Freud, Jung, and current issues.* New York: Prometheus.

Schwartz, S. E. (1995). Jungian analytical theory. In D. Capuzzi & D. R. Gross (Eds.), *Counseling and Psychotherapy,* (pp. 137–169). Upper Saddle River, NJ: Merrill/Prentice-Hall.

Chapter 7

DEVELOPMENTAL/PSYCHODYNAMIC THEORISTS

One of the greatest contributions of Freud's work was his ability to attract to his ideas people who were, themselves, brilliant and innovative thinkers with a deep interest in human development and psychology. Adler and Jung, discussed in Chapters 5 and 6, are probably the two whose work has had the greatest impact on current concepts of counseling and psychotherapy. However, many others have played a significant role in both the evolution of psychoanalytic theory and in its use today. This chapter focuses on five individual theorists and one group of theorists who served this important function: Helene Deutsch, Karen Horney, Harry Stack Sullivan, Anna Freud, Heinz Kohut, and the object relations theorists. It will also briefly consider the developmental concepts of John Bowlby. Many terms have been used to label these theorists. In this book, they will be collectively described as developmental/psychodynamic theorists because of their integration of both psychodynamic and developmental concepts in their work.

Because this chapter focuses on many theorists, unlike most of the other chapters in this book, its structure and organization differ. Discussion of each approach consists of three sections:

1. Brief biographical information on the theorist(s)
2. A review of the important concepts associated with each theory, highlighting their impact on current theory and practice
3. A summary, highlighting the strengths and weaknesses of the treatment system and its current status

The skill development section later in the chapter teaches interpretation, a technique associated with these theorists.

HELENE DEUTSCH

Helene Deutsch contributed important ideas about the psychological development of women. A colleague of Freud's, she initially agreed with most of his concepts. However, over her lengthy career, she shaped and modified many of Freud's ideas so that they reflected the special characteristics of women's development and took account of the importance of both the mother-daughter bond and women's maternal role. Although Deutsch's ideas may seem dated today, readers should view her in the context of her time; she bridged Freud's limited understanding of female development and our present understanding of it.

Biography of Helene Deutsch

Born Helene Rosenbach on October 9, 1884, in Przemysl, Poland, Deutsch was the youngest of four children. Reportedly, she adored her father but had a negative relationship with her mother (Sayers, 1991; Thompson, 1987). This childhood identification and closeness with her father was later reflected in her relationship with Freud, who became an admired father figure (Webster, 1985).

Deutsch was a pioneer from the start: she was one of the first female medical students at the University of Vienna, which she entered in 1907. Initially, her professional interests lay in pediatric medicine and helping children with intellectual and emotional disabilities. But by the time of her marriage to Felix Deutsch and her graduation from medical school, her interests had shifted, and she joined the staff of the University of Vienna's psychiatric clinic.

Deutsch was frustrated here by both the low standing of psychiatry in Vienna and the many limitations on the roles of women physicians. Consequently, in 1918, she became one of the first women to join the Vienna Psycho-Analytical Society and began a year of psychoanalysis with Freud. Despite her subsequent differences with him, the two worked closely until 1933, and Freud exerted considerable influence on Deutsch's thinking (Williams, 1987).

In 1935, Deutsch, her husband, and her only child, Martin, emigrated to Boston, Massachusetts, where she taught at Boston University, practiced at Massachusetts General Hospital, and was active in the Boston Psychoanalytic Institute. She wrote, taught, and practiced until her death in 1982. At the age of 89, she published her memoirs, *Confrontations With Myself: An Epilogue* (1973), a cap to her very productive life.

Helene Deutsch's Theories

Deutsch's contributions are primarily theoretical. As a practicing analyst, she adopted most of Freud's strategies, and her writings added little to our knowledge of interventions. However, she understood her clients differently from Freud, and therein lies her important contribution.

Deutsch's Revisions of Freudian Psychoanalysis   Deutsch was uncomfortable with Freud's patriarchal emphasis, particularly his concepts of penis envy and the Oedipal conflict. Her work revised both of these key concepts.

According to Deutsch, Freud's theory that girls suffer from a castration complex because they believe they have lost a penis and thus are envying males is too narrow. Although she believed in the existence of what she called the genital trauma, she did not think that it always played a fundamental part in female development and their adult conflicts. She broadened Freud's concept of penis envy to refer to a general tendency toward envy, which she believed was experienced by all children when they think others receive love, attention, or other qualities they desire.

Deutsch also suggested that the genital trauma could be a positive force in female development, contributing to the development of both sexual and maternal drives (Roazen, 1985). She believed that the experiences of intercourse, pregnancy, motherhood, and breast feeding enabled women to resolve the genital trauma and achieve emotional health and fulfillment. Identification with the child also helped them overcome the trauma of their own birth (Thompson, 1987).

In addition, while Freud emphasized the Oedipus complex and the impact of the son's fear and envy of the father on development, Deutsch placed more attention on the connection with the mother. She did not think it was healthy for girls to replace the mother with the father as their primary love object; rather, she felt that the challenge for girls was to establish a bond with the mother that was close, that served as a basis for the girls' own development, but that was not overly restrictive. According to Deutsch, emotional disorders often resulted when the tie to the mother did not allow the girl sufficient freedom to develop and failed to offer her a role model and guide for positive development. Deutsch believed that phobias, for example, could reflect a displaced jealousy of the mother's ability to become pregnant and that anorexia nervosa could reflect an overinvolved maternal identification (Sayers, 1991).

The Feminine Core   Deutsch emphasized biology and constitutional predispositions in her theory. She suggested that women inherently have a feminine core composed of three traits: narcissism, passivity, and masochism (Wimpfheimer & Schafer, 1977).

Today *narcissism* has negative connotations. However, as Deutsch used the term, it could be either positive or negative. Healthy narcissism involved loving and valuing the self, having self-esteem and self-respect, and being inner-directed rather than allowing others to control one's life. Unhealthy narcissism, on the other hand, was characterized by self-centeredness, insecurity, feelings of inferiority, intolerance of criticism, and a constant need for others' approval and affirmation to counteract that inferiority. People with unhealthy narcissism have particular difficulty handling rejection or disappointments in intimate relationships (Wisdom, 1990).

Healthy narcissism is especially important during adolescence; it facilitates development of a strong ego as well as the individuation and integration of the personality. Healthy narcissism serves an important protective function: it promotes the instincts for self-preservation, contributes to women's strong intuitive powers, and guards women against the dangers of excessive masochism.

For Deutsch, *passivity* was a central attribute of femininity,—an attitude of receptive waiting and expectancy (Williams, 1987). Her emphasis on this characteristic stemmed both from the biological (the man entering the woman during sexual intercourse) and the social (the man being the initiator and pursuer who provided the woman with financial and social status, typical in Deutsch's era). Deutsch credited women's passivity with the development of their concern with relationships, their ability to make subjective judgments based on emotions, their sensitivity, their capacity for love and tenderness, their insight and intuition, their emphasis on harmony rather than conflict, and their propensity for fantasy. Today, important thinkers such as Carol Gilligan (1993) have affirmed these positive traits in girls and women as well as Deutsch's belief that females and males have fundamental differences in personality that must be kept in mind and understood by clinicians, teachers, and others.

Feminine *masochism,*, according to Deutsch, allows women to accept more suffering than men do, enabling them to endure childbirth, menstruation, and other painful and uncomfortable experiences. Masochism is linked to an inhibition of aggression but does not encompass a wish to experience punishment, suffering, guilt, or humiliation. Healthy narcissism serves the function of guarding women against excessive masochism and preventing unnecessary suffering.

Clinicians today might dislike and question Deutsch's terminology. However, her concepts continue to have validity and are not in conflict with current research on female development.

Female Development   Deutsch believed that the goal of women's development was to become a mother and that women had both maternal instincts and maternal love that enabled them to be successful and happy in that role (Sayers, 1991). Healthy development throughout the life span enabled women to establish rewarding lives for themselves, which allowed them not only to become mothers but to preserve their self-esteem and individuality.

As young children, important developmental tasks for girls include individuating from the mother while still retaining a positive and loving connection to her, establishing a positive relationship with the father, and channeling the active-aggressive components of their personalities into directions that contribute positively to their adult development (Deutsch, 1944). Girls who identify with an active and empowered image of their mothers seem particularly likely to develop good self-esteem (Sayers, 1991). Some identification with males also is seen as desirable, especially in helping girls develop their objective and rational capacities and balance the feminine core. On the other hand, according to Deutsch, people who failed to establish close attachments to parental figures tend not to develop adequate superegos and instead develop what Deutsch called "as if" personalities that are unstable, other-directed, and lacking in a solid sense of self (Sayers, 1991).

Puberty revives girls' early sexual and bisexual feelings toward both parents, feelings that need further resolution in adolescence. Forming rewarding friendships with other girls during childhood and adolescence is especially important in resolving these feelings.

Deutsch paid considerable attention to women's biological milestones and responses, including menstruation, intercourse, orgasm, pregnancy, childbirth, breast feeding, and menopause, which she believed was a very difficult transition. She wanted women to participate actively in the birth process and disapproved of physicians' widespread use of medication, which dulled women's awareness during delivery. Despite the great value Deutsch placed on motherhood, she acknowledged that many women had achievement-oriented goals and addressed the importance of integrating these with their maternal goals. In her forthright discussion of such topics, she was ahead of her time and paved the way for our current understanding of women's development and conflicts.

Deutsch had some interesting thoughts about the development of a lesbian sexual orientation. She believed that women with such a sexual orientation sought to re-create the gratifications of the early mother-child relationship in their connection with other women (Thompson, 1987). This concept is thought-provoking, although it has not been substantiated by research.

Current Status

Best known for her two-volume *The Psychology of Women* (1944), Deutsch has made an impact not only on psychoanalysis but on an understanding of women's development from a psychodynamic perspective. Although probably few clinicians today would describe her work as the primary influence on their practice, it continues to be read by those receiving training in psychoanalysis and by scholars of women's development. Consistent with her view of healthy female development, she made an important contribution to her field while being a wife and mother. Through her insight into the development of her women clients and herself, she shaped our knowledge of females, enhanced the relevance of psychoanalysis to women, and opened up new avenues for research and thinking.

KAREN HORNEY

Like Helene Deutsch, Karen Horney initially believed strongly in the ideas of Freud and wrote papers in support of his work. However, as her clinical experience grew, she developed her own ideas that, like Deutsch's, laid the groundwork for some of our most important concepts of human development and psychotherapy.

Biography of Karen Horney

Karen Horney was born in Hamburg, Germany, on September 16, 1885. She received her medical degree from the University of Berlin, trained as a psychoanalyst, and began a practice in 1919. Her own analysis was with Karl Abraham and Hans Sachs, leaders in their field. In 1909, Horney married and subsequently had three daughters.

Horney, like Deutsch, broke ground for women in psychoanalysis. She was the first woman teacher at the Berlin Psychoanalytic Institute (Sayers, 1991). Between 1923 and 1935, she wrote a series of papers that critically examined the relevance of Freud's theories to women's psychosocial development. During the 1960s, these papers were embraced by proponents of the feminist movement because of their enlightened view of women (Eckardt, 1991).

In 1932, Horney moved to the United States to become the assistant director of the newly established Psychoanalytic Institute of Chicago and subsequently become involved with the New York Psychoanalytic Institute, where she encountered some difficulties. Described as a complicated person who elicited strong and often contradictory reactions from others, she directly challenged Freud's work in her book *New Ways in Psychoanalysis* (1939), which apparently led to her disqualification as instructor and training analyst at the New York Institute (Eckardt, 1984; Ewen, 1993). In response, she resigned from the institute and formed the American Institute of Psychoanalysis. Horney served as dean of this organization, which is still in existence.

Horney died of cancer on December 4, 1952. She left a substantial body of work reflecting her broad and timely interests in topics such as women's development and social and cultural influences.

Karen Horney's Theories

For Horney, as for Deutsch, Freudian psychoanalysis served as a baseline from which her thinking evolved. Her early works focused on an analysis of Freud's theories with her own revisions. This ultimately evolved into her mature work, which studied human nature and development in both men and women and paid particular attention to culture.

Human Nature and Self-Realization   Horney's view of human nature is positive and optimistic, more consistent with the ideas of Alfred Adler and the humanistic theorists than with Freud's. She suggested that the purpose of life was actualization of the real self, the repository of the healthy conscience and values that promoted the best interests of all humanity (Paris, 1994). Self-realization involved developing one's innate capacities, emotions, and interests. Horney believed that people who achieve self-realization are self-aware and responsible and able to make sound judgments and decisions. They seek healthy relationships and care about the welfare of others while maintaining their own integrity.

According to Horney, our potential for growth and self-actualization is present at birth. Children whose environment is nurturing and harmonious, promoting their constructive and healthy development, will move toward self-realization (Williams, 1987). However, children raised in an aversive environment, especially one that does not meet their strong needs for security, are likely to develop in a pathological direction. They may develop neuroses that lead them toward unrealistic and idealized self-images rather than help fulfill their inherent potential.

Neurosis and Basic Anxiety   The drive for security, according to Horney, was a more powerful force than either the sexual or the aggressive drive. She believed that hostile, threatening, and unfriendly environments compound children's natural insecurity and lead them to develop a basic anxiety, including feelings of helplessness, isolation, and anger. This, in turn, leads to neurotic conflicts involving a repressed and apparently insoluble dilemma (Horney, 1945). For example, a person might want the closeness of relationships yet believe that people are untrustworthy. Neurotic conflicts are expressed indirectly through characteristics such as inconsistency, indecisiveness, fear of change, shyness, sadistic and vindictive behavior, and unexplained fatigue.

Horney (1945) believed that in an effort to cope with their neuroses people gravitate toward one of three styles of relating to others:

1. *Moving toward people* involves seeking safety through the protection of others, becoming compliant and self-effacing so that others will meet our strong dependency needs, blaming ourselves for all our interpersonal difficulties, and suppressing our own needs.
2. *Moving against people* is characterized by seeking mastery and domination over others, externalizing blame, being arrogant and vindictive, caring only about ourselves, exploiting and manipulating others, and feeling superior.
3. *Moving away from people* is reflected by avoidance of interpersonal contact, withdrawal and detachment, feelings of uniqueness and differentness, pursuit of self-sufficiency, numbing of emotions, and avoidance of rules and restrictions.

Extreme versions of these styles are unsatisfying because they restrict growth and lead to impoverished relationships and self-hatred (Williams, 1987). Emotionally healthy people do not need to use exaggerated and inflexible styles of relating to others but deal with the world in balanced and integrated ways that promote positive self-esteem, rewarding relationships, and personal development.

Selves and Self-image   Horney believed that people have four competing selves (Paris, 1994):

> (1) the real or potential self;
> (2) the idealized or impossible self;
> (3) the despised self, which results from recognizing that we fall short of the idealized self; and
> (4) the actual self, all we are at a given time. The more self-actualizing we are, the more congruence there is between the real self and the actual self.

For people who do not develop good self-esteem and a sense of wholeness, the idealized image typically is the dominant one. Designed to enhance feelings of worth and provide a sense of identity, the idealized self-image actually leads people to feelings of self-contempt because of their failure to live up to this image. In a self-destructive effort to convince themselves that they really are their idealized selves, people may develop unrealistic and grandiose views of their accomplishments and believe that they are entitled to glory and special recognition. Horney calls this pattern a "pride system" that in reality promotes disappointment and self-hatred rather than true pride.

Although efforts to achieve the idealized self-image inevitably fail, people develop strong guidelines about what they must do in their efforts to reach this goal. Horney spoke of the "tyranny of the should" (Horney, 1950; Paris, 1994, 1996), designed to make us over into our idealized selves. (This concept surfaces again in Albert Ellis's work, discussed in Chapter 17.) Horney described four patterns of shoulds (1950):

> 1. Self-effacing people believe they should be grateful, humble, trusting, and giving.
> 2. Arrogant-vindictive people believe they should be in charge and independent, attack before being attacked, and not trust others.
> 3. Narcissistic people think they should be supremely competent, admired by all, and accept no limitations.
> 4. Detached people believe they should not need or expect anything out of life.

Female Development   Horney, like Deutsch, paid considerable attention to the development of girls and women. However, Horney's work was much more concerned with women's current personality structures and their social context than with their early childhood experiences, and she believed that change could be effected by empowering women and modifying their social roles (Symonds, 1991). Similarly, she placed far more emphasis on the female's desire for love, sex, and motherhood than on envy of the male anatomy (Horney, 1967).

Horney (1935) viewed feminine masochism differently from Deutsch, believing that it arose from neurotic conflicts related to the subordinate role of women in society. According to Horney, masochism was culturally rather than biologically determined; and unlike Deutsch, she believed that healthy development in women was not characterized by masochism.

Impact of Culture and Society   Horney placed great emphasis on the role of culture and environment in shaping personality. She believed that people's innate characteristics were not fixed but were possibilities shaped through reciprocal interaction with their environments (Williams, 1987). Conflicts can arise because of inconsistencies in a culture that are transmitted from parent to child (Strean, 1994). For example, conflicts in American society include competition versus love of humankind and autonomy versus arbitrary rules and laws. Horney's holistic philosophy emphasized the importance of understanding people in context. To reflect this point of view, she and Erich Fromm developed a culturalist school of psychoanalysis that recognized the importance of cultural and familial roles and messages in shaping personality (Sayers, 1991).

Horney's Psychotherapy   Horney's system of psychotherapy is an optimistic one. She believed that through treatment people can unearth and resolve their deeply repressed inner conflicts, freeing their innate constructive forces to grow and develop. She believed that with help people can give up their idealized images and find satisfaction in seeking actualization of their real selves (Ewen, 1993).

According to Horney, the clinician's role is to help people become aware of their conflicts without being overwhelmed by them (Rossano, 1996), facilitate both emotional and intellectual insight, and help reawaken a person's capacity for self-realization and joy. To accomplish this, the clinician works collaboratively with the client (Strean, 1994). Techniques of free association, analysis of dreams, countertransference and transference, empathy, and education are important in both recovering the past and unravelling the personality structure. Considerable attention also is paid to exploring the social context and life situation of the client.

Current Status

Horney's theories are probably more studied than practiced. However, she broke ground in many important ways, and the Association for Advancement of Psychoanalysis (AAP), which she founded, still promotes her ideas. Horney's definition of emotional health, "a state of inner freedom in which the full capacities are available for use," is compatible with our views today (Paris, 1994, p. 115). Her analysis of women's development as separate and distinctive from men's is similarly up-to-date (Miccolis, 1996; Rubin, 1991). So is her emphasis on cultural and interpersonal factors. In addition, many of her concepts such as the tyranny of the shoulds, self-actualization, the idealized self-image, basic anxiety, and neurotic styles of relating to the world have influenced the development of humanistic psychology and continue to facilitate our understanding of people. As Rubin (1991) says,

> Perhaps Horney's greatest contribution was and remains her wonderful optimism as regards the human condition. Horney believed that people are basically "good." She believed that sickness made them "bad" to themselves and others. She believed that people could get better, that is, healthier. She believed that people have the capacity to change and to grow in a healthy direction all of their lives. (p. 316)

HARRY STACK SULLIVAN

Harry Stack Sullivan is the first American-born clinician to be discussed in this book. Although his ideas, like the others in this chapter, draw heavily on Freud's (Grey, 1988), his emphasis on relationships and concern with the relevance of psychoanalysis to the general population led him to develop theories and approaches that reflect fast-paced, interactive American society rather than European culture (Mitchell, 1986). While Sullivan's ideas were very influential, the novelty and complexity of his work often caused others to misunderstand his theories and view them as too radical (Greenberg & Mitchell, 1983).

Biography of Harry Stack Sullivan

Harry Stack Sullivan was born on February 21, 1892, in Norwich, New York, the only child of a Catholic family living in a Protestant community. He experienced many personal difficulties, culminating in what he viewed as a schizophrenic episode during his freshman year in college (Ewen, 1993). He recovered from this and went on to receive his medical degree in 1917 from Valparaiso University of Indiana. After serving in the medical corps during World War I, he worked in several government and psychiatric hospitals in the Washington, DC, area where he focused his attention on the treatment of people diagnosed with schizophrenia. His work with this population had a great influence on the subsequent development of his theories.

In 1931, Sullivan moved to New York to further his training in psychoanalysis and establish a successful private practice, modifying traditional analysis according to his own ideas. He served as president of the William Alanson White Foundation, founded the still-thriving Washington School of Psychiatry, and initiated the journal *Psychiatry*. Because his ideas were controversial and diverged greatly from Freud's, many psychoanalysts felt they needed to choose whether to align themselves with Sullivan or Freud.

Sullivan died on January 14, 1949. Although his writings fill seven volumes, most of them were published posthumously.

Harry Stack Sullivan's Theories

Like many of the other developmental/psychoanalytic theorists, Sullivan valued the contributions of Freud but disagreed with him in fundamental ways. For Sullivan,

Freud was too pessimistic, too inflexible, too quick to theorize without supporting data, and too prone to overlook the importance of relationships. Sullivan developed his own school of psychoanalysis—called Interpersonal Psychoanalysis—to address these shortcomings and communicate his own ideas.

Interpersonal Relationships   Sullivan's theory can be thought of as a drive theory, with the search for relatedness being people's primary drive. Relationships, providing intimacy and approval, can counteract anxiety and serve as a primary source of tension reduction. Intimacy, according to Sullivan, is as strong an interpersonal drive as sexual desire (Chapman, 1978). Both have the power to bring people together in powerful unions that relieve tension and provide gratification. Intimacy occurs when people feel that the welfare of another individual is as important to them as their own well-being.

Sullivan believed that relationships proceed according to what he called the *principle of reciprocal emotions:* people enter a relationship with expectations of positive or negative outcomes, the relationship evolves in healthy or unhealthy ways, and each person's needs are met or unmet. The reciprocity of behaviors and attitudes determines the course of the relationship.

Sullivan believed that pathology resulted from unhealthy relationships (Sullivan, 1953). Excessive maternal anxiety, loneliness, failure to find satisfactory peers as children, and other relationship problems can impair self-esteem and the development of healthy relationships in adulthood.

Personality Development   Sullivan, like Horney, had a positive view of human nature, seeing it as pliable and adaptive. He believed that people have a natural tendency toward mental health, which he defined as achieving a balance between the pursuit of satisfactions and the pursuit of security (Ewen, 1993).

Sullivan has described several important components of the personality:

- The *self-system* includes all the security systems and maneuvers a person usually employs to defend against emotional discomfort and anxiety. These actions largely define who the person is (Chapman, 1978). Security measures of the self-system evaluate behaviors and aspects of ourselves as good-me (those that provide positive feelings), bad-me (those that were punished or disapproved of in childhood), and not-me (parts of the self that were ignored or neglected). These evaluations are based on our perceptions and derive from how others regard us; they give form to our personalities.
- *Personifications* are mental images of ourselves and others that grow out of our interpersonal experiences (Strean, 1994). Although they are rarely accurate, these images help us organize and make sense of our experiences. Stereotypes are personifications that are shared by a group of people.
- *Dynamisms* are relatively enduring patterns of energy transformation that characterize people's relationships and emotional functioning and are intended to reduce anxiety and increase satisfaction. These habitual reactions have a physiological origin but flow through interpersonal actions (Chapman,

1978). A hungry child asking to be fed reflects a dynamism, as does a person making sexual overtures toward another person.

Anxiety, Tension, Security, and Euphoria   Sullivan believed that what he called euphoria, a state of total well-being and equilibrium, was the ideal human condition, while tension was the polar opposite (Ewen, 1993). Anxiety, caused primarily by disturbances in relationships, creates tension that disrupts equilibrium. Williams (1994) described anxiety as the fuel that propels people to engage in security operations to minimize tension and create feelings of security, comfort, and self-esteem. According to Sullivan, safe relationships are people's primary source of security.

Stages of Development   According to Sullivan, development before adulthood consists of six stages characterized primarily by social maturation (Strean, 1994). Sullivan's view of development is another reflection of the great emphasis he placed on the importance of relationships. According to Sullivan, healthy development through the following stages gives people the tools they need to form relationships that will reduce anxiety and increase security:

1. *Infancy.* The self-system, personifications, and autonomy begin.
2. *Childhood.* The self-system becomes more coherent. Children recognize that not everyone will treat them well.
3. *Orientation in living.* Children become part of groups, learn to cooperate and compete, and begin to develop ideals and insight.
4. *Juvenile stage.* Children need confidants of the same gender to be their good friends.
5. *Early adolescence.* Heterosexual activity and sexual desire develop, leading to conflicts between opposing needs.
6. *Late adolescence.* Privileges, responsibilities, and satisfactions in interpersonal living all become important as the person moves toward developing mature adult relationships.

Strategies of Psychotherapy

Sullivan viewed all psychological dysfunction as resulting from faulty interpersonal processes. Consequently, he focused his treatment on correcting people's harmful perceptions of themselves through the interpersonal process of psychotherapy (Strean, 1994). Clinicians are both experts in interpersonal relations and participant observers in the process, bringing their own personalities and concerns into the treatment room, which can facilitate or impede communication. The relationship of the client and the therapist, then, is a primary component of treatment.

According to Sullivan (1954), clinicians should have a sincere desire to help, great respect and empathy for their clients, as well as a strong interest in them. Clinicians should ensure that the sessions progress well, that meaningful work takes place, and that clients keep their anxiety at manageable levels.

Awareness is one of the primary goals of Interpersonal Psychoanalysis. Sullivan believed that if people have a good understanding of their interpersonal relationships and the reciprocal processes in those relationships, they will be able to lead reasonably satisfying lives. Developing that awareness involves extensive examination of clients' life histories from varying viewpoints, so that clinicians and clients can reach a consensus about the nature and importance of the events in clients' lives. This brings thoughts and feelings to the surface and facilitates the development of clarity in thinking as well as new insights, perceptions, experiences, and ways of relating. In other words, "The goal is for the patient to abandon sick dynamisms and to substitute healthy ones in their place" (Chapman, 1978, p. 101).

Sullivan placed great emphasis on drawing conclusions based on solid data and observations, and this is reflected in his use of consensus to determine meaning. Achieving consensual validation was necessary because people's perceptions often involve what he called *parataxic distortion,* which occurs when people's feelings, behaviors, and interactions are colored and distorted by their unhealthy early childhood relationships and their private logic and images (Sullivan, 1947). Treatment seeks to help people explore these distortions, especially those that are reflected in the clinician-client interaction, and to shift from parataxic to syntaxic modes of thinking and perceiving that are less influenced by early childhood experiences.

Many aspects of Sullivan's system of treatment are innovative and contemporary. He stressed the importance of the therapeutic alliance and viewed therapy as a learning process. He believed that his task was to remove obstacles so that people could realize their natural tendency toward health, and emphasized the importance of nonverbal communication. In addition, he paid attention to cultural background and differences, avoided giving advice, and recognized that brief therapy and flexible treatment schedules could be very beneficial. He advocated short and simple interpretations and believed that clinicians should thoroughly understand what they were doing and what their goal was—in effect, planning treatment (Shainess, 1978). For Sullivan, when people's views of themselves were consistent with the consensually validated viewpoints that had evolved in treatment, treatment was completed and people could now use their own resources to pursue more rewarding lives (Levenson, 1992).

Current Status

Sullivan is considered one of the most influential figures in psychoanalysis (Greenberg & Mitchell, 1983). His work has had an impact on ego psychology, self psychology, and family systems therapy (Siegel, 1987). He maintained a deep respect for the uniqueness and power of the individual and for the limitations of psychotherapy. De-emphasizing the importance of dreams, free association, the libido, and transference in treatment, he focused on the importance of relationships, perceptions, anxiety, and learning.

Anna Freud, daughter of Sigmund Freud, was her father's colleague as well as his care-giver in his later years. However, she was also a creative and innovative theorist and clinician who focused on child development and analysis and the ego defense mechanisms. Her study of the impact of trauma on children is particularly relevant today.

Biography of Anna Freud

Anna Freud was born on December 3, 1895, the youngest of Sigmund Freud's six children and the only one to become a psychoanalyst. She first worked as a teacher but quickly shifted her interest to psychoanalysis. In 1922, she qualified to become a psychoanalyst after presenting a paper to the Vienna Psycho-Analytical Society. Current ethical standards for therapists clearly were not in place when Anna Freud began to practice. During the early years of her career, she was psychoanalyzed by her father and treated the children of family friends.

Initially, Anna Freud focused her practice on adults. However, her involvement in teaching, rescue work with children and families during World War I, and care of her nephew after her sister Sophie's death led her to focus on treating children and adolescents. Anna Freud believed strongly in direct observation and assessment of children, the need to understand child development, and the importance of social interest as well as the necessity of working with both healthy and troubled children. She combined these interests when she established an experimental nursery designed to serve Vienna's poorest families and provide a vehicle for study of the second year of life and the initial separation of the child from the mother (Sayers, 1991). Although the Nazis closed the school, Freud continued her work after she emigrated to London, where she opened the Hampstead War Nurseries for children who had been orphaned or separated from their families during World War II. Subsequently, she developed the Hampstead Child Therapy Clinic for both research and treatment.

Although Freud's training was primarily experiential rather than academic, she wrote numerous books on subjects such as family law and the impact of war on children. Her most important book may be *The Ego and the Mechanisms of Defense* (Freud, 1946), an 80th birthday present for her father.

During her long life, Anna Freud witnessed the growing influence and importance of her own work as well as her father's. She died on October 9, 1982.

Anna Freud's Theories

Anna Freud contributed greatly to our understanding of children and the ego defenses. Although Sigmund Freud's ideas formed the foundation of her own, she clearly established personal areas of specialization. Because her primary interest was in helping young children and because, unlike Melanie Klein (discussed later in this chapter), she did not believe that traditional psychoanalysis was effective with young children, Freud's work emphasizes a supportive and educational treatment approach rather than an analytical one.

Child Development   Developmental thinking was fundamental to Freud's work. She believed that children mature along a basic trajectory—from the infant's dependency on the mother to the adult's emotional self-reliance. This line of development can be divided into three processes: maturation of drives and ego functions, adaptation to the environment and building object relationships, and organization and integration of intrapsychic conflicts (Strean, 1994). The interrelationships, congruence, and progression of these processes determine whether a child's development is normal or unhealthy. Periods of imbalance or regression often signal problems in maturation, although Freud recognized that adolescent turmoil was normal and usually required time rather than psychotherapy (Crain, 1992).

The strengthening of the ego so that it gradually gains control over the id allows children to mature from primary process, instinctual, id-governed behavior to the secondary process, ego-driven behaviors and experiences of adults. The role of the mother, according to Anna Freud, is usually the most important determinant of ego development. The presence of the mother during the second half of the child's first year of life is especially important; at that time, children have more than a physical need for the mother. Freud believed that the presence of a constant maternal object and a reciprocal mother-infant relationship during that time was essential for development of the child's healthy capacity for attachment (Tyson & Tyson, 1990). Thus, she suggested that orphaned or displaced children should reside with relatives or foster families rather than in institutions and that hospitalized children be allowed to have a parent stay with them.

Child Psychoanalysis   Freud conceived of child psychoanalysis as a method of understanding and asking questions that leads to the emergence of the child's inner experiences and internal world (Mayes & Cohen, 1996). She recognized that children rarely have an active wish for treatment. Rather, they cooperate with treatment primarily for three reasons (Freud, 1965):

1. They trust and believe in an adult whom they perceive as helpful and interested.
2. They wish to please the clinician.
3. They view the clinician as a sort of understanding and safe parent.

These attitudes needed to be nurtured in order to address children's reluctance to engage in treatment (Edgcumbe, 1985).

Freud viewed the process of child analysis as different from adult analysis in some important respects. She believed that children often cannot benefit from direct interpretation but can gain more from the use of stories about toys or other children. She recognized that behavior that appears maladaptive might reflect a child's best effort to cope with environmental stressors. In addition, what might be resistance in an adult may be a developmentally appropriate response in a child. Children have difficulty with free association and often lack the words to express themselves clearly. Consequently, the clinician has to take a more active role to facilitate children's self-expression and articulate the connection between their symptoms and the content of sessions. Freud's treatment of children usually focused on current life events rather than transference and repressed material.

Role of Environment   Anna Freud was very aware of the role of environment in children's lives and believed that clinicians must pay attention to children's environment. She emphasized the need to establish a treatment alliance with the child's parents and understand the child's social and family situation.

Freud did not believe that analysis was the cure for all children's problems. She believed that it was primarily designed to treat internal and internalized conflicts, not problems due essentially to external causes (Sayers, 1991). Freud saw the impact of environmental factors in her work with children who had been orphaned and separated from their parents during World War II. She had great compassion for these children and sought to help them but did not view analysis as the best treatment for such externally caused difficulties. According to Freud, efforts to change the environment as well as supportive interventions were often more appropriate to facilitate development and address the after-effects of external events such as inadequate parenting and environmental traumas. At the same time, she believed that analysis could be useful in helping children who had incorporated social and external events into their psychic structure and emotional lives (Mayes & Cohen, 1996).

Assessment   Freud believed strongly in the assessment of both emotionally healthy and troubled children as a way of identifying the hallmarks of age-appropriate development and establishing a baseline for determining the progress of a particular child's development. She maintained a flexible concept of normal development, recognizing that individual variations and progressive and regressive swings in development were often normal. She sought to obtain a balanced picture of children's development, focusing on areas of positive growth and adjustment as well as areas of impairment. To help her work, she developed several tools and assessment procedures, including the Diagnostic or Metapsychological Profile and the Hampstead Psychoanalytic Index, which systematized the process of gathering information on children's development (Sandler, 1996; Solnit, 1983).

Ego Defenses   Freud's work focused on the ego. However, she believed that an effective clinician stayed equidistant from the id, the ego, and the superego, allowing all three components to surface without making judgments or choices (Strean, 1994).

One of Freud's major contributions was her comprehensive description of nine ego defense mechanisms: regression, reaction formation, undoing, introjection, identification, projection, turning against the self, reversal, and sublimation (Sandler & Freud, 1985). She believed that people used defense mechanisms to cope with anxiety stimulated by either unacceptable drives from the id or harmful threats and commands from the superego. As a result of these ideas, Freud shifted the emphasis of her treatment approach from the drives to the ego defenses, which, according to Gabbard (1990), "anticipated the movement of psychoanalysis and dynamic psychiatry away from neurotic symptom formation and toward character pathology." (p. 22).

Strategies of Intervention   Although Freud's work focused primarily on children and has particular relevance to the treatment of young people, she believed that psychoanalysis of adults could be enhanced by understanding and reconstructing childhood developmental issues (Yorke, 1983). Consequently, her work has meaning for all clinicians.

Freud's concept of therapy emphasized several perspectives that are compatible with treatment today. She believed in the importance of the therapeutic alliance, saying, "To be in contact is so important, and to interpret does not always mean to be in contact" (Freud, 1983, p. 119). She advocated an optimistic and holistic perspective: "In treatment, you work with the healthy side of the child and you work with the ill side—you don't only work with the ill side, but you trust that the healthy side will come to your assistance, although it may not be there or it may not be strong enough" (p. 125). She emphasized the importance of clinician flexibility, letting treatment follow the needs of the child and perhaps suggesting a game to reduce a child's anxiety.

Current Status

Not all therapists have accepted Anna Freud's ideas. Melanie Klein, for example, often disagreed with her, which led to a split in the British Psychoanalytic Society. Their differences offer insights into some of debates regarding effective child therapy. Freud disagreed with Klein's belief that the nonverbal aspects of transference and countertransference reflect the mother's relationship with the preverbal infant. Freud also disputed Klein's contention that neurosis in infancy inevitably leads to neuroses in adults. In addition, Freud advocated a preparatory stage, readying children for treatment, which Klein believed was unnecessary. Unlike Klein, Freud recognized that analysis was not always appropriate and was particularly unsuitable for very young children and for those with practical problems. Her more moderate and reasonable stance has led to her triumph in child analysis; even today, her methods dominate the field in the western world and continue to be consistent with current thinking about children and their appropriate treatment. (Sayers, 1991).

Anna Freud's ideas paved the way for other theorists and clinicians to focus on the bond between the child and the parent. Particularly important is research on attachment theory, increasingly acknowledged as a key variable in human development. The object relations theorists, including John Bowlby and his important work on attachment theory (Bowlby, 1978; Greenberg & Mitchell, 1983), are discussed next.

According to Sayers (1991), Anna Freud "left a legacy of child analysis, ego psychology, and psychoanalytic observations on pediatrics, developmental assessment, and childcare policy" (p. 198). Furthermore, "Her innovative thinking and active collaboration in child care and health and in education and the law, in addition to her extraordinary capacity to be practical in providing care for children caught up in 'experiments' of nature and man-made catastrophes were brilliant applications of psychoanalytic theory in the service of children and their parents" (Solnit, 1997, p. 7).

Clearly, current writers continue to acknowledge Freud's great contributions and their impact on counseling and psychotherapy today. Her writings have left their mark. Those on child rearing include *Beyond the Best Interests of the Child* (Goldstein, Freud, & Solnit, 1973) and *Before the Best Interests of the Child* (Goldstein, Freud, & Solnit, 1979); those on the impact of war on children include *War and Children* (Freud & Burlingham, 1943) and *Infants Without Families* (Freud & Burlingham, 1944). Also important are her pioneering work on child and adolescent analysis and development; her emphasis on health as well as pathology and on the ego and its defenses; her collaboration with professionals in child care, health, education, social welfare, and the law; and her belief that all people dealing with children must have practical as well as theoretical training. A web page created by the London-based Anna Freud Center, (http://www.annafreudcentre.org/) exists to educate others about Freud's work.

THE OBJECT RELATIONS THEORISTS

Although it seems complicated at first glance, object relations theory offers clinicians many useful tools and concepts. In general, object relations theorists emphasize the past through exploring people's early childhood relationships and the present by attending to the client-clinician interaction as it evolves. Observing what is occurring in the therapeutic relationship can give clinicians information about what clients have experienced in past relationships, while understanding of the past can shed light on present interactions.

The central concept of object relations theories is that development and individuation depend on the nature of people's early relationships, particularly the relationship the child has with the mother or primary caregiver. That relationship is critical because it is so linked to emotional gratification (Cashdan, 1988). Object relations theory sees the early mother (or primary caretaker) and child experience as the template for relationship patterns that follow. For these theorists, then, "the critical events that shape people's lives occur not at five or six years, but at five or six months!" (p. 24). Transference (projective identification) and countertransference processes are the keys to understanding those early relationships.

Many names are associated with the development of object relations theory. This section offers an overview of the backgrounds and ideas of some of the most important, including Melanie Klein, W. R. D. Fairbairn, D. W. Winnicott, Margaret Mahler, Edith Jacobson, Otto Kernberg, and John Bowlby.

Melanie Klein

Melanie Klein is generally regarded as the mother of object relations theory (Cashdan, 1988). Her work as an analyst grew out of her fascination with Sigmund Freud's work and her own experience in analysis. Like Anna Freud, Klein focused her work primarily on the application of psychoanalytic principles to the treatment of children. After practicing in Budapest and Berlin, she relocated to England when Ernest

Jones, Freud's colleague and biographer, invited her to share her work. Klein wrote and practiced in England until her death in 1960 (Greenberg & Mitchell, 1983).

Klein was a transitional figure, who shifted the focus of psychoanalysis away from drive theory and toward the importance of early relations. Although her failure to successfully integrate drive theory and object relations theory probably explains why most of her ideas are not currently accepted, she contributed several important concepts to psychoanalysis.

Klein believed that during the second quarter of the first year of life (when the child is three to six months of age), the infant develops the capacity to internalize objects and integrate fragmented perceptions of the caregiver. These *internalized objects,* based on very early relationships, color people's perceptions of their later interpersonal reactions. Fantasies and anxieties stemming from a person's internal object world form the underlying basis for his or her later moods, behaviors, and self-images.

Another interesting concept is Klein's idea that people have two fundamental positions: paranoid-schizoid and depressive (Schafer, 1994). The *paranoid-schizoid* position stems from infants' natural fearfulness, or paranoia. In an attempt to ward off danger, infants separate good objects and feelings from bad objects and feelings. Klein's interest in this pattern evolved into what she called *splitting,* referring to splits in the ego as well as in the conceptual and emotional organization associated with persecutory anxiety and the paranoid-schizoid position. In this position, people's emotional focus is on aggression and other-directed destructiveness, manifested through envy and grandiosity and characterized by defenses such as splitting and projective identification. Splitting is currently viewed as a defense used by people with borderline personality disorders as well as other emotional difficulties in which they tend to view themselves, others, and their life experience in extremes: as either all good or all bad.

The *depressive* position reflects people's concern that images of and connections with the internalized objects are threatened by internal conflicts. The depressive position is characterized by the defense of regression; people in this position focus on emotions such as love, understanding, empathy, reparation of the internalized object, guilt, and desire.

How these positions are manifested in an individual vary throughout life as the person grows. More mature people primarily manifest the depressive position, which is never fully overcome (Scharff & Scharff, 1992).

Klein also believed that play in children is comparable to free association in adults, reflecting unconscious material. This viewpoint is now well accepted in child psychoanalysis (Weisberg, 1994). Klein's ideas about the connection between internalized objects and interpersonal relations also has been accepted, although in a modified form.

W. R. D. Fairbairn

W. R. D. Fairbairn is another object relations theorist of some importance. Fairbairn's writings during the 1940s were influential because of their clear description of the shift in psychoanalysis from the drive/structure model to the relational/structure model (Greenberg & Mitchell, 1983). He modified the work of both Sigmund Freud and Melanie Klein. According to Cashdan (1988),

> Fairbairn's object relations are more purely relational than Klein's in that real interactions rather than fantasy are afforded primary consideration. Despite his retention of traditional analytic terminology, Fairbairn was one of the first to give meaning to the object relational contention that an ego or true self never develops outside the context of interpersonal relationships. (p. 12)

Fairbairn disagreed with Freud, stating that the infant was not so much "pleasure-seeking as object-seeking" (Summers, 1993, p. 226). He also disagreed with Klein, emphasizing the dependency needs rather than the destructive fantasies in a child's relationship with the mother. According to Fairbairn, human experience and behavior derive fundamentally from the search for and maintenance of contacts with others (Greenberg & Mitchell, 1983). Emotional development is characterized by a maturational sequence of relationships. Pathology can occur when the ego seeks to perpetuate the old hopes and ties of the internalized object, when strong attachments to bad objects are in place, and when fragmentation of the ego occurs. On the other hand, emotional health is reflected in an ego that retains a sense of wholeness and achieves positive relationships with real external objects.

D. W. Winnicott

D. W. Winnicott was a British pediatrician and child psychiatrist. His contributions, which come from the relational/structure model, center around the struggle of the self to establish both an individuated existence and intimate contact with others. Winnicott moved quite far from Sigmund Freud's emphasis on drives and instincts and instead elaborated on the importance of the child's relationship with the mother.

Winnicott believed that the presence of good-enough mothering was necessary for mental health. Adequate mothering allows the emergence of a healthy creative self and facilitates the shift from the dependency of the infant to increasing independence. The mother serves many essential functions for the infant. She provides a *holding environment* that contains and experiences the infant in which the mother offers security and serves an object for the child's love and aggression. The caregiver's physical holding of the child allows the baby to become psychologically organized as it sorts and reacts to physical touch. The mother also *mirrors* the child's experiences, validating them and allowing the development of a stable and unique self. In a *moment of illusion*, the infant experiences a oneness with the mother who meets his or her needs, giving the child a sense of omnipotence that contributes to healthy and integrated development. Also promoting the child's individuation and independence is *transitional space*, the growing physical distance between the mother and the child that allows the child room to discover and learn, and *transitional objects* such as blankets and teddy bears, which represent the mother and afford the child a sense of control and contract with the object mother while being separate from her. Transitional objects are frequently used now in treatment to ease separation and facilitate individuation in clients, especially those who are dealing with experiences of abuse.

The mothering experience can promote maladjustment as well as health. According to Winnicott, unhealthy maternal expectations can lead to the emergence of a false self in the child based on illusion and fragmentation, which both conceals and protects the true self. Regression can also result when the parenting is inadequate, leading the child to search for needed but missed relationship experiences.

Margaret Mahler

Margaret Mahler began her career as a pediatrician in Vienna. Her experience with both healthy and troubled children led her to appreciate the significance of the child's early attachment to the mother and to observe and describe the pattern of the young child's bonding to the mother. Mahler, too, elaborated on the significance of the early childhood object relation and emphasized the implications of that relationship for the person's later interpersonal experiences. She believed that the benchmark of healthy development was movement from embeddedness in the symbiotic mother-child relationship to the achievement of a stable, individuated identity within a realistically perceived world of other people. Mahler called this process *separation-individuation* or *psychological birth* and detailed its stages (Greenberg & Mitchell, 1983):

1. The *autism* of the infant who has no concept of others outside of the self
2. *Symbiosis* with the caregiver
3. Initial *differentiation* in the latter part of the first year of life
4. *Practicing* the beginnings of autonomy
5. The *rapprochement subphase* (between 18 and 24 months of age), when the child struggles with the conflict between need for the mother and need for separation
6. The *phase of libidinal object constancy*, which reflects an integration of the drives and the good and bad object representations and allows formation of stable concepts of the self and others throughout the life span (Greenberg & Mitchell, 1983).

Edith Jacobson

Jacobson's major contributions to object relations theory focused on the importance of phenomenological principles—the impact of people's individual perceptions of their worlds. She believed that people's experiences of themselves in their environments, their representational worlds, are linked to their object relations. Within the representational worlds, people's self-images are formed through the processes of introjection and projection of characteristics of the object images. The images are based on experiences of gratification and dissatisfaction with the mother.

Otto Kernberg

Kernberg's work has moved object relations theory even further away from Freud's drive theory. He emphasized the interactive nature of the self and the importance of relational factors in shaping the person. He believed that people are innately object-related and social from early development onward. Kernberg theorized that people have three kinds of internalization systems that shape who they are:

1. *Introjection,* which is the earliest and most primitive system
2. *Identification,* in which an image of the self is colored by an image of the object in a specific role
3. *Ego identity,* in which the introjections and identifications are organized in a coherent and integrated way to provide a sense of self

Kernberg's writings have made a strong contribution to our understanding of personality disorders, particularly borderline and narcissistic personality disorders (Kernberg, 1985). He reported using a modified psychoanalytic approach with some success to help clients develop a more accurate sense of reality. Kernberg's approach is interpretive, focusing on basic issues such as anger, envy, self-sufficiency, and demands of the self and others in reality and in transference.

John Bowlby

John Bowlby is currently one of the best-known object relations theorists. Bowlby believed that a strong causal relationship existed between children's attachment to their parents and their later capacity to form affectional bonds and experience positive emotional development. The main variable in this connection is the extent to which children's parents provide them with a secure base that allows growth and exploration.

Bowlby's clinical approach reflected his emphasis on attachment. He believed that, like a good parent, clinicians need to respect and encourage clients' desire to explore the world and make their own decisions. He believed that the essence of treatment was to help people understand the nature and development of representational models of attachment figures that were governing their perceptions, expectations, and actions and, if indicated, to help them modify those in light of more recent experience (Bowlby, 1978).

Bowlby's ideas have provided the basis for many articles and research studies supporting and extending his concept of attachment. For example, McClure and Teyber (1996) used Bowlby's work on attachment as the basis for their development of what they called the multicultural-relational approach, emphasizing the importance of a sound and sensitive therapeutic relationship with a diverse client population.

Overview of Object Relations Theory

Object relations theories seek to explain the effects of early experience on development in terms of internalization of representations of that experience with emphasis on objects (other persons). These representations are of both actual and fantasized experiences and include an investment of emotions or energy attached to the experience. These internal representations affect people's later perceptions of and capacity for forming external relationships as well as their sense of themselves. Object relations theorists believe that symptoms such as anxiety and depression reflect the nature of people's problems with object relations and corresponding threats to their sense of self.

Despite their shared emphasis on object relations, the theorists we have discussed had considerable differences of opinion. The British Psychoanalytic Group reflected these differences by dividing their curriculum into the *A* group (Freudian) and the *B* group (Kleinian). Winnicott began the *C* group, which saw value in both of the other groups. Object relations theorists were also divided according to national lines. For example, the British group (including Klein, Fairbairn, and Winnicott) placed great emphasis on transference and countertransference, while the American group (including Mahler and Kernberg) was more interested in ego functioning and adaptation (Scharff & Scharff, 1992).

Intervention Strategies   Freudian psychoanalysis forms the backdrop for object relations therapists. Many of their approaches are drawn from that school of thought, and their work typically entails long-term and intensive analysis. However, changes in emphasis, application, and technique distinguish object relations therapists from more traditional Freudian analysts.

Although both groups paid attention to transference, for the object relations therapists, transference (or projective identification, as it was also called) was viewed as a part of the internalized object or the self that was projected onto the therapist. The internal object relationship was then believed to be re-created in the clinician-client relationship, where it would be reworked to allow modification of the internalized object (Scharff & Scharff, 1992).

Establishing a positive therapeutic alliance was much more important to the object relations theorists than it was to traditional psychoanalysts. Just as an important element in the mother's role is to provide nurturing and care, so are those elements perceived as important in the therapeutic process. According to object relations theory, clinicians should deliberately introduce these and other elements into therapy to facilitate the transference. In a sense, the therapist becomes a good-enough mother, providing a holding environment for people who may never have had adequate parenting. Affective exchanges between clinician and client bring the internal object relationships into the here and now, allow the client to reexperience those relationships, and promote insight and change.

Resistance in clients is viewed as reflecting a rigid transference, growing out of the client's strong need for a particular type of object relationship. This leads to the client's inability to relate to the clinician in ways that are flexible and reflect present rather than past relationships. Resistance is a way for people to keep painful emotions and fantasies buried in the unconscious to protect the self from the threat they pose. Clinicians can reduce resistance by acknowledging and accepting clients' internal worlds and by being patient, consistent, safe, and available.

Understanding countertransference as well as transference is important in object relations theory. Countertransference is viewed as an inevitable product of the interaction between the client and the therapist and a source of important clues to the nature of the transference relationship (Greenberg & Mitchell, 1983). In understanding and dealing with their countertransference reactions, clinicians should be clear about whether those reactions stem largely from interactions with a client or from the clinicians' own issues and experiences.

Assessment is another important treatment ingredient in object relations therapy. The clinician, in collaboration with the client, assesses the person's development; unconscious patterns; internalized object relationships; and underlying anxieties, defenses, and projective identifications. A thorough assessment is necessary to pave the way for well-timed and accurate interpretations that will make a difference.

Interpretation is a primary route to change. Through analysis and interpretation of transference and countertransference, past and present experiences, and the manifestations of the unconscious, people work through their internalized and unconscious emotions and relationships. *Working through* is the process of obtaining clarification and resolution of projective identification patterns by experiencing them over and over at progressively higher levels of development (Scharff & Scharff, 1992). This enables people to develop the capacity to transcend old patterns and have genuine emotional contact with others. As Fairbairn (cited in Greenberg & Mitchell, 1983) stated, "The analytic process is understood not as consisting of a resolution of unconscious conflict over pleasure-seeking impulses, but as a process through which the capacity for making direct and full contact with real other human beings is restored." (p. 156). When this is accomplished, and when people can have loving relationships, cooperate with and perceive others accurately, have empathy and concern for others, and manage their own stress, they are ready for their analysis to terminate.

Current Status

Certainly, modern clinicians are aware of weaknesses in the ideas of the object relations therapists. Probably most glaring is their lack of emphasis on the role of the father. However, when these theories were developed, traditional family patterns with the mother as a child's primary caregiver were the norm. In addition, the birth process as well as breast feeding naturally gave the mother an essential role in the child's life. Other shortcomings of object relations theory include

- Complex ideas and vocabulary, sometimes compounded by a lack of clarity in definitions and the many differences of opinion among theorists
- An excessively narrow focus on issues of infantile dependence and inadequate mothering that downplays the impact of individual differences and incompatibilities between mother-child dyads
- A view of people as relatively passive victims of parental deficiency.

On the other hand, objects relations theories have made many important contributions to counseling and psychotherapy and are, in fact, connected with current clinical thinking in some important ways. In recent years, research by Bowlby (1978, 1988) and others has affirmed object relations theorists' emphasis on the importance of the child's developing a positive attachment to the mother. Many believe that the pervasiveness of attachment problems in western society is growing because of the high divorce rate, high stress in our daily lives, and parents' demanding and busy schedules. This, in turn, has been implicated as a factor in the growing rates of youth violence and family instability.

Other contributions of object relations theory to modern counseling and psychotherapy include

- The link it established between developmental theory and psychoanalytic practice (Weisberg, 1994)
- The emphasis it placed on making sure that the therapeutic situation is a safe place, a holding environment and a place of containment, that enables people to meet the challenges of emotional growth without being engulfed by troubling emotions
- The recognition of the importance of both countertransference and transference, the person of the therapist, the therapeutic alliance, and attention to the here-and-now clinical situation.

Object relations therapy has a wide application and is being used with individuals, couples and families (Scharff, 1989); in play therapy, art therapy, and group therapy; and for treatment of substance misuse, anorexia nervosa, personality disorders (especially borderline personality disorder), and even psychosis (Scharff & Scharff, 1992). Thomas and Garske (1995) have advocated the use of this model for people with disabilities, believing that it can provide insight into barriers to adjustment and ways to help people deal effectively with disabilities.

HEINZ KOHUT

Although Heinz Kohut's work grew out of Freudian psychoanalysis (as did the work of everyone discussed in this chapter), his self psychology moved the field toward its next major phase of development: humanistic, existential, and other theories that focus on emotion and sensation (see Part 3). Kohut's emphasis on empathy, current experience, and the importance of taking a holistic view of people as well as his groundbreaking work on narcissism made essential contributions to counseling and psychotherapy.

Biography of Heinz Kohut

Born in Vienna, Austria, in 1913, Kohut was an only child. Even in his youth, he was interested in medicine, and he received his medical degree in 1938. After a brief psychoanalysis, he began to focus his work on psychiatry and neurology. He completed his residency at the University of Chicago and became a U.S. citizen in 1945. In 1948, he married Betty Meyer, a social worker.

During the 1950s, Kohut established a successful clinical practice, which gave him experience on which to base his developing ideas. He has been described as meticulous but playful; he had the ability to invest himself heavily in his work as a clinician, teacher, researcher, writer, and leader in his field but also to set limits and to enjoy the moment (Stozier, 1985). Until 1965, Kohut was a leading spokesperson for Freudian psychoanalysis. However, his ideas about narcissism and his book *The Analysis of the Self* (1971) created a rift between him and other leading analysts of his time. This, coupled with his mother's development of paranoid delusions and her death in 1972, led him to engage in considerable self-analysis and creative thought and writing. Kohut died in 1981, leaving behind a considerable body of work.

Heinz Kohut's Theories

Lynch (1991) has described Kohut's self psychology:

> The patient needs to verbalize and experience fully the core deficits of the self structure (as exemplified in the kind of transferential response which develops). The therapist needs to take the transferential response and remain empathically immersed with the patient to learn fully about the nature and extent of the deficits and their genetic origins. Through the process of understanding and explaining, the therapist helps the patient achieve a new and lasting level of strength and maturity for what once was an enfeebled, vulnerable psychological self. (p. 25)

This quotation captures the essence of self psychology: using empathy and interpretation, clinicians explore early developmental deficits reflected in the transference relationship to help people emerge from their unhappy conditions and find joy and empowerment.

The Self Kohut, like the object relations theorists, placed great emphasis on the early relationship of young children and their parents. He ultimately developed a concept of the self as evolving out of this relationship and having a primary influence on development. In his framework, this unified and observable self was the focus of analysis rather than Freud's ego, id, and superego (Cocks, 1994). A strong self allows us to tolerate and successfully handle the successes and failures in our lives, while a deficient self is developmentally frozen and highly prone to fragmentation (Gabbard, 1990; Kohut & Wolf, 1978). The self structure, which begins at 18 months of age, has three poles (Lynch, 1991):

1. The *grandiose self*, which needs confirmation, validation, and mirroring responses from others
2. The *idealizing self*, which reflects the internalized and idealized selfobject derived from early relationships and leads to formation of goals and ideals for the self
3. The *twinship sector*, which seeks mutuality and equality in relationships with others as well as sharing of values and preferences

Kohut's concept of the selfobject is broader than the internalized object discussed by the object relations theorists. They referred almost exclusively to children's internalization of their image of the mother, while Kohut used *selfobject* as a generic term for our intrapsychic experiences of others, our mental representations of them experienced as part of the self or in service of the self. Selfobjects are needed throughout our lives. These internalized images constantly change and mature to provide us with a sense of ourselves, self-esteem, soothing, and validation, and to meet our needs for mirroring, idealizing, and twinship (Gabbard, 1990). Maturation and emotional health are reflected by our ability to use more appropriate and growth-promoting selfobjects.

View of People   Self psychology is based not on efforts to contain the drives but on understanding and promoting people's development in the context of a responsive environment so that they can achieve their positive potentials (Lachmann & Beebe, 1995). For Kohut, feelings of sexuality and aggression, appropriately moderated, are part of our normal development and integral parts of ourselves, not the primary source of our difficulties.

According to Kohut (1982), traditional psychoanalysis views a person with emotional difficulties as the "guilty man"—a person trapped in a conflict between the drives of the id and the constraints of the superego. Instead, Kohut speaks of the "tragic man," "attempting, and never quite succeeding, to realize the program laid down in his depth during the span of his life," his failures overshadowing his successes (p. 402). He viewed the tragic man as typically the product of an unempathic mother and an absent father. A representation of both men and women with emotional difficulties, the tragic man has the potential for growth, joy, adjustment, and fulfillment but consistently fails to reach that potential (Cocks, 1994).

Empathy, providing affirmation and mirroring, is essential to development of the healthy self. Initially, children need empathy from their parents to promote the development of the children's psychological strengths (Cocks, 1994). However, empathy is later sought from others and is an essential ingredient of the therapeutic relationship. This thinking reflects Kohut's emphasis on the present—what he called the *experience near* as distinguished from the *experience far,* which refers to the id, ego, and superego and to early childhood experiences. Kohut believed that, although past experiences certainly have a profound impact on our development, it is the present or here-and-now experiences that lead to their resolution.

Narcissism and Other Clinical Syndromes   Kohut perceived narcissism, one of the central concepts of his later work, as existing on a continuum (Nicholson, 1991). Healthy narcissism allows people to value themselves and their needs and to have self-confidence. Pathological narcissism often results when healthy development of a cohesive self is blocked. Unhealthy narcissism involves an unstable self-concept, grandiose fantasies of self-importance, a sense of entitlement, and an inability to think of others as anything but need-gratifying objects. Pathological narcissism can be reflected in a broad range of symptoms, including depression, anxiety, hypochondriasis, misuse of drugs and alcohol, acting out, and dysfunctional sexual experiences as well as fragmentation of the self and lack of a zest for life (Wolf, 1994).

Kohut believed that unhealthy narcissism was at the root of many people's emotional difficulties and that it could be modified through treatment.

Kohut also identified a number of clinical syndromes that he often saw in treatment, including the fragmented self, the overstimulated self, the overburdened self, and the understimulated self (Nicholson, 1991). In addition, he described some character or personality types, including the mirror hungry, ideal hungry, alter-ego hungry, contact shunning, and merger hungry. Kohut linked these syndromes and character types to particular early experiences and symptoms and suggested treatment strategies for each. This information is useful in helping clinicians understand many of the personality disorders and other longstanding and pervasive unhealthy patterns that clients manifest and facilitates efforts to plan strategies that are likely to be effective in treating these challenging disorders.

Strategies of Intervention

In self psychology, treatment focuses on a client's subjective experiences and meanings, enabling the clinician to enter the client's world as much as possible (Donner, 1991). From that vantage point, clinicians address the condition of the self, including symptoms, developmental deficits, intrapsychic conflicts, and relational and behavioral difficulties, with the ultimate goal being development of a healthy and cohesive self.

Empathy   Kohut viewed empathy as essential to effective treatment. Self psychology theorists believe that clinicians should take a nurturing role; emphasize active and open listening; and provide acceptance, understanding, and explanations or interpretations to facilitate the unfolding of the client's subjective world. Clinicians constantly reflect the essence of what clients have said, and clients' confirmation or rejection of these reflections allows clinicians to truly understand clients' inner reality.

Clinicians avoid judging and view even narcissistic needs as developmentally understandable rather than immature and self-centered. Resistance as well as symptoms are viewed as efforts to protect the vulnerable self and maintain some sense of internal cohesion. Clinicians' obvious interest in clients and their valuing of clients' words increase client investment in treatment and encourage disclosure of painful and unacceptable material.

Transference   Clinicians' empathy for clients facilitates the development of transference and clarifies the needs of that relationship. In an idealizing selfobject transference, the vulnerable client perceives the clinician as a source of strength and safety who is able to respond to unmet developmental needs, including mirroring, idealizing, and twinship (Lachmann, 1993). Clients' needs reflect those that were frustrated in the course of development, and the transference is viewed as a reactivation of the selfobject experience. Empathy allows clinicians to contain and rebuild the selfobject reflected in the transference relationship. Techniques such as *optimal frustration* and *optimal responsiveness* allow clients to change their internalizations, incorporating the functions provided by the clinician, so that clients develop an inner sense of self-competence that allows them to deal successfully with frustrations and nurture themselves. Kohut discusses this process in *The Restoration of the Self* (1977) and *How Does Analysis Cure?* (1984).

Current Status

During the 1980s and 1990s, Kohut's concepts were expanded on and substantiated through empirical research on infant development (Lachmann & Beebe, 1995). His work also has gained in influence because of our increasing attention to personality disorders and the sound ideas that his work provides for treating them (Meares, 1996). Not only is Kohut's work relevant to treatment of narcissistic and other personality disorders, but it also has demonstrated its value in treating depression and anxiety (Nicholson, 1991), eating disorders (Bachar, 1998), and the impact of abuse (Hirschman, 1997). Self psychology also seems to have value in treating people with psychoses and borderline personality disorders, although the approach needs to be adapted in such cases.

Kohut's emphasis on empathy and the importance of the clinician-client collaboration, his understanding of narcissism and the role it often plays in emotional disorders, and his phenomenological perspective, emphasizing people's subjective reality, are important contributions not only to the practice of depth psychotherapy but also to the development of humanistic approaches to counseling and psychotherapy. His work bridges Freudian psychoanalysis and the person-centered and existential counseling approaches discussed in Part 3. He provides a view of understanding and helping people that is analytical in nature but at the same time consistent with the current clinical emphasis on early attachments; subjective reality; and the importance of promoting resilience, optimism, and empowerment in clients. Kohut's view of the tragic man captures the pitfalls of our ambitious and hurried society and enhances the timeliness of his theory.

SKILL DEVELOPMENT: INTERPRETATION

Interpretation is one of the fundamental skills of psychoanalysis and is employed by all of the clinicians discussed in this chapter. Interpretations provide people with an alternative frame of reference for viewing a problem or situation. Interpretations can link a current reaction that may appear superficial or unimportant with a past experience that has considerable depth and significance.

Interpretations often reflect insights that clinicians have into clients' motives and behaviors that may not yet be in clients' awareness. For that reason, practitioners must deliver interpretations with great care. Ideally, questioning and giving information can be used to enable clients to make their own interpretations. Timing is another critical variable in effective presentation of interpretations; they should be presented when people seem ready to accept and understand them. Clinicians also should be very clear about what they hope to accomplish in making an interpretation. Although it may enhance clinicians' self-esteem to realize that they are insightful and have drawn important connections between pieces of information that clients have presented, interpretations, of course, should never be self-serving or primarily for the purpose of demonstrating the clinician's skills. Rather, they should be used to move clients forward in positive ways such as helping them gain insights that will enhance their self-esteem, empower them, help them make better choices, facilitate their efforts to manage and change their emotions, and improve their interpersonal and other behaviors. Finally, presentation of interpretations should never create an adversarial situation in which clinician and client are in conflict or engaged in a debate about who is right. Generally, interpretations are most successful if they are presented tentatively as information for clients to think about and discuss. If interpretations are not meaningful to clients, clients should have the right to reject them without being made to feel as though they are cowardly, unintelligent, or fearful of change. Using language carefully and thoughtfully can contribute to the successful delivery of interpretations.

CASE ILLUSTRATION

Consider the following pair of dialogues between Roberto and his counselor. Dialogue 1 has many shortcomings that Dialogue 2 is designed to overcome. Think about the strengths and weaknesses in each dialogue and what you can learn from them about the use of interpretations. Assume that the clinician's interpretation is accurate but don't assume that everything the clinician says reflects sound treatment. The exercises in the next section will give you an opportunity to analyze these dialogues.

DIALOGUE 1

Roberto: I just don't understand what's wrong with Edie. She has a wonderful daughter and husband. Why can't she be contented?

Clinician: Your intolerance of Edie's wish for change reflects your enmeshed childhood relationship with your own mother. You wanted your own mother to dote on you, and she did. Now you cannot accept Edie because she is different from your internalized object of your mother.

Roberto: I'm not sure what you're talking about; but I know Edie is not my mother, and I try to see her as an individual.

Clinician: Yes, but your unconscious needs are causing you to sabotage your relationship with Edie.

DIALOGUE 2

Roberto: I just don't understand what's wrong with Edie. She has a wonderful daughter and husband. Why can't she be contented?

Clinician: I wonder how Edie's role compares with the one your mother took when she had young children?

Roberto: Oh, my mother was very different from Edie. She devoted her whole life to her children. Me especially. I think I'm her favorite. She was so happy with her family. I don't understand why Edie doesn't feel that way.

Clinician: So your very positive experience with the nurturing you received from your own mother and the joy she took in her role as mother make it especially hard for you to understand Edie.

Roberto: Yes, I guess that's true. But Edie loves Ava, and she's so sad that we couldn't have more children. Shouldn't she feel happy that she has a home and family?.

Clinician: I can certainly understand why this would be puzzling to you and maybe even make you angry sometimes because Edie doesn't seem to be the kind of mother you think she should be.

Roberto: Yes, I guess I don't want to admit it to Edie, but I suppose she senses my anger. I'm trying to help her find herself, and I realize that times have changed and not all women feel like my mother did, but it still bothers me sometimes. I want Ava to have the best possible mother . . . like I did.

Clinician: I can hear you really struggling with a conflict inside yourself. On the one hand, you want to help Edie figure out what would make her happy; but on the other hand, you are concerned that it might keep Ava from having the good mothering you had.

Roberto: Yes, that's really it.

Clinician: Could it also be that sometimes you feel angry and almost deprived because Edie is not giving you the caring that your mother taught you to expect from a woman?

Roberto: Well, . . . I don't know. . . . I mean, I'm a grown man; I don't need anybody to mother me anymore. I can take care of myself.

Clinician: You certainly have become very self-sufficient. Yet sometimes most of us still can feel that little child inside us who wants a loving mother to ease our fears and tell us how special we are.

Roberto: Isn't there something wrong with a grown man having those feelings?

Clinician: I don't think so, especially if we can recognize those feelings and use them in ways that help us.

Roberto: Well, I guess I do feel that way sometimes. Every once in a while I get this feeling like I'm a scared kid, like I just skinned my knee, and I want somebody to tell me it's all right. But that's a fantasy; there's nobody to wipe my eyes and wash my knee and make everything all right. And my problems now go way beyond a skinned knee.

Clinician: It sounds like it's hard for you to let yourself talk about those feelings and even to have those feelings. But from what you're saying, they are there sometimes, and maybe they are having an impact on your relationship with Edie and your expectations of her.

Roberto: You know, you may have something there. I never thought about any connection between my feelings toward Edie and the kind of mother I have. What can I do about that?

EXERCISES

Large-Group Exercises

1. Discuss the two dialogues you have just read. Consider the following dimensions of the delivery of each dialogue: content, language, purpose, timing, impact on clinician-client relationship, how large a part the client played in the

interpretation process, and overall effectiveness. Consider ways in which the second dialogue might have been made even better.

2. Have each student list what he or she perceives as the three greatest contributions of the theories presented in this chapter as well as the three concepts that seem least acceptable. List these on the board, identifying areas of agreement among students. Discuss the thinking behind the choices.

3. The leading thinkers in psychoanalysis disagreed among themselves. Stage one or both of the following discussions. Participating students are encouraged to do some research on the theorists whose ideas they will represent.

   • Select three people to represent Sigmund Freud's ideas. Select three people to represent the ideas of the developmental/psychodynamic theorists. The two groups should debate the respective merits of their positions, focusing especially on the importance of drives versus relationships in human development.

   • Select six people, one to represent each of the major theories or theoreticians in this chapter (Deutsch, Horney, Sullivan, Anna Freud, object relations, and Heinz Kohut). Assume they have met at the annual meeting of the International Society for Psychoanalysis. Allow approximately 45 minutes for them to engage in a discussion in front of the class about their respective ideas on how early development affects later development. After the discussion, allow time for the class to process the discussion and ask questions of the "experts" to obtain clarification about their ideas.

Small-Group Exercise

Divide into your groups of four students. One dyad should assume the roles of clinician and client, with the client being Edie or Ava. Do a 10-ten minute role play in which the client discusses her early relationships with her parents and her current social and self-esteem difficulties. Using information already available about Edie and Ava, the clinician should make at least two interpretations, linking the past and the present.

The two observers should take notes on the effectiveness of the interpretation and of the role-play as a whole. Then the four should discuss the nature, language, timing, purpose, and impact of the interpretations, focusing particularly on ways in which they might be improved.

Individual Exercises

1. Think about your relationships with your parents. What kind of parents do you think they were when you were very young? You may be particularly likely to have some insights into this if you had the opportunity to observe them parenting your younger siblings or if you completed the exercise on early recollections in Chapter 5 on Alfred Adler. Write a paragraph in your journal in which you discuss ways in which the parenting you received as a young child might be affecting your current expectations and behaviors in relationships.

2. As you have learned in this chapter, Harry Stack Sullivan suggested that people go through a series of stages in their interpersonal development. Think

about your development during each of the stages described on page 131 and list an experience you had during each stage that was typical of your relationships at that time. Write about the progression of interpersonal stages in your own life and how your present relationships might be a logical outgrowth of those patterns.

SUMMARY

This chapter reviewed six theories or theorists: Helene Deutsch, Karen Horney, Harry Stack Sullivan, Anna Freud, the object relations theorists, and Heinz Kohut. All began their careers as psychoanalysts by embracing the ideas of Sigmund Freud, but all departed from Freud's ideology as they matured and developed their own ideas. All de-emphasized the role of drives in human development and placed considerable emphasis on very early parent-child relationships and attachment. Most believed that children internalize images of their parents and that those images have a significant impact on their sense of themselves and their subsequent relationships. Although most of these theorists continued to view the development and analysis of the transference relationship as important, they also believed in the collaboration of clinician and client and advocated the use of empathy, acceptance, and other affective and humanistic interventions to enhance the impact of therapeutic interpretation and accelerate the process of treatment. Nearly all of these theorists continue to be read and studied. Their influence has been great not only on shaping psychoanalysis but on other theories that will be discussed in this book.

RECOMMENDED READINGS

Helene Deutsch

Wimpfheimer, M. J., & Schafer, R. (1977). Psychoanalytic methodology in Helene Deutsch's *The Psychology of Women. Psychoanalytic Quarterly, 46,* 287–318.

Karen Horney

Paris, B. J. (1994). *Karen Horney: A psychoanalyst's search for understanding.* New Haven: Yale University Press.

Harry Stack Sullivan

Chapman, A. H. (1978). *The treatment techniques of Harry Stack Sullivan.* New York: Brunner/Mazel.
Grey, A. L. (1988). Sullivan's contributions to psychoanalysis: An overview. *Contemporary Psychoanalysis, 24,* 548–576.

Anna Freud

Sandler, A. (1996). The psychoanalytic legacy of Anna Freud. *Psychoanalytic Study of the Child, 51,* 270–284.

Object Relations Theorists

Cashdan, S. (1988). *Object relations therapy: Using the relationship.* New York: Norton.

Kernberg, O. F., & Clarkin, J. F. (1992). Treatment of personality disorders. *International Journal of Mental Health, 21,* 53–76.

Scharff, J. S., & Scharff, D. E. (1992). *Scharff notes: A primer of object relations therapy.* Northvale, NJ: Aronson.

Weisberg, I. (1994). Linking theory to practice: Melanie Klein and the relational revolution. *International Journal of Communicative Psychoanalysis and Psychotherapy, 9,* 77–84.

Heinz Kohut

Kohut, H., & Wolf, E. S. (1978). The disorders of the self and their treatment: An outline. *International Journal of Psycho-Analysis, 59,* 413–425.

Lachmann, F. M. (1993). Self psychology: Origins and overview. *British Journal of Psychotherapy, 10,* 226–231.

Other

Sayers, J. (1991). *Mothers of psychoanalysis: Helene Deutsch, Karen Horney, Anna Freud, Melanie Klein.* New York: Norton.

Chapter 8

TRANSACTIONAL ANALYSIS

Like the work of Heinz Kohut and several of the other theorists discussed in Chapter 7, transactional analysis (TA), developed by Eric Berne, has its roots in traditional psychoanalysis but reaches toward the humanistic approaches. TA de-emphasizes the unconscious and the transference relationship and instead focuses on responsibility, emotional health, and social relationships throughout our lives (Clarkson, 1993). Nevertheless, Berne does maintain that human development is largely formed in the early years and that parental messages have great importance. In addition, echoing the ideas of Alfred Adler, Berne believes that people form life scripts in childhood that guide their lives. TA succeeds in updating and translating psychoanalytic concepts into language that is useful, meaningful, and accessible and gives people helpful ways to conceptualize and change their behaviors and patterns.

THE PERSON WHO DEVELOPED TRANSACTIONAL ANALYSIS

Eric Berne was born in 1910 in Montreal, Canada. His father, a physician, died when Berne was nine years old, and he was raised by his mother. He received a medical degree from McGill University and completed his psychiatric residency in the United States, training under Erik Erikson, whose work was discussed in Chapter 4.

Berne was interested in both traditional psychoanalysis and the work of Wilder Penfield, whose research on electrical stimulation of the brain led him to believe that people could reexperience previous thoughts and emotions in a vivid way (Poidevant & Lewis, 1995). Drawing on both influences and seeking to reduce the complexity of psychoanalysis to make it appropriate for use with the average person, Berne developed TA. His first book on the his theory, *Transactional Analysis in Psychotherapy,* was published in 1961 and was soon followed by *Games People Play* (1964), which became a bestseller and led to widespread interest in and application of his ideas. Berne died of coronary failure in 1970, having published 8 books and 64 articles.

THE DEVELOPMENT OF TRANSACTIONAL ANALYSIS

The most rapid development of TA occurred during the last 15 years of Berne's lifetime (Dusay & Dusay, 1989). From 1955 to 1962, Berne focused on delineation of the ego states. During the mid-1960s, he developed his ideas on transactions and games, culminating in the publication of *Games People Play*. Script analysis was his focus during the last phase of his work. Since his death, others, notably Thomas Harris and the Gouldings, have continued to develop and promote Berne's ideas, refining and elaborating his work. Probably the most important development since Berne's death is the integration of TA with both Gestalt therapy and psychodrama.

Although Berne's theory is complex, the concepts he uses are clear and understandable. Our ability to gain immediate insight into our own lives simply through a review of Berne's ideas makes his concepts particularly appealing.

Human Development and Ego States

Berne, like his teacher Erik Erikson, suggested that people evolve through eight developmental stages (Poidevant & Lewis, 1995; Sapp, 1997). Although Erikson's influence is evident, Berne put his own stamp on the stages through his emphasis on the development of the three ego states: parent, adult, and child.

- *Stage 1,* from birth to age one, is the time when the child ego state begins to evolve. The *child ego state* evolves into three parts that contain the early experiences, the emotions, the intuitions, inquisitiveness, and the capacity for both joy and shame. The child ego state may talk in superlatives and focus on *I* ("I want" or "I don't like that"). Nonverbal characteristics include tears, whining, giggling, and squirming. All people are born with a *natural child* that is dependent, spontaneous, and lovable. During the first year we witness the development of the three parts of the child ego state: the adapted child, the free child, and the little professor. The *adapted child* tends to be inhibited, well behaved, socialized, conforming, and sometimes self-critical. The *free child* encompasses the original spontaneity and intuitiveness of the natural child and is playful, joyful, and exuberant. The *little professor* is a precursor of the adult ego state. It is curious and inquisitive, prompting children to learn and explore their surroundings. However, the little professor can also be didactic and rigid.
- *Stage 2* extends from age one to age three and is characterized by the initial development of the adult and parent ego states that continue to evolve until children are about six years of age. These two ego states are shaped primarily by children's social interactions, particularly the injunctions and restrictions that are placed on their behavior.

    The *adult ego state* is like a computer; it is objective and rational, emphasizing logic over emotion. It processes information, integrates messages from the other ego states, and solves problems. This ego state typically assumes a listening and inquisitive stance, seeking to understand and be understood. It is straightforward, gives opinions, and asks questions. It is a mediator, a referee, and a decision maker. It cannot erase material contained in the parent or child ego states, but it can silence or minimize the input from those states.

    The *parent ego state* has two parts: the nurturing parent; which provides support, affirmation, and caring; and the critical parent, which makes judgments, disapproves and criticizes, and sets standards. The critical parent grows out of the rules, reprimands, praise and rewards that children receive from parents, teachers, and other authority figures and reflects their conceptions of right and wrong (Harris, 1967). The parent ego state tends to use words such as *always, never,* and *should* and focuses on *you* ("You need to clean your room" or "You aren't doing a good job"). Nonverbal signs include pointing, sighing, and a raised voice. The parent ego state may provide clear guidelines or give mixed messages, particularly if the person's parents communicate conflicting values and traditions. The parent ego state includes two parts: (1) the *nurturing parent* is caring, protective, comforting, and praising but sometimes overprotective; (2) the *critical parent* is controlling, demanding, critical, limiting, powerful, and sometimes dogmatic.

- *Stage 3*, extending from ages three to six, continues the development of the ego states. During these years, children learn basic life skills, including toilet training, self-care, and ways to interact with others and begin to develop their own value systems, derived from the values they see reflected in people who are important to them. Messages which children receive from others as well as their own experiences in negotiating their world and developing their independence continue to shape the ego states.

- *Stage 4* occurs at age six, an important age in TA thinking. Berne believed that by this age the three major ego states (parent, adult, and child) are developed, although they will continue to evolve as the person matures. Children have also developed characteristic ways of relating to their environments, as reflected in their scripts (discussed later in this chapter).

- *Stage 5* encompasses the period between ages 6 and 12. Although by stage 4 the ego states have evolved enough to shape personality, Berne believed that their development continues at a slower rate during stage 5. Children's educational experiences as well as their increased interpersonal contacts, especially with peers and teachers, contribute to changes in the ego states. The adult ego state is particularly likely to show growth during this stage.

- *Stage 6* includes the period between ages 13 and 16, the years of puberty. The child ego state often develops rapidly during this stage and may be manifested by rebellion and conflict between both the internal child and parent ego states and between children and their parents, who represent the parent ego state.

- *Stage 7* is the time of late adolescence. For most people, the adult ego state gains the ability to moderate the rambunctiousness of the child ego state and achieve greater balance among the three ego states. Collaboration among the ego states promotes the maturation and need fulfillment of the individual.

- *Stage 8* is adulthood. Ideally, people have achieved psychological maturity. They function independently; make wise decisions; and have a healthy balance of parent, adult, and child ego states. Although the ego states, of course, continue to interact and imbalances may occur, people in stage 8 generally have a sense of purpose and direction that is advanced by the joint efforts of the ego states.

Clearly, Berne's parent, adult, and child ego states bear considerable similarity to Freud's concept of the superego, the ego, and the id. However, while Freud emphasized the unconscious nature and determinants of these elements of the personality, Berne located them in the conscious or preconscious and viewed them as observable in people's behaviors and interactions. Berne also differed from Freud in believing that these states evolve throughout life, although he, too, emphasizes development during the first five years. Finally, Berne focused on parental messages rather than frustrated drives as instrumental in forming the ego states.

Ideally, the three major ego states (parent, adult, and child) are in balance in the personality. However, if one or more dominates while others are blocked, if a person relies too heavily on one ego state, or if one ego state contaminates or intrudes on another, the person is likely to develop difficulties, especially in interpersonal communication and relationships. For example, the person who has too little adult is likely to be illogical, while the person with too much adult will probably be uninteresting (Dusay, 1972; Dusay & Dusay, 1989). Similarly, the person with too little free child is likely to be constricted and rigid, while the person with too much free child may be irresponsible.

Structural Analysis of Ego States

Part of TA involves a structural analysis of the relative strengths of a person's ego states. According to this approach, the ego states encompass a constant amount of psychic energy so that when one ego state increases in intensity, others must lose energy. Creating an egogram, or diagramming the energy balance of the ego states with a bar graph, provides a clear illustration of an individual's personality. For example, consider the egogram in Figure 8-1, which was completed for Anna, a 27-year-old woman who sought counseling for job-related problems. Her presenting concerns included difficulty meeting deadlines, managing time, and following through on projects. Anna had difficulty appreciating the seriousness of her supervisor's concerns and instead insisted that taking extra time off for vaca-

FIGURE 8-1   Anna's egogram

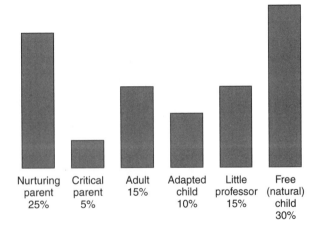

tions, making personal telephone calls from her desk, and refusing to bring work home were all essential to her mental health.

Transactions

Transactions are the basic units of behavior. They involve an exchange of strokes, a communication or acknowledgment, between two people. TA describes three types of transactions characterized by the source of the transaction, its target, and the replying ego state:

1. *Complementary transaction.* The target and the replying ego states are the same, and the reply is directed to the source ego state. Complementary transactions can be diagrammed by parallel lines (see Figure 8-2).

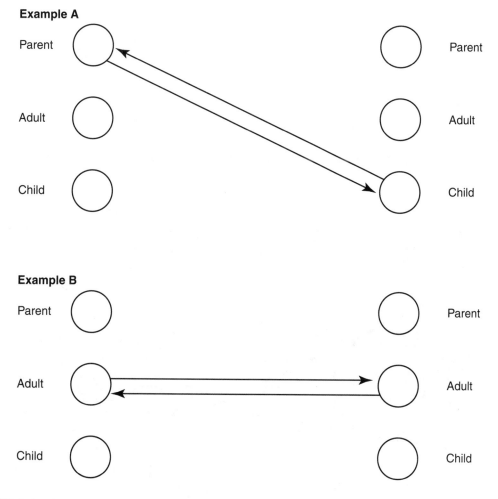

FIGURE 8-2 Complementary transactions

Example A

Parent (source ego state) to child (target ego state):   Please pick up your toys.

Child (replying ego state) to parent (target of reply):   All right, I will.

Example B

Adult to adult: I am interested in buying a car like the one you bought. Will you tell me about your car?

Adult to adult: It was very expensive, and I wasn't sure it would be worth the money, but the car has been very reliable and a pleasure to drive.

2. *Crossed transaction.* Here, the target ego state and the replying ego state are not the same. Consequently, the lines on the diagram are crossed (see Figure 8-3).

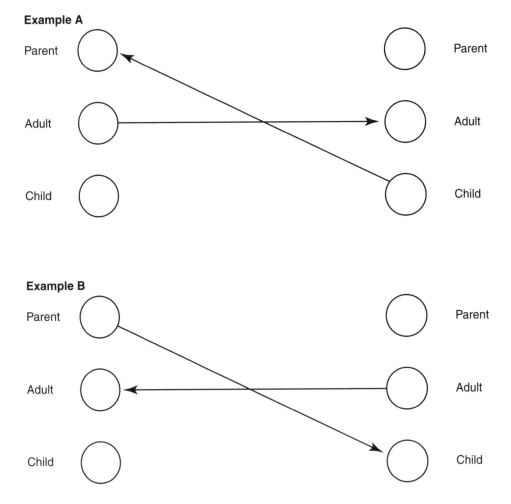

FIGURE 8-3   Crossed transactions

Example A

Adult to adult: It's cold out. Do you want to get your coat?

Child to parent: Don't tell me what to do!

Example B

Parent to child: Your desk is a mess. Aren't you ever going to clear off that junk pile?

Adult to adult: You know, I realized the other day that my desk really has become a mess. I'm planning to clear it off as soon as I finish this project.

3. *Ulterior transactions.* This transaction takes place on two levels of communication simultaneously: an overt or social level and a covert or psychological level. It involves more than one ego state as a source or target of a communication (see Figure 8-4).

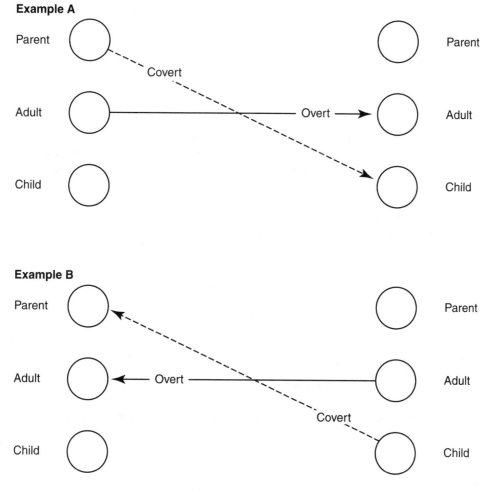

FIGURE 8-4 Ulterior transactions

Example A (Person 1 to Person 2, a few minutes after Person 2 arrives home late)

Adult to adult (overt message):   Is it after 11 p.m. already? I don't know where the time went tonight.

Parent to child (covert message):   I want to be sure you know I noticed that you came in after your curfew. Don't expect an extended curfew this weekend!

Example B (Person 2 to Person 1)

Adult to adult (overt message):   Yes, it is after 11. Excuse me; I need to read my e-mail.

Child to parent (covert message): There she goes again, ready to give me a hard time because I came in a few minutes late. I'll go into my room so she won't bother me.

The overt transactions in these last examples appear to be complementary transactions from adult to adult. However, the covert transactions are actually from parent to child and from child back to parent, as the thoughts behind the words reflect.

Clearly, complementary transactions are most likely to lead to interactions and relationships that are clear, open, and rewarding. People say what they mean and can understand what other people are saying. Any disagreements are evident and can be addressed.

Crossed transactions may be relatively clear to the outside observer but are very disconcerting to the participants. The responses people receive usually are very different from what they anticipated, and they may feel as if they are not being heard and understood. Animosities are common in this type of transaction.

Ulterior transactions are the most problematic: the overt communication is incongruent with the covert communication, and conversation is not meaningful or successful because neither person really knows what is in the mind of the other. A continuing pattern of ulterior transactions is likely to lead to a highly dysfunctional relationship or one that is terminated.

Strokes and Injunctions

Children's emotional development as well as the early development of their ego states are largely determined by the messages and responses they receive from their caregivers. Berne identified two types of messages. *Strokes* are positive messages and are best when they are unconditional, while *injunctions* (negative strokes) express disapproval and dislike and include criticisms and prohibitions. Positive and negative strokes may be verbal (such as words of praise and criticism) or nonverbal (such as a hug, a slap, or a lack of eye contact). According to Berne (1961), strokes are the basic motivation for human interaction; and even negative strokes are preferred to no strokes—that is, being ignored and discounted.

Parental strokes most important in forming the ego states as well as shaping transactions, life positions, scripts, rackets, and games (all discussed later in this chapter). Children who are encouraged and receive a substantial amount of positive, unconditional, and affirming messages are likely to develop in healthy ways and have a sound balance among their ego states (Massey, 1995). Although some injunctions are necessary, children who receive an overabundance of negative messages, are lacking in strokes and neglected or ignored, or receive many conditional strokes (e.g., "You are very pretty when you sit quietly") are unlikely to develop in positive ways. Particularly affected is their child ego state, which may become suppressed and inhibited or self-centered and out of control. People whose lives are ruled by a great many *shoulds* usually are people who heard many *don'ts* (negative injunctions) while they were children. Massey (1995) has summed up the impact of strokes: "Permissions foster the differentiation of the real self whereas injunctions promote anxiety-ridden fusion or symbioses" (p. 278).

Basic Life Positions

According to Harris (1967), people develop a basic life position that reflects the value they perceive in both themselves and others. These positions are revealed in people's thoughts, feelings, and behaviors about themselves and others (White, 1995). Harris (1967) described four possible life positions:

1. *I'm not OK; you're OK.* Harris (1967) believed that this is the most common pattern of early childhood. Young children cannot meet their own needs and so perceive themselves as weak and helpless. They seek strokes from others who appear powerful and in control. This position is appropriate for young children but can cause difficulties if they maintain it as they mature. In this position, people typically feel guilty, depressed, powerless, and inferior to others, although they long for acceptance and appreciation. Some may be envious of others and may try to compete but never believe that they are good enough. Others withdraw and feel unworthy of attention and relationships. People who assume this life position often have been abused or neglected. Their lack of positive strokes has made it difficult for them to feel good about themselves. They may have a very limited free child and a rigid adapted child, believing that they must always follow the rules to gain any acceptance. On the other hand, they may act out, viewing themselves as unworthy of positive strokes and preferring negative strokes to none.

2. *I'm OK; you're not OK.* This position also might characterize people who were abused or neglected and who received a lack of positive strokes. However, these people were able to survive through self-stroking. Although this position probably helped them endure a difficult childhood, they grow up believing that other people can only offer them harm and that they must rely totally on themselves. These people may react to others in angry and punitive ways and have a sense of entitlement and a grandiose view of themselves. They blame others for all their difficulties and have little empathy or love for them. They may engage in criminal behavior or abuse of others.

3. *I'm not OK; you're not OK.* This is the most negative of the four positions, characterizing the most difficult group of people to help through treatment. Typically,

they were severely deprived of strokes while they were growing up. Consequently, they become hopeless and see no value in themselves or others. They may see suicide as the only solution to their problems.

4. *I'm OK; you're OK.* In this position, people feel positive about themselves and the people in their lives. While they need strokes, they can be warm and loving and reciprocate those strokes. Harris viewed this as the healthiest of the four positions. Adults with this position value their own needs but also respect the needs of others. As a result, they are good partners in both their relationships and their work and often become social activists or take on other roles that promote the welfare of society. These people focus on win-win situations and have a good balance among their ego states.

Variations on these positions have been suggested by modern TA theorists. White (1995), for example, believes that children are born in an "I'm OK; you're irrelevant" position and then move to another position, depending on the nature of their parenting and early childhood experiences. Although Harris viewed children as starting from the more negative "I'm not OK; you're OK" position, he, too, believed that most children soon move away from their original positions. He hypothesized that by the time children are three years of age, they have either become fixed in the position where they began, (usually "I'm not OK; you're OK") or have moved to another position (generally either "I'm OK; you're not OK" or "I'm not OK; you're not OK"). The amount and nature of the stroking they receive as young children determines which position is finalized. They are unlikely to move out of one of these positions unless they make a conscious choice to change and to move into the fourth position, "I'm OK; you're OK." Education on and analysis of people's life positions can help them make this kind of deliberate decision to change.

Scripts

Like Alfred Adler (see Chapter 5), TA theorists believe that, as a result of early childhood experiences, people develop scripts that guide them through life. These scripts are shaped primarily by the internalized strokes and injunctions that they received as children and reflect their life position. The scripts are a belief system that lead people to envision life as a sort of ongoing drama in which the actors may change but the plot and the role of the person with the script does not change. Woollams and Brown (1979) described three characteristic scripts or roles:

1. *Persecutor.* These people give others primarily negative strokes, believing themselves to be superior to others.
2. *Rescuer.* These people can give positive strokes but dispense them conditionally, reflecting their belief that they know more than others and should judge and educate them.
3. *Victim.* These people assume a helpless stance and allow others to direct their lives.

Time Structuring and Games

Berne (1963, 1964) described five ways in which people spend their time with others. Listed in order of complexity, these include rituals, pastimes, games, intimacy, and activity. All serve the purpose of reducing tension, obtaining strokes, avoiding an unpleasant situation, and maintaining equilibrium. *Rituals* are routine, repetitive behaviors such as the greetings we give people when we come into the office or our behavior in a place of worship. *Pastimes* also include conversation and activities that are rather predictable and straightforward, such as talk during dinner. *Games* were of particular interest to Berne and will be discussed separately. *Intimacy* involves an exchange between two people who are both in an "I'm OK, you're OK" position and might include an open and sharing conversation with a friend or a mutually rewarding sexual experience. *Activities* involve dealing with external reality such as arranging to have housecleaning done or running a business.

According to Berne (1964), "A game is an ongoing series of complementary ulterior transactions progressing to a well-defined, predictable outcome" (p. 48). Games are basically dishonest, and the people playing the games use manipulation, deception, or trickery to achieve a pay off. Although some games are socially acceptable and do little harm, others destroy relationships and even lives. In *Games People Play* (1964), Berne described a great variety of games. He found that the most common game played between spouses is what he called "If It Weren't For You," in which one partner blames the other for all of his or her disappointments and failures. This may help the accusing spouse feel better but, of course, is likely to lead to an unhealthy relationship.

Berne believed that most people have great difficulty with true intimacy and clear and open communication, so they rely heavily on games. Games reflect the balance of our ego states as well as our life positions. For example, the man who constantly blames his wife for all of his failures is likely to have a weak adult ego state and a life position of "I'm OK; you're not OK." Most of his communications come from his child ego state and are directed at his wife's parent ego state.

Berne used the term *rackets* to characterize the habitual feelings that emerge in the aftermath of a game. For example, the husband in the previous example might tend to feel self-pity. These feelings probably stem from childhood and reflect his life script, in which he has the role of a victim. Other common rackets include the anxiety racket and the suicide racket. James and Jongeward (1971) described the way in which people accumulate rackets as *stamp collecting*, gathering enough demonstrations of their racket to justify a major pay-off. For example, the husband might use his accumulation of self-pity rackets to justify having an extramarital relationship or an alcoholic binge.

TREATMENT USING TRANSACTIONAL ANALYSIS

Although TA comes from psychoanalytic roots and does rely heavily on analysis, its concepts and vocabulary are much easier to understand. Similarly, its goals and the nature of the client-clinician relationship differ from traditional psychoanalysis.

Goals

The goal of TA is not insight into the unconscious but autonomy. According to Berne (1964), this is comprised of awareness, spontaneity, and intimacy. In addition, TA seeks to help people move into an "I'm OK; you're OK" position, achieve balance among their ego states, and make healthy use of their time, keeping games to a minimum.

Therapeutic Alliance

Just as the goals differ between traditional psychoanalysis and TA, so does the therapeutic alliance. In TA, clinicians assume a very flexible role, adapting to the needs of the clients and the treatment process. Clarkson (1993) delineated four roles of clinicians who use TA:

1. *Mutual person-to-person, I-you relationship.* Clinicians are very much present in the session, working to build rapport and sharing their ideas and perceptions to facilitate treatment. They do not sit behind the couch either literally or figuratively but seek to establish an adult-to-adult relationship with their clients.

2. *Working alliance.* The collaboration between clients and clinicians is important. Both participate actively and share responsibility for the treatment. The clinicians provide education on the language and concepts of TA and guide the therapeutic process. Clients are expected to be open, responsible for themselves, and willing to take risks to make positive changes.

3. *Transference-countertransference.* Although encouraging and analyzing transference is not an important part of TA, this treatment system, like psychoanalysis, continues to recognize the importance of transference and countertransference in the therapeutic relationship. Clinicians are particularly alert to the possibility that the way in which clients communicate with them may reflect patterns that date back to childhood.

4. *Reparenting or reparative relationship.* This clinician role is controversial and must be used with great care. In a reparative relationship, clinicians take on a parent-like role, providing strokes in an effort to compensate for the lack of positive strokes clients received as children.

Contracts

Contracts are viewed as an important component in TA (Dusay & Dusay, 1989). They clarify the nature of the treatment process and affirm the roles and responsibilities of clinicians and clients. Dusay and Dusay recommend that these contracts have the following four elements:

1. Mutual assent to engage in the therapeutic process and to the goals and procedures involved.

2. A statement of clinicians' competencies, emphasizing their role as facilitators of change.
3. A legal and ethical statement of the goals of treatment.
4. Clarification of the compensation due to clinicians and the terms of payment.

Consent-to-treatment agreements such as these are now standard in many therapeutic relationships. However, TA was one of the first approaches to emphasize the importance of such an agreement to maximize the establishment of a collaborative and effective clinician-client relationship.

How People Change

According to Harris (1967), people are prompted to change when they are hurting or bored or discover that they can change. If clients are not motivated to change, part of the clinician's task is helping them see that their lives can be better if they choose to change and demonstrating to them that it is possible to change through counseling and psychotherapy.

Woollams and Brown (1979) identified seven stages of treatment in the TA model: motivation, awareness, the treatment contract, deconfusing the child, redecision, relearning, and termination. Treatment involves considerable information gathering, exploring with clients their early family background, the strokes they have received, their intrapsychic processes, the important people and factors in their current life, and their social and cultural context (Massey, 1995). Once information has been gathered, clinicians and clients collaboratively seek to organize that information so that it makes sense in TA terms. The goal is to obtain a clear picture of the following:

1. The balance of the ego states forming the personality
2. The nature of the person's transactions with others
3. The games and rackets in which the person engages
4. The person's basic position (e.g., "I'm not OK; you're OK")
5. The person's life script

By analyzing and understanding this information, people can become more aware of their patterns and why those patterns have developed. This, in turn, frees people to modify patterns and choose healthier ways of relating to others. It enables them to form a more positive picture, both of themselves and of the people in their lives: an "I'm OK; you're OK" position.

Gouldings' Redecision Therapy

Goulding and Goulding (Goulding, 1987; Goulding & Goulding, 1979) integrated TA and Gestalt therapy (discussed in Chapter 13) into what they called redecision therapy. The basic premise of redecision therapy is that early life decisions are reversible if people reexperience them both intellectually and emotionally. This approach to treatment helps clients return to their childhood states, reexperience their early life situations, have a corrective emotional experience, and emerge from that experience with new decisions about how they will lead their lives. Clients and clinicians then collaborate to implement those new decisions in the present. Key questions in redecision therapy are "What do you want to change today?" and "What are you going to do differently now?" (McClendon & Kadis, 1995). Primary goals of this approach include helping people gain more autonomy and zest for life.

Redecision therapy uses the concepts and terminology of TA but often integrates them into treatment in ways that reflect the Gestalt model (Gladfelter, 1992). For example, group therapy is the primary mode of treatment in redecision therapy. Although group members do not interrupt the treatment of any individual in the group, the process of learning from the work of another allows them to benefit too. In addition, clients are often asked to act as if they are important people in their lives in order to understand the transactions and strokes in those relationships. For example, a person may be asked to assume the role of one of his or her parents and to talk to the clinician about that person's life. This allows the client to get in touch with his or her own parent ego state and better understand its impact.

APPLICATION OF TRANSACTIONAL ANALYSIS

Although TA no longer attracts the widespread interest and popularity it did in the 1960s and 1970s, it continues to have a strong following. Today, the International Transactional Analysis Association has more than 10,000 members (Sapp, 1997). The *Transactional Analysis Journal* is a current publication of that association that contains articles relevant to TA as well as useful information about the application of TA to various client groups and the integration of TA with other theoretical models. In addition, many clinicians who do not view TA as their primary theoretical orientation integrate its concepts and techniques into their work. The combination of TA and Gestalt therapy seems to work particularly well, with TA emphasizing the cognitive and analytical aspects of the person and Gestalt drawing in the affective parts.

The applications of TA are broad and varied. It is used in individual and group counseling, corporate settings (Dusay & Dusay, 1989), and family and couples counseling. Massey (1995), for example, believed that TA could be a useful vehicle for understanding family patterns and described a model for integrating TA and family systems counseling. Massey found that by helping family members understand the intergenerational messages they had received as well as their basic life positions, ego states, and transactions, they could become more aware of each other's expectations and styles of interaction. Script analysis also provides a way in which to help people look at how they operate in a social context and the choices they make in the family. Harris (1967) believed that helping a couple understand their own and each other's balance of ego states could help them assess their compatibility and the strengths and weaknesses in their relationship. TA also has been used in educational and preventive ways in an effort to avert or ameliorate emotional difficulties by giving people tools to help them understand their beliefs about themselves and others and the ways in which they communicate. Books such as *Staying OK* (Harris & Harris, 1985) and *TA for Kids* and *TA for Tots* (Freed & Freed, 1974a, 1974b) have been used to promote emotional health through TA.

Diagnostic Groups

TA seems most likely to be helpful to people who are either in a learning environment or willing to take the time to learn the concepts and vocabulary of the approach. Candidates for treatment seem to be people with at least average verbal skills and insight who have self-esteem and interpersonal difficulties. Ideally, they should be psychologically minded and be motivated toward personal growth. Although TA has been used with people with severe emotional disorders, it seems better suited to people with longstanding but mild to moderate difficulties.

Culturally Diverse Groups

TA should be used carefully with people from non-western cultures because of its emphasis on the early childhood origins of problems and its complex, lengthy, verbal, and analytical nature. The approach may be inappropriate for people from cultures in which it is unacceptable to question parental messages. At the same time, use of TA has the potential to promote understanding of family and societal messages and injunctions that may differ among cultures and cause conflicts for people who have immigrated from one country to another.

EVALUATION OF TRANSACTIONAL ANALYSIS

Overall, TA's primary contribution is its revision of traditional psychoanalytic concepts, simplifying and modernizing them so they promote optimism and understanding. TA has provided a way for clinicians to address the impact of early childhood experiences and messages that is more comprehensible and acceptable to many people than is traditional psychoanalysis. TA's emphasis on the clinician-client contract and the collaborative therapeutic relationship offers an appealing alternative to the detached stance of the traditional analyst.

Another strength of TA is its emphasis on health and its belief that people want to have a zestful life, full of rewarding, open relationships. TA theorists attribute problems not to pathology but to lack of education and strokes and take the optimistic stance that people can find the tools they need to make and implement more fulfilling choices.

As with most approaches to treatment, the research on the effectiveness of TA is limited. Miller and Capuzzi (1984) reviewed a substantial number of studies of TA that had been conducted in either clinical or educational settings. The studies reviewed showed that in educational settings TA was successful in improving self-esteem, social status, and internal locus of control in elementary-age students; behavior and attendance in high school students; and self-esteem and internal locus of control in college students. The results of studies of TA used in clinical settings is less clear, in part because of the studies' methodological flaws. TA does seem beneficial in some cases, especially when combined with behavior counseling strategies and when the client-clinician match is a good one. TA seems especially effective when used in groups in educational settings and when attitudinal changes are desired. Beyond that, few generalizations can be made.

The usefulness of TA is enhanced by efforts to combine it with other approaches to treatment; clinicians need not become wedded to the TA model but may borrow elements of the approach and integrate them with Gestalt, behavioral, and other orientations to treatment. As long as clinicians do not use TA in ways that are rigid and dogmatic or that overemphasize the jargon, the approach has a great deal to offer.

SKILL DEVELOPMENT: IDENTIFYING STROKES AND INJUNCTIONS

Sources of pride and shame in our lives as well as aspects of ourselves that we neglect or suppress often reflect the parental strokes and injunctions we experienced as children. According to TA theory, aspects of ourselves that received positive strokes are likely to be prized, aspects that received injunctions tend to be viewed as bad or undesirable, while aspects that received neither strokes nor injunctions are typically ignored or neglected. The following are important aspects of ourselves that may have been the target of strokes and injunctions:

1. The body, bodily functions, and sexuality
2. Intelligence
3. Interpersonal skills
4. Special skills and talents
5. Behavior
6. Overall self-assessment

People can be helped to discern the messages they received as children and be aware of the impact of those messages on their current functioning. The first step in gaining this awareness is identifying the strokes and injunctions they give themselves. Once those messages have been identified, they can be linked to messages people recall or believe they received as young children. Finally, they can choose to revise any negative messages, consciously taking steps to incorporate new and more affirming messages about themselves into their lives.

Consider May, a 48-year-old single woman who sought counseling shortly after the death of her mother. She felt alone and isolated and wanted help with socialization. She also reported confusion about her sexual orientation. May was asked to identify the messages she gave herself as well as those she recalled receiving from her parents about the six important aspects of herself (just identified):

The Body, Bodily Functions, and Sexuality

- *My viewpoint:* I don't like my body. I look all right when I have clothes on, but otherwise I can't stand to look at my body. I've never had a sexual relationship.
- *Parental message:* My mother would always say, "Don't stuff your face. You'll turn into a fat cow." And I guess I did. She never talked about sex. Whenever she would see a love scene on television, she would turn the TV off. I got the message that she thought sex was dirty, but she never said anything. I never saw my parents hug or kiss. I never heard them express love toward each other.

Intelligence

- *My viewpoint:* I did graduate from college, so I guess I must be at least average, but I see so many people who are smarter than I am. I'm afraid to speak up; I might say something dumb.
- *Parental message:* My parents made it clear they wanted us to do well enough to pass our courses so we couldn't cause them any problems, but then when I did pass, they never said anything. My sister wasn't as good a student as I was, and I remember my father yelling at her about her low grades; but as long as I passed, I knew they were satisfied.

Interpersonal Skills

- *My viewpoint:* I'm shy, and I don't get along very well with people. They just sort of tolerate me, but I think they find me boring. I don't know how to hold a conversation, especially with men.
- *Parental message:* I remember my mother saying that children should be seen but not heard. "Don't make a fool of yourself," she would say. "Don't criticize anyone. Just keep your mouth shut."

Special Skills and Talents

- *My viewpoint:* I've always been a good cook. And I work hard. I'm very responsible.
- *Parental message:* I used to help my mother in the kitchen. She didn't say much about it, but she would always take extra helpings when I cooked. My sister just opened cans when it was her turn to cook, and my parents wouldn't eat much of her cooking. My mother tried to get dinner on the table at six P.M. when my father came home from work. I would always watch the clock to make sure the dinner would be ready on time. A couple of times she even praised me for getting dinner ready early.

Behavior

- *My viewpoint:* I was always well behaved, always neat and clean, and I still am. I watch other people to figure out the right thing to do, like at restaurants, and I try to do what you're supposed to do.
- *Parental message:* My father was a banker in our town. Everyone knew him. My parents always said, "Don't embarrass your father. Whatever you do reflects on him. Make sure you are always well behaved; act like a lady." I always did. They would tell my sister she should act more like me.

Overall Self-Assessment

- *My viewpoint:* Well, I guess I'm a good person. I never deliberately hurt anyone. But I really don't have much going for me.
- *Parental message:* My mother would tell me that I was her special girl because I helped her so much. I did that from when I was a toddler until my mother died. But she also told me I would always need her to help me too. I don't know what to do now that she is gone.

Although, of course, May could not recall parental messages from her first few years of life, the messages she recalls receiving from her parents, which probably reflect those very early messages, clearly have shaped how she sees herself. In areas such as cooking, her behavior, and her contributions to her mother, she apparently received positive strokes and now feels fairly positive about those aspects of herself. She received injunctions related to eating and weight gain, her communication and assertiveness skills, and her self-sufficiency; these are areas in which her self-esteem is low. May received little information about love and sexuality from her parents, although she inferred a negative viewpoint. This explains, at least in part, why intimacy has never been a part of her life. You will be given an opportunity to apply the skill of analyzing strokes and injunctions in the exercises later in this chapter.

CASE ILLUSTRATION

Here we consider Edie's egogram (see Figure 8-5). The balance of her ego states makes sense in light of her early relationships and messages. Her strong critical parent probably stems from her grandmother, who was abusive toward Edie, and her mother, who became a single parent and had little time for her children. Edie did develop some nurturing parent because of the close relationship she had with her father and her sister, who did give her love and positive strokes. Edie's adult is relatively

FIGURE 8-5 Edie's egogram

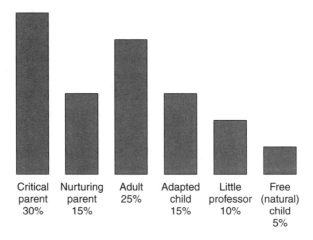

| Critical parent 30% | Nurturing parent 15% | Adult 25% | Adapted child 15% | Little professor 10% | Free (natural) child 5% |

strong; she is usually able to make rational decisions and deal with the world in mature ways. Her constricted behavior as a child is reflected in her own adapted child; she is very concerned about doing the right thing. Edie's curiosity, her spontaneity, and her zest for life are very circumscribed, as reflected in the low levels of her little professor and free child.

Edie's transactions come primarily from her critical parent, although when dealing with areas that are not highly charged, she can make good use of her adult. With Roberto, who has little critical parent and a strong free child, communication is often difficult. Edie speaks from her parent to his child; and more often than not, Roberto reacts in rebellious and childlike ways.

Edie's life position is "I'm not OK; you're OK." She usually believes that other people are better than she is in some way. However, when she gets close to people, she usually finds they do not meet the ideals she has set for them, and this can lead to criticism and disillusionment.

Edie's life script is a discouraging one: "Bad things keep happening to me. There is nothing I can do to prevent that. Although I may be able to fight hard and keep some of the bad things from destroying me, I will not win in the long run. But I must still be on guard."

Although Edie's relatively strong adult allows her to communicate in ways that are clear and straightforward some of the time, she does engage in games. One is "Courtroom" (Berne, 1964), which she commonly played during couples therapy. She often came to sessions armed with a list of everything Roberto had done wrong since the previous session, intent on convincing the clinician that she was right and Roberto was wrong and should be reprimanded.

Particularly because Edie is an intelligent person who is motivated to change and improve her relationships with her family, understanding these dynamics will probably be very helpful to her. According to TA, after becoming aware of these patterns, Edie has the option of electing to make a change, an option she is likely to take.

Exercises

Large-Group Exercises

1. Discuss the differences and similarities between TA and Freudian psychoanalysis. What are the strengths and weaknesses of each model? Which do you prefer and why?
2. Analyze Roberto from a TA perspective. Based on what you know about him, discuss and develop hypotheses about the following:
   - Roberto's egogram and how the strokes and injunctions he received as a child contributed to its development
   - The nature of his typical transactions
   - His basic life position
   - His life script
3. Diagram the following transactions. Indicate whether each is complementary, crossed, or ulterior. See Figures 8.2, 8.3, and 8.4 for examples.

Example A

Shopper: The shirt I bought here faded in the laundry. I would like my money back.

Salesperson: You people always have something to complain about.

Example B

Person 1:   I'd like you to come up and see my etchings tonight. (Underlying message: I would like the opportunity to be alone with you so that I am in a more powerful position.)

Person 2:   I'm not sure if I have enough time. (Underlying message: I know what you are after, but I don't want to play that game.)

Example C

Father: Remember, son, your curfew is midnight.

Son: No problem; I'll be in well before then.

Example D

Student: Professor, I was just devastated when I got a *C.* I studied so hard; I just feel awful (starts to cry).

Professor: I know how hard you worked. Let me review your exam. I'm sure I can find a few extra points to improve your grade.

Example E

Student: Professor, I was just devastated when I got a *C.* I studied so hard; I just feel awful (starts to cry).

Professor: I can see this exam was a challenge for you. Let's go over it to make sure you understand the material so that maybe you can do better next time.

Small-Group Exercises

1. Working in your small groups, create one example to illustrate each of the following: complementary transaction, crossed transaction, and ulterior transaction.
2. Divide into your groups of four. While one dyad observes and prepares to provide feedback, the other dyad should assume the roles of client and clinician. The clinician should help the client prepare an egogram reflecting the relative strengths of his or her ego states. Then discuss the impact this has on the person's everyday functioning. Spend about 15 minutes on this exercise.

   Observers should provide feedback on the following:
   • The understanding both people have of the egogram
   • The therapeutic alliance
   • The use of questions to promote exploration

- Strengths of the role play
- Suggestions for improving the role play

Individual Exercises

1. Summerton (1992) suggested that our family, social, and work groups can be described in terms of clusters of roles. Typical clusters include the following:
- Persecutor, rescuer, and victim
- Stage manager (the organizer), spectator (the observer), sniper (the attacker or defender), savior (solves problems and brings justice), and the scapegoat (carries the blame for others)

   Apply one of these clusters (or a cluster of your own creation) to your family, determining which role best fits each person. Now apply one of the clusters to either a social or a work group that is important to you. Think particularly about your own role and whether you might want to make some changes in that role. Write about this in your journal.

2. Think about the four life positions ("I'm OK; you're not OK"; "I'm not OK; you're OK"; "I'm not OK; you're not OK"; "I'm OK; you're OK"). Decide which one best reflects your own life position. Write about ways in which that position may reflect the strokes and injunctions you received as a child.

3. Listen to the conversations you have during the day. Write down at least three transactions that seem especially powerful or meaningful to you. Then determine which ego states are the source, target, and recipient of each transaction. Finally, determine whether each transaction is complementary, crossed, or ulterior.

SUMMARY

Although it is derived from psychoanalytic theory, transactional analysis is an optimistic approach that emphasizes people's drive toward emotional health and their ability to decide to make changes in their lives. TA theorists believe that the amount and nature of strokes and injunctions people receive in early childhood are the major determinants of their personalities, leading them to make early and enduring decisions about themselves and their relationships. The balance among people's ego states (critical and nurturing parent; adult; adapted child, little professor, and free child) forms their personalities and motivates behavior. Transactions between people are the basic unit of analysis in this model. Stemming from the ego states, interpersonal transactions may be complementary, crossed, or ulterior; and they shape relationships. Repetitive games and rackets also affect the sort of relationships people have.

Clinicians practicing TA believe that by age six people have established a life position ("I'm OK; you're not OK"; "I'm not OK; you're OK"; "I'm not OK; you're not OK"; "I'm OK; you're OK"). Overall, people's lives are guided by their life position and a script formed early in life that leads them to repeat and live out early childhood experiences.

Through TA, people can gain insight into these longstanding patterns and decide to change, using the tools they have learned from this model. They can develop more autonomy and joy in their lives as well as strong and functional parent, adult, and child ego states. As Harris (1967) stated, "As long as people are bound by the past, they are not free to respond to the needs and aspirations of others in the present." Although this approach focuses on the individual, it also acknowledges the importance of groups, families, and social contexts. According to Harris, "Society cannot change until persons change" (p. 279).

RECOMMENDED READINGS

Berne, E. (1961). *Transactional analysis in psychotherapy.* New York: Grove.

Berne, E. (1964). *Games people play.* New York: Grove.

Goulding, M. (1987). Transactional analysis and redecision therapy. In J. L. Zeig (Ed.), The evolution of psychotherapy (pp. 285–299). New York: Brunner/Mazel.

Harris, T. A. (1967). *I'm OK—You're OK.* New York: Avon.

Massey, R. F. (1995). Theory for treating individuals from a transactional analytic/systems perspective. *Transactional Analysis Journal, 25*(3), 271–284.

Chapter 9

BRIEF PSYCHODYNAMIC THERAPY

The final theory to be discussed in Part 2 is brief psychodynamic therapy (BPT). Like all of those reviewed in this part of the book, the approach has its origins in Freudian psychoanalysis. However, BPT also has been influenced by Anna Freud's ego psychology, developmental psychology, object relations theories, Kohut's self psychology, Sullivan's interpersonal theories, and family systems concepts (Strupp, 1992). Compared to traditional psychoanalysis, BPT is much more compatible with today's clinical emphasis on the establishment of specific goals, efficiency of treatment, and an interactive and collaborative clinician-client relationship. BPT usually is time-limited, focuses on a specific crisis or problem, establishes circumscribed goals, and uses a broad and flexible array of interventions. What makes this approach psychoanalytic or psychodynamic is the assumption that a person's focal problem in some way reflects or repeats earlier issues in that person's family of origin (Messer & Warren, 1995). Clinicians who practice BPT believe that, by addressing in treatment both the current focal conflict and its origins, people's presenting concerns can be resolved so they can become better able to deal with similar issues in the future. This approach is not appropriate for all people or problems but requires careful assessment to determine whether people are suitable for treatment by BPT.

The Development of Brief Psychodynamic Therapy

Several names are associated with the early development of BPT. Freud's work, of course, provides the basis for this approach. Although he saw many of his patients for years, even he sometimes conducted brief therapy. For example, in only six sessions, he successfully treated conductor Bruno Walter for cramps in his arm (Weisberg, 1993).

Others credited with laying the groundwork for this approach include Sandor Ferenczi and Franz Alexander. Ferenczi, from Budapest, was one of Freud's original followers. Ferenczi objected to the passive stance assumed by traditional psychoanalysts and sought a more active, efficient approach to treatment (Messer & Warren, 1995). He encouraged clients to face their fears, advocated a narrower focus of clinical attention, and believed that clinicians should assume an active role in the treatment process.

Alexander, practicing at the Chicago Institute for Psychoanalysis in the 1940s, viewed therapy as a "corrective emotional experience" designed to promote new learning (Weisberg, 1993, p. 106). Rather than seeking to elicit transference, he suggested that clinicians use their insights into clients' potential transference reactions to behave in ways opposite to those likely to provoke transference. In this way, clinicians could provide people with a different experience, one designed to heal rather than reopen old wounds (Messer & Warren, 1995). Alexander experimented with short-term treatment, focusing more on current life problems than on past issues and on understanding and building the strengths of the ego. He believed that, to be worthwhile, treatment should make a difference and sought to enable people to apply what they learned in treatment to their lives outside of therapy.

Many names are associated with modern applications of BPT, which began in the 1960s (Demos & Prout, 1993). They include the following:

- Habib Davanloo (intensive short-term dynamic psychotherapy)
- Peter Sifneos (short-term anxiety-provoking therapy)
- David Malan (Tavistock system of short-term dynamic psychotherapy)
- Lester Luborsky (time-limited dynamic supportive-expressive psychotherapy)
- James Mann (time-limited psychotherapy)
- Hans Strupp (time-limited dynamic psychotherapy)
- Gerald Klerman (interpersonal psychotherapy).

We will consider the distinguishing features and contributions of some of these approaches later in the chapter, once we have reviewed the commonalities of BPT. However, the names of these approaches in themselves reflect their nature. They are brief, intensive, and active and pay considerable attention to emotions and relationships.

IMPORTANT THEORETICAL CONCEPTS

Although BPT can be "dynamic and uncovering" (Weisberg, 1993, p. 105), it differs from traditional psychoanalysis in some important ways:

1. Strict criteria are employed for selection of suitable clients.
2. BPT is relatively brief, with a time limit, a specific termination date, or number of sessions often fixed at the start of therapy. Treatment is almost never longer than one year and usually lasts less than six months (Demos & Prout, 1993).
3. The client-clinician relationship differs from that of traditional psychoanalysis. The clinician is more active and challenging, using interpretation but discouraging regression. In addition, client and clinician sit face to face to promote interaction in a reality-based relationship.
4. The focus is on specific conflicts identified early in treatment.

Underlying Theory

According to BPT, emotional difficulties often result from people's inability to deal successfully with unacceptable feelings or impulses. When their ego defenses fail to mediate between their drives and the demands of external reality to suppress or modify unacceptable feelings, anxiety arises that causes problems. Clinicians using BPT believe that early intrapsychic experiences form enduring patterns in the mind and that these patterns show up in current difficulties, which typically reflect a repetition of early childhood factors (Strupp, 1992).

For example, a woman might find herself frequently attracted to married men who either reject her or take advantage of her. This may re-create her early relationship with her father, who was both seductive and rejecting, and her own inability to move beyond that relationship. Her ego defenses have been unsuccessful in mediating between her drive toward an intimate relationship with her father and the social unacceptability of such a relationship. Because these feelings have not been suppressed or modified in positive ways, the woman is caught in a conflict. She sabotages her efforts to find a rewarding relationship and is unhappy and frustrated about this pattern, but she is unable to modify her impulses to allow herself to establish a mutually rewarding relationship with an appropriate partner.

According to most BPT approaches, by strengthening the ego so that it can control the self-destructive impulses of the id, making the unconscious conscious, and helping people gain insight and resolve conflicts, clinicians can help clients break out of their repetitive dysfunctional patterns and grow and mature in healthy ways. Essential ingredients for change include emotional release, a corrective emotional experience with the clinician, and acquisition of greater insight. As people succeed in connecting with their clinicians, expressing their emotions, and understanding themselves better, energy that has been bound up in defensive and self-protective maneuvers is now freed to enable them to move forward in positive ways.

Selection of Appropriate Clients

Advocates of BPT all seem to agree that their approach is suitable for only a limited group of people. Davanloo (1980), for example, found that only 30 to 35% of people seeking treatment in outpatient settings were good candidates for his version of BPT. To determine whether a person is likely to benefit from BPT, a thorough initial assessment is essential. Some clinicians meet with prospective clients for an extensive history taking and evaluation that may last for up to three hours and make some trial interpretations before deciding whether to accept the person for treatment. Those who meet the following selection criteria and have a positive response to the trial are likely to be accepted as clients, while others are probably referred for treatment via another approach.

The following 10 qualities are perceived as desirable in people treated with BPT (Demos & Prout, 1993; Horowitz, et al., 1984; Messer & Warren, 1995):

1. Psychological-mindedness, or the ability to be introspective, report thoughts and feelings, recognize that symptoms are psychological in nature, and gain insight
2. Above-average intelligence and a capacity for new learning
3. Presentation of a circumscribed chief complaint that can be understood through BPT
4. Motivation toward change and growth, not just motivation toward symptom relief
5. A history of at least one trusting, meaningful relationship in childhood
6. Capacity to form a flexible and collaborative relationship with the clinician
7. Ability to handle strong emotions and anxiety-provoking material
8. Flexible defenses, at least some of which are mature ones
9. Ability to listen to, consider, and make use of interpretations
10. Capacity to be open, honest, and curious

On the other hand, people who are not motivated to understand themselves better, have strong dependency needs or other barriers to establishing sound therapeutic relationships, have rigid and immature defenses, and have complex and deeply entrenched issues are not likely to be suitable clients for BPT.

The Process of BPT

Horowitz et al. (1984) identified two triads that are important areas of focus in BPT. The first, the *impulse–defense triad,* includes current and recently ended relationships outside of treatment, past real or imagined relationships, and the transference relationship to the clinician. The second, the *triad of insight,* includes a drive or impulse, the injunction or threat that makes the impulse dangerous or unacceptable, and the defense used to reduce the anxiety that arises from the impulse. Exploration of these triads, leading to insight into their nature, can promote new learning and positive changes in people's lives.

Phases of BPT

Sifneos (1979a) identified five phases of treatment that are typical of most models of BPT:

1. *Patient-therapist encounter.* Client and clinician develop rapport and build a therapeutic alliance. They identify a feasible and mutually agreeable focus of treatment, an emotional problem that is related to the client's core difficulties. The clinician begins to develop a psychodynamic formulation to explain the difficulty. Client and clinician prepare a written statement of their goals and probable accomplishments in treatment.
2. *Early treatment.* This phase emphasizes the importance of reality in BPT. Clients' positive transference reactions are confronted to curtail regression, while they are encouraged to distinguish magical and wishful thinking from reality.
3. *Height of treatment.* The primary thrust of this phase is to link present problems to the past. Although the past is explored in BPT, it is only examined in relation to the current focal problem. Anger and anxiety toward the clinician are common during this phase, leading to manifestations of resistance. Transference may be explored when resistance is evident to facilitate understanding of clients' discomfort and reduce their resistance. Clients are encouraged to make increasing use of new ways to solve problems.
4. *Evidence of change.* Clients become able to generalize and apply what they have learned through treatment. Positive changes may be noted in symptom reduction, improved problem solving, and enhanced interpersonal skills.
5. *Termination.* Initial goals have been sufficiently met for client and clinician to determine that treatment should end. Efforts are not made to expand goals or to effect significant personality change; clinicians remain aware of the limitations of treatment. Rather, clients are congratulated on their efforts and accomplishments, and treatment is brought to a close with clients' awareness of work they can continue on their own.

TREATMENT USING BRIEF PSYCHODYNAMIC THERAPY

Brief psychodynamic therapy is not associated with a broad range of distinctive techniques. Rather, it draws heavily on analysis, interpretation, and other strategies associated with traditional analysis and uses additional techniques flexibly as needed. However, some generalizations can be made about the procedures and strategies associated with BPT.

Goals

BPT seeks to resolve specific conflicts as well as promote overall growth. Specific goals typically target the resolution of a focal conflict such as independence versus dependence, activity versus passivity, diminished versus positive self-esteem, and unresolved versus resolved grief (Mann & Goldman, 1982). Growth-related goals include promoting understanding and change in people's inner experiences and facilitating their application of that learning so they can live their lives more successfully (Strupp, 1992). Although symptom reduction is also important, that is usually accomplished when people make a conscious link between their symptoms and their early developmental experiences. In addition, clinicians seek to give people the insight and tools they need to continue exploration of their conflicts and their interpersonal contexts so they can resolve them more effectively and make better adjustments and decisions (Weisberg, 1993).

Therapeutic Alliance

Strupp (1992) said of BPT, "What may be the most therapeutic is the patient's experience of the therapist as a significant other whose feelings, attitudes, and values are *introjected,* thus effecting *corrections* of the patient's experience with significant others in his or her early life" (p. 25). According to BPT, formation of a positive relationship with the clinician can help people to reexperience and handle successfully experiences they had not handled well in the past, thereby enabling them to move out of maladaptive patterns. The corrective experience of the therapeutic alliance can enable them to compensate for the deficits in their early childhood relationships and form healthier relationships in the present. In addition, internalization of the clinicians' attitudes and behaviors toward clients can help clients treat themselves more positively. Clearly, a great deal of responsibility rests on the clinician in this model; consequently, personal therapy is recommended for those who practice BPT.

In addition to being able to provide a corrective emotional experience, clinicians should also be skilled in empathic listening, caring and compassion, understanding, interpretation, confrontation, and teaching. Clinicians play a very active and collaborative role in this model, developing rapport as quickly as possible to gain some influence in treatment (Koss & Butcher, 1986).

Specific Strategies

Neu, Prusoff, and Klerman (1978) have provided a list of six categories of interventions, organized from the simplest to the most complex, used in treating depression through BPT:

1. Support, empathy, and exploration to promote ventilation and expression of emotions
2. Active probing to elicit material
3. Clarification, rephrasing, and questioning to highlight inconsistencies
4. Direct advice
5. Examination of alternatives and probable consequences to facilitate decision making
6. Interpretation, designed to promote self-awareness and insight into patterns, defenses, and motivations

Although interpretation is an important tool in BPT, the internalization of the client's relationship with the clinician is even more important. Consequently, considerable emphasis is placed on the here-and-now interaction of client and clinician, the transference relationship, and the role of the clinician as a participant observer (Messer & Warren, 1995). Attention is also paid to process as well as the link between the focal conflict and past developmental issues. Symptoms are viewed as coping efforts, and a broad range of interventions is employed to help people discard their symptoms and learn new and more effective ways to cope with stress, challenges, and disappointment, particularly in their relationships.

Specific Models

Although many names are associated with BPT, several stand out because of their writings and theoretical contributions (Demos & Prout, 1993). Their approaches to BPT all share the general characteristics of the model as discussed previously in this chapter. However, each theorist has developed his own variation, which we will consider briefly here.

Davanloo's Intensive Short-Term Dynamic Psychotherapy   Davanloo's approach to BPT is one of the earliest models and, not surprisingly, also the one that is closest to traditional psychoanalysis (Davanloo, 1979, 1980). His model emphasizes interpretation of drives and defenses, as does Freud's, but Davanloo uses very active and confrontational techniques to elicit underlying thoughts and feelings and reveal the unconscious. He places particular emphasis on analysis and interpretation of the interconnections among the transference relationship, other current relationships, and past relationships. He believes that 30 to 35% of clients seen for outpatient treatment can be treated successfully by his approach, including people with depression, anxiety, and personality disorders.

Sifneos's Short-Term Anxiety-Provoking Therapy Sifneos has focused on treating people with a wide range of anxiety disorders, interpersonal problems, and physical problems that seem to have an emotional cause (Sifneos, 1979b, 1984). People with unresolved issues of separation and loss dating back to early childhood seem to respond especially well to this model. A written agreement, including both a hypothesis about the nature of the client's difficulties and outcome criteria, is used to guide treatment. Sifneos's treatment model typically involves using intense and direct interpretations that can initially raise anxiety, hence the name of this approach. Education about the nature and dynamics of emotional difficulties and their resolution is also an important component.

Malan's Tavistock System of Short-Term Dynamic Psychotherapy Malan's approach, too, is characterized by interpretations that often are anxiety-provoking as well as by the identification of a central focus to treatment. He advocates a more detached stance than does either Davanloo or Sifneos and places particular emphasis on the transference-parent link (Demos & Prout, 1993).

Luborsky's Time-Limited Dynamic Supportive-Expressive Psychotherapy Luborsky and his colleagues (Luborsky, 1984; Messer & Warren, 1995) focus on the conflict between people's interpersonal wishes and their fears or expected outcomes, leading to the identification of a *core conflictual relationship theme* (CCRT). The CCRT reflects habitual ways in which people view and interact with others that cause difficulty. This approach is more supportive than those just discussed; interpretations are delivered only when people seem ready to hear and understand them, and symptoms are viewed as efforts to cope and solve problems.

Mann's Time-Limited Psychotherapy Mann's approach more closely resembles object relations theory and self psychology, (discussed in Chapter 7), than it does Freudian psychoanalysis (Demos & Prout, 1993). Mann believes that problems of passivity, dependence, and low self-esteem typically originate in the child's early separation from the mother. Consequently, treatment emphasizes the connection between early separation issues and present concerns. Goals include improvement of self-esteem and self-reliance. Support and empathy, which can enhance self-esteem, are more important in this model than they are in most versions of BPT. Psychotherapy via Mann's model is limited to 12 sessions.

Strupp's Time-Limited Dynamic Psychotherapy Strupp, working with Binder and others at Vanderbilt University, has drawn heavily on both object relations theory and the work of Harry Stack Sullivan in formulating his approach. The primary goal of Strupp's approach is to improve interpersonal relationships. Focusing on the client-clinician relationship and finding a central maladaptive interpersonal pattern are key ways in which this treatment system helps people improve their relationships (Najavits & Strupp, 1994; Strupp, 1992). Initially, treatment concentrates on present relationship patterns, but it then shifts to exploring early origins of difficulties once current patterns have been identified and understood. The role of the clinician is exploratory and positive. Strupp and his associates found that the quality of the therapeutic alliance in this approach is strongly related to outcome; therapists who are perceived as warm, affirming, and protective of their clients have more positive outcomes.

Klerman's Interpersonal Psychotherapy Interpersonal Psychotherapy (IPT) is a form of brief psychodynamic therapy designed specifically for the treatment of depression (Klerman, Weissman, Rounsaville, & Chevron, 1984). In a large study conducted by the National Institutes of Mental Health, IPT was found as effective as antidepressant medication and cognitive behavior therapy in the amelioration of depressive symptoms (Elkin et al., 1989). Another approach influenced by Sullivan's ideas, IPT emphasizes social and interpersonal experiences. It recognizes the importance of the unconscious and of early childhood interactions but gives more attention to current relationships and patterns, social roles, and coping skills.

According to IPT, "A disrupted, unloving relationship between a child and its parent or parent substitute can increase the child's vulnerability to depression as an adult (p. 55)." Once the vulnerability has been established, stressful interpersonal experiences in adulthood can lead to the onset or recurrence of depression. On the other hand, IPT theorists believe that strong social bonds can reduce the likelihood of depression.

This model encourages use of a broad range of strategies including support, questions to elicit emotion and content, interpretation, advice giving, education, clarification, feedback on communication, information on decision-making skills, behavior-change techniques, role playing, and use of the therapeutic relationship. In addition to depression, common concerns that seem to benefit from treatment via IPT include abnormal grief, conflicts in interpersonal roles and relationships, role transitions such as divorce and parenthood, and interpersonal skill deficits. Although clinicians play an active role, clients are encouraged to take as much responsibility as possible for their treatment.

APPLICATION OF BRIEF PSYCHODYNAMIC THERAPY

Brief psychodynamic therapy is a major approach to treatment that is in widespread use in one form or another. In 1986, 19% of clinicians reported that their primary theoretical orientation was psychodynamic, second only to eclectic/integrative approaches (Prochaska & Norcross, 1994). Although this percentage probably has declined somewhat since the 1980s, psychodynamic therapy remains a powerful force.

Considerable research has substantiated the value of BPT (Demos & Prout, 1993). The NIMH study just cited above has probably attracted the most attention and seems to have contributed greatly to the use and importance of this model. Crits-Christoph (1992) conducted a meta-analysis of 11 studies of BPT that lasted at least 12 sessions. That review found that people treated with BPT showed considerable reduction in symptoms compared to people on a waiting list for treatment. This finding applied to people with a broad range of difficulties. Clearly, the approach has proven its value. As Messer and Warren (1995) state, we have "good evidence for the efficacy of BPT" (p. 103).

Diagnostic Groups

BPT is a sound treatment approach for many disorders of moderate severity. Research has substantiated its value in treating depressive disorders, personality disorders, trauma-related disorders, grief, substance use disorders, physical complaints of psychological origin, and others.

However, BPT is not suitable for all people or all disorders. Used alone rather than with medication or other approaches to treatment, it usually will not be the best approach for people with psychotic disorders, bipolar disorders, and severe personality and substance use disorders.

The selection criteria listed previously in this chapter should be kept in mind when determining whether BPT should be the treatment of choice. Particularly suitable are people who are intelligent, insightful, interested in increasing their self-awareness, and open to change and who have mature defenses, a focal complaint that is central to their concerns, and a history of at least one close, positive relationship (Horowitz, et al., 1984). In other words, people who are relatively healthy and well functioning seem to respond particularly well to this approach.

Culturally Diverse Groups

Whether BPT is appropriate for people from nonwestern cultures is an unanswered question. Some will be uncomfortable with the probing, interpretation, and exploration of early childhood issues that are part of most versions of BPT. However, because clinicians who practice BPT do not advocate the relative anonymity of the classical analyst and typically do emphasize empathy, support, and the importance of the clinician-client relationship, BPT is likely to appeal to a wider range of clients than is Freudian analysis. In addition, although BPT does not say much about the importance of culture, its emphasis on relationships and on problem solving enables practitioners to incorporate attention to cultural context as well as family and other significant relationships.

EVALUATION OF BRIEF PSYCHODYNAMIC THERAPY

The theorists who developed BPT have made a very important contribution through their efforts to build on the strengths of Freudian psychoanalysis and enhance that model through approaches that make it more efficient, more acceptable to many people, and more compatible with modern counseling and psychotherapy's emphasis on brief treatment and relationships. According to Weisberg (1993), BPT works as well as conventional/classical psychoanalytic therapy; saves time and money; and is more suitable for people in crisis as well as for many people with interpersonal problems, career concerns, difficult decisions, and disorders of mood and anxiety.

At the same time, some concerns and criticisms have been voiced. BPT's sometimes confrontational and authoritarian nature and its emphasis on early childhood issues can elicit anger, dependency, and even regression. Its short-term nature can result in a superficial sort of treatment that ameliorates symptoms but does not sufficiently address underlying concerns. In addition, the research of Najavits and Strupp (1994) suggests that the quality of the clinician-client relationship and the interpersonal qualities of the clinician may be at least as important as specific concepts and interventions. Despite these concerns, BPT promises to be one of the most important treatment approaches of the early 21st century.

The development of BPT continues. Research is ongoing to provide further information on the most therapeutic ingredients of this model and the conditions under which it is most likely to be effective. In addition, specific approaches to BPT, such as Klerman's Interpersonal Psychotherapy, are being developed to treat specific groups of disorders. By tailoring the application of this rich and flexible approach, its value seems likely to grow even further over time.

SKILL DEVELOPMENT: IDENTIFYING A FOCAL CONCERN

Identifying a focal concern is important in BPT and can also improve effectiveness and clarify the direction of other approaches to treatment. The focal issue in BPT usually reflects dysfunctional interpersonal interactions and patterns that occur again and again in a person's life. These patterns are often linked to early childhood experiences, especially formative aspects of people's lives such as their early childhood attachment to and separation from their primary caregivers.

Whether or not clinicians seek an early childhood origin for focal concerns, analysis of present interactions can provide understanding of the dysfunctional patterns these concerns perpetuate. Luborsky and Mark (1991) sought to identify what they called the core conflictual relationship theme (CCRT), their version of the focal concern, by listening for patterns in three key areas: "the patient's wishes from the other person, the other person's actual or expected responses, and how the patient responds" (p. 119). By eliciting examples of relationship difficulties and examining these three areas for similarities and patterns, clinicians can arrive at a tentative formulation about the nature of people's focal interpersonal concerns. This can be shared with clients, modified if necessary, and written down as a statement of the focus of treatment.

The following example illustrates the identification of a focal concern or CCRT for Julie, a divorced woman with a five-year-old son, who sought counseling for interpersonal problems, especially in relationships with her parents, her ex-husband, and her boyfriend. Julie complained that these people did not really seem to care about her and treated her unfairly. When she was asked for examples of her relationship difficulties, Julie produced the following, with accompanying analysis according to the three key areas identified by Luborsky and Mark:

Example 1: Asking my parents for financial help

- *What I wish for from the other person:* I had worked up a detailed budget of my monthly expenses. It took me a long time to do that. It clearly showed that I needed at least $1,000 more a month. I wanted my parents to provide that.
- *The actual or expected response:* Although I thought my parents would make up the difference between what I got from my ex and what my expenses were, instead they talked about my getting a part-time job. All they agreed to do is pay for after-school child care and gas for my car until I find a job.
- *My reaction:* I feel really hurt and angry. I don't know if I can manage a job and a child. My parents don't understand how hard it is to be a single parent, and they don't seem to care. They had it easy. They always had each other and never had to struggle like this. If I didn't need them to baby-sit so I can take a break every once in a while, I wouldn't even let them see Danny. Then they would feel sorry.

Example 2: Telling Danny to clean up his room before bedtime

- *What I wish for from the other person:* I think he should just do it. You know that T-shirt that says, "Because I'm the mom." Well, that's what I want. I tell him to clean up his room, and he should do it.
- *The actual or expected response:* Oh no, not Danny; he always has to give me a hard time. I think he's putting things away; and then as soon as I leave his room to do the dishes or something, he's playing with his toys.
- *My reaction:* Who does he think I am? His slave? I've sacrificed a lot for that kid, and the least he can do is mind me. So I yelled at him and gave him a time out.

Example 3: Learning that before the divorce my husband loaned his brother some money without discussing it with me

- *What I wish for from the other person:* I said to him, "Where are your priorities? Your own family needs money, and you lend it to your brother so he can start another business that will fail." I wanted him to see he that had made a mistake and that he should try to get the money back.
- *The actual or expected response:* Well, I didn't know if he would really ask for the money back, but at very least I thought he would see he was wrong and would promise not to do it again. No way! He just said, "I didn't tell you because I knew what you would say, and I really wanted to help my brother."
- *My reaction:* Well, I knew what really happened. He wanted his parents to think he was so great. He was more concerned with pleasing them than with helping us. I was really mad, so I took some money out of the checking account and bought a really expensive dress. Then when he asked me about it, I said, "You think you can do whatever you want with our money. Well, so can I."

Although more information should be obtained to conclusively establish the presence of patterns, these three examples provide enough information to allow the development of a hypothesis about Julie's focal conflict or CCRT. These examples suggest that on one level, Julie views herself as special and deserving of treatment that reflects her specialness. When people do not automatically treat her as special, particularly when she asks for something and is refused, she becomes very angry and even punitive. The conflict arises because under the surface she seems to have considerable self-doubt. She questions her ability to be both a parent and an employee, perceives her husband as valuing his parents' opinions more than hers, and even feels powerless in her role as mother to her son. Behind her unrealistic demands and expectations is a woman who needs others to reassure her of her importance. Not surprisingly, as a young child, Julie apparently received little affirmation and affection from her parents. The primary way in which she got some attention was by throwing a temper tantrum, paralleling her current behavior. In addition, Julie's transference relationship with her clinician reflected her need for special treatment to counteract her doubts. She soon requested telephone conversations between sessions and reduced fees.

Analysis of Julie's CCRT and the similarities in the triad of her current relationships, her past relationships, and her transference to the clinician all shed light on patterns related to her focal relationship concern. Once these patterns have been understood and worked through, Julie might be able to make changes that will improve her relationships and help her feel better about her role in them.

CASE ILLUSTRATION

The following dialogue between Roberto and his counselor illustrates several aspects of brief psychodynamic therapy:

- The stance of the therapist as supportive but also confrontational, analytical, and educational
- The clinician's efforts to identify a focal conflict reflecting dysfunctional relationship patterns
- Recognition of commonalities among Roberto's past relationships, his present relationships, and his relationship with the clinician

Clinician: Roberto, you look very upset.

Roberto: Yes, I am. Edie and I had another one of those fights. I give her everything she wants. . . . I don't know what more I can do.

Clinician: Tell me about what happened.

Roberto: Well, we were having a birthday party for Ava with the family. Her family and my family were coming for dinner, and Edie had been cooking all day. I had asked her yesterday what I could do to help, and I did everything she told me. I went to the jeweler to pick up the gift Edie had ordered, I got the wine and some of the groceries, I even vacuumed the house. So that morning I sat down to read my e-mail, and next thing I know she's standing there screaming at me: "I do all the work around here. Who do you think you are? Glued to your computer as usual." Yada, yada, yada. So I said to her, "Look, just give me 15 fifteen minutes to finish this, and then I'll come down." Not good enough for her. She goes off again. So I just left before I really lost it.

Clinician: Sounds like you felt angry that she expected you to do even more than you had already done and wouldn't give you a few minutes for yourself.

Roberto: Yeah, my e-mail is part of my work. If I don't take care of that, no job, no money.

Clinician: So her behavior just doesn't make sense to you. You know, this makes me think of our discussion of how much your mother expected of you and how unreasonable it sometimes seemed.

Roberto: Yeah, I can see that. I would be trying to get my homework done and the younger kids would be screaming, and she'd say, "Roberto, would you feed the baby and then take your brothers out to play so I can get something done around here?" What about me? When was I going to get my homework done? Yeah, I didn't like that either, but I just did it.

Clinician: So in both cases, you were doing a lot to help a woman, but it felt like there was no time for your needs.

Roberto: Yeah, I'm always supposed to be the strong one. Roberto, fix this, do that, pay this bill. And I do it. But when is it my turn?

Clinician: Yet in a way, it must feel good to be the strong one. I wonder if you might give people the message that you can handle anything because you enjoy having them see you as very capable?

Roberto: I guess so. It's like I'm strong and they're weak and they really need me. But then it gets to be too much.

Clinician: Perhaps we saw a similar pattern in our work together. You know, a couple of times when the phone rang here, you said, "Go ahead, doc, get the phone. It's okay." And when I was sick for a few weeks and had to cancel our sessions and I asked you how you felt about it, you said that it was fine; but I noticed that you seemed irritated and less open in the next few sessions. It seems hard for you to acknowledge that

you have any needs, but you do; and they can build up and come out in ways that hurt you and other people.

Roberto: Yeah, well, everybody has needs, but I've always been able to take care of myself.

Clinician: Yes, you have been very self-sufficient and take great pride in that. But maybe sometimes your need to be strong backfires and hurts you and those you care about.

Roberto: Well, that could be right, but I don't want to turn into a wimp. I like who I am. Are you telling me to be different?

Clinician: I'm certainly not telling you to be a wimp! I don't think you could do that if you tried. But, you know, sometimes part of being strong is recognizing that we can't do everything ourselves and being able to let other people know what we need and that we want a more mutual relationship.

Roberto: That's a new way to think about things. How could I have handled the problems around Ava's party differently?

At this point in the session, Roberto has gained some insight into patterns that have shown up in old relationships, current relationships, and his relationship with his clinician. He has been given some information to help him view his need to be strong in a different light. He is now ready to explore these patterns further and to consider ways to make some shifts that will allow him to maintain his image of himself as a strong caretaker but also will help him articulate his own needs appropriately. Accomplishing this should lead to more mutuality in his relationships and enable him to avoid the anger and frustration he experiences when his needs are ignored for too long.

EXERCISES

Large-Group Exercises

1. Discuss the differences and similarities between traditional psychoanalysis and brief psychodynamic therapy, listing them on the board. Then select five students to represent the traditional model and five to represent BPT. Have the two groups of students engage in a debate in front of the class in response to the question, "Which of these two approaches has more to offer today's clinicians?"

2. Conduct a group interview of Edie. One student should assume the role of Edie and should sit or stand in front of the class. Each student should then have the opportunity to ask Edie one or two questions. The goal of the interview should be an identification of Edie's focal conflict or CCRT. After the round-robin interview has been completed, analyze the information elicited from Edie, focusing on the following:
   - The *impulse-defense triad,* including current and recently ended relationships, past real or imagined relationships, and the transference relationship
   - The *triad of insight,* including the aim or impulse, the injunction or threat that makes the aim dangerous or unacceptable, and the defense used to reduce the anxiety that arises from the impulse
   - The focal conflict

3. Consider the criteria described in this chapter that indicate whether a person is likely to be a good candidate for BPT. Apply them to Edie to determine whether she would be appropriate for treatment via this model.

Small-Group Exercises

1. Divide into your groups composed of two dyads. The role play for this chapter should be a 15–20 minute interview designed to identify the client's focal conflict or issue. Once each role play has been completed, all four participants should engage in identifying the repeated patterns that emerged and defining the focal issue. Time should also be taken to provide feedback to the interviewers about the following:
   - Ability to elicit the focal conflict
   - Therapeutic alliance
   - Use of open questions and other intervention strategies
   - Strengths of the role play
   - Suggestions for improvement

2. The role of the clinician who practices BPT is a varied and flexible one, including use of confrontation, support, exploration, and education. Each group of four students should engage in four brief role plays of approximately five minutes each. Rotate the roles of client and clinician so that each of the four students has an opportunity to take on each of these two roles. Each role play should be characterized by the clinician relating to the client in a different way as follows:

Role Play 1: Clinician is supportive.
Role Play 2: Clinician is exploratory.
Role Play 3: Clinician is confrontational.
Role Play 4: Clinician is educational.

For the client role, group members may choose to be themselves, or they can take on the persona of one of the clients described in this book or of someone they know. Discuss the differences and similarities among the four role plays.

Individual Exercises

1. In this chapter, you learned to identify a core conflictual relationship theme (CCRT). Identify and list three important interactions you have had with others, at least one of which should have occurred at least five years ago. Next, examine the pattern used in the "Skill Development" section's example about Julie. Analyze your interactions in a similar way. For each, consider the following:

   What you wish for from the other person
   The actual or expected response
   Your reaction

   Now try to identify common patterns among these three interactions and develop a written hypothesis about the nature of your CCRT.

2. Brief, time-limited treatment has elicited much debate among mental health professionals. If you were to enter counseling, would you prefer open-ended, extended treatment or brief, time-limited treatment? Write about what you think your treatment would be like in each case, highlighting benefits and limitations you would expect to experience with each type.

Summary

Brief psychodynamic therapy, derived from traditional Freudian psychoanalysis, grew out of the work of Alexander, Ferenczi, and others, who found that length and depth of analysis were not clearly correlated with amount and stability of gains (Horowitz et al., 1984). BPT is typically much shorter than traditional analysis, often has a fixed time limit, and centers on a focal concern or core relationship pattern that seems linked to the person's symptoms. While clinicians practicing BPT assume that early childhood experiences, especially attachment to and separation from caregivers, are related to current relationship issues and do pay attention to the transference relationship, their primary focus is on present relationships and ways to help people lead more rewarding lives. Goals are clear and circumscribed; clinicians are active and flexible; and strategies are designed not only to promote insight but also to elicit feelings, promote new learning, and change behavior. Research supports the value of this approach in treating a broad range of mild to moderately severe difficulties, notably depression.

RECOMMENDED READINGS

Demos, V. C., & Prout, M. F. (1993). A comparison of seven approaches to brief psychotherapy. *International Journal of Short-Term Psychotherapy, 8,* 3–22.

Klerman, G. L., Weissman, M. M., Rounsaville, B. J., & Chevron, E. S. (1984). *Interpersonal psychotherapy of depression.* New York: Basic Books.

Luborsky, L. (1984). *Principles of psychoanalytic psychotherapy: A manual for supportive-expressive treatment.* New York: Basic Books.

Messer, S. B., & Warren, S. (1995). *Models of brief psychodynamic therapy.* New York: Guilford.

Strupp, H. H. (1992). The future of psychodynamic psychotherapy. *Psychotherapy, 29(1),* 21–27.

PART THREE

TREATMENT SYSTEMS EMPHASIZING EMOTIONS AND SENSATIONS

Chapter 10
Overview of Emotions and Sensations

Chapter 11
Carl Rogers and Person-Centered Counseling

Chapter 12
Existential Therapy

Chapter 13
Gestalt Therapy

Chapter 14
Emerging Approaches Emphasizing Emotions and Sensations

Chapter 10

OVERVIEW OF EMOTIONS AND SENSATIONS

"How are you?" Most of us hear this question many times each day—when we arrive at work, when we see our friends at school, when we go into meetings, when we answer the telephone, when we return home, and at many points in between. People all around us are asking about our feelings. We don't always answer this question honestly; we may simply participate in a ritual and respond, "I'm fine. How are you?" However, sometimes we give an honest answer, at least to ourselves, and talk and think about our feelings.

We express our feelings, either intentionally or inadvertently, many times a day; and many more times a day we have feelings that we do not disclose. Our emotions are an essential part of who we are. Expressions of emotion can bring people closer or drive them apart; they contribute to our professional success and can be part of the reason we fail at a job. Emotions such as guilt, hopelessness, and anxiety can be symptoms of mental disorders, while those such as joy, pride, and love may reflect our mental health.

Although emotions often lead people to seek counseling or psychotherapy, clinicians differ on the importance of dealing with feelings in treatment just as they disagree on the importance of dealing with past experiences (discussed in Part 2). Some clinicians and theorists believe that helping people identify, express, understand, and manage their emotions and sensations is the key to successful treatment, while others believe that emotions are governed by thoughts and that treatment efforts will be most productive if clinicians de-emphasize feelings and focus on cognitions. Whether you believe thoughts produce feelings or feelings produce thoughts, emotions inevitably play an important part in the treatment process.

In Part 1 you learned about the BETA model, which reflects the four important areas of focus in counseling and psychotherapy (background, emotions, thoughts, actions) and provides the structure of this book. Part 2 focused on systems of treatment that emphasize the importance of background. In Part 3 we focus on systems that emphasize emotions and sensations. In addition to paying particular attention to feelings, the treatment systems discussed in this part of the book are experiential in that they view as important what people have observed, encountered, or undergone. Similarly, they can be thought of as phenomenological because of the importance they ascribe to how people view themselves and their world.

Carl Rogers, more than anyone else, made emotions an important aspect of treatment; and we consider his theory, person-centered counseling, in Chapter 11. Chapter 12 focuses on existentialism. At least as much philosophy as psychotherapy, this approach, developed by Viktor Frankl, Rollo May, and others, emphasizes the importance of feeling that our lives are meaningful and that we have a purpose. We consider Fritz Perls's approach, Gestalt therapy, in Chapter 13. This approach pays particular attention to physical sensations and the messages they give to both ourselves and others. Chapter 14 introduces narrative therapy, constructivist therapy, feminist therapy, transpersonal psychotherapy, and focusing (developed by Eugene Gendlin). These systems of treatment have not yet been fully developed but do include concepts and techniques that emphasize emotions, are phenomenological, and have been gaining attention in recent years. Familiarizing ourselves with these emerging approaches can enrich our work as clinicians, help us deal more productively with our clients' feelings, and contribute to our understanding of new directions in counseling and psychotherapy.

DIMENSIONS OF EMOTIONS AND SENSATIONS

Feelings can take many forms. They can be emotional or physical, or a combination of the two. Examples of emotional feelings include sadness, apprehension, grief, anger, and discouragement. Examples of physical feelings include queasiness, headaches, muscle tension, shaky hands, and chills. Often physical and emotional feelings go together. For example, when we feel sad, we often lose our appetite, we may feel tired and heavy, or want to eat too much. On the other hand, when we feel happy, we may feel light and buoyant, relaxed, and very alert.

Feelings can be overt or covert, or a combination of the two. Overt feelings are evident to other people, either because they are expressed in words or because non-verbal clues reveal the feelings. For example, a person can express anger by saying, "You make me really mad when you do that," or by scowling, raising a fist, shouting, or making an obscene gesture. Covert feelings are kept inside and are not revealed. Sometimes when we give a presentation, attend a party where we know few people, or go into a situation such as a dissertation defense where we know others will be judging us, we experience considerable anxiety and tension. However, we often try to conceal those feelings so that we can make a positive impression. Fear of rejection and disapproval, shame about our feelings, and unawareness of our emotions may lead us to conceal or even deny our feelings.

Feelings may be both overt and covert—for example, when we share only a part of our feelings. Before a final examination begins, nearly everyone feels some apprehension and anxiety. However, some students may conceal the enormity of their feelings so that they do not seem to be any more fearful than most of the other students.

Feelings can be positive, negative, or neutral. Some emotions such as contentment, happiness, and amusement usually are positive. Others such as worry, rage, and disappointment are negative. Still others such as curiosity and sleepiness may be neutral. Of course, categorizing feelings as positive, negative, or neutral may be much more complex. Emotions that usually fall into one category may be experienced differently by a particular person. For example, George enjoyed feeling rage; it gave him a sense of power and control, and he liked to intimidate others. Sharon, on the other hand, viewed pride as a negative emotion; she had been brought up to be self-effacing and was afraid that people would disapprove or expect too much of her if she had significant accomplishments. Emotions may also be both positive and negative. For example, Karen did not like the sadness and lethargy she felt when she was depressed, but she did enjoy the extra attention she received from her family.

The intensity of emotions varies greatly depending on the person and the circumstances. Our anger may be mild when someone takes a parking spot that was justifiably ours but intense when we discover that our home has been burglarized. Be sure to consider intensity when assessing people's feelings. Emotions themselves may be appropriate, yet their intensity can cause misunderstandings and relationship difficulties.

People may be aware or unaware of their emotions and sensations. Likely to be particularly troublesome are emotions that are evident to others and that guide our behaviors and reactions but that are largely out of our awareness. For example, Fred felt envious of Charleton, his supervisor, but had difficulty recognizing those feelings and admitting them to himself. However, whenever the opportunity arose, he spoke negatively of Charleton to others, avoided working late, and fabricated excuses so he would not have to go on business trips with his supervisor. Charleton sensed Fred's displeasure and tried to talk with him about it, but the conversation was not a productive one. Although Fred received a satisfactory performance evaluation from his supervisor, he was not recommended for a promotion; his lack of understanding of the reasons for this contributed further to his resentment toward Charleton.

Feelings that are unacceptable to people or out of their conscious awareness usually are especially challenging in treatment. They may not emerge or be available for discussion until a solid rapport between the client and the clinician has been established.

Appropriateness of feelings is another important dimension, affecting how we are perceived by others and our relationships with them. In assessing appropriateness, consider the connection of the context and the precipitant of the feelings to the nature and intensity of the feelings. A wedding, for example, provides a context that can elicit a variety of emotions, both appropriate and inappropriate. The nostalgic tears of the mother of the bride, the pride of her father, the love of the groom, the joy of the bride, the shared happiness of the wedding party, and the pleasure, perhaps coupled with some mild envy, experienced by some of the guests are all classic and appropriate emotions. Inappropriate emotions such as the groom's obvious anger at the cost of the wedding, the noisy grieving of the bride's former suitor, or the rudeness of the servers when someone requests tea instead of coffee are particularly intrusive because of the context of the wedding. Emotions that may be acceptable in one context may be offensive in another. Context, as well as the immediate precipitant for an emotional response, then, determine how people and their emotions are perceived and the impact they have on others.

Congruence is another variable to keep in mind when assessing emotions. Congruence reflects the unity or consistency with which people express their emotions. When feelings are expressed congruently, verbal and nonverbal clues to emotions all give the same message. A person expressing words of love, for example, probably will speak softly, maintain good eye contact, and have an open and welcoming posture. However, if the person who is expressing words of love has poor eye contact, an angry and loud tone of voice, or a tense and closed posture, conflicting and confusing emotions are communicated. The receiver may not know what to believe, only pay attention to part of the message, misinterpret the message, or discredit the message because of its delivery. People sometimes unknowingly sabotage their efforts to communicate their feelings to others by giving such mixed and confusing messages. Self-observation and feedback can help people to increase the congruence, clarity, and impact of their emotional messages.

Finally, emotions may help or hurt people depending on the variables we have discussed. Expressing our emotions can enhance our lives and our relationships, move us toward achievement of our goals, and increase the pleasure we take in our lives. They can also do harm and can contribute to failed relationships, physical symptoms, unsatisfying careers, and unrewarding and unsuccessful lives. When assessing emotions, our own as well as those of our clients, family, friends, and associates, consider the eight dimensions of expression of feelings:

> 1. Emotional, physical, or a combination
> 2. Overt, covert, or a combination
> 3. Positive, negative, or neutral
> 4. In or out of awareness
> 5. Level of intensity
> 6. Appropriateness for context and stimulus
> 7. Congruence
> 8. Helpful or harmful

Being aware of these dimensions can help us to better understand the nature and impact of feelings and to find ways to modify emotions and their expression if they are not helping us.

THE IMPORTANCE OF EMOTIONS IN COUNSELING AND PSYCHOTHERAPY

The most common disorders treated in both inpatient and outpatient mental health settings are mood disorders, characterized primarily by depression. People typically seek treatment because they have feelings that are uncomfortable, painful, or confusing and they want clinicians to help them stop feeling bad. Emotions or feelings, then, are usually what motivates people to seek help. Even in their initial telephone call to schedule an appointment, people will explain, "I feel so bad. I'm thinking about killing myself," or "I feel worried all the time and can't stop worrying," or "My husband tells me I'm too angry and I need to do something about it," or "My stomach hurts, and the physicians can't find anything wrong with me. Can counseling help?" Even when people's presenting concerns seem to focus on actual or anticipated events or experiences, feelings typically underlie those experiences. For example, the woman who says, "My boss is threatening to fire me if I don't shape up," is probably thinking, "I'm terrified that I'm going to lose my job, but I'm also furious at my supervisor." The man who asks, "How can I get my wife off my back about my drinking? I've got it under control," may be feeling apprehensive about his ability to stop abusing alcohol and ashamed of his drinking. The teenager who complains, "My parents are from Korea and they don't understand what it's like to be a young person in America," may feel caught between his longing for the acceptance of his peers and his love and respect for his parents.

Because emotions typically lead people into treatment, clinicians' recognition and acknowledgment of those feelings can engender hope and optimism in clients, even in the first few minutes of treatment. Consider the following two openings:

Example 1
Client: I called for an appointment because I've been feeling very depressed and discouraged. Nothing seems to be going right.

Clinician: What specifically led you to make an appointment now?

Example 2

Client: I called for an appointment because I've been feeling very depressed and discouraged. Nothing seems to be going right.

Clinician: Sounds like you're feeling pretty hopeless. I wonder what specifically led you to make an appointment now?

Even though both clinicians ask the same exploratory question, the second clinician shows empathy for the client and acknowledges the importance of the person's feelings. The clinician's use of the word "hopeless" will probably lead the client to reflect further on the feelings that have been expressed and perhaps to understand them better. The first clinician, on the other hand, sounds very businesslike and, by failing to attend to those opening emotions, may seem uncaring and uninterested in the client.

Recognizing and dealing productively with feelings in treatment can accomplish the following goals:

1. The clinician can help clients to feel heard.
2. By letting people know that they hear and understand them, clinicians build rapport and join with their clients in a collaborative relationship focused on helping the clients.
3. Clients who believe that their clinicians hear and understand them seem more likely to have confidence in those clinicians and to feel optimistic that treatment can help them. This, in turn, is likely to enhance the effectiveness of treatment.
4. Clinicians who attend to their clients' emotions and sensations are likely to feel more caring toward those individuals; to know, as fully as possible, the pain and unhappiness that the clients are experiencing; and to appreciate them as unique human beings.
5. Because people's presenting problems and symptoms usually involve negative feelings, promoting clients' expression and understanding of those feelings can allow them to find ways to change the antecedents, the personal meaning, the nature, and the expression of the feelings, leading to relief of symptoms.
6. Many people not only experience painful emotions but berate themselves for having those feelings even though they may be very understandable. Discovering that their feelings are normal and understandable can be very reassuring.
7. By assessing the nature and intensity of people's feelings, clinicians can formulate specific treatment goals and interventions and can measure progress.

SKILL DEVELOPMENT: ANALYZING AND RESPONDING TO EMOTIONS

Here we consider three interrelated skills:

- Analysis of the nature and dimensions of emotions
- Reflection of feeling and meaning
- Communication of empathy

Analysis of Emotions

Previously, we discussed the following eight dimensions of emotions:

1. Emotional, physical, or a combination
2. Overt, covert, or a combination
3. Positive, negative, or neutral
4. In or out of awareness
5. Level of intensity
6. Appropriateness to context and stimulus
7. Congruence
8. Helpful or harmful

The following example illustrates how the expression of a feeling can be analyzed according to these dimensions.

> **Edie:** Roberto and I had another big blow-up yesterday. We were expecting his family for dinner in an hour, and I had tons more to do. I had asked him to help, but, there he was, locked away in his office with his computer. I marched down to the basement, pounded on the door, threw it open, and then gave him a piece of my mind. I was so mad that I knocked all the books and papers off his desk. I guess I got through to him because he shut off his computer right away and ran for the vacuum to help clean up the house. He really did work hard for that last hour. But somehow it didn't make me feel any better. I just felt like crying.

Nature of Edie's Feelings: Anger, Sadness

1. *Emotional, physical, or a combination.* Anger is emotional (feels mad) and physical (pounds on door, yells, pushes books and papers off desk). Sadness is emotional.
2. *Overt, covert, or a combination.* Anger is overt. Sadness initially is covert but then surfaces.
3. *Positive, negative, or neutral.* Both emotions are negative.
4. *In or out of awareness.* Edie seems to be aware of both emotions but has little understanding of the sadness underlying her anger.
5. *Level of intensity.* Anger was very intense. Sadness was moderate.
6. *Appropriate to context and stimulus.* Edie's anger seems to be an overreaction to the situation and probably reflects pent-up rage related to past conflicts and disappointments. The stimulus for the sadness is unclear and needs exploration. The underlying and unexpressed sadness probably contributed to the extreme nature of the anger.
7. *Congruence.* Although Edie's verbal and nonverbal expressions of anger were congruent, her conflicting emotions of anger and sadness do not fit together well and are confusing her.
8. *Helpful or harmful.* Although Edie did succeed in getting Roberto's immediate help and attention, the intensity of her anger was probably destructive to their relationship.

This analysis suggests ways in which counseling could help Edie deal with her emotions:

- Promoting her awareness of warning signs of her rage so that she can choose to express it differently
- Promoting her awareness of the complexity of her feelings, especially the link between her anger and her sadness, so that she can pay more attention to the sadness and perhaps express her feelings more fully
- Helping her recognize the potentially harmful nature of her expression of emotion
- Enabling her to gain insight into the intensity and incongruence of her emotions, probably reflecting other sources of anger and sadness beyond the present context
- Teaching her more constructive ways to manage and express her anger

The exercises later in the chapter will give you an opportunity to analyze emotions according to these eight dimensions and to use that information to suggest ways in which to help people deal with their emotions.

Reflection

Reflection is a process that identifies and feeds back to people the underlying or important meaning that emotions or experiences have for them. Reflections, using words different from those used by the client, give another perspective on emotions and experiences. Reflections are intended to deepen people's awareness of those emotions and experiences, promote thought and insight, let people know that they are heard and understood, and encourage further discussion and self-exploration.

Two types of reflection have been identified in the counseling and psychotherapy literature: reflection of feeling and reflection of meaning. The following examples clarify the nature of these reflections:

Client: For the first time, I handed in my assignment on schedule. Even though I worked very hard and followed the plan we had developed, I didn't think I could do it, but I did!

Reflection of feeling: I can hear that you feel very proud of yourself.

Reflection of meaning: This sounds like a real milestone for you.

Both of the interventions are potentially effective because they do not simply repeat the client's words but use language that enhances his awareness and demonstrates that the clinician is attuned to the client. The reflection of feeling contains a word that labels the client's emotion—pride, in this case. The reflection of meaning captures the significance this experience has for the client: succeeding, at least once, in overcoming his procrastination. Although the two interventions probably will take the session in somewhat different directions, both may solidify the client's feeling of accomplishment, help him feel good about his success, and help him become aware of how he achieved this milestone and can generalize those behaviors to other experiences.

The effectiveness of these reflections becomes particularly clear when they are contrasted with other types of interventions, such as the following:

Open question: How did you manage to do that?

Closed question: When did this happen?

Suggestion: I suggest you write down exactly how you did this so that you can try to repeat this success.

Self-disclosure: I'm really impressed!

Interpretation: It seems that once you became comfortable seeing yourself as a success, your behavior started to change.

Restatement: So you worked hard and finally met the deadline.

Previous chapters have already familiarized you with open and closed questions and interpretations, so you know that these often are appropriate and helpful interventions. That is also true of suggestions, restatements, and self-disclosure, which will be discussed in later "Skill Development" sections of this book. Not only do all six types of interventions have a place in counseling and psychotherapy, but all six are potentially therapeutic and helpful. However, none of them accomplishes the purpose of reinforcing the client's gains quite as well as the reflections do. Although the other responses might be good as follow-up interventions, a reflection with a positive emphasis seems most powerful in this case.

What if a reflection is not on target and does not really capture the client's emotions? That happens to the best clinicians, no matter how carefully they are listening. Usually, a reflection that is not accurate does not harm the treatment process as long as the clinician-client relationship is open and supportive enough so that the client can correct the reflection. Consider the following interaction:

Client: For the first time, I handed in my assignment on time. Even though I worked very hard and followed the plan we had developed, I didn't think I could do it, but I did!

Clinician: Sounds like you feel elated that you were able to work so hard.

Client: Well, that's not exactly it. I usually work hard, but most of the time it just feels like I'm spinning my wheels. Somehow this time I set a reasonable schedule for myself, I didn't get into that perfectionistic thinking, I did a good-enough job, and I was able to finish on time.

Clinician: So hard work wasn't really what made the difference. It was setting realistic expectations for yourself and seeing the strengths in what you did that led to your success.

Client: Yes, that's it.

Although the clinician missed the mark slightly in her first intervention, the intervention was still helpful. It prompted the client to think about what had contributed to his success, express that to the clinician, and hear a second intervention that demonstrated the understanding he wanted. In addition, exchanges such as these can give people practice in making themselves clear to others and ensuring that they are understood.

Communicating Empathy

Communicating empathy is probably the most important benefit of making sensitive and accurate reflections of meaning and emotions. Empathy involves feeling deeply connected to people, being sensitive to the nuances in their words and nonverbal cues, sensing and almost experiencing their emotions, and successfully communicating that awareness to the clients. Empathy is very important in building rapport between client and clinician and establishing a collaborative therapeutic alliance. Typically, people who feel that their counselors and psychotherapists understand and care about them are more optimistic that their treatment will help them, more willing to disclose intimate personal information, more agreeable to trying new experiences and behaviors, and more likely to achieve their treatment goals. As we discussed in Chapter 2, empathy is an important aspect of the clinical relationship and plays a vital part in determining the success of the treatment.

Empathy and sympathy are sometimes confused. Sympathy is characterized by feeling sorry for people. This can make them feel pitiful, helpless, and hopeless. Empathy, on the other hand, gives people the message that their feelings can be understood and accepted, which is empowering rather than demeaning.

Although reflections of meaning and reflections of feelings, designed to communicate empathy as well as promote self-awareness, are only one of many interventions that clinicians use, they are an essential part of their repertoire of skills. Consider the following dialogue with Ava in which the clinician emphasizes the use of reflections to communicate empathy:

Ava: My mom and dad told me I should meet with you today. I don't really know why.

Clinician: You sound a little apprehensive about coming in to talk with me.

Ava: Yes, I guess I am. I've seen movies about therapists, and they usually had a couch. I was afraid I would have to lie down on a couch, but you don't even have one here.

Clinician: So this is different from what you expected and maybe not quite so scary.

Ava: Yes. But I still don't know what to do.

Clinician: This is all kind of a mystery to you.

Ava: Yes. My mom said I should just come in and talk about my family. I guess I could do that.

Clinician: Sounds like that might be a comfortable place for you to start.

Ava: Well, I know my mom and dad have been seeing you for a while. They fight a lot. I just try to stay out of the way. I go to my room, but I wish I could make them stop fighting.

Clinician: It must be pretty upsetting to you when they fight.

Ava: Yes, I worry that they might get a divorce. My friend Carrie's mom and dad got a divorce, and it was awful. I never know whose house she's at when I want to call her.

Clinician: So divorce looks like a pretty bad thing to you, and you wish you could do something to make sure your mom and dad don't get divorced.

Ava: Yes, but when I ask my mom about it, she just says, "Don't worry about it. We both love you, and we'll always take good care of you." What kind of an answer is that?

Clinician: You sound angry that your parents are not really telling you what's going on.

Ava: That's true. I'm not a baby anymore. I just had my 10th birthday. I could understand what's going on, and maybe I could help them. I could earn more money mowing lawns; I could do better in school; I could bother them less. If they would only tell me what to do, I would do it.

Clinician: I can hear how much you love your parents and wish with all your heart that you could help them to be happier together.

Ava: (tearfully) Yes, that's exactly how I feel.

This dialogue demonstrates how using reflections of feeling and meaning to communicate empathy can help people to feel comfortable in treatment, share feelings that are hard for them to talk about, feel understood, and begin to make good use of the treatment process. Staying with a person's emotions and showing awareness, acceptance, and understanding of them can go a long way toward helping that person.

EXERCISES

Large-Group Exercises

1. Analyze the following statement of feelings according to each of the eight dimensions discussed previously in this chapter:

   - Emotional, physical or a combination
   - Overt, covert or a combination
   - Positive, negative, or neutral
   - In or out of awareness
   - Level of intensity
   - Appropriateness to context and stimulus

- Congruence
- Helpful or harmful

Roberto: (speaking in a loud voice and occasionally banging his fist on the table) I really love Edie, but I just can't seem to get through to her. I do everything I can to show her how much I care. I work hard; I help around the house; I'm a good father to Ava; I don't drink; I don't run around with other women. I said all this to her, but, no, it's not enough for her. She says, "But you don't understand my feelings." So I say, "I don't know what you're talking about. I tell you I love you. That's *my* feeling. But you don't understand my feelings either."

Based on your analysis of Roberto's feelings, how do you think treatment focused on his feelings could be helpful to him? Identify at least three goals that you would have for helping him deal with the emotions he has expressed in this example.

2. Write reflections of meaning and reflections of feeling in response to the following five statements. Then discuss your responses as a class, listing on the board two or three helpful responses to each statement. For each of the five statements, discuss whether a reflection of feeling or a reflection of meaning would be more helpful to the client.

Client A: Losing my job was the last straw. What else is going to happen? I feel like I'm jinxed.

Client B: I didn't have a good time at the party. I felt like everyone was watching me, waiting for me to do something stupid. That's the last time I'll put myself in a situation like that.

Client C: You know, it meant a great deal to me when you called me after my surgery. I was feeling pretty scared, but somehow knowing that you were there and wanted to talk to me really turned things around, and my situation didn't look so bad after all.

Client D: I love to be outside in the springtime, to get away from the mess at home. It makes me forget about all my problems. I get this sort of religious feeling.

Client E: I've been telling my wife for years that she doesn't make me feel special, that she takes me for granted. She never seemed to hear me. Then out of the blue, she makes me a surprise birthday party. Well, I couldn't believe it. It was like I was king for a day.

Small-Group Exercises:

1. Divide into your groups of four, composed of two dyads. Each dyad should engage in a 10-minute, role-played, counseling interview. The person playing the client should talk about how he or she spent the previous weekend, emphasizing discussion of feelings. The person in the clinician role should facilitate the

discussion, relying as much as possible on reflection of feeling and reflection of meaning to promote dialogue as well as the client's self-awareness. Tape-record the interview. Play back the recorded interview after it is completed so that the group can identify whether or not each intervention is a reflection of meaning or feeling and can discuss the impact of each intervention.

2. Each dyad should role-play another interview, remaining in the same roles and focusing on the same topic. This time, however, the interviewee should say little about emotions, while the interviewer should avoid using reflections whenever possible. Discuss the process of each of the two interviews. How did the participants feel about their roles? Which interview was more challenging and why? Which interview was more rewarding and why? What was the impact of each interview on the client-clinician rapport? What other important differences did you notice between the two interviews? What did you learn from this exercise?

Individual Exercises

1. We express emotions many, many times throughout each day. Listen to yourself and write down in your journal at least three statements of feelings that you have heard yourself make. Then select one of them—ideally, an expression of feelings accompanied by some discomfort—and prepare a written analysis of your statement according to the eight dimensions of feelings. What did you learn about yourself and the way in which you express your feelings from this analysis? Be your own counselor and suggest at least two ways you might have improved on your expression of feelings so that you would have communicated your emotions more clearly to others and been better understood.

2. Select a two-hour time period in the next few days in which you will make a conscious effort to use more reflections of feeling and reflections of meaning in your everyday conversations. Be aware of how it feels to use these skills, whether your reflections seem to produce any changes in your interactions with others, and the kinds of responses your use of reflection elicits. Write about this experience in your journal.

Summary

This chapter reviewed the place and importance of emotions and sensations in counseling and psychotherapy. It also provided a list of eight dimensions that can help clinicians understand and analyze feelings. Skill development included analyzing expressions of feelings, using reflections of meaning and reflections of feelings, and communicating empathy.

Chapter 11

CARL ROGERS AND PERSON-CENTERED COUNSELING

More than anyone else, Carl Rogers is associated with systems of counseling and psychotherapy that emphasize emotions. As much a philosophy as a theory of how to help people, Rogers's person-centered theory was built on a strong humanistic base. Unlike the early psychoanalytic approaches, which tend to be deterministic, viewing people as shaped largely by early parental messages, powerful drives, and the unconscious, humanism views people as capable and autonomous, with the ability to resolve their difficulties, realize their potential, and change their lives in positive ways. The task of the clinician is to build a relationship with clients that will promote their self-esteem and empower them so that they can use their own strengths and flourish.

THE PERSON WHO DEVELOPED PERSON-CENTERED COUNSELING

Carl Rogers was born in 1902 and spent his childhood in the midwest, first in Chicago and later on a farm. He described his family as religious fundamentalists (Rogers, 1980). Rogers was raised to be judgmental of behaviors and attitudes that conflicted with his parents' values. His family rarely shared personal thoughts and feelings. Rogers reported that he had little social contact with children other than his brothers and viewed himself as distant and aloof.

Rogers's family had instilled in him the importance of hard work, the scientific method, and a sense of responsibility, values that were reflected in his academic pursuits. He was an outstanding student who valued academic accomplishment. College and graduate school, however, were periods of great transition for him. Initially majoring in agriculture, he soon realized that following the career path reflected by his family background was not right for him, and he changed his focus first to history, then religion, and finally clinical psychology. Rogers completed his undergraduate work at the University of Wisconsin and began to study for the ministry at Union Theological Seminary in New York City but transferred to Columbia University, where he received a Ph.D. degree in psychology in 1931.

These changes in career direction seemed to parallel Rogers's growing awareness of the importance of social relationships and of sharing thoughts and feelings. His experiences as a camp counselor, a trip to China as part of the World Student Christian Federation Conference, his dating experiences, and his marriage immediately after college all contributed to his evolution from a person with a rigid and judgmental view of others to one who appreciated the individuality of each person while believing strongly in the importance of world peace and the interconnections of all humankind.

Rogers's career after 1931 reflected a growing involvement with people and the development of his theory of counseling and psychotherapy. He initially worked with children in Rochester, New York, and later was a faculty member at Ohio State University and the University of Chicago. From 1963 until the end of his life, he promoted his ideas through the Center for Studies of the Person in La Jolla, California. During his later years, he focused on using his theories to reduce interracial tensions and promote world peace. He was nominated for a Nobel Peace Prize shortly before his death.

Rogers broke his hip as a result of a fall in 1987, underwent surgery, but died of heart failure several days later. Rogers was an active leader in his profession until his death. His own words capture well the sort of life he led: "I do not know when I will die, but I do know that I will have lived a full and exciting eighty-five years!" (Rogers, 1987, p. 152).

According to Cain (1987a), Rogers was the embodiment of the theory he had developed, "the most attentive, careful, and sensitive listener" he had ever known (p. 284). Rogers's habits of hard work, self-discipline, organization, and concentration continued throughout his life. He enhanced these strengths with his optimism, his sense of self-actualization, and his ability to be open to experience and live in the moment. He was not afraid to express ideas that were new and innovative and was deeply committed to improving the world. His life and his ideas are inseparable. As he stated (Rogers, 1961), "Experience is, for me, the highest authority. The touchstone of validity is my own experience. No other person's ideas, and none of my own ideas, are as authoritative as my experience. It is to experience that I must return again and again, to discover a closer approximation to truth as it is in the process of becoming in me" (pp. 23–24).

THE DEVELOPMENT OF PERSON-CENTERED COUNSELING

According to Seeman (1990), the evolution of Rogers's theories closely mirrored his own development as a person, with his ideas growing richer as his insight, personality, and compassion deepened. His conceptual development seems to fall into five periods: the 1940s, the 1950s, the 1960s, and the 1970s and 1980s (Zimring & Raskin, 1992).

When Carl Rogers published his first major work, *Counseling and Psychotherapy* (1942), the field was dominated by two systems of treatment: psychoanalytic/psychodynamic approaches and behavioral approaches. Rogers criticized both systems for their lack of scientific methods (perhaps reflecting his upbringing) and for their assumption that clinicians know best and should tell clients what they are thinking and feeling and how they should change. Instead, he proposed what he called *nondirective counseling* in which the primary role of the clinician is to help people express, clarify, and gain insight into their emotions. According to Rogers, acceptance and reflection are a clinician's primary tools; he omitted elaborate interventions and diagnostic procedures because of their lack of proven validity. Even theory was minimized in Rogers's early writings; practice and experience were what mattered to him.

His second stage of development was marked by the publication of *Client-Centered Therapy* (1951). Although Rogers maintained his basic emphasis on the importance of people's emotions, the book signaled several important changes in his thinking. To begin with, he renamed his approach *client-centered therapy,* a reflection of his realization that treatment cannot, and probably should not, be completely nondirective. He now saw the clinician's role as more active and important and believed that by communicating accurate empathy, congruence, and acceptance, clinicians can create an environment conducive to helping people make positive changes. These three core facilitative conditions—empathy, congruence, and acceptance—became hallmarks of Rogers's work.

In the 1960s, he began his third developmental period (Zimring & Raskin, 1992), again signaled by the publication of a major work, *On Becoming a Person* (1961). The book introduced Rogers's conception of healthy and fully functioning people: those who are open to experience, appreciate and trust themselves, and are guided by an inner locus of control rather than by an effort to please or impress others. Such people view their lives as a process and value lifelong growth. Rogers's interest in promoting people's healthy development led him to extend his reach beyond the clinical setting. For example, he promoted the idea of student-centered teaching to encourage teachers to better understand and adapt their methods to the needs of their individual students. Encounter groups based on Rogers's ideas were a widespread way to use his approach to promote positive development (Rogers, 1970). His work during the 1960s also continued to reflect his interest in research. He was particularly involved in studying those elements of the client-clinician relationship and the therapeutic process that are most likely to facilitate positive change.

The last two decades of his life, the 1970s and 1980s, reflected a continued broadening of his ideas and their application. The term *client-centered* was replaced by *person-centered*. Because Rogers's focus was no longer only on the clinical relationship, the new term better represented his concern with all of humanity. His methods were now used not only in treatment of individuals but also in families, business and administration, education, crosscultural settings, conflict resolution, and, perhaps most important to Rogers, the promotion of world peace.

Throughout his professional career, Rogers continued his efforts to help people feel powerful and in control of their lives while encouraging them to respect the rights of others to their own feelings of power and competence. His person-centered theory evolved out of the belief that people have within themselves "vast resources for self-understanding" and for developing their self-concepts and their self-direction, but "these resources can be tapped only if a definable climate of facilitative psychological attitudes can be provided" (Rogers, 1980, p. 49).

IMPORTANT THEORETICAL CONCEPTS

For Carl Rogers, understanding, appreciating, and relating to others in positive ways were the ultimate goals. The theory of person-centered counseling reflects this.

Person-Centered Theory and Humanism

Humanism has been defined as "a style of thought or attitude which makes the human central, important, valuable, crucial, pivotal, wonderful, powerful—even miraculous" (Barton, 1992, p. 332). Rogers's ideas embody that humanistic perspective. He perceived people as being basically strong and capable and trusted their ability to handle their difficulties, grow and develop, and realize their potential. Consistent with this point of view, he believed that the goal of treatment was to affirm and empower people so that they have enough trust and confidence in themselves to make use of their innate resources.

Human Potential

Implicit in person-centered theory is a strong belief in the dignity and worth of each individual. Practitioners believe that people must be appreciated and accepted for themselves, not shaped to fit a mold. They believe that people have a right to their own thoughts and opinions, should be free to construct their own lives, and are fundamentally good and trustworthy. They believe in the human potential—in the inherent tendency of people to develop in positive ways that enhance and maintain themselves and humanity (Cain, 1987a).

An important aspect of the human potential is people's tendency toward self-actualization: their natural inclination to move in the direction of expansion, growth, and health. Rogers's concept of self-actualization was similar to ideas advanced by Karen Horney (discussed in Chapter 7) and Abraham Maslow (discussed in Chapter 12). However, only person-centered counseling views self-actualization as a practical and functional goal for treatment (Bozarth & Brodley, 1991). Rogers believed that actualizing occurs throughout all aspects of the person as he or she seeks to develop in holistic and unified ways. Actualization is constant, manifesting itself throughout a person's life; it is directional, toward self-realization, fulfillment, and perfectionism; and it involves a tendency toward autonomy and self-regulation. Although actualization is a universal tendency, each person's path to it is unique.

Conditions of Worth

According to person-centered theory, people who manifest behaviors that are inconsistent with the ideals of human potential and actualization have probably not received the acceptance and affirmation that all people need to become fully functioning. As a result, they are likely to become defensive and poorly integrated and develop incongruencies and conflicts within themselves.

Unlike the psychoanalytic and psychodynamic theorists, Rogers paid little attention to the childhood origins of people's difficulties. However, he did believe that people need to experience certain conditions in their world that enable them to move toward actualization and realization of their potential (Dolliver, 1995). Environments that are overprotective, dominating, or intimidating exert a negative influence on children's development and make it difficult for them to feel free and powerful and develop positive self-esteem. Children who receive conditional messages, telling them they are only worthwhile if they fit the needs and purposes of others, learn to devalue themselves and their experiences and emotions (Barton, 1992; Rogers, 1961). Children who grow up in such negative environments have a high likelihood of developing into adults who are timid, inhibited, conformist, or angry. On the other hand, children who receive unconditional positive regard—the message that they are special and wonderful just because of who they are, not because of their importance to another or of any specific behaviors or characteristics they do or do not manifest—are far more likely to become actualizing and fully functioning adults.

Although Rogers (1980) acknowledged the harm that an aversive background can do to a person's development, he was ever optimistic: "Individuals have within themselves vast resources for self-understanding and for altering their self-concepts, basic attitudes, and self-directed behavior; these resources can be tapped if a definable climate of facilitative psychological attitudes can be provided" (p. 115). The goal of person-centered treatment is to provide that climate of acceptance and unconditional positive regard, counteract the negative messages that people might receive, and enable them to develop positive self-esteem and realize their potential as actualized and fully functioning people.

The Fully Functioning Person

Rogers's concept of the fully functioning person reflects his ideal of emotional health. Three personality dimensions are particularly characteristic: openness to experience, living with a sense of meaning and purpose, and trust in self and others (Bozarth & Brodley, 1991). People with these characteristics are moving and growing in positive directions, have a sense of their place in the world, feel comfortable with and connected to other people, have an internal source of evaluation, and channel their lives in ways that are productive and rewarding. They are not driven by a need to please or outdo others but strive to meet their own high standards for themselves. They manage their lives well, have positive self-esteem, are proud of who they are, and feel actualized.

Rogers's image of the fully functioning person has considerable importance in person-centered treatment, and helping people become fully functioning is a fundamental treatment goal. Clinicians can educate their clients about the nature and importance of becoming a fully functioning person and establish goals and plan interventions that will move people toward becoming fully functioning. In addition, Rogers believed that clinicians, too, should move toward becoming fully functioning. This concept can help us to lead our own lives in positive ways and become role models for our clients.

Phenomenological Perspective

Person-centered theorists are phenomenological in their thinking. They believe that each person has his or her unique perception of the world. That perception determines the person's beliefs, behaviors, emotions, and relationships. According to Rogers (1951), "The organism reacts to the field as it is experienced and perceived. This perceptual field is, for the individual, reality" (pp. 483–484).

Because all the choices we make in our lives stem from our perceptions, we are, in effect, the focus of our universe. Rogers believed that each individual exists at the center of a constantly changing world of experience. Even when we believe we are being objective, our subjective perceptions determine the direction of our lives.

For example, assume that a group of people in an office hears a loud noise. Timi, who delights in social gatherings, believes the noise is a balloon bursting at a nearby office party and wishes she were there rather than in her meeting. Kahing attributes the noise to a car backfiring and is reminded that he has put off having repairs done on his own car. Tom, who experienced combat when he was in the military, thinks the noise might be gunfire and suddenly feels apprehensive, while Alice is so immersed in her work that she does not even hear the noise. This example illustrates how people can distort, interpret, and organize objective information based on their perceptions of the world, with those perceptions leading to thoughts ("I really should get my car repaired"), behaviors ("I'm going to check out that party"), and emotions ("I feel afraid").

Every moment of the day, we have perceptions that evolve out of our experiences and influence all aspects of our lives. Understanding ourselves, our relationships, and our clients depends on our awareness and acceptance of these subjective perceptions. Only by understanding people's perceptions of reality can we fully appreciate others and the ways in which they direct and organize their lives.

Consistent with his strong emphasis on phenomenology and people's internal frame of reference, Rogers held that he wanted nothing but clients' own experience to inform their treatment (Dolliver, 1995). He believed that no authority, including the clinician's, should take precedence over the use of clients' direct experience. Correspondingly, he drew heavily on his own experience and perceptions both in his interactions with clients and the development of his theories.

TREATMENT USING PERSON-CENTERED COUNSELING

Although the use of specific strategies of intervention is not an important part of person-centered counseling, goals and the therapeutic alliance are both vital. Person-centered counseling is more a way of being with clients and giving them conditions that will facilitate change than it is developing a specific treatment plan.

Goals

In the early 1960s, Rogers became interested in bettering his understanding of the process of person-centered counseling. To do this, he spent many hours listening "as naively as possible" to recorded sessions (Rogers, 1961, p. 128). He found that during the early sessions of treatment, people were characterized by remoteness, rigidity, and a limited awareness of their inner selves. By the end of treatment, however, people were able to live in and experience the present and trust both themselves and the therapeutic process.

A central goal of person-centered counseling, then, is to facilitate people's movement along this path toward trust and the ability to be in the present moment. Other goals include promoting self-awareness, empowerment, optimism, self-esteem, responsibility, and autonomy. Development of these strengths, in turn, helps people build an internal locus of control, become more aware of external reality, become more congruent in their presentation, make better use of their potential, become more able to manage their lives and resolve their concerns, and become more actualized. Rogers's approach does not focus on the resolution of specific presenting problems but on developing fully functioning people who are capable of creating rewarding lives and dealing successfully with whatever joys and challenges they encounter.

Therapeutic Alliance

The person of the clinician and the relationship of the client and the clinician are the essential ingredients for change (Barton, 1992). Not only do clinicians need to establish a positive therapeutic alliance, but they also need to communicate the core therapeutic conditions, which we discuss in this section.

Role of the Clinician   Person-centered counselors view people in a very positive light. They appreciate and accept their clients on their own terms. They believe that people are capable and powerful, possessing the abilities they need to resolve their difficulties. These clinicians assume that people have a natural tendency toward growth, self-regulation, and self-knowledge (Bozarth & Brodley, 1991). They focus on their clients' strengths rather than their deficiencies, their successes rather than their failures, encouraging them to move forward with their lives so that they reach the goals of becoming more actualized and fully functioning.

Person-centered counselors have great faith in their clients. As a result, they do not need to probe the unconscious, direct people's activities, point out their errors, or even teach an array of new skills. Because they believe in people's freedom and ability to be responsible, create meaning in their lives, and make positive choices, person-centered clinicians do not need to give people a program to follow. Instead, what they need to do is create an environment that allows people to trust themselves and make good use of their potential. Counselors' acceptance and understanding of their clients, their respect for clients' subjective experiences, their valuing of clients, and their full and active participation in the treatment process empowers those clients. The trust their counselors have in them is contagious, and they begin to feel more self-confident themselves, enabling them to find and use their strengths and abilities to help themselves.

The role of the person-centered clinician is a rewarding but demanding one. Clinicians must have great self-awareness as well as the ability to be fully present and use themselves as an instrument of change. According to Barton (1992), "Rogerian technique and attitude liberate therapists to become a full, resonating, affective, thinking, imagining, listening, and speaking presence. They come to inhabit fully their client's worlds" (p. 334).

Client-Clinician Relationship   Rogers (1967) stated, "Significant positive personality change does not occur except in a relationship" (p. 73). His view of this relationship evolved over many years (Rogers, 1961). In his early writing, he described a distant and impersonal therapeutic relationship, perhaps reflecting his own upbringing. However, in 1955, he wrote, "I launch myself into a relationship. . . . I risk myself. . . . I let myself go into the immediacy of the relationship where it is my total organism which takes over" (Rogers, 1955, p. 269). By the 1960s, he acknowledged that while he initially feared being trapped by a close and loving involvement with his clients, he now found a close client-clinician relationship to be something he valued that added to the lives of both participants (Rogers, 1961).

Clinician and client are conceived of as two equal and capable human beings who become collaborators in a shared journey in which both grow and are enriched by the process. Clients and clinicians work together in close and positive ways to empower clients to make changes that will result in their living full and actualized lives. Clinicians may challenge, encourage, and promote self-exploration but are always supportive, caring, and trusting of the client's natural tendencies toward growth and actualization. According to Rogers (1961), "If I can provide a certain type of relationship, the other person will discover within himself or herself the capacity to use that relationship for growth and change, and personal development will occur" (p. 33).

Core Therapeutic Conditions

Consistent with the great emphasis Rogers placed on the importance of the clinician in the therapeutic process is his belief that effective clinicians have several qualities that they are able to communicate to their clients. These qualities help create a positive client-clinician relationship and increase clients' confidence in their ability to direct their lives in positive ways.

Genuineness To create a positive and trusting relationship, clinicians must know themselves well, like and be comfortable with themselves, and have good awareness of how they are perceived by others. This self-awareness allows them to really be themselves in the counseling relationship and communicate honesty and openness.

This does not mean that clinicians should share with clients their personal stories and experiences but that what they do share with clients comes from the heart. Thoughtful and relevant self-disclosure certainly is part of this model. For example, a clinician might say, "I am concerned that you may not have thought about all aspects of that decision," or "I can really share your joy in that accomplishment." This gives the client the opportunity to consider another perspective and receive feedback.

Clinicians' genuineness promotes clients' trust and openness, establishes a relationship that is free of deception and hidden agendas, and provides a positive role model. For some clients, this sort of relationship is new and can help them see that such relationships are possible in other settings.

Congruence Congruence and genuineness are closely related. People who are congruent transmit messages that are clear and coherent; their inner and outer selves are consistent. Incongruent messages, on the other hand, are difficult to decipher because they contain mixed messages and inconsistencies. In a congruent message of affection at the end of a first date, for example, a person might say, "I really enjoyed spending time with you," while smiling, looking directly into the person's eyes, and extending a hand. An invitation to get together again might follow. In an incongruent message, the words might reflect liking, but the body language might involve poor eye contact and a tense posture. In addition, the person may not initiate any further contact, even after promising a follow-up telephone call.

Incongruent messages lead to confusion and mistrust and can interfere with the establishment of positive relationships, including the therapeutic alliance. If clients believe that they cannot really count on their clinicians to be consistent and clear, they may have difficulty knowing how to act and what to disclose about themselves. Their own messages may become indecipherable as they strive to address all possible meanings in the clinicians' unclear messages.

Clearly, congruence in communication is important in treatment. This, again, requires considerable openness and self-awareness on the part of clinicians as well as sensitivity to clients' reactions. Clinicians must realize, for example, that clients' tendency to interpret information subjectively may lead them to think that a yawning counselor is bored with them. While clinicians may not be able to suppress their yawns, they can be aware of the possible impact of their sleepiness and say something like, "I noticed you looked dismayed a few minutes ago when I yawned. I'm sorry to be yawning. The thunderstorm kept me awake last night. How did you react when I yawned?" Whatever the therapeutic situation, clinicians need to be aware of both their verbal and their nonverbal messages, maintain consistency between the two, and address clients' reactions if they do inadvertently give confusing or potentially negative messages. (Transactional analysis, discussed in Chapter 8, would conceive of this as using complementary transactions rather than crossed or ulterior ones.)

Immediacy   To maximize their ability to be genuine and congruent, clinicians must be in the present moment, aware of and attuned to their environment and interactions. Person-centered counseling focuses on the here and now and emphasizes present interchanges between client and clinician. Reactions to current interactions can be explored and verified or modified if appropriate. Exploration of the client's reaction to a yawn is an example of immediacy that can shed light on that person's typical way of perceiving the world.

According to person-centered clinicians, discussion of past events and emotions largely reflect client's subjective perceptions rather than the reality of those experiences. Consequently, a focus on the past limits the clinician's opportunity to become involved in the client's experiences and participate in the client's world. Exploration of the past, then, is viewed as far less useful in person-centered treatment than is discussion of the present.

Acceptance   Rogers's writings emphasize the importance of what he called unconditional positive regard: caring about, respecting, liking, and accepting clients for who they are without placing any requirements on them to act, feel, or think in certain ways to please their clinicians. Communication of warmth and positive regard is essential to helping people like themselves and feel powerful enough to successfully cope with their difficulties and become more fully functioning.

Unconditional positive regard does not mean that clinicians must view everything people do or think as wise and appropriate but simply see that they are doing the best they can at the present time. Current child-rearing practices advocate focusing feedback and evaluation on the behavior, not on the child. For example, parents are encouraged to say, "You did a great job picking up your toys," rather than, "You're such a good girl for cleaning your room." Similarly, person-centered clinicians are consistent in their acceptance of and confidence in the person, although they might express concern about that person's choices. Rather than saying, "You seem to be an angry person," they might say, "You sounded angry when I could not change our appointment time."

Communication of acceptance and unconditional positive regard helps people believe that they are fully worthy and can trust their own feelings, beliefs, and ideas. It can counter devaluing messages they have received throughout their lives. It allows people to recognize that they might want to change certain aspects of their behavior or modify their thoughts or feelings while still viewing themselves as likable and worthwhile people. Knowing that they will be accepted no matter what also enables them to disclose aspects of themselves that cause them to feel shame or discomfort without fear that the clinician will contribute to their already negative feelings. Rogers (1980) believed that the more therapists are able to prize and value people for who they are in the present, the more likely it is that positive change will occur.

Empathic Understanding   As Rogers (1980) stated, "Simply to listen understandingly to a client and to attempt to convey that understanding are potent forces for individuals' therapeutic change" (p. 50). This kind of listening is empathic understanding: the accurate sensing of what people are experiencing, feeling, and communicating and the ability to let people know they are heard in this way. Rogers viewed this process of sensitive, accurate, and active listening; deeply grasping the subjective world of another person; and transmitting understanding of that world to enhance a person's own self-awareness as the most powerful force for change.

Empathy is very close to reflection (described in Chapter 10), although it usually refers to understanding of emotions while reflection is broader. However, empathy is not very close to sympathy. Sympathy can make people feel pitiful and can communicate a distance between the sympathizer and the other person, while empathy brings people closer together in a shared experience. Empathy opens the door for further discussion, usually at a deeper level, and is likely to be empowering. Sympathy, on the other hand, encourages people to view themselves as wounded victims and limits productive conversation. The following example illustrates the difference:

> **Client:**   I can't believe I got the lowest grade in the class on the exam. I hope no one finds out.
>
> **Sympathy:**   I'm so sorry you did so poorly on the test.
>
> **Empathy:**   I can hear the deep sense of shame you feel about your grade.

The dialogue with the sympathetic clinician is likely to further entrench the client's negative self-evaluation. That dialogue might continue like this:

> **Client:**   I can't believe I got the lowest grade in the class on the exam. I hope no one finds out.

> **Clinician:** I'm so sorry you did poorly on the test.
>
> **Client:** Yes, I am too. I guess I'm just too dumb to learn physics. I better give up on going to med school.
>
> **Clinician:** That's really a shame.
>
> **Client:** Yes, I don't know how I'll ever tell my parents.
>
> **Clinician:** How unfortunate that you might have to do that.

In this dialogue, the client seems to be in a downward spiral and has no sense of empowerment or competence.

Empathic understanding, on the other hand, often leads clients and clinicians to develop hypotheses that promote self-awareness and positive change. For example, the conversation with the empathic clinician might continue as follows:

> **Client:** I can't believe I got the lowest grade in the class on the exam. I hope no one finds out.
>
> **Clinician:** You seem to feel a deep sense of shame about your grade.
>
> **Client:** Yes, I do feel ashamed. I just always screw things up.
>
> **Clinician:** You're sounding very angry with yourself.
>
> **Client:** Yes, I am. I mean, it's not just school. I screwed up my relationship with Judy. I screwed up my job by getting that report in late.
>
> **Clinician:** You're blaming yourself for all those things. Help me understand that better. I wonder if you ever felt like you screwed things up in our work together?
>
> **Client:** Yes, I did. Remember when I paged you when you were on vacation? I was so upset about my father's heart attack and so much wanted to talk to you that I forgot you were away. I felt ashamed there too.
>
> **Clinician:** Sounds like you felt you were imposing on me and weren't worth a few minutes of my time. I wonder how you thought I reacted to your call?
>
> **Client:** Well, you didn't sound annoyed and really tried to help me. Somehow I still felt I had done a dumb thing.

The use of empathy, as well as immediacy and acceptance, has enabled the client to begin to disclose feelings of low self-esteem. The clinician can now generate some hypotheses about the client's view of the world and himself and the impact this has on his relationships. Awareness of his phenomenological field or world view as well as the unconditional positive regard communicated by the clinician is likely to facilitate the client's positive change.

Other Strategies

Many of the systems of psychotherapy and counseling discussed in this book rely heavily on specialized strategies such as word association, dream analysis, and modification of cognitive distortions to further the treatment. Because the heart of person-centered counseling is the therapeutic relationship, strategies such as these as well as elaborate assessment tools are rarely used. They are viewed as unnecessary and as detracting from the client-clinician relationship. All interventions in person-centered treatment should be designed to promote the therapeutic relationship and enhance the client's awareness and empowerment (Kelly, 1997). Open questions (described in Chapter 3); reflections of emotion and meaning (described in Chapter 10); and paraphrases, minimal encouragers such as "umm-hmm," "how so?" and repetition of a key word (described in Chapter 24) are probably the most used interventions in person-centered counseling. Other interventions include closed questions (discussed in Chapter 3), interpretation (discussed in Chapter 7), self-disclosure (discussed later in this chapter), and caring confrontation (discussed in Chapter 21).

Nondirectiveness

Rogers originally called his approach nondirective counseling, emphasizing the importance of the client's, rather than the clinician's, taking the lead and being the focus of the treatment process. Although Rogers later changed the name of his approach to person-centered counseling, the nondirective aspects of this approach still merit attention.

Grant (1990) described two types of nondirective counseling, instrumental and principled nondirectiveness. *Instrumental nondirectiveness* is the technique of allowing clients to take charge of the therapeutic process. Although person-centered counselors sometimes use this approach, most seem to believe it is more realistic and helpful to play a more active part in the treatment.

Grant views principled nondirectiveness as integral to person-centered treatment. He defines it as not forcing self-expression, insight, or change in clients but providing "the therapeutic conditions in the belief that they are expressions of respect and with the hope that the client will make use of them" (p. 78). Person-centered clinicians do not manipulate change; rather, they create a favorable psychological environment that is conducive to change. Although they are always respectful of and responsive to the needs of their clients, they are not simply passive recipients of client input but are instrumental in developing therapeutic conditions that are conducive to client growth. According to Grant, it is this principled nondirectiveness, rather than instrumental nondirectiveness, that is compatible with Rogers's vision of person-centered counseling.

APPLICATION OF PERSON-CENTERED COUNSELING

Person-centered counseling has evolved since the 1980s, with changes in both its popularity and its application.

Current Use

Clinicians who describe themselves as primarily person-centered are now likely to use a broader array of interventions than Rogers described in his writings. This is due, at least in part, to the increasing severity of problems that most clinicians confront. No longer are counselors and psychotherapists focusing their attention primarily on issues of personal growth and fulfillment; now they are much more likely to be helping people deal with physical and sexual abuse, drug and alcohol problems, violence, and incapacitating depression and anxiety. Cognitive and behavioral techniques (discussed in Parts 4 and 5) have demonstrated their effectiveness in ameliorating problems of this nature, while person-centered counseling has not.

Although person-centered counseling is now likely to be integrated with other approaches to treatment and the number of pure person-centered clinicians has almost certainly declined, Rogers's humanistic view of people and his approach to treatment lives on. Prochaska and Norcross (1994), for example, reported that while only 8% of counselors and 1% of clinical psychologists in the United States viewed person-centered treatment as their primary theoretical orientation, making it tied for last place in a list of 11 theoretical orientations, the combination of humanistic and cognitive approaches was the second-most frequent combination of theoretical orientations and the combination of humanistic and behavioral approaches was fourth. In addition, person-centered principles have been used in career counseling, play therapy, and management training.

Rogers predicted that various separate schools of psychotherapy, including person-centered counseling, would gradually disappear as the field shifted toward more integrated models (Kelly, 1997). Indeed, this prediction seems to hold true particularly for person-centered counseling. Although the model may, unfortunately, be too gentle for use with many of the challenging problems presented by today's clients, the genuineness, caring, and empathy that characterize person-centered treatment have left their mark on the field and have been incorporated into a wide range of other approaches to treatment. In addition, some clinicians espouse what is called relationship-centered counseling, an approach that has its roots in humanism and person-centered counseling but employs a broader and more eclectic array of clinician interventions (Kelly, 1997).

Application to Client Groups

A pure version of person-centered counseling seems best suited to people who have an interest in personal growth and development, have not made good use of their potential, and feel that their lives are not fulfilling. Ideal candidates are likely to be people who have fairly good emotional resources hampered by low self-esteem, lack of confidence in themselves and others, and negative and distorted views of the world. These people are not in crisis, nor do they have severe mental disorders; but they do believe that they can find more fulfillment in their lives.

Combining person-centered counseling with another approach to treatment can enhance the usefulness of this approach. For example, an active version of person-centered counseling can help build rapport and increase motivation in people who are resistant to treatment. In addition, the respectful and accepting nature of person-centered counseling, coupled with its phenomenological perspective, makes it an appropriate part of the treatment for people from a wide range of ethnic, cultural, and socioeconomic backgrounds. The person-centered approach can facilitate their involvement in counseling, reduce any threat they may perceive in that process, and enable clinicians to get to know clients better before moving ahead with more active interventions.

At the same time, many people enter treatment seeking solutions to their problems. They view clinicians as the experts and expect to be told what to do. People with this frame of reference may well be disappointed at the slow pace and unstructured nature of this model and may question the competence of clinicians who use it. For such people, a more active and focused model will probably better meet their needs and increase the likelihood that they will make a commitment to and benefit from treatment.

Whether or not person-centered counseling is the best model of treatment for a particular person or problem, the concepts of respect, empowerment, genuineness, and empathy can be integrated into almost any therapeutic approach. In that way, the application of person-centered treatment is very broad.

EVALUATION OF PERSON-CENTERED COUNSELING

Rogers's person-centered theory has made an immeasurable contribution to the fields of counseling and psychotherapy. As Cain (1987a) stated, Rogers's views of the human potential and the role of the clinician "literally shook the beliefs of therapists of many persuasions and professions" (p. 286). His vision of a collaborative therapeutic alliance and a supportive, accepting, listening, and caring clinician provided an important alternative to the anonymity of the Freudian analysts and the directiveness of the early behaviorists. Rogers humanized the role of the clinician and taught us that while techniques certainly matter, the clinician's' demonstration of the core conditions in the context of a positive therapeutic alliance is the most important strategy for change.

Strengths

Rogers's belief in the dignity and worth of each individual and the ability of people to heal themselves offers a view of people that is up-to-date and optimistic. It also is consistent with western culture, which prizes independence, self-direction, and individuality. Although Rogers's thinking does seem to reflect American ideals, many aspects of his theory are relevant to a diverse and multicultural society (Freeman, 1993):

- His emphasis on people's right to their own opinions and thoughts
- The importance he placed on respect, genuineness, acceptance, and empathy in counseling
- His focus on clients' own experience and frame of reference
- His attention to the need for clinicians to listen and truly understand their clients
- His encouragement of clinicians to take a responsive stance toward clients
- His interest in relationships and commonalities among people
- The attention he paid to the immediacy of the counseling situation

These attitudes seem pertinent to our work with all people, regardless of cultural background.

Rogers's work also was important in demystifying psychotherapy. As he stated, person-centered counseling revolutionized treatment by opening the "field of psychotherapy to public scrutiny and research investigation" (Rogers, 1980, p. 48). Through his extensive writings for both mental health professionals and the general population; demonstrations, tapes, and transcripts of his sessions; and his emphasis on education and the widespread need for person-centered relationships in many contexts, Rogers gave us an accessible and comprehensible brand of counseling. Person-centered counseling is welcoming, affirming, growth-promoting, and respectful, encouraging people to be all that they can. It does not seek to control behavior or delve into the secrets of the mind. Rogers's ideas have found wide appeal because they explain "basic aspects of the way in which the person's own capacity for change can be released and ways in which relationships can foster or defeat such self-directed change" (Rogers, 1980, p. 50).

Rogers's ideal of the client-clinician relationship has infiltrated and influenced all theories of counseling and psychotherapy. Stiles et. al. (1996), for example, found that support, provided through the therapeutic relationship, is the clinical intervention that is most highly rated by both psychodynamic-interpersonal and cognitive behavioral clinicians. Similarly, its humanistic and phenomenological emphases reflect great appreciation of individuality and diversity and have been incorporated into many other treatment approaches.

Limitations

Despite its enormous contribution, Rogers's theory has limitations. The following are common criticisms:

- It is overly simplistic.
- Clinicians may misunderstand this model and believe they can just listen and reflect, failing to provide the depth of understanding that facilitates change.
- Person-centered counseling fails to draw on developmental, psychodynamic, behavioral, and other approaches that enhance understanding of people.

- Listening and caring are not enough.
- This approach is inappropriate for people who are not motivated toward change or do not have the capacity for or interest in making productive use of their sessions.
- It is not useful with people manifesting significant pathology.
- Acceptance of clients may further entrench their self-destructive thoughts, emotions, and behaviors and lead to passivity and complacency.
- The unconditionally positive clinical relationship does not prepare people to deal with the real world.
- This approach is too leisurely and unfocused; people who are in crisis or prefer a more active, structured, and efficient approach may feel uncomfortable or disappointed.
- Person-centered theory lacks techniques designed to help people solve their problems.
- The emphasis on the individual, internal evaluation, and the core conditions may make this model unsuitable for people from cultures that emphasize the community and external evaluation and do not value relationships characterized by the core conditions.
- Although this approach claims to value the uniqueness of the individual, it does have a clear picture of the fully functioning person that may tend to mold people in a given direction.
- Research on the effectiveness of this model has been inconclusive, limited, and methodologically flawed.

Certainly, these criticisms all contain some truth. Listening and caring are often not enough to facilitate change. However, as Quinn put it (1993), "But how are we as therapists to know when it is best for our clients to be held and supported and when to be confronted and contradicted? The answer for us as therapists is the same for us as parents, educators, lovers, and friends. We must be willing, in Rogers's words, to learn to live out of the deepest recesses of our physiological and emotional beings" (p. 18).

Contributions

Research, such as that discussed in Chapter 1, continues to support the importance of the client-clinician relationship, particularly the client's perception of that relationship, in effecting positive change. Rogers has not only focused attention on the importance of that relationship but has given clinicians the guidelines and tools they need to establish positive and growth-promoting relationships with clients. Although thousands of clinicians have been influenced by Rogers, relatively few now view themselves as primarily person-centered clinicians (Cain, 1987a). However, his ideas live on in the relationships most seek to have with their clients, even though treatment may be further enhanced by interventions and ideas derived from other systems discussed in this book.

Rogers's work is well known internationally (Cain, 1987b). His writings have been translated into 12 languages, and he is viewed not only as a leader in the fields of counseling and psychology but also as a peacemaker. His ideas have formed the basis for the work of Thomas Gordon, founder of Effectiveness Training, Inc., used in training more than 1.25 million parents, teachers, adolescents, and leaders in 25 countries through Parent Effectiveness Training (Gordon, 1970), Teacher Effectiveness Training (Gordon & Burch, 1974), and Leader Effectiveness Training (Gordon, 1983). In addition, organizations based on Rogers's theory, such as the Center for Studies of the Person in La Jolla, California, continue to promote and teach his ideas. Clearly, as Rogers (1980) himself said, he "expressed an idea whose time had come" (p. 49).

SKILL DEVELOPMENT: CLINICIAN SELF-DISCLOSURE

Because the clinician is encouraged to be fully human and present in the moment in person-centered counseling, a practitioner using this approach often engages in self-disclosure. Although self-disclosure probably is less common in most other models of counseling and psychotherapy, all clinicians use it at one time or another.

Using self-disclosure is risky for many reasons. It can shift the focus of the session away from the client and onto the clinician, damage the client-clinician relationship, and give clients the message that the clinician wants them to fill some of his or her own needs.

However, research has found that many benefits can result from judicious self-disclosure. According to Knox, Hess, Petersen, and Hill (1997), clinician self-disclosure received high client ratings for helpfulness. It enhanced the therapeutic alliance and enabled clients to feel less alone, more hopeful, and less troubled. It encouraged the use of clinicians as role models and led clients to share more of themselves in sessions. Self-disclosure enhanced clients' appreciation of clinicians' humanness and did not result in any loss of status for the clinicians.

The following guidelines should be kept in mind when clinicians consider self-disclosure:

1. The purpose of a self-disclosure should always be to advance the progress of the treatment. For example, self-disclosure might be designed to

- *Enhance the collaborative nature of the client-clinician relationship.* I'm impressed that you were able to accomplish the two tasks we agreed on, especially when you had such a challenging week.
- *Provide useful feedback.* Your sense of humor seems to be a strength you use very well!
- *Normalize a client's reactions.* I would have been pretty angry, too, if that had happened to me.
- *Provide a different perspective.* I understand that you believe your husband was justified in hitting you when you were late picking him up because of traffic. However, it would be hard to convince me it was justified.

Inappropriate purposes of self-disclosure include

> - *Obtaining information to meet the clinician's personal needs.* I understand you work for a roofing company. What do you think I should do about that leak in the ceiling?
> - *Working out the clinician's own problems.* You know, I had a date stand me up not long ago also. Let me tell you about that, so we can figure out how I should have handled the situation.
> - *Controlling the client.* I confronted my father about his abuse, and it really improved our relationship. I think you should confront your father too. I'm sure it will help you.
> - *Just making conversation or filling up time.* Terrible weather, isn't it? Do you think that hurricane will hit us?

When contemplating a self-disclosure, be aware of exactly why you are using this strategy and what you expect it to accomplish. Being aware and deliberate about self-disclosures will help avoid risks. If you are in doubt about using a self-disclosure, the safest choice is generally to find another way to accomplish your purpose.

2. Conciseness is essential in self-disclosures. Lengthy stories about oneself can detract from the client's train of thought and shift the focus of the session from the client to the clinician. Brevity should be a goal in delivering a self-disclosure. If more information needs to be provided, that can be done in a follow-up statement, but make the initial statement brief and assess its impact before proceeding.

3. Timing of a self-disclosure is important, as it is with any intervention. The self-disclosure should fit in smoothly with the conversation and be clearly linked to the immediate focus of the session unless the clinician has the specific purpose of disconcerting or redirecting the client. By their nature, self-disclosures can be distracting and can interrupt the flow of the session. Thus, if an opportunity for a contemplated self-disclosure has passed, wait for another opportunity or use another type of intervention rather than intrude on the session.

For example, consider the clinician who says, "I know you've moved onto talking about your mother now, but I wanted to remind you of the impact that the Vietnam War might have had on your father's choices. I know it had a great impact on me at the time." While this intervention might be helpful, it seems more likely to reflect the clinician's own needs and is intrusive.

4. Focus is another important aspect of self-disclosure. Whatever clinicians share about their lives and their reactions to what clients have said must be in the service of helping the clients. Focus should remain on the clients and their concerns, and any information about the clinician should be secondary. If clinicians sense that the focus of the session is shifting to them, they need to take steps to restore attention to the client.

5. Self-disclosures should be relatively impersonal, although there are exceptions to this guideline. Some clinical settings deliberately employ clinicians who

have dealt successfully with problems similar to those faced by clients seen in that setting. This is particularly common in drug and alcohol treatment programs. Under these circumstances, clinicians typically are expected to serve as role models and to talk about their efforts to overcome their own difficulties. In most other clinical settings, however, counselors and psychotherapists are not encouraged to talk at length about their personal problems. In general, self-disclosure should primarily include clinicians' immediate reactions to material presented by the client or relatively neutral and superficial information about the clinician such as the fact that she came from the same part of the country as the client or he, too, has trouble resisting chocolate brownies. Clinicians do not usually discuss highly charged and personal issues such as current conflicts in their marriage or their history of sexual abuse.

6. The core conditions discussed by Rogers should be evident in self-disclosures. In other words, clinicians should demonstrate genuineness and congruence in their self-disclosures and always communicate acceptance and caring for their clients.

The exercises later in this chapter will give you an opportunity to refine your skills in self-disclosure.

CASE ILLUSTRATION

The following dialogue between Edie and her counselor illustrates many principles of person-centered treatment, including active listening, communicating empathy, valuing and empowering the client, modeling genuineness and congruence, and focusing on the present. Edie is working on her relationship with her mother and step-father:

Edie: I feel so angry at my mother! Ava and I were visiting her and in came Pete, her husband. I could smell the liquor across the room. And my mother said nothing. How could she be like that?

Clinician: You're feeling pretty frustrated that she can't assert herself.

Edie: Yes, and to expose Ava to that. . . .

Clinician: You wish she could have done something to protect Ava.

Edie: Yes, but she never does.

Clinician: Never?

Edie: Yes, she's always been like that.

Clinician: I wonder if you are thinking about her not protecting you from your stepfather and the pain that caused you.

Edie: Yes, it's affected my whole life.

Clinician: I can sense the very deep hurt that's still there for you.

Edie: I feel like crying just thinking about that. How could anyone abuse a helpless child?

Clinician: I have trouble understanding that too. We may never be able to understand why you were abused. But perhaps we can find a way for you to protect Ava.

Edie: You know how much I want to, but I don't know where to start.

Clinician: Even thinking about what happened must make you feel like that helpless child again. But you have accomplished so much in your life . . . coping with cancer, succeeding in school, having a family. . . . Perhaps you can find a way to protect Ava.

Edie: I have thought about it.

Clinician: So you did have some ideas?

Edie: Yes, several. One idea was not to see my mother or her husband anymore. That would protect Ava, but it seems so drastic.

Clinician: I guess part of you would like to just get away from this difficult situation, but that seems to you like too big a step.

Edie: Yes, sometimes I do feel like never seeing them again, but that seems very childish. My mother is a victim of Pete, just as I was. I also thought about setting some limits, telling her that if Pete is angry or drunk, I'll just have to leave, even if it seems rude.

Clinician: It sounds difficult for you to even think about doing anything that might hurt your mother's feelings, and yet I agree with you that protecting Ava is essential.

Edie: Yes, I know it is. But somehow it's very hard for me to stand up to my mother. I can't imagine myself telling her what I just told you.

Clinician: It really frightens you to stand up to her. Yet I have seen you assert yourself very successfully with Roberto in ways that let him know what you needed but still conveyed your love for him. How would it feel to speak to your mother in that same way?

Edie: Well, I would be scared, but I think I can do it. It's for Ava.

Clinician: Yes, and maybe for you too. I suspect you would feel very proud of yourself if you could follow through on this plan.

Edie: That's true. I am starting to feel that I can protect Ava, stand up for myself, and still have a close relationship with my mother. Wouldn't that be something?

EXERCISES

Large-Group Exercises

1. Discuss the strengths and limitations of the dialogue in the case illustration. What would you change, if anything, to improve on this segment of a counseling session?
2. Identify, in the dialogue, examples of the following key elements of person-centered counseling:

- Active listening
- Communicating empathy
- Reflection of feeling
- Reflection of meaning
- Valuing and empowering the client
- Genuineness
- Focusing on the present
- Self-disclosure

3. Create a round-robin dialogue. One person, professor or student, stands or sits in front of the class and assumes the role of Roberto or another hypothetical client. This client should talk about a time when he or she had very strong emotions and should engage in a dialogue with the class, with each student in turn making one comment or intervention. Interventions should reflect person-centered treatment, with each successive intervention building on the previous one. Following the dialogue, the class should discuss the overall nature of the role-played interview and its strengths and limitations.

Small-Group Exercises

1. Divide into groups of four students. Each dyad should engage in a 10-minute client-clinician role play, building on previous dialogues that you have had with your partner. Use self-disclosure at least twice and try to communicate empathy as often as possible when assuming the role of clinician.

   After each dialogue, the group of four should discuss the overall nature of the dialogue and its strengths and limitations, providing feedback to each clinician on the following:

   - The nature and effectiveness of self-disclosures
   - Communication of empathy
   - Therapeutic alliance
   - Strengths of the role play
   - Ways in which it might have been improved

2. Most clinicians agree that person-centered counseling is not an appropriate treatment approach for all people. Discuss how you would screen people to determine their suitability for this mode of treatment. Develop a list of 5–10 questions you would use to help you determine whether this treatment system is suitable for a particular person. Then develop a list of 5–10 criteria that suggest a client's suitability for person-centered treatment.

Individual Exercises

1. Develop and write in your journal an appropriate self-disclosure in response to the following client statements and questions:

   Client A: There must be something really wrong with me. Everybody else seems to love parties, but I hate going into a big room full of strangers.

   Client B: I finally had a great weekend. I woke up early, took a walk, then had brunch with a friend and went to that great Georgia O'Keeffe exhibit at the museum.

   Client C: I feel really embarrassed that my parents found out I had too much to drink last night and had to have someone drive me home. Did anything like that ever happen to you when you were younger?

Client D: My older brother hits me and pushes me whenever we are alone. Yesterday, when he pushed me, I fell down and really hurt myself. I don't know what to do. I'm afraid he'll get into trouble if I tell anyone.

Client E: It feels like once I let people know I'm a lesbian, that changes all their reactions to me and they don't see me as a person anymore. Sometimes I think that happened here too. When I told you my partner was a woman, your expression changed, and I sensed that you disapproved of me.

2. Listening is something we often take for granted, not realizing that it is quite an art. For the next hour of time when you will be interacting with people, try to be very conscious of your listening skills. Use the verbal listening skills of reflection and communication of empathy to let people know you are listening. Maintain good eye contact. Monitor your verbal and nonverbal messages to be sure they are congruent and that you are coming across as genuine, caring, and accepting. Write about this experience in your journal.

SUMMARY

Carl Rogers's person-centered counseling, first developed in the 1940s and 1950s, is a humanistic and phenomenological approach to treatment that prizes the dignity and worth of all people as well as their potential to resolve their own difficulties. The primary source of healing comes from the therapeutic alliance. By demonstrating core conditions such as active listening, empathy, caring and acceptance, genuineness, and congruence, clinicians promote clients' feelings of empowerment and esteem and help them to mobilize their abilities to help themselves. Ideally, counseling moves people along a path of growth toward actualization of their potential, helping them to become fully functioning people. This approach, which emphasizes the present moment rather than past problems, revolutionized thinking about psychotherapy. Although person-centered treatment is no longer widely used as a primary approach to counseling and psychotherapy, its emphasis on the interaction of the client and the clinician has influenced nearly all current approaches to psychotherapy and has helped us recognize that the success of any approach to treatment can be accelerated through a positive client-clinician collaboration.

RECOMMENDED READINGS

Cain, D. J. (1987). Carl R. Rogers: The man, his vision, his impact. *Person-Centered Review, 2*(3), 283–288.

Patterson, C. H. (1990). On being client-centered. *Person-Centered Review, 5*(4), 425–432.

Rogers, C. R. (1951). *Client-centered therapy: Its current practice, implications and theory.* Boston: Houghton Mifflin.

Rogers, C. R. (1961). *On becoming a person.* Boston: Houghton Mifflin.

Rogers, C. R. (1980). *A way of being.* Boston: Houghton Mifflin.

Chapter 12

EXISTENTIAL THERAPY

Existential therapy embodies many of the values and viewpoints of Carl Rogers's person-centered counseling. According to Vontress (Epp, 1998), "Existential philosophy for me fills in where Rogers left off. It defines the issues that must be broached in counseling in broad strokes: love, death, suffering, and meaning." (p. 3).

Existential therapy is more a philosophy than a structured treatment system. It seeks to help people face the painful uncertainties of life, take responsibility for their choices, and create meaning in their lives. In this way, existential therapy helps people to become self-actualized and experience a deep, perhaps even spiritual, connection with other people and their world. These goals are accomplished through the special relationship between the clinician and the client, the primary vehicle for change in existential therapy, as it is in person-centered counseling.

THE PEOPLE WHO DEVELOPED EXISTENTIAL THERAPY

Many names are associated with the development of existential therapy, including Victor Frankl, Rollo May, Irvin Yalom, James Bugental, Ludwig Binswanger, and Medard Boss. The ideas of theoreticians and philosophers such as Abraham Maslow, Soören Kierkegaard, Friedrich Nietzsche, Martin Heidegger, Paul Tillich, and Martin Buber were also key to the development of this approach. In addition, writers including Albert Camus, Jean-Paul Sartre, Franz Kafka, and others have helped to shape existentialism. Following are brief biographies of the three men—Victor Frankl, Rollo May, and Irvin Yalom—who are most strongly associated with existential therapy today.

Victor Frankl

Victor Frankl was born in 1905 in Vienna, Austria, and received both M.D. and Ph.D. degrees from the University of Vienna. Before the Second World War, he was a practicing physician. Between 1942 and 1945, however, he was a prisoner in the Nazi concentration camps in Dachau and Auschwitz. His mother and father, his brother, and his first wife and their children all perished in the camps. Of course, these experiences had a profound impact on Frankl's thinking. Although his interest in existential thought began before his imprisonment, his difficult years in the concentration camps impressed on him how important it is for people to have meaning and purpose in their lives. For Frankl, his purpose became surviving his imprisonment so that he could tell others about those experiences and the terrible outcomes of war and hatred. *Man's Search for Meaning* (Frankl, 1963) is a powerful description of his experiences and existential struggles and what he learned from them (Wawrytko, 1989). In that book, he quotes Nietzsche: "He who has a why to live for can bear with almost any how" (p. 121) and "That which does not kill me, makes me stronger" (p. 130). These quotations reflect Frankl's own triumph over tragedy, his ability to make meaningful the terrible losses and experiences he endured.

Frankl called his approach to treatment *logotherapy,*—therapy through meaning. Barton (1992) said of logotherapy, "It presupposes that the freedom to make meanings belongs to the human world essentially, and that all human beings have regions in which they can take up freedom and make meaning." (p. 338). Frankl believed that even under the most difficult circumstances, people have choices. The essential task of the clinician is to help people discover the parts of their lives where they possess freedom and to develop the ability and will to use that freedom to transform and make meaning of their lives.

Frankl's writings as well as his lectures throughout the world certainly made his life a meaningful one. In addition, he married again in the late 1940s and reportedly found personal as well as professional success. He lived until 1997, continuing to write throughout his life about the most important aspects of all our lives, including meaning, love, work, and society (Frankl, 1978, 1987, 1992).

Rollo May

Rollo May was born in 1909 into a family of six children and spent his childhood in Ohio and Michigan. A practicing psychoanalyst, he studied with Alfred Adler in Vienna and was influenced by both Adler and European existential thought. In addition, May's own difficult life, including an unhappy childhood, two unsuccessful marriages, and serious illness, contributed to the development of his ideas.

May's writings brought existentialism to the United States (May, Angel, & Ellenberger, 1958). His work initially focused on the anxiety he believed all people experience as we struggle with the difficulties of growth and change, our aloneness in the world, our apprehensions about death, and the courage required to pursue goals of independence and growth (May, 1950). Also important to him were people's roles in and relationships with their society, reflecting Adler's emphasis on social responsibility. His book *Love and Will* (May, 1969) became very popular and greatly increased general awareness of existential concepts that May believed were relevant to all our lives. As he stated (May, 1990a), "I do not believe there is a special school of therapy to be put in a category of 'existential.' I think existential, rather, refers to an attitude toward human beings and a set of presuppositions about these human beings." (p. 49). Like Frankl, Rollo May lived a long and productive life, dying in 1994 at the age of 85.

Irvin Yalom

Born in 1931 in Washington, DC, Irvin Yalom grew up in a small apartment over his parents' grocery store. His escape from the poverty and danger of his inner-city neighborhood was the library, where he developed a continuing love of reading. Yalom was trained as a psychiatrist and completed his residency at Johns Hopkins University. After some years in the army, he became a professor of psychiatry at the Stanford University School of Medicine. He and his wife Marilyn, a scholar of women's studies and French literature, have four children and five grandchildren.

Yalom is a prolific writer on both existentialism and group psychotherapy. He has also written books for the general reader that describe his treatment of people who are coping with existential issues. As Yalom (1989) stated in *Love's Executioner and Other Tales of Psychotherapy*, "I have found that four givens are particularly relevant to psychotherapy: the inevitability of death for each of us and for those we love; the freedom to make our lives as we will; our ultimate aloneness; and, finally, the absence of any obvious meaning or sense to life. However grim these givens may seem, they contain the seeds of wisdom and redemption." (pp. 4–5).

In *Existential Psychotherapy* (1980), Yalom identified the basic difference between Freudian psychoanalysis and his own concept of existentialism. Freud viewed people as struggling with a conflict between the instinctual strivings of the id and the socialized forces of the ego and superego, while Yalom saw our conflicts as stemming "from the dilemma of a meaning-seeking creature who is thrown into a universe that has no meaning" (p. 9). He continues to lecture and write about his ideas as well as his practice of psychotherapy, as reflected in his recent book, *Momma and the Meaning of Life: Tales of Psychotherapy* (1999).

THE DEVELOPMENT OF EXISTENTIAL THERAPY

Although existentialism as a philosophy has evolved since the 19th century, existential therapy arose in Europe during the 1940s and 1950s. Social, political, and scientific events during those years clearly contributed to the development of this approach. According to Bauman and Waldo (1998), the two great wars led to a "pervasive sense of alienation and meaninglessness." Growing industrialization and urbanization of society, as well as scientific advances, contributed to this dehumanization. Even psychology, dominated at that time by psychoanalysis, seemed to "conceptualize the person as an assemblage of parts often struggling against one another." (p. 15). People needed a force that would restore their sense of humanness as well as help them cope with their concerns about the meaning of life in the face of the devastation, isolation, and death that resulted from the two world wars. Existentialism, along with its close relative, humanistic psychology, evolved in response to that need.

The works of Frankl and May were widely read in the United States during the 1950s and 1960s. Interest in existential therapy has been kept alive by the more recent writings of Yalom, Bugental, Vontress, and others, although attention to the approach seems to have declined over the years. This may be because of the growing importance of accountability in treatment and the corresponding growth of attention to more structured and empirically validated systems of treatment such as cognitive behavioral therapy.

As with person-centered counseling, relatively few clinicians report that their primary theoretical orientation is existential therapy. However, existentialism continues to exert an influence today, particularly on our conception of the clinician's role and the realization that, for many people, counseling and psychotherapy are not just tools for solving problems but ways to give meaning to lives that lack purpose or fulfillment.

IMPORTANT THEORETICAL CONCEPTS

The theory underlying existential therapy focuses not on the treatment process but on the universal issues that people face. Through their understanding of these issues, clinicians can connect with people on a very deep and personal level and help them change their lives so that they offer more meaning and fulfillment.

Dimensions of the Human Condition

For existentialists, the human condition is a difficult one. Life has no inherent meaning and is replete with sadness and loss. They believe that the following aspects of the human condition are typically at the root of emotional difficulties:

- *Inevitability of death.* From childhood, we realize that our death is inevitable, as are the deaths of our loved ones. No matter how gifted we are, no matter how special our lives are, death is the outcome for everyone. The fear of our ultimate nonbeing can cast a pall over people's lives and make them seem pointless.
- *Existential alienation.* Although we may surround ourselves with colleagues, friends, and family, we are ultimately alone. No one can truly understand us or sense our thoughts and feelings as we ourselves do. No one can rescue us from the inevitability of death or from many of the other losses we will experience in our lives. Some seek to fuse with and become dependent on others in an effort to counteract their sense of alienation, but those efforts will inevitably fail because they detract even further from people's sense of themselves and the purpose of their lives. Loneliness is often most acute when we are with other people and are aware of our lack of a true connection with them.
- *Meaninglessness.* According to existential theory, "Meaninglessness is the dreaded answer to the existential questions 'What is the meaning of life?' 'What difference do I really make?' 'What is the purpose of the struggles?' " (Frank, 1995, p. 217). The only certainties in our lives are birth and death. Beyond that, life seems to be a random process, and only we can make sense of it. The inherent meaninglessness of life can lead to feelings of hopelessness and discouragement and a sense of emptiness; we may be tempted to give up on our lives.
- *Anxiety and guilt.* Existential anxiety is viewed as an inevitable part of the human condition. It is much deeper than anxiety about one's career or health. Rather, it is "a deep feeling of unease that arises from our awareness of the givens: our existence is finite, we are mortal, and there is no purpose but the ones we create for ourselves" (Bauman & Waldo, 1998, p. 19). Existential anxiety stems from our realization that we have both the freedom to create and the responsibility for creating a worthwhile existence for ourselves in the limited time we have on earth. That is a daunting prospect for most of us!

Existential guilt results when we fail to take responsibility for making our lives meaningful and worthwhile and realize that we have not become what we might have. It reflects our awareness that we have not fully realized ourselves as human beings and have allowed our lives to be controlled by chance and circumstance. We may not realize or be able to articulate the reasons for our feelings of guilt; but for many, an underlying sense of deep guilt and regret pervades our lives.

Depression often is the result of efforts to defend against existential guilt and anxiety and avoid the task of making our lives meaningful. Yalom (1980) found, for example, that among people nearing death, depression was greatest in those who had not created meaningful lives, while those who felt satisfied with the lives they had created for themselves were more able to accept death.

Human Development and the Development of Emotional Difficulties

Existential therapists do not dispute the importance of the early years of development, the child-parent relationships, and the unconscious but relate those factors to existential concerns. Frankl, for example, believed that what he called neurotic difficulties often stem from an upbringing in which parents were punitive and deprived children of their sense of freedom (Barton, 1992). Similarly, existential therapists do not concern themselves with the unconscious sexual and aggressive drives that fascinated Freud or the internalized objects that interested the psychodynamic/developmental therapists. Instead, they concentrate on the unconscious conflict between people's wish to escape the givens of the human condition and lose themselves in lethargy and denial and their wish to achieve fulfillment despite the challenges and responsibilities that achievement entails. For the existentialists, emotional difficulties basically stem from failure to deal successfully with the inevitabilities of the human condition and to transcend them by creating a meaningful and authentic life for oneself.

Existential therapists pay attention to development throughout the life span and do not limit their focus to the early childhood. They view life as a process of creating our own histories, with each choice and phase shaping and contributing to the next. Existence is never static; people are always becoming something new, striving to move toward their possibilities and making their lives worthwhile.

Dasein

Existentialists speak of *dasein*—defined as being present, being in the world. According to Bauman and Waldo (1998, p. 16), "The term dasein acknowledges that human beings exist, have consciousness, and are responsible for their own existence." (p. 16). According to May, "Man (or Dasein) is the particular being who has to be aware of himself, be responsible for himself, if he is to become himself. He also is that particular being who knows that at some future moment he will not be: he is the being who is always in dialectical relation with non-being death." (May et al., 1958, p. 42). The concept of dasein is complex and elusive but seems to reflect people's ability to simultaneously live in the present, be conscious, and take responsibility for making their lives meaningful while realizing fully that death will inevitably end their efforts.

Concept of Mental Health

Clement Vontress, a contemporary existential counselor, defined mental health as "being in balance and harmony with one's inner-self; with one's friends, family and colleagues; with one's physical environment; and with one's spirituality" (Epp, 1998, p. 9). Existential therapists emphasize the importance of experiencing the unity of self and world. They also believe that people who are not simply passive victims of circumstances but become the architects of their own lives reflect emotional health. As Paul Tillich (1961), an existential philosopher, stated, "Man becomes truly human only at the moment of decision" (p. 39). Whatever difficulties we encounter in our lives, we always have choices. According to May (1990b), "No matter how great the forces victimizing the human being, man has the capacity to know that he is being victimized and thus to influence in some way how he will relate to his fate." (p. 270). A clear example is Victor Frankl's ability to make choices and find purpose, even in his terrible years as a prisoner in concentration camps.

Potentials of the Human Condition

The inevitabilities of the human condition, as discussed previously, seem to present a bleak picture of life. However, existentialism has optimism and hope because of the potential all people have to transcend those inevitabilities.

Awareness   People have the capacity for awareness of both themselves and the world. The greater our awareness, the more possibilities that are open to us and the more successfully we can address our fears and anxieties. Although awareness will not always bring us pleasure or peace, it allows us to recognize the limitations and challenges of our lives and make choices that can make them as worthwhile as possible.

Years ago, people often were not told when they had a terminal illness because of the general belief that they were better off not knowing about their condition. However, that decision deprived them of the capacity to make meaningful choices about how they would live out their lives and encouraged inauthenticity and deceptive relationships. Now people are almost always told the truth about their medical conditions so they can make choices such as whether or not to take medication that may hasten their deaths but relieve their pain.

Authenticity and Intimacy   Authenticity has been described as "the kind of existence human beings have when they accept the responsibility for choosing the direction of their lives and they base those choices on values determined through increasing self-awareness" (Bauman & Waldo, 1998, p. 19). In *The Search for Authenticity* (1965), Bugental describes three essential features of authenticity:

1. People are aware of themselves and their relationships with the world.
2. They make choices, knowing that decisions are the inevitable consequences of responsibility.
3. They take responsibility for their choices, recognizing that awareness is imperfect, and sometimes leads to unanticipated results.

In other words, taking responsibility for making choices based on awareness reflects authenticity and allows people to live more fully in the present and be fully themselves in their relationships. People whose decisions are based on denial, the wishes of others, or dependence are not truly living in the present; they may be driven by past losses or acting out of a hope for future gains. In addition, they are wearing a "mask of inauthenticity" that prevents others from really knowing who they are (Frank, 1995, p. 214).

Freedom and Responsibility   Yalom (1980) identified three aspects of freedom: choice, action, and change. Once people accept that they have freedom, no matter what their circumstances are, they have responsibilities:

- To be aware of themselves and their options
- To consider their past history and their future potential
- To exercise courage and thought in making changes and choices

No longer can we view our decisions and behaviors as purposeless and accidental; no longer can we make excuses for ourselves and shift blame. The responsibility that accompanies freedom is the responsibility for our own lives and the recognition that ultimately we alone are in charge of them. The enormity of that realization can be frightening but also can be empowering, if only we can use our freedom in positive and growthful ways.

Self-Actualization   Self-actualization is an important concept for existential therapists, as it is for person-centered clinicians. Abraham Maslow (1954, 1968) probably best described the nature of self-actualization. He advanced the idea that each person has an essential nature, part of which is universal and part of which is unique to that individual. Maslow (1954) believed "that full healthy and normal and desirable development consists in actualizing this nature, in fulfilling these potentialities, and in developing into maturity along the lines that this . . . essential nature dictates, growing from within rather than being shaped from without" (p. 340). Self-actualization is a natural process that leads people toward growth and fulfillment.

However, self-actualization can be blocked by a variety of factors including a cultural or family background that inhibits creativity, a repressive environment, and overwhelming fear and guilt. People who fail to achieve self-actualization typically experience feelings of shame, defeat, and anxiety and a perception of life as meaningless (Frank, 1995; Yalom, 1980).

Making Meaning   Existential therapists believe that life has the potential to be meaningful if people use their capacities to bring purpose, worth, and meaning into their lives. According to May (1969), our will to love and to live gives us meaning. Our awareness, our recognition that we have freedom, our authenticity, and our progress toward self-actualization all enable us to know and confront potentially disturbing aspects of ourselves and our world, such as the inevitability of death and our ultimate aloneness, and to transcend them through the meaning we create in our lives.

Meaning is the purpose and logic of our lives and often is reflected in the patterns of choices people make. Dreams, visions, and fantasies also provide clues to help people discern the meaning in their lives. Some people have socially meaningful goals, such as Carl Rogers's efforts to increase world peace; others have competitive goals such as breaking a world record or creative goals such as writing a novel. But most people find meaning in daily activities such as raising emotionally healthy children, planting beautiful gardens, volunteering to help people who are homeless, or establishing a rewarding business.

Because life itself is a process, we are in a constant state of emerging and evolving, becoming more fully ourselves, and making meaning of each day as well as of the entirety of our lives. According to the existentialists, it is this journey that makes us human.

TREATMENT USING EXISTENTIAL THERAPY

Existential therapy is a process in which two people embark on a journey to help the client cope more effectively with the inevitable conditions of life and make better use of the potentials of humankind. This approach makes minimal use of techniques but relies heavily on the person of the clinician to effect change.

Goals

The fundamental goal of existential therapy is helping people find value, meaning, and purpose in their lives. Treatment does not seek specifically to change behaviors or ameliorate symptoms. In other words, "The purpose of psychotherapy is not to 'cure' the clients in the conventional sense, but to help them become aware of what they are doing and to get them out of the victim role" (May, 1981, p. 210).

To reach this goal, existential therapists help people confront their deepest fears and anxieties about the inevitable dimensions of life. Reviewing and reflecting on their histories can facilitate this process, especially if it helps people identify barriers that they perceive as impeding their movement toward authenticity and living a life that reflects their values and priorities. In addition, treatment helps people become aware of the freedom they do have, recognize their options, and make choices that will lead them toward self-actualization and meaningfulness in their lives.

Therapeutic Alliance

As the primary vehicle for facilitating change, clinicians who practice existential therapy have a great deal of responsibility. Their own values are very much a part of the treatment process. They advocate freedom and responsibility (Barton, 1992), encourage people to confront their fears, and promote their efforts to make meaningful choices. In keeping with their emphasis on personal freedom, existential clinicians do not hold back their views. They express their own values and beliefs, give advice, use humor, and make suggestions and interpretations but always allow clients the freedom to determine how they will use this input. As Bugental (1987) put it, "The therapeutic alliance is the powerful joining of forces which energizes and supports the long, difficult, and frequently painful work of life-changing psychotherapy. The conception of the therapist here is not of a disinterested observer-technician but of a fully alive human companion for the client" (p. 49).

Existential therapists recognize that to understand their clients' deepest thoughts and feelings about issues such as death, isolation, and guilt, they need to be with their clients as fully as possible. According to Yalom (1980), clinicians should, "implicitly and explicitly, wonder about the patient's belief systems, inquire deeply into the loving of another, ask about long-range hopes and goals, and explore creative interests and pursuits." (p. 471). They must communicate respect, support, encouragement, and concern and be genuine, open, and available.

Martin Buber (1970) believed that relationships can reflect several possible levels:

1. I to I relationships, in which other people are almost irrelevant; I am all that matters
2. I to it relationships, in which people are viewed as objects in transient interactions
3. It to it relationships, in which people have little sense of self
4. We to we relationships, involving a lack of individuality and primarily characterizing children's relationships
5. Us to them relationships, in which others are viewed as either chosen or rejected, special or lacking, in or out of favor; us (those in good favor) are all that matters
6. I to you relationships, involving two people who view each other as separate individuals
7. I to thou relationships, in which people have the deepest respect for each other as well as a great sense of relatedness.

I to thou relationships are the most profound and meaningful kind. Therapists who can create this type of relationship with their clients are truly sharing a journey with them and empowering their clients through the strong and honoring connection between client and therapist (Bugental, 1978).

Maintaining relationships of this magnitude and intensity can be very demanding of clinicians. As Frank (1995) stated, "Making several such painful journeys with clients is bound to affect practitioners at a very personal level. . . . Being an existential counselor or therapist means being open to continued learning and awareness because existential helping operates at an intense level of involvement." (p. 222).

The Process of Treatment

Because existential therapy is not problem- or crisis-focused and involves the establishment of a deep relationship between client and clinician, it is almost never time-limited or rushed. Typically, no clear stages or transitions can be identified in the treatment. However, the process generally begins by promoting the clinicians' understanding of the clients and the clients' awareness of themselves and their world. Clients are encouraged to talk about their values, beliefs, and assumptions; their histories and backgrounds; and the choices they have made as well as the choices they believe they cannot make. Throughout this process, clinicians listen closely so they can comprehend the clients' views of the world and gradually help them express their deepest fears and take greater responsibility for their lives.

The middle phase of treatment enables people to use the information they have shared about themselves to find meaning in their lives, develop a sense of purpose, and value their lives. Therapist interventions encourage client authenticity during this process.

Treatment moves toward a close when people are able to implement their awareness of themselves and move forward to establish a more meaningful life. They have learned that they cannot eliminate anxiety from their lives but have found ways to live full lives despite anxiety about the inevitabilities of the human condition. In addition, they are progressing along a path that seems natural and right for them, one that is moving them toward self-actualization.

An important and challenging aspect of the termination process is the client's separation from the clinician. This can be a reminder of the inevitability of endings and is often difficult for both client and clinician. However, if clients and clinicians can be present in the moment, authentic, and aware of their reactions to the end of treatment, the termination process itself can help people face and cope effectively with their fears, making even the end of therapy a process that fosters growth.

Specific Intervention Strategies

The primary interventions in existential therapy—use of the person of the clinician and the client-clinician relationship—have already been discussed. However, the approach also uses some other interventions.

Being in the World   May (May et al., 1958) used the term *being in the world* to refer to the importance of clinicians' understanding as fully as possible not only clients' objective world but also their subjective one. The term includes three modes of being: being in the physical world, being in the world of interpersonal relationships, and being in the personal and psychological world. May believed that therapy needs to focus on the interaction of these three modes, helping people to keep them in balance. Being in the world is compromised for both client and clinician if one mode is overemphasized while the others are excluded from attention.

Symbolic Growth Experience   Both Frankl (1963) and Maslow (1968) emphasized the importance of intense experiences in promoting learning and growth. Maslow referred to these as peak experiences. Frick, building on the ideas of Frankl and Maslow, described a model, the Symbolic Growth Experience (SGE), to explain the relationship between experience and the discovery of meaning. Frick (1987) defined the SGE as "the conscious recognition and interpretation of the symbolic dimensions of an immediate experience leading to heightened awareness, discovery of meaning, and personal worth." (p. 36). The exploration of an SGE has four steps:

1. People are educated about the concept of the SGE.
2. They select an important past experience and explore its importance and symbolism in their lives.
3. They are helped to clarify the meaning in the experience.
4. They have a clearer sense of meaning and are able to repeat their use of these strategies to understand the significance of other experiences.

We will explore an SGE in more detail later in this chapter.

Frankl's Logotherapy and Paradoxical Intention   Victor Frankl (1978) termed his particular version of existential therapy *logotherapy*—"therapy through meaning" (p. 19). He believed that even well-functioning people sometimes feel that life is meaningless and experience a sense of emptiness. He referred to this as "the unheard cry for meaning" (p. 20). Through treatment, he helped people recognize the depth of their need for meaning, reassured them that all people can create meaning in their lives, and supported them in their efforts to find the sense of purpose and meaning they craved.

Frankl believed that fears tended to escalate through a vicious circle in which fears evoke symptoms that in turn increase the fears. For example, the person who fears heights avoids them; because of the avoidance, anticipatory anxiety develops, the heights become increasingly frightening in the person's mind, and the avoidance as well as the fears increase. As Frankl (1978) put it, "The fear of fear increases fear" (p. 116).

To break this cycle, he recommended a technique called *paradoxical intention* in which clinicians encourage clients to do or wish for the very thing they fear most. For example, one woman was afraid to leave her house lest she faint. Frankl instructed her to go outside and try her best to faint. Not surprisingly, she was unable to faint. His intervention succeeded in both reducing her fear and strengthening her courage by changing the meaning of her fear of fainting. No longer was it a terrible, embarrassing experience that she must avoid at all costs; now it was something that was acceptable. As Yalom (1980) stated, "When we take ourselves out of the lie and become distant spectators, things cease to matter." (p. 478).

Yalom (1980) believed that this principle extended to people's search for meaning: "I believe that the search for meaning is similarly paradoxical: the more we rationally seek it, the less we find it; the questions that one can pose about meaning will always outlast the answers" (p. 482). Finding meaning is a lifelong process of facing our fears, developing awareness, and making choices. Paradoxical intention is one technique that can help people in that process.

Dereflection   *Dereflection* is a type of paradoxical intervention that can help people deal with feelings of meaningless. Developed by Frankl, it involves telling people to focus less on themselves and more on finding meaning outside of themselves (Yalom, 1980). Encouraging people to focus on something other than themselves helps to reduce self-absorption and anxiety and facilitates their efforts to find meaning in their lives.

Inventories Based on Existential Theory

Several inventories have been developed based on existential theory. Although none has yet demonstrated strong evidence of validity (Frank, 1995), they may still be useful if used cautiously and for discussion rather than assessment.

Reker (1994), for example, developed both the Life Attitude Profile—Revised (LAP-R), a 48-item measure of meaning and purpose in life, and the Sources of Meaning Profile (SOMP), a 16-item scale of how meaningful respondents find various aspects of their lives. In studies using these inventories, he determined that "individuals who find meaning from sources transcending self-interests experience a great degree of purpose, coherence, and ultimate meaning in life, supporting Frankl's theoretical view" (p. 49). In a study of people ranging in age from 16 to 93, Reker also found that the older group of people reported higher levels of life purpose compared to people in their middle and younger years and that having a strong sense of personal meaning seemed to play a role in protecting and enhancing health in older people.

Other inventories linked to existential therapy include the Purpose of Life Test, developed by Crumbaugh and Maholic to measure meaning; the Life Regard Index developed by Battista and Almond (Yalom, 1980); and scales to measure avoidance of existential confrontation and confrontation of death (Thauberger, Thauberger, & Cleland, 1983). Clearly, existential theory yields a rich source of variables that might be usefully assessed. However, more research is needed to demonstrate the validity of inventories designed for this purpose.

APPLICATION OF EXISTENTIAL THERAPY

Like person-centered counseling, existential therapy is the primary theoretical orientation of a relatively small number of clinicians. However, its themes of meaningfulness, authenticity, freedom, and responsibility continue to have great relevance. The more our lives seem controlled by technology, the more we hear about terrorism and school violence, and the more we are troubled by our own overcommitted lifestyles, the more many of us search for meaning and purpose in what we do and struggle to maintain a sense of freedom and authenticity. The growing emphasis on spirituality in counseling and psychotherapy is also consistent with an existentialist viewpoint. Although it does not advocate any specific religion or religious beliefs, existentialism reminds us of the importance of having a sense of meaning that transcends our immediate and finite lives. Whether that meaning comes from traditional religion, the spirituality of nature, watching a child grow, or another source, existentialism can help people cope with the challenges of the 21st century.

Specific Groups

Quite a few studies have looked at the impact of existential therapy on specific client groups. Although the number and power of these studies are not sufficient to firmly establish the treatment system's effectiveness, research does suggest broad application for existential therapy.

Eisenberg (1989), for example, used Frankl's logotherapy as well as other humanistic and emotionally oriented interventions (e.g., Rogers's core conditions, meditation, relaxation) to treat people incarcerated in an Israeli prison. Participants were helped to increase their awareness, find meaning and alternatives in all situations, and use their guilt as a catalyst for positive change. They were encouraged to make a conscious choice to "straighten themselves out" (p. 90) and to be more open and authentic. A theme of treatment was this existential message: "Place one thing above everything else: To master life under all circumstances. This foremost self-transcending endeavor immunizes against despair. By forgetting yourself, by transcending yourself, you become truly human" (p. 90). The treatment approach yielded positive results and has continued to be used in this setting.

Schwartzberg (1993) applied existential concepts to the study of HIV-positive gay men, certainly a group of people struggling with fears of death and the meaning of life. Common issues of irreparable loss, isolation, powerlessness, and punishment as well as clients' efforts to find spiritual growth and meaning in the face of their diagnosis suggested that existential concepts and therapy would be very relevant to such a population.

These two studies reflect the type of person and situation for whom existential therapy seems ideal:

- People coping with life-threatening and chronic illnesses.
- Those who have suffered losses of all kinds, such as bereavement, disappointments in relationships, and failure to achieve their goals.
- Those whose lives have challenging limitations, such as people who are incarcerated, people with disabilities, and people living in poverty.
- People at a crossroads in their lives who are looking for direction, such as those who have been recently divorced, have retired, or have graduated from college.

Although existential theory seems especially relevant to these four groups, this system of treatment has relevance to all of us, whether or not we are actively struggling with issues of meaning. Nearly all people, at one time or another, reflect on the significance of their lives, on who they really are and who they want to become, and on issues of closeness and authenticity in relationships. Whether or not existential therapy is used as the primary mode of intervention with a given person, its concepts have a place in all client-clinician relationships, especially with people who are open to new ideas and who are struggling with issues addressed by existentialist thinkers.

Culturally Diverse Groups

Some have raised questions about the appropriateness of existential therapy in treating a multicultural population because of its European origins, its abstract and theoretical nature, and its lack of focus on solving immediate problems. Vontress, however, argues that existential treatment is very suitable for people from all cultural backgrounds (Epp, 1998). He reminds us that philosophers from Asia and other nonwestern areas have addressed issues of the meaning of life for many more years than western philosophers have. He believes that because of its focus on issues that all people face such as death, suffering, love, and loneliness, existential counseling can help all people find meaning and harmony in their lives and is, indeed, "a universal philosophy of humankind" (p. 7).

Diagnostic Groups

Because of its lack of specific interventions, its focus on philosophical issues rather than on concrete problems, and its emphasis on the client-clinician relationship and thoughtful and open dialogue, existential therapy seems most appropriate for people who are coping with relatively mild disorders that do not need rapid relief. People with longstanding, pervasive anxiety (generalized anxiety disorder) or depression (dysthymic disorder) seem especially likely to benefit from this approach to treatment, probably combined with interventions designed to reduce specific symptoms. People with the milder personality disorders such as dependent, avoidant, narcissistic, and histrionic personality disorders also might benefit from this approach, probably after they have made some progress via other modes of treatment. Looking at the ways in which they have made choices and the meaning of their lives so far might enable clients with these disorders to live their lives more deliberately, create more meaning in their lives, and be more authentic in their relationships.

Existential therapy also might be helpful to people who are coping with chronic or recurrent mental disorders such as major depressive disorders, schizophrenia, and substance use disorders at times when their symptoms are not prominent. For these people, too, looking at the direction of their lives, perhaps seeing that their lives have lacked meaning, might enable them to find more powerful ways to cope with their difficulties and make the most of their lives.

EVALUATION OF EXISTENTIAL THERAPY

Like all approaches to counseling and psychotherapy, existential therapy has both strengths and limitations. In addition, we must keep in mind the limited research on this approach when considering its appropriate use.

Limitations

Existential therapy relies heavily on developing a strong client-clinician relationship and on verbal communication. It is an individualistic approach in which the clinician offers little structure or direction. It takes a stance that responsibility, choice, and self-determination are desirable but does not offer specific steps and has few strategies for intervention. Treatment may be a leisurely and lengthy process. Because of these limitations, many people may be skeptical of its value, reluctant or unable to engage in the thinking and self-exploration that it requires, and find its underlying philosophy unacceptable. Of course, clinicians need to respect those feelings and select carefully the people for whom treatment via existential therapy is recommended.

Strengths

At the same time, the approach has many strengths. Its greatest contribution is probably not as a separate approach to psychotherapy and counseling but as a philosophy of human development that can be infused into other systems of treatment. This idea was advanced by May and Yalom (1995), who stated that their primary objective was the integration of the theory's goals and concepts into all approaches to psychotherapy. They wanted all clinicians to become more aware of the importance in treatment of issues of choice, meaning, and self-actualization and of the therapeutic alliance. May and Yalom believed that this process was already well underway. Certainly, few would argue with the premise that counseling and psychotherapy should promote people's overall wellness, help people live fully and authentically, and encourage them to take responsibility for their lives, making more positive and deliberate choices and creating meaning for themselves (Bauman & Waldo, 1998).

Contributions

Existential therapy has made many important contributions to the fields of counseling and psychotherapy. Like person-centered counseling, it has emphasized the great importance of a collaborative, respectful, and authentic client-clinician relationship. Current research has given ample support to the connection between the treatment alliance and the outcome of treatment. Existential therapy has broadened the reaches of psychotherapy beyond pathology and symptoms and legitimized inclusion in the treatment process of deep and philosophical issues such as existential anxiety, isolation, fear of death, self-actualization, and the meaning of life.

In addition, although existential therapy de-emphasizes techniques, Frankl's paradoxical intention has attracted the attention of clinicians from many systems of treatment. Family therapists and cognitive behavioral counselors, in particular, have appropriated this intervention in their work and find it to be a powerful tool for change, although one that must be used with great care.

SKILL DEVELOPMENT: VALUES CLARIFICATION

Understanding people's values is relevant to existential therapy as well as to other treatment approaches. Our values are an important aspect of our identity and affect the choices we make. Our success in leading lives that are consistent with our values is strongly connected to the meaningfulness of our lives and our sense of fulfillment.

Values can be expressed, manifested in our daily activities, and assessed via inventories. Ideally, people's expressed, manifest, and assessed values will all be congruent. However, sometimes discrepancies emerge, particularly between expressed and manifest values. This can lead people to feel unfulfilled and unmotivated.

Wanda, for example, expressed values of maintaining close interpersonal relationships, spending time in nature, and demonstrating her creativity. However, her manifest values were quite different. She worked long hours as a manager in a bank and made a high salary but had little time for her friends and her leisure activities. In addition, she lived in a small apartment in an urban setting. Her place of residence did not allow her to grow a garden, make space for her painting, or have much contact with the beauty of nature. Not surprisingly, Wanda reported that she was unhappy with her life and felt particularly unmotivated at work.

Seeing the discrepancy between her expressed and manifest values prompted her to take a more honest look at her values. She realized that the security and income of her job were important values to her but that she was neglecting the interpersonal and creative values that also mattered. She was able to transfer to a bank in a more rural area and purchased a small house. These changes allowed her more time and opportunity for hiking, painting, and gardening. Although Wanda did have to take a cut in pay, she was able to maintain an adequate and stable income and decided that the loss in income was more than offset by her ability to realize some of her other values.

Expressed Values

Looking at values from several perspectives clearly can provide useful information. The usual place to start is with people's expressed values. This might involve asking questions such as the following:

1. What do you view as the most important and meaningful parts of your life?
2. What accomplishments have you had that make you particularly proud?
3. If you had only one year to live, how would you want to use your time?
4. What do you view as your three most important values?
5. If you were to write a brief biography of yourself for publication in a national magazine, what information would you include?

Of course, these questions can be modified and adapted to ensure that they are well received by a particular client.

Manifest Values

Manifest values are reflected in the ways in which people lead their lives, including their personal and professional activities, how they distribute their time, their lifestyles, their objective accomplishments, and their disappointments. Questions such as the following can elicit manifest values:

1. Describe a typical day (or week or month) in your life.
2. If someone who did not know you read a biography of your life, what would that person view as your greatest accomplishments? Your greatest disappointments?
3. Assume that you have approximately 16 waking hours each day. Tell me the number of hours you typically spend in each of the following roles and what you usually do in that role:
   - Spouse/partner/friend
   - Parent
   - Career person
   - Leisurite
   - Life manager (e.g., shopping, cleaning, paying bills)
   - Other roles
4. If you could redistribute your time among these roles, what changes would you make?
5. How have your activities and the way in which you spend your time changed during the past 5–10 years?
6. When you awaken in the morning, what parts of your life do you look forward to and engage in as much as possible and what parts do you avoid whenever you can?
7. What do you enjoy doing when you are on vacation?

Inventoried Values

Many inventories, both standardized and nonstandardized, are available to assess values. Sometimes paper-and-pencil or computerized inventories promote more objective responses than do questions such as those just listed. The following is a simple written assessment of values that can be used to obtain another perspective on what is important to a person. Either of the two sets of instructions can be used with the accompanying list of values depending on which seems more likely to engage a person's interest and cooperation. Discussion of the person's responses should follow completion of the inventory to clarify the information provided.

> *Instructions 1:* Review the following list of values. Place a checkmark by all of the values that are important to you. Then review the values that you have checked and list, in priority order, the three that are most important to you.
> *Instructions 2:* Assume that you have $1,000 to spend at an auction of values. Review the following list and decide how you will allocate your money. Allo-

cating too little to any one value may mean you will lose the auction for that value, but allocating too much to a value limits how much you can allocate to other values.

List of Values
Achievement
Beauty
Career success
Child rearing
Creativity
Fame
Friendship
Health and fitness
Helping others
Independence
Learning and knowledge
Love and romance
Nature/outdoors activities
Order
Possessions
Power
Prestige and admiration
Security
Variety
Wealth

CASE ILLUSTRATION

The following dialogue illustrates a clinician's use of a Symbolic Growth Experience (SGE) with Edie. As you have learned, there are four steps in processing a SGE:

1. People are educated about the concept of the SGE.
2. They select an important past experience and explore its importance and symbolism in their lives.
3. They are helped to clarify the meaning in the experience.
4. They have a clearer sense of meaning and are able to repeat their use of these strategies to understand the significance of other experiences.

Assume that Edie has already been educated about the concept of the SGE, as discussed previously in this chapter. As you read this dialogue, observe how exploration of the significance of past experiences helps her develop a greater sense of meaningfulness in her life as well as understanding of some of her emotions and choices. Also note the existential clinician's role.

Clinician: Edie, I see great sadness on your face today.

Edie: Yes, the weekend was tough. I told you that Roberto and I were planning to attend my 20th high school reunion. I bought a new dress, got my hair styled, picked out pictures of Ava to show off. I thought it would be wonderful, but it was horrible.

Clinician: How did something you were so looking forward to bring you so much pain?

Edie: You remember my telling you that when I was 10 years old, I was diagnosed with cancer. No one thought I would survive, except maybe my father. I had chemotherapy and lost all my hair. And I took steroids to help with the nausea and that made me gain weight. There I was, disgusting-looking, maybe dying . . . and I was supposed to go to school, if I could drag myself there. The other children would make fun of me, laugh at me, call me baldy. I know they didn't understand, but it was so awful.

Clinician: That must have been such a difficult time for you, not only coping with cancer but also with the teasing. How is the reunion connected with that?

Edie: I guess I wanted to show everyone that I had survived, that I was attractive now and had a family. But when I got to the reunion, all those feeling I had when I was 10 came back to me.

Clinician: So in your mind, the reunion was to be a sort of life-affirming experience, but somehow it was just the opposite. What sense do you make of that?

Edie: I don't know.

Clinician: Edie, you have talked quite a bit about the impact cancer had on your life and your concern that it might recur despite the doctors' reassurances. I wonder if that strong fear of death has never left you and the reminder of the reunion intensified that fear.

Edie: That's true. You know, when I hit the 10th anniversary of my cancer diagnosis, the doctors said I was cured, but I never really believed it.

Clinician: And you're still living as though death is imminent.

Edie: Yes, I am. I felt like a fake at the reunion. How could I present myself as a woman who had survived when I knew inside that I was really dying?

Clinician: Most of us have a great deal of anxiety about death, but for you, of course, it is particularly strong because you did have a brush with death. How do you think this fear affects your life now?

Edie: I worry a lot about dying before Ava is grown. She needs me so much, and I don't want to abandon her. I try to do all I can for her while I still have time, but I never feel like I can do enough. Roberto can't understand. He says I pamper her and I should stop, but she's my only child. I couldn't get pregnant again because of the cancer. It's a miracle I got pregnant with Ava. She's like a gift from God.

Clinician: I hear you saying so many important things. Ava's birth and your role as a mother seem to have really given meaning to your life, and you want to make the most of that. But I also hear a sense of urgency, a fear that time might run out for you before Ava can take care of herself, and that terrifies you.

Edie: Yes, I still feel like I'm a walking time bomb, and it's just a matter of time before the cancer catches up with me again. Why can't Roberto understand that?

Clinician: It sounds like you feel very alone. I think one of the hardest things about being human is that no matter how much other people love and care about us, they can't really know what its like to feel the way we feel. That can be very lonely.

Edie: That's true. I know Roberto loves me and Ava, but he never does seem to really understand me. Maybe I've been too hard on him and expected too much.

Clinician: What could you choose to do differently?

Edie: Instead of blowing up at him, I could remind myself that he hasn't been through what I have, that there's no way he could really understand, and that's all right. I have a better awareness of myself now that I understand why I treat Ava the way I do.

Clinician: How does the way you treat Ava fit with the great importance in your life of being a good mother?

Edie: Well, I certainly love her and do all I can for her. Roberto says it's not good for her, though—that she needs more independence and confidence in herself.

Clinician: I know your anxiety makes it hard for you not to do everything possible for Ava and, as we discussed before, to be a different parent to her than your parents were to you. Could it be that your anxiety is making it hard for you to see any value in what Roberto is saying?

Edie: You mean that I'm scared something bad will happen to Ava if I don't keep a close watch on her? Yes, I guess I can be overprotective . . . and I know that's not really good mothering. I certainly want her to feel confident and good about herself, not the way I felt when I was growing up.

At this point, Edie has developed a clearer idea of the meaning, for her, of both her experience with cancer and the recent reunion. She is more aware of the impact that her fear of death and her sense of aloneness have on her. She has gained some clarification about the primary purpose of her life—to stay alive so that she can continue to be a good parent to Ava—and has begun to increase her awareness of both her own behavior and the possible validity of Roberto's words. She is now in a better position to make choices that will truly help her to move toward the meaning she has created in her life, to feel more self-actualized, and to improve her relationships with both Ava and Roberto.

EXERCISES

Large-Group Exercises

1. Discuss the differences and similarities between person-centered counseling and existential therapy. What differences do you note in the clients for whom each approach is suitable?
2. Conduct a values auction in class based on the list in the "Skill Development" section.
3. Are clinicians who focus primarily on profound issues of the human condition doing people a great service, or are they doing them a disservice by

de-emphasizing the immediate problems and symptoms that have led people to seek treatment? Create a debate in the classroom, with a small group
of people taking each side of the this question.

4. Engage in a round-robin counseling dialogue, with one person assuming the
   role of either Roberto or another hypothetical client and the class assuming
   the role of the clinician. Dialogue should focus on helping the client create a
   greater sense of meaning in his or her life.

Small-Group Exercises

1. Divide into your small groups of four students. Each dyad should have an opportunity to assume clinician and client roles for a dialogue of approximately
   15 minutes long. The client in each dialogue should present an experience in
   his or her life that was probably a Symbolic Growth Experience (SGE). The clinician should help the clients explore the importance of that experience and
   the connection it has to the meaning the client has created in his or her life.
       Feedback about the dialogue should focus on the following:

   - Ability to incorporate existential issues into the dialogue
   - Clarification of the meaning of the SGE
   - Use of empathy
   - Use of questions
   - Therapeutic alliance

2. Engage in another role-played counseling session following the format in Exercise 1. This time, focus on values clarification, exploring both expressed and
   manifest values. Questions listed previously in this chapter can be used to facilitate the discussion. Feedback on the dialogue should address the list of
   focus points in Exercise 1.

Individual Exercises

1. Write a paragraph in your journal about the meaning or purpose you have
   created in your own life. Then list three choices you have made recently. Write
   another paragraph, discussing whether or not they were congruent with the
   purpose of your life.
2. List your three greatest fears. Do they reflect the fears that seem important in
   existentialist theory? Consider the impact they have on your life. Write down
   a change you might make to reduce their negative impact.
3. Victor Frankl's paradoxical intention is one way to help people address their
   fears. Think about a way to use this intervention to help yourself. Write down
   your plan so that you will be committed to following through. Be sure that you
   take care of yourself and do not take any unwise risks.

SUMMARY

Existential therapy grew out of a European society devastated by two great wars. It seeks to help people deal with the deep and powerful issues that affect everyone. More a philosophy than a system of treatment, the approach addresses troubling dimensions of the human condition such as the inevitability of death and loss, existential alienation, meaninglessness, and guilt. Clinicians and their relationships with their clients are the primary instruments of change; establishment of a genuine, caring, supportive, and authentic client-clinician relationship is essential in this treatment model. Existential therapy enables people to find their potential for self-actualization, awareness, and relatedness, which can help them make wise and responsible choices and create meaning in their lives.

People interested in continuing to learn about existential therapy might contact

Society for Existential Analysis
School for Psychotherapy and Counselling
Regent's College
Inner Circle, Regent's Park
London, England NW1 4NS

This organization publishes the *Journal of the Society for Existential Analysis* and provides training in this mode of treatment.

RECOMMENDED READINGS

Bauman, S., & Waldo, M. (1998). Existential theory and mental health counseling: If it were a snake, it would have bitten! *Journal of Mental Health Counseling, 20*(1), 13–27.
Bugental, J. F. T. (1987). *The art of the psychotherapist.* New York: Norton.
Bugental, J. F. T. (1990). *Intimate journeys.* San Francisco: Jossey-Bass.
Frankl, V. (1963). *Man's search for meaning.* Boston: Beacon.
May, R. (1969). *Love and will.* New York: Norton.
Yalom, I. D. (1980). *Existential psychotherapy.* New York: Basic Books.
Yalom, I. D. (1989). *Love's executioner and other tales of psychotherapy.* New York: Basic Books.

Chapter 13

GESTALT THERAPY

Gestalt therapy encompasses many of the concepts of both existential therapy and person-centered counseling. It emphasizes the importance of the therapeutic alliance and is phenomenological, experiential, humanistic, and optimistic. Promoting awareness and responsibility are important aspects of Gestalt therapy. The present receives more attention than the past in this model; and of course, exploring and experiencing emotions and sensations are integral.

What distinguishes this approach from others is its emphasis on the *Gestalt*, which Laura Perls (1992) defined as "a structured entity that is more than and different from its parts. It is the foreground figure that stands out from its ground, it 'exists' " (p. 52). According to Gestalt therapists, people experience psychological difficulties because they have become cut off from important parts of themselves such as their emotions, bodies, or contacts with others. The purpose of Gestalt therapy is to help people become aware of these neglected and disowned parts and restore a sense of wholeness, integration, and balance.

Gestalt therapy was developed primarily by Fritz Perls with his wife Laura Perls. Erving and Miriam Polster have also made important contributions to Gestalt therapy. Widely used during the 1960s and 1970s, it continues to have many followers and to influence other approaches to treatment.

THE PEOPLE WHO DEVELOPED GESTALT THERAPY

Frederick Perls, known as Fritz Perls, was born in 1893, the middle child and only son of a middle-class Jewish family living in Berlin, Germany. Although Perls apparently was not always a motivated student, he succeeded in receiving an M.D. degree with a specialization in psychiatry in 1920 (Perls, 1969b). Interested in becoming a practicing psychoanalyst, Perls relocated to Vienna, the home of Sigmund Freud, to be trained, where he met many of the leaders in his field. He studied with Karen Horney and was psychoanalyzed by both Horney and Wilhelm Reich, who emphasized the importance of using the body to promote understanding and personal growth (Wulf, 1998).

In addition to his training and analysis, Perls was also influenced by World War I. During the war, he served as a medical corpsman, a powerful personal experience. After the war, he worked with the neurologist Kurt Goldstein at the Frankfurt Neurological Institute, a treatment facility for people who had suffered brain injuries. Both experiences led Perls to reflect on the workings of the human mind, on Gestalt psychology, and on better ways to help people (Simkin, 1975; Wheeler, 1991). Even early in his career as a psychoanalyst, he was becoming disenchanted with that mode of treatment as well as with behaviorism.

The versatile and extroverted Perls also worked as an actor in the 1920s. He later reported that his experiences in the theater gave him an understanding of and appreciation for the importance of nonverbal communication, an essential aspect of Gestalt therapy.

In 1930, Fritz Perls married Laura Posner, a concert pianist and dancer (Serlin, 1992). While Fritz Perls emphasized independence and confrontation, Laura Perls advocated support and connections. She studied existentialism with Martin

Buber and Paul Tillich, drawing on this background as she became involved in the development of Gestalt therapy with her husband.

When Hitler came into power, the couple decided to leave Europe, relocating first in Holland and then in South Africa, where Fritz Perls served as a captain in the South African Medical Corps. During his years in South Africa, he outlined his theory of personality integration, which later became Gestalt therapy (Simkin, 1975). In 1946, the couple immigrated to the United States, where Fritz published *Gestalt Therapy: Excitement and Growth in the Human Personality* (Perls, 1951). In 1952, he established the Gestalt Institute of America.

The most important impetus for the growth of Gestalt therapy was Fritz Perls's work at the Esalen Institute in Big Sur, California, between 1962 and 1969. He became best known there for his use of the "hot seat" in his workshops and soon was regarded as an innovative and charismatic advocate of the human potential movement.

His personality enhanced the popularity and success of Gestalt therapy. An outspoken free spirit, unafraid to challenge and reject established traditions and procedures, both Perls and his work were in tune with the 1960s, when many people were seeking more fulfillment in their lives and new ways to live. As he stated, "The meaning of life is that it is to be lived; and it is not to be traded and conceptualized and squeezed into a pattern of systems. We realize that manipulation and control are not the ultimate job of life" (Perls, 1969a, p. 3).

Fritz Perls died in 1970, when the popularity of Gestalt therapy was at its height. Many clinicians abandoned more traditional systems of treatment in favor of this exciting approach, while others incorporated elements of Gestalt therapy into already-established approaches to treatment. After Fritz's death, Laura continued his work until her death in 1990, and followers are still developing and refining this approach.

Particularly important are Erving and Miriam Polster. Both served for many years as co-directors of the Gestalt Training Center in San Diego and were on the faculty of the School of Medicine of the University of California, San Diego. The Polsters expanded on the ideas of Fritz Perls, emphasizing the importance of theory to increase the credibility of this treatment system (Polster & Polster, 1973). According to the Polsters, Gestalt therapy can be a major integrative force in society, ameliorating common human concerns and increasing meaning and creativity in our lives.

THE DEVELOPMENT OF GESTALT THERAPY

Like many of the systems of counseling and psychotherapy discussed in this book, Gestalt therapy has its roots in Europe. The work of a group of Gestalt psychologists in Berlin, including Max Wertheimer, Kurt Koffka, and Wolfgang Kohler, laid the groundwork for Gestalt therapy with their studies of perception and integration of parts into perceptual wholes. These theorists believed that understanding knowledge in "units of wholes, Gestalten" is more useful to the expansion of knowledge than dissecting the parts (Wulf, 1998, p. 86). In other words, they believed that the whole is greater than the sum of the parts. They also viewed people as having a natural tendency toward closure and equilibrium, which leads them to think in terms of wholes rather than parts.

Although the Gestalt psychologists may have provided the name and a basic premise for Gestalt therapy, Perls drew on many sources of knowledge in developing his treatment system, including psychoanalysis and existentialism, which were powerful forces in Europe during the first part of the 20th century. Although his work clearly is a significant departure from psychoanalysis, he recognized the importance of Freud's work and was influenced by other analysts, including Karen Horney, Wilhelm Reich, and Otto Rank.

Wulf (1998) described Rank's therapy as "centered on the will and the ego-functions as autonomous organizing forces inside the individual. He demands re-experiencing and repeating instead of remembering, which inevitably implies an active role of the therapist." (p. 86). Certainly, these concepts are mirrored in Perls's insistence on the importance of the present experience and the involved and committed role of the clinician.

Jacob Moreno's psychodrama, along with Perls's own experience as an actor, also influenced the development of Gestalt therapy. Psychodrama encouraged people to work out personal difficulties by creating dramatizations of problematic situations such as a family fight. With the help of a therapist, members of the audience assume the family and other roles and give the protagonist an opportunity to relive and change painful experiences. Feedback from observers enhances the impact of the process and gives them vicarious benefits. Perls's techniques, including the empty chair, role plays, group feedback, and perhaps even the hot seat, were probably influenced by Moreno's ideas, as was Perls's emphasis on spontaneity, creativity, and enactment (Wulf, 1998).

During Perls's lifetime, the highly charged techniques associated with his approach received considerable attention because of their use at Esalen, their powerful impact, and their application to encounter groups, which were in widespread use during the 1960s and early 1970s. However, since that time, Gestalt therapy seems to have become less sensational and more solid. The integration of techniques from Gestalt therapy and transactional analysis, (discussed in Chapter 8) seem particularly important in establishing Gestalt therapy as not just a collection of exciting and highly charged interventions but a treatment system with many contributions to make to the fields of counseling and psychotherapy.

IMPORTANT THEORETICAL CONCEPTS

Although Perls often used terminology that differed considerably from that used by existentialist and person-centered clinicians, his theoretical concepts are in many ways consistent with those treatment systems. However, Perls and his associates added their own ideas, which distinguish Gestalt therapy from both person-centered and existential approaches. In addition, the strategies used in Gestalt therapy, (discussed later in this chapter) represent a considerable departure from existential and person-centered systems, which both make minimal use of strategies of intervention.

View of Humankind

Perls was a humanist who had an optimistic and empowering view of people. Like other humanists, he placed the greatest importance on self-actualization: "Every individual, every plant, every animal has only one inborn goal—to actualize itself as it is" (Perls, 1969a, p. 33). He believed that people were basically good and had the capacity to cope with their lives successfully, although he recognized they sometimes needed help.

According to Perls, healthy individuals engaged productively in the tasks of survival and maintenance and intuitively moved toward self-preservation and growth. As Enright (1975) stated, "The basic assumption of this therapeutic approach is that people can deal adequately with their own life problems if they know what they are and can bring all their abilities into action to solve them." (p. 22). Gestalt therapy seeks to help people develop awareness, inner support, and self-sufficiency so that they can recognize that the capacities they need to help themselves lie within themselves rather than in a partner, title, career, or clinician.

Wholeness, Integration, and Balance

As its name implies, Gestalt therapy emphasizes the importance of wholeness, integration, and balance in people's lives. According to Simkin (1975), "Man is a total organism functioning as a whole, rather than an entity split in dichotomies such as mind and body." (p. 4). Perls (1969a) said of the human organism, "We *have* not a liver or a heart. We *are* liver and heart and brain and yet, even this is wrong—we are *not* a summation of parts but a *coordination* of the whole. We do not have a body, we *are* a body, we *are* somebody." (p. 6).

Polarities   Unfortunately, many personalities lack wholeness and are fragmented (Korb, Gorrell, & Van de Riet, 1989). People with such personality structures are aware only of some parts of themselves and deny or cut off other parts. For example, people who believe they must always be independent may deny the part of themselves that craves support and wants to express grief over a loss, while people who believe that their intellect is their greatest gift may cut themselves off from their bodies.

To some extent, this fragmentation and denial of parts of the self stems from a drive toward homeostasis. People have difficulty dealing with ambiguity or disequilibrium and prefer stability and cohesiveness. This may lead them to exclude from awareness the parts of themselves that seem incongruent or cause discomfort in a misguided effort to force equilibrium. Some men, for example, deny the sensitive and aesthetic aspects of their personalities because they view them as conflicting with their image of themselves as strong and masculine.

People's need for homeostasis also leads them to view themselves and their world in terms of *polarities*, or extremes. The world may seem easier to understand if we categorize people as either good or bad, lazy or productive. However, these polarities generally reflect internal or interpersonal conflicts. To truly achieve wholeness, people must become aware of and integrate their polarities, especially the polarities of the mind and the body. Unless we accomplish that, the neglected or rejected side of the polarity is likely to build barriers against our efforts toward growth.

Figure-Ground   Although people strive for homeostasis, the world is always in flux, always changing. As a result, people constantly experience needs that create disequilibrium and then respond to those needs in an effort to restore balance. We are hungry, so we eat to restore balance. We are tired, so we nap to feel rested.

Perls used the concept of the *figure-ground* to clarify this constant flux. The world around us is the ground, or background, of our lives. However, as we go through the day, we cannot possibly attend to every facet of our experience. Rather, certain elements come to the foreground, depending on our needs. These are the figures that emerge. For example, when we go into the kitchen to get a drink, we are focused on that need. The refrigerator, the container of milk, and a glass are the figures, or foreground, that we notice as we pursue our efforts to drink a glass of milk. We barely notice the vase on the counter or the cat on the floor. However, if the cat jumps up on the counter and knocks down the vase, the figure-ground changes; the glass of milk recedes into the ground, and the broken vase becomes the figure.

Most of us experience another example of this figure-ground shift when we are in a restaurant where background music is being played. For the most part, we are oblivious to that music. However, when our favorite singer or a melody that is meaningful to us is played, figure and ground change; the music moves into the foreground.

Ego Boundary   Just as the figure-ground relationship changes, so does the ego boundary. Perls (1969a) described the *ego boundary* as "the organism's definition in relation to its environment, . . . [and] this relationship is experienced both by what is inside the skin and what is outside the skin, but it is not a fixed thing" (p. 7). The two phenomena of the fluid ego boundary are identification and alienation. Identification, as with our parents, our bodies, our jobs, and our values, brings those aspects of our lives into our ego boundaries, while alienation, as from other people, their beliefs, or parts of ourselves, leads us to view those aspects as outside our ego boundaries. According to Perls (1969a), "So the whole idea of good and bad, right and wrong, is always a matter of boundary, of which side of the fence I am on." (p. 9).

Gestalt therapy, like the other approaches discussed in Part 3, is *phenomenological*: it recognizes that people's perceptions of a given situation can vary widely; that even within a person perceptions are likely to change; and that our perceptions have a great influence on our thoughts, emotions, and behaviors. Perceptions also play a major role in shaping our ego boundaries. For example, people with low self-esteem and a confused sense of self commonly have weak ego boundaries. They overidentify with other people in an effort to feel more like them and gain a sense of belonging. However, they tend to have difficulty distinguishing their own needs and feelings from those of other people and may erroneously assume that other people feel exactly as they do. On the other hand, people with rigid ego boundaries tend to have difficulty bringing new experiences and relationships into their lives and may feel very different and separate from other people. Inflexibility, particularly in response to change, is often a problem for them.

Homeostasis versus Flux   Perls used a great many terms, including figure-ground, ego boundary, and polarities, to refer to the constant state of flux that he believes people experience. These terms may be less confusing if we consider the property they all share: posing threats to our efforts toward homeostasis. Clearly, people cannot achieve a state of fixed homeostasis and then freeze the action. Our lives are always changing. However, through awareness of and identification with all aspects of ourselves, we can deal successfully with flux and still have a sense of integration and wholeness. As Simkin (1975) stated, "Organismically balanced individuals have the capacity to experience intellectually, emotionally and sensorially." (p. 7).

Awareness

For Gestalt therapists, awareness is an essential element of emotional health: "Awareness per se—by and of itself—can be curative. Because with full awareness you become aware of this organismic self-regulation, you can let the organism take over without interfering, without interrupting; we can rely on the wisdom of the organism." (Perls, 1969a, p. 17). Awareness is both a hallmark of the healthy person and a goal of treatment.

Several possible causes have been identified for people's lack of full awareness. Preoccupation is one of the foremost. We may be so caught up with our pasts, our fantasies, our perceived flaws or strengths that we lose sight of the whole picture and become unaware. Another reason for lack of awareness is low self-esteem: "The less confident we are in ourselves, the less we are in touch with ourselves and the world, the more we want to control." (Perls, 1969a, p. 21). Low self-esteem makes it difficult for people to trust themselves, to allow the natural health and strength of the organism to move toward growth and self-actualization. Rather, people with low self-esteem typically set out to deliberately control themselves and others in an effort to realize an idealized self-image rather than to truly actualize themselves. The result is often exactly the opposite of what is intended.

Environmental Contact   Human beings engage in many efforts to achieve awareness, and contact with the environment is one of the most important. Contact is made through seven functions: looking, listening, touching, talking, moving, smelling, and tasting (Polster & Polster, 1973, pp. 129–138). Contact is necessary for growth; when we make contact with other people or aspects of our world, we must react and change. The experience of contact teaches us about ourselves and our environment and helps us to feel a part of our world while defining more clearly who we are. People who avoid closeness with others and seek to live isolated and circumscribed lives may believe that they are protecting themselves, but, in reality they are preventing their growth and actualization.

Perls (1969a) identified five levels or stages of contact:

1. *The phony layer.* People play games, assume roles, react in stereotyped and unauthentic ways, and are insincere.

2. *The phobic layer.* They avoid pain, hide their real selves to prevent rejection, act out of fear, and feel vulnerable and helpless.
3. *The impasse layer.* Having passed through the first two layers, people do not know what to do next. They feel stuck, believe that they cannot help themselves to change, and seek help from others.
4. *The implosive layer.* People become aware of ways in which they have limited themselves and begin to experiment with change, to deal with unfinished business, lower defenses, and move toward greater integration. A sort of death occurs at this layer as people really connect with possibilities and give up the old layers. The implosion turns into an explosion in the fifth layer.
5. *The explosive layer.* People experience reintegration and wholeness, become their authentic selves, gain access to great energy, feel and express emotions, and move toward actualization.

Perls referred to these stages as the *five layers of neuroses* (Korb et al., 1989). Treatment often involves a progression through the layers, peeling away each layer to expose the next healthier layer as people truly become their authentic, actualized selves, capable of full contact with the environment, other people, and themselves.

Here and Now   Another way to increase awareness is to live in and be conscious of the present moment rather than live our lives tied to the past or in hopes of a better future. According to Perls (1969a), "Nothing exists except the here and now.... The past is no more. The future is not yet. . . . You should live in the here and now" (p. 44). When we are centered in the present, we are more likely to be congruent—to have our minds, our bodies, and our emotions integrated. When we are not fully in the present, we may be fragmented. For example, our emotions may be stuck in past hurts and our thoughts may wander to future anticipations while we talk with people in the present. When we are not centered in the present, we give mixed messages to others, have a poorly integrated sense of ourselves, and have difficulty making contact because we are not fully present.

Responsibility   Like the other theorists discussed in Part 3, Gestalt therapists place considerable importance on accepting responsibility for our own lives rather than giving over that power to others or blaming and resenting others for our disappointments. Gestalt therapists believe that people must make their own choices rather than allow others to choose for them.

Perls's focus, in keeping with the climate of the 1960s, was on the individual; but modern Gestalt therapists have modified the concept of responsibility so that it refers to the importance not only of taking care of ourselves but also of recognizing that we are part of a society, that we are interdependent, and that we must recognize the impact we have on the lives of others. Achieving a healthy balance between contact with others and self-sufficiency is an essential aspect of emotional health. To achieve that balance and act in responsible ways, we must have awareness, which is at the core of so many aspects of the healthy person.

The Nature of Growth Disorders

Of course, not all people are emotionally healthy. Although Perls sometimes used the term *neurosis* to describe emotional problems, he stated that these difficulties should more accurately be referred to as "growth disorders" (Perls, 1969a, p. 30). This term describes people who are denying or rejecting aspects of themselves and their environment, are not living in the present, are not making fulfilling contact with others, lack awareness, and are not self-actualized. They are stuck at a point in which the environment is no longer giving them the support they need to grow and mature, but they do not yet have sufficient confidence in their own resources to take responsibility for themselves. They feel guilty and resentful and tend to hold onto the past, blaming their parents and others for their failure to grow. Their ego boundaries are probably either diffuse or rigid.

Avoidance and resistance keep people trapped in this unhealthy state. They avoid dealing with uncomfortable feelings, remain unaware, and circumscribe their lives to minimize flux or change. They make extensive use of ego defenses such as projection of disowned aspects of themselves onto others, distraction, failure to set boundaries between themselves and others, and withdrawal from their surroundings. Wholeness, integrity, freedom of choice, and actualization are sacrificed to the illusion of safety and homeostasis. Such people do not allow themselves to be aware of, anticipate, and cope successfully and flexibly with the natural and constant changes in their lives. Rather, they persist in their unsuccessful defensive maneuvers to avoid change. Paradoxically, as Perls observed, people who operate in this way actually experience greater turmoil and discomfort than do those who are aware of the here and now and can use their own powerful resources to manage their lives.

People who are not developing in healthy ways often have a great deal of unfinished business. According to Perls (1969a), "our life is basically practically nothing but an infinite number of unfinished situations—incomplete Gestalts. No sooner have we finished one situation than another comes up." (p. 15). Most of us are familiar with our never-ending lists of tasks to be done; as soon as one item is crossed off the list, another takes its place. Unfinished business is inevitable. Healthy people may be disconcerted by the constant unfinished business in their lives but learn to use their resources to deal with it effectively.

People with growth disorders, however, are overwhelmed by unfinished business, particularly resentments and unexpressed emotions. Because they are alienated from many aspects of their environments and themselves, they cannot deal effectively with the demands of their lives, and so they accumulate more and more unfinished business. Their energy is sapped by their unproductive efforts to cope, leaving them depleted of the resources they need to live their lives successfully. People whose lives are overwhelmed by unfinished business typically feel stuck or blocked and may experience physical symptoms (Enright, 1975). Their current issues tend to mirror unresolved issues from the past and are never finished because they are not addressed in the here and now. One of the major goals of Gestalt therapy is to help people become aware of their backlog of unfinished business and bring it to closure—finish it so that they are able to live more fully in the present.

TREATMENT USING GESTALT THERAPY

Unlike person-centered counseling and existential therapy, Gestalt therapy includes a rich array of techniques and strategies that have been developed to facilitate the treatment process. Many can also be incorporated into other treatment systems. These strategies have been developed to further what Perls, Hefferline, and Goodman (1951) identified as the four major emphases in their work:

- To pay attention to experience and become aware of and concentrate on the actual present situation
- To maintain and promote the integrity and interrelationships of social, cultural, historical, physical, emotional, and other important factors
- To experiment
- To encourage creativity

Goals

Many of the treatment objectives of Gestalt therapy are similar to those of person-centered counseling and existential therapy. However, others are unique to this approach. Typical goals include:

- Promoting attention, clarity, and awareness
- Helping people live in the here and now
- Enabling people to bring closure to their unfinished business
- Increasing people's appreciation of and access to their own considerable resources
- Helping them depend less on outside support
- Promoting responsibility, appropriate choices, and self-sufficiency
- Facilitating people's efforts to have meaningful contact with all aspects of themselves, other people, and their environment
- Promoting self-esteem, self-acceptance, and self-actualization
- Reducing polarities in people's lives, particularly the polarity of the mind and the body
- Developing the skills people need to manage their lives successfully without harming others
- Improving people's sense of wholeness, integration, and balance

According to Perls (1969a), "The difference between Gestalt therapy and most other types of psychotherapy is essentially that we do *not* analyze. We *integrate*." (p. 70). The ultimate aim of Gestalt therapy is to promote the natural growth of the human organism and enable people to live aware and actualized lives—not just to solve problems or promote adaptation but to help clients feel more fulfilled and whole.

How People Change

Gestalt clinicians believe that awareness is the primary vehicle in the process of change. If people can gain awareness of their unfinished business (the areas in which they are blocked and alienated) and their own strengths and resources, they can move forward toward growth and actualization. Particularly important is awareness gained through the body since, according to Gestalt theory, most people have a tendency to overemphasize intellectual awareness and ignore the messages from the body and the senses.

As with all of the treatment approaches in Part 3, the role of the clinician and the therapeutic alliance are essential to effecting change. In addition, Gestalt therapists use dreams and a wide range of other exercises and experiments to create an environment that is conducive to learning and change.

Therapeutic Alliance

Like existential therapists, Gestalt therapists seek to create an I-thou relationship with clients in which both client and clinician are fully present in the here and now (Korb et al., 1989). Gestalt clinicians strive to be genuine and fully aware of their own feelings, experiences, and perceptions. They do not urge or persuade people to change or tell them how they should be. Rather, they establish a climate that promotes trust, awareness, and a willingness to experiment with new ways of thinking, feeling, and acting.

Clinicians and clients enter into a partnership in which clients take an active role. They are encouraged to take responsibility for themselves and decide for themselves how they will use the information that emerges in their sessions.

As long as clients are fully present and aware in the sessions, clinicians do not interrupt people's efforts to deal with their concerns (Enright, 1975). However, when a clinician observes that a client's attention is wandering, that incongruencies are emerging, or that a person seems fragmented or out of contact, the clinician will call the client's' attention to these phenomena. The clinician makes this observation without interpretation or judgment, simply to provide information that is likely to refocus attention, create awareness of blocks, and help people maintain constant contact with their present activities and experiences. Instead of trying to figure out what is emerging from their clients, Gestalt therapists focus on listening and helping clients find their "own way through the pauses and blocks" (Enright, 1975, p. 22).

Experiments

One task of Gestalt therapists is suggesting experiments or learning experiences for their clients. These are individually tailored to each client, although certain formats are common. Because they are intended to promote awareness and bring problems and unfinished business into the present where they can be resolved, these experiments should not be threatening or negative. Instead, they should be positive and growth-promoting. Presentation of suggested experiments should always be respectful, inviting, and carefully timed. While confrontation may be used to encourage involvement in experiments, clients are never demeaned and can always choose whether or not to involve themselves in the experiments.

Experiments might take the form of enactments, role plays, homework, or suggested activities for clients to accomplish between sessions (Polster & Polster, 1973). For example, a Gestalt therapist suggested to a withdrawn and guarded woman who wanted to have closer relationships with people that she tell a friend something about herself that would surprise and please the friend. Spending time thinking about what she would tell the friend promoted the woman's self-awareness, while the eventual sharing increased the closeness between the woman and her friend.

Use of Language

Language plays an important part in Gestalt therapy. By choosing their words carefully, clinicians can create an environment that is likely to encourage change.

"What" and "How" Questions   In this treatment approach, questions usually begin with "what," "how," or sometimes "where" but rarely with "why." Questions such as "What are you experiencing when you stamp your foot?" and "How does it feel when you stamp your foot?" are more likely to keep the client in the present moment and promote integration than are questions such as "Why are you stamping your foot?" "Why" questions typically lead to a focus on past experiences and manifestations of resistance.

I Statements   People in Gestalt therapy are encouraged to own and focus on their own feelings and experiences rather than talk about other people (they) or events (it). Statements beginning with "I" such as "I feel angry" and "In the dream, I am lost" encourage ownership and responsibility as well as integration. Statements such as "My mother made me angry" and "My dream was about being lost" take the focus off the client and the present moment and are likely to promote fragmentation and externalizing of responsibility.

Emphasis on Statements   Although questions certainly are a part of Gestalt therapy, clinicians typically prefer statements. For example, they are more likely to say, "I am experiencing a loss of contact between us," than "Where has your attention gone?" The immediacy and direct person-to-person contact of a statement is more likely to create the sort of client-clinician relationship that is seen as desirable. Questions, on the other hand, are reminiscent of a teacher-student relationship in which there is a power differential that may undermine the therapeutic partnership. Talking *with* someone rather than *at* someone is critical in building a connection.

The Present Tense   Even if clients are talking about past events, Gestalt clinicians encourage them to focus on their present experience of the events—to bring events into the room and into the moment. This fosters awareness as well as a true connection with the clients' experience of the events.

Encouraging Responsibility   People are encouraged to take responsibility for themselves, their words, and their behaviors to facilitate their efforts to move toward integration. Language can be used to further that goal. For example, the clinician might suggest that people begin their sentences with the phrase, "I take responsibility for . . . " to help them recognize and accept their feelings. They might also be encouraged to apply to themselves statements they have made about others to facilitate awareness of their projections. For example, the woman who says, "My sister only thinks of herself," might be asked to say, "I think only of myself," and then talk about what feelings this brings up for her. Another way to encourage people to take responsibility for themselves and their behaviors is for clinicians to help them make the implicit explicit. For example, a woman assured her husband that she would be happy to accompany him to church as he requested. However, each Sunday she told him that she had work to do and could not find the time to go to church with him. Her therapist encouraged her to make her implicit feelings explicit by stating, "I really don't want to go to church with you; I feel uncomfortable and out of place there because it is not the religion I was brought up to believe."

Dreams

Dreams occupy an important place in Gestalt therapy. Perls viewed dreams as the royal road to integration rather than the royal road to the unconscious, as Freud had viewed them. Perls believed that the parts of a dream represented projections or aspects of the dreamer. Awareness comes from assuming the various roles or parts of the dream and enacting the dream as though it is happening in the present.

For example, a man had a dream about a rabbit being chased across a field by a fox but escaping into a burrow. Freud, of course, would focus on the unconscious meaning of the conflict between the fox and the rabbit and the possibly sexual significance of the burrow. Perls, on the other hand, would encourage the man to assume the roles of each of the salient parts of the dream. One at a time, the client would enact the roles of the frightened rabbit, the menacing fox, the open field, and the protective burrow, speaking the thoughts and feelings that arise for him in each role. For example, he might say, "I am that rabbit, running scared, afraid that I will be swallowed up. I am always running for cover, safe just in the nick of time, but knowing that I might not make it the next time."

This approach to understanding dreams puts the client in charge of the process rather than the clinician. It also allows people to take responsibility for their dreams, see their dreams as part of themselves, have a greater sense of integration, and become aware of thoughts and emotions reflected in the dream that they might otherwise disown.

Fantasy

Fantasies, like dreams, are often used to help people become more self-aware. Clinicians might use guided imagery to enable people to take a journey into their imaginations. For example, they might be encouraged to imagine themselves walking through a beautiful place, looking around to see who is with them, and deciding what to do in that situation. Clinicians might make the fantasy more productive by asking questions to promote exploration and suggesting actions the person might take in the fantasy.

As with dreams, Gestalt therapists generally assume that the parts of the fantasy represent projections or aspects of the person. When the fantasy is completed, clinicians encourage people to process the experience by becoming the parts of the fantasy and speaking as though they are each part. This technique, like exploration of dreams, often helps people become more aware of and in contact with their feelings and more able to express those emotions.

Fantasies also can be used to bring closure to unfinished business. For example, a woman who had undergone surgery was left with some very negative feelings about her surgeon and a need to have her surgery redone. When she called to express her feelings to the physician, the physician failed to return her telephone calls. To help her reach closure, her clinician led her on a guided fantasy trip in which she expressed her feelings to the physician and affirmed her ability to take care of herself and have the unsatisfactory surgery corrected by another physician.

Role Play

Role play, in a variety of forms, is an essential tool of Gestalt therapists. Although Perls was influenced by Moreno's psychodrama, Gestalt therapy rarely uses other people to play roles, in part because that might encourage fragmentation. Rather, an empty chair is more often used to represent a role.

In a common type of role play, two chairs are used, with each representing an aspect of a person's life. The chairs might represent the client and another person such as a parent or friend; or they might represent two parts of the person, perhaps the intellect and the body. The chairs might also represent parts of a person's dream or fantasy, physical symptoms the person is having such as a headache, or conflicting emotions such as love and anger. The client spends time sitting in each chair and talking from the perspective represented by that chair. The dialogue that emerges from the conversation between the two chairs often yields honest but previously unspoken or unacknowledged feelings. This, in turn, creates what has been described as an "ah-ha" experience: the shock of recognition in which people gain new emotional awareness and understanding. They also become more able to integrate both parts of the dialogue and claim their ownership. The case illustration in this chapter demonstrates the use of the empty chair technique.

Top Dog/Underdog

Perls believed that "we constantly harass ourselves with . . . the top-dog/under-dog game where part of ourselves attempts to lecture, urge, and threaten the other part into 'good behavior' " (Fagan & Shepherd, 1970, p. 4). The top dog makes judgments and tells the underdog how it should feel, think, or act, as if it were a sort of superego or conscience. The underdog, on the other hand, tends to be meek and apologetic but does not really try to change. Although the top dog may seem more powerful, the underdog really has control by refusing to change or cooperate despite feelings of guilt. In addition to having both top dog and underdog within them, some people try to cast another person into the role of top dog while they assume the role of the guilty but ineffectual underdog. Some clients may even seek such a relationship with their clinicians, creating a hierarchical and nonproductive relationship.

The empty chair technique can be used to raise awareness of the top dog/underdog game and encourage integration of both parts of the self as well as promote change. A teenager named Mary, for example, had been overweight since early childhood. She blamed her overeating on her mother, who constantly criticized Mary's weight. In reality, the conflict lay within Mary. Her top dog told her that she was a worthless, unattractive person who must lose weight immediately, while her underdog, like a rebellious child, refused to develop healthy eating habits despite guilt and low self-esteem related to her eating. Using two chairs, Mary alternately assumed the roles of her top dog and underdog, coming to recognize the polarities represented by both positions and the underdog's sabotage of the tyrannical top dog. This awareness enabled her to see the harm she was doing to herself, own her eating behavior rather than blame it on her mother, reduce her resistance to addressing her unhealthy weight, and make some reasonable changes in her behavior.

The Body As a Vehicle of Communication

Gestalt therapy seeks to give people a sense of wholeness, enabling them to access and be aware of their thoughts, emotions, and physical sensations. Many people have fairly good awareness of their thoughts and their emotions. However, they tend to ignore or cut themselves off from their bodily sensations. Consequently, Gestalt therapists tend to pay particular attention to the messages of the body.

Three strategies are especially useful in focusing attention on the body:

1. Therapists try to remain alert to bodily messages. If they notice that a part of a person's body may be in a reactive state, such as fingers tapping on a table or a leg strenuously swinging, they will call attention to the movements and ask about their message. A clinician might say, for example, "I notice that your leg began swinging when we started to talk about your relationship with your sister. What is your leg saying?" or "Become your leg and give your leg a voice. What is your leg feeling?"

2. Another strategy is to help people locate their emotions in their body as a way to help them more fully experience their feelings. A clinician might say, "You have told me that you feel rage toward your sister. Show me where you are experiencing this rage?" Once the client has located the rage, perhaps in her stomach, the clinician can explore the physical sensations that the client is experiencing and enable her to more fully connect with and express her feelings.

3. When they observe body movements or symptoms, clinicians often encourage clients to exaggerate them. For example, a clinician might say, "I notice you are tapping your foot. I would like you to exaggerate the tapping, do it as hard as you can, and then talk about what feelings come up." The technique of exaggeration or repetition can also be applied to a tone of voice or a meaningful phrase that the person uses. This intervention seems to focus attention on where energy is located and can succeed in releasing blocked energy.

Groups

Gestalt therapy lends itself very well to use in both individual and group counseling. The feedback and support from both the clinician and the group members can accelerate the process of awareness and empowerment. Members can also learn vicariously from each other. The use of this treatment approach in a group setting has led to the development of several other useful techniques.

Hot Seat   Fritz Perls's work at the Esalen Institute emphasized the use of the hot seat in a group setting. This powerful technique brought him considerable attention, and it was widely adopted by encounter groups during the 1960s and 1970s. The hot seat is a chair placed in the middle of the group, usually with a box of tissues nearby since sitting in the hot seat often evokes strong emotions. Group members volunteer to work, one at a time, spending 5–10 minutes sitting in the hot seat and becoming the center of the group's attention. When people are in the hot seat, they are encouraged to express and stay with their feelings. Feedback from the group on their body language and verbal messages promotes their awareness of themselves and their feelings.

Making the Rounds   When making the rounds, people in the hot seat say something to each member of the group, perhaps identifying something they want from that person or something in him or her that reminds them of themselves. Alternatively, group members might take turns giving people in the hot seat feedback, perhaps on their strengths in an effort to empower them. Like many of the other experiments used in Gestalt therapy, this is a powerful technique that is likely to have an enduring impact on people.

APPLICATION OF GESTALT THERAPY

Gestalt therapy is a powerful, action-oriented approach. Its success depends largely on the establishment of a trusting and collaborative relationship between client and clinician and, correspondingly, the client's willingness to take some risks and engage in experiments that may elicit strong emotions and new awareness. Because it is usually a forceful approach to treatment that can have a great impact, Gestalt therapy should be used with considerable thought and care. While it is not appropriate for treatment of many disorders and people, it is well suited for some.

Diagnostic Groups

According to Laura Perls (1992), Gestalt therapy "is not useful in working with very disturbed people and not usable at all with the real schizophrenic or paranoid patient." (p. 51). For people to truly engage in the essential I-thou relationship and safely participate in highly charged and dynamic experiments, they must have a good measure of emotional health. Consequently, Gestalt therapy is not suitable for people in urgent crisis, those who are out of touch with reality, those who are not able to make true contact with another person, those who are unwilling to consider taking any responsibility for themselves and blame others for all their difficulties, and those who are very fragile. It is also not designed to help people who only want counseling for a specific problem such as an unrewarding job.

On the other hand, Gestalt therapy seems like a sound approach for many people who seek treatment because they realize they are not living their lives fully, feel detached and uninvolved, or feel so wrapped up in the pressures of daily life that they no longer have a sense of joy. These people may have been diagnosed with dysthymic disorder (a longstanding, moderately severe depression), generalized anxiety disorder (pervasive anxiety about many aspects of their lives), or mild dysfunctional personality patterns or traits. Gestalt therapy also seems well suited for people who channel their emotional concerns into their bodies. Such people might be diagnosed with somatoform disorders (often called psychosomatic illnesses) in which they report physical complaints that have no medical basis.

People with eating disorders including anorexia nervosa and bulimia nervosa also may benefit from Gestalt therapy. Angermann (1998) found that people with eating disorders tend to have distorted perceptions of their bodies; dichotomize themselves, perhaps separating mind and body; have problems with contact and boundaries in relationships; and be weighed down by unfinished business. Appropriate goals for people with eating disorders might include increasing awareness of both physical and emotional states, promoting integration of the self and self-image, bringing closure to unfinished business that is creating blocks to growth, and reducing barriers to making healthy contact with others in addition to changing eating habits.

An article by Alexander and Harman (1988) opens other possible applications. They used this approach to help middle school students deal with the suicide of a classmate. Although little has been written about the use of Gestalt therapy with children and adolescents, sensitive application of interventions by skilled clinicians might be very helpful. In addition, although Gestalt therapy is not generally designed to help people in crisis, Korb et al. (1989) believe that it is appropriate for brief therapy, especially in conjunction with a contract that narrows the focus of treatment. Its present orientation as well as Gestalt therapy's use of powerful experiments such as the empty chair can quickly bring all aspects of an issue into awareness and encourage closure as well as growth.

Diverse Client Groups

Because of its emphasis on the individual and the importance of adapting experiments and interventions to the particular person, Gestalt therapy can be used with a broad range of client groups. At the same time, some clients, particularly those from non-western cultures, may be uncomfortable with the confrontational nature of this approach as well as its attention to nonverbal aspects of communication. They also may be reluctant to engage in a collaborative relationship with the clinician, preferring to view the counselor as the expert. The Gestalt emphasis on dreams, fantasies, and symbols also may be foreign to many people and incompatible with their orientation to the world. Consequently, care should be taken when using Gestalt therapy to ensure that it is well received.

Gestalt therapy does seem especially well suited to some groups of clients. Enns (1987) suggested integrating Gestalt and feminist therapy (discussed in Chapter 14), believing that the Gestalt approach could be very useful in empowering women, promoting their self-awareness and establishment of healthy interpersonal boundaries, and facilitating their expression of denied or suppressed emotions. Livneh and Sherwood (1991) concluded that Gestalt therapy could be a rich source of help for people with disabilities, promoting their responsibility for themselves, self-awareness, and integration of the mind and the body. Certainly, many other useful applications can be found for this versatile approach to treatment.

Current Use

Although Gestalt therapy is no longer as popular as it was in the 1960s and 1970s, it seems to have firmly established its place among the important systems of counseling and psychotherapy. It has influenced and is often integrated with a broad range of other treatment systems, especially transactional analysis (Polster & Polster, 1993). In addition, Gestalt therapy itself has changed in recent years. Jacobs (1989) reported that Gestalt therapists have become even more aware of the importance of the client-clinician relationship and strive to establish a true I-thou relationship. At the same time, they have de-emphasized the importance of techniques, while the use of Gestalt therapy in encounter groups and workshop demonstrations has declined. Gestalt therapy continues to develop in the work of many individual practitioners and at Gestalt Institutes in Cleveland, San Diego, and Los Angeles as well as those in Israel, Canada, France, Chile, and other parts of the world. Although in a sense, Fritz Perls *was* Gestalt therapy during his lifetime, his ideas have attracted many followers and have lived on after his death.

EVALUATION OF GESTALT THERAPY

Like other treatment approaches, Gestalt therapy has both strengths and limitations. Because of its powerful nature, clinicians need to be particularly aware of its limitations and appropriate use.

Limitations

Saner (1989) did not believe that Gestalt therapy was universally or cross-culturally valid: "Is this focus on individual Gestalt formation an indication of theoretical choice or a general reflection of individualism so typical of white American middle class society?" (p. 58). Polster and Polster (1993) addressed other possible short-comings, expressing concern about the risk of oversimplification as well as neglecting important past concerns in the service of promoting immediacy. They also wondered if some clinicians are more concerned with replicating the charismatic style of Fritz Perls than finding their own way to use this approach and really understanding its underlying theory and philosophy. Gestalt therapy also runs the risk of overemphasizing emotions and ignoring cognitions, which in recent years have been found to be very important determinants of emotions and vehicles for modifying feelings.

In addition, Gestalt therapy tends to evoke strong emotional reactions. In one group therapy session, a woman in the hot seat became so anxious that she lost control of her bladder, which led her to experience great shame and social withdrawal. Thus, just as this approach has the power to do great good, it also has the power to do great harm. Its strategies are appealing and may seem deceptively simple but in reality require a skilled and experienced clinician who can determine their appropriate use, guide people through the treatment process, and protect them from harm. This seems more likely to happen if clinicians do not try to take on the powerful guru-like role embodied by Fritz Perls but temper that role with support, education, exploration of cognitions as well as emotions, and greater recognition of the importance of clients' culture and background. In addition, combining Gestalt techniques with those from other approaches, including feminist and cognitive behavioral therapy, can reduce the risk of overemphasizing emotions and create a less highly charged treatment environment.

Strengths

Despite these limitations, Gestalt therapy has many strengths. It is a philosophy of life, growth, and change and also provides specific ways in which to help people realize that growth. It respects the individual and seeks to adapt treatment to the needs of each person. Its emphasis on process and the client-clinician relationship are consistent with current understandings of how counseling and psychotherapy effect change. Gestalt therapy is a compassionate approach that seeks to empower people and enable them to have more joy and fulfillment in their lives.

Contributions

Gestalt therapy has certainly made many contributions to the fields of counseling and psychotherapy. The concepts of immediacy and wholeness as well as the importance of mind-body integration are particularly important and have been assimilated into other theoretical systems (Polster & Polster, 1993). Similarly, many innovative strategies, including the empty chair, the emphasis on nonverbal messages, Perls's approach to processing dreams in treatment, and I statements, have achieved wide acceptance in a broad range of mental health disciplines. In addition, the work of Gestalt therapists, along with that of the person-centered and existential theorists, established the importance of phenomenological, experiential, and humanistic approaches to treatment as well as the realization that the therapeutic alliance is probably our most important tool for change.

SKILL DEVELOPMENT: GESTALT DREAMWORK

People often bring dreams into their treatment sessions. They have a sense that the dreams are important but do not know how to make sense or meaning out of them. Theorists have suggested several approaches to using dreams in treatment. Freud emphasized the importance of the dream as a reflection of unconscious wishes and conflicts that need to be brought into consciousness. Jung wrote about the importance of identifying and using the archetypes and symbols in dreams (see Chapter 6). Perls dealt with dreams in a more present-oriented way, viewing them as projected aspects of the person.

Dreams are a powerful but complex vehicle of communication. They can be a fruitful source of information and can promote awareness, but dreamwork can also be harmful. Because dreams have a mystical quality, some people tend to place too much emphasis on dreams and their interpretation. They may even believe that dreams are prophetic. Consequently, clinicians should exercise great caution when helping people make sense of their dreams and be sure not to impose their own ideas or interpretations on the client.

The approach to dreamwork used by the Gestalt therapists seems less likely to cause harm or impose ideas on people than do more interpretative and analytical approaches. However, even in Gestalt dreamwork, clinicians should be supportive and guide the client through the process, making sure that no unfinished business remains to trouble the person. Many examples of dreamwork are included in *Gestalt Therapy Verbatim* (Perls, 1969a).

The following four steps reflect Gestalt dreamwork:

1. The person presents the dream, using the present tense in the narration. Recurrent or emotionally charged dreams seem particularly fruitful sources of information.
2. The elements of the dream are identified. Gaps or omissions may also be noted and may have meaning.
3. With the guidance of the clinician, the client assumes the roles of each element of the dream and speaks about the emotions and experiences of that element.
4. The clinician and the client work together to make sense of the dream in light of what is already known about the person, integrating the messages of the dream into the person's self-image and seeking to increase self-awareness.

The following is a brief illustration of the four steps of Gestalt dreamwork:

Step 1: Narration of dream

Client: I walk into my office, and I see that my desk is clear. All the papers are gone. And all the books on the shelf are different. Instead of my technical books, there are books on history and theater and art. I think that the housekeeper must have moved everything around.

Step 2: Identification of elements of the dream

Clinician: What are the elements in this dream?

Client: Well, I'm in the dream. Also my office, my desk, and the new books.

Clinician: You also refer to your technical books, which are no longer in the office, and the housekeeper who you believe has made the change.

Step 3: Becoming the elements of the dream

Clinician: Be the desk.

Client: I am the desk. I am a beautiful antique wooden partner desk. But usually no one can see how beautiful I am because I am covered with papers. Now I have no papers; I am empty.

Clinician: Empty?

Client: Yes, I know I am beautiful, but I feel exposed, unnatural. Somehow I like it better when I am covered with papers even though I look like a mess.

Clinician: Describe the way the desk looks.

Client: I have beautiful carvings. My finish is old but still shiny. I am wide and have space for two people even though only one person is using me now.

Clinician: Now be the new books.

Client: What are we doing here? We don't belong in this office. No one will ever read us here in this office. We have so much to offer, but we will never be appreciated.

Clinician: Now be the old books that are no longer on the shelf.

Client: We are tired and old and dog-eared. We have done our job well, but now we've just been stuffed away somewhere. No one will pay attention to us any more.

Clinician: I'd like you to repeat what you just said but use I instead of we.

Client: I am tired and old and dog-eared. I have done my job well, but now I've just been stuffed away somewhere. No one will pay attention to me any more.

Step 4: Making sense of the dream

Clinician: You are looking sad as you speak.

Client: Yes, I feel like those old books. You know, I have started to think about retiring, and I wonder if my life will have any meaning anymore. My whole life has been my work.

Clinician: I'd like you to be the beauty of the desk now.

Client: Yes, I am beautiful, but no one notices. I guess the housekeeper notices when she dusts. Maybe that's why she cleared me off. But I feel so exposed.

Clinician: Repeat that.

Client: I feel so exposed. I know that I have beauty; I have something to offer, but I have kept it hidden for so long. I am afraid to show who I am.

Clinician: So someone else has to do it for you?

Client: Yes, the housekeeper in the dream. But maybe I can do it for myself.

This dream seems to have brought into awareness polarities within this client, her identification with her intellectual side, and her alienation from her creative and physical aspects. She has also become aware of her reliance on others to bring out the neglected aspects of herself and begins to feel powerful enough to do that independently. Of course, this is just a beginning step in helping this person deal with her separation from important aspects of herself, but it is a powerful beginning that she seems to find useful.

CASE ILLUSTRATION

The following dialogue illustrates the use of the empty chair technique with Roberto. This is one of the most powerful and widely used of the Gestalt strategies.

Clinician: Roberto, you have talked about feeling like there is a split within you between your tough side and your caring side and how hard it is for you to express that caring side. I have set up two chairs here, one to represent your tough side and one to represent your caring side. I would like you to role-play each side of you while sitting in the chair that represents that side.

Roberto: All right. Well, I'll start out with the tough side. That's the easy one. I was the biggest bully on the block.

Clinician: Would you talk in the present?

Roberto: Okay. I am the biggest bully on the block. No one messes with me. I have quite a reputation. My father is very proud that I can take care of myself. I protect the younger kids too.

Clinician: Now change seats.

Roberto: Well, here I am, in the caring seat. I'm not sure what to say. I do care deeply about my family, Edie and Ava. I make sure they are safe, that we have enough money, that Ava goes to a good school. But they say that's not enough. I feel invisible. No one seems to see me and all that I do.

Clinician: What do you look like?

Roberto: I am small and weak.

Clinician: Continue to be the caring side and talk to the tough side in the empty chair.

Roberto: I really feel overshadowed by you. I try to let people know I'm here, but you're all they notice.

Clinician: Now change chairs and have the tough side talk to the caring side.

Roberto: I know you're there, but I want to keep you in my shadow. What will it do to my reputation if people see you? They won't think I'm the tough guy anymore.

Clinician: Change chairs and continue the conversation.

Roberto: Yes, I know your tough reputation is very important to you. But I'm important too. Without me, you don't get along very well with people. Edie gets mad at you, and Ava goes off and cries. You need me even if you don't know it. I don't want to be as big as you, but maybe you could let me grow a little bigger.

Clinician: How could the caring side grow?

Roberto: It . . . I could exercise. That's how the tough side got so big. Practice. If I could keep the tough guy from sitting on me every time I try to show my face.

Clinician: Can you tell him that?

Roberto: Yeah. Hey, tough guy, how about giving me a little space? I won't take over any of your turf. You don't

have to be afraid of me ruining your reputation. I have a great deal of respect for you. You worked hard to get where you are. Can you give a little guy a chance?

Clinician: Change chairs again and respond.

Roberto: Yeah, I guess I could do that. As long as we agree that I run the show, I'm in charge . . . at least for now.

Roberto clearly has a top dog and an underdog as well as a polarity within himself. His tough side has served him well, and he is identified strongly with that aspect of his personality; but he has all but cut himself off from his caring side. This dialogue has increased his awareness of these polarities and the negative impact his neglect of his caring side has had on his life. Although he continues to be apprehensive about revealing the caring side, he has made some movement toward integrating the two sides and allowing them to coexist. He has also begun to recognize that he does not need to choose between the two.

EXERCISES

Large-Group Exercises

1. You have now had the opportunity to learn about three approaches to counseling and psychotherapy that emphasize the importance of emotions and sensations. Discuss the similarities and differences among person-centered counseling, existential therapy, and Gestalt therapy. List them on the board and then discuss which approach is more appealing to you and which has more to offer clients.
2. Review the illustration of the use of the empty chair with Roberto. Using this dialogue as a starting point, discuss how a Gestalt therapist would continue to work with him. What blocks and impasses do you see in Roberto? From what you know about him, can you identify other polarities that he might be struggling with in addition to the tough/caring polarity? What unfinished business do you think he has? What do you imagine Roberto would look like if his body expressed his emotions? How would he sit? What would his eye contact be

like? Would he have characteristic gestures? Plan some experiments you might suggest to Roberto to promote his awareness and integration.

3. Look around you at your clothes, your books and other possessions, and the contents of the classroom. Pick an object with which you identify. Write down the object as well as a few I statements, speaking from the point of view of the object, such as "I am a chalk board. I am blank and impressionable. I have little character myself but am there to reflect the ideas of others." Have some volunteers share their objects and accompanying statements with the class.

Small-Group Exercises

1. Divide into your groups of four students in two dyads. Each dyad should have an opportunity to assume client and clinician roles and engage in a 10- to 15-minute exploration of a dream according to the above model in the "Skill Development" section. The clinician should try to use interventions that are characteristic of Gestalt therapy. As always, clients should take care of themselves. Clinicians should not confront, interpret, or pressure clients.

   Feedback should focus on the following areas:

   • Presentation and clarification of the dream
   • Use of questions and other interventions that reflect Gestalt therapy
   • Nonverbal messages of both client and clinician
   • Therapeutic alliance
   • Strengths of the role play
   • Ways in which the dialogue might have been improved

2. Each dyad should engage in an exercise using the empty chair technique. The person in the client role should identify an internal or external conflict that can be represented by two chairs. With the help of the person in the clinician role, the client should engage in a 10-minute dialogue between the two people or aspects that represent the conflict. Try to bring closure to the experience.

   Feedback following the exercise should focus on:

   • The effectiveness of the empty chair exercise
   • Use of questions and other interventions that reflect Gestalt therapy
   • How Gestalt therapy might help the client deal with the polarity that has been presented
   • Nonverbal messages of both client and clinician
   • Therapeutic alliance
   • Strengths of the role play
   • Ways in which the dialogue might have been improved

3. In the large group, ask for volunteers to lead the participants on a guided fantasy. Then divide the class into groups, with one volunteer for each group. Ideally, each group should have approximately six to eight participants. Allow

approximately 15 minutes for the guided fantasy and another 15 minutes for participants to share and process their reactions to the experience.

Individual Exercises

The individual exercises in this chapter are especially challenging. If you want to engage in these exercises but have difficulty doing so, you might seek some help from your professor, a counselor, or someone else you trust.

1. Observe your own body language, your eye contact, the way you sit, the way you use your hands, and any other body movements you display. What messages do they seem to give? What can you learn about yourself from your body language? Did you notice any incongruities between your verbal and your nonverbal messages? Think about whether your body language reflects any polarities or disowned parts of yourself. Write about this in your journal.
2. Write down a dream that you have had. Identify the parts of the dream. Write down what each element of the dream would say if it had a voice. What might you learn about yourself from this exercise?
3. Think about a criticism you recently made of someone else. Turn the statement around so that you apply it to yourself. For example, instead of saying, "My friend is a very irresponsible person," say "I am a very irresponsible person." Think about whether the new statement has any truth to it. Write about this in your journal.

SUMMARY

Fritz Perls developed Gestalt therapy in the 1950s. Like the other theories discussed in Part 3, it is humanistic and phenomenological and pays particular attention to emotions and sensations. The concept of Gestalt implies that patterns and wholes are important to people; and Gestalt therapists believe that we all have a natural drive toward integration, homeostasis, and actualization. However, people sometimes deny or become alienated from parts of themselves or their world. This can lead to fragmentation, an overload of unfinished business, and what Perls termed a growth disorder.

Gestalt therapy is an active approach that emphasizes the importance of a trusting, collaborative, I-thou relationship between client and clinician. The security offered by that relationship enables people to engage in growth-promoting experiments developed by the clinician to meet the needs of each client. Techniques such as dreamwork, the hot seat, the empty chair, the fantasy trip, the use of I statements, a focus on "what" and "how," and attention to nonverbal communication all help to move people toward the goals of Gestalt therapy, which include awareness, integration, and actualization.

For more information, readers can contact

The Center for Gestalt Development
P.O. Box 990
Highland, New York 12528
(914) 691-7192

The center publishes both a directory of Gestalt practitioners and the *Gestalt Journal*. It is also the headquarters of the Association for the Advancement of Gestalt Therapy, a membership organization for people interested in this approach to treatment.

RECOMMENDED READINGS

Korb, M. P., Gorrell, J., & Van de Riet, V. (1989). Gestalt therapy: Practice and theory (2nd ed.). New York: Pergamon.

Perls, F. (1969a). *Gestalt therapy verbatim.* Lafayette, CA: Real Person.

Perls, F. (1969b). *In and out of the garbage pail.* Lafayette, CA: Real Person.

Polster, E., & Polster, M. (1993). Fritz Perls: Legacy and invitation. *Gestalt Journal, 16*(2), 23–25.

Stephenson, F. D. (Ed.). (1975). *Gestalt therapy primer: Introductory readings in Gestalt therapy.* Springfield, IL: Thomas.

Chapter 14

EMERGING APPROACHES EMPHASIZING EMOTIONS AND SENSATIONS

As in all dynamic fields, new systems and strategies of counseling and psychotherapy continually emerge while established approaches undergo expansion and revision. This chapter, which concludes Part 3, introduces five emerging approaches that emphasize emotions and sensations: narrative therapy, constructivist therapy, feminist therapy, transpersonal therapy, and focusing-oriented therapy. At present, they are not fully developed treatment systems, and the literature does not provide substantial evidence of their successful use. However, they have a great deal to offer when used either on their own or in combination with other approaches. Over time, one or more of these approaches may well achieve the status of an established system of counseling and psychotherapy.

Selection of approaches included in this chapter (and in chapter 18, which focuses on emerging approaches emphasizing cognitions) was based on both a review of the recent literature and discussions with clinicians and academicians. Approaches were selected that showed promise of adding a new dimension or perspective on the treatment process and enhancing its effectiveness. Particular attention was given to strategies that are consistent with postmodern thinking about counseling and psychotherapy and are both holistic and sensitive to issues of diversity, individual difference, and people's multiple roles and perspectives.

NARRATIVE THERAPY

According to narrative therapy, people are interpretive beings who make meaning of their world through the language of their own stories and their understanding of those stories (Gottleib & Gottleib, 1996). This highly phenomenological approach takes the stand that people's views of themselves and their world come from the stories about their lives that they have made a part of themselves. Narrative theorists believe that through exploration, deconstruction, and revision of these stories, people can shift their perceptions, leading to greater empowerment and the ability to successfully manage their lives.

According to this approach, problems are manufactured in a social, cultural, and political context rather than being intrinsic to or inherent in the person (Monk, 1997). Consequently, narrative therapy can be useful not only to individuals but also to couples and families and can apply to a broad range of concerns.

The Development of Narrative Therapy

Unlike most of the approaches discussed so far, which have developed primarily in western Europe or the United States, narrative therapy has its roots in Australia in the work of Michael White and David Epston. However, clinicians and researchers throughout the world have shown interest in its application and study.

Important influences on the primary developers of narrative therapy include Gregory Bateson and Michael Foucault. Bateson suggested that to be able to detect and acquire new information, people must engage in a process of comparison in which they distinguish between one set of events or body of information and another

(Monk, 1997). Building on this concept, White discovered that by drawing people's attention to subtle changes in their lives, he could foster new insights, promote empowerment, and help people develop clearer and more effective ideas on how to resolve their difficulties.

Foucault's writing on the equation of knowledge and power led White to address the damaging effects of encouraging people to adjust and comply with stereotyped standards of behavior that could undermine their efforts to lead a life of their own design (Monk, 1997; White & Epston, 1989). White believed that only through knowledge could people truly be the authors of their own lives.

In several important ways, narrative therapy represents a departure from conventional counseling and psychotherapy. White has been described as a "therapeutic anthropologist" (Lee, 1997, p. 5) and refers to himself as a consultant. He does not seek to heal or fix people but to learn about them, understand them, and provide a different and helpful perspective. Narrative therapy has been characterized as *postmodern* because it perceives people as having many selves and promotes their liberation from constraining definitions (Parry & Doan, 1994). Another new perspective is narrative therapy's *constructivist* nature, which emphasizes the concept that our personal realities and self-images are not absolute but are created and maintained by our societies and ourselves. In a sense, narrative therapy has taken the phenomenological emphasis of the other treatment systems discussed in Part 3 one step further; not only do narrative therapists believe that people's perceptions determine their realities, but they believe that changing people's perceptions is the best route to facilitating their positive development.

Theories and Strategies

Lee (1997) has summarized this approach to treatment:

> The narrative perspective attempts to address the human dilemma of existence in a postmodern world by focusing on the linguistic and discursive ways that people construct their lives. It assumes that humans are interpretive beings in the phenomenological sense, active in the interpretation of everyday life and in the attribution of meaning through stories or self-narratives. (pp. 5–6)

In other words, narrative therapists believe that people's lives are created and interpreted through stories: the ones they hear, the ones they create in their own minds, and the ones they tell and retell. Consider the following example. Suki, a young woman from an Asian background, sought counseling because of her difficulty trusting others, her inability to form close relationships, and what she termed her "self-hatred" that led her to cut herself repeatedly. Suki's mother had told her the following story many times since Suki was a young child:

> When I became pregnant with you, I was living with your father. He was a terrible man. He beat me, he stayed with other women, and he took all the money I had. I wanted so badly to leave him. When I found out I was pregnant, I was devastated. I thought I would never be able to escape. So I went to a wise woman in the village and asked her to help me abort you. I did everything she told me, but it didn't work. I went back to her, and

she told me other things to do. I did everything again, but it still didn't work. Then I decided that this baby was meant to be. I packed up everything I could carry and ran away. I found my way to the home of my aunt, who took me in and helped me until you were born.

Hearing this story over and over again led Suki to adopt a negative view of herself and her world. She perceived herself as unwanted by both her father and her mother. She saw herself as a burden to her mother and viewed men as abusive and untrustworthy. She believed that she could only survive if she avoided closeness and intimacy with others; but at the same time, she viewed herself as unworthy of survival and thought that everyone would have been happier if the abortion had been successful. Her self-injurious behavior and her inability to trust others reflected the views of herself and the world that had grown out of the story her mother had told her so often. Although Suki's mother later married an American man who brought Suki and her mother to the United States and was a loving father to Suki, the story continued to have an impact. Clearly, stories give messages and are, in a sense, the road maps of our lives. Narrative therapy was used to help Suki change those messages and improve her life.

The Therapeutic Alliance   In narrative therapy, the clinician is a consultant in a partnership. Clients are the experts on themselves and their stories, while the clinician is the expert on narrative therapy. The two are co-authors, sharing the responsibility for shaping the treatment process (Winslade, Crocket, & Monk, 1997).

Narrative therapists place great emphasis on being respectful of clients' strengths. Although clinicians do share their own stories and perceptions, they assume a tentative stance, never prescribing or judging. Concepts such as resistance, denial, and mental disorders, which may give the clinician the upper hand, are not a part of narrative therapy. According to Monk (1997), "This way of working requires therapists to squarely face the moral and ethical implications of what it is they create in their interactions with their clients. They can no longer hide behind a 'truth-based theory' in accounting for their ethical behaviors." (p. 26)

Clinicians encourage and facilitate, help people appreciate themselves, and give them a sense of playing an important part in the therapeutic relationship. Clinicians use careful listening, reflection, summarization, and paraphrasing to help people listen to themselves in a new way, give them ownership over their right to create themselves, and hear themselves speak in ways that engender courage, hope, and resourcefulness (Winslade et al., 1997). All stories are accepted as legitimate and important. Only the clients have the right to make and accept changes to their stories, although clinicians often suggest alternative viewpoints and seek to elicit stories of power and resourcefulness.

Nature of the Stories   People have a large repertoire of stories that they carry with them. However, these stories tend to fall into several categories. Many people have a single dominant story that shapes who they are, as did Suki's story (Parry & Doan, 1994). This story typically acts as a sort of tyrant that censors and changes people's other stories and can send those stories into oblivion. These lost, unnoticed, or marginalized stories also need to be told and may serve the person better than the dominant story does, particularly if the lost stories present unique outcomes: portraying a life in which the presenting problems are either solved or absent. However, what White (1986) called *specifications of personhood*—the information in the stories that tells people how to behave as individuals or family members—act as restraints and keep people stuck inside and limited by their dominant stories.

For example, Suki's stepfather told her stories about how she used to make up poems when she was a young child and how much he enjoyed reading her poems. However, as long as her single dominant story was in control, Suki paid little attention to the stories her stepfather told her, which reflected appreciation for her intelligence and creativity. Accessing that neglected story and others helped Suki value herself and use her intelligence and creativity to relate more successfully to others.

Eliciting Stories   People produce many stories spontaneously and typically enjoy telling stories. However, those stories that support the dominant theme are usually the ones that are closest to the surface and most accessible. Narrative therapists have some strategies they can use to encourage people to tell a wider variety of stories (Carr, 1998):

- They may ask people to tell alternative stories about a single event or emotion.
- They may suggest that people create a story as if they were another person or had assumed a different perspective.
- They may suggest that people extend their stories into the future.
- They may ask people to tell stories in which they are more powerful than their problems.

Deconstruction of Stories   Before stories can be changed, they must be taken apart, analyzed, and understood. Narrative therapists use several strategies to accomplish this, with their goals being to identify themes and metaphors that are prominent in the stories, enable people to recognize the influence the stories have had on them, and help people see that they did not totally create their stories themselves.

White (1992) speaks of landscapes of consciousness and landscapes of action. *Landscapes of consciousness* are the backdrops of values, feelings, motives, beliefs, and attitudes that recur in a person's stories. *Landscapes of action* are the sequences of behaviors related to events in people's lives that similarly pervade and keep appearing in a person's stories. Questions help people identify, reflect on, determine the meaning of, and perhaps effect changes in these landscapes. In Suki's stories, the landscapes of consciousness generally reflected hopelessness, sorrow, and pain. People in her stories usually experienced rejection and loss. In the landscape of action, Suki was usually withdrawn and ineffectual.

Mapping is another approach designed to help people reflect on their stories. Clients' presenting problems are identified and linked to their stories, illustrating how their problems emerge and are handled in the stories.

Externalizing is the process of creating a separation between people and their stories and problems. Problems are discussed as problems rather than the people being viewed as problems. Instead of saying, "I am unable to have close relationships," a person might be encouraged to say, "Developing close relationships is a problem I have struggled with in my life." Externalization is facilitated by helping people identify the threads connecting many stories and the assumptions they suggest about the self and the world. Once externalization occurs, access points for changing the story can be identified.

This process of externalization seems to conflict with the emphasis of the Gestalt therapists on the importance of helping people own and take responsibility for their difficulties. However, narrative therapists believe that the process of externalizing and objectifying problems reduces feelings of failure and self-blame, decreases unproductive discussion about who is at fault for the problem, allows people to view their difficulties in new ways, reduces blocks to action and change, and opens the way for people to reclaim their lives from their problems (White, 1988–1989). Instead of believing they are the problem, people can mobilize their resources to combat the problem, which is now separate from who they are. They can establish a new perspective on their problems and themselves, seeing themselves as competent and powerful people who have some problems that need to be addressed rather than people who are problem-ridden and flawed.

Revisioning and Reauthoring Once the stories have been told and deconstruction has begun, the stories can be modified, or revisioned. Revisioning refers to both changing the story and changing people's visions of their lives. The two are inseparable; as people come to see more clearly the rules and meanings that govern the old stories, their vision changes, a new interpretation of their lives emerges, and the stories can be revisioned. As revisioning proceeds, it provides opportunities for further deconstruction, which in turn allows for more story revisioning. Gradually, alternative stories that offer exceptions to the dominant story emerge, and other perspectives become available for incorporation into the stories. White (1989) referred to this as the *insurrection of subjugated knowledge.*

Reauthoring can now take place. Possibilities for thoughts, actions, and emotions are expanded as therapists and clients share new descriptions of old stories (Gottlieb & Gottlieb, 1996). People have come to understand their meaning constructions and can move toward a more productive version of their self-narratives in terms of their feelings about themselves and their relationships with others (Lee, 1997).

Through revisioning and reauthoring, people can develop alternative and preferred self-narratives extending into the future, in which the self is viewed as more powerful than the problem (Carr, 1998; White, 1995). People are now ready to solidify their gains and share them with others.

Therapeutic Documents Therapeutic documents are materials generally prepared by the clinician in collaboration with the client to reinforce and provide evidence of accomplishments. Both client and clinician decide on the form for the documents, how they should be prepared, when and how they should be consulted, and with whom they should be shared (Carr, 1998). The documents may take the form of literary productions such as personal letters, lists, reports, certificates and awards, news releases, personal declarations, letters of reference, or manifestos that articulate people's problems, contradict the dominant plots of their lives, and suggest ways for them to deal with these problems (White & Epston, 1990). An exchange of letters between client and clinician is another form of documentation; these may be used to promote clients' reflection and to put their ideas and alternatives into a concrete form that can be retained as a resource.

Importance of the Social Network   Narrative therapists are very aware of the importance of people's social and cultural contexts and incorporate them into treatment in several ways. Of course, the origins of many stories lie in people's social systems. Stories may be passed from one person to another, shaped along the way, and come to people as a legacy from their families. Clients are encouraged to recognize the family origins of some of their stories and to find people in their social and family networks who have similar experiences and problems. Drawing on those relationships and learning about ways in which other people have addressed similar problems can provide support, resources, and education about problem solving.

Because of the importance of people's social systems in creating and forming their stories, narrative therapists also make use of social systems to promote and solidify people's revisioned stories. Clients may be encouraged to tell their new stories to an outsider witness group composed of significant members of their social system who are chosen to hear and witness the new self-narrative (Carr, 1998). This public declaration helps solidify changes and puts others on notice to expect people to reauthor their lives.

Clinicians practicing narrative therapy also view it as important to encourage clients to share their learning with others. In what has been called the bringing-it-back process, people are encouraged to prepare a written account of their new knowledge and behaviors to share with future clients who have similar difficulties. The authors of the written accounts are then invited in person to share the narratives of how they solved their problems (Carr, 1998). These innovative procedures not only help the new clients but solidify and reinforce the gains of those who have made progress through treatment.

Current Status

Narrative therapy views human problems as arising from and being maintained by oppressive stories that dominate people's lives. Therapists using this approach seek to develop a deep understanding of people through their stories and enable them to reauthor their stories as well as their lives. A collaborative client-clinician relationship, the empowering of the client, and the use of the social network are all essential in this approach.

Because the approach is not focused on specific types of problems and is deeply respectful of people's ownership of their own lives, it can be useful with a broad range of clients and concerns. For example, narrative therapy has been used successfully with delinquency, bullying, and other conduct problems in children; with people coping with eating disorders; for addressing marital conflict; with survivors of childhood abuse; for people coping with grief; and for people diagnosed with schizophrenia (Carr, 1998).

A description of the use of this approach in treating people who misuse alcohol makes clear its distinctive characteristics (Winslade & Smith, 1997). Rather than accept the stance of Alcoholics Anonymous and have people internalize their problem ("I am an alcoholic"), clinicians help them to externalize the problem, give it a name (Al), and then divorce him. In this way, people separate themselves from a close identification with alcohol and are in a better position to combat its influence. In addition, rather than assuming the role of expert and teaching people skills to change their behaviors, clinicians help clients discover and use the knowledge they already have about ways to deal with the problems alcohol has brought into their lives. By using their own resources, creating new stories, and making better use of relationships, people are helped to make changes and overcome their problems.

Narrative therapy seems particularly well suited for the treatment of people who have been victimized and disenfranchised by others, such as women, the elderly, and individuals from some ethnic and cultural groups (Drauker, 1998; Kropf & Tandy, 1998; Lee, 1997). Drauker (1998) wrote about using narrative therapy with abused women: "A therapy that challenges sociopolitical conditions that contribute to violence, highlights women's personal insurrections against these conditions, and supports the reauthoring of their life stories should be considered as a potentially useful approach for women who have been victimized throughout their lives" (p. 168) Similarly, when used with older people, narrative therapy can be positive and life-affirming, transforming stories that are based on loss and worthlessness into those that reflect a rich and full life. Narrative therapy can also provide a respectful way to understand people from diverse cultural backgrounds, giving them the opportunity to tell the stories of their lives and revision those stories in ways that give them greater power and control but also are consistent with the values and beliefs of their cultures.

Although narrative therapy clearly has value for a broad range of people, clinicians must still take care when applying the approach. It may be unsuitable for people who are not able to engage in a coherent conversation because of their poor contact with reality, for those who are seeking a quick solution to a specific problem or are in crisis, and for those who anticipate receiving little benefit from treatment. In short, like all approaches to counseling and psychotherapy, narrative therapy has limitations but does offer a new perspective on the treatment process as well as considerable promise.

CONSTRUCTIVIST PSYCHOTHERAPY

Constructivist psychotherapy (or constructivism) and feminist therapy, discussed next, bear considerable similarity to narrative therapy. Some theorists consider narrative therapy a form of constructivist therapy.

Although both constructivist therapy and feminist therapy attend to thoughts and behaviors as well as emotions, they are discussed in Part 3 of this book because they are strongly phenomenological and experiential. Like narrative therapy, both constructive therapy and feminist therapy focus on people's perceptions of themselves and their worlds. These approaches adopt the postmodern assumption that there is no such thing as universal, objective knowledge and that our perceptions reflect the language, values, and beliefs of our particular community or social system. Both are holistic and seek to understand people fully and from many perspectives.

The Development of Constructivism

George Kelly (1955) was the first to write about the principles of constructivism in *The Psychology of Constructs*. He suggested that people have a system of constructs and symbols that reflect their views of themselves and their world. His book proposed ways to elicit and modify the content and structure of those constructs. Kelly's work, discussed further in Chapter 16, emphasized cognitions. However, his work has been expanded by modern constructivist theorists.

Today, Robert Neimeyer and Michael Mahoney are the names most strongly associated with constructivism. Both have contributed to the development of constructivist theory and its use as an approach to psychotherapy.

Theories and Strategies

According to Mahoney (1988a), "Constructivist theories recognize that psychological realities are inherently private, even when they are shared collectively, and that the forum of psychological change lies in the domain of those dynamic processes referred to as the self" (p. 9). He further stated, "Psychological construction refers to a family of theories that share the assertion that human knowledge and experience entail the (pro)active participation of the individual" (p. 2).

This is reminiscent of the classic tale of the blind men encountering an elephant. Each touched a different part of the elephant and so described the elephant in a different way. Their perceptions of the elephant were colored not only by their direct and limited contact with the elephant but by their own life experiences and interactions, which gave them the language and comparisons they used to help them understand what the elephant was like.

We, too, have a reciprocal relationship with our world. We bring our past perceptions and experiences with us as we encounter and assess new experiences; those assessments, in turn, affect the nature of the new experiences and of our own development and sense of self. A key concept in constructivist therapy is that personal identity is socially constructed.

For example, Suki, discussed previously in this chapter, viewed people as untrustworthy and aloof and herself as having little to offer. This led her to avoid contact with others and, in turn, contributed to their lack of interest in her. When she began college, she felt out of place and excluded by the other students, not recognizing the part that her construction of the world played in determining her isolation.

View of Problems   Constructivist clinicians view problems as an expression of a discrepancy between people's adaptive capacities and the current demands of their environment (Mahoney, 1988b). Adaptive capacities that developed in response to prior challenges may not have the flexibility or characteristics people need to cope with current situations and so need to be modified.

Therapeutic Alliance The therapeutic alliance in constructivist treatment is a strongly collaborative one. As Mahoney (1988b) stated, "Constructivist psychotherapy is a very intimate and personalized exchange between human beings" (p. 308). Client and clinician differ only in terms of roles and training. In treatment, both embark on an exploration. Clinicians do not direct the process or seek to persuade, analyze, or instruct. Rather, they use reflection, elaboration, and metaphor to advance a process. They are coinvestigators, helping people "construct more coherent and comprehensive self-theories or as coauthors assisting clients in the identification and revision of central themes in their personal narratives" (Neimeyer, 1993, p. 230).

Process of Treatment Constructivism views people in positive and optimistic terms, seeing them as "pro-active, goal-directed, and purposive organisms" (Neimeyer, 1993a, p. 223). People operate according to the knowledge they possess, which reflects their construction of their experiences and actions. Knowledge is evolutionary and changes with new experiences and shifts in perception. A central goal of constructivist treatment is to help people develop possibilities, to recognize that experiences have a variety of alternative meanings and interpretations. People's knowledge can then be assessed and either changed or validated, leading to knowledge that allows more satisfying ways of being.

Treatment initially begins with a focus on current problems and distress, then shifts to an exploration of patterns or recurrent difficulties, and finally moves to an understanding of underlying processes or constructions that contribute to the perpetuation of patterns. Both successful and unsuccessful ways to address problems provide useful information that can guide people to develop more rewarding ways of being and coping.

Constructivist approaches to clinical practice situate the self in the social context (Neimeyer, 1993a) and take the perspective that people can only be understood and helped if attention is paid to that context. Constructivist therapists draw on many other treatment systems to advance their efforts to really get to know their clients and promote clients' self-awareness. Constructivist clinicians pay considerably more attention to background than do other treatment systems discussed in Part 3 of this book and believe that early attachment plays an important part in shaping who we are. They also attend to thoughts and actions as well as emotions to help people achieve a sense of integration (Mahoney, 1988a).

Everything that people bring with them is construed as reflecting who they are and providing information on how people are managing their lives. Both positive and negative emotions, for example, are viewed as people's efforts to make meaning out of their experiences and as something to work with rather than against. Resistance is similarly viewed as an understandable form of self-protection.

Language is an important focus in constructivism; it is through language that people make meaning. As Lynch (1997) stated, language not only labels human experience; it forms it.

Constructivist treatment is viewed as more creative than corrective. It seeks to help people change what Neimeyer (1993b) called their core ordering processes, which operate at primarily unconscious levels and shape their emotions, perceptions, thoughts, and actions. However, because these core ordering processes are difficult to access, the focus of treatment is on exploring people's subjective reconstructions of their lives.

Current Status

Constructivist therapy has captured the attention of many clinicians because of its compatibility with modern clinical thought. It appreciates the importance of the individual in society, diversity, and the client-clinician collaboration. It is respectful and optimistic, viewing people's efforts to cope as sources of knowledge that can be used to promote positive change. It is holistic and flexible.

Although research is still limited on the effectiveness of this relatively new approach, constructivism is being applied to a wide range of concerns and settings. It is being used in schools to promote active, social, and creative learning (Perkins, 1999). It has been adapted for use with couples and families (Neimeyer & Neimeyer, 1994). It has also been used to treat a broad range of problems and mental disorders, including attention-deficit disorder, posttraumatic stress disorder, and grief (Neimeyer & Stewart, 1996). The *Journal of Constructivist Psychology* has been developed to promote and disseminate the rapidly expanding research on this approach to treatment.

FEMINIST THERAPY

Feminist therapy was originally developed by Helene Deutsch, Karen Horney (discussed in Chapter 7), and other psychodynamic and developmental theorists in reaction to what they perceived as Freud's lack of understanding of women. Feminist therapy seeks to acknowledge and counteract women's limited and often inferior roles and to broaden and legitimize women's perspectives. However, as this approach has evolved, it has recognized that both genders are harmed when they are constrained by narrow and hierarchical roles and relationships. Despite its name, feminist therapy has the potential to help both men and women change themselves and their societies and act together to make a difference (Forcey & Nash, 1998).

Underlying Concepts

Feminist therapy has been strongly influenced by humanistic and phenomenological approaches as well as by cognitive therapy and existentialism. Like constructivism, it postulates that the external and internal worlds of women, the subjective and objective, are interconnected and that both must be part of the therapeutic process (Day, 1992).

Many feminist therapists view women as oppressed by their culture. According to Vindhya (1995), cultures that are patriarchal in nature identify "masculinity with values associated with individualism—like self-sufficiency, competition, separation—

while femininity is identified with community—affective relations of care, mutual aid, cooperation" (p. 75). Such cultures typically value masculine characteristics over the feminine ones and view women as secondary to men.

Feminist therapy seeks to help women value their traditional roles while deconstructing the discriminatory aspects of their societies and recognizing that they need not be limited to the roles of mother, wife, and caregiver or have an identity that is restricted to the spiritual, nurturing, and emotional (Lewis, 1992). This approach emphasizes the here and now and the importance of self-actualization and both individual and group empowerment. It promotes women's efforts to construct language, stories, and symbols drawn from their own experiences that strengthen and expand possibilities. It stresses the importance of relationships that respect diversity and that are nonhierarchical. Inclusiveness and plurality rather than discrimination are advocated. Particular attention is paid to the unique roles of women such as motherhood and the mother-daughter bond in a way that recognizes their great value and also gives women the message that biology need not be destiny, that they can be the architects of their lives (Lewis, 1992). This approach seeks to give women a shared view of their social position and a sense of community with other women while affording them greater power as well as new possibilities and ways of seeking knowledge.

Current Status

Feminist therapy has considerable potential for both good and harm. Narrowly construed or misperceived, it can contribute to anger and distance between the genders. However, if the true message rather than the name of this approach is emphasized, its value to both genders becomes evident. This is an approach that is growing in importance because of its emphasis on the human potential and people's ability and right to make choices that will enable them to live their lives in rewarding ways.

The current literature on feminist therapy has emphasized the application of this approach to special populations, including African American and Chicana women and adolescent girls. Research on the interface of gender-related perspectives and those growing out of age and cultural background should contribute greatly to our understanding of diversity and our ability to help a wide range of people feel more successful and self-actualized. Like narrative therapy and constructivist therapy, feminist therapy has made an important contribution to our thinking and is expected to continue to advance our knowledge of human development, knowledge, and growth.

TRANSPERSONAL THERAPY

Transpersonal psychotherapy represents an effort to integrate western and eastern approaches to personal growth and change (Holden, 1993). With its emphasis on spirituality and transcendence, it has been characterized as a fourth force in psychology, with the first three being psychoanalysis, behaviorism, and humanism. Many see this approach as particularly well suited to addressing today's problems of violence, addiction, and alienation, which may reflect spiritual impoverishment, lack of purpose and meaning, and a failure to recognize the interconnection of all living beings (Cowley, 1993). We consider transpersonal psychotherapy here because of its connection to humanism, its emphasis on experiences and sensations, and its phenomenological stance.

The People Who Developed Transpersonal Therapy

Many names are associated with the development of this approach. Carl Jung (discussed in Chapter 6) is its philosophical parent, while Abraham Maslow is credited with originating transpersonal psychology in the United States (J. M. Holden, personal communication, October 22, 1999). Maslow (1971) hypothesized that people have a hierarchy of needs that include, in sequence, physiological needs, safety, belonging, self-esteem, self-actualization, and transcendent self-actualization. Lower-order needs must be met before people can direct their efforts toward achievement of higher-order needs. Maslow's work initially focused on promoting people's efforts to achieve self-actualization. However, he later came to believe that a step beyond self-actualization existed: transcendent self-actualization. He also concluded that peak or transcendent experiences were instrumental in enabling people to move toward this state. A central goal of transpersonal psychotherapy is helping people achieve a higher state of consciousness, which for Maslow was transcendent self-actualization.

Roberto Assagioli (1965, 1991), an Italian contemporary of Freud, was one of the early theoreticians in transpersonal psychology, which he called psychosynthesis. Assagioli believed that people have seven levels of consciousness:

1. The lower unconscious, including fundamental drives and urges as well as dreams and repressed material
2. The middle unconscious, including readily accessible unconscious material
3. The higher unconscious or superconscious, including inspiration and higher feelings such as altruism
4. The field of consciousness, or material in awareness
5. The conscious self, or awareness of ourselves
6. The higher self, which is a sort of synthesizing center
7. The collective unconscious, similar to that described by Jung

Wilber (1996, 1999), an important modern theoretician in transpersonal psychology, believed that human development involved a progression through three successive stages toward increasing differentiation and transcendence:

1. The prepersonal or pre-egoic stage characterizes newborn and young children who are in the process of developing a sense of themselves. Adults still at the prepersonal level have not developed a strong sense of self. An example is people diagnosed with borderline personality disorders.

2. The personal or egoic stage characterizes the years from late childhood through adulthood and is as far as most people develop. In this stage, the self is based in rationality and functions reasonably well in the world but does not reflect higher states of consciousness.

3. The transpersonal or transegoic stage, beyond the personal or the ego, unfolds in later adulthood, if at all. It is characterized by expanded consciousness that includes the transpersonal experiential domain, which provides depth and richness to people's lives. People in this stage can make use of transrational processes involving intuition and mystical and paranormal experiences.

These stages are considered sequential; people cannot successfully skip a stage. In fact, if people immerse themselves in the transpersonal domain before having a well-developed ego, psychopathology results (J. M. Holden, personal communication, October 22, 1999).

Janice Miner Holden (1993, 1996) also has made an important contribution to transpersonal theory. Her work operationalizes transpersonal psychology and offers useful guidelines to clinicians using this theory.

Important Theoretical Concepts

According to Atwood and Maltin (1991),

> [transpersonal psychotherapy] creates psychological health, which is defined as the ability to live in harmony with oneself and nature, to understand one's relationship to the universe, to show tolerance and compassion to one's fellow human beings, to endure hardship and suffering without mental disintegration, to prize nonviolence, to care for the welfare of all sentient beings, and to see a meaning and purpose in one's life that allows one to enter old age or to face death with serenity and without fear. (p. 374)

Transpersonal psychology assumes that all people have the potential to transcend the usual limitations of the ego and attain higher levels of consciousness that will give much greater meaning and fulfillment to their lives.

Assumptions

The following assumptions characterize transpersonal therapy (Tart, 1992):

- The universe has a purpose.
- People are more than their physical being.
- People are part of and interdependent with the rest of the world. All beings are interrelated.
- People have a function or purpose.
- People are here to understand and fulfill their place in the universe, not to make the universe fit them.
- People have the potential for higher levels of awareness but generally have not realized this potential.
- To grow, people must question and modify.
- Both rational and experiential knowledge are important.
- Intuition is a powerful cognitive faculty and can be developed.
- Spiritual growth is an essential need for everyone.

The Process of Change

Transpersonal theorists emphasize the value of integrating transpersonal concepts and approaches into the entire range of more traditional approaches to counseling and psychotherapy, although transpersonal therapy seems to differ from traditional treatment in many respects. Conventional treatment systems emphasize the importance of striving to make the unconscious conscious, controlling our thoughts, strengthening the ego, and working toward clear goals. Transpersonal theorists, on the other hand, believe that, once realized, goals need to be transcended; that people need first to develop strong egos and then detach from them, thereby losing their self-centeredness and feeling more connected to the universe.

Despite these apparent inconsistencies, the transpersonal approach does not challenge the assumptions of more traditional approaches. In fact, it embraces those assumptions as completely relevant at the pre-egoic and egoic levels. The transpersonal approach asserts, however, that another level of experience and functioning exists beyond the egoic level. Rather than saying no to the pre-egoic and egoic domains, the transpersonal approach says, "yes, and there's more" (J. M. Holden, personal communication, October 22, 1999).

Transpersonal theory suggests shifts in orientation that can facilitate movement toward a higher level of experience and functioning. After reasonable success with seeking power, we need to be open to experience. After achieving the capacity for clear and logical thinking, we need to be open to intuition and spontaneity. After developing our capacity to modify and direct our feelings, we need to feel and experience them. In an apparent paradox, transpersonal theory holds that only by letting go of power and control and abandoning our driven and goal-directed ways can we achieve more responsibility for our lives as we move toward higher levels of consciousness and fulfillment.

Feelings are viewed as important in transpersonal therapy, as they are in other humanistic theories. Transpersonal theorists believe that both positive and negative feelings are valuable and should be recognized and accepted (Atwood & Maltin, 1991). They also perceive people as responsible for both their behaviors and their emotions (J. M. Holden, personal communication, October 22, 1999).

Learning and change come from present experiences. Of greatest importance are experiences of altered states of consciousness that involve a sense that we are transcending our usual boundaries. Holden (1996) offered the following description of these experiences: "Transpersonal experience is a spontaneous, transient experience involving perception or action that *transcends* the ego boundaries of space and/or time, and which is, paradoxically, perceived as authentic or potentially authentic by the experiencer's ego with consensus reality intact" (p. 7).

For most people, transpersonal experiences are hard to explain and just seem to happen, although they can be facilitated by a variety of circumstances. There are two categories of transpersonal experience: mystical experiences, involving a sense of other-worldliness and higher consciousness; and paranormal experiences—meaningful, inexplicable experiences involving the everyday world, such as predicting events accurately and gaining information about people from objects (Holden, 1996).

Transpersonal experiences such as these give people access to their higher selves and their deepest resources of creativity as well as to reality that goes beyond human knowledge. Insight, intuition, and sudden awareness are important aspects of these experiences and often lead to a paradigm shift or a new way of viewing the world. Mystical experiences, for example, are typically characterized by positive emotions such as joy, love, and peace; convey a sense of unity and spirituality; and often lead to positive changes in attitude and self-image.

Blocks to Development

Holden (1993) identified four impediments to people's personal and transpersonal development that keep the higher self "repressed or undeveloped" and prevent people from having transcendent experiences (p. 8). She refers to these as the four *I*s:

1. Innate (genetic/physiological) factors
2. Cognitive immaturity
3. Inexperience limiting knowledge of options
4. Impotence (internal and external constraints on access to options)

The four *I*s are reflected in a person's style of adaptation. They need to be assessed and addressed in treatment to alleviate blocks to growth. In addition, Holden recommends assessing people's physical, interpersonal, intrapersonal, and transpersonal realms. By *transpersonal*, she refers to people's sense of connectedness to a higher power either within themselves or outside themselves.

Treatment

Like existential therapy, transpersonal psychotherapy is more a philosophy than a set of interventions. However, writings since 1990 place greater emphasis on application and do provide many useful guidelines.

Goals Transpersonal psychotherapy seeks to promote people's spiritual development. According to Cowley (1993), "Prime concerns . . . are the search for ultimate values, peak or mystical experiences, and unitive consciousness and the legitimation of spiritual practices" (p. 527). Goals include increased feelings of self-worth and self-acceptance, a greater sense of spirituality and hope, increased appreciation of life and caring for others, a decrease in materialism, more inner-directedness, a greater sense of meaning, and increased knowledge and feelings of freedom. Through this approach, people are helped to lose their self-centeredness and develop "global awareness, a knowledge of one's place in the universe" (Atwood & Maltin, 1991, p. 372), in order to develop the "ability to live in harmony with oneself and nature" (p. 374). People can resolve past pain, anger, and disappointment and replace them with peace and harmony. They can achieve spiritual awareness and enlightenment, a transcendence of the self, and an appreciation of the unity of all things.

Therapeutic Alliance   The process of change associated with transpersonal psychotherapy can be disconcerting and even painful because it involves movement into new and unfamiliar areas. People may experience disorientation and disintegration (Holden, 1993). Because transpersonal treatment can be a challenging process, the role of the clinician and the therapeutic alliance are very important.

The core conditions of empathy, genuineness, respect, and caring (described in Chapter 11) are essential in the transpersonal clinician. Creation of a safe therapeutic environment is also important. As with the other approaches in Part 3, collaboration between client and clinician is integral to treatment. Both clinicians and clients are expected to learn and develop from this process.

Clinicians are viewed as more advanced students of enlightenment—educating, facilitating, offering help, and guiding clients but never directing, forcing, or imposing. Their role is to facilitate transpersonal experience and enhance the benefits of that experience. They are carriers and agents, not sources of enlightenment. This approach encourages clinician self-disclosure: these clinicians often choose to share their own transpersonal experiences. However, whether or not to self-disclose is up to each clinician.

Because transpersonal therapy is a challenging process, clinicians should be experienced and have sound training in the established approaches to treatment. In addition, clinicians using this approach should have undergone considerable personal and spiritual development (Holden, 1993). If at all possible, they should have experienced transpersonal techniques themselves before suggesting them to their clients.

Interventions   According to Holden (1993), "Transcendence can occur through the sensory modality of new experience. . . .this results in disintegration of the old pattern and reintegration of a new, more inclusive and gratifying one" (p. 15). People in transpersonal therapy typically need "some sort of psychological or contemplative practice that will provide the practitioner with direct experience of transpersonal phenomena," an altered state of consciousness (Walsh, 1992, p. 41). Interventions also seek to develop in people qualities that are necessary to deepen awareness, including patience, a nonjudgmental attitude, acceptance of things as they are, and comfort with ambiguity (Atwood & Maltin, 1991).

Holden (1996) described four broad approaches to transcendental treatment, which are especially useful for helping people address spiritual concerns and issues. The overall purpose of these approaches is to help clients stay in touch with spiritual material without being overwhelmed by it so that they can experience and integrate its benefits.

1. *Grounding* is used if clients' functioning is diminished because they are overwhelmed by their spiritual experiences. It is a way to narrow people's focus of attention to outer reality only. Grounding can be accomplished through physical exercise, problem solving, concentration on daily tasks and activities, and focusing (discussed later in this chapter).

2. *Centering* helps people derive benefits from spiritual experiences or material. It brings attention to inner reality while maintaining outer awareness. Techniques

for centering include deep breathing, physical relaxation, quieting exercises, biofeedback, yoga, meditation, massage, and focusing.

3. *Opening* reduces concentration on both outer and inner reality to help people attend to spontaneous and emerging inner experiences—to facilitate a "passive surrender of deliberate thought" (Holden, 1996, p. 20). Techniques include trance induction and transpersonal methods such as meditation, guided imagery, hypnosis, Reiki and other energy methods, biofeedback, and focusing.

4. *Processing* integrates both inner and outer spiritual experiences into the ego using focusing as well as therapeutic dialogue.

Many other techniques can also can be productively incorporated into transpersonal psychotherapy. They include writing down dreams and transpersonal experiences in a journal, writing a spiritual autobiography, Rolfing and other approaches to body work, and a day of complete silence.

Meditation   Meditation is the intervention most associated with transpersonal therapy and has received most attention and study. Meditation has been described as voluntary redirection and self-control of attention. It "may promote inner calm, loving kindness toward oneself and others, access to previously unconscious material, transformative insight into emotional conflicts, and changes in the experience of personal identity" and can enhance concentration, memory, and coping (Bogart, 1991, p. 383).

Meditation typically is preceded by 5–10 minutes of preparation that might include muscle relaxation, stretching, deep breathing, and scanning the body for strong sensations. Then "the instructions for meditation can be put very simply: Calmly attend to a simple stimulus. After every distraction, calmly return your attention—again and again and again" (Smith, 1986, p. 67). The focus of attention might include a relaxing sound or word, a visual image such as a candle or a picture of a child, the process of breathing deeply and slowly, or a repetitive movement such as walking.

Many types of meditation have been developed. Probably the best known is transcendental meditation (TM). Research has shown that TM can promote improvement in variables such as affective maturity, integrative perspective of self and world, resilient sense of self, and inner-directedness (Alexander, Rainforth, & Gelderloos, 1991, p. 191).

Another type of meditation is mindful meditation, which involves being in the present moment as much as possible—concentrating one's full, undivided attention on the details of everyday life. In mindfulness, "attention is focused upon registering feelings, thoughts, and sensations exactly as they occur, without elaboration, preference, selection, comments, censorship, judgment, or interpretation" (Holden, 1993, p. 384).

Application

Because this is one of the newer approaches to psychotherapy, information on the appropriate use of transpersonal therapy is still emerging. However, some tentative conclusions can be drawn.

Appropriate Clients   When people come to counseling with inadequate functioning that reflects pre-egoic or egoic stages of development, more traditional treatment approaches should be used (J. M. Holden, personal communication, October 22, 1999). Transpersonal therapy seems particularly well suited to people with spiritual concerns or goals (Cowley, 1993). They might include people who feel a lack of direction or meaning in their lives, those whose current spiritual practices are unsatisfying, those who believe that their lives will be enhanced by experiences that go beyond their own awareness of reality, those who have had spontaneous transpersonal experiences that do not fit into their existing world view, and those who feel that life must have more to offer them.

Because transpersonal therapy is a flexible approach that can be tailored to meet the needs of the individual and because transpersonal clinicians do not coerce people to change, this approach is suitable for a broad range of people. Its emphasis on the spiritual dimension may appeal to people from many cultural groups who may be uncomfortable with more traditional approaches to treatment that focus on exploring the past and disclosing thoughts and feelings but neglect the importance of spirituality.

At the same time, transpersonal therapy is a powerful approach that can create chaos in people's former views of themselves and their world. It also can precipitate a spiritual crisis and can expose people to experiences that are confusing and disconcerting. Consequently, this approach should be used only with relatively healthy and well-functioning people who have well-developed egos and can tolerate ambiguity and address the profound questions and experiences that may arise. This treatment system does not seem appropriate for people who lack a sound grasp on reality, are looking for magical solutions to all their problems, or are very fragile or suicidal. Just as this approach seems more suited for use by advanced clinicians, so it seems best for clients who already have experienced considerable growth and development, are managing their lives relatively well, but are now ready to take the growth process to a higher level.

Current Status   Although few approaches to psychotherapy and counseling have been well researched, there is a "glaring lack of evidence" regarding the effectiveness of transpersonal therapy (Holden, 1993, p. 18). With the exception of transcendental meditation, which has been studied quite a bit, most of the other interventions have not yet proven their value. This is especially important because some of the interventions (e.g., past life regression) are controversial and, in the wrong hands, can be used in harmful and misleading ways.

Perhaps more than any other approach discussed in this book, transpersonal therapy has the potential for misunderstanding and exploitation. Practitioners have been accused of both overemphasizing traditional religious beliefs and advocating practices that violate conventional religion. Used by well-trained and experienced clinicians, this approach allows people to develop their own spirituality and simply guides and facilitates their growth. However, in the wrong hands, the approach may be dangerous. Before engaging in transpersonal therapy, training, or supervision, people should be sure to investigate the credentials of those with whom they will be working. They should also obtain enough information about these clinicians' treatment approaches to be sure that they are compatible with the professional literature on transpersonal therapy as well as ethical and legal practices for counselors and psychotherapists.

Although a relatively small number of clinicians seem to identify themselves as transpersonal therapists, many more draw heavily on the interventions associated with this approach. Strategies such as meditation, yoga, and visual imagery have been used to enhance a broad range of treatment approaches. Although transpersonal therapy has not yet made a place for itself among the mainstream approaches to treatment, interest is growing, as is the integration of aspects of this approach with other systems of treatment.

Evaluation

The strengths of transpersonal therapy are similar to those of existential therapy. Transpersonal therapy gives people a sense of meaning and purpose and of an interconnection with the rest of the world. It advocates values such as altruism, peace, joy, and love that have the potential of ameliorating many of the problems both in people's lives and in the world as a whole. This is an optimistic approach that emphasizes people's potential for higher levels of awareness and views our lives as unending growth processes. Such messages can be empowering and prompt people to better themselves and their lives. The rich array of strategies designed to promote transpersonal experiences can be fruitfully incorporated into many other approaches. In addition, the approach's emphasis on the importance of spirituality has contributed to a growing recognition that spirituality, broadly defined, is an appropriate focus of attention in treatment and that ignoring or refusing to acknowledge its place in people's lives does clients a disservice.

On the other hand, the approach has many limitations connected primarily to lack of research on its use and the powerful interventions it uses. Also, there is a pervasive lack of clarity in the literature on transpersonal therapy; writings are often complex and laden with terminology that seems unfamiliar and disconcerting to many readers. In sum, while this approach is indeed emerging and must prove itself, it has expanded people's thinking on approaches to psychotherapy and may indeed make a considerable contribution. People interested in learning more about the approach are strongly encouraged to do some additional reading and speak with clinicians and others who have experience in transpersonal psychotherapy. Further information can also be obtained from

The Association for Transpersonal Psychology
45 Franklin Street, #313
San Francisco, CA 94102
(415) 863-9941

The Institute of Transpersonal Psychology
744 San Antonio Road
Palo Alto, CA 94303
(650) 493-4430

The Spiritual Emergent Network
California Institute of Integral Studies
9 Peter Yorke Way
San Francisco, CA 94109

FOCUSING-ORIENTED PSYCHOTHERAPY

Focusing-oriented psychotherapy was developed by Eugene Gendlin, a professor of psychology at the University of Chicago. Holden (1996) found focusing useful in promoting grounding, centering, opening, and processing, all aspects of transpersonal psychotherapy. Focusing-oriented therapy is an experiential approach to treatment that, like Gestalt therapy, places considerable emphasis on the body as a source of information. More than a technique yet less than a system of treatment, focusing-oriented therapy is a potentially valuable addition to more fully developed models of counseling and psychotherapy, particularly transpersonal therapy.

The Nature of Focusing-Oriented Psychotherapy

According to Gendlin (1996), people grow and develop by taking what he called *experiential process steps.* These steps begin when people sense a source of information somewhere between the conscious and the unconscious: the place "where crying comes from" (p. 23). Initially, the message or information is unclear; but gradually complex bodily sensations are likely to arise, reflecting something unresolved, an unclear edge.

Gendlin called this edge the *felt sense,* but his description of it is rather vague. It seems to be an intense and meaningful experience, always new and different, that has a bodily, physical quality. Information from the felt sense often is more reliable than information from emotions or cognitions. Feelings, perceptions, thoughts, and memories may be associated with a felt sense. People seem to recognize when they are in touch with their felt sense, although the phenomenon is difficult to describe.

Gendlin suggested that connecting with the felt sense, a sort of transcendent function or intuitive sense, may bring people closer to being themselves. Connecting with and attending to their felt sense moves them in the direction of change and growth.

Focusing is a process that allows people access to the felt sense. The heart of focusing-oriented psychotherapy, focusing is a way of directing attention inward and learning from the messages of the body. Becoming skilled in the use of focusing requires approximately eight three-hour training sessions. However, Gendlin (1996) believed that "even therapists who do not know focusing can markedly improve therapy with some proportion of their clients, simply by asking how what is being discussed makes them feel *in the middle of the body* and then waiting quietly for the client to sense there. Therefore, this is worth trying with every client" (p. 1). Gendlin (1996) viewed the body as an inner touchstone and believed that having people check their bodily messages can help determine the impact of treatment and guide its direction. When focusing, people seek an entry point into their bodies, a way to find the edges, "that unclear, implicitly intricate mass of experience from which the steps of a process of experiential change can come" (p. 69).

Therapeutic Alliance

Gendlin (1996) believed that, "interpersonal interaction is the most therapeutic avenue" (p. 283). He advocated clinicians' use of active listening, acceptance, and genuineness to provide a safe and steady human presence that is willing to be with the client fully. Although clients are viewed as in charge of the direction of treatment, clinicians and clients ideally move forward together.

Strategies

After clinicians explain the process of focusing, clients are encouraged to relax, think about a problem or concern, and see what comes up for them without judging or screening their responses. Passive attention seems to work best: people pay attention to what emerges, gradually honing in on and following one's feeling without putting it into pictures or words. People are encouraged to be receptive to whatever comes up and to stay with and next to the feeling.

Once people are truly experiencing the feeling, clinicians might suggest they make space for it, allow it to come further into awareness, and try to find new words or images that capture the message of the feeling that has arisen (Hackney & Cormier, 1996.) People can imagine a mural of the feeling and then try to identify and repeat to themselves one true thing about their problem. Finding an image, word, or phrase that fits the problem can promote exploration and awareness. An entire session might be spent on experiencing, translating, and applying the information from the felt sense, particularly encouraging people to allow energy and positive new feelings to come into the body as they arise.

Although some people have no difficulty engaging in this process, others find it foreign. For these people, Gendlin (1996) suggests beginning at the bottom: "Put your attention into your right foot inside your shoe" (p. 71). He then gradually directs the person's attention up through the body, encouraging awareness of bodily sensations. For most people, the felt sense is most easily experienced in the middle of the body.

Strengths and Limitations

The sort of body work that is reflected in focusing-oriented psychotherapy can easily be integrated with other treatment systems as well as strategies such as role play and visual imagery. Focusing offers a source of information that may be helpful to many people, particularly those who have difficulty verbalizing emotions.

At the same time, people may feel disappointed in themselves if they cannot readily engage in focusing. They may have trouble deciphering the messages of the body and may rely too heavily on the clinician's perceptions of their experiences. Although focusing seems simple and straightforward, using this technique effectively requires training, experience, and considerable sensitivity. This approach seems less dangerous than some others associated with transpersonal therapy. However, it, too, has potential for both harm and good.

People interested in obtaining more information on focusing can contact

The Focusing Institute
34 East Lane
Spring Valley, NY 10977

This organization is a worldwide network of people interested in focusing. It holds an annual conference and publishes a journal, *The Folio,* as well as other publications related to focusing.

SKILL DEVELOPMENT: GUIDED IMAGERY

Visualization or guided imagery is an important strategy in transpersonal therapy. It is also widely used in cognitive and behavior therapy (discussed later in this book) and can be productively incorporated into almost any system of treatment. Imagery can reduce anxiety and facilitate relaxation, promote a sense of empowerment and control, improve problem solving and decision making, ameliorate pain and other physical symptoms, and help people transcend and develop new perspectives on themselves and their lives.

Encouraging Cooperation with Visualization

Although most people are eager to try any treatment strategies that seem likely to help them, some view guided imagery and other nontraditional techniques as silly, worthless, or even threatening. To encourage cooperation, people should be given a rationale for whichever strategy is being used and should be encouraged to approach it with a playful, curious, open attitude. Clinicians might say something like, "I don't know whether guided imagery will be helpful to you, but many people find it helpful and relaxing. I'd be curious to see how you react. How about if we try it? You can let me know if you want to stop at any point, but you may discover some new and interesting things about yourself." In addition, clients should be given as much control over the process as possible and helped to see that this is not some mysterious process that is being done to them but their inner resources coming to the fore. Timing of the guided imagery and its duration and intensity should be carefully adapted to the needs of the individual. Imagery is especially likely to be well received if it appeals to a person's dominant sense (visual, auditory, tactile, or olfactory) (Siegel, 1990).

Visualization is most powerful if it is practiced and used between sessions. Tape recordings can be made of the guided imagery sessions to be played daily as well as before stressful events to help people cope more effectively. Practicing as little as three to five minutes a day, in the same comfortable place, seems to greatly facilitate the process of visualization (Fanning, 1990). The best times to use this process are upon wakening and before falling asleep. Keeping an arm slightly raised during the visualization can keep the person awake during the imagery if that is a concern.

The Process of Guided Imagery

The following steps are typical of a guided imagery session (Seligman, 1996b, pp. 88–95):[1]

1. The clinician promotes the client's relaxation via deep breathing, muscle tension and release, or other techniques.
2. The person imagines a peaceful, relaxing scene in which he or she feels secure, whole, and healthy. This can be a familiar place or an imaginary place.
3. The person is given the opportunity to find a wise inner guide; means are provided in the image for the guide to appear (e.g., on a path, from behind a rock, through a door). The guide offers a channel for messages from the unconscious (Fanning, 1988). The first time a possible guide appears, the person should visualize greeting the visitor and asking whether he or she is the person's guide. If the answer is no, the person should ask for the guide to be sent.
4. The person presents a question or a task to the inner guide.
5. The guide assists the person with the task or question, usually either providing more information and ideas or facilitating a decision.
6. The person visualizes him or herself as empowered and successful at dealing with the task or question.
7. The guide departs. The person says good-bye, thanks the guide, and affirms that he or she can summon the guide whenever that would be helpful.
8. The person gradually leaves the peaceful scene and returns to the room.

In the following example, a clinician takes a person through a second session of guided imagery. The nature of the guide and the images are based on information that arose for the client during the first imagery session.

Clinician: Now I would like you to relax your body and sink deeply into your chair. Uncross your arms and legs and gently let your eyelids close. Pay attention to your breathing and breathe deeply and from your diaphragm, in and out, in and out, feeling your diaphragm move deeply with each breath . . . Take full, deep, slow breaths, . . . and with each breath, you will feel all the tension,

[1]Adapted from Seligman, L. (1996). *Promoting a Fighting Spirit*. San Francisco: Jossey-Bass. Copyright 1996, Jossey-Bass. Adapted/reprinted by permission of Jossey-Bass, Inc., a subsidiary of John Wiley & Sons, Inc.

all the stress flowing away, . . . feel all your muscles relax, your head, . . . your face, . . . your shoulders, . . . your arms, . . . your hands; feel the tension being released. Now relax your chest, . . . your lower body, . . . your legs, . . . and your feet. Feel the breath flowing through your body, relaxing all your muscles. Now when you feel ready and relaxed, I'd like you to return to that special place, that beautiful lush forest where you feel as strong as the strongest tree. Look around you, and you will remember how happy you feel here, how calm and peaceful you are, surrounded by the tall, green trees and the tall mountains, how happy you are to be back here. Now as you look around, you will see your inner guide, the fox, coming out from behind the tree. He has been waiting for you to call on him, always ready to help you. I'd like you to greet your guide; and when the two of you are ready, you will once again go on a journey.

The question you have decided to work on with your guide is whether to end your marriage because your husband refuses to seek help for the difficulties you two are having. Explain your question to your guide so that your guide can help you as much as possible.

When you are ready, you and your guide may walk down the path you see before you, going toward the yellow house with three rooms that you visualized in our last session. Being in that house with your guide may give you information about the decision that is worrying you. As you approach the house, look at it carefully. Be on the alert for information and messages all along this journey.

When you approach the house, decide how you will enter the house and go into the first room you see. This is the room of problems in your marriage: the abuse, the untruthfulness, and the alcohol. Be aware of your feelings, both in your body and in your heart, as you look around this room. Look at the furniture, the walls, any windows you might see, any decorations in this room. Remember that your guide is there to help you deal with this experience. Take the time to really experience this room.

When you are ready to go to the next room, let me know by raising a finger. . . . Now you are entering the next room. This is the room of joys in your marriage, your children, your home, the close and intimate times you have had with your husband, the security that is so important to you. Be aware of your feelings, both in your body and in your heart, as you look around this room. Look at the furniture, the walls, any windows you might see, any decorations in this room. Remember that your guide is there to help you deal with this experience. Take your time to really experience this room.

When you are ready to go to the next room, let me know by raising a finger. . . . Now you are entering the next room. This is the room of your life, the joys and the disappointments, the wholeness of your life. Again, look around the room. Be aware of your thoughts and feelings. Be open to any messages and information that come up while you are here. Even if it doesn't seem to make any sense, whatever comes up for you may be important and meaningful. You may see a container in this room; you can use that to bring back with you all the experiences, thoughts, emotions, and sensations you experience while you are in this house. Remember that your guide is there to help you.

When you are ready to leave the house, let me know by raising a finger. . . . Now you and your guide may leave the house, pausing briefly outside the house to look back and reflect on all you learned, all you gained from this journey. . . . It's time to say good-bye to your guide for now, but you know that he is always there to help you. Every time you open the front door to your house, it will remind you of your guide, and you will know that he is always with you.

Now look around the forest and be aware of how capable and strong you feel, knowing that whatever steps you take, they will be the right ones for you. You will be able to take those steps with the assurance that you have explored all your choices and all the rooms of the house and have found the choice that seems to be the best one for you. Think about all you have accomplished so far and all you are proud of, your children, your graduation from college, your furniture making, and the person you are.

When you are ready, I'd like you to gradually come back to this room, slowly open your eyes, and remember where you are. Now I'd like you to draw a picture of the images you had, and then we can talk about what came up for you during this visualization.

This guided imagery was carefully planned to include 10 important elements:

1. Relaxation
2. Images that promote a sense of control, hope, competence, and empowerment
3. Reassurance, strength, and support provided by the inner guide
4. Reminders of the guide's availability
5. Images that promote greater awareness (the house with three rooms)
6. Encouragement to notice emotions, sensations, and thoughts
7. An opportunity for synthesis, decision making, and closure
8. Reminders of the person's previous successes and accomplishments
9. An image of the person as successfully resolving the concern
10. Processing and reinforcing of the guided imagery without judging the person, the images, or the person's success in creating images

Uses for Visualization

Following are some of the helpful ways to use visualization in counseling and psychotherapy:

1. The threat and discomfort presented by an aversive experience can be reduced by imagining the experience in a way that is ridiculous, desensitizes the person to the threat, or changes the threat into something positive. A child who was fearful about giving a talk in front of her class gained confidence by imagining the other students all dressed as cheerleaders, applauding her performance.

2. Imagery can provide a mental rehearsal for coping with challenging experiences. Meichenbaum (1985) suggested that such imagery should include the experience of stress as well as successful coping with the stressor; imagining only mastery or success without the presence of the stressor and the challenge of coping seems to

provide a less realistic and less useful image. People can imagine a movie of themselves successfully performing feared acts, thereby identifying and reinforcing desired behaviors.

3. Brigham (1994) suggested the use of what she called a transformational fantasy. Here the clinician guides the client on a symbolic journey, typically walking down a strange road, seeing a house, and exploring the house. Dialogue used during the session encourages the person to describe and explore reactions to the scene. Brigham believed that the scene symbolized the person's life and that the house, its rooms, doors, hallways, and other features, gave information about the person. She used this strategy successfully with people who were coping with cancer; it can be used productively with people coping with any significant life event or turning point.

4. Imagery can provide positive distraction. Creation of an absorbing and readily accessed fantasy or series of images can decrease a person's rumination and provide a tool for reducing anxious images and messages.

5. Reliving a scene through the imagination can help people retrieve their feelings and reassess their behaviors in relation to an experience. Processing a troubling or powerful event in the mind can help people understand it more clearly and view their reactions from a different perspective.

6. Imagery, using the inner guide, can be used to find answers to difficult questions. Fanning (1988) called this receptive visualization. The guide might be asked for advice, or a dialogue with the guide can help people find answers to their questions.

7. McWilliams and McWilliams (1991) suggested having a person imagine hosting a gratitude party in which all the people and events for which he or she can be grateful are reviewed. This technique can promote optimism and a positive outlook, as can an image that projects a person into a positive time in the future.

CASE ILLUSTRATION

This case illustrates the use of focusing with Roberto. Assume that the strategy was explained to him before the focusing began. Focusing, developed by Eugene Gendlin, was described previously in this chapter.

Clinician: Roberto, I'd like you to focus on the middle of your body. Take some time to feel any sensations that come up for you there, and then tell me about it.

Roberto: Middle of my body? You mean my stomach?

Clinician: Anywhere at the center of your body where you feel sensations.

Roberto: Well, this seems sort of ridiculous, but I do have these funny feelings like in the pit of my stomach. Maybe what people talk about when they say they have butterflies in their stomach.

Clinician: There's something there?

Roberto: Yes, I don't know how to explain it.

Clinician: Focus on the butterflies and talk about the sensations.

Roberto: Tingly, sort of like a scared feeling too. Like things jumping or flying around out of control. Now the feeling is changing, getting worse, things rumbling around, almost like a volcano before it blows. Hot; lava bubbling all over.

Clinician: Can you focus on that volcano, make space for it so you can really feel it?

Roberto: I'm not sure I want to. It scares me.

Clinician: It's up to you whether you want to keep feeling that sensation.

Roberto: I think I should. There seems to be something here.

Clinician: You might just try to tap it lightly to see what comes up for you.

Roberto: Yeah, I can do that. . . . First, I thought this was butterflies in my stomach; but when I went deeper, there was this rumbling volcano, seething, dangerous.

Clinician: Stay with it, really sense the feelings.

Roberto: I'm getting more comfortable with the feelings now; they feel more familiar, like part of me.

Clinician: Try to make space for the feelings; give them a friendly reception and see what comes up.

Roberto: Be friendly to a volcano, hmmm. Okay, I guess I know what you mean. This is all part of me, and I need to accept it.

Clinician: What is coming up for you now?

Roberto: I can feel that the volcano is part of me, inside me, like when I lose my temper. I feel like I can't control it or like Edie made me lose my temper but it's really all inside me. Even if I am like a volcano sometimes, it's really just me, and I can sense when I'm about to explode. Those blow-ups I have; they feel more like they belong to me.

Clinician: Try to stay next to that rumbling, see what comes up.

Roberto: Yeah, I guess I'm close to exploding these days. I'm really fed up with Edie, sort of like the volcano ready to explode.

Clinician: Tell me what the rumblings feel like now.

Roberto: Well, I guess I sort of let off steam by talking about it. The rumblings don't seem so loud now, not ready to blow anymore.

Clinician: Let those sensations come through, stay with them.

Roberto: I can see that the hot feeling is cooling off; I guess I'm cooling off. I suppose I am like that volcano sometimes. That doesn't sound like it's the way I want to be, to have an active volcano inside me.

This exercise in focusing has enabled Roberto to reach his feelings of anger in a new way. Because of this, he seems more open to realizing the harm his anger can cause as well as the control he does have over it. Although only a beginning, this realization may enable him to understand and manage his anger more successfully.

EXERCISES

Large-Group Exercises

1. The approaches described in this chapter (narrative therapy, constructivism, feminist therapy, transpersonal therapy, focusing) are controversial and may

have elicited some strong reactions as you read about them. Each member of the class should take five minutes and write spontaneously about his or her reactions to these approaches. Read several of these aloud to the class and then engage in a class discussion of your reactions to the approaches. Be sure to listen to others' ideas, even if they conflict with your own.

2. This is an exercise in mindfulness. Give a cookie to each member of the class. Eat the cookie slowly. Try to be as aware of the experience as you can—noticing the textures, the smells, the tastes, and the way you approach the process of eating the cookie. Try to tune out all distractions, focusing only on the experience of savoring the cookie. Then engage in a discussion of that experience.

3. Select someone to lead the class in a guided visualization. Begin the session with relaxing diaphragmatic breathing and then spend approximately 15 minutes in the visualization. The script may be similar to the one provided in this chapter, or an alternate script may be used. After the visualization, draw a picture of the image that was most powerful for you. Some time should be allowed for the class to discuss and process the experience.

Small-Group Exercises

1. Divide into your groups of four people in two dyads. Each dyad should have the opportunity to engage in a focusing exercise, following the guidelines provided in this chapter. If time allows, reverse roles so that each person experiences the process of focusing. Then discuss the experience so that client, clinician, and observers all have the opportunity to talk about what the focusing experience was like for them as well as its benefits and shortcomings.

2. One member of each dyad should lead his or her partner in a guided visualization. Spend 10–15 minutes in the relaxation and visualization phase and then allow 5–10 minutes for discussion. Process the experience so that client, clinician, and observers all have the opportunity to talk about what the visualization experience was like for them as well as its benefits and shortcomings.

3. Take about 10 minutes to write a brief story that is meaningful to you about the community in which you grew up. Share that story with the other three members of your group and discuss what picture emerges of your background and your experiences in this community.

Individual Exercises

1. Write your spiritual autobiography in your journal, describing important spiritual experiences that you have had in your life. If you feel comfortable doing so, share your writing with someone to whom you feel close.

2. Choose a word or an image that is meaningful to you, ideally one that helps you to feel peaceful and optimistic. For one week, spend 15 minutes a day

meditating on that word or image. If your mind wanders, simply bring it back to the image you have chosen. Think about what this experience is like for you and write about it in your journal. You may want to use this as an opportunity to initiate regular meditation.

3. Choose one hour of your time when you will be engaged in fairly routine activities. Use this as an opportunity to experience mindful meditation, trying to be very aware of all of your thoughts, emotions, sensations, and activities. When the hour is over, write about the meaning this experience had for you. Be sure to consider how this differed from the way you usually go about your daily activities.

Summary

This chapter provided information on five approaches to counseling and psychotherapy: narrative therapy, constructivist therapy, feminist therapy, transpersonal therapy, and focusing-oriented therapy. Narrative therapy is a phenomenological approach, suggesting that people's conceptions of themselves and their lives come from the stories they have made a part of themselves. By helping people to explore, understand, and modify their stories, clinicians can enable them to revision and reauthor their lives.

Constructivist psychotherapy and feminist psychotherapy have many similarities to narrative psychotherapy. All three are phenomenological approaches that focus on people's perceptions of themselves and their worlds. Both constructivist psychotherapy and feminist psychotherapy are holistic, attending to background as well as emotions, thoughts, and actions. They view people in a social context and believe that each person has a private and subjective psychological reality that has grown out of his or her life experiences. Constructivism emphasizes the reciprocal relationship we have with our world and helps people understand their underlying constructions and expand their interpretations and possibilities. Feminist psychotherapy seeks to help both men and women overcome rigid gender roles. This approach encourages people to appreciate the special attributes of their gender while expanding their options and promoting empowerment and egalitarian relationships.

Transpersonal therapy emphasizes the importance of spiritual growth, the interrelationship of all beings, and the potential of all people to achieve higher levels of awareness. By creating experiences and conditions that are likely to release intuition and creativity, clinicians can help people to move toward transcendent self-actualization and spiritual development.

Focusing is a strategy that encourages people to attend to their bodily sensations and use them as a reliable source of information about themselves and their lives. Often used in transpersonal therapy, focusing can also enhance a broad range of treatment systems. All five approaches emphasize emotions and sensations, and all offer new and emerging ways for clinicians to treat their clients more effectively.

RECOMMENDED READINGS

Boorstein, S. (Ed.). (1996). *Transpersonal psychotherapy* (2nd ed.). Albany: State University of New York Press.

Gendlin, E. T. (1996). *Focusing-oriented psychotherapy*. New York: Guilford.

Day, G. L. (1992). Counseling for women: The contribution of feminist theory and practice. *Counseling Psychology Quarterly, 5,* 373–384.

Holden, J. M. (1993). Transpersonal counseling. *TCA Journal, 21*(1), 7–23.

Mahoney, M. J. (1988a). Constructive metatheory. I: Basic features and historical foundations. *International Journal of Personal Construct Psychology, 1,* 1–35.

Mahoney, M. J. (1988b). Constructive metatheory. II: Implications for psychotherapy. *Journal of Consulting and Clinical Psychology, 61,* 299–315.

Monk, G., Winsland, J., Crocket, K., & Epston, D. (Eds.). *Narrative therapy in practice: The archaeology of hope.* San Francisco: Jossey-Bass.

Tart, C. T. (1992). *Transpersonal psychologies.* San Francisco: HarperCollins.

White, M., & Epston, D. (1990). *Narrative means to therapeutic ends.* Adelaide, Australia: Dulwich Centre.

PART FOUR

TREATMENT SYSTEMS EMPHASIZING THOUGHTS

Chapter 15

OVERVIEW OF THOUGHTS

Thoughts, like emotions and sensations, are our constant companions. We wake up thinking about our plans for the day, fall asleep reviewing the day's experiences, and have a myriad of thoughts in between. The term *stream of consciousness* has been applied to the constant flow of thoughts we all have.

Part 4 focuses on approaches to psychotherapy that view thoughts and cognitions as the primary avenue to change—the third of the four elements in the BETA model (background, emotions, thoughts, actions). Cognitive psychologists and counselors believe that thoughts lead to emotions and behaviors and that, through awareness and modification of their thoughts, people can effect significant changes in their feelings and actions.

As an illustration, consider the examples of Paula and Carmen. Both were single women in their early 30s who had graduated from college and been employed in professional positions for the past 10 years. Both had saved their money and recently achieved a longstanding goal of purchasing a town house. Both were preparing to move into their new homes by spending a weekend painting and wallpapering. What distinguished the two women in this example were their thoughts about the experience.

While she was painting, Paula thought, "Here I am, all alone, with no one to share my life. I will never find the sort of partner I am looking for. Buying this house and having to do all this work myself really confirms that I will spend the rest of my life all alone."

Carmen, on the other hand, thought, "It's hard to believe I really did this all myself, bought the house I have been dreaming of for 10 years. My parents and my friends didn't think I could accomplish this on my salary, but I did. And here I am painting and wallpapering. I never did anything like this before, but the house looks great. The colors I chose are wonderful. I can't wait to invite people over to dinner in my new home."

Not surprisingly, Paula felt depressed after she moved into her new home. She rarely invited friends to visit, made little effort to meet her neighbors, and viewed her purchase as a sign of her unhappy future. Carmen, on the other hand, entertained friends and neighbors, felt proud of the purchase and decoration of her home, and became even more optimistic about achieving her next important goal—a graduate degree. The differences in the thoughts the two women had about their purchase of a home led to very different emotions and behaviors. If Paula were to seek counseling from a cognitive therapist, that clinician would help her express, reality-test, dispute, and modify her cognitions to effect changes in her emotions and actions.

This chapter describes two major systems of cognitive treatment. The first, cognitive therapy, was developed by Aaron Beck and his associates and has attracted considerable attention since its development. Many procedures and clinical tools are associated with this approach, making it very useful in the treatment of a broad range of disorders and problems. Extensive research has demonstrated the value of cognitive therapy. The second, Albert Ellis's rational emotive behavior therapy (REBT), was really the first major approach to counseling and psychotherapy that focused attention on the importance of thoughts. Ellis's pioneering efforts established a solid foundation for future theoreticians. In this chapter, we also consider three emerging approaches that focus on changing thought patterns: eye movement desensitization and reprocessing (EMDR), neuro-linguistic programming (NLP), and thought-field therapy (TFT). Their innovative techniques to disrupt and change thought patterns have greatly enhanced the power of clinical work.

USE OF COGNITIONS IN COUNSELING AND PSYCHOTHERAPY

Focusing treatment on thoughts has many advantages and benefits. As a primary emphasis of treatment or in combination with other theoretical approaches, cognitive theories of counseling and psychotherapy are powerful and flexible approaches with broad application.

Thoughts are readily accessible. We typically have only limited awareness of the myriad of thoughts running through our minds. However, when we pay attention to our thoughts about a particular subject, we typically have little difficulty becoming cognizant of them and articulating them.

Asking people about their thoughts is usually less threatening than asking them about their feelings. People are used to being asked questions such as, "Do you think it will rain today?" "What do you think about the president's speech?" and "Who do you think will win the game?" Most people have little hesitation in responding to such questions and do not find them intrusive or inappropriate. On the other hand, asking questions about emotions, beyond the routine "How are you feeling today?" may seem like prying into issues that are too personal.

Cognitions seem more amenable to change and analysis than feelings are. Thoughts can be written down, examined, tested, disputed, and modified. For example, assume Pablo is at home reading a book when the doorbell rings. He thinks, "I bet that is my brother wanting to borrow some money." He feels unhappy and apprehensive. The reality of his thought can easily be tested; all he needs to do is answer the door and see who is there and what that person wants. If it is not his brother, Pablo's thought will change, leading to a change in his emotions. However, focusing initially on Pablo's emotions and trying to change his apprehensions about a visit from his brother will probably be a more complex process; emotions often feel amorphous, difficult to identify, and even harder to explain and analyze.

Changing thoughts can be a relatively rapid process. Experiencing positive gains early in treatment can increase people's motivation and optimism, which can accelerate the course of treatment.

Learning to identify, dispute, and change thoughts can be empowering. Those skills can give people a greater sense of control over their lives and provide highly effective strategies for addressing problems.

Focusing on thoughts may enable clinicians to work successfully with a broad range of clients. Treatment that emphasizes thoughts is likely to be comfortable for and make sense to a wide range of clients. Particularly important, a focus on thoughts can make the counseling process more comfortable for people who are not used to sharing their emotions, including some men, many older people, and people from Asian and other cultural backgrounds who view expression of emotions to a relative stranger as inappropriate, weak, or conflicting with their upbringing and self-images.

Finally, Beck and others have extensively researched cognitive approaches to treatment, and the effectiveness of cognitive therapy has been well established.

Martin Seligman (1995), for example, found that cognitive therapy was very successful in treating depression as well as some types of eating and anxiety disorders. Francine Shapiro and her colleagues found that eye movement desensitization and reprocessing (discussed in Chapter 18) was effective in treating posttraumatic stress disorder.

SKILL DEVELOPMENT: ANALYZING AND MODIFYING COGNITIONS

People have thoughts, emotions, and behaviors. When a person relates a problem or concern, one of these is likely to be more accessible or prominent than the other two. Harold was very upset about an interaction with his wife, Carol, which occurred when Harold's younger brother was dying of cancer. Review the following three ways in which Harold might describe this interaction with his wife:

Description 1: We were supposed to take our vacation when I found out that Louis was dying. I talked to the doctors, who said he only had a few weeks to live. I tried to be there for Louis. I told Carol that I wanted to postpone the vacation, so we put it off for a month. Louis was failing but was still alive then, so I suggested we postpone the vacation again. Carol just wouldn't consider it. So I went on the vacation even though it was not what I wanted to do. Louis died while we were in Spain. We flew right home for the funeral.

Description 2: We were supposed to take our vacation when I found out that Louis was dying. I was just devastated when I found out. I couldn't bear the idea of going on a vacation while he was dying. I felt enraged when Carol refused to postpone our vacation a second time, but I was afraid I would lose my marriage if I didn't comply with her wishes. Louis died while we were in Spain. I felt so guilty that I hadn't been there with him.

Description 3: We were supposed to take our vacation when I found out that Louis was dying. All I could think of was that I needed to be with him when he died. When Carol refused to postpone our vacation the second time, I thought she didn't care anything about me, that she only thought about her own needs. But I believed that it would hurt my marriage if I didn't go on the trip with her. Louis died while we were in Spain. I thought that I would never be able to forgive myself for not being with him.

Eliciting Actions, Emotions, and Thoughts

Each of these descriptions has a different focus. Description 1 focuses on actions, Description 2 on emotions, and Description 3 on thoughts. When seeking to elicit and analyze thoughts, it is useful to obtain all three aspects of a person's reactions. Start with the most accessible of the three (thoughts, emotions, or actions) and ask about the other two, writing them down concisely and checking with the client to make sure that the important thoughts, feelings, and behaviors have been captured accurately.

Burns (1980) referred to this process as the triple column technique. The strategy involves eliciting people's actions, thoughts, and emotions in relation to a particular situation and asking them to rate the intensity of their thoughts and feelings. A 0–100 rating scale can be used to assess the strength of people's emotions and the extent of their belief in their thoughts. This approach is particularly helpful in providing a baseline for use later in determining whether the intensity of people's thoughts and feelings have changed as a result of treatment.

For Harold, his description of his actions, thoughts, and emotions and the accompanying rating of his thoughts and emotions looked like this:

Identifying Actions

Clinician: Describe the actions you took in response to this situation.

Harold: I persuaded Carol to postpone our vacation once; but when I asked her to postpone the vacation a second time, she refused. I went to Spain with her.

Identifying and Rating Thoughts

Clinician: Identify the thoughts you had in response to this situation. Then, on a 0–100 rating scale, with 100 representing absolute belief, indicate how much you believe your thoughts.

Harold: (1) I thought Carol didn't care about my feelings when she wouldn't postpone the vacation: 95.

   (2) I believed it would cost me my marriage if I didn't go on a vacation with Carol: 90.

   (3) I think I am a terrible person for abandoning my brother: 99.

Identifying and Rating Feelings

Clinician: Identify the emotions you had in response to this situation. Then, on a 0–100 rating scale, with 100 representing the strongest possible emotion, indicate how strongly you are experiencing the feelings you reported.

Harold: (1) Devastated by my brother's death: 99.

   (2) Fearful of losing my marriage: 95.

   (3) Guilty that I had left my brother: 92.

Assessing the Validity of the Cognitions

The next step is to help the client find ways of determining whether the cognitions have validity. The clinician's role is not to criticize or devalue the cognitions but to maintain an objective stance and help the client determine how to go about evaluating the veracity of the cognitions.

Moorey and Greer (1989) described five approaches to evaluating and modifying cognitions:

1. *Testing reality.* Assess the accuracy of the thought, using past experiences, research, logic, and other sources of information. Harold might consider whether his

wife's past behavior supports his cognition that she doesn't care about his feelings. He also might talk with his wife about his interpretation of her insistence on their taking a vacation while his brother was dying.

2. *Seeking alternative explanations.* Clinician and client brainstorm other possible and usually more positive explanations. For example, Harold considered the possibility that his wife felt a strong need for a vacation and was afraid to travel without him as well as the possibility that she felt a vacation would help him deal with his brother's dying.

3. *Decatastrophizing.* This involves identifying the most negative possible outcome or interpretation of a cognition and then assessing its likelihood, probable impact, and possible solutions. For Harold, this would be the thought that his wife no longer loved him and that their marriage was over. Although this thought was very painful, articulating the thought allowed him to see that he could survive the end of his marriage even if it would be difficult for him.

4. *Reattribution.* The process of reattribution helps people recognize that factors outside of themselves might be the cause of their difficulties, thereby reducing their feeling of self-blame. Harold was a deeply spiritual man with great faith in both God and the human spirit. He came to believe that perhaps the timing of his brother's death had a purpose or meaning. He considered the possibility that his brother chose to die when he was away to spare Harold the pain of seeing his brother die.

5. *Distraction.* Focusing on other thoughts and activities can prevent people from ruminating excessively and being depressed by their negative thoughts. Harold might have been encouraged to use his rewarding involvement in his work to distract him whenever he felt overwhelmed by negative thoughts and memories related to the death of his brother. Of course, this technique should not be used excessively or exclusively; that might prevent people from successfully changing their dysfunctional thoughts.

Harold found the process of reattribution (as just described) very helpful. In addition, he decided to engage in some reality testing. Although Carol sometimes seemed insensitive to his needs, when he pointed them out to her, she usually showed concern for his feelings. Viewing her as indifferent to his feelings, then, was not consistent with his history with her. Assisted by the clinician, he planned a conversation with Carol to try to gain a better understanding of her insistence on a vacation and her perception of their marriage. Carol told Harold that she had been very concerned about his health and believed that Louis would survive for at least another month. She thought that Harold, who had been with his brother night and day during his illness, needed to get away. When Louis died while they were on vacation, Carol realized that she had made a mistake but thought that she would only make matters worse if she told Harold that. She reassured him that, although they did have some difficulties in their marriage, she was not considering a divorce and was willing to seek help for their marriage.

Identifying an Automatic or Core Cognition

Often, an automatic or core cognition underlies specific thoughts. This automatic cognition is a more general statement that serves as a sort of screen for how people view their world and themselves. Identifying these automatic cognitions can help people apply what they have learned from assessing a specific cognition to other thoughts and situations in their lives. Acknowledgment of the automatic cognition can help people see that their specific cognitions may not really be valid.

One of Harold's automatic cognitions was "I must please other people, or they will reject me since I really don't have very much to offer them." After identifying this cognition, he was able to see that, in part, his inability to assert himself with his wife was related to his own low self-esteem. He recognized how this automatic cognition colored many aspects of his life and often led him to make choices that he later regretted. It also prevented him from letting other people really get to know him and curtailed the closeness and intimacy in his relationships.

Categorizing the Cognitive Distortions

Dysfunctional or distorted cognitions can be categorized (Beck, 1995; Burns, 1989). Following is a list of types of cognitive distortions, illustrated by statements that Harold might make:

- *All-or-nothing thinking.* If I don't do everything in my power to please my wife, she will leave me.
- *Overgeneralization.* Relationships just don't work out for me. My high school sweetheart dumped me. My first wife was unfaithful. I know my marriage to Carol is doomed too.
- *Mental filter.* I know that Carol said she wanted to work on our marriage and said that she loved me, but my first wife said those things too. I don't think I can really trust what Carol is saying.
- *Disqualifying the positive.* Yes, it's true that I spent every day for a month with Louis when he was dying. I made sure he had good care; I brought hospice workers in to help him; I even got a lawyer to come to the hospital so he could have a will prepared. I know I made a difference for him. But the bottom line is I wasn't there when he died. What good is all the rest if I wasn't there for him when he needed me most?
- *Jumping to conclusions.* Carol and I had a big fight this morning, and now she's over an hour late coming home from work. I think she's left me.
- *Magnification/minimization.* Carol told me that she wanted diamond earrings for her last birthday, but I forgot. Instead, I got her some pearls. She was really disappointed. How could I have forgotten something that was so important to my wife? Why would she want to stay married to me?

- *Emotional reasoning.* My sister told me she made sure Louis was comfortable when he was dying, and she was with him all the time until he died. She said Louis understood why I left. But I still feel awful. We were so close; it must have been harder for him without me there. No matter what my family says to me, I still feel so guilty for leaving Louis.
- *"Should" and "must" statements:* A good husband should do everything he can to please his wife. I should try harder to be the sort of husband that Carol wants.
- *Labeling and mislabeling.* I'm a loser. Nothing I do works out. No matter how hard I try, I'm just a failure.
- *Personalization.* Maybe Louis would have lived longer if I had been there. I think I gave him a reason to go on. He had already lived much longer than the doctors expected, and who knows how long he could have kept going. It's my fault that he died when he did.
- *Catastrophizing.* If Carol leaves me, my life is not worth living. I won't be able to go on.
- *Mind reading.* I know Carol doesn't understand my concern for my family. She probably just thinks I can't stand up for myself.
- *Tunnel vision.* I can't do anything to please Carol.

Becoming familiar with these categories of cognitive distortions can help people identify, understand, and dispute their own cognitive distortions. In addition, this list can reassure people that having cognitive distortions is very common and that dysfunctional thinking can be changed. This reassurance can relieve some of their self-blame and enable them to take on the role of detective, seeking clues to cognitive distortions rather than judging themselves.

Harold's original cognitive distortions can be categorized as follows:

1. I thought Carol didn't care about my feelings when she wouldn't postpone the vacation: *jumping to conclusions.*
2. I believed it would cost me my marriage if I didn't go on a vacation with Carol: *all-or-nothing thinking.*
3. I am a terrible person for abandoning my brother: *mislabeling and magnification.*

Disputing and Replacing Cognitions

Once the distorted cognitions have been identified, discussed, and categorized, they can be disputed. Client and clinician work together to find alternate cognitions that have more validity and are likely to be more helpful to the client. These are written down as replacements for the original cognitions. Harold revised his cognitions like this:

1. "I thought Carol didn't care about my feelings when she wouldn't postpone the vacation" was replaced with "Although I felt hurt when Carol refused to postpone our vacation, I can see that she was doing what she thought was best for both of us."

2. "I believed it would cost me my marriage if I didn't go on a vacation with Carol" was replaced with "Although I believed at the time that I had to go on a vacation with Carol to save my marriage, I can see now that my marriage is stronger than I thought. We do have some problems but we are both committed to our marriage and willing to work on the problems."

3. "I am a terrible person for abandoning my brother" was replaced with "I still regret deeply that I was not there when my brother died, but I can see that I did a great deal for him throughout his life and especially after he got sick. I had no way of knowing that he would die during the 10 days we were away. If I had known that, I would not have left him."

Rerating Thoughts and Feelings

The final step is rerating the original thoughts and feelings to assess whether and how much their intensity has changed. Harold came up with the following reratings:

Thoughts

Clinician: On a 0–100 rating scale, indicate how much you believe your thoughts.

Harold: (1) I thought Carol didn't care about my feelings when she wouldn't postpone the vacation: 30.

(2) I believed it would cost me my marriage if I didn't go on a vacation with Carol: 15.

(3) I am a terrible person for abandoning my brother: 45.

Feelings

Clinician: On a 0–100 rating scale, indicate how strongly you are experiencing the feelings you reported.

Harold: (1) Devastated by my brother's death: 75.

(2) Fearful of losing my marriage: 40.

(3) Guilty that I left my brother: 50.

Harold has experienced considerable change. Although he is, of course, still grieving over the death of his brother and regrets that he was not present when his brother died, he is beginning to forgive himself and even to come to terms with his brother's death. Significant change is evident in his perceptions of both his wife's feelings toward him and the stability of his marriage. Success in collaborating with his wife to improve their marriage should help him feel even more secure in his marriage and more positively about himself and his relationship with his wife.

Review of Steps in Analyzing and Modifying Cognitions

1. Elicit and write down actions, emotions, and thoughts related to a troubling experience.
2. Rate the intensity of the thoughts and emotions on a 0–100 scale.
3. Assess the validity of the cognitions.
4. Identify any automatic or core cognitions.
5. Categorize the cognitive distortions.
6. Dispute and replace dysfunctional cognitions.
7. Rerate the intensity of thoughts and emotions.

CASE ILLUSTRATION

The case of Harold has already illustrated the process of eliciting, identifying, assessing, disputing, and modifying cognitive distortions. Consequently, what we consider here is only the first part of a case illustration; the exercises that follow will enable you to complete the picture.

This dialogue with Edie is designed to elicit cognitive distortions. Look for them as you read.

Edie: I'm really glad we had an appointment today. I've been so worried. I think Roberto may be involved with another woman.

Clinician: What led you to think that?

Edie: Well, he always has his cell phone on. But yesterday I tried to call him for hours, and it was turned off. And then he put on a sports jacket and tie today when he left for work. He never dresses up like that. I started to think that maybe he's trying to impress someone.

Clinician: Those thoughts must have been upsetting. What other thoughts did you have about this?

Edie: You know that my father was unfaithful to my mother. I thought,

here we go again. It's happening to me now. I'm just like my mother. I can't make my marriage work. I'm doomed.

Clinician: So it seemed like the past was repeating itself. How have you and Roberto been getting along lately?

Edie: Actually, pretty well, but that makes me suspicious too. He gave me a beautiful gift for Mother's Day. He's probably just feeling guilty. But who would want to stay married to me? All I do is complain. I'm not much of a wife. And forget about sex. . . .

Clinician: What feelings do all these thoughts bring up for you?

Edie: I feel pretty hopeless. Here we've been seeing you for months, and I thought there was some hope of keeping our family together, but it doesn't look that way. I feel scared. How will I manage without Roberto?

Clinician: This situation must be very frightening. What actions are you going to take?

Edie: What can I do? If I ask Roberto about it, it might just bring the situation to a head and he'll decide to leave. Maybe if I just pretend I don't notice what's going on, he'll decide to stay married to me . . . until the next woman comes along.

Clinician: Do you know of other extramarital relationships that Roberto has had?

Edie: No, he must hide them pretty well.

EXERCISES

Large-Group Exercises

Using the dialogue with Edie, go through the following steps of cognitive therapy:

1. List Edie's prominent thoughts, feelings, and planned behaviors. Try to hone in on her central thoughts, summarizing them in 3–5 cognitions.
2. From what you know about Edie and her reaction to this situation, rate the likely intensity of her thoughts and feelings on the 0–100 scale.
3. Again, from both this dialogue and what you know about Edie, identify one or two underlying automatic core cognitions.
4. Using the list of cognitive distortions presented in the "Skill Development" section, identify the nature of each of the distortions you identified, including both specific and core cognitions.
5. Develop a plan to help Edie assess the validity of her cognitions. Draw on the suggestions of Moorey and Greer discussed previously in this chapter as well as your own ideas.
6. Assume that your work with Edie has been successful. Write rational responses or restatements to replace each of her cognitive distortions. When developing these, be sure to use language that is likely to be acceptable to Edie.
7. Rerate the dysfunctional thoughts and feelings as you think Edie might do after her successful counseling.

Small-Group Exercises

1. Form into your groups of four with two dyads. Each person should have the opportunity to role-play both clinician and client roles. Engage in a role-played counseling session approximately 15 minutes long focused on identification and modification of cognitive distortions. Use the steps in the "Large-Group Exercises" to guide the process of the session. After each dialogue, allow about 10 minutes for feedback to the person in the clinician role as well as discussion of the process of the session.
2. Identify the type (or types) of cognitive distortion reflected in each of the following examples. As a small group, discuss ways you would help each person assess the validity of his or her statement:

Person A: My physician didn't call to tell me the test results. She probably has bad news and doesn't want to tell me.

Person B: My agency didn't get the grant we had applied for. My colleagues did such a good job writing the proposal. It was probably the budget I prepared that ruined it for them. I thought I was asking for too much money, but I wanted to be sure the project would succeed.

Person C: I was doing great on my diet, but then I went to Gary's wedding and made a pig of myself. I just know I'll gain back all the weight I lost. It's hopeless for me to even try to get myself in shape.

Person D: I really should visit my mother every day. It's hard for me because she has dementia and doesn't recognize me, but a daughter should see her mother as often as she possibly can, no matter what.

Person E: I was having a great time on my date with Nur until I made a real fool of myself. We were at an amusement park, and she wanted to go on this ride that went up and down and around and around. I didn't really want to, but I thought, "If she wants to go, I should go too." I started to feel really sick on the ride; and as soon as we got off, I had to run for the bathroom. You can imagine the rest. I was so humiliated. She'll never go out with me again. She's probably telling everyone what a wimp I am.

Person F: The other girls avoid me because they know that my mother works in the school cafeteria. I know she needs a job and wanted one that would let her be home with me when I'm not at school, but she's ruining my life. I'll never be popular or have lots of friends like Jessica. Her mother doesn't have to work at all and drives a Jaguar when she picks her up after school.

Individual Exercises

1. Identify a recent experience when you had strong emotions. Identify the emotions, actions, and thoughts that accompanied the experience. Do any of the thoughts seem to be cognitive distortions? Try to identify at least one cognitive distortion that you had in relation to the experience. Write down the distortion in your journal. Then, in writing, go through the steps of rating, classifying, assessing, disputing, replacing, and rerating the cognition(s).
2. We all have thoughts, emotions, and actions. Observe yourself as you go through the day. Which of these categories is most accessible to you? Are you most likely to discuss thoughts, feelings, or actions with other people? Which of the three is most likely to worry you and stay in your mind? Write out your answers in your journal.

SUMMARY

This chapter reviewed the importance of thoughts in understanding and counseling people. It also provided guidelines, examples, and exercises to teach you how to elicit, rate, classify, assess, dispute, replace, and rerate distorted cognitions. The skills you have learned in this chapter will provide a foundation on which to develop your understanding of cognitive approaches to treatment as presented in the remaining chapters of Part 4.

Chapter 16

AARON BECK AND COGNITIVE THERAPY

Cognitive therapy has grown rapidly in importance over the past 25 years and is now recognized as one of the major approaches to counseling and psychotherapy. The foundations of cognitive therapy were established by Albert Ellis (discussed in Chapter 17). However, the work of Aaron T. Beck and his colleagues really fueled the growth of this approach. We discuss their treatment system first because it is more structured and organized than Ellis's and provides a clearer introduction to cognitive therapy.

Cognitive therapy is a phenomenological model similar to person-centered counseling, existential therapy, Gestalt therapy, and the other approaches discussed in Part 3. However, cognitive therapy focuses on the meaning that people give a situation through the way they think, not feel, about it. Although cognitive therapy recognizes that both emotions and background are important and worthy of attention in treatment, it views thoughts as the primary determinant of both emotions and behaviors as well as of mental disorders and psychological health. Cognitive therapists believe that the basic material of treatment is people's transient automatic thoughts and their deeply ingrained and fundamental assumptions and schemas. Once these have been discovered and identified, clinicians can draw on a wide variety of interventions to help people test and modify their cognitions. Replacing dysfunctional cognitions with those that are more accurate and helpful enables people to deal more successfully with their immediate difficulties and lead more rewarding lives. Inventories, suggested tasks, life skill development, and other strategies are used to advance the goals of cognitive therapy. This is a well-organized, powerful, usually short-term approach that has proven its effectiveness through a large number of research studies.

THE PERSON WHO DEVELOPED COGNITIVE THERAPY

Aaron T. Beck, the man behind the development of cognitive therapy, was born in 1921 and raised in New England. He was the fifth and youngest child of Harry Beck and Elizabeth Temkin Beck, Russian Jewish immigrants to the United States (Weishaar, 1993). Two of the five children born to this family died in infancy, apparently contributing to emotional problems in Beck's mother. He perceived her as depressed, unpredictable, and overprotective—very different from his calm father.

Beck himself had many difficulties during childhood. He was often ill, missing many days of school. As a result, he was forced to repeat a grade, leading him to develop negative views of his intellectual abilities. In addition, his serious illnesses left him with many anxieties and phobias, including a blood/injury phobia, a fear of public speaking, and a fear of suffocation. Beck used reasoning to alleviate these anxieties and was apparently successful since he went on to study surgery as part of his medical training and give many presentations throughout his life. A connection seems probable between his early experiences with both anxiety and depression in his family and the later focus of his work, which was primarily on treating those disorders.

Beck graduated from Brown University and Yale Medical School, where he studied psychiatry. Although he was trained in psychoanalysis, he had little faith in that approach to treatment, even during the early years of his career. At the University of

Pennsylvania Medical School, Beck, an assistant professor of psychiatry, engaged in research designed to substantiate psychoanalytic principles. Instead, his work led him to develop cognitive therapy, which has since been the focus of his teaching, research, writing, and clinical work. He has spent most of his professional career at the University of Pennsylvania, where he established the Beck Institute for Cognitive Therapy and Research, which focuses on the study and development of cognitive therapy.

Beck married Phyllis Whitman, now a superior court judge in Pennsylvania. They have four children, including his daughter Judith Beck, whose writings on cognitive therapy are discussed in this chapter.

THE DEVELOPMENT OF COGNITIVE THERAPY

According to Moss (1992), the roots of cognitive therapy lie in the ideas of the Stoic philosophers of ancient Greece and Rome. Epictetus's belief that people are disturbed not by things but by the view they take of them is particularly relevant.

George Kelly's (1955) personal constructs psychology was a modern precursor of cognitive therapy. Kelly was one of the first theorists to recognize the role of beliefs in controlling and changing thoughts, emotions, and actions. He suggested that people each have a set of personal constructs that offer them a way to make sense of and categorize people and experiences. These constructs operate like scientific hypotheses, enabling people to make predictions about reality. When their predictions are not borne out or when people recognize that their personal constructs may be harmful to them, they may seek alternative constructs (Hergenhahn, 1994).

Albert Ellis was the first clinician to become well known for his emphasis on thoughts as the route to changing emotions and behaviors. Rational emotive therapy (RET), which he developed in the 1950s, quickly became an important alternative to Freudian psychoanalysis and Rogers's person-centered counseling. However, while Ellis's dynamic and sometimes abrasive style certainly brought attention to RET, the system also became associated with Ellis's personal style. For some people, the sound theory and interventions of RET were overshadowed by Ellis's personality, probably limiting the system's popularity.

Like Ellis, Aaron Beck was trained as a psychoanalyst but soon became disenchanted with that mode of treatment and gravitated toward an approach that emphasized cognitions. Beck drew on the ideas of George Kelly, Alfred Adler, and Karen Horney as he sought to find a way to help people that was more efficient and effective than psychoanalysis. Working at the University of Pennsylvania in the 1960s, Beck and his colleagues initially had the goal of developing a structured, short-term, present-oriented, problem-solving approach to the treatment of depression (Beck, 1995). *Cognitive Therapy of Depression* (Beck, Rush, Shaw, & Emery, 1979), which describes the results of this work, had a powerful impact on the field of psychotherapy. It offered a clear and structured approach to the treatment of depression, the symptom clinicians most often see in both inpatient and outpatient treatment. Beck and his colleagues provided evidence that cognitive therapy was considerably more effective in treating depression than antidepressant medication.

Beck has acknowledged a strong debt to Ellis's work (Weishaar, 1993). At the same time, Beck's personal style, as well as the development of his theory, differ considerably from Ellis's style and clinical ideas. Beck has sought to enhance the importance of his system of cognitive therapy through research, clinical application, and writing. In demonstrations and videotapes, he appears reserved and thoughtful, a researcher at least as much as a clinician. Through his books and articles, he has continued to expand the application of cognitive therapy and validate its effectiveness. *Anxiety Disorders and Phobias* (Beck & Emery, 1985) applies cognitive therapy to anxiety disorders, while *Cognitive Therapy of Personality Disorders* (Beck, Freeman, & Associates, 1990) applies it to personality disorders.

Two other names should be mentioned for their contributions to the development of cognitive therapy. Aaron Beck's daughter, Judith S. Beck, has been working with him for many years. Now director of the Beck Institute for Cognitive Therapy and Research in Philadelphia and professor at the University of Pennsylvania, she continues the development of cognitive therapy through her writings and research (Beck, 1995). In addition, David Burns's writings, primarily *The Feeling Good Handbook* (1989), a self-help book based on cognitive therapy, have greatly increased awareness of this treatment system and provided many inventories and interventions that enhance its usefulness.

IMPORTANT THEORETICAL CONCEPTS

Judith Beck (1995) has summarized cognitive therapy: "In a nutshell, the *cognitive model* proposes that distorted or dysfunctional thinking (which influences the patient's mood and behavior) is common to all psychological disturbances. Realistic evaluation and modification of thinking produces an improvement in mood and behavior" (p. 1). The purpose of cognitive therapy is to teach people to identify, evaluate, and modify their own dysfunctional thoughts and beliefs.

View of Human Development

Cognitive therapists believe that many factors contribute to the development of dysfunctional cognitions, including people's biology and genetic predispositions, experiences throughout their life span, and their accumulation of knowledge and learning. According to Beck et al. (1990), "We speculate that these dysfunctional beliefs have originated as the result of the interaction between the individual's genetic predisposition and exposure to undesirable influences from other people and traumatic events" (p. 23). Distorted cognitions begin to take shape in childhood and are reflected in people's fundamental beliefs, making them more susceptible to problems related to life events that "impinge on their cognitive vulnerability" (p. 23). Although this approach focuses on the present, an extensive intake interview is recommended so that clinicians have a good understanding of their clients' history, development, and background (Beck, 1995).

Unlike most theorists who focus on emotions (discussed in Part 3), cognitive theorists also value the importance of making an accurate diagnosis of any mental disorders that are present in their clients. Using the guidelines for a multiaxial assessment in the *Diagnostic and Statistical Manual of Mental Disorders* (DSM) (American Psychiatric Association, 1994), clinicians determine whether a client's symptoms meet the criteria for a mood disorder, an anxiety disorder, a personality disorder, or another mental disorder. Cognitive theory suggests that each mental disorder is characterized by relatively predictable types of underlying cognitive distortions. For example, feelings of depression typically stem from thoughts of loss. An accurate diagnosis can therefore facilitate identification of those distortions and of ways to change them. It also can guide clinicians' efforts to gather information so that they can better understand their clients. For example, discussion of childhood experiences is probably important in treatment of people with personality disorders, and discussion of traumatic experiences is essential for people diagnosed with posttraumatic stress disorder. However, discussion of past experiences is less likely to be important in the treatment of people with disorders that are mild, brief, transient, and recent, such as adjustment disorders.

Although cognitive theorists focus primarily on thoughts, they take a holistic perspective of people and believe that learning about and understanding their feelings and behaviors also is important (Beck et al., 1990). According to cognitive theory, the three areas are largely interdependent, with problems or change in one area spilling over and affecting the other two (Persons, 1989). Having a comprehensive understanding of people is particularly useful in helping clinicians develop effective interventions that target all three areas of functioning: thinking, feeling, and acting.

According to cognitive theory, psychologically healthy people are aware of their cognitions. They can systematically test their own hypotheses and, if they find they have dysfunctional and unwarranted assumptions, can replace them with more functional beliefs that lead to more positive emotions and behaviors.

Principles of Cognitive Therapy

The following important principles characterize the practice of cognitive therapy (Beck, 1995; Beck & Emery, 1985; Beck et al., 1990):

- Cognitive therapy is based on the finding that changes in thinking lead to changes in feeling and acting.
- Treatment requires a sound and collaborative therapeutic alliance.
- Treatment is short-term, problem-focused, and goal-oriented.
- Cognitive therapy is an active and structured approach to treatment.
- Cognitive therapy focuses on the present, although attention is paid to the past when indicated.
- Careful assessment, diagnosis, and treatment planning are integral.
- This is a psychoeducational model that seeks to promote emotional health and prevent relapse by teaching people to identify, evaluate, and modify their own cognitions.

- This approach uses a broad range of techniques and interventions to help people evaluate and change their cognitions.
- Inductive reasoning and Socratic questioning are particularly important in helping people accurately assess their cognitions.
- Task assignments, follow-up, and client feedback are important in ensuring the success of this approach.

Levels of Cognitions

Cognitions can be categorized according to four levels: automatic thoughts, intermediate beliefs, core beliefs, and schemas. In cognitive therapy, treatment typically begins with automatic thoughts and then proceeds to identification, evaluation, and modification of intermediate and core beliefs and finally of schemas.

Automatic thoughts are the stream of cognitions that constantly flow through our minds. As we go through our day, situation-specific thoughts spontaneously arise in reaction to our experiences: "I don't think I'll ever be able to get all that work done; I think I'll eat a healthy lunch today; I don't think I should call my father back yet; I'm going to help Bill with his homework tonight; that man makes me think of my brother"; and on and on. When people are encouraged to pay attention to their thoughts, they become accessible and people can articulate and evaluate them.

Automatic thoughts mediate between a situation and an emotion. Consider the following example:

> *Situation:* Man learns that his sister has been in town but did not call him.
> *Automatic thought:* She found out that I am unlikable and didn't want to spend time with me.
> *Emotion:* Sadness

What caused the emotion, sadness, was not the situation itself but the man's automatic cognition or the meaning he made of the situation. Understanding people's automatic thoughts is important in helping them change their emotions.

Intermediate beliefs often reflect extreme and absolute rules and attitudes that shape people's automatic thoughts. For example, the intermediate beliefs of the man in the previous example might include "A sister should call her family when she is in town" and "Being ignored by your sister is a terrible thing."

Core beliefs are central ideas about ourselves that underlie many of our automatic cognitions and usually are reflected in our intermediate beliefs. Core beliefs can be described as "global, overgeneralized, and absolute" (Beck, 1995, p. 167). They typically stem from childhood experiences, are not necessarily true, and can be identified and modified. Core beliefs reflect our views of the world, other people, ourselves, and the future. They may be positive and helpful such as "I am likable," "I am a capable person," and "The world is full of interesting and exciting opportunities and people." However, they can also be negative, such as "People only care about themselves," "The world is a dangerous place," and "I make a mess of everything." Most negative core beliefs can be categorized as *helpless core beliefs* such as "I am weak" and "I am a failure" or as *unlovable core beliefs* such as "I am not good enough" and "I am bound to be abandoned" (Beck, 1995, p. 169).

As clinicians get to know and understand their clients and hear a series of automatic thoughts, the clinicians can begin to formulate hypotheses about a client's core belief. At an appropriate time, clinicians can share this hypothesis with the client for confirmation or disconfirmation, along with information on the nature and development of core beliefs. Clients are encouraged to view their core beliefs as ideas rather than truths and to collaborate with their clinicians to evaluate and change their core beliefs.

Schemas have been defined as "cognitive structures within the mind" that encompass the core beliefs (Beck, 1995, p. 166). Beck viewed them as "specific rules that govern information processing and behavior" (Beck et al., 1990, p. 8). Schemas are idiosyncratic and habitual ways of viewing what Moss (1992) termed *the cognitive triad:* ourselves, the world, and the future.

People have many schemas that act as mental filters, affecting the way in which they perceive reality. Common types of schemas are personal, familial, cultural, religious, gender, and occupational (Beck et al., 1990). Schemas have content as well as structural qualities such as breadth, flexibility, and prominence. They may be activated by a particular stimulus or lie dormant until triggered ("Controversies," 1993). For example, a person may have a danger schema that gives the message, "The world is a dangerous place. Avoid any possible danger." This schema is usually latent but can be activated by threats to that person's safety.

When a schema has been activated, it readily incorporates any confirming information and tends to neglect contradictory information. For example, when people have a depressed view of themselves, they accept any negative information they receive about themselves and overlook anything positive. Schemas become amenable to analysis and modification after people have experienced some positive change as a result of assessing and altering their automatic thoughts and core beliefs. Beck viewed schema work as the heart of the therapeutic process (Beck et al., 1990).

Cognitive therapy seems to operate at several levels, seeking to elicit and change people's symptoms as well as their underlying schemas. Once healthy thinking has been restored, clinicians can move to the next level of intervention: enabling people to develop the skills they need to monitor, assess, and respond to their own cognitions as well as lead their lives more successfully.

The Process of Treatment

Treatment via cognitive therapy usually is time-limited, 4–14 sessions long, for relatively straightforward problems (Beck, 1995). Sessions are carefully planned and structured to maximize their impact and efficiency. People complete inventories and intake questionnaires before beginning treatment. Clinicians review these before the first session in order to be well prepared.

Each session has clear goals and an agenda. Judith Beck (1995, pp. 26–27) has recommended 10 procedures for an initial session:

1. Establish an agenda that is meaningful to the client.
2. Determine and measure the intensity of the person's mood.
3. Identify and review presenting problems.
4. Elicit the person's expectations for treatment.
5. Educate the person about cognitive therapy and the role of the client in this approach.
6. Provide information about the person's difficulties and diagnosis.
7. Establish goals.
8. Recommend tasks and homework between sessions.
9. Summarize the session.
10. Obtain the client's feedback on the session.

Throughout the session, clinicians promote development of the therapeutic alliance and seek to build trust, rapport, and an attitude of collaboration while encouraging realistic hope and optimism.

Subsequent sessions follow a similar structure. They typically begin with an assessment of the person's mood, focusing particularly on changes. Next, the foundation for the session is established by making a transition from the previous session to the current one; clinicians ask about clients' learning from and reactions to the previous session and obtain an overview of the clients' week, highlighting any important happenings. This facilitates establishment of an agenda for the session, which always includes reviewing homework. The central part of the session focuses on items on that agenda, with clinicians eliciting and assessing thoughts as well as emotions and actions related to the identified issues. Each session concludes with the planning of new homework, a summary of the session, and feedback from clients on the session and the process of treatment. Ending the session on a positive note is important to promote optimism and continued motivation.

Cognitive therapists make sure to explain to clients the nature and purpose of the sessions' structure. Clients seem to find that structure to be reassuring. They know what to expect and typically believe that this plan will help them as it has helped others. Of course, an agenda may be modified if needed, perhaps if a crisis has occurred; but any changes are planned when the agenda is determined at the outset of each session rather than randomly.

TREATMENT USING COGNITIVE THERAPY

Not surprisingly, cognitive therapists carefully specify goals for their treatment, and they draw on a rich array of interventions to achieve them. Information on the strategies of cognitive therapy is likely to be useful to clinicians from any theoretical background, who can incorporate these ideas into their work.

Goals

The overall goal of cognitive therapy is to help people identify errors in their own information-processing systems and correct them. To accomplish this, clinicians help people identify both their immediate (automatic) and global (core) thoughts and beliefs as well their associated emotions and behaviors; evaluate the validity of these thoughts; and modify them if indicated. Throughout treatment, people are taught to use this process for themselves and also to develop skills and attitudes they will need to think more realistically and lead more rewarding lives.

Clinicians and clients collaborate on determining goals. Once identified, goals are written down, with copies made for both client and clinician. Goals are referred to regularly to assess progress. (For more detailed information on goal setting, see the "Skill Development" section in Chapter 22.) Having clear, specific, and measurable goals is an important component of cognitive therapy and increases the likelihood that clients and clinicians work collaboratively with a shared objective in sight.

Therapeutic Alliance

Cognitive therapists emphasize the importance of a trusting and collaborative client-clinician partnership (Beck et al., 1990). Although cognitive therapy does not focus primarily on feelings, the emotional connection between client and clinician is not disregarded or viewed as unimportant. On the contrary, an essential role of the therapist is communicating support, empathy, caring, warmth, interest, optimism, and the other core conditions that form a successful therapeutic alliance in treatment. Cognitive clinicians make great efforts to really know and understand their clients and welcome the opportunity to serve as their role models.

Cognitive therapists seek to be nonjudgmental; they do not tell people their thinking is irrational or argue with them about the merits of their thoughts. Rather, they enable clients to develop the skills they need to make their own judgments and choices. To accomplish this, clinicians take on the roles of teacher, scientist, co-investigator and truth seeker, encouraging people to search for accurate and realistic information (Moss, 1992). Clinicians also have the responsibility for orienting clients to treatment and helping them develop realistic expectations and goals for that process. Clinicians focus on and reinforce successes and attribute progress to clients' efforts and growth.

Unlike psychodynamic therapists, cognitive therapists do not seek to elicit or provoke transference reactions. However, if clients do manifest transference, clinicians will address it as part of treatment to more fully understand and help the clients. Flexibility in role seems to characterize the cognitive therapist.

Persons (1989) found that both technical interventions and relationship factors made "independent contributions" to the success of cognitive therapy (p. 160). Although a positive client-therapist relationship alone was not sufficient to help people reach their goals, it was a necessary ingredient in the treatment system.

Cognitive Distortions in Clinicians

According to Persons (1989), clinicians should be alert to the possibility that they may have distorted cognitions related to their role as clinicians. Common examples include "If the therapy fails, this means I'm an incompetent therapist" (p. 209); "The patient won't be able to cope with this failure" (p. 210); and "If I terminate the treatment, the patient will feel rejected or abandoned" (p. 211). Clearly, clinicians as well as clients are prone to dysfunctional thinking and should monitor the nature and accuracy of their thoughts.

Case Formulation

Before cognitive therapists move forward with interventions designed to modify cognitions, they take the time to develop a case formulation, reflecting in-depth understanding of the client. According to Persons (1989), a complete case formulation includes six elements:

1. List of problems and concerns
2. Hypothesis about the underlying mechanism (core belief or schema)
3. Relationship of this belief to current problems
4. Precipitants of current problems
5. Understanding of background relevant to development of the core belief or underlying mechanism
6. Anticipated obstacles to treatment

Such a thorough case formulation allows clinicians to develop a treatment plan that is likely to be successful. As part of treatment planning, cognitive clinicians identify the best points for initial intervention, treatment strategies that are likely to be helpful, and ways to reduce anxiety and other possible obstacles to progress. In general, treatment initially focuses on overt automatic cognitions related to the client's presenting problems and, as progress is made, moves to identification and assessment of underlying core beliefs and schemas.

Eliciting and Evaluating Cognitions

The "Skill Development" section of Chapter 15 reviewed ways for clinicians to help clients identify and evaluate their cognitions. Although we review these procedures here, readers should refer back to Chapter 15 for additional information.

Eliciting Cognitions   Judith Beck (1995) suggests a basic question to elicit people's thoughts: "What was going through your mind just then?" (p. 81). Once one thought is presented, it may lead to production of other thoughts. Especially important are thoughts that are truly automatic, appear repeatedly in conjunction with a variety of experiences, and have a negative impact on the person. Beck uses what she calls a dysfunctional thought record to facilitate identification and modification of thoughts (p. 126). This record includes six items:

1. Date and time of the situation
2. The situation that elicited thoughts (including physical responses present at that time)
3. Automatic thoughts and extent of belief in those thoughts, rated on 0–100% scale
4. Emotions and their intensity, rated on 0–100% scale
5. Adaptive responses, including identification of nature of distortion, modified cognition, and rerating of response
6. Outcome, including revised beliefs, ratings of automatic thoughts, current emotions and intensity ratings, and actions

The first four items are completed initially, as in the following example:

1. Monday, 9/27
2. The school called to tell me that my son had been seen breaking into the school over the weekend. He was accused of vandalizing the computer room. I felt a knot in my stomach; I felt lightheaded and tense all over.
3. I am a failure as a parent: 95% belief rating. My son is a hopeless criminal, and it's my fault: 90% belief rating.
4. Anxious: 95% intensity; sad: 85% intensity

Assessing the Validity of Cognitions   Once the cognitions have been elicited and placed in context, people can assess the validity of their cognitions. Beck and Emery (1985) have suggested a five-step process called A-FROG to determine if one is thinking rationally. This involves assessing thoughts according to the following criteria:

A: Does it keep me *alive?*
F: Do I *feel* better as a result of this thought?
R: Is the thought based on *reality?*
O: Does it help me in my relationships with *others?*
G: Does it help me achieve my *goals?*

If "yes" is not the answer to all of these questions about a given thought, that thought may well be dysfunctional and distorted.

Guided Discovery   Cognitive therapists make extensive use of skillful questioning and experiments to guide people in a process of discovery in which they can test the reality of their thoughts. Questioning and experiments are powerful techniques that must be used with care. Therapists should never act as though they know better than the client, should not engage in debates or arguments with clients, and should remain neutral on whether a thought is distorted. The clinician's role is simply to help clients find the truth.

The following dialogue illustrates the use of questioning to help the client in the previous example assess the logic and validity of her thoughts:

Clinician: One thought you had was that your son was a hopeless criminal.

Client: Yes.

Clinician: What led you to have that thought?

Client: Well, it sounds like he committed a crime.

Clinician: Yes, he may have. Does he have a history of criminal behavior?

Client: No, not at all. He's always been very well behaved.

Clinician: So this is the first time he has been suspected of breaking the law?

Client: Yes.

Clinician: And what is your definition of a hopeless criminal?

Client: Well, I guess it's someone who repeatedly breaks the law, who can't be rehabilitated.

Clinician: And does that sound like your son?

Client: No. I guess I overreacted when I said I thought he was a hopeless criminal.

Clinician: And what about your thought that you are to blame for his behavior. What led you to think that?

Client: Well, I'm his parent. Aren't I the biggest influence in his life?

Clinician: Yes, your role is certainly an important one. How might you have encouraged him to become a criminal?

Client: I don't know what you mean.

Clinician: Well, I wonder if you have engaged in criminal behavior yourself.

Client: No, of course not.

Clinician: Perhaps you condoned criminal behavior or didn't try to teach him the difference between right and wrong?

Client: No, just the opposite. I have very strong values, and I always tried to transmit them to my son. When he misbehaved, I really tried to talk to him about what was wrong with his behavior and teach him how to act differently.

Clinician: I'm confused, then, about how you might have been the cause of his criminal behavior.

Client: Well, I guess I was just feeling bad and wanted to find an explanation. But I can see that I certainly never taught him to break the law.

Experiments designed to test hypotheses stemming from faulty thinking are another approach to helping people evaluate the reality of their cognitions. In the previous example, the client might use her statements "My son is a hopeless criminal" and "I am to blame for my son's criminal behavior" as hypotheses. Clinician and client would then develop experiments or ways to test these hypotheses. The client might talk with her son about the reasons for his behavior, talk with school personnel about this incident as well as about her son's usual behavior at school, and read about criminal behavior.

A third approach to raising questions about cognitions is seeking alternative explanations. For example, the boy might have been erroneously accused of breaking into the school. Even if he had committed the crime, mitigating factors might have played a part, such as his being forced or coerced to engage in the break-in.

The following are additional approaches that cognitive therapists use to help people evaluate the reality of their cognitions:

- Asking clients how another person whom they respect would think about the situation
- Asking them what they would say if their child or best friend had the thoughts they are having
- Using humor or exaggeration to take an idea to its extreme
- Helping people see that they are catastrophizing to counter their tendency to anticipate the worst
- Encouraging people to imagine their worst fears and then think of ways to deal with them so the fears have less power over them
- Reattributing actions or outcomes to another cause or person so that people see other possible explanations for a situation
- Helping people find a middle ground to counteract extreme or polarized ways of thinking
- Redefining or reconceptualizing a problem so that it seems more amenable to change
- Decentering, or helping people see they are not really the cause of the problem or the center of attention

Labeling the Distortion   Evaluation of distorted cognitions can be facilitated by categorizing and labeling the distortions. This helps people see more clearly the nature of their unrealistic thinking, reminds them that other people have had similar distorted cognitions, and gives them a tool for assessing subsequent thoughts.

As we discussed in Chapter 15, the nature of a dysfunctional or distorted cognition can be described according to the following categories (Beck, 1995; Beck & Weishaar, 1995; Burns, 1989):

1. *All-or-nothing or polarized thinking:* viewing a situation in terms of extremes rather than on a continuum. "Either my son is innocent, or he is a hopeless criminal."
2. *Overgeneralization:* drawing sweeping conclusions that are not justified by the evidence. "I am a failure as a parent because my son was arrested."
3. *Mental filter (selective abstraction):* focusing selectively on negative details and failing to see the broad picture. "I know my son has been a good student and

has not caused any problems in the past, but all I can think about is that he broke the law."

4. *Disqualifying the positive:* paying attention only to negative information. "What good are all my efforts to be a good mother if this is the result?"

5. *Jumping to conclusions (arbitrary inferences):* drawing hasty and unwarranted conclusions. "My son must be guilty. Someone saw him hanging around the school late that night."

6. *Magnification/minimization:* making too much of the negative or devaluing positive information. "My son stole a candy bar from another child when he was four. He must have been destined to become a criminal."

7. *Emotional reasoning:* believing that something is true because it feels that way; paying no attention to contradictory evidence. "I just feel like this is my fault, and no one can convince me it isn't."

8. *"Should" and "must" statements:* having definite and inflexible ideas about how we and others should behave and how life should be. "I should never have let Kevin get his driver's license. I should have made sure I met all his friends. I should have been a better mother to him."

9. *Labeling and mislabeling:* fixing an extreme, broad, and unjustified label on someone. "Kevin is a hopeless criminal."

10. *Personalization:* assuming inordinate responsibility for events or others' behaviors. "My son and I had an argument about his curfew three days before the school break-in. If I hadn't yelled at him, this probably never would have happened."

11. *Catastrophizing:* predicting a negative outcome without considering other possibilities. "I just know Kevin will be sent to prison for this. How will I ever be able to face my friends again?"

12. *Mind reading:* attributing negative thoughts and reactions to others without checking whether they are present. "My husband will never forgive Kevin for this. He'll disown him."

13. *Tunnel vision:* focusing only on the negative aspects of a situation. "I can't do anything right as a parent. There I was, eating dinner, while my son was breaking into the school. How could I not have known what was going on?"

Assessment of Mood

Assessing mood is an important part of cognitive therapy for many reasons. Troubling emotions are often the reason people seek treatment. Consequently, upsetting emotions are likely to be close to the surface and presented early in the treatment process. Those feelings can point the way to identification of distorted cognitions. In addition, monitoring the nature and intensity ratings of people's emotions provides important evidence of progress, while improvement in mood can enhance clients' motivation and optimism.

Cognitive therapists use structured approaches to assess emotions, as they do to assess thoughts. One of Aaron Beck's major contributions to the field of psychotherapy is the development of concise and brief inventories that provide a quick measure of the nature and intensity of those emotions that are most likely to be troubling to people. These include the Beck Depression Inventory (BDI), the Beck Anxiety Inventory (BAI), the Beck Hopelessness Inventory, and the Beck Scale for Suicidal Ideation. Published by the Psychological Corporation, these inventories each take only a few minutes to complete. Any or all of these might be administered before a person begins treatment to obtain a sort of emotional baseline. If elevated scores are obtained on one or more of the inventories, repeated administrations of that inventory every few sessions can allow client and clinician to track and quantify changes in emotions. An even more rapid assessment of emotion can be obtained using an informal 0–100 scale of severity or intensity of a specific mood such as anger, jealousy, or sadness. Clients can rate themselves on these scales at the beginning of each session.

Changing Cognitions

The last two steps in Judith Beck's (1995) dysfunctional thought record include

1. Helping people to formulate new cognitions that are more realistic and adaptive
2. Determining treatment outcome by asking people to rate their belief in the new cognitions, identify and rate their emotions, and determine actions that will be taken in light of the altered thinking

Clinicians work closely with clients to restructure their cognitions and help them find the words that express their new cognitions accurately and realistically and in ways that are compatible with their emotions. This process involves helping people deepen their beliefs in their revised cognitions and make those cognitions part of themselves.

Once again, cognitive therapists draw on a wealth of strategies to accomplish these goals. While many of these techniques are primarily cognitive in nature, others are behavioral and will be addressed further in Part 5. The following are some of the strategies that enhance the work of cognitive therapists (Seligman, 1996a):

- *Activity scheduling* can give people the opportunity to try out new behaviors and ways of thinking and encourages them to remain active despite feelings of sadness or apprehension. Particularly helpful in alleviating depression and anxiety are experiences that bring people feelings of both pleasure and mastery (Burns, 1989). Learning a new and interesting skill and having a good time can contribute to improved moods and clearer thinking.
- *Mental and emotional imagery* (discussed in Chapter 14) can help people envision and try on new ways of thinking and feeling. They might imagine themselves coping successfully, changing parts of an image, or repeating an image to reduce its emotional charge. A man who has always thought of himself as uninteresting, for example, might imagine himself telling fascinating stories to an admiring audience.
- *Cognitive and covert modeling* is a strategy in which people rehearse a new behavior mentally and then create a cognitive model of themselves performing

that behavior successfully. Some athletes use this technique as a way of improving their skills in their sport. A woman married to a verbally abusive husband used this approach to rehearse asserting herself to her husband, making it easier for her to stand up to him when he spoke to her in a demeaning way. A variation is for people to imagine themselves as someone they admire and then tackle a challenging situation as if they were that person.

- *Thought stopping* can be useful when people are having difficulty ridding themselves of persistent thoughts that they view as distorted or harmful. Thought stopping involves saying, "Stop!" either aloud or subvocally each time the unwanted thought recurs and deliberately replacing it with a more positive thought. Over time, the thought is likely to diminish in frequency and intensity.

- *Diversions or distractions* also can help people reduce their negative thinking. A woman who had been diagnosed with a life-threatening illness had a good prognosis but still had constant thoughts that she would certainly die. To distract herself from her troubling thoughts of death, she mentally catalogued each item in her extensive wardrobe, beginning the mental list again each time the negative thoughts returned.

- *Self-talk* is a technique in which people repeat to themselves many times a day positive and encouraging phrases that they have identified as helpful, such as "Don't let fear control you. You can do it." In essence, they are giving themselves a pep talk.

- *Affirmations* are closely related to self-talk. An affirmation is a sort of slogan that is positive and reinforcing. People can post these in prominent places such as the refrigerator or the bathroom mirror where they will see them frequently and be reminded to shift their thinking. An adolescent girl chose as her affirmation "You have great potential and will realize that potential someday." Keeping those words in mind helped her think positively about some of the challenges in her life.

- *Diaries* of events, realistic and distorted cognitions, emotions, and efforts to make positive changes can increase people's awareness of their inner and outer experiences. These written records can provide important material for discussion in sessions and serve as a way to track both progress and difficulties.

- *Letter writing* can serve as an avenue for exploring and expressing thoughts and feelings. The woman whose son was accused of breaking into his school might benefit from drafting a letter to her son expressing her thoughts and feelings. The letters need not be mailed but can be used as the focus of a session.

- *Systematic assessment of alternatives* (cost-benefit analysis) is an approach that is useful in helping people make decisions or choices. They begin by listing their options and examining the pros and cons of each one. Then they assign numbers on a 1–10 scale showing the importance of each advantage and disadvantage. Finally, they total the numbers assigned to the pros and cons of each option. For example, a man considering a career change used this approach to help him decide whether to remain in his secure, well-paying position in computer technology or pursue his lifelong goal of becoming a counselor.

- *Relabeling or reframing* experiences or perceptions can help people think differently about them. For example, a woman who had few dating experiences at age 35 stopped thinking of herself as a failure and instead focused on viewing herself as a late bloomer.
- *Role playing* can help people actualize some of the new thoughts they have about themselves. For example, a man who was developing more positive thoughts about himself and his abilities role-played sharing his accomplishments with his friends, asking his supervisor for a raise, and inviting a colleague to join him for lunch.
- In *rational emotive role play,* clients play the emotional part of the mind while clinicians play the rational part; the two then engage in a dialogue (Beck, 1995).
- When *role playing dialogue between old and new thoughts,* clients use two chairs (as described in Chapter 13) to represent both their old and their new thoughts. By moving from one chair to another, they can engage in a dialogue between the two groups of thoughts. This can help people clarify the changes in their thinking and solidify their more rational thoughts.
- *Distancing* involves projecting into the future to put a problem in perspective and diminish its importance. A woman realized that getting a *B* in a college course would mean little to her in 10 years.
- *Bibliotherapy,* or reading about other people who have coped well with experiences similar to the client's, can help a person modify his or her thinking.
- *Graded task assignments* are activities that clinicians ask clients to complete between sessions. Starting with easy assignments that guarantee success, clinicians gradually make tasks more challenging over time so that people continue to learn from them and feel a sense of mastery and accomplishment. You will learn more about such assignments later in this chapter.

Termination and Relapse Prevention

Like the other phases of cognitive therapy, the concluding phase is also carefully planned and structured to achieve the primary goal of helping people become their own therapists and successfully apply what they have learned through treatment. Sessions are scheduled less frequently, typically shifting to every other week, then to once a month, then to every three months for at least a year (Beck, 1995). This gives people the opportunity to test their skills and cope with almost inevitable setbacks while still staying in contact with their clinicians.

Normalizing setbacks and stressing the importance of ongoing learning can enable people to cope with future disappointments successfully. Life skills such as assertiveness, decision making, coping strategies, and communication skills, which have probably been taught throughout the treatment process, are reviewed and solidified. Progress is also reviewed, with every effort made to help clients accept credit for and take pride in their accomplishments. Clinicians address any concerns that clients have about termination and obtain feedback from clients about the treatment process. Finally, clients and clinicians work together to develop plans and directions that clients can use to continue their progress on their own.

APPLICATION OF COGNITIVE THERAPY

Cognitive therapy has established itself as one of the leading approaches to counseling and psychotherapy. Because Aaron Beck and his colleagues, as well as other cognitive therapists, encourage and engage in extensive research on the impact of this approach, its effectiveness has been more clearly demonstrated than that of most other treatment systems.

Diagnostic Groups

Research during the past 20 years has established the effectiveness of cognitive therapy in treating a broad range of mental disorders. One of the first important indications of the power of this system of treatment came from Smith, Glass, and Miller's (1980) meta-analysis of more than 400 studies on psychotherapy outcome. They concluded that cognitive therapy had a broad range of effectiveness and a particularly strong impact on the treatment of fear and anxiety, specific phobias, and problems in overall adjustment. Cognitive therapy has also demonstrated its effectiveness in alleviating chronic pain, adjustment disorders, social fears, and performance anxiety (Dattilio & Freeman, 1992). Arntz and Van Den Hout (1996) reviewed multiple studies of the treatment of panic disorder via cognitive therapy and found that it had a strong positive impact on both the frequency of attacks and the fear of future attacks; 75–90% of people treated for panic disorder with cognitive therapy were panic-free after treatment.

Extensive research documents the importance of cognitive therapy in the treatment of depression. Probably the most compelling is a study by the NIMH Treatment of Depression Collaborative Research Program (Elkin et al., 1989), which found that, for treatment of moderately severe depression, cognitive therapy was somewhat better than interpersonal therapy (discussed in Chapter 9) and much better than medication alone. Dobson (1989) reviewed 27 separate studies using cognitive therapy to treat depression and concluded that cognitive therapy is significantly better than psychodynamic therapy, person-centered therapy, behavior therapy, and medication. Research by Hollon and Najavits (1988) found that the relapse rate for people treated for depression by cognitive therapy was 30% compared with 60% for people treated via medication.

Beck et al. (1990) have described a plan for using cognitive therapy to treat personality disorders. Linehan and Kehrer (1993) report success in using dialectical behavior therapy, a cognitive behavioral approach, in treatment of people with borderline personality disorders. Although research is still limited on the use of cognitive therapy with personality disorders, distorted thinking is characteristic of people with those disorders, suggesting the likelihood that cognitive treatment will be effective.

Many other disorders also seem likely to respond well to treatment via cognitive therapy, although further research is needed to conclusively demonstrate its effectiveness. Eating disorders, including anorexia nervosa and bulimia nervosa, seem likely to benefit because they often involve underlying depression and a distorted self-image. Judith Beck (1995) reports that, in combination with medication, cognitive therapy has been used successfully to treat people with schizophrenia and bipolar disorders. She also reports good results in using cognitive therapy to treat people with posttraumatic stress disorder, obsessive-compulsive disorder, and substance use disorders.

Cognitive therapy has been used with children and adolescents as well as adults. It has successfully improved the social skills of children with attention deficit/hyperactivity disorder (Cousins & Weiss, 1993; Rapport, 1995). It has also been used to help young people with disruptive behavior disorders manage their anger (Lochman, White, & Wayland, 1991) and improve their problem-solving skills (Kazdin, 1997).

Diverse Client Groups

Because cognitive therapy targets some of the most common concerns presented for treatment—depression and anxiety—it is useful with a broad range of not only disorders but also clients. It is likely to be well received by most people because it is a clear and logical approach and not intrusive. Cognitive therapy does not require people to share intimate details of their past, focus extensively on their emotions, or engage in analysis of dreams or other activities that may be uncomfortable for them. It is an empowering and nonthreatening approach. In addition, cognitive therapy draws on an extensive array of interventions and can readily be adapted to the needs of a particular person.

Because this approach is respectful, addresses present concerns, and does not require disclosure of emotions and experiences that may feel very personal, cognitive therapy is likely to appeal to people from a wide variety of cultural backgrounds. It seems especially suitable for people for whom sharing thoughts is more natural and acceptable than sharing emotions. This characterizes many people from Asian backgrounds. In addition, Thomas (1992) found that cognitive therapy was particularly useful in exploring negative cognitions and engendering hope in African American clients.

At the same time, cognitive therapy is, of course, not for everyone. It requires people to assume an active and collaborative role in the treatment process. In addition, it stresses present-oriented, relatively time-limited treatment. The goal of cognitive therapy is not greater self-awareness but greater ability to think clearly and cope with life's challenges. Consequently, people who are interested in a long-term treatment system that focuses on development of insight and self-awareness may view this therapy as superficial and inadequate for their needs. In addition, people who are reluctant to participate fully in their own treatment, not willing to complete tasks between treatment, intellectually limited, and not motivated to make some changes may not be good candidates. At the same time, high intelligence or motivation is not required for people to benefit from this approach; people who do not meet those criteria should not automatically be viewed as unsuitable for treatment via cognitive therapy (Haaga, DeRubeis, Stewart, & Beck, 1991). Careful screening of clients as well as discussion with them about the nature of cognitive therapy can help clinicians determine if a client is an appropriate candidate for treatment.

Current Status

According to Aaron Beck (1993), by the mid-1980s cognitive therapy had achieved the status of a system of psychotherapy. It had a theory of personality and psychopathology, a teachable and testable model of psychotherapy with techniques to implement the theory, and a body of research documenting its effectiveness. Its efficacy had been supported with a broad range of populations; in both inpatient and outpatient settings; and in individual, couples, family, and group therapy formats. Cognitive therapy has been used with all ages, from preschool children to the elderly (Beck, 1995). Its use has been refined and expanded, and its effectiveness continues to grow. All clinicians should be familiar with the powerful and important concepts of cognitive therapy.

EVALUATION OF COGNITIVE THERAPY

Although cognitive therapy has a great deal to offer, it also has limitations. Keeping these in mind can help clinicians maximize the effectiveness of this treatment system.

Limitations

Cognitive therapy is demanding of both clients and clinicians. Clinicians must be organized, comfortable with structure, and willing to use inventories and forms to elicit and assess clients' concerns and progress. They must be knowledgeable about learning theory, behavior therapy, diagnosis, and the impact of the past on the present and able to draw skillfully on a broad range of interventions. Clients must be willing to complete homework between sessions and participate actively in their own treatment. Planning, effort, and motivation can make a great difference in the success of cognitive therapy. Both clients and clinicians should be aware of the commitment required by this approach.

Strengths

Cognitive therapy has many strengths. Its clear and carefully planned structure facilitates both teaching and research on the effectiveness of this treatment system. It is a versatile approach that can be modified and adapted to address a broad range of people and disorders. Its time-limited nature makes it efficient and appealing to many people, while its use of long-term follow-up provides a safeguard against relapse. Its emphasis on building a collaborative client-clinician alliance, providing task assignments between sessions, giving the client credit for progress, reinforcing positive changes, and teaching skills is empowering. This approach is designed not just to resolve immediate problems but to enable people to manage their lives successfully. Although mastery of cognitive therapy is not as simple as it seems, with training and experience most clinicians can easily learn and use it effectively.

Contributions

Cognitive therapy has made many important contributions to counseling and psychotherapy. Aaron Beck's work, in particular, has emphasized the importance of research and evidence of effectiveness. This has led to increased research throughout the helping professions as well as development of treatment manuals designed to provide some uniformity to treatment and facilitate assessment of efficacy. Cognitive therapy's use of case formulation and treatment planning is compatible with today's emphasis on goal setting and accountability in treatment and has established a standard that other treatment systems are expected to follow. The wealth of techniques and interventions that have grown out of cognitive therapy provide useful ideas for all clinicians. Cognitive therapy's emphasis on the importance of the therapeutic alliance has helped to dispel the myth that cognitive and behavioral therapists are indifferent to the nature of their relationships with their clients. On the contrary, they recognize that a positive and collaborative therapeutic relationship is an essential ingredient of treatment. Perhaps the most important contribution of cognitive therapy is the message that analysis and modification of distorted cognitions are important ways to help people change. While emotions, actions, and background should never be ignored in treatment, helping people develop more realistic cognitions is an effective and efficient way to help them reach their goals.

SKILL DEVELOPMENT: PLANNING AND PROCESSING HOMEWORK

The mere mention of homework as an integral part of treatment can bring up negative images for both clinicians and clients—memories of deadlines, failures, and blame for poor performance. However, homework, or what Beck has called task assignments, can also be a great asset to treatment; it can help people feel empowered, encourage them to take credit for their gains, and accelerate the treatment process. According to Judith Beck (1995), "Cognitive therapy patients who carry out homework assignments progress better in therapy than those who do not" (p. 248). The guidelines that follow can help make homework a positive experience for both clients and clinicians.

Terminology

For some people, the words *homework* and *assignment* have negative connotations. They also imply that the clinician/teacher is telling the client/student to complete a requirement. This can create a hierarchy rather than a collaboration, which is undesirable in cognitive therapy. Finding more acceptable language can help. Terms such as *tasks, between-session projects,* and *suggested activities* may be more acceptable. Clinicians should seek to use language that will elicit a positive response from clients.

Determining the Assignment

Collaboration Clients and clinicians should collaborate in determining assignments. Although suggestions may first come primarily from clinicians, clients should have the opportunity to shape the tasks in ways that make them more meaningful. They should also have the right to accept or reject any suggested assignments. As clients begin to progress and become more familiar with the treatment process, clinicians may encourage them to suggest tasks they find meaningful.

Relating Assignments to Sessions Clinicians should clarify for clients the rationale behind each assignment. The assignments should be logically related to the session so that their value is clear and they continue the progress of the session. For example, a woman who expressed thoughts of self-blame related to the abuse she and her younger sister received from their mother was urged to draft a letter to her mother, expressing her thoughts and feelings about the mother's abuse of the sister. The woman was able to think more clearly about the injustice of the abuse toward her sister than about her own abuse. The letter assignment was intended to help her become more aware of those thoughts so she could eventually believe similar thoughts about her own abuse. This letter was not actually mailed but served as a learning experience.

Making Assignments Specific Assignments should be specific so that clients know exactly when and how to complete them. This helps reduce resistance and barriers to performance of the assignment. For example, rather than suggesting that a client "have more contact with friends this week," the assignment might involve "having telephone conversations of at least five minutes with two friends on Wednesday evening and inviting at least one of them to have lunch with you."

Ease of Accomplishment Assignments should be easy to accomplish. This, too, reduces clients' resistance and makes it more likely that people will complete the tasks. In addition, their success in accomplishing the tasks will help them feel empowered and optimistic about their treatment. Graded task assignments, which gradually increase in difficulty, are particularly useful in helping people build on past successes and confront increasing challenges. Again, clinicians should plan carefully when making tasks more difficult, always seeking success. Assigning tasks that are too hard for clients or that bring up strong negative feelings are likely to undermine the treatment process and increase clients' self-doubts.

Practicing Tasks in the Session Clinicians can increase the likelihood of clients' completing suggested tasks by starting or practicing a task in the session before asking people to complete tasks on their own. For example, a person who wanted to stop thinking negative thoughts about his failure to graduate from college with honors was encouraged to deliberately think the negative thoughts in the session and then practice using thought stopping followed by an affirmation to curtail his negative ruminating. Coaching and encouraging him through this process in the session increased his motivation to use these skills outside of the session.

Addressing Possible Barriers   Clinicians should address possible barriers to accomplishment of assignments as well as potential negative outcomes to prevent them from interfering with the treatment process. Elinor, a young woman who had been adopted as an infant, had successfully modified cognitions about her unlovableness. Her newfound confidence led her to decide to contact her biological mother. She and her counselor spent time talking about the possible reactions her mother might have to receiving a letter from Elinor to prepare her to handle any outcome. In addition, the clinician helped Elinor focus on the personal achievements that enabled her to take this step rather than look to the outcome of the reunion to determine whether this experience was a success or a failure. Role play and cognitive rehearsal are particularly useful strategies for helping prepare people for challenging tasks.

Minimizing Excuses   Clinicians also should plan assignments so that they minimize the likelihood of excuses. For example, "If I go out to dinner with my mother and if she orders a glass of wine, I will tell her my thoughts about her excessive use of alcohol" is not a good assignment. It has too many ifs and possible pitfalls. Create assignments that depend on the client rather than on other people or external circumstances.

Addressing Clients' Reactions   Clinicians should address clients' reactions to the concept of homework assignments. Some people have a strong need for perfection, may fear failure or judgment, or may be very eager to please the clinician (Persons, 1989). Clinicians should explore clients' feelings about completing task assignments, making sure that clients understand the reason for the homework and know that they and their homework will not be judged by the clinician. Keeping the clients' reactions to homework in mind when suggesting or processing tasks should increase the likelihood that they will make a positive contribution to treatment.

Offering Options   For people who are beginning treatment or who may be apprehensive about completing assignments, offering options can be helpful. For example, identifying three tasks but encouraging a client to complete only two of them gives the person an added measure of control that can reassure the person that this is not school where all assignments must be done.

Writing Down Assignments   Task assignments should be written down, by either the client or the clinician, in a place where the client can easily locate them. Some clinicians have space on the back of their appointment cards for assignments, some give clients a form at the end of each session that lists their suggested tasks, and others have clients bring a notebook or date book to each session to record their homework for the week. Clinicians should also note the homework in their own records so that they can follow up appropriately in the next session.

Processing Homework

Clinicians should be sure to discuss and process homework in the session after it has been suggested. Most clients invest considerable effort into their tasks and want to share their accomplishments with their clinicians. Not only is processing the homework likely to improve clients' self-esteem and cooperation with the completion of future tasks, but it also helps identify and reinforce the learning that has come from the task and draws on that in planning the agenda for the session as well as the next suggested task.

Of course, clients will not always complete homework, and their experiences with assignments may not always be rewarding. Even under these circumstances, the homework can be viewed as a learning experience so that something positive always emerges from the homework. For example, in an effort to develop her social skills and relationships, Mary joined a cooking class. Unfortunately, traffic problems delayed her arrival at the class. When she got there and saw that the class was already in progress, she became very anxious and left the class. Although this disappointed her, she could take credit for making an effort to attend the class and learned that she needed to plan her next social experience more carefully to maximize her comfort level. The experience also gave Mary an opportunity to identify an automatic thought, "I am a failure at whatever I undertake," and replace it with "I was wise to know that coming into the class late was too much for me. I can learn from this and be more successful next time."

Homework can be a rewarding and reinforcing experience for clients and provide an opportunity for clinicians to use their creativity and understanding of clients to tailor meaningful, interesting, and growth-promoting experiences. One clinician who made regular use of written homework reported that many of her clients kept a file of their assignments over the course of treatment and viewed them as a reflection of how much they had accomplished.

CASE ILLUSTRATION

This case applies many of the strategies of cognitive therapy to Edie, who came to a session upset because she had not received a promotion at work. Assume that she and her clinician have already made use of cognitive therapy in their sessions so that Edie is familiar with this mode of treatment.

Edie: I had really been hoping to get promoted when the position as assistant head of the library opened up. I should have known they wouldn't hire me.

Clinician: I can hear that this is very upsetting to you. Let's take a close look at some of your reactions. When did this happen?

Edie: Just yesterday, February 23rd.

Clinician: And fill me in on the situation.

Edie: The assistant head of our library resigned, and the position was announced. I put in my application, really hoping for the job and the promotion. But they hired someone from outside our library system.

Clinician: That must have been a real disappointment for you. What physical sensations did you have when you heard the news?

Edie: I felt like I was going to cry, but I didn't want to do that in the middle of the library.

Clinician: What thoughts went through your mind when this happened?

Edie: I'm really a loser. No matter how hard I try, I fail. Everybody must be laughing at me behind my back.

Clinician: On a 0–100% scale, how much do you believe each of those thoughts?

Edie: I'm really a loser: 90%. No matter how hard I try, I fail: 95%. Everybody must be laughing at me behind my back: 80%.

Clinician: So you have a pretty strong belief in all of them. Tell me what emotions you had when you learned you would not receive the promotion and what the intensity rating of those emotions would be on the 0–100% scale.

Edie: I felt disappointment and sadness: 99%; and hopelessness: 95%.

Clinician: Now let's take a closer look at these beliefs. How about starting with the last one, "Everyone must be laughing at me behind my back," which you gave the lowest rating. What reactions did you get from people when the name of the new assistant head was announced?

Edie: I only told two people that I was applying for the job in case I didn't get it. One of them came right over to me and she said, "You should have gotten that job. Nobody knows this library better than you. They just hired that other person because she has a doctorate and they thought she was a big deal."

Clinician: When you think about what was said to you, what thoughts come up for you?

Edie: Well, I guess I was exaggerating when I said everyone was laughing at me. Most people didn't even know I wanted that job. I just felt so embarrassed that I hadn't gotten the

position. And my friend could be right. I don't have a doctorate, and the advertisement did say doctorate preferred.

Clinician: What about your statement that you fail at everything you do? Let's evaluate that statement.

Edie: That one sounds like an exaggeration too. I did feel like a failure though.

Clinician: Let's look at the other side of the coin. Tell me some things at which you have succeeded.

Edie: I generally do a good job as a mother. I know I do well at the library; I even got an award from the county.

Clinician: Anything else?

Edie: I'm a pretty good ice skater. And I write pretty well. I even managed to learn to use the computer system at the library. That wasn't easy.

Clinician: So there are many aspects of your life where you have succeeded. If you were to say what percentage of the things you do are successful, what would you say?

Edie: I guess at least 75%.

Clinician: So you succeed at most of what you do.

Edie: Yes, that seems true.

Clinician: Let's go back to your original beliefs. How would you rate them now on the 0–100% scale?

Edie: I'm really a loser: 40%. No matter how hard I try, I fail: 30%. Everybody must be laughing at me behind my back: 20%.

Clinician: So there's been a big change. From this list of types of cognitive distortions, what distortions are reflected by your statements?

Edie: I can see emotional reasoning: feeling like people were laughing at me just because I felt so embarrassed. And overgeneralization: calling myself a failure and a loser because I had this one disappointment. I guess I was also discounting the positive: ignoring all the things I do well.

Clinician: How would you respond to those initial beliefs now?

Edie: Well, I don't think many people are laughing at me. If they are, well, they'll be sorry I didn't get the job. No one knows the library as well as I do. And I'm not a loser. I don't succeed at everything I try, but I do have a pretty good track record; 75% isn't bad at all.

Clinician: What emotions are you feeling now?

Edie: Disappointment, about 75%; but sadness and hopelessness are way down to about 50% and 20%. In fact, I heard about a job at another library that I think I'll look into.

Clinician: Let's come up with some homework to help solidify the work you've done today. Any ideas on what might be useful?

Edie: Yes, if I do start to feel like a failure, I can use that thought-stopping technique you taught me. Maybe an affirmation would help too.

Clinician: What would be a good one?

Edie: How about "I succeed at least 75% of the time"?

Clinician: Is that positive enough for you?

Edie: If it were too positive, I wouldn't believe it. This works for me.

Clinician: All right. How can you remind yourself of that affirmation?

Edie: I'll write it down and put it in my date book so I'll see it every time I look at my calendar, which I do often.

Clinician: How about writing it down now, and let's both make note of the homework you agreed to do this week.

Edie: Sure. And I'll also make a note to myself to get some information about that other job opening.

EXERCISES

Large-Group Exercises

1. On the board, list the types of cognitive distortions. Then, focusing on Roberto or any other hypothetical client, generate at least one example of each type that might reflect the client's thinking.
2. Select at least three of those cognitive distortions and discuss ways in which you would help modify those beliefs. Consider what strategies you would use to enable the person to evaluate each thought.
3. For each of the following cognitive distortions, come up with at least three alternative interpretations or attributions that might be used to raise questions about the validity of the belief.

Person A: Susan told me she would call me on Sunday morning to arrange to meet for brunch. Now it's the afternoon. She didn't really want to spend time with me but was just afraid to tell me. I'll never be able to make a good friend. I'm so unlikable.

Person B: When the principal announced that I had won the math award, my teacher gave me a really funny look. She probably wanted Nancy to win. Nancy does get better grades than I do. It's just a fluke that I won that award.

Person C: I had a business trip to the town where my nephew goes to college and called him to see if we could get together. He just told me he was too busy right now and couldn't get off the phone fast enough. I know the family has felt differently about me since I let them know I was gay. My brother probably told him not to have anything to do with me any more. We used to be so close, but I guess he can't deal with my being gay. He did call me back later and apologize for being so abrupt, but the damage had already been done. I know what he was really feeling.

Small-Group Exercises

1. Form into your small groups of four people in two dyads. Each dyad should have an opportunity to role-play both client and clinician roles. Allow 10–15 minutes for each role play. The client should open the session by talking about an upsetting experience. The role of the clinician is to guide the client through the following process:

> - Identify date, time, situation, and accompanying sensations.
> - Identify two automatic thoughts, write them down, and rate how much each is believed on the 0–100% scale.
> - Identify the accompanying emotions and rate their intensity on the same scale.
> - Use some of the strategies you have learned in this chapter to help the client evaluate the cognitions.
> - Replace any distorted cognitions with more adaptive responses, and rate how much each of those is believed.
> - Rate the belief in the original cognitions.
> - Identify and rate the intensity of the current emotions.
> - Decide on a homework task to solidify the learning in the session.

Allow time for group members to share feedback after each role play has finished. Feedback should look at both general counseling skills and the process of taking the client through the previous steps and should focus on both strengths and suggestions for improvement.

2. After all the role plays are completed, list the distorted cognitions that were generated in the group. Then review the types of distorted cognitions and identify which type characterizes each distorted cognition on the list.

3. As a group, develop an appropriate affirmation for each of the clients in the previous role plays.

Individual Exercises

1. Becoming your own therapist is an important aspect of cognitive therapy. Writing your responses in your journal, analyze your thoughts and emotions after an upsetting experience. Follow the format in Small-Group Exercise 1. Label and dispute your thoughts, identifying tasks you can use to help modify your thoughts and emotions.

2. Develop, write down, and use an affirmation that sounds right to you and will help you meet your goals.

3. Identify an upcoming experience that presents difficulty for you—perhaps public speaking, meeting new people at a business or social gathering, or asking someone for something. Engage in the process of cognitive rehearsal in which you imagine yourself successfully handling the experience. Rehearse the experience in your mind at least three times. Write about your reactions to this exercise.

Summary

Cognitive therapists believe that the most effective way to help people make positive changes is by enabling them to identify, evaluate, and, if indicated, modify their thoughts. While attention is also paid to emotions and actions, distorted thoughts are the target of treatment. Developed by Aaron Beck and his associates, cognitive therapy is a time-limited, structured approach that offers specific plans for change, gives people clear explanations of all steps in the treatment process, and teaches skills that empower people and promote their emotional well-being. Clients and clinicians work collaboratively in this process, with the clinicians who are guiding the process drawing on an extensive array of creative interventions to promote and reinforce positive change. Task assignments, inventories, and forms are used extensively and contribute to the clarity and impact of cognitive therapy. Research conducted by Aaron Beck and others has proven the effectiveness of cognitive therapy with a broad range of mental disorders and clients. It is especially effective in treating depression and anxiety.

Training in cognitive therapy is widely available. The following is a good place to begin gathering additional information on education and resources:

Beck Institute for Cognitive Therapy and Research
GSB Building
City Line and Belmont Avenues, Suite 700
Bala Cynwyd, PA 19004-1610
(610) 664-3020

Information also can be obtained from

Center for Cognitive Therapy
1101 Dove Street, Suite 240
Newport Beach, CA 92660-2803
(714) 964-7312

Although many of the journals in psychology and counseling include articles on cognitive therapy, two focus specifically on treatment via this approach: the *Journal of Cognitive Psychotherapy* and the *International Cognitive Therapy Newsletter.* In addition, you can order the Beck inventories discussed in this chapter from

The Psychological Corporation
555 Academic Court
San Antonio, TX 78204
(800) 211-8378

RECOMMENDED READINGS

Beck, A., Freeman, A., & Associates. (1990). *Cognitive therapy of personality disorders.* New York: Guilford.
Beck, J. S. (1995). *Cognitive therapy: Basics and beyond.* New York: Guilford.
Dattilio, F. M., & Freeman, A. (Eds.). (1992). *Comprehensive casebook of cognitive therapy.* New York: Plenum.
Persons, J. B. (1989). *Cognitive therapy in practice.* New York: Norton.

Chapter 17

ALBERT ELLIS AND RATIONAL EMOTIVE BEHAVIOR THERAPY

Another important theory of counseling and psychotherapy that emphasizes thoughts—rational emotive behavior therapy (REBT)—was developed by Albert Ellis in the 1950s. Ellis has continued to be the primary advocate and spokesperson for this approach, although many other clinicians have become practitioners of REBT. Like Aaron Beck's cognitive therapy, REBT takes the position that people's cognitions are the primary source of their difficulties. Although rational emotional behavior therapists believe that thoughts, emotions, and behaviors are interrelated and interdependent (Bond & Dryden, 1996), they view changing cognitions and self-statements so that people think more rationally as the most effective route to improving all three areas of functioning. In particular, REBT hones in on "self-defeating absolutistic beliefs" (Nielsen & Ellis, 1994, p. 327).

As you will learn, cognitive therapy and REBT have much in common in terms of their theories of human development, approaches to effecting change, and strategies used. Both treatment systems take a structured approach to facilitating change while emphasizing the importance of the human element in treatment. As Ellis (1992) has stated, REBT "tries to combine a tough-minded scientific attitude with a down-to-earth humanistic approach to psychotherapy" (p. 357).

However, the two also have some key differences. REBT uses a somewhat different approach to disputing and modifying distorted cognitions. Persuasion and teaching, along with gathering evidence, are important strategies for the rational emotive behavior therapist. More important, REBT addresses change on two levels: general REBT focuses on resolving immediate and practical concerns, while elegant REBT "helps people achieve an intensive, profoundly philosophical and emotional change" (Ellis, 1995a, p. 1). We will discuss these two types of REBT later in this chapter.

THE PERSON WHO DEVELOPED RATIONAL EMOTIVE BEHAVIOR THERAPY

Albert Ellis, the originator of REBT, was born in 1913 in Pittsburgh. He moved to New York as a young child and has lived there for most of his life. Ellis's family of origin included an independent mother, a father who cared about the family but was often absent, and a younger brother (Weinrach, 1980). Ellis was apparently the family favorite and got along well with the others in his family, although in many ways he had a difficult childhood. At an early age, he perceived his family as "pretty crazy" and has stated that he basically raised himself from the age of seven (p. 159). In addition, Ellis, like Beck, was sickly as a child and was hospitalized many times, usually for nephritis. To overcome these difficulties, he determined not to be miserable about his circumstances and maintained strong positive thoughts about his own competence and worth (Ellis, 1997). Thus, at an early age he learned to believe that the way in which people think can enable them to overcome adversity.

In the 1940s, Ellis received his M.A. and Ph.D. degrees in clinical psychology from Columbia University and began practicing as a marriage, family, and sex therapist. Believing that psychoanalysis was the way to help people achieve the most profound change, he obtained training as a psychoanalyst with an emphasis on the work of Karen Horney (Ellis & Dryden, 1997). However, his dissatisfaction with the inefficiency of that approach as well as his readings in Greek and Asian philosophy led him to search for a way to treat people that focused on their thoughts.

Ellis began practicing what he initially called rational therapy in 1955, founded the still active Institute for Rational Emotive Therapy in 1959 to offer both treatment and training in this approach, and published the first of his many works on REBT in 1962. Since then, he has had an illustrious career advancing his system of treatment. A prolific writer, he has published more than 700 papers and 55 books and monographs. He has received many awards, including the Distinguished Professional Psychologist Award in 1974 and the Distinguished Professional Contributions Award in 1985, both from the American Psychological Association. In a 1991 survey, Canadian clinical psychologists chose Ellis as the most influential psychologist (Ellis, 1997). American clinical psychologists and counselors ranked him second, after Carl Rogers but before Sigmund Freud.

Ellis is very open about discussing his personal life and often uses himself as a role model in his work. A classic story he has told about himself is that, as a young man, he was apprehensive about asking women for dates. In an effort to overcome his fears, he forced himself to approach 100 women and invite them out. Although all refused, this experience of forcing himself to do repeatedly what he feared most apparently enabled him to overcome his anxieties. Ellis's shame-attacking exercises (discussed later in this chapter) recall this experience. Ellis has had two brief marriages, which both ended in divorce. However, for more than 30 years he has lived with Janet Wolfe, a psychotherapist who also writes about and practices REBT.

Now approaching his 90th year, Ellis is "partially disabled with diabetes, tired eyes, deficient hearing" and other disabilities (Ellis, 1997, p. 17). Reportedly, he uses REBT to cope with these difficulties, and he continues to write, lecture, and practice. A typical work day extends from 9:30 A.M. to 11:00 P.M. In a given week, he might see 80 people for individual counseling and another 40 for group therapy at the Psychological Clinic of the Albert Ellis Institute. Each year, Ellis also gives several hundred talks about his work.

Ellis is a man with a strong personality. Windy Dryden, another leading proponent of REBT, has described him as abrasive, humorous, and flamboyant. Ellis's direct manner and his frequent use of colorful language always make an impact; many people are impressed, while others are offended. In studying REBT, keep in mind that one need not emulate Ellis's style to practice successfully the important treatment system he has developed.

THE DEVELOPMENT OF RATIONAL EMOTIVE BEHAVIOR THERAPY

Now more than 40 years old, rational emotive behavior therapy has undergone some development over the years, although its basic premise—that emotions and behavior can best be modified by changing thinking—has not changed.

Early influences on REBT's development include Buddhist and Taoist philosophy and writings on the philosophy of happiness, secular humanism, and behaviorism. Alfred Adler's emphasis on the social system, belief in the importance of goals and purpose, and use of live demonstrations are also apparent in REBT. In addition, some of Karen Horney's concepts, especially her ideas about the power of the *shoulds* in our lives, had an impact on what Ellis originally called rational therapy.

Ellis has changed the name of his theory twice. In 1961, he changed it from rational therapy to rational emotive therapy, indicating that this approach did pay attention to feelings. This modification may, at least in part, have responded to the popularity of Carl Rogers's ideas, which emphasized the great importance of emotions. Although Ellis always paid considerable attention to behavior, especially as a vehicle for reinforcing and implementing changes in thinking, RET did not become rational emotive behavior therapy until 1993 (Ellis, 1995b). This most recent name change clearly reflects REBT's belief that, although thoughts are emphasized, emotions, behaviors, and thoughts are intertwined and inseparable. To maximize success, treatment must attend to all three areas (reflected by Parts 3, 4, and 5 of this book).

Although the theory and strategies associated with REBT have evolved over the years, one of the greatest changes is the conception of REBT as two-tiered. *General REBT* is used with all clients to target immediate presenting concerns. *Preferential* or *elegant REBT* seeks deep philosophical changes and is used only with people who seem able to benefit from it. According to Ellis and Dryden (1997), general REBT is comparable to cognitive therapy, while preferential REBT goes beyond it, seeking to help people effect long-lasting and profound change.

Since its initial development, the theories and strategies of REBT have become less absolute and more compatible with postmodern and less structured treatment approaches, including narrative therapy and existentialism. Interventions have become more varied and eclectic. In addition, greater attention is paid to getting to know and understand the background and viewpoints of each client.

IMPORTANT THEORETICAL CONCEPTS

Like cognitive therapy, REBT focuses on helping people identify, evaluate, and modify dysfunctional cognitions. However, rational emotive behavior therapists differ from cognitive therapists following Beck's approach in terms of the approaches they use and their conception of healthy development.

Human Development and Emotional Health

According to REBT, dimensions of psychological health include the following (Ellis, 1995a; Ellis & Dryden, 1997, pp. 18–19):

- Self-interest, or valuing oneself
- Social interest, or caring about others and recognizing that contributing to the world enhances our own happiness
- Self-direction and personally meaningful goals and direction
- High frustration tolerance so we are not devastated by disappointments
- Flexibility, allowing us to adapt to changes
- Acceptance of uncertainty and ambiguity
- Involvement in long-range absorbing creative pursuits; commitment to something outside oneself
- Ability to think in a clear, logical, scientific, and rational way
- Awareness, acceptance, and appreciation of oneself and others
- Willingness to take sensible risks, experiment, and be reasonably adventurous
- Long-range hedonism, or the ability to enjoy the present as well as the discipline to defer immediate gratification and seek pleasure in the future
- Recognition that we cannot always be totally happy and that life will not always go exactly as we hope
- Taking responsibility for one's own emotional difficulties

Although REBT emphasizes the importance of the individual, it also recognizes that we all live in a social context and must attend to the needs of our society as well as ourselves.

Self-Acceptance   Self-acceptance is an important concept in REBT. Theorists believe that emotional difficulties often are found in people with conditional self-acceptance; they value themselves only because of their accomplishments rather than because of their basic worth as a person. When they experience failures or disappointments, their self-esteem plummets. They cannot separate "performance from personhood" (Barrish, 1997, p. 73), and believe "I am what I do" and "If I fail, I am a bad, worthless person." According to Ellis, people should have a realistic sense of their strengths and weaknesses and take pride in their achievements. At the same time, they will feel happier and have more stability in their lives if they can accept, value, and believe in themselves even when they are disappointed in their behaviors or in events in their lives. REBT teaches people to assess their thoughts and behaviors, not themselves.

Barrish (1997) extended this concept to child-rearing practices and emphasizes the importance of parents' contributions to developing children's self-esteem. Consistent with REBT, Barrish suggested that parents give their children messages such as "I value you even when I don't agree with you or am disappointed with your performance" and "I am proud of what you did," praising the act rather than judging the intrinsic value of the person. By recognizing that people are fallible and not equating the worth of the child with the child's accomplishments, parents can help their children value themselves unconditionally.

Origins of Emotional Disturbance REBT suggests that because irrational thinking is so widespread, people must have a strong biological tendency to think dysfunctionally and believe that life should go their way. However, people do vary in their propensity to think irrationally, in part due to their backgrounds, in part due to their innate styles of thought. Rational emotive behavior therapists recognize that childhood difficulties and traumas may contribute to a person's tendency to think and act in ways that reflect those early problems. Emotional disturbance, then, results from a combination of one's predisposition toward irrational thinking and one's life experiences.

According to REBT, emotional disturbance is usually characterized by underlying anxiety. Ellis (1991) described two levels of anxiety. *Discomfort anxiety* is linked to situational problems such as phobias and recent losses, while *ego anxiety* results when people's sense of self is threatened and includes strong feelings of guilt and inadequacy. These two levels of anxiety seem to parallel the two levels of REBT, with general REBT being sufficient to treat discomfort anxiety but preferential REBT needed for ego anxiety.

Despite its somewhat fatalistic viewpoint and its recognition of the impact of biological, social, and other forces on human development, REBT maintains an optimistic view of human nature. It emphasizes will and choice and perceives people as having inborn drives toward self-actualization as well as irrational thinking (Bernard, 1995). This treatment system perceives people as being able to exercise choice, see that their thoughts are responsible for disturbing them, and actively and continually work toward positive change (Ellis & Dryden, 1997).

Underlying Theory

With its focus on the perceptions and responsibility of the individual, REBT is rooted in secular humanism. According to Ellis (1992), secular humanism is "opposed to religious, mystical, and spiritual humanism. Secular humanism is relativist, skeptical, and nondogmatic and emphasizes the best and most practical aspects of the scientific method together with human choice and meaningfulness" (p. 349). Secular humanists view people as unique individuals who usually value and choose to live in interdependent social groups. They see people as neither good nor bad but simply human; only people's acts are evaluated. People who adopt a philosophy of secular humanism typically are concerned with social systems and advocate peace, fairness, and democracy. They seek possibilities and alternatives rather than absolute truths.

REBT and Religion Because of his criticism of certain types of religious beliefs, Ellis and REBT have sometimes been seen as opposed to conventional religion. This reflects a misunderstanding of Ellis's viewpoint. Ellis and Dryden (1997) describe REBT as compatible with a Christian viewpoint in that it "condemns the sin but not the sinner" (p. 3). What REBT does criticize is any type of belief system, religious or other, that is dogmatic, rigid, and antihumanistic. This should not be construed to mean that Ellis and REBT are opposed to religion; in fact, they recognize that belief in a higher power and involvement with a religious community can help people find a personally meaningful direction in their lives. REBT clinicians are only opposed to what they perceive as irrational and harmful belief systems: those that are absolutist rather probabilistic (Weinrach, 1980).

REBT and Other Treatment Systems Rational emotive behavior therapists view their work as compatible with many of the modern approaches to counseling and psychotherapy. The importance they place on the intrinsic value of each individual is similar to Rogers's unconditional positive regard. The importance they attribute to each person's finding a personally meaningful and rewarding direction is consistent with existentialism. REBT is a phenomenological approach that maintains that people's views of reality are the source of their disturbance; this is compatible with narrative therapy and constructivism. Of course, great overlap exists between Beck's cognitive therapy and Ellis's REBT. However, Ellis has been critical of transpersonal approaches to treatment, viewing them as antihumanistic because of their mystical and unscientific aspects (Ellis, 1992).

Thoughts As the Route to Change According to REBT, people need to recognize and accept that they are largely responsible for creating their own emotional problems (Ellis, 1988). Regardless of when and how the problems began, theorists believe that emotional problems stem primarily from irrational beliefs. As Shakespeare wrote, "Things are neither good nor bad but thinking makes them so" (DiGiuseppe, 1996). Rational emotive behavior therapists have found that, through hard work and practice, people can change their absolute and irrational beliefs and correspondingly alleviate their emotional difficulties.

Of course, REBT recognizes that traumatic experiences can have a profound impact on people. Nevertheless, even for people who have been traumatized, the focus of treatment is on present thoughts—on gently helping people accept their experiences, stop blaming themselves, and focus on the present and the future rather than the past.

REBT also recognizes the role of early experience in human development. However, this approach does not focus extensively on the roots of people's difficulties. Instead, the focus is on people's current beliefs and related actions that are keeping their disturbances alive (Bernard, 1995). Clinicians use forceful and creative approaches to help people identify and dispute their irrational beliefs and maintain that positive results are obtained when people gain awareness of their irrational beliefs and take successful action to change those beliefs. Like cognitive therapists, clinicians practicing REBT seek to give people the skills they need to become their own therapists—to enable them to use the methods of REBT throughout their lives to identify and change their self-destructive thoughts.

Insight Insight into the origins of problems and emotional disturbance is not an essential part of REBT. Not only is insight viewed as insufficient for change, but it is seen as potentially harmful, leading to self-blame and immobilization. However, insight related to the principles of REBT is important. Ellis (1988) has described three levels of this type of insight, which he believes are necessary for people to make positive changes:

1. The insight to see that we choose to upset ourselves
2. The insight to see that we acquired our irrational beliefs and to see how we continue to maintain them
3. The insight to see that we need to work hard to change

Present Focus   REBT focuses on present thoughts rather than past events. Although clinicians recognize the significance of the past, they discourage lengthy, indepth exploration of people's backgrounds and the origins of their thoughts (Ellis, 1995a). Instead, they believe that a present-oriented focus is more meaningful to people, more likely to enhance rapport, and in keeping with the idea that people's current thoughts and behaviors are what keep their self-defeating thoughts alive, whatever the origins of those thoughts.

Emotions   Clinicians using REBT do not spend a great deal of time exploring emotions and certainly do not seek to change them directly. However, they do recognize that awareness of people's emotions can help both clients and clinicians identify clients' irrational beliefs and succeed in effecting change in those beliefs. Clinicians also encourage people to recognize how their emotions contribute to their overall disturbance.

Ellis (1986) distinguished between inappropriate/self-destructive emotions and appropriate/nondefeating emotions. *Self-destructive emotions* are enduring, immobilizing, and nonproductive; reflect overreactions to stimuli; and lead to negative self-images. Examples include rage, shame, guilt, hatred, self-criticism, anxiety, and depression. On the other hand, *appropriate emotions* are transient, manageable, proportioned to the stimulus, and preserving of self-acceptance. They include emotions such as annoyance, regret, disappointment, criticism of one's behavior, concern, and sadness. Of course, we all have negative reactions when we experience disappointments. However, our thoughts about those disappointments determine whether we develop emotions that are inappropriate and self-destructive or appropriate and nondefeating.

Behavior   Although the word *behavior* has only recently been added to the approach's name, REBT has always paid great attention to people's behaviors (Ellis, 1995b). However, like emotions, behaviors are viewed as a secondary focus of treatment. They can be a vehicle for assessing progress and modifying and reinforcing thoughts and are a prime target of homework assignments. Although behaviors, emotions, and thoughts are seen as having a reciprocal relationship, thoughts are viewed as the primary route to change. Changing thoughts and accompanying self-statements will lead to changes in both actions and emotion.

Irrational Beliefs

Ellis and Dryden (1997) have identified six types of beliefs:

1. *Nonevaluative observations.* A person is running toward a bus that is pulling away from the curb.
2. *Nonevaluative inferences.* The person is probably trying to catch the bus.
3. *Positive preferential evaluations.* My friend keeps smiling and patting my hand as we talk, so I presume she is enjoying my company.
4. *Positive musturbatory evaluations.* I am always an entertaining conversationalist, so I am a wonderful person.
5. *Negative preferential evaluations.* Because my friend keeps fidgeting and looking at her watch, I presume that she is bored by my company.
6. *Negative musturbatory evaluations.* Because I have not succeeded in holding my friend's interest, I am boring and a failure. That is just awful and unbearable.

The first two types, nonevaluative observations and inferences, are neutral and nonjudgmental beliefs that Ellis (1984) has called cold cognitions. Positive and negative preferential evaluations may or may not be accurate, but they are grounded in reality, reflect preferences rather than convictions, and are not absolute or exaggerated. Consequently, they can be viewed as rational beliefs and warm cognitions. However, positive and negative musturbatory evaluations involve overgeneralization, judgments of self and others, and absolutes. Negative musturbatory evaluations are also characterized by what Ellis and Dryden (1997) have called "awfulizing" and "I-can't-stand-it-itis" as well as by shoulds and oughts and condemnation of self and others (p. 12). These are the hot cognitions that lead to disturbances, problems, and emotional difficulties. The three major musturbating belief systems that follow reflect thoughts and demands about the self, others, and the world (Ellis, 1984, p. x).

1. I am no good unless I act perfectly and receive everyone's love and approval.
2. You are no good unless you always treat me well.
3. Life is not good unless it goes the way I want it to go.

According to DiGiuseppe (1996), irrational beliefs are usually characterized by at least one of the following themes: awfulizing, global evaluations of human worth and self-criticism, demandingness, and frustration intolerance.

REBT, then, identifies thoughts and beliefs as either rational beliefs (rB) or irrational beliefs (iB). Irrational beliefs often include words such as *should, ought,* and *must* and may include immediate demands. Common issues reflected by these beliefs include success and approval, justice and comfort (Bernard, 1995). Irrational beliefs are typically absolutes about oneself, other people, or one's circumstances. They tend to be evaluative and judgmental and view life in extremes. They are logically incorrect, inconsistent with empirical reality, and prevent people from attaining their goals (Maultsby, 1984).

The types of common irrational beliefs identified by clinicians practicing REBT are very similar to those described in Chapter 16 and include the following 12 categories (Ellis & Dryden, 1997, p. 12):

1. All-or-none thinking
2. Jumping to conclusions and non sequiturs
3. Fortune telling
4. Focusing on the negative
5. Disqualifying the positive
6. Allness and neverness
7. Minimization
8. Emotional reasoning
9. Labeling and overgeneralization
10. Personalizing
11. Phonyism (seeing oneself as a phony or imposter)
12. Perfectionism

Examples of iBs include beliefs such as these:

Vince: I must have a date for New Year's Eve by tomorrow, or I will be the laughing stock of my fraternity.

Martin: My supervisor should appreciate me more and is a jerk for not seeing how hard I work.

Natasha: I ought to spend every evening with my family and am a terrible mother if I don't do that.

Here are rational versions of the same beliefs:

Vince: I would really like to have a date for New Year's Eve so that I can join my friends in that celebration.

Martin: I believe that my supervisor is not really familiar with my work and so is not giving me the appreciation I would like.

Natasha: My family and I would enjoy spending more time together, and I believe that would be helpful to my children.

The irrational beliefs above are extreme statements that are likely to promote negative emotions and difficulties in relationships. They do not facilitate problem solving or constructive action because they view success or failure in extreme terms, are demanding, and blame people rather than assess a situation rationally. The rational beliefs, on the other hand, reflect preferences, hopes, and wishes. They do not judge but look at possibilities. Problem solving and constructive action are facilitated because, without extremist thinking, many options and solutions are available. Vince can take steps to find a last-minute date but still may be able to celebrate the holiday with his friends even if he doesn't have a date. Martin can make plans to acquaint the supervisor with the quality of his work. Finally, Natasha can review her schedule to build in more time with her family while not demanding perfection from herself. Ellis (1995b) defined a rational belief as a "cognition that is effective or self-helping, not just empirically or logically valid" (p. 85).

Identifying, Disputing, and Modifying Irrational Beliefs

Like cognitive therapy, REBT uses a structured format for identifying, disputing, and modifying irrational beliefs—a six-step plan represented by the letters *ABCDEF* (Ellis, 1995a, 1995c). The REBT Self-Help Form is sometimes used to facilitate this process. The form lists common irrational beliefs to help people identify their Bs. To illustrate the *ABCDEF* model, we will consider Martin's beliefs about his supervisor.

A, the first step, is identification and description of the *activating event.* This is the external and objective source of discomfort, the experience that initiates the process of irrational thinking and precipitates the negative thoughts, emotions, and behaviors.

> *Martin A:* "My supervisor gave me an average rating on my evaluation."

B is the person's *belief* about the activating event, evaluating that stimulus as positive, negative, or neutral. The belief may be rational or irrational. REBT holds that people may not have a choice about experiences or activating events but do have a choice about their beliefs related to those activating events. However, before efforts are made to change an irrational belief, clinicians identify and evaluate it.

> *Martin B:* "My supervisor should appreciate me more and is a jerk for not seeing how hard I work. It is awful that I work so hard and am not valued as I ought to be."

C stands for the *consequences* of the belief. Of course, the activating event itself can produce negative consequences; but according to REBT, beliefs mediate between events and consequences, with beliefs being a major determinant of most consequences. Those consequences are likely to be unhealthy and self-destructive if the belief is irrational. They typically include inappropriate and self-destructive emotions (e.g., rage, anxiety, depression) and inappropriate and self-destructive behaviors (e.g., excessive use of alcohol, blaming self and others, withdrawal). Initial consequences of a belief can lead to subsequent negative and reinforcing consequences that themselves become activating events. For example, if Martin expressed his anger toward his supervisor in loud and attacking ways and the supervisor reacted with further disapproval, Martin's irrational beliefs and negative emotions would probably be reinforced (Wessler, 1986). Rational beliefs usually lead to healthier and more constructive consequences such as appropriate emotions (e.g., disappointment, annoyance) and appropriate behaviors (e.g., taking effective steps to change the situation or distract oneself with exercise or a creative pursuit).

Martin C: Martin experienced anger, shame, and anxiety about losing his job. His behaviors included berating his supervisor.

D, or *dispute,* is the next step in the process. Questions about the belief are used to determine whether it is rational or irrational. In general, clinicians should begin by focusing on irrational beliefs that refer to immediate situations and then move to more generalized and abstract irrational beliefs, comparable to Beck's core beliefs and schemas.

Gandy (1995, p. 39) suggested the following four questions as keys to determining whether or not a belief is irrational:

1. Logic—"Where is the logic that this should not have happened to me?"
2. Empirical evidence—"Where is the evidence that this condition should not have happened to me?"
3. Pragmatic/functional—"How will holding this belief help me achieve my goals?"
4. Constructing an alternative rational belief—"What is an alternative belief that would better help me achieve my goals?"

Later in the chapter, we will talk more about ways to dispute irrational beliefs. A wide variety of strategies are used to help people contest their iBs. Many are similar to the strategies used by cognitive therapists (discussed in Chapter 16). However, REBT clinicians are more likely to rely on persuasion, teaching, and techniques that elicit strong emotions than are cognitive therapists, who rely more on logic. Ellis, for example, is well known for his powerful statements and humorous songs, which he uses to help people see the irrational nature of their thoughts. Strategies to dispute irrational beliefs can draw on cognitive, behavioral, and emotional approaches to change.

Martin D: For Martin, all three are relevant. Cognitive approaches might involve examining the logic of his belief including the nature and adequacy of the supervisor's information on Martin's performance and whether or not receiving an average evaluation was truly awful or simply undesirable. Ellis would probably also use emotional methods, pointing out Martin's awfulizing, his tendency to catastrophize, and his musturbating: his need to have his life be exactly as he wishes. Ellis might encourage Martin to feel appropriate and nondestructive emotions such as annoyance and disappointment, which would contribute to rational thinking, rather than shame and anger, which are self-destructive and inappropriate emotions. Behavioral strategies, such as Martin's having a meeting with his supervisor, providing her with additional information about his work, and planning an outing or creative project to help him focus on more rewarding aspects of his life, might also be helpful.

E, the fifth step, stands for *effective,* describing the desired outcome of the disputation. The outcome is likely to include both effective rational beliefs and an effective new philosophy.

Martin E: After disputing his beliefs, Martin came up with some more rational beliefs: "Although I am disappointed that my evaluation was average, it is not the end of the world. I see that I can take some steps to familiarize my supervisor with my work and hopefully obtain a more positive evaluation next time."

F, the last step in the process, represents the *new feelings and behaviors* that result from the effective rational beliefs. At this stage, too, interventions are used to promote change.

Martin F: Martin reported the following emotions and behaviors: "I do still feel disappointed with the evaluation, but I am no longer devastated or depressed. I feel optimistic that my next evaluation will be better. I will meet with my supervisor so that is likely to happen."

Although the *ABCDEF* process may seem simple and straightforward, changing irrational beliefs to rational ones is a challenging and complex process. It requires effort and practice on the part of the client as well as well-chosen and skillfully used interventions on the part of the clinician. The process can be complicated by the tendency of many people to have secondary level disturbances: to feel bad about feeling bad. This creates several layers of irrational beliefs that need attention. In addition, people sometimes prefer to stay with the comfort of their familiar discomfort rather than risk the unknown discomfort of change (Ellis & Dryden, 1997). They also may value the sympathy, attention, and other secondary gains they receive as a result of their problems.

The Nature of Sessions

Sessions in REBT tend to follow a relatively predictable plan. A typical session includes 10 steps similar to those in a session of cognitive therapy (Walen, DiGiuseppe, & Dryden, 1992, p. 65):

1. Old business from the previous session
2. Checkups on mood, behavior, symptoms, and medication
3. New business, especially any major life changes
4. Follow-up on homework
5. Establishing the agenda for the sessions
6. Doing the work according to the *ABCDEF* format
7. Summarizing the work that has been done
8. Assignment of new homework
9. Eliciting feedback on the session
10. Closure

Certain additional steps at the beginning and end of the treatment process are also invaluable in ensuring the success of REBT. Clinicians typically begin by explaining the theory of REBT, familiarizing clients with the procedures that will be used and with what is expected from them as clients. Although clinicians who practice REBT are less likely to use a structured assessment process with many inventories than are cognitive therapists, they, too, engage in an assessment process during the first few sessions of treatment, exploring clients' history and background, thoughts, emotions, behaviors, and symptoms. Once that has been accomplished, most clients need help in recognizing that they largely create their own disturbance, understanding that psychological difficulties often stem from irrational beliefs, and seeing that they have the ability to change their beliefs and alleviate their difficulties.

By the end of treatment, clients should have internalized the *ABCDEF* process, learned to evaluate and dispute their own beliefs using a variety of strategies, and be prepared to continue that process throughout their lives (Ellis, 1995a). Follow-up meetings facilitate people's efforts to continue the process of REBT on their own. Relapse prevention is especially important for people who have made significant philosophical changes through elegant REBT and may need help in continuing to maintain those changes.

While REBT is often a relatively brief treatment process, clinicians generally do not predetermine the number of sessions. Rather, treatment lasts as long as necessary to help people accomplish their goals. Efficiency rather than brevity is valued.

Neenan and Dryden (1996) have identified six common errors or pitfalls for clinicians who practice REBT:

1. Skimming the surface and moving too quickly to dispute beliefs
2. Focusing on beliefs other than those held by the client (such as the supervisor's view of Martin)
3. Failing to obtain enough information about the client's emotions
4. Not paying attention to clues that provide important information
5. Automatically moving through the *ABCDEF* process without sufficiently addressing the needs of a particular person
6. Not giving enough depth to each part of the process, especially exploration of the activating event and the beliefs

This list emphasizes the importance of not underestimating the depth and complexity of REBT.

TREATMENT USING RATIONAL EMOTIVE BEHAVIOR THERAPY

Like cognitive therapists, clinicians who practice REBT draw on a wide range of strategies.

Goals

REBT is a goal-oriented treatment system that focuses on outcomes such as reduction in symptoms and changes in beliefs. It de-emphasizes processes such as development of insight and self-awareness. Although it acknowledges that enabling people to become more aware of their thoughts and language is important, REBT is primarily concerned with helping people learn skills that promote more rational thinking, lead to greater happiness and self-acceptance, and enable them to enjoy their lives more (Ellis, 1995a). It seeks to help people "make themselves elegantly effective, including less *disturbable*" (Ellis, 1995a, p. 3).

Therapeutic Alliance

Clients and clinicians have a collaborative relationship in REBT. Clients are expected to assume considerable responsibility for planning and implementing their treatment, just as they are encouraged to take considerable responsibility for their difficulties. Clinicians teach clients about rational and irrational thinking; help people identify, dispute, and modify their irrational beliefs; and facilitate their efforts to develop a more rational philosophy of life. Although problem solving is part of treatment, REBT clinicians go beyond problem solving and seek to enable people to establish more balanced, logical, and rewarding lives.

The role of clinicians in REBT is somewhat different from their role in cognitive therapy, perhaps because of the model established by Albert Ellis. Rational emotive behavior therapists are more of a presence in the treatment process, often using their influence on clients to effect change, whereas cognitive therapists tend to assume a more neutral role. Clinicians in REBT do not hesitate to use persuasion, praise, exaggeration, instruction, humorous songs, and anecdotes from their own lives to enable people to think more rationally and make positive changes. According to Ellis (1992), clinicians should not be blank screens but highly active, genuine, and directive, revealing much of their own lives and relating it to clients openly and directly as long as they always maintain a professional rather than personal relationship with their clients.

Ellis and Dryden (1997, p. 29) have suggested that clinicians practicing REBT should be

- Structured but flexible
- Intellectually, cognitively, and philosophically inclined
- Active and directive in their style
- Comfortable using behavioral instruction and teaching
- Not troubled by fear of failure and willing to take thoughtful risks
- Emotionally healthy, accepting themselves and others as fallible
- Practical and scientific rather than mystical and magical
- Comfortable with a variety of interventions

Clinicians assume many roles. They are teachers, role models, confidence builders, cheerleaders, and motivators. They strive to communicate acceptance and caring to their clients, helping them to both overcome problems and lead happier lives.

Establishment of mutual liking and rapport is less important in REBT than it is in many other approaches to treatment (Ellis, 1995a). Ellis cautions against clinicians' becoming gurus and creating a situation in which clients change to please the clinician rather than themselves. In REBT, self-acceptance is more important than clinician acceptance. While clinicians do not judge their clients, they may well judge their behaviors. Ellis has often told clients he does not like some of their behaviors and would not want to befriend them in social situations—certainly a powerful message.

However, all clinicians practicing REBT do not seek to emulate Ellis. According to Walen et al. (1992), "RET therapists have many different yet effective styles" and do not need to replicate Ellis's (p. 42). Walen et al. have found that rapport and empathy are compatible with being active and directive and view rapport as important in the treatment process, growing over time as clients and clinicians work together. Adapting REBT to the needs of a particular client is essential to effective treatment (Weinrach, 1995).

Interventions

REBT therapists draw on a wide range of interventions and strategies to help people change. Although some are strongly associated with REBT, most are similar to those used by cognitive therapists and have been described in Chapter 16.

Disputing Irrational Beliefs   Probably the most important group of strategies are those designed to dispute people's irrational beliefs. Beal, Kopec, and DiGiuseppe (1996) have described four strategies of disputation:

1. *Logical disputes* identify magical thinking and leaps in logic in people's thinking. For example, "Just because your sister seemed quiet and distracted when she visited you on her birthday, it doesn't logically follow that she doesn't want to continue a close relationship with you."

2. *Empirical disputes* focus on the accumulation of evidence. For example, "You told me that after her visit, your sister called to tell you what a good time she had and suggested that you visit her soon. You also told me that your sister is often quiet. When we examine this evidence, there is little reason to believe that your sister is withdrawing from you. In fact, the evidence suggests just the opposite."

3. *Functional disputing strategies* focus on the practical consequences of people's beliefs, looking at whether their beliefs are getting them what they want. For example, "Believing that your sister is withdrawing from you seems to be making you withdraw from her and is bringing up memories of past wrongs you believe she has done to you. This belief doesn't seem to be helping you rebuild your relationship with your sister, as you want to do."

4. *Rational alternative beliefs* offer a viable alternative belief. For example, "I know your sister is going through a difficult divorce. I wonder if another possible explanation for her quietness could be that she felt sad because she wasn't spending her birthday with her husband."

Beal et al. (1996) also describe four disputing styles:

1. A *didactic style* is explanatory, educational, and efficient but involves giving information rather than dialogue. For example, "Marnie, I think you may be jumping to unwarranted conclusions about the significance of your sister's behavior. Keep in mind that she is still recovering from her divorce and that may be affecting her mood."

2 A *Socratic style* involves questioning to promote client reasoning. This is the most common REBT clinician technique. For example, "What do you make of your sister's call and her invitation to visit? . . . Do those behaviors seem to suggest that she is withdrawing from your relationship?"

3. A *metaphorical style* uses analogies, especially from the person's own experience, to dispute beliefs. For example, "Your reaction to your sister's visit reminds me of the time you believed your supervisor was dissatisfied with your work because she did not offer you a ride to a conference. Then later you learned that she had to leave the meeting early because of a medical appointment and so was not able to give you a ride. I think that was the same month you received a top evaluation from your supervisor."

4. A *humorous style* disputes the belief in a lighthearted way. Clinicians should be sure never to make fun of a person, only their thoughts and behavior. For example, "So let's see. . . . It sounds like you are equating the number of words a person speaks to you with how much they like you. How about for the next day you count how many words each person you encounter says to you. Then we can determine which one likes you best."

The four strategies of disputation and four disputing styles can be combined to form 16 different ways in which clinicians can approach the process of disputing beliefs. This great variety of strategies allows clinicians to adapt their approaches to disputing beliefs to the needs of a particular client as well as their own personalities.

Other Intervention Strategies   Ellis (1995a) believes that active, directive, and vigorous strategies lead to more rapid change. Strategies used by REBT clinicians can be categorized according to whether their focus is primarily cognitive, behavioral, or affective, although cognitive techniques are almost always combined with behavioral or emotive ones (Ellis, 1995a, 1996; Ellis & Dryden, 1997). The following list organizes many of the interventions used in REBT according to whether they target thoughts, behaviors, or emotions:

Cognitive Strategies
- Detecting, disputing, debating, and modifying irrational cognitions
- Writing to express and explore thoughts and feelings
- Teaching the difference between rational and irrational beliefs
- Confronting irrational beliefs
- Identifying disadvantages to particular thoughts, actions, and feelings
- Socratic questioning

- Reducing thinking to absurdity
- Reframing a situation by changing labels and language
- Promoting tolerance to counteract I-can't-stand-it-itis
- Listing ways to cope with the worst that might happen
- Rating experiences on a continuum to counteract awfulizing
- Generating alternatives
- Distracting oneself
- Using visualization and imagery
- Rating degree of conviction in beliefs and then rerating after change
- Formulating, writing down, and repeating rational coping statements
- Problem solving
- Decision making
- Using hypnotherapy
- Being persistent; accepting no denials or excuses
- Projecting into the future to gain perspective
- Encouraging acceptance of oneself and others as fallible human beings
- Encouraging a focus on happiness

Behavioral Strategies

- Promoting relaxation
- Staying with uncomfortable activities until the discomfort diminishes
- Desensitizing or reducing fears via graduated exposure to feared situations
- Engaging in shame-attacking exercises (potentially embarrassing experiences such as singing loudly on a bus to insulate oneself against feelings of shame)
- Creating challenging situations and then coping with them
- Role playing
- Reversing roles; clinician takes on client's irrational beliefs, and client talks clinician out of those beliefs
- Using two chairs to represent a rational and an irrational belief; person enacts a dialogue between the two beliefs, moving from one chair to another
- Acting as if a person is someone else; stepping out of character
- Reading self-help books and listening to tapes (especially those by Albert Ellis) intended to effect change
- Training in skills such as assertiveness or communication
- Taking reasonable risks
- Teaching REBT to others
- Rewarding or penalizing oneself
- Socializing
- Planning rewarding activities and involvement in an absorbing interest or long-range pursuit

Affective Strategies

- Flooding or inundating a person with a particular feared or overvalued stimulus until it loses its power

- Imagining the worst that might happen
- Telling emotionally powerful stories, metaphors, and parables
- Using emotionally charged language
- Persuading
- Eliciting inappropriate emotions via imagery and then practicing changing them
- Singing rational humorous songs such as Ellis's "I'm Just Wild about Worry" to elicit and change emotions
- Using humor
- Encouraging will power and determination to change
- Promoting unconditional clinician and self-acceptance

Strategies such as these may be incorporated into homework assignments or used within sessions. As in cognitive therapy, use of task assignments is viewed as an essential part of treatment and is planned collaboratively. This promotes client responsibility, builds optimism, and facilitates progress.

Although this array of strategies seems very comprehensive, certain strategies are discouraged in REBT (Ellis & Dryden, 1997):

- Strategies that create dependency (e.g., excessive therapist warmth, focusing on transference)
- Those that do not promote rational thinking, such as unrealistic positive thinking
- Those that are inefficient, such as lengthy exploration of a client's history and activating events
- Those that promote only immediate improvement, such as catharsis or encouragement to discharge anger
- Prolonged use of strategies that deflect people from working on their underlying difficulties, such as overreliance on distraction and relaxation
- Unscientific techniques, such as faith healing and mysticism
- Strategies that focus on changing activating events rather than beliefs
- Strategies that have not received adequate empirical support

APPLICATION OF RATIONAL EMOTIVE BEHAVIOR THERAPY

REBT is a well established and widely used approach to treatment. It is used in a variety of ways and is appropriate for a broad range of people, although not everyone is a suitable candidate.

Group Therapy, Family Counseling, Demonstrations, Marathons

REBT is a very flexible approach. It is appropriate for use in both group and family counseling. Ellis and Dryden (1997) describe the use of rational emotive behavior couples therapy, focused on common irrational beliefs about relationships such as "My partner should always know intuitively what I want" and "Romantic love will always endure." Treatment goals include both resolving disturbances and increasing relationship satisfaction. REBT can be particularly useful in helping family members realize they have little power to change others but need to take responsibility for themselves. It also is recommended for helping people deal with a severely disturbed family member; treatment encourages the family to accept that person as a fallible human being and enables them to increase the happiness in the family.

REBT is particularly well suited for treatment in a group setting, which offers participants an opportunity to observe and try out behaviors and to share feedback and reactions. Group members are encouraged to take responsibility for helping each other as well as themselves. Ellis and Dryden (1997) recommend a group of 8–10 participants that meets weekly for 2 1/4 hours for at least six months. However, groups as large as 20 or 30 people can also be successful. People who are reasonably well functioning can begin their treatment in a group setting, whereas 5–15 sessions of individual REBT are recommended first for people who are shy or have other significant interpersonal difficulties. REBT has also been used for time-limited groups focusing on the development of communication and other specific skills.

Marathon group sessions of 10–14 hours, with a 4-hour follow-up in 6–10 weeks, have also been conducted using REBT (Ellis & Dryden, 1997). These groups make extensive use of experiential exercises to promote rapid self-disclosure and accompanying changes in cognitions, behaviors, and emotions.

For many years, Ellis has conducted Friday-evening demonstrations of his work at the Albert Ellis Institute in New York City. Sometimes attended by more than 200 people, these presentations have contributed to the popularity of REBT.

Diagnostic Groups

REBT is well suited for treatment of many mild to moderately severe mental disorders, including depressive disorders, anxiety disorders, and adjustment disorders. Little has been written about its use with personality disorders. However, like cognitive therapy, elegant or preferential REBT seems likely to help people with some of the milder personality disorders (e.g., avoidant and dependent personality disorders) make important and pervasive changes. Because of its forceful and directive nature and its emphasis on client responsibility, REBT does not seem appropriate for people with psychotic disorders or other severe mental disorders or for people who are highly suicidal or very fragile. In addition, REBT should be used with great caution, if at all, for people who have had traumatic childhood experiences or problems with impulse control and substance use (Ellis & Dryden, 1997). People who are unwilling to complete homework, manifest narcissistic or histrionic symptoms or rebellious behavior, have severe intellectual limitations, or have an extremely low frustration tolerance also do not seem to be good candidates.

Special Populations

Just as clinicians vary in their comfort with the active and directive stance of REBT, so do clients vary in their reactions. People who are highly motivated, fairly resilient, pragmatic, logical, and tough-minded are most likely to enjoy this energetic and interactive approach and appreciate the characteristic directness and humor of the REBT clinician. Garfield (1995) suggested that REBT is particularly likely to be well received by people who are externally oriented, intelligent, well-educated, and articulate. Solomon and Haaga (1995) found this approach quite successful with people who tend to intellectualize.

Janet Wolfe (1995), Albert Ellis's partner, has found REBT very useful with women. According to her, REBT "helps women deal with the shoulds, self-rating, and love-slobbism inherent in female sex role messages" and enables them to "take steps to increase their social, economic, and political power" (pp. 161–162). She found that REBT couples therapy can also help men as well as women negotiate new gender roles.

Ellis's own discussion of his disabilities as well as the efforts of REBT to help people stop dwelling on their difficulties and make the most of their strengths make this approach well suited to treatment of people with disabilities. Its emphasis on unconditional self-acceptance also seems useful with this population.

REBT has been used with young people as well as adults for both therapeutic and educational purposes. Manuals have been developed for using REBT preventively with children and adolescents in school settings (Vernon, 1989a, 1989b).

Although Ellis and other proponents of REBT acknowledge the importance of the social system and people's cultural background, little attention is paid in the literature to adapting this approach to the needs of a culturally diverse client group (Weinrach, 1996). Nielsen and Ellis (1994) caution clinicians not to attack beliefs that are strongly anchored in people's ethnic, religious, and cultural backgrounds unless they are clearly self-defeating. Of course, Ellis and Nielsen state that people should never be humiliated or demeaned during treatment. At the same time, REBT takes a strong stand against dogmatic and mystical beliefs. This may well be offensive to people with strong religious affiliations, especially those who do not come from a Judeo-Christian background and those who perceive the source of their strength as coming from a higher power (Ellis, 1995a).

Clinicians are encouraged to exercise great care in using REBT with people from nonwestern backgrounds, especially those whose cultures stress interdependence, privacy, and respect; those who may not have the background needed to appreciate the humor and linguistic subtleties of REBT; and those whose religious and spiritual beliefs may conflict with REBT's pragmatic stance.

EVALUATION OF RATIONAL EMOTIVE BEHAVIOR THERAPY

Weinrach (1995, 1996), a leading spokesperson for REBT, has suggested that it has not received the acceptance in the profession that it deserves. In part, he attributes this to misconceptions that this approach ignores emotions, advocates harsh confrontation, lacks depth, overemphasizes hedonism, and neglects rapport in the therapeutic relationship. Some of these misconceptions can be explained by REBT's strong association with the personality of Albert Ellis. While Ellis's outspoken style may have initially contributed to REBT's popularity, that association may now deter some people from practicing or seeking treatment through this approach. This seems like a disservice to REBT, which has many strengths and can easily be adapted to both the styles of the clinician and the needs of the client.

Limitations

Nevertheless, REBT does have limitations that should be kept in mind. Its use with particular diagnostic groups and people from diverse cultural, religious, and ethnic backgrounds has not been well studied or delineated. Although the approach does offer some standardized questionnaires and inventories, more tools to facilitate analysis and modification of cognitions would be useful (Bernard, 1995). In addition, REBT sometimes seems to pay too little attention to clients' history and move too rapidly toward promoting change; clinicians should be sure to allow adequate time to assess and understand people before moving forward.

Strengths

REBT has many strengths. An efficient approach, it is likely to lead to rapid reduction in symptoms as well as philosophical change. It teaches and empowers people to help themselves after treatment has ended. Its theory is relatively clear and straightforward. Because it draws on a broad range of techniques and interventions, REBT can be adapted to a wide variety of people and problems and used for prevention and psychoeducation as well as treatment.

Although most of the writing on REBT is theoretical and clinical, many empirical studies of its impact have been conducted. DiGiuseppe (1996) reported that more than 240 studies were conducted before 1995, and many have been conducted since. A review of 31 outcome studies using controls found significant improvement immediately after treatment with REBT relative to no treatment (Solomon & Haaga, 1995). These conclusions are typical of research on the impact of REBT. Lyons and Woods (1991) concluded, "The results demonstrated that [REBT] is an effective form of therapy. The efficacy was most clearly demonstrated when [REBT] was compared to baseline and other forms of controls. The differences among comparisons of [REBT] to CBM (Cognitive Behavior Modification) and Behavior Therapy were not significant" (pp. 367–368). Although REBT cannot be said to be superior to other cognitive and behavioral approaches to treatment, it has clearly demonstrated its effectiveness.

Contributions

Probably REBT's most important contribution is raising awareness of the importance of thinking in people's lives and the need to attend to and change thinking in treatment. Information on the differences between rational and irrational thinking, the *ABCDEF* model, and the broad range of interventions associated with REBT have shaped the fields of psychotherapy and counseling, leading to the development of Beck's cognitive therapy as well as other approaches that focus on cognitions. SMART Recovery, a self-help group grounded in REBT for people with substance use problems, is another outgrowth of this theory. An alternative to Alcoholics Anonymous (AA) and other 12-step programs, SMART Recovery diverges from AA in its belief that people are not always in the process of recovering but can actually recover from drug and alcohol abuse and dependence. In addition, unlike AA, which emphasizes the importance of a higher power, SMART Recovery focuses on personal responsibility for effecting change.

In 1998, nine members of REBT's International Training Standards and Review Committee met to discuss the future of this approach. Each member made predictions about REBT's future 25–50 years after Albert Ellis's death. (He was 85 years old at the time of the meeting.) Most believed that REBT's impact on counseling and psychotherapy would continue to be great. However, several, including Wolfe and Weinrach, whose writings we have discussed in this chapter, anticipated that REBT would eventually become integrated into a more general theory of cognitive behavioral therapy.

Whether or not this integration occurs, REBT is currently a widely used and important approach. REBT centers are located in 10 countries throughout the world (Ellis & Dryden, 1997); and Albert Ellis continues to practice, write, and spearhead its development.

SKILL DEVELOPMENT: RATIONAL EMOTIVE IMAGERY

Ellis and Maultsby developed the technique of rational emotive imagery (REI) to help people practice changing their unhealthy and inappropriate negative emotions into healthy and appropriate ones (Ellis & Dryden, 1997). Clinicians teach clients the steps in this exercise during a session in which they can learn and practice REI. Then they encourage clients to spend at least 10 minutes a day practicing REI on their own.

REI includes the following steps (Thompson, 1996):

1. *Visualize an unpleasant activating event.* "Picture yourself or fantasize, as vividly and intensely as you can, the details of some unpleasant activating experience (A) that has happened to you or will likely occur in the future" (Thompson, 1996, p. 115).

For example, "I had met a man over the Internet; Gary was his name. We communicated over the computer for more than a month and then finally decided to meet. We agreed that, no matter what, we would have a pleasant time—just have dinner together and get better acquainted. I was very apprehensive. I hadn't had a date in 12 years, since I married my ex-husband. I can see myself standing in front of the museum, waiting for Gary to show up. I was cold but I didn't want to put my coat on because I wanted him to see my pretty dress. I think being anxious made me feel even colder. So there I was, shivering, feeling like I could hardly breathe. Then this man walks by real close to me, looks me up and down, and keeps walking. I just knew it was Gary because he told me what he looked like."

2. *Experience the unhealthy negative emotions.* As you vividly imagine the experience, let yourself feel any strong emotions that come up for you—the *C*, or emotional consequence of this experience. Really feel those feelings, get in touch with them, and for a few minutes fully experience them. Don't try to avoid the feelings or change them; just face them and feel them.

For example, "I felt sick to my stomach. I felt disgusted with myself. I just wanted to disappear into a hole in the ground. I felt so repulsive. I felt overwhelming shame. And then I felt rage at Gary. How could he have made me feel so bad?"

3. *Changing the emotions.* After you have allowed yourself to feel these disturbing emotions for a few minutes, push yourself to change those feelings so that you feel different inside. Change them so that instead of feeling those unhealthy and inappropriate emotions such as rage, shame, and depression, you feel emotions such as disappointment or annoyance. You can do this. Keep pushing yourself and working at it until you start to experience a shift in your feelings, a new emotional consequence.

For example, "This is hard, but I'm sort of doing it. I do feel really annoyed; I got this new dress and took time off work so I could get ready, and then this jerk doesn't even speak to me. I guess I feel disappointed too. He seemed so nice over the Internet. I thought maybe this would really turn into a special relationship."

4. *Examine the process.* You are succeeding in changing your emotions from the self-destructive ones of shame and anger to new and appropriate feelings of disappointment and annoyance. When we look at how you made that happen, we will see that you have in some way changed your belief system (*B*), which mediates between the activating event (*A*) and the emotional consequence (*C*). Let's identify both the old and the new beliefs.

For example, "At first, I was thinking, 'You are really a hopeless failure. It's unbearable that I was stood up like that—so humiliating.' And I felt so angry at Gary. We had an understanding, and he should not have treated me so badly. But then I started to think about it differently. Nobody but me knew what was going on. It wasn't a public humiliation. And I sure learned something about Gary fast. It's a good thing I didn't really get interested in him and then discover what a rat he was. I do still feel really annoyed that I wasted all that time and effort, and I'm disappointed that things didn't work out. But I guess I just got carried away with my romantic fantasies. I think I'll find other ways to meet people besides the Internet."

5. *Repetition and practice.* Keep repeating the process. Imagine the scene, bring up the disturbing feelings, and then deliberately push yourself to change your feelings so that you feel displeased and disappointed but not disturbed. I encourage you to practice this exercise at least 10 minutes a day until you can easily bring up the activating event and the disturbing feelings and then, just as easily, change those into feelings that are not harmful to you.

6. *Reinforcing the goal.* It may take a few weeks, but before too long you will find that when you bring up the activating event, you will automatically and easily experience the feelings of displeasure and disappointment rather than rage and shame.

7. *Generalization of skills.* Then you can use this same technique for other situations. If you find that an activating event brings up strong and disturbing emotions, imagine the event and then push yourself to change those feelings to ones that reflect displeasure rather than disturbance. Once you have done this, identify both the disturbing irrational belief and the rational belief that enabled you to change your emotions.

CASE ILLUSTRATION

In this case illustration, the clinician works with Ava following the *ABCDEF* model. Ava begins the session by expressing disturbing and upsetting feelings about an interaction she recently had with her parents.

Clinician: Ava, tell me about the situation or activating event [*A*] that led you to feel so disturbed.

Ava: This awful thing happened to me at school. I had gym class, and I was in such a hurry to get dressed and catch the bus that I forgot to zip up my skirt. I went out in the hall like that. Some kids were looking at me, but I didn't know what was wrong. Then one boy started to sing, "Zip-a-dee-do-da." Then I got it. I was so ashamed. All I wanted to do was go home and tell my mother. But when I got home, she was on the phone with my grandmother and couldn't be bothered with me. "I'm busy now," she said. "Go out and play with your friends." That was the last thing I wanted to do. So I just took the dog and went up to my room. I wanted to die so that I wouldn't ever have to go back to school again.

Clinician: Tell me some more about the feelings [emotional consequences/*C*] you had when all this happened.

Ava: Well, I told you I felt ashamed, like I was the big joke of the school. I bet all the kids will be talking about me tomorrow. It was so awful! And then when I got home, even my mother didn't care. I felt horrible, like nobody loved me, like I was just a hopeless mess.

Clinician: I can hear that you had some strong negative emotions, feeling ashamed and rejected and unlovable, that were really disturbing you. Ava, remember we talked about irrational beliefs last week. Let's take out that list I showed you of common irrational beliefs [*B*] and figure out if any of them reflect the thoughts you were having in reaction to this incident.

Ava: I certainly had this thought: "I am a bad or worthless person when I act weakly or stupidly." And then when my mom was too busy to talk to me, I thought this one, "I need to be loved by someone who matters to me a lot," and this one, "I am a bad, unlovable person if I get rejected." I thought this one too: "It's awful or horrible when major things don't go my way." I also thought, "My mom doesn't really love or care about me."

Clinician: So many of the thoughts on the list really hit home for you. It seems like you had two groups of thoughts: one about not being loved by your mother and another about feeling worthless and devastated when the kids teased you about forgetting to zip your skirt.

Ava: Yes, that's right.

Clinician: Let's start with the first group, thoughts about your mom not really loving you and your feeling unlovable. Have there been other times when you needed to talk to your mom and she was there for you?

Ava: Yes, almost always.

Clinician: Then just because your mom was in a phone conversation and couldn't talk to you this one time, does it logically follow that she doesn't love you [logical dispute]?

Ava: Well, she should have known I really needed to talk to her.

Clinician: How should she have known that [empirical dispute]?

Ava: I don't know. I guess I didn't really tell her that.

Clinician: Then does it logically follow that if she didn't want to talk to you at that time, that she doesn't love you?

Ava: No, I know she loves me. I was just disappointed that she wasn't there for me. It made me feel like she didn't love me.

Clinician: I wonder if the thought that she doesn't love you is helping you or hurting you [functional dispute]?

Ava: Well, it's making me feel pretty bad, and it kept me from talking to her when she finally got off the phone, so I guess it's hurting me.

Clinician: Could there be other explanations for her not wanting to talk to you at that time [rational alternative]?

Ava: Yes, she was on the phone with her mother. It sounded like

Grandma's husband had wrecked her car. I guess my mom really needed to try to help her.

Clinician: So can you tell me a thought that seems to be a more accurate reflection of your interaction with your mother?

Ava: Yes. My mom loves me, but I can't expect her to read my mind or be there for me every minute. She really does her best to help me when I'm upset, but Grandma needed her then [effective rational belief].

Clinician: And how are you feeling now?

Ava: I still feel really disappointed that my mom was on the phone when I needed to talk to her. I felt so hurt that I never did tell her what happened.

Clinician: What can you do about that now?

Ava: I guess I could go home and tell her about it now. I think that would help me to feel better [new feelings and behaviors].

This process has helped Ava change her beliefs about the activating events, resulting in changes in her feelings and behaviors. Her level of disturbance and the absolute nature of her thoughts have both changed, and she is no longer devastated by her interaction with her mother. That allows her to take constructive action to communicate her concerns to her mother. Ava's second group of thoughts are addressed in the exercises that follow.

EXERCISES

Large-Group Exercises

1. Review Ava's second group of irrational beliefs, including "I am a bad or worthless person when I act weakly and stupidly" and "It's awful or horrible when things don't go my way." Use the four disputing strategies (logical, empirical, and functional disputes and rational alternative) to dispute her beliefs. Then formulate effective rational beliefs that might replace Ava's irrational beliefs and identify new feelings and behaviors that are likely to result from her new beliefs. Suggest homework that Ava might do to help reinforce these positive changes.

2. Ellis believes that REBT is incompatible with the theory of transpersonal therapy (discussed in Chapter 14). Based on what you have learned about both theories, discuss their differences and similarities and whether the two really do conflict. Can you think of ways to resolve that conflict and integrate the approaches?

3. Considerable overlap exists between REBT and Beck's cognitive therapy. Discuss the similarities and differences between those two approaches. Assess whether the two really are distinct theories or whether the differences are largely minor and semantic.

Small-Group Exercises

1. Form into your groups of four students in two dyads. Each student should have the opportunity to assume both the role of the clinician and the role of the client. Each dyad should engage in a role play in which the client begins by describing a disturbing experience. The clinician should follow the *ABCDEF* model in counseling the client. Allow approximately 15 minutes for each role play, followed by 5–10 minutes of feedback from the observing dyad. Feedback should focus on the use of the *ABCDEF* format as well as the nature of the therapeutic alliance.

2. Following the format in Exercise 1, engage in role plays using rational emotive imagery (illustrated in the "Skill Development" section) to practice changing emotions by changing thoughts.

3. Drawing on your knowledge of diverse groups, discuss which cultural groups are likely to be favorably disposed to REBT and which are likely to be uncomfortable receiving treatment via this approach. What sort of screening would you do to determine people's suitability for treatment with REBT?

Individual Exercises

1. Write briefly in your journal about a time during the past week when you felt upset or disturbed. Identify and dispute your irrational thoughts using the *ABCDEF* format. Write your responses to each step in the process.

2. Identify a personal goal you have for yourself this week. Drawing on the list of strategies used in REBT, assign yourself two or three homework tasks to help you reach your goal.

SUMMARY

Rational emotive behavior therapy, formerly known as rational emotive therapy, was developed by Albert Ellis more than 40 years ago. REBT takes the position that people disturb themselves by their irrational beliefs and that changing those beliefs to rational ones will reduce people's levels of disturbance and lead to positive changes in emotions and behaviors. General REBT emphasizes problem solving, while elegant or preferential REBT goes beyond problem solving and aims toward deep philosophical change. Sessions typically focus on a six-step process to modify cognitions: identifying the activating event (A), identifying irrational beliefs (B), looking at the negative consequences (C) of those beliefs, disputing (D) the beliefs, replacing them with effective rational beliefs (E), leading to changes in feelings (F) and behaviors. Clinicians practicing REBT typically adopt an active, directive, and vigorous style and make use of a broad range of strategies to effect rapid change.

More information on training in REBT as well as publications on this theory can be obtained from

The Albert Ellis Institute
45 East 65th Street
New York, New York 10021-6593
(212) 535-0822

RECOMMENDED READINGS

Bernard, M. E. (1995). It's prime time for rational emotive behavior therapy: Current theory and practice, research, recommendations, and predictions. *Journal of Rational-Emotive and Cognitive Behavioral Therapy, 13*(1), 9–27.

Ellis, A. (1995). *Better, deeper, and more enduring brief therapy.* New York: Brunner/Mazel.

Ellis, A., & Dryden, W. (1997). *The practice of rational emotive behavior therapy* (2nd ed.). New York: Springer.

Walen, S. R., DiGiuseppe, R., & Dryden, W. (1992). *A practitioner's guide to rational-emotive therapy.* New York: Oxford University Press.

Chapter 18

EMERGING APPROACHES EMPHASIZING THOUGHTS

Clinical experience and research have led many people to appreciate the importance of thinking in human development and functioning. This chapter reviews some of the emerging treatment approaches emphasizing thoughts: eye movement desensitization and reprocessing, neuro-linguistic programming, thought field therapy, and cognitive therapy of evaluation. With the possible exception of eye movement desensitization and reprocessing, these have not yet, and may never, become fully developed treatment systems. However, they go beyond techniques and reflect the most current thinking on treatment focused on changing thoughts.

The current status of the treatment approaches discussed in this chapter vary considerably. Two (thought field therapy and cognitive therapy of evaluation) are still in their infancy and have not yet been well described or substantiated in the literature. Neuro-linguistic programming has been used for many years and has experienced a recent resurgence in growth and interest but has not yet been well supported in the literature. While eye movement desensitization and reprocessing is a relatively recent addition, it has received considerable empirical support and seems likely to become an essential clinical tool. These approaches all require specialized training that goes beyond the scope of this book. Thus, descriptions are relatively brief in comparison to descriptions of the more established systems of counseling and psychotherapy presented in this book. The goal of this chapter is to introduce readers to these approaches and perhaps excite some interest and curiosity rather than actually teach them, with the hope of prompting some readers to investigate the approaches and perhaps study them further via training and additional readings.

EYE MOVEMENT DESENSITIZATION AND REPROCESSING

Eye movement desensitization and reprocessing (EMDR) has received considerable attention in recent years. EMDR uses directed eye movements and other guided tracking procedures to accelerate people's processing of negative information and enable them to deal with that information in new ways that promote their emotional health.

The Development of EMDR

EMDR was discovered in 1987 by Francine Shapiro (1995), a senior research fellow at the Mental Research Institute in Palo Alto, California. As she was walking in the park, Shapiro noticed that some disturbing thoughts she was having had become less upsetting. She attributed this to her spontaneous eye movements and began to investigate whether those movements could indeed help people process troubling memories and thoughts more effectively.

Shapiro originally called her approach *eye movement desensitization* (EMD) and focused her attention primarily on treating people who had traumatic experiences. Her first study (Shapiro, 1989) focused on a group of 22 people between the ages of 11 and 53, all of whom had traumatic memories such as rape, molestation, and war experiences as well as pronounced symptoms such as flashbacks, sleep disturbances, and relationship difficulties that had lasted at least one year. All were treated with

EMD, as it was known then, which included the clinician's guiding the client in a series of directed eye movements. Following procedural guidelines, people moved their eyes rapidly back and forth 25–30 times, following the movements of the clinician's hand. This series of movements was repeated again and again for 15–90 minutes, while a brief dialogue between client and clinician between each series enabled the clinician to monitor the clients' progress and guide their attention. Outcome measures indicated that, after only a single session of treatment, people reported considerably less anxiety, cognitive shifts toward more positive beliefs about themselves, and an amelioration of symptoms.

Since that time, EMDR, as it was renamed in 1990, has been greatly refined and its use expanded. Extensive research has led to changes in the timing of the procedure, the development of structured formats for evaluation of progress, and clearly defined protocols for treatment (Shapiro, 1995). In addition, EMDR was found to be effective not just for treatment of posttraumatic stress disorder but for a wide range of disorders. Other bidirectional techniques, including tones in alternate ears, lights flashing on alternating sides of a bar, and tapping on alternating sides, have been found as effective as the original eye movements.

Important Theoretical Concepts

EMDR holds the optimistic view that people have an innate system that enables them to process information to a healthy resolution. However, sometimes this system becomes unbalanced or blocked, and negative memories are held in the nervous system in ways that are harmful to the person. EMDR is a complex approach that uses bidirectional stimulation and other interventions to facilitate the processing of the memories, the transformation and integration of the negative emotions linked to the memory, and the modification of self-destructive cognitions. Learning as well as new positive cognitions result from this process and are available for future use (Shapiro, 1995).

The exact mechanism that underlies the impact of bilateral stimulation is unclear. However, the use of bidirectional eye movements has been linked to the function of rapid eye movements during sleep or the rhythmical eye movements that often accompany periods of deep concentration and problem solving (Shapiro & Forrest, 1997). In all of these, eye movements seem to be linked to cognitive processing and integration of the functioning of the two hemispheres of the brain. By artificially inducing the eye movements and linking them to disturbing memories, EMDR may, in effect, speed up the derailed information-processing system and allow the memory to progress rapidly through the neural networks in positive ways.

EMDR is based on an information-processing model and can be a very important and powerful element in a treatment plan. It is generally integrated with and draws on a wide range of approaches to psychotherapy. EMDR has its roots in cognitive therapy with its stress on information processing and modification of beliefs. EMDR also reflects psychodynamic approaches in its use of free association and catharsis. Shapiro (1995) views EMDR as also being person-centered because, during the treatment process, the clinician generally assumes a neutral role and, other than directing the eye movements, lets the client guide the treatment process.

In some instances, the clinicians assist their clients by directing their attention in ways that mimic effects that would be achieved with spontaneous processing. The cognitive interweave is one of the most powerful techniques used in EMDR to facilitate information processing and reinforce new learning. It can be very helpful in enabling people to process information differently, to see new possibilities and viewpoints. The following dialogues present examples of cognitive interweaves:

> *Example 1:* A man who was sexually abused as a young boy had the negative cognition "I'm spoiled goods." To help increase the validity of his positive cognition, ("I'm okay as I am"), the clinician asked him to imagine that his son had been sexually abused at that same age and to consider whether he would view the son as spoiled goods (Shapiro, 1994, p. 22).
>
> *Example 2:* A young woman with an eating disorder was having great difficulty believing that she could overcome her eating disorder. In the course of her EMDR treatment, she spoke of how well her recently deceased grandmother had known her and the great faith her grandmother had had in her. To help increase the validity of her belief in her positive cognition ("I am a worthwhile person and can control my weight and my eating"), the clinician asked, "What would your grandmother who knew you so well have to say about your ability to overcome your eating disorder?"

Strategies

Developing client-clinician rapport and a trusting relationship seems at least as important for clinicians using EMDR as it is for those using other approaches to treatment. The directed eye movements seem strange, questionable, and even threatening to many clients. Their willingness to participate in this treatment approach and their ability to benefit from EMDR is, in large measure, connected to the trust they have in their clinicians. In addition, EMDR can lead troubling and traumatic memories to surface, risking the retraumatization of people under treatment. Strong clinical skills as well as a positive therapeutic alliance between client and clinician are indicated to address these possibilities.

The Eight Phases of EMDR The process of EMDR includes eight phases (Shapiro, 1996):

1. *Establishing the foundation.* EMDR is recommended for people who are relatively stable and are not in danger of suicide or in crisis. Before the EMDR phase of the treatment begins, clinicians spend some time taking a client history and exploring presenting problems and symptoms. At the same time, they develop rapport with the client, creating a safe place and making sure that the person is a suitable candidate for EMDR.

2. *Client preparation.* The clinician explains the nature, theory, and goals of EMDR to the client. The eye movement process is demonstrated briefly and the client taught to use a "stop" hand signal or an image of a safe place if the treatment ever becomes too difficult. Client's expectations and fears are elicited and addressed if needed.

3. *Assessment.* The clinician obtains the following information from the client in preparation for treatment:

- Identification of a presenting issue or troubling memory
- A visual image or picture that represents the worst part of the memory or issue
- A negative cognition or self-statement that the client currently holds about the self that goes along with the picture and incident, similar to the irrational beliefs addressed in rational emotive behavior therapy and including statements such as "I cannot stand it," "I am stupid," "I am not lovable," and "I am a bad person"
- A positive cognition or self-statement that captures what the person would like to believe about the self when the picture or incident is recalled (e.g., "I can handle it," "I deserve love," and "I am a good person")
- The validity of the positive cognition (VoC), reflecting how true that statement feels to the person, rated on a 1–7 scale, with 1 representing completely false and 7 completely true
- The emotions associated with the incident or picture
- The person's rating of his or her level of disturbance on a 0–10 subjective units of distress (SUDS) scale, with 0 reflecting no disturbance and 10 the highest disturbance
- The location of body sensations associated with the disturbance and their location in the body

4. *Desensitization.* A series of directed eye movements or other bidirectional stimuli helps the person process the disturbing issue or recollection. The client is instructed to bring up the disturbing picture and the negative cognition and to notice accompanying bodily sensations when beginning each series of bidirectional stimulations. The clinician checks in with the client briefly between each series to determine what is coming up for the person. The clinician is reinforcing, caring, and encouraging during this phase but maintains a detached stance, intervening little during the desensitization process to allow the client's own brain to produce the associations necessary for resolution.

5. *Installation.* When the SUDS rating is low (ideally 0 or 1) and the VoC rating is high (ideally 6 or 7), the installation phase is used to reinforce the results, linking the positive cognition with the initial memory. (If the EMDR needs to be stopped before these ideal levels are reached, relaxation and other procedures are used to tide the person over until the next session.)

6. *Body scan.* The person scans the body, identifying any residual discomfort that may need to be reprocessed.

7. *Closure.* Debriefing is the focus of this phase, with client and clinician reviewing and processing the experience. Exercises such as visualization of a healing light stream may be used to return the client to a state of equilibrium. Self-control techniques might also be taught to help the client maintain self-control and self-mastery between sessions. The clinician encourages the client to keep a log during the week of any relevant memories, thoughts, or experiences.

8. *Reevaluation.* Reevaluation occurs at the beginning of each subsequent session. The client's log as well as any consequences and progress associated with the EMDR session are processed. The reevaluation phase helps clinicians determine whether treatment should further address the previous target memory or issue, progress to additional EMDR protocols, use other ancillary procedures, or move toward closure.

The Importance of Training   Although this process may seem simple, EMDR is a complex and powerful tool. No clinician should use it without adequate training. The EMDR Institute offers a basic two-part training. Each training program is about 20 hours long and includes lectures, demonstrations, and supervised practice.

Application and Current Status

EMDR is rapidly growing in importance in counseling and psychotherapy. Its effectiveness as part of a treatment program for people with posttraumatic stress disorder (PTSD) is well established (Wilson, Becker, & Tinker, 1995). A meta-analysis of all psychological and drug treatments for PTSD found that EMDR was not only effective in treating this disorder but was more efficient than other treatments (Van Etten & Taylor, 1998). Division 12 (Clinical Psychology) of the American Psychological Association recently added EMDR to a list of empirically validated treatments effective with PTSD (Chambless et al., 1998), and the International Society for Traumatic Stress Studies declared it effective for treating PTSD (Foa, Keane, & Friedman, 2000). In addition, EMDR shows promise in the treatment of a broad range of other disorders, including depression, anxiety, substance use, sexual dysfunction, and somatoform disorders (Manfield, 1998). It is also used to help people deal with their emotional reactions to life-threatening illnesses such as cancer and AIDS (Shapiro & Forrest, 1997). EMDR has been used successfully with children as well as adults (Tinker & Wilson, 1999).

On the surface, EMDR seems to be an almost magical process that diverges considerably from mainstream approaches to treatment. Perhaps to demystify the approach, Francine Shapiro has placed great emphasis on the importance of research on EMDR. Consequently, many empirical studies have been done. For a treatment strategy that is little more than a decade old, EMDR has an impressive record of demonstrating success. More than 30,000 clinicians have been trained in this approach (Shapiro, 1995), and further growth in the use and application of EMDR is anticipated. Research also is expected on the integration of EMDR with other approaches to treatment.

Information on EMDR can be obtained from

EMDR Institute
P.O. Box 51010
Pacific Grove, CA 93950
(408) 372-3900
Website: http://www.emdr.com

EMDR International Association (EMDRIA)
P.O. Box 141925
Austin, TX 78714-1925
(512) 451-5200

Neuro-linguistic Programming

Neuro-linguistic programming (NLP) was initially developed in the 1970s by John Grinder, a linguist, and Richard Bandler, a mathematician and student of psychology (Kamp, 1996). According to de Luynes (1995), "NLP embraces an attitude based upon a curiosity about people and how they do the things they do, supported by a methodology—a way of thinking about people and the process of communication—and a technology, to obtain well-defined and ecological results" (p. 34). NLP theorists believe that people's internal representations (thoughts and images) determine their repertoire of choices and behaviors. Identifying patterns in those internal representations and consciously changing or manipulating them can lead to specific behavioral outcomes (Grey, 1991).

The Development of NLP

John Grinder and Richard Bandler, working at Santa Cruz University in the 1970s, believed that psychotherapy research overemphasized pathology and did not pay enough attention to what people did right and what enabled them to function well (Kamp, 1996). In an effort to focus on excellence and learn more about effective treatment, they embarked on a study of three outstanding clinicians: Virginia Satir, Fritz Perls, and Milton Erickson. They found that the styles of these clinicians had certain commonalities. All three seemed gifted with intuition (a great ability to read their clients) and intervention and response skills that made a difference.

Drawing on a variety of disciplines including cybernetics, linguistics, behaviorism, family and systems theory, personality theory, and communication, Bandler and Grinder sought ways to teach those skills that the master therapists all possessed. Their findings highlighted the following:

- Methods for operationalizing the intuitive skills of excellent therapists
- The discovery that people who function well pay much more attention to their desired outcome than they do to analyzing and discussing the problem; once the problem has been clarified, they put their energy into defining in detail an ideal resolution

Both findings—the importance of focusing on outcome and the process of nurturing intuition—are integral to NLP. Bandler and Grinder's first book, *The Structure of Magic* (1975), presents the results of their research on excellence.

Important Theoretical Concepts

The name of this approach, neuro-linguistic programming, reflects three essential concepts in this model (de Luynes, 1995, p. 34):

1. *Neuro.* All behavior is the result of neurological processes.
2. *Linguistic.* Neural processes are represented, ordered, and sequenced into models and strategies through language and communication systems.
3. *Programming.* The components of a system are organized or programmed to achieve specific outcomes.

According to NLP (Kamp, 1996), people learn to react in certain ways to specific situations and develop automatic patterns, or *programmes,* in both their neural system and their language. These programmes constitute most of people's daily responses to themselves, others, and their environment and form the personality. When these programmes were originally put into place, they worked more successfully than any other approach in a person's repertoire. Over time, however, these automatic responses become deeply entrenched. People generally do not stop to evaluate them or seek to change them unless they conclude that the responses are causing them difficulties.

The primary goal of NLP is to help people become conscious of their internal representations of reality and the ways in which those representations are reflected in their linguistic patterns (Sterman, 1990). According to NLP, people experience internal and external events through sensory modes including visual, auditory, kinesthetic (touch), olfactory (smell), and gustatory (taste) modes. Change is made primarily through these sensory modes, leading to modification of linguistic patterns.

NLP is a phenomenological approach that takes the position that people respond to their maps or pictures of reality, not to reality itself (de Luynes, 1995). Although people typically react as though the meaning of their communication is what they intend that meaning to be, NLP focuses on outcomes and suggests that the meaning of people's communications is really reflected in the responses they receive from others.

For example, Anita suggested to her friend Jennifer, who had recently been diagnosed with cancer, that Jennifer should lose weight and eat more healthful foods to improve her immune system. Anita intended to be helpful and express caring; however, Jennifer experienced her message as hurtful and intrusive and responded by avoiding contact with Anita. Regardless of Anita's good intentions, Jennifer's response to the message determined its meaning.

According to NLP, people are responsible for the responses they receive to a communication. Although Anita did not desire the response she received from Jennifer, her message was the cause of the response. Anita was operating according to deeply ingrained internal representations of friendship, illness, helping, and her role in relation to her friends, which led her to communicate, both verbally and nonverbally, in ways that Jennifer saw as belittling and unsupportive. If clinicians practicing NLP were to work with Anita, they might help her become more aware of her internal representations and how they contribute to the responses she receives from her communications. Then, by identifying the responses and outcome she desires, they would help Anita modify her internal representations as well as the nature of her communication.

Assumptions   NLP is an encouraging and optimistic approach that assumes a positive view of people and the world. The following are some of its basic assumptions (de Luynes, 1995; Isaacson, 1990; Sterman, 1990):

- People have the resources they need to make changes.
- People always make the best choice available to them at the time.
- All behavior serves a purpose, but that purpose may be unconscious.
- No one is wrong or broken; by finding out how a person functions now, change can be facilitated.
- There is no such thing as failure, only feedback; all responses can be used.
- An organism naturally moves toward well-being.
- Mind and body are part of the same system; changing the body can change the mind, and changing the mind can change the body.
- Anything can be accomplished by breaking tasks into small-enough chunks.
- The world is a place of abundance that provides the resources and opportunities for continued growth and development.
- People already have all the resources they need in their lifetimes; they just need help in accessing those internal resources.

The Process of Facilitating Change   Isaacson (1990) described NLP as a systems model that seeks to change behavior by identifying conscious and unconscious internal representations and patterns and intervening, both verbally and nonverbally, through the sensory modes. By increasing and expanding people's internal representations, NLP enables them to construct a repertoire of internally generated choices that are effective in eliciting and dealing with desired outcomes in a wide variety of life situations.

To maximize their effectiveness, people are encouraged to use all aspects of themselves, including the rational mind, intuition, the emotions, and the body. Thus, people acquire the ability to consider situations from different perspectives and develop multiple descriptions that increase their appreciation of the various interpretations and responses other people make.

Bandler and Grinder (1975) have described a six-step process of change via NLP, illustrated here with the example of Anita, introduced previously:

1. Identify the pattern to be changed.

Anita grew up in a family that expressed little empathy but overemphasized advice and viewed illness as a weakness. Anita internalized the views of her family and applied them to her friends.

2. Establish communication with the part of the person responsible for the pattern. Once established, use sensory systems as well as internal and external representations to begin to change the pattern.

Anita accessed and explored her internal representations of illness, her image of herself as a friend, her auditory and visual processing of information, and her linguistic style.

3. Determine the positive function of the pattern and separate the pattern from that function since all behaviors serve some positive function.

In Anita's family, giving advice was one of the few acceptable ways to connect with and show concern for another person, the original purpose of Anita's behavior toward Jennifer. However, Anita was able to separate pattern from function by recognizing that her behavior no longer accomplished its goal.

4. Access a creative part of the person and generate new behaviors to accomplish the positive function.

Using her creative strengths, Anita was able to develop some skill at empathy and communication of warmth and concern, which she perceived as more likely to accomplish her goal of connecting with and expressing caring and support for her friends.

5. Connect the new response with the relevant context for change, using all representational sensory modes to reinforce the change, and ask the creative part of the self if it is willing to take responsibility for using the new alternative behaviors when appropriate.

Techniques including reframing and anchoring (discussed later in this chapter) helped Anita link her new response to the context for change. Reframing allowed her to view her new behaviors as meeting her friends' needs rather than communicating pity, which was how she initially and negatively viewed empathy. Drawing on multiple sensory modalities, she visualized herself looking Jennifer in the eye, listening carefully to her concerns, putting her hand on Jennifer's shoulder, and communicating heartfelt caring. An anchor, clasping her hands, helped Anita easily retrieve this scenario and the good feelings it brought her.

6. Do an ecological check, asking whether any part of the person objects to using the new alternative behaviors. If the answer is yes, return to Step 4 for revision of the behaviors.

Anita reported that the new behaviors were appealing and that she was eager to try them out in context. She believed enough in the value of the planned change to be convincing in her verbal and nonverbal communications.

These six steps reflect a very simplified and streamlined version of NLP. This is a complex approach that draws heavily on a broad range of theories. Readers are encouraged to study this approach more fully to appreciate its depth and richness.

Strategies

NLP uses an extensive array of strategies to promote change. Many have a neurological basis and are consequently very different from those used by other approaches to treatment. Although a detailed discussion of the many interventions associated with NLP is beyond the scope of this book, a brief overview of some of the most important can introduce readers to NLP practice.

- *Rapport* between client and clinician is essential, as it is in most approaches to treatment (Grey, 1991).
- *Pacing* enhances rapport by sharing the client's view of the world, emphasizing language and sensory modalities that reflect the client's preferences (Lankton, 1980). For example, a clinician might say to a client who uses the visual modality more than others, "Can you see the benefit of that?" and "Can you visualize yourself engaged in the new behavior?" To a client who emphasizes the auditory modality, the clinician might say, "I hear what you are saying," and "Listen carefully to your description of the behavior."
- *Feedback* and monitoring, both verbal and nonverbal, are integral parts of NLP, helping people become conscious of slight changes in their physiological and mental reactions and continue to fine-tune their actions and reactions (Kamp, 1996).
- *Leading* people from one sensory channel to another can promote awareness and give them new experiences and useful tools. As Lankton (1980) described this strategy,

A therapist might, for instance, be matching a client who was representing a difficult problem kinesthetically. At an appropriate moment, with enough rapport built, the therapist may pace and lead the client from the kinesthetic channel to a visual one by remarking, "I certainly know how you feel about being unable to get a handle on things (kinesthetic), but has there ever been a time when you had a different perspective and were able to see things clearly (visual)?" (pp. 62–63)

- *Calibrating* links a person's internal state with his or her external behavior and makes sure that the two are consistent. Close attention to language and sensory channels, as expressed by the client and used by the clinician, is important in helping people align verbal and nonverbal messages.
- *Reframing* is enhanced by calibrating. Reframing is the process of creating "a framework in which all parts of the system are aligned toward achieving the desired outcome" (Dilts, 1983, p. 32). It gives people a different and typically more integrated perspective.
- *Anchoring* associates a stimulus with a particular experience and can facilitate assessing resources to address problems. For Anita, the stimulus of clasping her hands was linked to the experience of clearly communicating concern and caring to her friends. When she clasped her hands (the anchor), the learning that she had acquired about better ways to communicate became accessible to her because of the link between those skills and the anchor.
- *Eye movements* reflect the way in which people process data. According to Grey (1991),

For most normally organized people, upward eye movements reflect visual processing, lateral eye movements reflect auditory processing, and downward movements represent either kinesthetic processing or indicate that the client is talking within. For most right-handed people, an eye movement up and to the left is a signal that they are attempting to access a visual memory. Movement up and to the right usually signals that the client is constructing a visual image. Auditory patterns follow the same left-right pattern, left for remembered, right for constructed" (p. 13)

- NLP therapists pay close attention to people's eye movements. They use this information to identify the sensory channels that people are using, facilitate their efforts to match their clients' sensory modalities, and enhance the process of calibration.

Application and Current Status

The literature provides examples of the application of NLP to a wide variety of people and groups. For example, it has been used to treat substance use disorders (Sterman, 1990), help people deal more effectively with traumatic experiences (Lankton, 1980), and improve family functioning. Although NLP has been available to clinicians for more than 20 years, it has not yet received strong empirical support. However, in recent years, interest in NLP seems to have increased, perhaps as a result of its connection in people's minds to eye movement desensitization and reprocessing, a newer and apparently very powerful tool. The concepts and tools of NLP are compelling and may well have considerable value to clinicians, but more research is needed to establish the value of this approach.

THOUGHT FIELD THERAPY

Thought field therapy (TFT) is another new and innovative approach. TFT is designed to change disturbing and intrusive thoughts and is one of several new energy-oriented approaches to treatment.

According to TFT, people have many thought fields, each with a focus and comprised of a circumscribed group of thoughts (Callahan & Callahan, 1997). Thought fields may be intrusive and present themselves frequently and automatically, or they may appear only when a person is reminded of a disturbing situation linked to that thought field. Disturbing thought fields have the capacity to trigger negative emotions such as fear and rage and are viewed as the fundamental cause of all negative emotions. These negative emotions are elicited when perturbations or instability occur in a disturbing thought field. The goal of TFT is to quiet the perturbations so that the body's nervous system no longer is activated by the disturbing thought field.

According to Callahan and Callahan (1997), "The precise explanation for why TFT works is still under development" (p. 261). They believe that the process causes slight modifications in the body's neurotransmitter systems that result in changes in the body's bioenergy system, leading to transformation of negative emotions.

The process of TFT begins by having people think about an unpleasant thought and then rate their emotional state on the subject units of distress (SUDS) scale. This provides a baseline rating. They are then directed to tap a specific sequence of accupressure points on the body such as the eyebrow, the cheek, or the collar bone while focusing on their upsetting thoughts and painful issues. Other activities such as humming, directed eye movements, and verbalizations such as "I accept myself even though I still have some of this problem" may accompany the process of tapping. TFT uses different algorithms for different problems. The SUDS rating is checked periodically and the TFT process repeated if necessary to lower the rating.

Proponents of thought field therapy have reported rapid success in treating problems such as PTSD, phobias, depression, guilt, grief, addictions, and anxiety. At present, however, TFT must be considered a highly experimental procedure. Research has not substantiated its value, nor has clear information yet emerged on its appropriate use. However, we consider TFT here because of recent attention to this and a variety of energy-related interventions. They are innovative and potentially fruitful approaches to effecting change and may prove their value over the next decade.

Information on thought field therapy can be obtained from

Gregory J. Nicosia, Ph.D.
Advanced Diagnostics, P.C.
4927 Centre Avenue
Pittsburgh, PA 15213
(412) 683-8378
Website: http://www.thoughtenergy.com

COGNITIVE THERAPY OF EVALUATION

Cognitive therapy of evaluation (CTE) has been described as a new cognitive therapy (Caro, 1991). Derived from a general semantics theory developed by Alfred Korzybski, CTE focuses primarily on how language affects perceptions and how changes in language can correspondingly change beliefs and emotions. This approach has been influenced by other treatment systems, including strategic family therapy, Fritz Perls's Gestalt therapy, Aaron Beck's cognitive therapy, and Albert Ellis's rational emotive behavior therapy.

CTE takes the position that most emotional problems are due to "wrong or inappropriate evaluations": people make judgments before obtaining the facts and then react to their words or judgments as though they were facts (Caro, 1991, p. 192). The theory of CTE is reflected by three premises:

1. Perceptions do not equal reality.
2. Interpretations depend on cognitive processes that are fallible.
3. Beliefs and cognitions are only hypotheses that need to be tested and may need modification.

CTE seeks to reeducate people so that they learn to put facts before words. Clinicians encourage clients to assume the role of scientist, search for facts before making judgments, and use language that is concrete and descriptive rather than emotional and evaluative. For example, a person is encouraged to say, "I am not doing as well as I would like in school," rather than "How could I have gotten a *C*? I'm really stupid."

CTE was developed primarily by researchers at the University of Valencia in Spain. Preliminary results suggest that 15–20 sessions may be effective in treating generalized anxiety disorder, panic disorder, and mood disorders. Although this approach may become a valuable addition to the list of approaches that emphasize thoughts, CTE has not yet been widely used or proven its effectiveness. Consequently, it should be viewed as a new and emerging rather than an established approach.

SKILL DEVELOPMENT: ANCHORING

Although many of the interventions associated with the approaches presented in this chapter require special training, some can be readily used and easily incorporated into other treatment systems. One is anchoring, a technique associated with neuro-linguistic programming. An *anchor* is defined as any trigger or stimulus that evokes a consistent response pattern from an individual. An example of a common anchor is the smell of fresh-baked cookies. For some, this scent evokes positive memories of childhood experiences, while for others it evokes feelings of sadness, loss, and longing for a family life they never had. The anchor itself is neutral; only the associated cognitions and emotions give the anchor meaning.

Anchors can occur in any of the sensory channels. The following are examples of anchors that are likely to evoke emotional responses:

- *Visual* (sight): seeing a stranger who resembles a loved one; photographs; pictures of familiar places; seeing places where very good or very bad experiences occurred
- *Auditory* (hearing): music, particularly songs that marked special occasions; the sound of someone's voice; the screech of car brakes that are reminiscent of an accident
- *Kinesthetic* (touch, feeling): touching clothing worn on a special occasion; holding a child; being touched in ways that are reminiscent of particularly good or bad experiences
- *Olfactory* (smell): a perfume usually worn by a loved one; the aroma of a particular food or flower; smells associated with particular places
- *Gustatory* (taste): eating food that is associated with important memories; smoking a cigarette after a good meal or a sexual experience; the first cup of coffee in the morning

Anchors can be internal or external or can be combined in a sort of chain reaction. For one woman, the song "Autumn Leaves" (an external anchor) made her think of her father, who had appreciated that song, and initially brought up positive feelings. However, when images of him came into her mind, she was reminded of his painful death and how much she missed him (an internal anchor), which led to feelings of sadness.

Anchors can be positive or negative. A man undergoing chemotherapy for cancer associated the smell given off by the heating unit in the doctor's office with his treatment. Whenever he was exposed to a similar smell, he became anxious and nauseated because of his exposure to the negative anchor. However, the same man created a positive anchor to help himself get through his treatments. He always brought a photograph album containing pictures of family vacations with him to his treatment and found that the positive feelings and thoughts associated with the photographs helped reduce his discomfort and anxiety during treatment.

Anchors can be spontaneous or planned. People are constantly exposed to unanticipated and unpredictable anchors throughout the day—stimuli that consistently elicit certain emotional responses. Anchors also can be planned and constructed so that they help people reach their goals. Both spontaneous and planned anchors can be important elements in treatment.

Although emotions sometimes seem to arise without cause or explanation, a trigger for the emotions can usually be identified. Clinicians can help people to identify the triggers for their emotions and then use that information to help them deal with the emotions more successfully. For example, the man who had undergone chemotherapy realized that he became anxious every time he went to the airport because the smell reminded him of his doctor's office and his difficult medical treatment. Once he became aware of this association, his trips to the airport became less disturbing, and his negative feelings even diminished over successive visits to the airport. Had the feelings continued to be very painful for him, he could have made the choice to avoid the airport or offset those negative feelings with some planned and positive anchors. Having knowledge of the link between triggers and emotions and thoughts they evoked can give people options and greater control of their lives.

Positive anchors can be planned to reinforce learning and growth. For example, the man who was diagnosed with cancer used visualization to help him relax, become more optimistic, and cope with his disease and its treatment. When he achieved a peaceful and hopeful state through his visualization, he anchored those feelings by clasping his hands in a prayerlike gesture. After practicing this connection a number of times, he found he could immediately bring up those peaceful and hopeful feelings by clasping his hands. At stressful times that did not give him the opportunity to use visualization, as when he was about to receive chemotherapy, he could clasp his hands and immediately experience positive feelings.

Clearly, anchoring has many possibilities as a useful adjunct to any form of treatment. Most people find it an easy and appealing tool to use and benefit from understanding and developing ways to help themselves via anchoring.

CASE ILLUSTRATION

Here, Edie illustrates the application of eye movement desensitization and reprocessing (EMDR). However, this reflects only a brief segment of treatment. The therapist and Edie have decided to use EMDR to help Edie deal with her troubling memories of the abuse from her grandfather.

The first and second phases of the EMDR treatment—planning the treatment and client preparation—have already been completed. Edie and the clinician have had five previous sessions so that some rapport has developed, Edie's history has been discussed, and the clinician has determined that Edie is ready for EMDR. The clinician has explained and demonstrated EMDR to Edie, has made sure her expectations are realistic, and has taught her how to stop the process and imagine a safe place if her memories become too disturbing. The dialogue begins with the third phase of EMDR, assessment.

Clinician: Edie, we have decided that you will be working on images and memories of times when you were abused by your grandfather. Can you describe a visual image or picture that represents the worst part of the memory?

Edie: Yes. I must have been about seven years old. I was in bed at my grandparents' house. My grandfather came in and lay down on the bed. Then he started touching me. He had locked my grandmother out of the house. I heard her outside, yelling and banging on the door, but she couldn't get in to help me.

Clinician: What is a negative self-statement that you have now about yourself that goes along with that incident?

Edie: I feel so dirty, so bad about myself because of what happened. I guess the statement would be "I am worthless."

Clinician: And what is a positive statement that reflects what you would like to believe about yourself when you remember that incident?

Edie: That I am a worthwhile person.

Clinician: On the 1–7 validity scale, with 1 representing completely false and 7 completely true, how true does the statement "I am a worthwhile person" feel to you now?

Edie: I guess about a 2.

Clinician: What emotions do you associate with the memory you described to me?

Edie: Disgust, depression, hatred of myself.

Clinician: How do you rate your level of disturbance on a 0–10 scale, with 0 reflecting no disturbance and 10 the highest?

Edie: A 7; no, maybe 8.

Clinician: And where in your body do you experience that disturbance?

Edie: Mainly in my stomach. It feels queasy. And my chest feels tight.

Phase 4, desensitization, begins. A series of eye movements occurs after each brief client-counselor dialogue.

Clinician: (after the first series of eye movements) What comes up for you now?

Edie: I can see myself lying on the bed and my grandfather coming into the room. I can hear my grandmother outside. It's awful. (eye movements)

Clinician: How about now?

Edie: The picture is getting less distinct, sort of fuzzy. (eye movements)

Clinician: And now?

Edie: Still fuzzier. (eye movements)

Clinician: What comes up for you now?

Edie: This is strange. It's like I'm up on the ceiling looking down on myself in the bed, and the image of the bed seems to be getting smaller. (eye movements)

Clinician: How about now?

Edie: The girl on the bed, me, is getting up off the bed. She's going out the bedroom door. (eye movements)

Clinician: And now?

Edie: My grandfather is still there on the bed, but I've left the room and I'm about to walk out the front door. (eye movements)

Clinician: What do you see now?

Edie: She . . . I've walked out the front door, and I'm out there with my grandmother. The two of us are getting into the car and driving away. (eye movements)

Clinician: How would you rate your level of disturbance now on the 0–10 SUDS scale?

Edie: Wow, it's really changed. I'd say it's down to a 4.

Clinician: And how about the rating of your self-statement "I am a worthwhile person"? On the 1–7 validity scale, how true does that statement feel now?

Edie: That's gone up. I'd say it's a 5.

Clearly, Edie is making progress in reprocessing the traumatic memory, as reflected by both the SUDS rating and the VoC rating. The EMDR process would continue at this point, seeking to reduce the SUDS score further and increase the validity (VoC) of the positive cognition. Once the SUDS score is a 0 or 1 and the VoC score is a 6 or 7, EMDR will be used to install and reinforce those results (Phase 5). This would be followed by a body scan to make sure that the unpleasant feelings Edie is experiencing in her stomach and chest have been alleviated (Phase 6). The session would close with a review of the experience (Phase 7). Edie would be encouraged to keep a log of her reactions and experiences between this session and the next, and the log would be used as part of the reevaluation process (Phase 8) in the next session.

EXERCISES

Because of the innovative and powerful nature of the approaches in this section and the need for specialized training before people can practice most of them, this chapter includes only large-group exercises.

Large-Group Exercises/Discussion Questions

1. EMDR, NLP, and TFT all involve procedures that have not yet been fully explained. Discuss how you feel about using approaches that are not well understood. What information would help you feel more comfortable about using these approaches? How could that information be obtained? How do you feel about using tools such as tapping and directed eye movements as part of the treatment process?

2. EMDR and NLP have been referred to as power therapies because of the great impact they can have on people. Although both approaches emphasize the importance of the client-clinician relationship, that relationship is primarily a context for the use of the interventions. This contrasts with approaches such as person-centered counseling and existential therapy, which emphasize the healing power of the therapeutic alliance. Which conception

of the therapeutic relationship is more comfortable for you and why? Which is more compatible with your view of the role of the clinician?

3. NLP and TFT have not yet been well researched. Develop a research study that would help determine the value of one of these approaches. This can help you reflect on how clinicians and researchers might go about the process of proving the effectiveness of a treatment system.

SUMMARY

This chapter has reviewed four emerging approaches that emphasize the importance of thoughts: eye movement desensitization and reprocessing, neuro-linguistic programming, thought field therapy, and cognitive therapy of evaluation. Of these four approaches, only EMDR has thus far been well supported by empirical research. However, all of the approaches, with their innovative use of language and interventions such as directed eye movements and tapping, have the potential to become powerful additions to the clinician's repertoire of skills.

RECOMMENDED READINGS

Bandler, R., & Grinder, J. (1975). *The structure of magic.* Palo Alto, CA: Science and Behavior Books.

Callahan, R. J., & Callahan, J. (1997). Thought field therapy: Aiding the bereavement process. In C. R. Figley, B. E. Bride, & N. Mazza (Eds.), *Death and trauma* (pp. 249–267). Washington, DC: Taylor & Francis.

Caro, I. (1991). An introduction to the cognitive therapy of evaluation. *Counselling Psychology Quarterly, 4,* 191–206.

de Luynes, M. (1995). Neuro-linguistic programming. *Educational and Child Psychology, 12,* 34–47.

Manfield, P. (Ed.) (1998). *Extending EMDR.* New York: Norton Professional Books.

Shapiro, F. (1995). *Eye movement desensitization and reprocessing.* New York: Guilford.

Shapiro, F., & Forrest, M. (1997). *EMDR: The breakthrough therapy for overcoming anxiety, stress and trauma.* New York: Basic Books.

PART FIVE

TREATMENT SYSTEMS EMPHASIZING ACTIONS

Chapter 19
Overview of Actions

Chapter 20
Behavior Therapy and Cognitive Behavior Therapy

Chapter 21
Reality Therapy

Chapter 22
Solution-Based Brief Therapy

Chapter 19

OVERVIEW OF ACTIONS

Part 5 emphasizes the fourth component in the BETA model: actions. The first three components of this model—background, emotions, and thoughts—were considered in previous parts of this book. Theories that emphasize behaviors and actions take the position that, because behaviors are overt and observable and have an impact on the direction of our lives as well as our thoughts and emotions, it makes sense to focus the treatment process on modifying behaviors.

Actions or behaviors shape our lives, as history and literature have shown. In "The Road Not Taken," poet Robert Frost (1962, p. 223) described a man standing where two roads diverge. After choosing to follow one path, the man reflected on his actions:

> Oh, I kept the first for another day!
> Yet knowing how way leads on to way,
> I doubted if I should ever come back.

Similarly, the film *Sliding Doors* portrays the profound difference just catching or barely missing a subway train makes in a woman's life. One choice leads to her discovery of her partner's infidelity, while the other leaves her unaware of his behavior. History provides with us many examples in which the actions of one person such as Julius Caesar, Martin Luther King Jr., Marie Curie, or Jonas Salk made a great difference in the lives of millions of people. In art, too, the music of Mozart and Martha Graham's dance innovations, for example, have had an impact on many lives and have shaped the fields of composition and dance.

The person who experiences feelings or has thoughts may be the only one who knows those feelings and thoughts; they can be kept private, and any given thought or emotion may not have an impact on the person's life. That is not the case with behaviors. Once we take action—choose which road to travel—we make an irrevocable move in a certain direction. In addition, the potentially public and observable nature of behaviors intensifies their meaning. Although background, emotions, and thoughts may underlie our behaviors, the actions we take are most likely to determine the direction of our lives and, to a large extent, our relationships with other people and the perceptions they have of us. Even a small act such as skipping breakfast to get to work early can have a profound impact on a person's life if it enables that person to miss having an accident on the highway, get acquainted with a new friend in the line at the employees' cafeteria, and make a positive impression on a supervisor who is deciding on promotions.

Sometimes people feel overwhelmed and immobilized when they consider the possible impact of their behaviors and seek to avoid making choices and taking action. However, inaction is an action in itself and does have consequences.

Part 5 focuses primarily on treatment systems designed to modify behaviors and actions. However, because behavioral approaches to counseling and psychotherapy are typically integrated with cognitive approaches, some chapters also pay attention to the integration of behavioral and cognitive approaches to change. Chapter 20 reviews the theory and strategies of behavioral counseling and psychotherapy, paying particular attention to Donald Meichenbaum's approach to cognitive-behavior therapy. Chapter 21 focuses on reality therapy as developed by William Glasser, which is particularly useful in settings such as schools, correctional institutions, and substance use treatment programs that emphasize changing behavior. Finally, Chapter 22 reviews solution-based brief treatment, an efficient approach to counseling and psychotherapy that helps people build on strengths and successes to effect change in their lives.

THE IMPORTANCE OF ACTIONS IN COUNSELING AND PSYCHOTHERAPY

Focusing on behavior change has many advantages in treatment, most of which are similar to the advantages of focusing on cognitions. However, an emphasis on behavior and actions has additional advantages as well as some drawbacks.

The Advantages of Focusing on Actions

Most counselors and therapists recognize that emotions, thoughts, and actions have reciprocal relationships. For that reason, regardless of whether or not clinicians focus primarily on behaviors, they should be aware of the potential benefits of paying some attention to clients' behaviors.

Behaviors As Presenting Problems   Presenting problems often focus on behaviors. People rarely seek treatment because of dysfunctional thoughts, although they sometimes seek help for negative emotions such as depression and anxiety. Most often, however, what impels them to seek help is an action or a behavior, either theirs or someone else's, that has upset them. Common behavioral concerns include overeating, unhealthy use of drugs or alcohol, poor impulse control, difficulty finding a rewarding job, and problems in forming and maintaining friendships. Because behaviors often prompt people to seek treatment, clients are more likely to feel heard and believe that treatment will be helpful if it, at least initially, focuses on the concerns that led them to seek help.

A focus on unrewarding or self-destructive behavior is particularly likely in treatment of people who are not self-referred for help. For example, people who are court-mandated to undergo treatment, encouraged to see the employee-assistance counselor at work, or brought for help by a concerned parent or dissatisfied partner are usually in treatment because their behaviors have violated the law or been unsatisfactory or troubling to another person. It is generally people's observable behaviors that lead to a referral for treatment, not their underlying thoughts or feelings.

The Accessibility of Behaviors   Behaviors are usually more accessible than either thoughts or emotions are. Think back to yesterday at this same time. It may be difficult for you to recall your thoughts and feelings, but you can probably remember where you were and what you were doing. You may have been listening to a lecture, driving home from work, or taking a nap. Because behaviors are linked to the structure of our days, we can usually retrieve them, whereas our thoughts and emotions may not be related to that external frame of reference and so may be far more difficult to recall.

Comfort in Discussion of Behaviors   Discussion of people's behaviors is likely to be far less threatening than a discussion of their early childhood experiences or their troubling emotions and somewhat less threatening than discussion of their cognitions. People are used to talking about their activities with their friends and colleagues but may have far less comfort and experience in talking about thoughts and emotions.

In addition, most actions are overt, open to observation by others, whereas thoughts and emotions are covert and often not obvious. Thus, questions about behaviors are likely to seem less intrusive than questions about emotions and cognitions. Few people, for example, would be uncomfortable with questions such as "What time did you get up this morning?" and "What did you say to your child when you learned he had lied to you?" although they might experience some discomfort with questions such as "What thoughts led you to stay in bed all day?" and "How did you feel when your child lied to you?"

Accuracy of Information   Discussion of behaviors is socially acceptable even among casual acquaintances, and people seem more able to present accurate information about their behaviors than about their emotions and cognitions. Having clear and valid information, especially at the beginning of treatment, is essential in facilitating development of realistic goals and a viable treatment plan as well as in developing a positive therapeutic alliance.

Ease of Measurement   Behavior is readily amenable to measurement and change. People can easily assess change in variables such as how many beers they drink each day, how often they get to the gym, how many hours they devote to work, and how much time they spend with friends. Because even small changes can readily be identified, people seeking to modify their behaviors can have rapid evidence of improvement. This, in turn, can be empowering and promote motivation, optimism, and compliance with treatment.

At the same time, if an incorrect diagnosis, case formulation, or treatment plan has been made, it will quickly be reflected in a lack of behavior change in response to treatment. This can show the clinician that a revision in treatment is needed, facilitating the development of a more effective treatment approach.

The Availability of Behavior Change Strategies   A broad range of behavior change strategies has been developed. This enables clinicians to individualize treatment plans, bring creativity to their work, and maximize the likelihood of success by tailoring treatment to a particular person.

Extensive Research Support   Because the impact of behavior change strategies is relatively easy to assess and because behaviorally oriented clinicians generally are favorably disposed toward empirical research, an extensive body of literature is available on the application and effectiveness of behavior therapy. Behavior therapy seems to have received more support in the literature than any other approach, not because it is necessarily superior to other treatment systems but because of the extensive research that has been conducted on this approach to treatment.

In 1995, a task force of the Division of Clinical Psychology of the American Psychological Association conducted a thorough review of the literature to identify treatment approaches that had been empirically validated (Division 12 Task Force, 1996). They identified 22 well-established treatments and 7 that were probably effective; as a group, these treatments were appropriate for use with 21 different mental disorders listed in the *Diagnostic and Statistical Manual of Mental Disorders* (DSM) (American Psychiatric Association, 1994). Nearly all of these were behavioral in nature. Another 8 well-established treatments and 19 probably effective treatments were added to the list in 1996; all but 5 were behavioral in nature. Clearly, behavior therapy has proven its value in treating a broad range of disorders and symptoms.

No Symptom Substitution   In the past, some clinicians expressed concern that treatment of one troubling behavior would simply shift the nature of the problem and that other undesirable behaviors would emerge. However, current research has demonstrated that this process of symptom substitution is not usually a concern (Myers & Thyer, 1994). In fact, generalizability seems to operate in a positive way; once people learn ways to modify one undesirable behavior, they usually are able to use those same strategies to change other unwanted behaviors.

The Limitations of Focusing on Actions

Although treatment systems that focus on behavior change have many advantages, they also have some shortcomings. Excessive emphasis on behavior can lead clinicians and clients to ignore thoughts and feelings that may need attention and be important in solidifying change. An exclusive focus on actions can lead to a superficial treatment process with results that are little more than cosmetic.

For example, Mimi sought counseling for a presenting problem of time management, expressing a wish to have more involvement with her husband and children. Underlying her presenting problem were feelings of self-doubt and low self-esteem, disappointment with her marriage, and fear that her husband was having an affair. Mimi's doubts about her marriage were exacerbated by her feelings of betrayal linked to having been sexually abused by her father when she was a child. Neglect of Mimi's thoughts and emotions, as well as her background, would have done her a disservice and probably have led to treatment that at best would have had very limited success and might have worsened her difficulties.

Several safeguards can minimize the likelihood that clinicians focusing on actions will miss important underlying concerns. First, they should conduct a comprehensive assessment of their clients via a thorough intake interview and appropriate inventories. This should help provide a full picture of clients and facilitate development of a treatment plan that is broad enough to address both presenting problems and relevant underlying concerns. Second, clinicians should closely monitor the progress of treatment; if rapid change is not evident, clinicians may not have adequately conceptualized a case and need additional information and a revised treatment plan. Third, behavior counseling should usually not be used alone. Combining behavior treatment strategies with cognitive approaches, in particular, makes behavior therapy a more powerful model of treatment as well as one that is likely to be effective in addressing a broader range of concerns.

SKILL DEVELOPMENT: PLANNING AND IMPLEMENTING BEHAVIOR CHANGE

Helping people make behavior change involves a series of relatively structured and predictable steps that can, of course, be adapted to meet the needs of a particular person or problem. We review these steps here, illustrating them with the example of Ernest, whose supervisor reprimanded him for getting to work late. These steps can be applied to a wide variety of undesirable behaviors, including overeating, substance misuse, poor time management, unsatisfactory performance at work or school, inappropriate expressions of anger, children's misbehavior, insufficient exercise, smoking, unwanted personal habits such as nail biting, and deficiencies in social skills.

Describing the Behavior

The first step in changing a behavior is describing that behavior in terms that are specific and measurable. If appropriate, both the undesirable behavior and the desirable change should be specified.

For example, Ernest's presenting concern was arriving at work late. First the undesirable behavior was explored in detail. Ernest worked full time and had a wife and three children. His days were full and demanding. He reported that he had little time to unwind; so after his wife and children were in bed, he would stay up until about 2:00 A.M. watching television so that he could have some time to himself. In the morning, he was tired and had difficulty rising early enough to help his wife get the children ready for school. As a result, mornings were usually very hectic. The children sometimes missed the school bus, meaning that Ernest had to drive them to school. Even when the children caught the bus, Ernest was usually at least 30 minutes late to work. Obtaining a full description of the undesirable behaviors made clear that Ernest's lateness was a complicated situation with many contributing factors.

Ernest excused his lateness by explaining that he often worked through his lunch hour and stayed late. However, he recognized that his job description stated that his working hours were 9:00 A.M. to 5:30 P.M. and that he was not adhering to those hours. The desirable change he sought was clear: arriving at work on time on a regular basis. However, he also hoped to find ways to manage the needs of his family more successfully and have more time for himself.

Establishing a Baseline

Once the problem behaviors have been clearly described, a baseline can be obtained, reflecting the severity and frequency of the behaviors before the inception of treatment. To determine the baseline, client and clinician must agree on the following:

1. *Ways to measure the behavior.* The two most common dimensions for measuring behavior are *frequency* (e.g., how many glasses of wine did a person drink in a day? how many times in one hour did a child get out of his seat at school? how many times a week did a man yell at his wife?) and *severity* (e.g., how late was the homework assignment? how much damage was caused by the nail biting? how much clutter has resulted from a person's hoarding behavior?). Describing the behavior in clear and specific terms facilitates its measurement. For example, the problem of a messy house is difficult to measure unless it is described as including a floor piled with clothes, six boxes that remain unpacked, and a mildewed shower.

2. *Ways to record the measurement.* Generally, people in treatment are encouraged to keep a record of their own behaviors. They can use a checklist, a diary, or another written record of the dimensions of the undesirable behavior. Ernest decided to use his date book to record his schedule for five days. He listed the times when the alarm went off, when he actually got out of bed, when he arrived at work, when he left work, and when he went to bed. For each day, he also wrote down a brief description of what he did between rising and arriving at work,

In his next session, Ernest reviewed his records with the clinician. Ernest set his alarm for 6:00 A.M. each morning but rarely arose before 6:30. He was 30–45 minutes late to work each day—twice because he had to drive his children to school; once because he was delayed by his daughter, who had misplaced her homework; once because the dog had an accident that required attention; and once because Ernest slept until 7:00 A.M. He left work between 6:00 and 6:30 P.M. Four out of five nights he watched television until nearly 2:00 A.M.

Establishing Goals

Goals should be clear, specific, measurable, and achievable. They should be logical outgrowths of the baseline information. Both clinician and client should understand and have a record of the goals, and both should agree that the client seems able to accomplish the goals without too much difficulty. Success in reaching goals is reinforcing and can encourage people to tackle more challenging goals, but goals that are not achieved can be discouraging and lead people to doubt themselves and their abilities. Consequently, goals should be designed to facilitate accomplishment rather than frustration. (Chapter 22's "Skill Development" section includes more information on goal setting.)

Although Ernest was eager to make changes so that he could get to work on time each day, the complexity of the problem as well as its severity, as reflected by the baseline, suggested that the goal should be approached gradually. Ernest's initial goal was defined as getting to work by 9:00 A.M. at least once during the next week and getting to bed by 1:00 A.M. at least three times during the week.

Developing Strategies

The next step in the process of changing behavior is developing individualized strategies that seem appropriate for both the client and the goal. Because Chapter 20 reviews many specific strategies, we will not repeat them here. However, clinicians should consider several categories of strategies when helping people move toward their goals.

Skill Development and Education   People often need to develop new skills and learn new information to help them change problem behaviors. These might include assertiveness and communication skills, parenting skills, time management, and others.

Impulse Control   Problems with impulse control are often a key element in an undesirable behavior. Ernest, for example, described himself as "addicted to late-night television" and had difficulty curtailing that behavior. Teaching people impulse-control strategies such as relaxation, distraction, avoidance of triggers that evoke the impulse, and others can facilitate behavioral change.

Reinforcement   Rewards can motivate people to achieve their goals, help them take pride in their accomplishments, and encourage them to take on more challenging goals. Rewards can take several forms. They can be social, such as encouragement and compliments from friends and family; intrinsic, such as the good feelings and improved health benefits a person experiences after losing weight or giving up smoking; or extrinsic, such as going out to dinner to celebrate or putting aside money for a desired object. Rewards are particularly likely to serve as a motivator if they are identified in advance and made contingent on the person's performance. As with goal setting, plans should be formulated so that the person is likely to receive a reward.

   Reinforcements can be delivered regularly (each time the desired behavior is emitted) or intermittently. Intermittent reinforcement can be particularly powerful. Lundin (1977) has described four schedules of reinforcement:

1. *Fixed-interval reinforcement* occurs on a regular schedule, such as a weekly paycheck or quarterly report cards.
2. *Variable-interval reinforcement* occurs at irregular intervals that average out to a specified time. For example, an animal might receive five treats in 75 minutes, averaging out to one every 15 minutes, but the intervals between the treats might vary from 5 to 30 minutes.
3. *Fixed-ratio reinforcements* are provided at a specified rate that depends on the number of responses made. For example, people working on an assembly line may be paid for the number of parts they put together rather than for the hours they work.
4. *Variable-ratio reinforcements* usually appear random and unpredictable to the recipient, although they are controlled or planned by the provider. Winning at the slot machines is an example. Variable-ratio reinforcements can be very powerful in encouraging responses because each response holds the promise of being the one that yields a substantial reward.

   Although penalties or punishments are sometimes used instead of rewards to shape behavior, rewards are generally more effective. They make the process of change a positive and empowering experience and promote motivation. In addition, if other people are dispensing the consequences, they are likely to be perceived positively if they are giving rewards but viewed negatively if they are providing punishments.

However, punishments can give a powerful and immediate message and do have a place in behavior change. Time-outs, for example, give misbehaving children an opportunity to calm down and reflect on their behavior. Yelling at a child who starts to run into traffic is certainly a powerful deterrent.

Natural consequences (discussed further in Chapter 21) are punishments that avoid some of the potentially harmful consequences of other types but still give a strong message. Natural consequences are designed to grow logically out of the undesirable behavior; for example, a boy who is neglecting his homework is required to keep a notebook in which his teachers write down the daily homework assignments for parent follow-up. The girl who uses six towels each time she bathes is made responsible for doing the laundry.

Planning   Planning is almost always an essential element of behavioral change. Planning enables people to specify exactly how and when they will modify their behaviors and can help them anticipate and overcome obstacles they might encounter in their efforts to make positive changes.

Commitment   Making a commitment to change as well as a public declaration of the intent to change can motivate people to follow through on their plans. Clinicians should be sure that their clients are really invested in the process of change and intend to give it their best effort. Their resolve can be further solidified through a written contract with the clinicians or by suggestions that clients share their goals with friends or family members who might be able to give them support and encouragement. Having a partner in a behavior change program, perhaps a friend who also wants to stop smoking or exercise regularly, can also be reinforcing.

Ernest and his counselor developed a series of strategies to help him reach his goals:

1. *Skill development.* Ernest had little knowledge of time management. Before he began his program of change, his counselor reviewed important principles of time management with him and suggested a book he might read on the subject. Ernest also received some information on the cumulative effects of inadequate sleep and was helped to realize the part that fatigue might play in his difficulties.

2. *Impulse control.* Ernest needed help in controlling his impulse to watch television. He reported that he typically drowsed in front of the television and lost track of time. He decided to set a timer to go off at 12:30 A.M. to remind him that it was time to shut off the television and get ready for bed.

3. *Planning.* Planning was important in helping Ernest change his behavior. Ernest determined that he needed to rise by 6:15 A.M. to get to work on time. He decided to set two alarms, one next to the bed for 6:00 A.M. and one across the room for 6:15 A.M. This allowed him a few welcome minutes to gradually awaken but made it likely that he would get out of bed at 6:15 to shut off the second alarm.

Although some of the crises that occurred in the mornings at Ernest's house were unavoidable, some could be averted by careful planning. Ernest and his wife agreed that before their children went to bed, they would organize their books, homework, lunch money, and other necessities for school to streamline their morning routine. The two older children, ages seven and nine, were asked to assume some responsibility for setting the table and putting out the breakfast food.

To help Ernest shift some of his relaxation time to an earlier hour, he and his wife agreed that they would alternate taking primary responsibility for the children each evening. While one person was in charge of baths and homework, the other could take an hour of quiet time to relax, read, or watch television.

4. *Reinforcement.* Ernest expected to receive some natural reinforcers for his behavioral change. He anticipated getting better evaluations from his supervisor, feeling more relaxed, and having a less harried home environment. In addition, he decided that, once during each week in which he achieved his goals, he and his wife would hire a sitter so they could go out to dinner as a couple. This reinforcer in itself seemed likely to contribute to Ernest's sense of relaxation and positive feelings about his family.

5. *Commitment.* Ernest and his counselor wrote up a contract of his goals and strategies. Ernest shared this with his wife and asked her for help with his efforts to change his behaviors.

Implementation

Once goals have been established and strategies determined, the plans for behavior change can be implemented. People should keep a record of their progress as they did when determining the baseline of their undesirable behaviors. They also should make notes about anything that facilitated or hindered the implementation.

Ernest found that he did well with the parts of his plan that were under his control but had difficulty persuading his children to help out in the morning and prepare for school the night before. He planned to ask the counselor for some help with this situation.

Assessment

At regular intervals, clients and clinician should monitor progress so that successes can be maintained and reinforced and any difficulties in the plan addressed. Prolonged experiences of failure should certainly be avoided. When discussing the outcome of clients' behavior change plans, clinicians should be encouraging and optimistic but not judgmental, critical, or blaming. People often do not fully achieve their goals. This should be viewed as an opportunity for learning and refining the plan rather than as a failure. People should not be encouraged to dwell on excuses or disappointments but congratulated on the efforts they made and the successes they had. Subsequent plans can be modified to address difficulties in the original plan.

Ernest got to work on time two days out of five and was no more than 30 minutes late on the other days. He succeeded in getting up by 6:15 every day and getting to bed by 1:00 A.M. on four out of five nights and felt that he could get to bed even earlier in the future without too much difficulty. He enjoyed the hour of quiet time in the evening, even though he and his wife only implemented that change on two evenings. Although the children made some progress in organizing themselves, they were having trouble accepting their new responsibilities.

Reinforcement

Assuming rewards have been built into the plan and some success has been achieved, people can now receive those rewards. Clinicians can also cautiously provide some social reinforcement, congratulating clients on their efforts and helping them to take pride in their accomplishments. In general, however, clinicians should encourage people to praise themselves rather than give praise directly; making positive as well as negative judgments is risky and can cast clinicians in an undesirable evaluative role.

Ernest felt very proud of his success and reported that he also felt somewhat less fatigued. In addition, his wife had complimented him for trying to reduce some of the chaos they typically experienced in the morning. He had already hired a sitter and made dinner reservations for himself and his wife.

Continuing the Process

This last stage of a behavioral change plan takes one of three directions:

1. If the plan had some shortcomings and clients did not reach their goals, client and clinician consider what revisions in goals and strategies are likely to lead to greater success. Considerable attention may be paid to the strengths and weaknesses of the original plan to determine how it needs to be improved.

2. If the plan was successful but the client has additional goals or wants to build on the accomplishments of the initial plan, client and clinician agree on new objectives and develop strategies to facilitate their accomplishment.

3. If clients are satisfied with their accomplishments, they work with their clinicians to solidify those gains and prevent relapse. Strategies such as involvement in a peer support group, ongoing self-monitoring, stress management, and periodic follow-up treatment sessions are common elements in a relapse-prevention plan.

Ernest thought he had made a good start toward accomplishing his goals but recognized that he had only begun to make a significant change in his behaviors. He and his counselor developed additional goals and strategies to help him continue his efforts. In addition, the counselor suggested some strategies Ernest could use to facilitate change in his children's behavior such as modeling, using praise and reinforcement, letting them choose their chores from a list, and reframing their new responsibilities as reflecting their evident maturity.

CASE ILLUSTRATION

As part of improving his overall health, Roberto asked his clinician to help him include more exercise in his life. Roberto reported that he was so busy at work that he had no time for physical activities, although the family did belong to a health club. The following dialogue illustrates the application of a behavior change plan to Roberto's presenting concern.

Clinician: Roberto, let's begin by getting a clear picture of the situation [description of behavior].

Roberto: All right. Well, I know I need more exercise to keep my weight down and for my overall health. My father was very overweight, and he had a heart attack when he was just a few years older than I am. So I know I need to make a change. I just can't seem to do it. I work such long hours and I travel a lot for work. At the health club, they told me I should get there at least three times a week, but that seems impossible.

Clinician: How much exercise do you get now [establishing baseline]?

Roberto: About all I do is get to the health club once a week on Fridays after work. But that's it.

Clinician: I wonder if you get any informal exercise like sports with the family or just walking?

Roberto: Not really. Once a week at the health club is about it. I don't see any way you can get me there three times a week.

Clinician: Perhaps we need to define our goals differently. What I'm hearing is that your goal is to get sufficient exercise, not necessarily get to the health club [establishing goals].

Roberto: Yes, that's true.

Clinician: Perhaps we can find more realistic ways to help you get that exercise. Exercise can be thought of in terms of frequency and duration. Using those terms, what would you see as an acceptable amount of exercise, not necessarily ideal?

Roberto: At the health club, they say that at a minimum you should get 20–30 minutes of exercise a day for at least three days a week.

Clinician: Does that seem like an initial goal that you would be comfortable with?

Roberto: It's a place to start, although I'd really like to exercise more than that.

Clinician: We can increase the goal later, but it sounds like you would feel all right about an initial goal of exercising at least 20 minutes at least three days a week.

Roberto: Yes.

Clinician: Did you know that you don't need to do that 20–30 minutes all at once? You can break that into segments of 10 minutes or so of exercise and achieve the same results. That might sound more manageable.

Roberto: Yes, it does. Ten minutes doesn't sound like much.

Clinician: I wonder if you have a way to build one or two 10-minute walks into your day?

Roberto: Yes, I could do that. If I park my car over at the picnic area sometimes instead of by the entrance to my office, that would give me a 10-minute walk at each end of the day. I could even take a 10-minute walk after lunch.

Clinician: I can hear that you're starting to generate some ideas. Remember that, at least at the beginning, we want to make this change fairly easy for you.

Roberto: Okay, I can make that lunch walk optional and only walk at lunch on days when I don't have too much work.

Clinician: Making the plan as specific as possible might help you to follow the plan. How about choosing the specific days when you will park your car by the picnic area?

Roberto: I could do Mondays and Wednesdays. Those days tend to be less busy; no regular meetings on those days.

Clinician: So you have identified two possible days to walk each week. Let's look at some possible obstacles. What if the weather is bad on those days?

Roberto: I guess if it's really bad, I could shift to the next day; but I'm no wimp. . . . I can walk even if it's cold or raining.

Clinician: It sounds like you are really determined to do this!

Roberto: Yes, I know I have to.

Clinician: I wonder if you can build in some recreational activity with your family for the weekend?

Roberto: That's a good idea. Before Ava was born, Edie and I used to take bike rides together. I wonder if I could talk her into that again. If not, I bet Ava would come with me, especially if I bought her a new bike.

Clinician: Sounds like that idea really appeals to you. When could you fit biking into your schedule?

Roberto: Either Saturday or Sunday afternoon would work.

Clinician: If you continue going to the health club on Fridays, park by the picnic area twice a week, and go biking on the weekend, then we have four days planned when you will exercise. Because of your travel and work schedule, it might make sense to include those four opportunities in the plan in case you do have to miss one. Then you can still reach your goal of three days a week.

Roberto: That sounds good, and some weeks I might even hit four.

Clinician: Let's come up with some strategies to help you [development of strategies].

Roberto: All right.

Clinician: Having some more information about exercise and its health benefits might be useful to you. That could motivate you and help you plan your exercise better.

Roberto: The health club has lectures on that, but I've never gone. I think they have the lectures on tape. I could borrow them.

Clinician: That sounds like a way to get some information. Let's write that down on our plan. Sometimes people have great intentions about exercise, but other things get in the way. How can we try to prevent that from happening?

Roberto: I'll make copies of the plan we're writing down, and I'll post it at home and work. I can tell Ava and Edie what I'm doing and ask them to help. If one of them went biking with me, I'd really enjoy it.

Clinician: Another strategy that can help is building in a reward for yourself if you accomplish your goal. Would you like to make that part of your plan?

Roberto: How about two pieces of apple pie each day that I exercise?

Clinician: Will that help you reach your goal?

Roberto: Just joking! Let's see what will help. . . . I could use a new bike, but that's big bucks.

Clinician: What about putting aside a certain amount of money each week that you succeed in reaching your goal?

Roberto: That should work. I could put away $10 a week. By the end of the year, I'll have that bike.

Clinician: Let's review the whole plan now to make sure it's clear and that you are comfortable moving ahead with the plan. As we go over the plan, let me know if you see any more obstacles that might get in the way of your following up on the plan. We can think of ways to prevent them from keeping you from your goals. I'd also like to suggest that you keep a record of your exercise for the next week as well as notes on any factors that helped or hurt your efforts to exercise as you have planned. We'll use that information next week when we assess how things went to see if we need to change the plan in any way.

Roberto: Sounds good to me.

EXERCISES

Large-Group Exercises

1. Develop a plan for changing each of the following behaviors:

   - Smoking
   - Procrastination
   - Children's tantrums
   - Overeating

   Your plan should include the following elements:

   - Describing the behavior
   - Obtaining a baseline
   - Establishing goals
   - Developing behavior change strategies such as skill development, impulse control, reinforcement, planning, and commitment
   - Assessment

2. This book includes chapters on treatment systems that emphasize emotions, those that emphasize thoughts, and those that emphasize actions. Discuss which group of theories is most appealing to you and why.

3. Behavior change strategies can be used to shape the behavior of another person. Discuss how clinicians might help parents learn behavior change strategies for use with their children.

Small-Group Exercises

1. Divide into your groups of four, composed of two dyads. Each dyad should engage in a 15-minute session in which the person playing the client presents an undesirable behavior that he or she actually wants to change. The person in the clinician role should take the client through the five steps in formulating a behavior change strategy (see the list in Large-Group Exercise 1). The process should culminate with a written contract. Tape-record the interview. Play back the recorded interview after it is completed so that the group can identify each of the five steps and provide feedback to clinician and client.

2. Each dyad should role-play another interview, remaining in the same roles, with the person in the client role presenting the same behavioral concern. However, this time, the clinician should explore emotions and thoughts related to the behavior and avoid use of behavior change strategies. Discuss the process of each of the two interviews. How did the participants feel about their roles? Which interview was more challenging and why? Which interview was more successful and why? What was the impact of each interview on the therapeutic alliance? What other important differences did you notice between the two interviews? What did you learn from this exercise?

3. After the role plays have been completed, list all the undesirable behaviors that were presented by the group. Discuss them one at a time, identifying at least three strategies that might facilitate changing each of the behaviors. Then discuss and address obstacles that might arise when efforts are made to change each behavior.

Individual Exercises

1. Nearly everyone has behaviors that he or she would like to change. Identify one of your behaviors that you view as undesirable. Be your own behavioral counselor and develop a plan to change that behavior. Your plan should include the following elements:

   - Describing the behavior
   - Obtaining a baseline
   - Establishing goals
   - Developing behavior change strategies such as skill development, impulse control, reinforcement, planning, and commitment
   - Assessment

2. Now implement the plan you have developed. Review your efforts to change your behavior. Reward yourself for any successes and think about how you might change your plan if it is not as successful as you had hoped.

3. Think about a time when you made an effort to change your behavior. Perhaps you went on a diet, tried to stop smoking, or set out to take a more active part in discussions at work or school. Identify the strategies you used to

change your behavior. Then assess the outcome. What factors were important in determining the outcome of your efforts? Now that you have learned about strategies to facilitate behavior change, what, if anything, would you have done differently? Write about this in your journal.

SUMMARY

This chapter has discussed the importance of focusing on behaviors in counseling and psychotherapy as well as some of the advantages that an emphasis on changing actions can bring to the treatment process. The chapter has also outlined a process for planning and implementing behavior change: describing the behavior, establishing a baseline, setting clear and realistic goals, developing helpful strategies, implementing the plan, and assessing the outcome.

Chapter 20

BEHAVIOR THERAPY AND COGNITIVE BEHAVIOR THERAPY

By the 1970s, behavior therapy, first developed during the 1950s and 1960s, presented a powerful challenge to the principles of psychoanalysis. Behavior therapy's focus on the present rather than the past; on observable behaviors rather than the unconscious; and on short-term treatment, clear goals, and rapid change had considerable appeal.

Behavior therapy has continued to play an important role in the fields of counseling and psychology. It offers clinicians a wealth of helpful strategies and is useful in a broad range of settings and with a diverse clientele. At present, however, behavior therapy is more likely to be integrated with cognitive therapy and other approaches to treatment than used alone.

This chapter introduces the principles of behavior therapy and describes many of the useful techniques associated with that approach. We pay particular attention to cognitive behavior modification and stress inoculation training (developed by Donald Meichenbaum), which integrate cognitive and behavioral approaches. Readers should keep in mind that the demarcation between cognitive and behavioral approaches is not clear and that the cognitive theories of Beck, Ellis, and others (discussed in Part 4) also pay considerable attention to behaviors and behavior change strategies.

The differences among the cognitive treatment systems, behavior therapy, and the cognitive behavioral approaches are primarily those of emphasis. Cognitive approaches focus primarily on changing thoughts; behavioral approaches concentrate on modifying actions; and cognitive behavioral approaches attend to both thoughts and actions.

The Development of Behavior Therapy

Unlike many of the theories discussed in this book, behavior therapy is not strongly associated with one or two names. Instead, many people have contributed in a variety of ways to the evolution of this approach. Some, like Eysenck, Lazarus, Wolpe, Dollard and Miller, Krumboltz, and Bandura, focused on applying behavior therapy and learning theory to people. Others, including Skinner, Harlow, and Pavlov, used principles of behavior change to shape the actions and reactions of animals but contributed to the use of this approach in psychotherapy and counseling.

B. F. Skinner

B. F. Skinner, an experimental psychologist, may be the best-known behavioral theorist. Skinner received many awards for his contributions to psychology from the 1950s until his death. He emphasized the orderliness of behavior and tried to find principles to describe and predict behavioral patterns as well as ways to modify behavior. His ideas are known as *operant reinforcement theory* (Skinner, 1969). This theory postulates that the frequency of a behavior being emitted is largely determined by the events that follow that behavior. Skinner used the process of *operant conditioning* to change the behavior of pigeons; he used rewards to gradually shape naturally emitted behaviors until the pigeons learned to peck at a red disc. Similarly, a child's behavior can be shaped through parental reinforcement; for example, parents who pay greatest attention to a child when he or she is misbehaving inadvertently reinforce the child's negative behavior.

Ivan Pavlov

In the early 1900s, Ivan Pavlov (1927), a Russian physiologist, identified and wrote about a type of learning that has become known as *classical conditioning*. His study of the process of using conditioning with dogs has become well known. He demonstrated that, by simultaneously presenting an unconditioned stimulus (meat paste) and a conditioned stimulus (the sound of a tuning fork), researchers could eventually elicit the dogs' response of salivation (originally elicited by the unconditioned stimulus, the meat) using the conditioned stimulus (the sound) because the dogs learned to associate the sound with the meat. We can see this principle in our daily lives; as we drive a familiar route to visit a good friend, our mood may change and we begin to experience cheerful feelings associated with the presence of the friend. The familiar route (the conditioned stimulus) has evoked our positive response because of its association with the unconditioned stimulus (the friend).

Pavlov also studied the process of *extinction*. The dogs in his study salivated for a time in conjunction with the sound of the tuning fork, even when the sound was no longer accompanied by the presentation of the meat. However, over time, the salivating response diminished and eventually disappeared as a response to the sound of the tuning fork without the accompanying meat paste.

John W. Watson

John W. Watson, an American psychologist, sought to use Pavlov's principles to change behavior in people. Watson (1925) rejected psychoanalysis, then the prevailing approach to psychotherapy, and proposed what he called *behaviorism,* an approach to treatment that was objective and took account of learning theory. Drawing on Pavlov's principles of classical conditioning as well as stimulus generalization, Watson demonstrated that an unconditioned stimulus (a loud bell), paired with a conditioned stimulus (a white rat), could lead a child to emit a conditioned response (startle) in reaction not only to a white rat but also to white cotton and Watson's white hair.

John Dollard and Neal Miller

Subsequent work by John Dollard and Neal Miller (1950) contributed greatly to the understanding of learning theory and paved the way for behaviorists to move into the arena of psychotherapy. Dollard and Miller identified four important elements in behavior: drive, cue, response, and reinforcement. In *Social Learning and Imitation* (Miller & Dollard, 1941), they wrote

What, then, is learning theory? In its simplest form, it is the study of the circumstances under which a response and a cue stimulus become connected. After learning has been completed, response and cue are bound together in such a way that the appearance of the cue evokes the response . . . The connection between a cue and a response can be strengthened under certain conditions. The learner must be driven to make the response and rewarded for having responded in the presence of the cue. (p. 1)

The more frequently the stimulus and the response occur together with the response being rewarded, the stronger is the tendency to emit the response when the stimulus occurs, leading to the development of a habit or habitual response. This is the essence of the *stimulus-response (S-R) concept,* which, according to behavior theorists, determines the behaviors that people have learned.

Assume that a young girl is growing up in an abusive environment. In an effort to avoid mistreatment (drive), the child responds to people moving toward her or focusing on her (the cue or stimulus) with withdrawal (the response). Because the withdrawal helps the child reduce the abuse she experiences (reward), the behavior of withdrawal is learned. As the child grows into an adult, her withdrawal from social involvement is generalized to settings outside the home and becomes habitual. In this way, behaviors that may no longer be helpful become deeply entrenched.

Dollard and Miller found that *counterconditioning* could reverse habits. This involves pairing the behavior to be changed with a strong incompatible response to the same cue. For example, if the person in the previous example were exposed to positive interactions with people that elicited pleasure and the wish to move closer to people, her habitual response of withdrawing from people would probably diminish.

Joseph Wolpe

In a similar vein, Joseph Wolpe (1969) suggested a concept called *reciprocal inhibition* in which the elicitation of a novel response brings about a decrease in the strength of a concurrent habitual response. A parent who makes a silly face to cheer up a child who is crying after a minor fall is a simple example; the silly face elicits amusement, which automatically reduces the sad emotions associated with the tears. Wolpe's ideas led to the development of *systematic desensitization,* a powerful tool that pairs relaxation with controlled exposure to a feared stimulus such as heights or dogs. This technique continues to be widely used, especially in treatment of phobias, and is discussed in detail later in this chapter. Wolpe also developed strategies that continue to be used to help people become more assertive.

Wolpe's work reflects the concept of *stimulus generalization.* When people learn to behave in a particular way in response to one stimulus, they often behave in that same way when presented with similar cues. For example, a child who is taught to be respectful of teachers is likely to behave in the same way around other authority figures. Sometimes behavior is overgeneralized and becomes inappropriate or unhealthy. Then people need to learn *stimulus discrimination*—the ability to distinguish among similar cues. For example, most of us have learned to confide in a small number of close friends but recognize that it is inappropriate to share too many details of our personal lives in a work environment (stimulus discrimination). However, some people share intimate details of their lives not only with close friends but with casual associates, perhaps reflecting inappropriate stimulus generalization.

Albert Bandura

Albert Bandura (1969) played an important role in the development of behavior therapy through his application of principles of both classical and operant conditioning to social learning. He found that learning and subsequent behavior change could occur vicariously through observation of other people's behaviors. This process, which Bandura called *modeling*, can elicit both positive and negative behaviors.

Modeling often has a beneficial impact. For example, observing someone we admire undertake a challenging task can reduce our fears and facilitate our efforts to perform the task. On the other hand, Bandura's experiments suggested that children who observed adults engaged in verbally and physically aggressive behavior were more likely to manifest that behavior than were children who had not been exposed to such models. These findings certainly have implications for understanding the apparent increase in violent behaviors in young people.

Current Development

By the 1980s, behavior therapy had established its place in psychotherapy, and its effectiveness was well substantiated by research. However, many clinicians were dissatisfied with traditional behavior therapy, which de-emphasized the importance of the therapeutic alliance, viewed the clinician as the authority, and sometimes seemed dehumanizing. As a result, the shape of behavior therapy began to change and has continued to evolve over the past 25 years. Collaboration of client and clinician has come to be valued as an essential element. The move to integrate behavior therapy and cognitive therapy (reflected in the work of Meichenbaum, Lazarus, Ellis, and Beck, among others) has broadened the application of this approach and made it less mechanical and more sensitive to the needs of the individual client.

IMPORTANT THEORETICAL CONCEPTS

Behavior therapy today is reflected in the following five models (Wilson, 1995):

1. *Applied behavioral analysis.* Derived from the work of B. F. Skinner, this approach looks at the impact of environmental events on behavior. Taking a scientific approach, it focuses on observable and measurable behavior.
2. *Neo-behaviorism.* Drawing on Pavlov's classical conditioning as well as stimulus-response theories, this approach focuses on the process of conditioning or learning responses.

3. *Social learning theory.* Based on the research of Bandura, this approach seeks to understand the interaction of cognitive, behavioral, and environmental factors in shaping behavior. Many strategies that clinicians use to improve feelings of self-efficacy and reduce learned helplessness reflect understanding of social learning (Seligman, 1990).

4. *Cognitive behavior therapy.* Reflected in the work of Meichenbaum, Ellis, and Beck, this approach looks at how cognitions shape behaviors and emotions. This treatment system makes use of both cognitive and behavioral strategies to effect change.

5. *Multimodal therapy.* Multimodal therapy, developed by Arnold Lazarus, is based on principles of behavior therapy but systematically integrates strategies from a wide range of approaches. (Multimodal therapy is discussed in detail in Part 6.)

Principles of Behavior Therapy

Regardless of which specific approach to behavior therapy they endorse, behavior therapists generally subscribe to the following principles and beliefs (Myers & Thyer, 1994; Stuart, 1998):

- Although genetics plays a role, individual differences are derived primarily from different experiences.
- Behavior is learned and acquired largely through modeling, conditioning, and reinforcement.
- Behavior has a purpose.
- Behavior is the major determinant of habits, thoughts, emotions, and other aspects of personality.
- Behavior therapy seeks to understand and change behavior.
- Therapy should be based on the scientific method and be systematic, empirical, and experimental. Goals should be stated in behavioral, specific, and measurable terms; and progress should be assessed regularly.
- The focus of treatment should generally be on the present. Even if behaviors are longstanding, they are maintained by factors in the present environment.
- However, behaviors must be viewed in context, and some exploration of the past is appropriate to provide that context and help people feel understood.
- Education, promoting new learning and transfer of learning to the natural environment, is an important aspect of behavior therapy.
- Strategies of behavior therapy need to be individualized to the particular person and problems.
- People need to take an active part in their treatment to successfully change their behaviors. Although clinicians are generally responsible for suggesting interventions, clients have primary responsibility for defining their goals and completing homework tasks. The treatment plan is formulated collaboratively, with both client and clinician participating actively in that process.

Some people think of behavior therapy as narrow, directive, and deterministic. However, Myers and Thyer (1994) and Stuart (1998) dispute those misconceptions, asserting that modern behavior therapy has both depth and breadth as reflected in the following concepts and practices:

- Although behavior therapists may focus on observable behavior, they interpret behavior broadly as anything an organism does, including thinking and feeling, and are interested in the total person.
- Behavior therapists recognize the importance of a collaborative and positive therapeutic relationship and the communication of encouragement as important in promoting learning and motivation.
- Although objectivity and the scientific method are valued, behavior therapists also recognize the importance of understanding and respecting individual differences.

The Development of Personality

According to behaviorists, when children are born, they have three basic building blocks of personality:

1. A number of primary drives, such as toward food and warmth
2. Specific reflexes, such as sucking and blinking
3. Innate responses to particular stimuli, such as escape or crying in reaction to pain

Beyond that, behavior therapists believe that personality is shaped through learning and maturation. New behaviors may be emitted accidentally, acquired after observation of others, or be the product of thought. Whether these new behaviors continue to be emitted frequently and become a habit or are rarely if ever produced depends largely on the conditions accompanying or following the behavior. Both maladaptive and healthy behaviors are learned because they have yielded positive reinforcement or led to a decrease in an aversive stimulus. In other words, messages provided by both internal reinforcements such as good or bad feelings and external reinforcements such as praise or punishment are the primary determinants of the development of a behavior.

Understanding Terminology

Understanding the terminology of behavior therapy can facilitate understanding of personality development as well as behavior therapy. Following is a review of important terms, illustrated by the experiences of Theresa, a 33-year-old woman who was receiving chemotherapy for breast cancer. Although we discussed some of these terms previously in this chapter, we review them here for clarification.

Theresa presented many issues related to her recent diagnosis. She had always been fearful of injections and found blood tests and intravenous chemotherapy very difficult. She had anticipatory nausea associated with her chemotherapy, becoming queasy when driving into the parking lot of the clinic where she received treatment, whether or not she was even scheduled for chemotherapy. In addition, although her prognosis was encouraging, Theresa constantly ruminated about the likelihood of her death.

Theresa's anticipatory nausea can be explained by *classical conditioning.* The *unconditioned stimulus,* the chemotherapy, elicited the *response* of nausea. Because that unconditioned stimulus was paired with the experience of driving up to the clinic, entering the parking lot became a *conditioned stimulus* that elicited the same response of nausea whether or not the unconditioned stimulus (the chemotherapy) was also present.

Theresa, like all of us, had a natural *drive* to avoid pain. When she was due to receive inoculations as a child, her parents had emphasized the unpleasantness of that experience and had *reinforced* her fears by paying special attention to her when she became fearful. As a result of this *operant conditioning,* her fear of injections became *habitual* and had evolved into a *phobia.* In fact, through the process of *stimulus generalization,* Theresa experienced inordinate anxiety in reaction to any medical appointment, whether or not it necessitated an injection. Her learned behavior reflected a *stimulus-response* model; because her fearful behavior had been rewarded when she was a child, Theresa demonstrated fear and avoidance (response) to the stimulus of any medical visit.

Her therapist used several behavioral treatment approaches to modify Theresa's responses. *Systematic desensitization* was used in the hope of *extinguishing* Theresa's excessive fear of medical visits and inoculations. An *anxiety hierarchy* was created, listing her fears in ascending order from the mildest fear (a visit to a dermatologist that would definitely not involve any discomfort) to the most frightening (a visit to the oncologist for chemotherapy). Beginning with the mildest fear, the therapist helped Theresa to relax and feel empowered while visualizing the frightening stimulus. This process of *reciprocal inhibition* paired relaxation and positive feelings with an aversive stimulus to decrease the strength of the fear response. Theresa was also taught to use both relaxation and *stimulus discrimination* to reduce her fears; she learned to relax when approaching medical visits and driving into the parking lot at the oncology clinic and reminded herself that not all medical appointments involved discomfort. *Counterconditioning* was used to help Theresa further reduce her fears; when she began to ruminate or felt anxious, she visualized herself triumphantly completing her chemotherapy and setting off on a trip to Bali that she was planning. The feelings of pride and optimism elicited by that image counteracted and reduced her apprehension. To make sure she could readily access this positive image, the therapist led Theresa through a process of *covert modeling* in which she mentally rehearsed how she would deal with her fears about her next chemotherapy treatment. Joining a support group of other women who were dealing with breast cancer also provided Theresa with an experience in *social learning and reinforcement* and gave her additional *role models.*

Steps in Treatment

Chapter 19 discussed the steps in a plan to effect behavior change. Although we review them here, readers will find more detailed information in that chapter. Once behavior therapists believe they have obtained enough information to have at least a basic understanding of their clients and to put their concerns in context, clinicians and clients collaborate in the development of a plan, generally characterized by the following seven steps:

1. • Conceptualize the problem.
   • Review the nature of the problem and its history.
   • Explore the context of the target (unwanted) behavior.
2. Obtain a baseline, reflecting the current frequency, duration and nature of the target behaviors.
3. Establish goals.
   • Make sure that goals are realistic, clear, specific, and measurable.
   • Make sure that goals are meaningful to the client.
   • State goals positively. For example, "Arrive at work on time at least twice this week" is a more appealing goal than "Avoid being late to work at least twice this week."
4. Develop strategies to facilitate change.
   • Change precipitating conditions that trigger undesirable behaviors.
   • Teach skills that can contribute to the change.
   • Review and enhance impulse-control strategies.
   • Use strategies such as modeling, rehearsal, and systematic desensitization to facilitate positive change.
   • Formulate appropriate reinforcement contingencies and, if indicated, meaningful consequences.
   • Carefully plan implementation of the change process as well as ways to monitor and record the outcomes of that process.
   • Make a written contract and encourage the client to share the commitment to change with others.
5. The client implements the plan.
6. • Evaluate the success of the plan.
   • Successes are emphasized and reinforced.
   • If necessary, the plan is revised.
7. Make plans to promote maintenance of gains and prevent relapse.

MEICHENBAUM'S COGNITIVE BEHAVIOR MODIFICATION

Behavior therapy is often integrated with cognitive therapy, as Donald Meichenbaum's work illustrates. Meichenbaum (1993) developed cognitive behavior modification (CBM) in an effort to integrate psychodynamic and cognitive treatment systems with the "technology of behavior therapists" (p. 202). He believed that no one of these treatment systems alone was sufficient to explain psychopathology and promote behavior change but that the combination could accomplish both goals.

Three assumptions of CBM clarify Meichenbaum's integration of cognitive and behavior therapies:

1. *Constructive narrative.* People actively construct their own reality; "reality is a product of personal meanings" (p. 203).
2. *Information processing.* People experience negative emotions because they distort reality as a result of cognitive errors and misperceptions.
3. *Conditioning.* Cognitions are viewed as covert behaviors that have been conditioned. Correspondingly, they can be deconditioned and modified through both external and internal contingencies (rewards or negative consequences), thereby strengthening new cognitions and changing attributions. Modeling, mental rehearsal, and other strategies are important in effecting cognitive change.

The Role of the Clinician

According to Meichenbaum (1993), the role of a cognitive behavior therapist is that of co-constructivist: helping people alter their stories and cognitions so they can build "new assumptive worlds" (p. 203). To accomplish this, treatment via CBM entails the use of cognitive interventions, such as Socratic dialogue and reframing, as well as behavioral interventions, such as development of coping skills and client self-monitoring. At the same time, cognitive behavior therapists believe that treatment should be demystified; techniques de-emphasized; and clients seen as active, knowledgeable, and responsible partners in their own treatment. Learning and self-help are encouraged, and feedback from the client is welcomed.

Stress Inoculation Training

Meichenbaum (1985) has developed stress inoculation training (SIT), a useful and effective cognitive behavioral treatment procedure. He described stress as "a cognitively mediated relational concept, reflecting the interaction between person and environment" (p. 3). Typically, people experience stress because of a perception that their life circumstances have exceeded their capacity to cope, to effectively use "behavioral and cognitive efforts to master, reduce, or tolerate the internal and/or external demands that are created by stressful transactions" (p. 3). SIT is an approach to reducing stress that assumes that if people can successfully cope with relatively mild stressors, they will be able to tolerate and successfully cope with more severe ones. In other words, as its name implies, SIT seeks to immunize people against the adverse impact of stress by helping them successfully handle increasing levels of stress. SIT usually consists of 12–15 weekly sessions plus additional follow-up sessions over 6–12 months.

SIT has three phases (Meichenbaum, 1985):

1. *Conceptualization.* Clients and clinicians develop a collaborative relationship. People are taught about the nature of stress; the relationship between stress and coping; and the roles that thoughts, actions, and emotions play in engendering and maintaining stress. Once people have some understanding of stress and factors that promote it, their stressful thoughts and experiences, as well as the antecedents and consequences of those thoughts and experiences, are explored via discussion and self-monitoring. Particular attention is paid to self-statements and to making people aware of their self-talk.

The initial goals of treatment are to translate the experience of stress into specific fears and problems that are amenable to solution and help people see that they have some control over their lives. Like Beck's cognitive therapy, SIT asks people to rate the severity of their fears on a scale of 0–100 subjective units of distress (SUDS).

2. *Skills acquisition and rehearsal phase.* Treatment then proceeds to address people's milder fears, helping them gather information, use coping self-statements, learn relaxation strategies, change their behaviors, or use other cognitive and behavioral strategies to reduce those fears. In addition, people are taught to effectively apply problem solving to their fears using the following five steps:

- Problem identification
- Goal selection, focusing on small manageable units of stress
- Development of alternatives
- Evaluation of each possible solution and its probable consequences
- Decision making and rehearsal of coping strategies, including modification of self-statements

3. *Application and follow-through.* In the third phase, people implement their plans to solve problems and reduce stress. This is followed by an assessment of the outcome and reinforcement of people's efforts and accomplishments. Strategies such as coping imagery and practice are used to solidify gains, apply learning to other problem areas and more significant fears, and help people to prevent or cope with relapses.

Learning the skills to reduce their fears as well as develop confidence from their initial success in managing stress can generalize and facilitate people's efforts to address others fears and problems successfully. Taking one step at a time and building on successes can make challenging situations manageable and foster self-esteem and more desirable cognitions and behaviors. In addition, encouraging people to have a sense of responsibility for their futures rather than their pasts during this phase of treatment can be very empowering.

TREATMENT USING BEHAVIOR AND COGNITIVE BEHAVIOR THERAPY

Behavior therapy makes substantial use of specific strategies and interventions. Although these are important ingredients of treatment, they should not overshadow the broad goals of the treatment system and the importance of the therapeutic alliance.

Goals

Behavior therapy, as its name implies, seeks to extinguish maladaptive behaviors and help people learn new adaptive ones. The following is only a partial list of goals that can be achieved through behavior therapy:

- Reduction in use or abstinence from drugs and alcohol
- Reduction of undesirable habits such as nail biting and pulling out one's own hair
- Improvement in social skills such as assertiveness or maintaining conversations
- Amelioration of fears and phobias such as fear of flying, apprehension about public speaking, and excessive fear of snakes
- Improvement in concentration, organization, and time management
- Reduction in undesirable behaviors in children such as tantrums, disobedience, acting out, aggressiveness, and difficulty going to bed
- Weight loss and improvement of health and fitness

In addition to such specific goals, behavior therapists also have the general goal of teaching people skills that will help them improve their lives. Consequently, skills such as decision making, problem analysis and resolution, time management, and relaxation are often incorporated into behavior therapy.

Therapeutic Alliance

Modern behavior therapists view it as essential to establish a positive and collaborative therapeutic alliance. In fact, some studies have found that cognitive behavior and behavior therapists outperformed psychodynamic/interpersonal therapists in terms of their ability to establish highly effective working alliances with their clients (Myers & Thyer, 1994; Raue, Goldfried, & Barkham, 1997).

A behavior therapist assumes many roles: teacher, consultant, advisor, devil's advocate, supporter, role model, encourager, and facilitator. Active listening, understanding, caring, respect, and concern all are part of a therapist's repertoire as well as presenting and enabling clients to make use of the principles of behavior therapy. Although behavior therapists encourage and reinforce positive change, they also value genuineness and professionalism. According to Jacobson (1989), "The therapist who offers unsolicited reassurance, arbitrary reinforcement, or deceptive acceptance will be acting in a self-defeating manner" (p. 93). These clinicians are cautious about giving advice and praise. They want clients to take credit for their positive changes rather than attribute them to their therapists. Symbolic of the genuine caring that behavior therapists have toward their clients was the American Humanist Association's 1972 selection of B. F. Skinner as Humanist of the Year.

Clients are expected to participate fully in the process of behavior therapy and take responsibility for presenting their concerns, identifying their goals, and implementing plans for change. Clinicians typically encourage their clients to try out new behaviors, complete tasks between sessions, self-monitor, and provide feedback to the clinicians. No longer is behavior therapy a process that one person does to another; rather, it is a shared endeavor.

Strategies and Interventions

Behavior and cognitive behavior therapists use a broad range of cognitive and behavior change strategies. These strategies are useful not only to behavior therapists but also to clinicians using other treatment systems who want to help clients hone in on and change behaviors.

Cognitive techniques have been discussed in earlier chapters of this book. However, to facilitate their integration into behavior therapy, they are listed here followed by the chapter number in which they are discussed in more detail. Behavior change strategies are also listed here, with an accompanying description.

Cognitive Strategies   Following are strategies to improve thinking:

- Ellis's *ABCDEF* model (17)
- Self-talk (16)
- Development and assessment of alternatives (16)
- Relabeling and reframing (16)
- Projecting into the future/distancing (16)
- Systematic decision making (17)
- Problem solving (17)

Following are strategies to curtail ruminating and repetitive self-destructive thoughts:

- Distraction (16)
- Thought stopping (16)
- Writing out thoughts, letter writing (16, 17)
- Flooding (17)

Following are strategies to improve coping skills:

- Cognitive and covert modeling (16)
- Visual imagery (14, 16)
- Graded task assignments (16)
- Bibliotherapy (16)
- Role playing (16)

Following are strategies to reinforce positive change:

- Affirmations (16)
- Focusing on the positive (17)
- Cueing, anchoring (18)

Behavioral Strategies   *Acting as if.* When confronting a challenging situation, people act as if they are someone else whom they view as capable of handling the situation effectively. Children undergoing medical treatments, for example, have coped more successfully with their treatments when they pretended to be their favorite superhero. Adults, too, can benefit from this empowering approach by acting as if they are an admired friend or colleague.

Activity scheduling. Planning activities that are rewarding and provide a sense of accomplishment can help people in many ways. Having a schedule can give them focus and direction, which can counteract inertia, confusion, and problems in decision making. It can limit excessive sleeping or television watching and prevent isolation. It can increase optimism and reduce depression by helping people realize that they can still enjoy their lives and be successful.

Activities designed to accomplish treatment goals are particularly valuable. For example, the person who is overwhelmed by a recent job loss is likely to benefit from preparing a realistic schedule of activities to find another job. The schedule should list the activities, when they will be performed, and how much time will be spent on each task.

Exercise and other forms of physical activity also can be very helpful. Research has shown that physical exercise can reduce depression and increase the secretion of endorphins that can improve feelings of well-being (Locke & Colligan, 1987).

Aversion therapy. Rewards rather than punishments or negative consequences are usually favored in behavior therapy because they enhance self-esteem, optimism, and relationships. However, sometimes linking undesirable behaviors with negative experiences can be a powerful motivator for behavior change. Of course, great care must be exercised in planning and implementing aversion therapy to be sure it does not have a negative emotional or physical impact and is respectful of people's rights and choices. Antabuse, an emetic used to discourage people from consuming alcohol, is an example of aversion therapy. Time-outs, used to modify children's behavior, are another form of aversion therapy, although their primary purpose is to give a child an opportunity to calm down and reflect rather than be a punishment.

Visual imagery sometimes makes use of aversion therapy. For example, a woman who wants to stop smoking might imagine herself having severe difficulty breathing or coping with a smoking-related disease. A young man who is contemplating suicide so that his girlfriend will feel guilty about ending their relationship may change his mind after imagining himself lying in his grave while she goes on to have a full and rewarding life.

Satiation or flooding—giving people excessive exposure to a negative stimulus or behavior—is another type of aversion therapy (see Chapter 17). For example, a woman who wants to stop smoking might be encouraged to smoke a large number of cigarettes in rapid succession until she feels ill. Flooding, like other forms of negative interventions, must be used with great caution.

Behavioral rehearsal. This strategy gives people an opportunity to practice a challenging task. The rehearsal might involve a role play with the clinician or a practice session with a friend. Tape-recording the rehearsal or observing oneself in the mirror while practicing the desired behavior offers opportunities for feedback and improvement.

Behavioral rehearsal can be used for a wide variety of experiences. Those that involve making or refusing requests and sharing both positive and negative feelings with others lend themselves particularly well to behavioral rehearsal. Examples include asking for a promotion, sharing feelings of love, requesting a change in a relationship, and refusing to serve on a committee. Behavioral rehearsal can also help people improve their social skills—for example, by practicing ways to initiate and maintain conversations or invite other people to join a client in social activities.

Biofeedback. Biofeedback involves the use of instruments that monitor bodily functions such as heart rate, sweat gland activity, skin temperature, and pulse rate and give people feedback on those functions via a tone or light. Biofeedback is particularly effective in reducing tension and anxiety and promoting relaxation. It also can have physical and medical benefits such as lowering blood pressure and promoting pain control.

Contracting. Establishing a clear agreement between client and clinician about the goals of treatment and the roles of both participants is an important component of behavior therapy. Contracting is usually done early in the treatment process. However, each time a new problem area is targeted for change, client and clinician can expand their contract to include additional objectives and procedures. This provides focus and motivation and can increase client cooperation with the treatment process.

Diaphragmatic breathing. Taking slow, deep breaths and focusing on the breathing process can be very calming and even induce sleep. This sort of breathing supplies the body with more oxygen, focuses concentration, and increases self-control and mindfulness. Abdominal, or diaphragmatic, breathing is particularly helpful. To accomplish this, people breath in through the nose, focusing on expanding the diaphragm with the intake of air, and then expel the air through the mouth. Counting to eight with each breath gives the breathing process a slow and relaxed pace (Golden, Gersh, & Robbins, 1992).

Expressive therapies. These approaches use art, dance, music, poetry, and other forms of creative self-expression to enable people to become more aware of and give form to their emotions. These techniques can be particularly successful with people who have difficulty verbalizing their feelings and concerns or may feel stuck or blocked in a certain area of their lives. Expressive therapies can be freeing and empowering and are useful with both adults and children.

Extinction. Extinction involves withdrawing the payoff of an undesirable behavior in hopes of reducing or eliminating it. For example, parents who give their children extra attention whenever they misbehave may be inadvertently reinforcing the undesirable behavior. Coaching the parents to pay attention to positive behavior and ignore misbehavior as much as possible is likely to reduce the negative behaviors.

Hypnosis. Hypnosis has been described as "essentially a state of heightened and focused concentration" (Breitbart & Passik, 1993, p. 67). This state of altered consciousness typically promotes greater relaxation, increased ability to access unconscious material and long-term memories, increased receptivity to suggestion, and an enhanced ability to take in new material (Carich, 1990; Fairchild, 1990). Hypnosis can increase feelings of well-being and promote insight and empowerment. It is particularly useful in treatment of people with anxiety disorders, phobias, or a history of physical or sexual abuse. Specialized training is necessary for clinicians to learn the concepts and strategies of hypnotherapy.

Modeling. Other people can be used as models, or clients can serve as their own models by making audio or video recordings of themselves engaged in positive and desired behaviors. Clinicians can serve as models, demonstrating target behaviors. In addition, people can be encouraged to observe others engaged in behaviors or activities that they would like to emulate, such as public speaking, conversing at social gatherings, or offering suggestions at a meeting. By observing these models and identifying the ingredients that make their behaviors successful, people can expand their repertoire of positive behaviors. People are most likely to be influenced by models who are similar to them in terms of gender, age, race, and beliefs; perceived as attractive and admirable in realistic ways; and viewed as competent and warm (Bandura, 1969).

Natural consequences. Discussed further in Chapter 21, natural consequences are the logical, and usually unpleasant, outcomes of undesirable behavior. For example, the child who fails to pick up her toys before dinner will be required to clean up her room later in the evening instead of watching her favorite television program. Getting fired for repeatedly coming to work late is another example of a natural consequence. Although natural consequences can be conceived of as punishment, they usually are preferable to arbitrary and contrived punishments because they have a logical connection to the undesirable behavior and give people a strong message about the implications of their behavior.

Reinforcements. The use of reinforcements or rewards can encourage behavior change, enhance learning, and solidify gains. Reinforcements should be carefully selected and planned; they should be meaningful and worthwhile to the person so that they are motivating and should be realistic and reasonable. For example, giving a child a video game for cleaning up his room once is not realistic, but setting aside $3 toward the purchase of a video game each week the child cleans his room five out of seven days probably is.

Adults can create their own reinforcement plans. One woman who was having difficulty paying her bills on time set aside one hour twice a week in which she would concentrate on organizing her finances. Each time she completed the hour of financial planning, she rewarded herself by going to the bookstore to buy a new mystery and spending the rest of the evening reading her book.

Relaxation. Relaxation is often combined with other techniques such as systematic desensitization, abdominal breathing, hypnosis, and visual imagery. Teaching relaxation strategies in the session and encouraging practice between sessions can facilitate people's efforts to reduce stress and anxiety and effect behavioral change. Several well-established relaxation strategies are available, including progressive muscle relaxation (sequentially tensing and relaxing each muscle group in the body); a body scan (tension in each part of the body is systematically assessed and released); and simple exercises such as head rolls, shoulder shrugs, and shaking one's body until it feels loose and relaxed.

Shaping. This technique is used to effect a gradual change in behaviors. People are taught to make successive approximations of desired behaviors, eventually leading them to develop new patterns of behavior. For example, people with social anxiety might follow these steps to improve their interactions with others:

1. Spend 5–10 minutes at a social gathering. Do not initiate any conversations.
2. Spend 5–10 minutes at a social gathering and greet at least two people.
3. Spend 15–20 minutes at a social gathering, greet at least two people, introduce yourself to at least one person, and ask a question of at least one other person.
4. Follow Step 3 and, in addition, engage in one brief conversation about the weather and compliment the host on the food.

Skill training. An important component of promoting behavioral change is teaching people the skills they need to modify their actions. A wide variety of skills can be taught through counseling and psychotherapy, including skills of use to nearly everyone (e.g., assertiveness training, decision making, problem solving, communication skills) and those serving the needs of a particular client (e.g., interviewing, anger management). Parents often benefit from learning to apply strategies of behavior change to interactions with their children. Bibliotherapy, or relevant readings, can supplement clinicians' efforts to help people develop new skills. Many books are available, for example, on assertiveness, self-esteem, parenting, and other aspects of positive development.

Systematic desensitization. One of the most powerful behavior change strategies, systematic desensitization is very useful in reducing fears, phobias, obsessions and compulsions, and anxiety. Systematic desensitization can be conducted in the imagination (imaginal desensitization) or in context (in vivo desensitization).

The first step is the construction of an anxiety hierarchy: a list of frightening stimuli ranked from the mildest to the most severe. The process begins by focusing on the mildest fear (perhaps standing in front of the open front door for a woman diagnosed with agoraphobia), pairing exposure to the stimulus with relaxation. When the person develops comfort with a given stimulus, the clinician moves to helping the person deal with the next most troubling stimulus on the list until even the greatest fears have been reduced to manageable levels. Continuing the desensitization process until a fear has been reduced is imperative; stopping the process while a fear is still great can actually increase rather than decrease apprehension. Practicing this approach between sessions can enhance progress.

Token economies. Particularly useful in group settings such as schools, day treatment programs, hospitals, and prisons, token economies are an effective and efficient way to change a broad range of behaviors in a group of people. Behavioral rules or guidelines must first be established and then understood and learned by all participants. These are generally written out and posted to maintain awareness of the guidelines. Then a system of assessing and recording each person's performance of the desired behaviors must be developed. This might be stars or marks on a chart or poker chips distributed at the end of the day when each participant's behavior is assessed. Finally, a system of rewards is developed.

The rewards should be clear, realistic, and meaningful to the participants and be given in ways that are fair and consistent. In a typical token economy, the stars, points, or poker chips can be used like trading stamps to earn privileges. For example, 2 points might be traded in for extra time watching television or talking on the telephone, 5 points might merit a trip to the movies, and 15 points might be traded in for a new CD. Opportunities should be provided for frequent redemption of rewards to provide reinforcement. In addition, social reinforcement (praise, words of approval, appropriate physical affection) should be paired with the material rewards to develop intrinsic motivation and internalization of the desired behaviors. Generalization of the behaviors outside of the therapeutic setting can promote their establishment.

APPLICATION OF BEHAVIOR AND COGNITIVE BEHAVIOR THERAPY

Behavior and cognitive behavior therapy has a broad range of applications. Used either alone or in combination with other treatment systems, their principles and strategies can be applied in almost any treatment setting and with almost any client or problem.

Special Populations

Behavior and cognitive behavior therapy has wide appeal. These approaches are easily understood and logical, respect individual differences, and can be adapted to a broad range of people and problems. As Stuart (1998) stated of behavior therapy, "Individual differences must be understood and respected. People want to be accepted for who they are, not only for who they could be" (p. 8).

Behavior and cognitive behavior therapy offers a considerable repertoire of interventions to address almost any concern. These approaches are not intrusive; they do not emphasize the unconscious, the early years of development, or the covert meanings of dreams and body language, all of which seem more likely to create discomfort than does attention to overt behaviors. People are typically more willing and able to talk about overt behaviors than they are to examine thoughts or emotions. Particularly for people from cultures that do not place great value on personal growth, insight, and self-expression and that discourage disclosure of problems to people outside of the family or community, behavior therapy is often the preferred approach.

Even for people who begin treatment with strong feelings of apprehension, doubt, and resistance, behavior therapy can be effective. It encourages people to play an active and informed role in their treatment, promotes learning and competence, and can produce rapid and positive results that are reinforcing.

Behavior and cognitive behavior therapy has been used in a wide variety of settings (Kazdin, 1994). For example, schools and correctional institutions as well as day treatment and in-patient treatment programs rely heavily on behavior therapy to teach and establish positive behaviors. In addition, behavior and cognitive behavior therapy can be used in family and group counseling as well as individual therapy. The reinforcement and modeling provided by the other group members makes the group setting especially well suited for behavior therapy. Many parents benefit from learning strategies of behavior change and using those strategies to shape their children's behavior. Although we may not even be aware of it, most of us use behavior change strategies in our everyday lives. When we reward ourselves with a snack after finishing a difficult chore, give a chronically late friend a message by deciding not to wait more than five minutes, buy a kitten for a child who is afraid of animals, or embark on a plan to improve our nutrition and exercise, we are using behavior change strategies. These approaches, then, have a great deal to offer a broad and diverse range of people.

Diagnostic Groups

Behavior and cognitive behavior therapy has demonstrated strong effectiveness in the treatment of mood disorders (Sexton, 1995a). Behavior change strategies such as activity scheduling and systematic decision making can reduce the severity of depression, counteract the inertia and confusion often associated with depression, and promote feelings of mastery and competence.

Behavior therapy and cognitive behavior therapy are also very useful in the treatment of many types of anxiety disorders. Systematic desensitization is a powerful tool in the treatment of agoraphobia and specific phobias such as fear of flying, fear of heights, and fear of snakes. People diagnosed with social phobia are likely to benefit from training in social skills involving instruction in assertiveness and communication, modeling, role playing, and practice. Thought stopping, distraction, and substitution of positive activities for negative ones have helped people cope with obsessive-compulsive disorders. In addition, aversion therapy, satiation, and flooding, used with great care, can also be useful in treatment of that disorder.

Linehan (1993) and her colleagues developed Dialectical Behavior Therapy (DBT), a variation on behavior therapy. A manualized version of DBT has been used primarily to treat people diagnosed with borderline personality disorder who were chronically suicidal and severely dysfunctional. DBT is characterized by four stages:

1. Development of commitment to treatment
2. Establishment of stability, connection, and safety
3. Exploration and emotional processing of the past
4. Synthesis of gains, including increased self-respect and achievement of individual goals

Follow-up of people treated with at least one year of DBT reflected considerable reduction in suicidal ideation, hospitalization, anxiety, and anger and increases in occupational and social adjustment (Linehan & Kehrer, 1993).

Behavior and cognitive behavior therapy has also demonstrated effectiveness with many other mental disorders and problems. Token economies and natural consequences have been used successfully to treat children and adolescents diagnosed with conduct disorders. Relaxation, activity scheduling, and time management all can be helpful to people with attention-deficit disorders. Behavior therapy has also demonstrated effectiveness in helping people diagnosed with mental retardation, impulse-control disorders, sexual dysfunctions, sleep disorders, and paraphilias. Behavior therapy plays a major role in the treatment of disorders characterized by dysfunctional eating such as bulimia nervosa and anorexia nervosa as well as disorders that involve unhealthy use of drugs or alcohol. Research also supports the effectiveness of behavior and cognitive behavior therapy in the treatment of people who are experiencing suicidal ideation (Carney & Hazler, 1998). Cognitive behavioral counseling has been shown to improve grade-point average, attendance, and self-concept in academically at-risk students (Sapp, 1994). Relaxation, hypnosis, and visual imagery have been used in behavioral medicine to reduce pain and help people cope with cancer, heart disease, and chronic and life-threatening illnesses.

Clearly, behavior and cognitive behavior therapy is useful in the treatment of a broad range of mental disorders and symptoms. Even disorders such as schizophrenia and some personality disorders, which are unlikely to be resolved through behavior therapy alone, benefit from the inclusion of behavior change strategies in the treatment plan.

Current Use

Behavior and cognitive behavior therapy has a well-established role in the treatment of a wide range of mental disorders and emotional difficulties as well as in the entire range of treatment settings. Because of their variety and flexibility, behavior change strategies can be used with almost anyone regardless of age, background, intellectual level, motivation, or problem. Not surprisingly, they are essential in the treatment of dysfunctional habits and behaviors, depression, and anxiety.

However, behavior therapy is generally not used alone; its combination with cognitive therapy is widespread. Behavior therapy can also be integrated into a broad range of other approaches, including psychodynamic therapy, Gestalt therapy, and person-centered counseling. Such combinations seem likely to deepen the impact of behavior therapy and ensure that changes resulting from treatment are not superficial.

EVALUATION OF BEHAVIOR AND COGNITIVE BEHAVIOR THERAPY

As with cognitive therapy, extensive research has been conducted on behavior therapy. The literature suggests that treatment focused on behavior can be very powerful and effective. Of course, it also has limitations.

Limitations

Most of the criticisms of behavior therapy focus on the possibility that it will accomplish only superficial and transitory gains. Emotions and insight may not receive the attention they merit in treatment. Clinicians may move too quickly to focus on behaviors and not fully explore the underlying antecedents and dynamics of those behaviors. For example, development of social skills may be emphasized in the treatment of a woman who is fearful of dating, with insufficient attention paid to her history of abuse. In addition, clinicians may become so caught up in the power of this approach that they neglect to help clients take adequate responsibility for their treatment and progress. As a result, people may feel manipulated and powerless rather than experience the growth in self-worth and competence that should emerge from treatment.

These limitations can be minimized by skilled clinicians who take a holistic view of their clients, seek to understand behavior in context, and remember the importance of empowering people. At the same time, behavior and cognitive behavior therapy is not the ideal approach for all clients. A focus on behavior relatively early in treatment can initiate progress and enhance motivation. However, for clients who have longstanding and deep-seated problems, perhaps stemming from an early history of abuse and inadequate parenting, psychodynamic and other approaches should probably be combined with behavior and cognitive behavior therapy. This combination can facilitate clients' development of insight and allow them to work through past concerns while also helping them make cognitive and behavioral changes. In addition, although behavior therapy can be helpful to people with psychotic and other severe disorders, medication and other interventions are also needed. Indeed, behavior therapy and cognitive behavior therapy are useful with almost all clients but often need to be combined with other treatment modalities to maximize their effectiveness.

Strengths

Behavior therapy and cognitive behavior therapy have many strengths. Both offer a straightforward approach to treatment that has both face and empirical validity. They are flexible and broad treatment modalities, offering a wide variety of useful interventions that facilitate their application to a wide range of people and problems. These approaches emphasize goal setting, accountability, and results. Thus, they remind clinicians that psychotherapy is not simply an interesting process to promote self-awareness but a place where people can change their self-destructive behaviors and relieve their emotional pain.

Although early versions of behavior therapy tended to ignore the importance of background and individual differences and sometimes seemed too directive and contrived, modern versions have acknowledged and addressed these shortcomings. Today, behavior and cognitive behavior therapists recognize that problems must be viewed in context. Clinicians explore the historical roots and antecedents of clients' concerns, strive to develop positive and collaborative therapeutic alliances with their clients, and seek to know and understand their clients as individuals. Clinicians practicing behavior and cognitive behavior therapy generally emphasize the importance of empowering people and helping them not only deal with immediate presenting concerns but also develop skills and strategies they can use in the future to lead healthier and more rewarding lives.

Earlier in its development, some clinicians dismissed behavior therapy, viewing it as a superficial approach likely to effect only transient improvement or, worse, shift symptoms from one problem area to another (symptom substitution). However, extensive research has largely dispelled these concerns. The outcomes of behavior and cognitive behavior therapy tend to be enduring; rather than leading to symptom substitution, behavior therapy is likely to lead to a generalization of positive change in which people spontaneously apply the skills they have learned to address one problem to other areas of concern. As Jacobson (1989) concluded of cognitive behavior therapy, there is "no doubt that the treatment is a powerful one" (p. 87).

Contributions

Behavior therapy, more than any other treatment system, has emphasized the importance of research on treatment effectiveness. Through their own research, behavior and cognitive behavior therapists have demonstrated the success of their work.

Behavior therapists' emphasis on goal setting, accountability, and outcome is very much in keeping with modern conceptions of counseling and psychotherapy. The requirements of managed care for treatment plans and progress reports, as well as clients' own demands for efficient and effective treatment, can readily be met through behavior and cognitive behavior therapy. In addition, these approaches have paved the way for other treatment systems to research their effectiveness, establish clear goals and interventions, and assess their impact.

Behavior therapy has also provided a foundation for the development of several other approaches—for example, reality therapy and brief solution-based psychotherapy (discussed in Chapters 21 and 22) as well as multimodal therapy (discussed in Part 6). The practice of behavior and cognitive behavior therapy is widespread, and articles on these approaches to treatment appear regularly in most psychotherapy and counseling journals.

SKILL DEVELOPMENT: SYSTEMATIC DESENSITIZATION

Systematic desensitization is one of the most powerful interventions in behavior therapy. It is particularly important in the treatment of phobias and excessive fears of certain situations such as socializing, flying, and public speaking. However, it is also useful in addressing other apprehensions and anxieties. For example, it has been used to reduce fear of surgery and chemotherapy in people who have been diagnosed with cancer.

Systematic desensitization involves gradually exposing people to the object of their fears while helping them relax. Relaxation and fear are incompatible responses; as a result, fear of a stimulus typically diminishes if relaxation can be achieved and maintained during exposure to that stimulus. However, this treatment can have a reverse effect if not well planned; premature exposure to frightening stimuli or exposure that is aborted while the fear is still high can increase terror of the stimulus. Consequently, careful pacing is essential to successful treatment using systematic desensitization.

Exposure to the frightening stimulus may occur in the imagination (imaginal desensitization) or the real world (in vivo desensitization). One is not clearly more effective than the other. The choice of whether to use imaginal desensitization, in vivo desensitization, or a combination of the two is determined primarily by the nature of the feared stimulus and the ease of creating a situation of controlled exposure to that stimulus. For example, imaginal desensitization, perhaps enhanced by pictures and films, would probably be necessary to treat someone with a fear of hurricanes, while in vivo desensitization could probably be used to help someone overcome an inordinate fear of dogs or balloons. A combination of imaginal and in vivo desensitization would probably work best for someone coping with a fear of flying.

Systematic desensitization typically follows a series of steps after one or more sessions have been spent on developing the therapeutic alliance, exploring the antecedents and symptoms of the fear, and discussing the person's history and present life situation so that the symptoms can be viewed in context. These steps are illustrated by the case of a young girl, Makita, age eight, who was frightened by balloons popping at a party and has since developed a phobia of balloons that prevents her from attending any parties or social gatherings where balloons might be present.

1. *Teach an effective relaxation strategy.* Makita was taught to relax by shifting her breathing to a pattern of slow abdominal breaths while focusing on her breathing. She was then taught to relax her body, progressing gradually down from her head to her toes, until her entire body felt relaxed.

2. *Establish an anxiety hierarchy.* A list of fear-provoking stimuli is developed and ranked according to the amount of fear each elicits. A 0–100 SUDS (subjective units of distress) scale can be used to obtain an initial rating of the fear associated with each item on the list and to facilitate ordering the list. Here is Makita's list:

Stimulus	SUDS Rating
Picture of a balloon	55
One small deflated balloon	60
A bunch of larger deflated balloons	67
One small inflated balloon	74
Several medium-sized inflated balloons	80
Several large inflated balloons	84
Gradually deflating a balloon	88
Popping one small balloon	95
Popping a group of large balloons	99

3. *Provide controlled exposure.* In vivo desensitization was used to help Makita overcome her fear of balloons because the object of her fears, balloons, could easily be brought into the treatment room. After helping Makita relax as fully as possible, her counselor brought out a picture of a balloon as she and Makita had agreed. With guidance from Makita, the picture was gradually moved closer to her and finally handed to her. She was encouraged to hold the picture and look at it until she felt her fear subside significantly. The SUDS (subjective units of distress) scale was used to track the level of the fear. This experience would be repeated as often as necessary, perhaps extended over several sessions, until Makita and her counselor thought she was ready to move to the next item on the list. The exposure and desensitization process must be carefully planned so that it does not raise anxiety but promotes feelings of self-confidence, optimism, and control.

Continuing the desensitization between sessions, with the help of a friend or a family member who has been coached by the clinician, can accelerate progress. Makita's parents were willing to help her continue her treatment at home, never exposing her to more than she had successfully handled in her counseling session.

Approximately five sessions were required to complete the desensitization process and reduce Makita's fears to a manageable level. Although she was able to deal with some of the fears on her list rapidly, several sessions were necessary to help her feel comfortable with the actual popping of a balloon. However, Makita and her family were able to celebrate her success by having a family party complete with balloons.

CASE ILLUSTRATION

As treatment of Edie, Roberto, and Ava Diaz progressed, the clinician realized that Edie's self-consciousness, her apprehensions about socialization, and her weak social skills were having an impact not only on Edie but on the rest of the family. Edie avoided talking to Ava's teachers and the mothers of her friends and was reluctant to accompany Roberto to office parties or on business trips because of her social discomfort. Consequently, she and her therapist decided to use Meichenbaum's (1985) stress inoculation training (SIT) to help her address her social difficulties. This approach integrates both cognitive and behavior change strategies. The process of using SIT with Edie had three phases.

CONCEPTUALIZATION

First, the clinician explained SIT to Edie, reviewing the interventions that would probably be used and describing how SIT was likely to help her. Once Edie's questions and concerns were discussed, she felt ready to cooperate with the process and was optimistic that it might alleviate her longstanding social discomfort.

Edie and her therapist then tried to clarify the nature of the problem and to establish realistic goals. Edie believed that people generally found her unappealing and uninteresting. She feared that if she risked exposure to social situations, she would experience painful rejection and humiliation. Using the SUDS scale, the extent of Edie's fears were assessed. Specific goals were identified, focused on reducing her fears of rejection and humiliation in social situations and increasing her participation in social conversations and activities.

SKILLS ACQUISITION AND REHEARSAL

Several techniques were used to help Edie overcome her fears:

1. She was helped to realize that at work, where she felt competent and her professional role was clear, Edie experienced little social anxiety and interacted well with others. She identified communication skills that served her well in her role as librarian and identified ways to transfer them to the social arena.
2. The therapist helped Edie dispute her belief that she would certainly be rejected and humiliated in social situations. This had not happened to her since adolescence, and she could report only two instances of ever having seen other people rejected and embarrassed in a social setting.
3. Edie further developed her social skills. She was given a book on assertiveness and communication and helped to identify and practice skills that seemed useful to

her. She and the therapist paid particular attention to role-playing ways to initiate and develop conversations.

4. Because she enjoyed reading, Edie sought out some literature on shyness as well as biographies of people who viewed themselves as having had social difficulties so that she could learn more about ways to cope with her social discomfort.

5. Edie identified a co-worker whose social skills she admired. She observed that person so she could identify her social strengths and use her as a role model. In addition, Edie tried to act as if she were that person when she role-played conversations in her treatment sessions.

APPLICATION AND FOLLOW-THROUGH

Beginning with small steps forward, Edie and the clinician generated alternative ways for her to apply her developing social skills and increased self-confidence. Edie considered volunteering at Ava's school, accompanying Roberto on a business trip, and throwing a small party. Although she anticipated engaging in all these activities in the future, she decided to begin by inviting the mother of one of Ava's friends to have tea with her after they dropped their daughters off at ballet class. Edie felt relatively safe with this woman and believed that meeting one person at a time with readily available topics of discussion (tea, the ballet class, their daughters) would provide an initial experience that was likely to be successful. A role play of social conversation over tea helped Edie feel well prepared for this venture.

After the tea, Edie processed the experience with her therapist, focusing on what she did well and identifying a few ways in which she might have improved on the experience. For example, she had gotten flustered when it was time to pay the check and saw that she needed to develop more comfortable strategies for dealing with that. Edie rewarded herself for her efforts, as well as for her success, and began to plan the next steps to improve her social skills.

EXERCISES

Large-Group Exercises

1. Although the value of behavior therapy has clearly been substantiated by research, some clinicians view it as less powerful than psychodynamic therapy. Discuss what thoughts and feelings might underlie this perception and then discuss your own reactions to and perceptions of behavior therapy.

2. Using your class as the target group, plan implementation of a token economy that might be useful in promoting learning in the class. Identify the behavioral goals, the system for tracking and recording performance, and the rewards for positive behavior.

3. Ava was troubled by fear of the dark and of being alone. Plan her treatment, using behavioral strategies. Be sure to view her presenting problem in the context of what you already know about her and her family. The treatment plan should include, but not necessarily be limited to, determining how to establish a baseline, setting specific goals, identifying treatment strategies, establishing rewards

or reinforcements, and determining how to track progress. In addition, consider whether it seems advisable to integrate other approaches with the behavioral interventions.

Small-Group Interventions

1. Divide into your groups of four students. Identify one person to lead the group in a relaxation exercise, beginning with abdominal breathing, continuing to progressive muscle relaxation, and ending with an anchoring of the feelings of relaxation. (The skill of anchoring was presented in Chapter 18.)
2. Following the guidelines for planning Ava's treatment (Large-Group Exercise 3) plan treatment for the following behavioral difficulties:
   - A 4-year-old refuses to go to bed on time and delays his bedtime by several hours each evening with requests for stories, drinks of water, and other attention.
   - A 33-year-old man reports family conflict as a result of his nightly consumption of 8–10 cans of beer.
   - A 52-year-old woman reports a range of difficulties, including overeating, being 50 pounds overweight, getting almost no exercise, and avoiding contact with friends because she is embarrassed about her weight.
   - A 42-year-old man describes himself as "addicted to sex." Although he is married and has a sexual relationship with his wife, he has had many extramarital affairs. His wife has warned him that she will end their marriage if this continues. He wants to continue his marriage but feels unable to control his sexual impulses.
3. Divide into your groups of four, composed of two dyads. Each dyad should engage in a 15-minute role-played counseling interview in which the person playing the client talks about a behavior he or she would like to change while the person in the clinician role follows the steps in stress inoculation training to help the client. Spend 10 minutes processing each role play after it is completed, providing feedback to both client and clinician on strengths and areas needing improvement. Feedback should focus on the following:
   - Conceptualization of problem
   - Skills acquisition
   - Rehearsal
   - Application

Individual Exercises

1. Identify a fear or a source of apprehension in your life. Following the guidelines presented in the "Skill Development" section of this chapter, develop a plan to use systematic desensitization to help yourself manage this fear more successfully. Write down the plan in your journal and then try to implement it.
2. Consider a behavior that you would like to increase, decrease, or change in your life. Develop a written treatment plan to help yourself implement that

change. The treatment plan should include, but not necessarily be limited to, determining how to establish a baseline, setting specific goals, identifying treatment strategies, establishing rewards or reinforcements, and determining how to track progress. Continue your learning by actually implementing the plan you have developed. Write in your journal about the successes and challenges you experience as you try to implement this plan.

3. Most of us automatically use behavior change strategies on ourselves and others without being aware of what we are doing. Monitor yourself for the next two days and list in your journal any behavior change strategies you use such as rewarding yourself for completing a difficult task, using a time-out with a child, or applying consequences when you are treated badly.

SUMMARY

Behavior therapy has evolved during the twentieth century from the research of B. F. Skinner, Ivan Pavlov, John W. Watson, Joseph Wolpe, and others. This treatment system takes the stance that behavior is learned and consequently can be unlearned. Behavior therapists are concerned about results; so they take the time to establish a baseline, develop interventions that are likely to facilitate behavioral change, use reinforcements to solidify gains, facilitate application, and monitor progress.

In recent years, behavior therapy has changed as its practitioners incorporate more attention to the whole person into their work, recognizing the importance of history, background, and context. In addition, through the work of Donald Meichenbaum and others, behavior therapy is often integrated with cognitive therapy, broadening and deepening its impact. Behavior therapy and cognitive behavior therapy have demonstrated strong effectiveness with a diverse range of people and problems.

The following association focuses its training and publications primarily on analysis and assessment of behavior and the use of behavior and cognitive behavior therapy:

The Association for Advancement of Behavior Therapy (AABT)
305 Seventh Avenue
New York, New York 10001
(800) 685-AABT

AABT publishes two journals, *Behavior Therapy* and *Cognitive and Behavioral Practice,* as well as directories of internships and training opportunities. It holds an annual convention for people interested in behavior and cognitive behavior therapy. AABT has more than 4,000 members, most of whom identify themselves as cognitive behavior therapists (Craighead, 1990).

Numerous other journals also focus on cognitive and behavior therapy, including *Advances in Behaviour Research and Therapy, Child and Family Behavior Therapy, Cognitive Therapy and Research,* and *Journal of Behavior Therapy and Experimental Psychiatry.*

RECOMMENDED READINGS

Cormier, W. H., & Cormier, L. S. (1991). *Interviewing strategies for helpers: Fundamental skills and cognitive behavioral interventions* (3rd ed.). Pacific Grove, CA: Brooks/Cole.

Kazdin, A. E. (1994). *Behavior modification in applied settings.* Pacific Grove, CA: Brooks/Cole.

Meichenbaum, D. (1985). *Stress inoculation training.* Elmsford, NY: Pergamon.

Meichenbaum, D. (1993). Changing conceptions of cognitive behavior modification: Retrospect and prospect. *Journal of Consulting and Clinical Psychology, 61*(2), 202–204.

Spiegler, M. D., & Guevremont, D. C. (1993). *Contemporary behavior therapy* (2nd ed.). Pacific Grove, CA: Brooks/Cole.

Stuart, R. B. (1998). Updating behavior therapy with couples. *Family Journal, 6*(1), 6–12.

Chapter 21

REALITY THERAPY

Reality therapy, initially developed by William Glasser in the 1960s, is solidly grounded in cognitive and behavioral theory and interventions. Like other cognitive behavioral approaches to treatment, reality therapy focuses on the present and seeks to help people make changes in their thoughts and actions that will enable them to lead more rewarding lives.

However, reality therapy is more philosophical than the cognitive behavioral approaches discussed in Chapter 20 and places greater emphasis on self-determination and process rather than results. This no-excuses approach places the responsibility on people themselves for both their difficulties and their joys instead of blaming their history, heredity, or society (Wubbolding, 1988). Helping people make choices that meet their needs without harming others and bring more happiness into their lives is the essence of reality therapy. As Glasser (1998) stated, "We choose *everything* we do, including the misery we feel" (p. 3).

Drawing heavily on cognitive and behavioral intervention strategies, reality therapists guide people through a process of change that promotes their awareness of their own needs; helps them recognize the essential ingredients of a rewarding life; and facilitates their efforts to establish goals, plan change, and monitor progress. Through this process, people can gain more control over their lives and take the steps they need to assume a responsible and rewarding role in society.

Reality therapy has been used in a wide variety of mental health settings. Schools and substance abuse treatment programs have been particularly attracted to this approach. According to Glasser, reality therapy can be effective with almost anyone, regardless of diagnosis or background. Although not all clinicians agree, reality therapy certainly has much to offer.

THE PERSON WHO DEVELOPED REALITY THERAPY

William Glasser was born in 1925 and grew up in Ohio. His family environment seems to have been a difficult one; Glasser (1998) reports that his father was occasionally violent, while his mother was overly controlling. Even as a young child, he recognized the incompatibility in his parents' relationship. This early history is particularly telling in light of Glasser's later emphasis on the importance of personal responsibility, not harming others, and the marital or partner relationship.

As a young adult, Glasser became a chemical engineer but later changed his career goals and entered medical school. He received his medical degree from Case Western Reserve University in 1953 and then trained as a psychiatrist at the Veterans Administration Center and the University of California.

Between 1956 and 1967, Glasser served as a consulting psychiatrist for the Ventura School for Girls, a prison school, operated by the California Youth Authority, housing 400 delinquent adolescents. This experience had a profound impact on his views of mental health and psychotherapy and was instrumental in leading him to develop reality therapy. Like Albert Ellis, Aaron Beck, and others who moved away from traditional models of treatment and focused on cognitive and behavioral approaches to change, Glasser found that traditional psychoanalysis offered little to help the girls and young women at the Ventura School. Consequently, he began to modify this approach and develop his own ideas, which soon proved much more successful.

Glasser concluded that many of the difficulties of the adolescents at the Ventura School stemmed from their failure to take responsibility for themselves and their lives and to act in ways that truly met their needs. Although they might have believed that they were seeking to meet their needs, the result—their involuntary stay at the Ventura School—was not the outcome they had sought. By helping the girls think more clearly about what their present needs really were, holding them responsible for their behavior, and playing an active and involved role in the treatment process, Glasser found he could be much more effective than he had been as a traditional psychoanalyst. Implementation of his ideas for change resulted in an 80% success rate.

Glasser's first book, *Mental Health or Mental Illness?* (1961), laid the groundwork for the development of reality therapy. *Reality Therapy* (1965) spelled out the principles that were and continue to be fundamental to reality therapy: that people who take responsibility for themselves and their behaviors and are aware of and able to meet their basic needs without harming others are likely to lead happy and fulfilling lives. Glasser's work always emphasized the importance of relationships as well as responsibility. He believes that a warm, accepting clinician is essential to the success of treatment, just as he believes that close and positive relationships are essential to mental health and fulfillment.

Relationships seem to have been important in Glasser's own life. His first marriage ended with his wife's death. He said he married his present wife after they checked the strengths of their needs and concluded that they were very compatible. Glasser's three children also play a significant role in his life.

Since the 1960s, Glasser has channeled his efforts into developing and expanding the scope of reality therapy. Focusing his writings and lectures on not only the application of reality therapy in treatment but also its inclusion in school and business settings, he has succeeded in establishing the approach's importance. Currently based at the William Glasser Institute in Chatsworth, California, Glasser continues to play an active role in the development of reality therapy.

Reality therapy found another important spokesperson in Robert E. Wubbolding, director of the Center for Reality Therapy in Cincinnati, Ohio; training director at the William Glasser Institute; and a faculty member at Xavier University in Cincinnati. Wubbolding has played an important role in both the development of reality therapy and its widespread acceptance. He is a prolific writer whose books include *Reality Therapy for the 21st Century* (2000), *Understanding Reality Therapy* (1991), *Using Reality Therapy* (1988), and *Expanding Reality Therapy: Group Counseling and Multicultural Dimensions* (1990), among others. His writings facilitate the implementation of reality therapy through their extensive use of case studies, exercises, and treatment protocols.

THE DEVELOPMENT OF REALITY THERAPY

Reality therapy began in the 1960s with three relatively straightforward concepts that Glasser (1965) labeled *reality, responsibility,* and *right and wrong.* He believed that all people have two basic human needs: relatedness (to love and be loved) and respect (to feel worthwhile to oneself and others). Those needs are intertwined and likely to be satisfied if people take responsibility for their lives and seek to fulfill their needs without depriving others of the ability to meet their own needs. Behavior that shows appreciation for both our own needs and those of others leads to feelings of self-worth and to rewarding relationships, thereby meeting the two basic needs. Such behavior also reflects awareness of reality, a sense of responsibility, and understanding of right and wrong.

Some aspects of Glasser's initial ideas have stayed the same while others have changed. His early writings placed considerable emphasis on ethical issues and de-emphasized individual differences. However, recent writings sound less judgmental and imply rather than insist on the importance of right and wrong in the therapeutic process. In addition, recent writings convey greater appreciation of individual differences, although reality therapy still draws generalizations about the causes and appropriate treatment of emotional difficulties. In addition, basic needs have expanded as have treatment procedures. (We discuss these points later in this chapter.) Nevertheless, Glasser's emphasis on responsibility, interpersonal relationships, and the importance of making choices and taking action that fulfills our needs has changed little. These concepts form the foundation of reality therapy.

Control Theory

In the 1970s, Glasser was introduced to the writings of Powers (1973) and others on control theory or control system theory. Glasser incorporated the concepts of control theory into reality therapy. He conceptualized people as driven by inner control systems in the brain that guide behaviors and emotions so that they are instrumental, moving people in directions that seem likely to fulfill their needs. According to Glasser (1984), "A control system acts upon the world and itself as part of the world to attempt to get the picture that it wants" (p. 39). Unfortunately, people's control systems can sometimes cause difficulties and conflicts by misdirecting their efforts toward goal attainment and leading them to seek to control others.

For Glasser, awareness and creativity were the keys to modifying our control systems and improving our lives. He believed that the first step is to become cognizant of the pictures in our heads that reflect our needs and wants. We can then become aware of what we are doing to reach those goals. By assessing the success and impact of our behaviors, we can determine whether change is warranted and, if so, use creative strategies to modify both our emotions and our behaviors. Although Glasser (1984) recognizes that some immediate, intense, short-term feelings do emerge spontaneously at moments of frustration or satisfaction, he is convinced that people can choose and control their long-term feelings.

Choice Theory

For many years, control theory was an integral component of reality therapy, and this treatment system became known as reality therapy/control theory. However, in 1996, Glasser determined that the theory underlying reality therapy was really choice theory rather than control theory. His view of the brain as a control system "aligning the external world to what we want as well as closing the gap between what we want and what we have" continues to be part of reality therapy (Wubbolding, 2000, p. xiii). However, choice theory—the recognition that people's choices of thoughts, emotions, and behaviors largely determine the quality of their lives—can really make a difference in people's lives. According to Glasser (1998), reality therapy can help people make better choices and improve their lives.

IMPORTANT THEORETICAL CONCEPTS

Clearly, reality therapy has evolved considerably over the years and has expanded its applications (Wubbolding, 1995b). At present, it is a well-developed treatment system that is used successfully in a broad range of settings.

Human Development

Reality therapy, like psychodynamic theories, maintains that current problems originate in childhood. According to Glasser (1998), problems begin during the early years when we encounter people who believe they know what is right for us. Because of our own youth, inexperience, and self-doubts, we accept this external control and come to believe that others make us feel or act as we do. However, "external control harms everyone, both the controllers and the controlled" (p. 7).

Instead, according to reality therapy, the key to rearing emotionally healthy children is surrounding them with loving and supportive people who enable them to experience freedom, power, and fun in responsible ways. Even in their early years, children's belief in themselves as well as their ability to identify and meet their needs in positive ways can be fostered, instilling attitudes and behaviors that will serve them well as they mature.

Where reality therapy departs from the psychodynamic approaches is in its emphasis on people's capacity to overcome their early difficulties. Reality therapy views people as basically self-determining. In Glasser's (1998) view, "We are rarely the victims of what happened to us in the past" (p. 3). However, if people have not learned to satisfy their needs during the early years, they may require psychotherapy, education, and other sources of help to enable them to develop new ways of feeling, thinking, and behaving.

Despite their recognition of the important formative influences of the early years, reality therapists tend to pay little attention to the past. Instead, they believe that conflicts and issues from the past find their expression in present unsatisfying relationships and behaviors and that treatment is most likely to succeed by focusing on the present manifestations of people's difficulties. According to Wubbolding (1991), "People are motivated to fulfill a current force inside of them. . . . early childhood conflicts, unconscious reasons, and external stimuli do not cause present behavior" (p. 21).

Five Basic Needs

Reality therapy holds that all people are born with five basic or genetic needs that are fixed at birth (Glasser, 1998). The relative strengths of these five needs give people their different personalities (Wubbolding, 1991):

1. *Belonging:* loving and being loved; having contact, connections, interactions, and relationships with people
2. *Power/achievement:* feelings of accomplishment and competence, self-esteem, success, and a sense of control over one's own life
3. *Fun/enjoyment:* enjoyment of life; the ability to laugh, play, and appreciate being human
4. *Freedom/independence:* the ability to make choices; to live without excessive and unnecessary limits or constraints
5. *Survival:* the essentials of life, including good health, food, air, shelter, safety, security, and physical comfort

Because these needs overlap, fulfillment of one may speed fulfillment of others. For example, people who have positive relationships are likely to have greater enjoyment of life. However, these needs can also be in conflict. People who channel great effort into the achievement of power or independence may have difficulty forming rewarding relationships.

Conception of Mental Illness

Mental illness, according to reality therapy, is actually people's failure to meet their needs in responsible and effective ways—overemphasizing some needs while neglecting others. According to Glasser (1998), people diagnosed with antisocial personality disorder, for example, generally focus on meeting their needs for power and freedom and fail to satisfactorily address their needs for love and enjoyment. Conventional diagnostic terminology is not central to reality therapy; instead, mental illness is conceptualized in terms of problems in choices, need satisfaction, and responsibility. Common symptoms of emotional difficulties include loneliness (rather than belonging); loss of control (rather than empowerment); boredom and depression (rather than fun); frustration, inhibition, or rebelliousness (rather than freedom); and illness or deprivation (rather than safety and security).

Conception of Mental Health

Reality therapy has a clear conception of emotionally healthy people: those who are successful in meeting all five of their basic needs. Emotionally healthy people accomplish this by choosing thoughts, feelings, and behaviors wisely and responsibly. In other words, their choices help them meet their needs while respecting the rights of other people to pursue fulfillment of their own basic needs. Furthermore, emotionally healthy people not only seek to improve their own lives but take steps to help others and make the world a better place for everyone (Wubbolding, 1991). Emotionally healthy people have a success identity rather than a failure identity (Glasser & Wubbolding, 1995). They have a solid and positive sense of themselves that reflects their own internal frames of reference; they do not derive their sense of themselves from the ways in which they are perceived by others.

Total Behavior and Motivation

As Glasser (1998) observed, all people can do at birth is behave. All aspects of functioning are linked to behavior. He calls people's overall functioning *total behavior*, which is composed of four inseparable components: acting, thinking, feeling, and physiology. Reality therapists believe that all behavior is chosen, that people can directly control the acting and thinking components that indirectly affect and afford them control over feelings and physiology. Glasser has compared the four elements in total behavior to the four wheels of a car, with acting and thinking represented by the front wheels. This emphasis on and attention to thoughts and behaviors makes reality therapy a cognitive behavioral approach to treatment.

Reality therapy takes the position that all human behavior is purposeful and directed at meeting one of the fundamental needs (Wubbolding, 1988). Although the five needs are universal, the specific wants that people pursue in an effort to meet their needs are particular to the individual. People are motivated to bridge the gaps between what they have and what they want to meet their needs. However, feelings such as loneliness and deprivation can limit the degree of people's motivation. Reality therapists seek to change those feelings not by directly addressing emotions but by changing thoughts about wants and needs as well as corresponding purposeful behaviors.

Quality Worlds

Glasser (1998) suggests that all people have quality worlds formed of pictures or images of the sort of life they would like to have, the people they want to be with, the possessions or experiences they would like to have, and the ideas and beliefs that they value. These pictures guide people's efforts to satisfy their needs and are linked to the success they have in meeting those needs. For example, if a woman with good work skills puts a promotion or a salary increase into her quality world, representing a way for her to meet her need for achievement, she is likely to have made responsible picture choices, and her related behaviors will probably be successful. However, if her way to satisfy her need for love is represented in her quality world by a picture of her best friend's husband, she is not making responsible choices and is unlikely to meet her needs.

Reality therapists believe that people can choose the pictures they put in their quality worlds. If they choose pictures that are unattainable or unlikely to meet their needs, they will probably experience frustration and disappointment. By becoming aware of their needs as well as the pictures in their quality world, people can make better, wiser, and more realistic choices; have greater control over their lives; and achieve success in fulfilling their needs.

WDEP System

The procedures involved in reality therapy are represented by the acronym WDEP, which includes four main elements: wants, direction and doing, evaluation, and planning. These are not sequential but can be applied in whatever way seems most likely to be helpful.

W: **Wants**   Reality therapists take time to explore clients' wants and the pictures in their quality world, focusing on what they want that they *are* getting, what they want that they *are not* getting, and what they are getting that they *do not want* (Wubbolding, 1995b). Keeping in mind that wants are linked to needs, clinicians also encourage clients to look at that connection by asking questions such as "How do you perceive your wanting to drop out of high school as meeting your needs?"

Reality therapy is a phenomenological approach in that it recognizes the role that perceptions have in behavior. It seeks to help people become aware of their perceptions so that they can modify them if appropriate. According to Wubbolding (1991, 1995a), perceptions pass through two filters. The lower-level filter, called the *total knowledge filter*, recognizes and labels perceptions, while the upper-level filter, *the valuing filter*, evaluates perceptions. Reality therapists facilitate this evaluation by suggesting that positive or need-satisfying perceptions be labeled as yellow, negative perceptions as red, and neutral perceptions as green. For example, "That is an attractive piece of jewelry" is a neutral or green perception; "I deserve that diamond more than she does" is a negative or red perception because it can lead to relationship difficulties; while "I'm delighted to share my friend's happiness about receiving a beautiful engagement ring" is a positive or yellow perception because it can contribute to the need for love and belonging. Becoming aware of and evaluating their perceptions can help people identify and make changes that will enable them to successfully meet their needs.

An aspect of the *W* in WDEP is helping clients want to make positive changes. Wubbolding (1995b, p. 408) identified five levels of client commitment to change:

1. I don't want to be here.
2. I want the outcome but not the effort.
3. I'll try; I might.
4. I will do my best.
5. I will do whatever it takes.

If people begin treatment at the first or second levels, an important goal of treatment is to help them see how they can benefit from changing their choices so that they can be led to the next level of commitment.

D: **Direction and Doing**   Reality therapists also devote considerable attention to exploring people's total behavior, including actions, thoughts, emotions, and physiology. Helping people be as specific as possible in describing their total behavior as well as looking at the direction of the behaviors is integral to this phase of treatment. The focus of reality therapy is on what people are doing, not why they are acting in certain ways.

E: **Evaluation**   With the clinicians' help, clients are encouraged to evaluate their behavioral direction, their specific actions, their perceptions and viewpoints, and the consequences of all these. As new directions, actions, and attitudes emerge, they, too, are evaluated. The evaluation process does not involve a judgment from either clients or clinicians about the goodness or badness of the dimensions under consideration. Instead, evaluation is based on whether behaviors and perceptions are realistic and helpful to the clients as well as to others. Clinicians might facilitate the evaluation process by asking thought-provoking questions such as "How realistic is it for you to expect that your daughter will never ask about her father's whereabouts?" and "What success have you had in using drugs as a way to build relationships and gain power and freedom?"

   Both the discussion of doing and the evaluation process focus primarily on the present and emphasize positive and successful aspects of people's lives. The past is discussed only in terms of its impact on the present. According to Wubbolding (1988), "We talk little about the past—we can't undo anything that has already occurred" (p. 41).

P: **Planning**   Reality therapists view planning as essential and encourage people to have long-range plans and goals that are subdivided into a series of short-term, realistic plans. As Wubbolding (1991) put it, "To fail to plan is to plan to fail" (p. 95). Plans should evolve from the process of self-evaluation and primarily reflect desired changes in wants and total behavior, especially in actions and thoughts. Wubbolding (1995b, p. 411) listed eight qualities of viable plans, represented by the acronym SAMI2C3. Plans should be *simple, attainable, measurable* and specific, *immediate* in implementation, *involving* the clinician in appropriate ways, *controlled* by the client, reflecting the client's *commitment,* and *consistent* or repeated.

   Successful planning is also facilitated by helping people decide whether dimensions of their wants and total behavior are important or unimportant and controllable or uncontrollable. Once they make those decisions, they can formulate realistic plans to change what they want, what they are doing, or both. Plans are most likely to succeed in making a difference in people's lives if they target areas that are both important and controllable.

   Usually, planning focuses on modifying and improving actions because that is the aspect of total behavior over which people have the greatest control. However, focusing on thoughts may provide a point of entry, enabling people to believe that making different choices in their actions will be beneficial. Reality therapists believe that feelings do not need to be addressed directly, although they can be important sources of information on wants and perceptions; if actions change, emotions will correspondingly change.

Planning and choice go hand in hand. The primary goals of planning are to help people make better choices and take more control of their lives. According to Glasser (1998), if people can make bad choices, they can make better ones.

Unlike some other approaches to cognitive and behavior therapy, reality therapy focuses more on process than outcome, more on the behaviors that are used to achieve desired results than on the achievement of the results themselves. This perspective offers two advantages: it encourages people to develop behaviors they can generalize to other situations and reduces the risk that people will view themselves as failures if they make better choices in their behaviors but do not immediately obtain their desired outcomes.

Importance of Relationships

Since its inception, reality therapy has viewed relationships as key to both development of difficulties and achievement of a more rewarding life. According to Glasser (1998), "People who have no close relationships are almost always lonely and feel bad" (p. 30). He views people's present relationships as the primary source of both happiness and misery.

Glasser (1998) is particularly interested in the marital relationship and suggests that the best marriages are between people with similar personalities. In addition, he believes that marriages are most likely to be successful if both people are low in their power and freedom needs and high in their needs for fun, love, and belonging.

Parenting is, of course, another important role in relationships. Glasser advocates loving children no matter what but suggests that parents may dislike the ways in which children behave and can let them know that some behaviors make loving them difficult. He cautions parents to avoid being punitive and judgmental, although he believes they do need to establish guidelines, rules, and limits for their children. Encouragement and praise are seen as far more helpful than censure. Like Adlerian therapists, reality therapists maintain that an essential element in good parenting is helping children learn from their mistakes, thereby turning disappointments into experiences of success rather than ones that are likely to promote feelings of failure.

TREATMENT USING REALITY THERAPY

As a cognitive behavioral approach to treatment, reality therapy makes use of many of the same strategies that have been discussed in other chapters in Parts 4 and 5. However, reality therapy is also characterized by its own set of goals, relationships, and strategies.

Goals

The fundamental goal of reality therapy is enabling people to have greater control over their lives by making better choices. Wise choices are perceived as those that meet the following three criteria:

1. They help people meet their innate needs and their specific wants, as reflected by the pictures in their quality world.
2. The choices are responsible, meaning that they not only help the person making the choice but also respect the rights of other people and contribute to their efforts to make wise choices.
3. The choices are realistic and are likely to be attained through sound planning.

The following goals are also important:

- People become able to form and sustain positive and mutually rewarding and respectful relationships.
- They develop a success identity rather than a failure identity.
- They have a consistent repertoire of healthy actions that enhances their total behavior by helping them think clearly, experience happiness and other positive emotions, and take steps to maintain their physical health.

Therapeutic Alliance

In light of the considerable emphasis that reality therapy places on the importance of relationships in people's lives, it is not surprising that a positive client-clinician relationship is viewed as an essential element in the treatment process. As Glasser (1975) stated, "The ability of the therapist to get involved is the major skill of doing reality therapy" (p. 22).

Bassin (1993) echoed those sentiments by stating that involvement with the client is the "most important and most difficult assignment in conducting reality therapy" (p. 4). Bassin, Glasser (1998), and Wubbolding (1988) suggest the following ways to achieve that involvement:

- Clinicians should maintain a warm, friendly, caring, respectful, and optimistic stance.
- Genuineness and authenticity are important in reality therapists.
- Clinicians should be teachers and listeners as well as friends and allies to their clients.
- Some limited self-disclosure from clinicians can facilitate involvement.
- Reality therapists make extensive use of the first-person pronouns *I* and *we* to emphasize the collaborative nature of the treatment process.
- Reality therapists do not pressure, judge, or coerce clients but motivate people through optimism, encouragement, support, and reinforcement.
- They negotiate clear commitments and contracts with their clients.
- Clinicians focus on the present and on behaviors rather than emotions.
- They ask *what* rather than *why* questions.
- Reality therapists ensure that clients evaluate their own behaviors and wants.
- Clinicians help people formulate realistic and viable plans.
- They avoid wasting time on excuses, moving forward rather than backward.

- If necessary, clinicians use consultation, continuing education, and follow-up to facilitate treatment.
- Reality therapists are firm and determined to help people. They never give up.

Clients and clinicians form a team to help the clients explore, evaluate, and revise their choices. Reality therapists tend to form more personal and friendly relationships with their clients than do clinicians from other treatment systems. Although reality therapists certainly do not advocate crossing boundaries specified by ethical standards, they are not adverse to talking about a sports event or giving a person advice about what to wear to a meeting or a party if those interactions seem likely to promote the client-clinician rapport and help people achieve their goals.

Although clinicians do not assume responsibility for telling clients what choices they should make or evaluating clients' behaviors, they do take considerable responsibility for the direction and success of the treatment. They promote motivation and commitment, guide the WDEP process, teach planning and other important skills, and use creativity and imagination to keep people involved and interested and give them new perspectives. Reality therapists consciously use active verbs such as *angering* and *depressing* to help people take responsibility for their emotions and behaviors. These clinicians do not hesitate to use caring confrontation, usually through thought-provoking questions, if they believe it will be helpful. They also represent the voice of society, reminding people of the reality of moral, legal, and ethical standards.

Reality therapists are very much human beings in the treatment process. They share their perceptions and experiences and ask for regular feedback. They pay little attention to transference and countertransference, viewing those processes as part of the past. Instead, they assume roles not as symbols of the past or blank slates but as people with skills and information they can use responsibly to help others.

Strategies

Reality therapists value creativity in their work as well as understanding, appreciating, and motivating each person. As a result, they draw on a broad range of interventions to promote their clients' involvement in treatment and bring energy and interest into the sessions. Included in their repertoire are most of the interventions used by cognitive and behavior therapists (discussed in previous chapters of Parts 4 and 5). However, reality therapists also have their own preferred interventions.

Metaphors   Reality therapists use metaphors, similes, images, analogies, and anecdotes to give clients a powerful message in a creative way (Wubbolding, 1991). These clinicians also listen for and use metaphors or themes that clients present. For example, one client whose hobby was fishing was told by his therapist that his efforts to meet his goals seemed like fishing without bait in a lake with few fish.

Relationships   Reality therapists believe that relationships are essential to the development of a rewarding life. Consequently, they encourage their clients to form relationships and coach them on ways to make those connections rewarding. According to Wubbolding (1991, pp. 55–57), the foundation of a strong relationship is time spent together, which has the following characteristics: it is effortful, valued by each person, enjoyable, focused on the positive, noncritical and nonargumentative, promoting awareness of each other, regular and repetitive but time-limited. As an example, he suggests taking frequent and regular walks with a friend as a way to build closeness.

Questions   Although reality therapists advocate evaluation of total behavior, they want that assessment to come from the clients themselves rather than from the clinicians. Reality therapists avoid telling people what is not working for them or how they should change. Rather, they use questions that are carefully structured to help clients take a close look at their lives and formulate their own evaluations of what does and does not need change (Wubbolding, 1991, p. 90). Examples include "Is what you are doing helping you?" "Is the plan you have made the most effective plan you are capable of formulating?" and "Is your present commitment to change the best or highest that you are willing to make?"

WDEP and SAMI2C3   As we have discussed, the concepts represented by these acronyms play an important part in keeping both clients and the treatment process focused and on track. WDEP (wants, direction, evaluation, planning) reflects the process of moving toward change by evaluating wants and direction and formulating plans. SAMI2C3 represents the elements that maximize the success of plans: simple, attainable, measurable, immediate, involving, controlled, consistent, and committed.

Positive Addictions   According to Glasser (1976), negative addictions or repetitive self-destructive behaviors such as misuse of substances, acting out, and depressing oneself reflect giving up and hopelessness. Such behaviors characterize people who either have never learned to meet their needs in effective and responsible ways or have lost that ability.

Glasser suggests that one way for people to reduce negative behaviors is to develop positive addictions. These are behaviors that provide mental strength and alertness, creativity, energy, confidence, and focus but do not dominate or control people's lives. Prime examples include regular exercise, journal writing, playing music, yoga, and meditation.

Developing a positive addiction generally requires six months to two years of regular practice, usually 45–60 minutes at a time. Glasser suggests the following guidelines for choosing and nurturing positive behavioral patterns:

1. The behavior should be noncompetitive and capable of being done alone.
2. The behavior should be able to be accomplished without inordinate mental or physical effort.
3. The behavior should have value to you.
4. The behavior should be one that you believe will lead you to improve in some way if you persist in it.
5. Avoid criticizing your performance of the behavior.

Using Verbs and "ing" Words   Because reality therapists want people to realize that they have considerable control over their lives and can choose their total behavior, these clinicians deliberately make extensive use of active verbs and "ing" words. Rather than describing people as angry, depressed, phobic, or anxious, they describe them as angering, depressing, phobicking, or anxietying. This implies that these emotions are not fixed states but actions that can be changed.

Natural Consequences   Reality therapists believe that people should be responsible and therefore should experience the consequences of their behaviors. For example, the adolescent who returned home after curfew may have to be grounded for the next weekend, and the woman who was never ready when her carpool arrived may be dropped from the carpool. Reality therapists do not advocate making excuses or special exceptions. At the same time, they are not punitive; rather than focusing on what people did wrong, they focus on what can people choose to do differently so that they do not have to suffer the negative consequences of their irresponsible and unrealistic behaviors.

Renegotiation   Client progress in all forms of counseling and psychotherapy is rarely smooth; occasional lapses or backsliding are the norm rather than the exception. When this occurs in reality therapy, clinicians use renegotiation to help people consider doing something different. Emphasis is on developing plans with a high likelihood of success and anticipating and rehearsing ways to cope with temptations to diverge from agreed-on plans and goals.

Paradoxical Interventions   Inspired by Victor Frankl, an existential therapist discussed in Chapter 12, reality therapists use paradoxical interventions. These creative interventions can encourage people to take responsibility for themselves. Paradoxical interventions typically take two forms (Wubbolding, 1988):

1. They relabel or reframe to promote choice and control. People might be viewed as lacking in skills rather than psychotic and their disappointments might be referred to as learning experiences rather than failures.
2. They involve paradoxical prescriptions. Reality therapists might encourage people to imagine the worst that might happen and find ways to cope with that; choose their symptoms rather than fight them; do the opposite of what is not working; or schedule a relapse. Of course, these prescriptions always reflect accepted ethical standards.

Skill Development   Education is an important aspect of reality therapy. Clinicians help people develop skills to help them fulfill their needs and wants in responsible ways. To facilitate this, reality therapists might teach people skills such as assertiveness, rational thinking, and planning. In addition, teaching people to develop positive addictions and other behaviors that promote nurturance and growth are important in this approach.

Reality therapy has been used in a wide range of settings. Particularly important is its widespread use in schools and its developing use in business and industry.

Schools

In light of reality therapy's origins in a correctional school, it is not surprising that Glasser (1969) has maintained a strong interest in the use of reality therapy in schools. He has sought to replace the punitive and judgmental atmosphere of many schools with an environment that is encouraging and reinforcing: "a good school could be defined as a place where almost all students believe that if they do some work, they will be able to satisfy their needs enough so that it makes sense to keep working" (Glasser, 1986, p. 15).

Glasser has suggested several approaches to effecting positive change in schools:

1. *Learning teams.* These are groups of two to five students of varying ability levels who study and learn together, motivated by their feeling of belonging in the group. Their goals include both learning new material and using whatever means they choose to convince their teachers that they have mastered the material. Teams should be changed regularly, and emphasis should be on cooperation rather than competition.

2. *Quality School Model.* This model proposes a reconceptualization of the school environment to eliminate coercion and promote cooperation, safety, consideration, and conservation (Schatz, 1995). Teachers strive to make course work useful and meaningful and to teach in a way that meets students' basic needs and contributes to their sense of fulfillment. Features of this model include year-round education to promote continuity, parent action teams to promote parental involvement in the schools, teachers and students sharing lunchtime and other activities, partnerships with businesses, elimination of bells to signal times, elimination of grading, peer tutoring in multi-age learning groups, open classrooms, emphasis on computer-aided learning and student portfolios, student-led conferences and businesses in the schools, and daily self-evaluations for staff and students. The model recognizes the importance of both psychological and academic growth and emphasizes a win-win perspective. This model has been adopted by a number of schools, and its efficacy is currently being studied.

Although only a small number of schools have fully implemented the Quality School Model, many have incorporated facets of reality therapy into their teaching and counseling programs. Murphy (1997) reviewed six studies of the use of reality therapy with varied student populations, including students with learning disabilities, students at risk, and Mexican-American students. Reality therapy programs were 4–12 weeks long. All the studies yielded some positive results, although they varied from one study to another. However, the diversity of the studies and the weak design of some led Murphy to conclude that, although reality therapy seems to enhance behavior and interest in school, more research is needed before firm conclusions can be drawn.

Stehno (1995) suggested ways for school counselors and other clinicians to apply reality therapy to classroom consulting. Rather than assuming the role of expert or coming from a medical model, Stehno suggests process or collaborative consultation, with teachers and consultants in a partnership to identify and resolve problems. This sort of consultation is characterized by five steps:

1. Becoming involved
2. Identifying wants
3. Identifying current behaviors and evaluating their success
4. Making a plan
5. Following up

Management

Glasser (1998) has also applied principles of reality therapy to management in business and industry. He distinguishes between *boss management,* which is authoritarian, judgmental, and punitive, and more effective *lead management,* which uses praise and encouragement and seeks to make work meaningful and rewarding to employees. His philosophy of leadership emphasizes collaboration, self-evaluation, choices, and competencies rather than rote learning. He suggests that tests used in both schools and work settings should not be given once to determine passing or failing but should be given repeatedly until people develop the skills they need to pass the tests.

Special Populations

Reality therapy is a flexible approach that has been used for individual, group, and family therapy and for a great variety of people and problems. It is widely used in schools, correctional institutions, and rehabilitation programs and is probably the most popular approach to treating problems of drug and alcohol use. Reality therapy also has been used in both inpatient and outpatient mental health settings (Wubbolding, 1995b).

Reality therapy seems well suited to a diverse and multicultural population, although writings on the use of this approach with various ethnic and cultural groups are limited. Reality therapy is phenomenological and is interested in getting to know people and understanding their world view and quality world. It seeks to help people identify their wants, evaluate themselves, and develop responsible plans to increase their success in achieving their wants. It is a respectful and humanistic approach that recognizes the importance of relationships and encourages people to help each other. The positive and action-oriented nature of reality therapy makes it appropriate for people who would be uncomfortable with a more conventional approach to psychotherapy—one emphasizing the unconscious, dreams, and transference.

Wubbolding (1990) has taught reality therapy in Asia, Europe, and the Middle East and has described ways to adapt this treatment system to other cultures. For example, he emphasizes the importance of looking at the particular balance of basic needs in each culture and suggests that "I'll try" be viewed as a firm commitment for people from Asian cultures.

Sanchez and Garriga (1996) have raised concerns about the application of reality therapy to some cultural groups. They point out, for example, that fatalism (the idea that some things are meant to happen regardless of what people do) is an important belief in Latino culture. Clinicians should exercise particular caution and sensitivity when using reality therapy with people whose belief system emphasizes a higher power, predestination and predetermination, and the value of an external locus of control. Sanchez and Garriga suggest speaking of a dual control framework with such clients, sharing action and responsibility with a higher power but still striving for an improved quality world and better need satisfaction.

Livneh and Sherwood (1991) suggest that reality therapy may be helpful to people coping with physical disabilities. Its encouragement of a success identity and emphasis on responsibility, autonomy, and self-efficacy seem likely to be empowering.

Diagnostic Groups

The literature suggests that reality therapists view their approach as useful with almost everyone, regardless of the nature of their backgrounds, problems, or mental health. Not only do reality therapists avoid using common diagnostic nomenclature, they dispute the validity of the concept of mental illness. Instead, they view people with diagnosable mental disorders as lacking the skills necessary to meet their needs. Glasser (1998) raises particular questions about the existence of repressed memories and the diagnosis of posttraumatic stress disorder. In addition, he minimizes the value of psychotropic medication: "Good psychotherapy precludes the need for [brain] drugs" (p. 88).

This lack of attention to the presence and diagnosis of mental disorders and lack of recognition that some disorders have a biological component and benefit considerably from medication is worrisome, especially since reality therapists have not provided adequate research to substantiate the value of this approach in treating a broad range of mental disorders. Although reality therapy may well be able to play a part in the treatment of many mental disorders, it seems best suited for mild to moderately severe ones, including adjustment disorders, anxiety disorders, mood disorders, impulse control disorders, substance use disorders, and conduct disorders. With severe disorders such as bipolar and psychotic disorders as well as with long-standing disorders such as personality disorders, reality therapy should be used with caution and will probably need to be combined with medication or other approaches to psychotherapy.

Evaluation of Reality Therapy

Like the other cognitive behavioral approaches to treatment, reality therapy has a great deal to offer clients and clinicians. However, it also has limitations.

Limitations

Reality therapy has some important shortcomings that clinicians should bear in mind. It pays only limited attention to helping people understand and deal with their environments and minimizes the importance of the past in people's development and difficulties. As a result, reality therapists may overlook some of the barriers and experiences that limit people's choices, and they may focus too much on symptoms. In addition, their disregard of the importance of diagnosis is not consistent with current professional guidelines and may lead to inadequate treatment and neglect of important areas of concern. Equating mental illness with lack of knowledge about responsible ways to meet one's needs is highly questionable. In addition, unskilled clinicians may use reality therapy as a vehicle for imposing their own values on clients and become too challenging and determined in their efforts to effect change. Finally, reality therapy has not paid sufficient attention to individualizing application of this approach, considering such variables as gender, ethnic and cultural background, sexual orientation, and level of functioning. All of these shortcomings may cause both clinicians and clients to have an unrealistically optimistic view of what can be accomplished by reality therapy alone and can lead to feelings of disappointment and failure if those expectations are not realized.

Strengths

Nevertheless, reality therapy has a great many strengths. It is a clear, straightforward approach to treatment that makes sense to most people. It is respectful, empowering, and encouraging and addresses fundamental issues in people's lives such as motivation, need satisfaction, and control. Reality therapy encourages clinicians to become involved with their clients in appropriate professional ways; this stance seems likely to be more appealing to many clinicians and clients than is the relative anonymity of the classic psychoanalytic therapist. Reality therapy's emphasis on the importance of both relationships and responsibility in people's lives is relevant and timely in light of prevalent problems of violence and family disruption. Also relevant is its emphasis on choice at a time when many people feel overcommitted and overprogrammed. In addition, reality therapy has a strong preventive component and offers sound and hopeful ideas for changes in schools and other institutions that are likely to make those environments more rewarding.

Research has documented positive outcomes for reality therapy, particularly in schools and therapeutic communities (Wubbolding, 1995b). In addition, quite a few studies are available that document the successful use of reality therapy with a variety of clients (Wubbolding, 2000). However, continued research is needed on the application of reality therapy to specific client groups so that clinicians have a clearer idea of the appropriate use of this approach.

Contributions

Reality therapy has made many contributions to counseling and psychotherapy. It has provided a clear and structured approach to treatment that is widely used in schools and rehabilitation programs. It has emphasized the importance of values in treatment and reminds clinicians not to neglect relationships and responsibility. It has enhanced appreciation of the collaborative therapeutic relationship and has helped broaden conceptions of the appropriate role of the clinician. Finally, it has focused attention on the need to help people engage in honest self-evaluation and make wise and responsible choices and plans.

SKILL DEVELOPMENT: CARING CONFRONTATION

Confrontation is a highly charged word that may seem incompatible with the supportive and encouraging role of the clinician. However, when done with caring and sensitivity, confrontations can help people more honestly and accurately evaluate their behaviors, have a better grasp of reality, and act in more responsible ways.

Confrontation can be defined as the process of noting discrepancies in a person's words and behavior and reflecting those discrepancies back to the person. Confrontation should never involve shaming, belittling, or attacking clients and should not precipitate a debate between client and clinician about who is right. In keeping with the guidelines of reality therapy, confrontation seems most likely to be effective if it is posed as a question that prompts people to reflect and self-evaluate rather than as a judgment.

Consider the following clinician statement:

> **Clinician:** Ronnie, you've told me that you and your fiancé are on a limited budget and are saving to buy a house, but you also told me that you bought a wedding gown that cost $3,000. Help me understand how those pieces of information fit together. How do you see your purchase of the wedding gown as helping you meet your needs?

The clinician has identified a discrepancy in the information that Ronnie has presented. This is reflected back to her in an unemotional and nonjudgmental way, with an invitation for Ronnie to make sense of this discrepancy.

Ronnie may respond in a variety of ways. She may have information that resolves the discrepancy: "I didn't tell you that my aunt gave me the $3,000 specifically to buy a wedding dress." She may open the door to further discussion of her values and choices: "This is the most important event in my life, and I want it to be as special as possible." Or she may reflect on her choices and make a self-evaluation: "I never put those two pieces together. Maybe it isn't such a good idea for me to spend so much on a dress. That's only important for one day, but the house will mean something to us for years." Whether or not Ronnie sees the situation as her clinician does is not important; what does matter is that she has an opportunity to clarify, reflect on, evaluate, and possibly change the choices she has made so that they better meet her needs. The exercises later in this chapter will give you an opportunity to develop some caring confrontations.

CASE ILLUSTRATION

Roberto consulted his therapist a few weeks before Thanksgiving because of family difficulties over last year's Thanksgiving. His therapist applied the WDEP and SAMI2C3 formats in the context of reality therapy to help Roberto develop a plan to make the holiday more rewarding this year.

Roberto: Thanksgiving last year was a disaster. I don't want a repeat of that.

Clinician: What did you do?

Roberto: Well, I came home early on the day before Thanksgiving, thinking I would like to have some extra time with Edie and Ava. I did have to bring some work home, and I wanted to get that done first, so I just said hello and headed over to the room where we have the computer. Before I know it, Edie flings the door open and is in my face about how I never help and am not really part of the family. I couldn't calm her down, so I just picked up my stuff and went back to the office. Who needs that! Of course, this spoiled Thanksgiving Day too; Edie and I just glared at each other for most of the day.

Clinician: So even though you came home early and were thinking of your family, somehow your actions backfired and wound up not meeting either your needs or your family's. When you think about the five basic needs that we have discussed before, how do you evaluate your efforts?

Roberto: You know, I can see that my thoughts and actions were at cross purposes. In coming home early, I was focused on my needs for love and fun; I really wanted to have a close, enjoyable time with my family. But I didn't give them that message. By going right to the computer, all Edie saw was me trying to meet my need for achievement. She didn't know I just had a little work to do and was then going to spend time with the family. I guess I really didn't try to see things from her perspective.

Clinician: So you have some new thoughts about what happened last year. What are the needs you want to focus on this Thanksgiving?

Roberto: Definitely fun and love and belonging.

Clinician: And what pictures do you have in your head about what that would look like?

Roberto: We would all get along. We'd all pitch in to cook dinner. We'd have some good food and good conversation. I'd make a fire in the fireplace. Then maybe we could do something fun like taking a walk or going to a movie.

Clinician: Let's develop a plan to try to help you make those pictures real. We've reviewed the eight steps in the SAMI2C3 model for making successful plans: simple, attainable, measurable, immediate, involving, controlled, consistent, and committed. What plan comes into your mind?

Roberto: I could come home early again on the day before Thanksgiving but not bring any work home. I could ask Edie if she needs any help. And I could suggest something fun to do after Thanksgiving dinner.

Clinician: How does that plan fit the criteria?

Roberto: It seems simple and attainable. I guess it's measurable; I can tell if I'm doing what I planned or not. I'm certainly committed to changing our holiday experience. But I'm not sure the plan is immediate; and I don't know how I could make it more involving, controlled by me, or consistent.

Clinician: So you've made a start at planning, but how could you modify the plan so that it meets more of the criteria?

Roberto: I could make it immediate by starting right now. I'll write down the plan and tell Edie about it when I get home. I could even ask her now if there are ways I could help, like shopping or cleaning the house. If I offer specific ways to help, I have more control over the plan, and I'm taking more initiative. Edie complains that I leave everything at home up to her, so taking initiative seems like a good idea.

Clinician: So you can see ways to make the plan more immediate and consistent as well as more under your control. Are there ways I could be involved in helping you carry out the plan?

Roberto: Maybe you could touch base with me sometime during the week to help me stay on track. I really want to, but sometimes I get so caught up with work. . . .

Clinician: How about if I telephone you on Tuesday to see how things are going?

Roberto: That would be great.

Clinician: Now let's look at the plan again to evaluate how well it promises to fulfill your needs and wants in realistic and responsible ways, and then you can write down the details of the plan.

EXERCISES

Large-Group Exercises

1. Although reality therapy has many strengths, it also presents some potential pitfalls, notably the risks that clinicians will become too judgmental, imposing their standards on clients, and that important diagnostic information will be neglected. Discuss the potential negative impact of these risks on the treatment process and then develop ways to minimize those risks while practicing reality therapy.
2. Glasser's Quality School Model suggests many innovative ways to improve education. Discuss ways in which that model could be applied successfully to your college or university. How would that improve the educational experience for you?

3. Reality therapy takes the stance that nearly all aspects of people's lives are under their control. Does this belief seem realistic and responsible? In what ways is it likely to be helpful to people? Hurtful to them?

4. Review the "Case Illustration" in this chapter. Identify in the dialogue the elements of the WDEP and SAMI2C3 formats.

Small-Group Exercises

1. Divide into your groups of four, composed of two dyads. Each dyad should engage in a 15-minute, role-played counseling interview in which the person playing the client presents a behavior he or she would like to change and the person in the clinician role uses the SAMI2C3 format to facilitate development of a plan to effect change. Feedback should focus on the use of the SAMI2C3 format as well as overall strengths and areas needing improvement in the role play.

2. Divide into your groups of four, composed of two dyads. Each dyad should engage in a 15-minute, role-played counseling interview in which the person in the clinician role helps the client discuss the balance of his or her five basic needs and identify one or more important ways in which he or she is seeking to fulfill each of the five needs. Feedback should focus on how successfully the clinician helped the client to explore balance and implementation of the five basic needs as well as overall strengths and areas needing improvement in the role play.

3. In your small groups, develop caring confrontations in response to the following client statements. Each group member should write out his or her responses individually before discussing them in the group and refining the responses. Evaluate the responses in terms of whether they are likely to facilitate client awareness and self-evaluation without sounding judgmental or negative.

Client A: My co-workers have been giving me grief because I've been getting to work late. They say they can't get started until they have my input on the project. But they don't understand that I'm a night person. I like to stay up late, and it's really hard for me to get up in the morning. My job is important to me, but I don't think it should matter so much when I get there.

Client B: My mother is just impossible. You know, she's nearly 80 years old and really can't live alone anymore. I offered to come up and help her move into one of those continuing care places. I suppose they're all awful, smelly and depressing . . . I've never been inside one . . . but what choice does she have? So, no, she doesn't want to do that. She didn't say it, but I bet she wants me to let her move in with me.

Client C: I can't believe what my stepfather did. When I was out, he went through my backpack and found some drugs I had in there. I told him I was just keeping the stuff for a friend; but of course, he didn't buy that. Now he's saying I need to go into a drug rehab program. What does he think I am . . . a drug addict? I just smoke a little pot once in a while. At least I don't go nosing around in people's personal possessions.

Client D: My supervisor said some things that really upset me. She said that people who get welfare payments are "ripping off the government" and "taking advantage of the middle class" and "getting a free ride." She doesn't know that I was on welfare when my husband left me with three young children. She's so wrong about what it's like to be on welfare. I wish I could straighten her out; but if I tell her about my background, she'll just write me off as one of those "welfare cheats." And she's usually very caring and understanding, so I know she didn't mean to hurt me. I'll just keep quiet about my reaction.

Individual Exercises

1. Identify a positive addiction that you would like to make part of your life. Write out a plan, following the SAMI2C3 format, to move toward establishing that positive behavior in your life.
2. Reality therapy stresses the key role that relationships play in both people's happiness and their misery. Write one or two pages in your journal about ways in which relationships have had a major impact on your feelings of well-being. Then identify two small and specific changes you would like to make in the way in which you relate to others. Write them down and consider making a commitment to implementing those changes.
3. Draw a picture of what comes up for you when you visualize the images in your quality world. Write a paragraph about what your drawing represents and means to you.

SUMMARY

Reality therapy, originated by William Glasser in the 1960s and developed primarily by Glasser and Robert Wubbolding, is an optimistic and encouraging treatment system that focuses on present thoughts and behaviors and helps people meet their basic needs more successfully by making better choices. Responsibility (fulfilling one's own needs in ways that respect other people's rights to meet their needs) is key to this approach as is the importance of positive relationships. Clinicians play an active and involved role in treatment, promoting self-evaluation and realistic and viable planning. Katz (1991) captured the essence of reality therapy: "When you behave the way you want to be then you will be that way" (p. 65).

RECOMMENDED READINGS

Glasser, W. (1965). *Reality therapy.* New York: Harper & Row.
Glasser, W. (1986). *Control theory in the classroom.* New York: Harper & Row.

Glasser, W. (1998). *Choice theory.* New York: HarperCollins.

Wubbolding, R. E. (1988). *Using reality therapy.* New York: Harper & Row.

Wubbolding, R. E. (1990). *Expanding reality therapy: Group counseling and multicultural dimensions.* Cincinnati: Real World.

Wubbolding, R. E. (1991). *Understanding reality therapy.* New York: HarperCollins.

Wubbolding, R. E. (2000). *Reality therapy for the 21st century.* Briston, PA: Accelerated Development.

Chapter 22

SOLUTION-BASED BRIEF THERAPY

Solution-based brief therapy has become an important treatment system in recent years. This approach emphasizes identifying solutions, rather than attacking problems, and then figures out how to reach those solutions (O'Hanlon & Weiner-Davis, 1989). It is usually brief, although progress is measured by results, not by number of sessions.

This treatment system is known by a variety of names, including solution-oriented therapy, solution-focused therapy, problem-focused brief therapy, solution-based brief therapy, and simply brief therapy. Although each of these names is associated with a particular approach to brief treatment, these models have much more in common than they have distinguishing features. We will pay some attention in this chapter to the distinctions among types of brief therapy but will focus primarily on the shared characteristics of all these approaches. The name used here for this group of treatment systems is solution-based brief therapy.

Solution-based brief therapy has much in common with reality therapy (Greenwalt, 1995). Both emphasize behavior change as the most effective and efficient way to help people improve their lives. Both focus on wants and goals, value planning, and seek to build on successes. Both de-emphasize the past but place considerable importance on the clinician's role in promoting positive change. However, solution-based brief therapy has historical influences, concepts, and strategies that set it apart from reality therapy and the other cognitive and behavioral treatment systems and enhance its power and appeal.

Clinicians at the beginning of the 21st century are experiencing considerable pressure from managed care, schools and agencies, clients, and themselves to be accountable and demonstrate results as effectively and efficiently as possible. Solution-based brief therapy, perhaps more than any other approach to treatment, accomplishes these goals. As a result, it has grown rapidly in popularity and become well established as an effective treatment system for certain types of problems and clients.

THE DEVELOPMENT OF SOLUTION-BASED BRIEF THERAPY

No one name is associated with the development of solution-based brief therapy, as Glasser is associated with reality therapy or Rogers with person-centered counseling. Rather, many ideas and people have played important roles in the evolution of this approach since it began to appear in the professional literature in the 1970s. However, Steve de Shazer, Bill O'Hanlon, and Michele Weiner-Davis, (all discussed later in this chapter) have probably made the greatest contributions to solution-based brief therapy as it is currently practiced.

Early writings on brief therapy in the 1970s and early 1980s include important contributions from Richard Fisch, John Weakland, and Paul Watzlawick, among others, who were involved with the brief therapy project of the Mental Research Institute (Fisch, Weakland, & Segal, 1982). Their vision of what can be called solution-based therapy is reflected in the following statement: "We try to base our conceptions and our interventions on direct observation in the treatment situation of *what* is going on in systems of human interaction, *how* they continue to function in such ways, and *how* they may be altered most effectively" (Weakland, Fisch, Watzlawick, & Bodin, 1974, p. 150). Their approach to treatment was generally limited to 10 sessions. Typical interventions encouraged people to reverse or alter what they were doing, not just do more of the same (O'Hanlon & Weiner-Davis, 1989).

Brief psychodynamic psychotherapy (discussed in Chapter 9) also contributed to the early development of solution-based brief therapy. This treatment system emphasized the importance of efficient and results-oriented psychotherapy and suggested that identifying a focal concern could help to narrow and streamline the therapeutic process. These strategies have subsequently become part of solution-based brief therapy, although unlike brief psychodynamic psychotherapy, solution-based brief therapy usually pays little attention to clients' past history.

Other forerunners included Milton Erickson and Gregory Bateson, also at the Mental Research Institute in Palo Alto, California (Gilligan, 1997). Erickson, who practiced from the 1920s to the 1970s, realized how important it was for people to have an open and receptive attitude toward change and new possibilities. He also recognized that people were more likely to be responsive to treatment if clinicians accepted and used whatever clients presented and focused on observable behavioral interactions in the present (Weakland et al., 1974). Solution-based brief therapy reflects Erickson's concepts in its orientation toward clients.

Behavioral and cognitive behavioral approaches to treatment provide the underpinnings of solution-based brief therapy. Those approaches demonstrated that focusing on and changing present actions and thoughts could have a profound impact on people's lives and that the resulting changes were typically enduring and generalizable. Cognitive and behavioral approaches to treatment also provided solution-based therapists with an extensive repertoire of interventions that could be used both within and between sessions to promote change.

Systems family therapy is another approach that contributed to solution-based brief therapy. The writings of Salvador Minuchin (Minuchin & Fishman, 1981) and other family therapists brought home the importance of considering the reciprocal relationships between client and environment and client and other people. Solution-based brief therapy emphasizes appreciation of the importance of circular or reciprocal relationships as well as linear relationships. Consequently, this treatment system pays considerable attention to people's social systems, including the therapeutic alliance, the family, the community, and the cultural group.

In the 1980s and 1990s, Steve de Shazer (1985, 1988), Bill O'Hanlon, and Michele Weiner-Davis (O'Hanlon & Weiner-Davis, 1989; Weiner-Davis, 1992) all made important contributions to this approach. Steve de Shazer, head of the Brief Family Therapy Center in Milwaukee, developed what he called *solution-focused brief therapy*. De Shazer probably is best known for his use of the miracle question (discussed later in this chapter). However, his contributions to brief therapy go far beyond that. De Shazer and his colleagues used a decision tree to determine which intervention to use with a client. They generally began treatment with a standard task such as suggesting that clients observe what was happening in their lives that they wanted to continue to happen and describe that in the next session. If the clients responded to such a straightforward task and completed suggested activities, treatment continued in a fairly traditional way. However, if people failed to complete suggested tasks, indirect treatment strategies were tried, such as the use of metaphors or paradoxical interventions. De Shazar and his colleagues are known for their creative use of clues or suggested tasks to help people find solutions to their problems. They also sometimes use a reflecting team that observes treatment sessions and interrupts with suggestions or ideas.

O'Hanlon and Weiner-Davis were influenced by the work of de Shazer but also made many of their own contributions through what they called *solution-oriented brief therapy*. Their treatment approach is designed to help people focus on their future goals and then determine the steps they need to take to reach them. They are unconcerned with how problems arose or how they are maintained but only how they will be solved. By creating images of what might be and raising awareness of potentials, they seek to produce a change in clients' viewpoints and actions, leading to solutions. O'Hanlon and Weiner-Davis view small changes as stepping stones to larger ones, and suggest that understanding follows rather than precedes behavior change.

Talmon's *Single Session Therapy* (1990), with its compelling title, brought further attention to brief therapy. Talmon does not actually propose that clinicians complete their work in one session; rather, his book is a reminder that effective interventions can begin in the first moment of contact with a client and that brief treatment, building on natural, spontaneous, and ongoing changes in people, can be very powerful. Talmon (1990) initiates treatment in his first telephone conversation with a client, saying, "Between now and our first session, I want you to notice the things that happen to you that you would like to keep happening in the future. In this way, you will help me find out more about your goals and what you are up to" (p. 19). This intervention is powerful because it changes people's focus from what is wrong to what is right and initiates the process of building on strengths.

This overview of important contributors to solution-based brief therapy is by no means exhaustive. Because this new approach is still evolving rapidly, the array of contributors will continue to grow and expand.

IMPORTANT THEORETICAL CONCEPTS

Solution-based brief therapy does not have many of the features associated with a well-developed system of counseling and psychotherapy. Its literature does not offer a detailed understanding of human development, nor does it address at length the impact of past experiences on present difficulties. It does not dwell on the nature of psychopathology.

These omissions might be interpreted to mean that solution-based brief therapy is an emerging approach rather than a full-fledged treatment system. However, these omissions are consistent with the nature of the approach, which pays little attention to the origins of people's difficulties and touches lightly, if at all, on their histories. Adopting an idea suggested by Albert Einstein, this treatment system maintains that a problem cannot be solved at the same level it was created. Therefore, solution-based brief therapy focuses on the present and the future rather than the past and emphasizes even small glimmers of health and positive change rather than past pathology (de Shazer, 1985).

Underlying Assumptions

Solution-based brief therapists assume that people's complaints involve behavior brought about by their world view. These behaviors are maintained when people do more of the same in the belief that there is only one right and logical thing to do. Brief therapists believe that minimal changes are usually all that are needed to effect progress since changes tend to have a self-perpetuating ripple effect. Clinicians base their ideas and suggestions for change on clients' conception of their lives without their symptoms. Suggesting a new possibility or frame of reference often is enough to prompt people to take effective action. Once behavior is changed, the whole system is different; small shifts in actions, then, can lead to important change.

Solution-based brief therapy assumes that people have the resources to resolve their difficulties successfully but that they have temporarily lost the confidence, direction, or awareness of resources they need to move forward. These clinicians usually find they do not need to know a great deal about a complaint to resolve it and do not seek to discover the cause or function of a complaint. Solution-based therapy wastes little time helping people figure out why they have been unable to address their problems successfully and carefully avoids giving people the message that they have been deficient or remiss in their efforts to help themselves. Instead, it assumes that people are doing the best they can at any given time. The thrust of treatment is to increase people's hope and optimism by creating an expectancy for change, no matter how small. In this way, people become more aware of what is working rather than what is not. As they become more cognizant of the possibilities for positive change, their feelings of empowerment and motivation increase correspondingly, creating a beneficial circle; positive change fuels people's belief that change can happen, which enhances their motivation and efforts to change, which in turn leads to more positive changes.

Solution-based therapists believe that change happens all the time, that things cannot *not* change. Often, all that is needed to help people is to enable them to notice and build on positive changes that are already happening.

According to solution-based therapy, reality is not fixed or static, and there is no one right way to view things. By helping people "negotiate a solvable problem" (O'Hanlon & Weiner-Davis, 1989, p. 56) or even "dissolve the idea that there is a problem" (p. 58), clinicians can enable people to set meaningful and viable goals and achieve rapid resolution of their complaints.

Stages in Treatment

Solution-based brief treatment typically proceeds according to seven stages (de Shazer, 1985):

1. *Identifying a solvable complaint* is an essential first step in treatment. Not only does it facilitate development of goals and treatment strategies, but it contributes to the process of change. Client and clinician collaborate and co-create images of the complaints in such a way that their solutions are in the client's hands. Clinicians

carefully phrase their questions to communicate optimism and an expectancy for change and to empower and encourage people. People's difficulties are viewed as normal and able to be changed. For example, clinicians might ask, "What led you to set up an appointment now?" rather than "What problems are bothering you?" or ask, "What do you want to change?" rather than "How are you going to change?"

Clinicians use empathy, summarization, paraphrase, open questions, and other active listening skills to understand the situation in clear and specific terms. They might ask, "How do you do anxiety?" "What would help me to really understand this situation?" and "How does this create a problem for you?"

In solution-based therapy, presenting complaints are not viewed as symptoms or disorders or evidence of pathology. Rather, they are thought of as a function of unsuccessful interactions with others or the mishandling of everyday experiences. People often believe that what they are doing is the only right and reasonable choice and keep trying harder and doing more of the same, even though they are unsuccessful. As a result, "the solution becomes the problem" (Weakland et al., 1974, p. 31). People may fail to take necessary action, take action when none is indicated, or take action in the wrong way. Clinicians assume that if people's actions and interactions change, their complaints can be alleviated (Fisch et al., 1982).

Like other behaviorally oriented treatment systems, solution-based therapy often uses scaling questions to establish a baseline and facilitate identification of coping and progress. For example, people might be asked, "Let's say 1 stands for how bad you felt when you first came to see me with this problem and 10 stands for how your life will be when you don't have to come back to see me anymore. On a scale between 1 and 10, where would you put yourself today?" (Berg & Miller, 1992, p. 362). This scale can also be used to assess specific areas of focus, including symptoms and relationships.

2. *Establishing goals* continues the treatment process. Clinicians collaborate with clients to determine goals that are specific, observable, measurable, and concrete. Goals typically take one of three forms: changing the doing of the problematic situation; changing the viewing of the situation or the frame of reference; and accessing resources, solutions, and strengths (O'Hanlon & Weiner-Davis, 1989). Again, questions are asked that presuppose success, such as "What will be the first sign of change? How will you know when this treatment has been helpful to you? How will I be able to tell?" Detailed discussion of positive change is encouraged to obtain a clear view of what a solution looks like to the client. (The "Skill Development" section of this chapter offers more information on goal setting.)

One of the most useful ways for solution-based clinicians to establish treatment goals is to use the *miracle question* (de Shazer, 1991): "Suppose that one night there is a miracle and while you were sleeping the problem that brought you to therapy is solved. How would you know? What would be different? What will you notice different the next morning that will tell you that there has been a miracle? What will your spouse notice?" (p. 113). This enables clients to imagine the possibility that their problems have been solved, instills hope, and serves as a foundation for discussing how to make the miracle a reality. Typically, people's responses to the miracle question provide clinicians with a wide range of potential solutions to the client's concerns.

Delivery of the miracle question is important to its success. Solution-based clinicians typically speak slowly, using an almost hypnotic tone of voice, when presenting this question. This is designed to engage clients and evoke openness and responsiveness. The miracle question also can be adapted so that it is compatible with the client's concept of the mythic or divine. Berg and Miller (1992), for example, suggest that the miracle might be presented as a magic pill, divine intervention, a silver bullet, or a magic wand, depending on the client's cultural and ethnic background.

Solution-based therapists accept and use whatever clients present (Gilligan, 1997). For example, when asked the miracle question, one woman replied, "The first thing I will notice is that my husband will have brushed his teeth before he comes back to bed for some romance." She had tried unsuccessfully to let her husband know that his morning breath bothered her, but increasing nagging yielded no results. After determining that both the woman and her husband were playful, the clinician suggested that the woman hide a toothbrush and toothpaste under her pillow and whip it out to brush her husband's teeth the next morning. She felt empowered by having something to do other than nag more, and tried this suggestion, which brought the message home to her husband and also introduced some humor into their interaction.

3. *Designing an intervention* is the point at which therapists draw on both their understanding of their clients and their creative use of treatment strategies to develop ways to introduce change, no matter how small. For example, clinicians might use reframing or relabeling to help people view their concerns differently and see hopeful possibilities or might suggest strategic tasks designed to accelerate the process of change.

Questions are used to prompt change, with language always designed to raise hope and emphasize the positive. Typical questions during this stage include "What changes have already occurred?" "What has worked for you in the past when you have dealt with similar situations?" "How did you make that happen?" and "What would you need to do to have that happen again?"

Esther sought counseling at the urging of her daughter after Esther's husband died suddenly. Esther had rarely left her apartment since the funeral more than a month ago. The clinician first questioned Esther about how she managed to take care of her banking and grocery shopping without leaving her apartment, congratulating her on her resourcefulness. The therapist then looked for similar situations that Esther had handled successfully. As a child, her daughter had been diagnosed with a learning disability; in getting her daughter the help she needed, Esther had read extensively about the nature and treatment of learning disabilities and became very active in her daughter's school, helping other parents find the resources they needed to help their children. Esther viewed this as one of her greatest accomplishments.

Reframing her month in seclusion as having been an excellent opportunity to understand how difficult it was to be widowed, the clinician cautiously raised the possibility that Esther might help others avoid some of the pain she had experienced by reading about ways to deal with loss and contacting a hospice program to share her insights. The therapist did not fall into the same patterns as Esther's daughter had: pressuring her mother to leave the apartment. Esther, who by now was rather bored at home, began to do some reading on bereavement and did telephone the hospice. When hospice workers invited her to attend a support group and perhaps become a peer helper, she took advantage of that opportunity, viewing the chance to help others as a good reason to leave her apartment.

4. *Strategic tasks* are typically used to promote change. These are generally written down so that clients can understand and agree to them. Tasks are carefully planned to maximize client cooperation and success. People are praised for the efforts and successes they have already had and for the strengths they can draw on in completing tasks.

Careful assessment of the client is essential in determining an appropriate task. De Shazer (1988) has identified three types of strategic tasks, each linked to the level of client motivation.

If clients are perceived as *visitors or window shoppers* who have not presented clear complaints or expectations of change, clinicians should only give compliments. Suggesting tasks prematurely is likely to lead to a failure experience that will jeopardize the treatment process.

If clients are viewed as *complainants* who have concerns and expect change but generally in others rather than themselves, clinicians should suggest observation tasks so that clients become more aware of themselves and their situations and more able to describe what they want. For example, the clinician might suggest, "Between now and our next appointment, I would like you to notice things that are happening in your life that you want to continue." Observation tasks require little client effort or motivation and, once suggested, usually are done almost automatically.

Finally, if clients are *customers* who want to take action to find a solution to their concerns, clinicians can suggest action tasks with the expectation that they will be completed. Tasks should both empower clients and effect a change in their complaints.

5. *Positive new behaviors and changes are identified and emphasized* when clients return after they have been given a task. Questions focus on change, progress, and possibilities and might include "How did you make that happen?" "Who noticed the changes?" and "How did things go differently when you did that?" The problem is viewed as "it" or "that" and as external to the client; this is designed to help people view their concerns as amenable to change, not as an integral part of themselves. (In this respect, solution-based therapy resembles narrative therapy, discussed in Chapter 14.)

Particularly during this stage of treatment, solution-based clinicians serve as a sort of cheering squad for their clients. They might provide compliments and highlight areas of strength and competence.

6. *Stabilization* is essential to help people consolidate their gains and gradually shift their perspectives in more open and hopeful directions. During this stage, clinicians might actually restrain progress, curtail people's plans, and perhaps even predict some backsliding. This gives people time to adjust to the changes they have made, promotes further success, and prevents them from becoming discouraged if change does not happen as rapidly as they would like.

7. Finally, *termination* of treatment occurs, often initiated by the clients, who have now accomplished their goals. Because solution-based brief therapy focuses on pre-

senting complaints and does not seek resolution of childhood issues or achievement of major personality change, it recognizes that people may well return for additional treatment in the future, and clients are reminded of that option.

At the same time, solution-based therapy is not just seeking to help people resolve immediate concerns. Through the process of developing confidence, feeling heard and praised rather than blamed, and finding their own resources to solve their problems, people treated through solution-based therapy can become more self-reliant and capable of resolving future difficulties on their own.

Timing

Most therapy or counseling relationships are relatively brief, whether or not that is planned. Budman and Gurman (1988) observed that the mean number of sessions is six to eight, with 80% of clients concluding their treatment by the 20th session and most of their positive changes occurring by the 8th session.

Solution-based brief therapy capitalizes on this pattern, and both clinician and client are aware from the outset that treatment is likely to be relatively short. Because solution-based brief therapy emphasizes present-oriented efficient treatment that seeks solutions to specific concerns, treatment usually requires fewer than 10 sessions. However, duration is not determined by some artificial conception of how long brief therapy is supposed to be; rather, treatment is as long as it needs to be to help people meet their goals and resolve their complaints. Brief therapists do not hesitate to extend the treatment process as long as positive change and forward movement are evident.

Solution-based brief therapists tend to be more flexible in scheduling appointments than are clinicians who follow most other theoretical approaches. Solution-based clinicians sometimes allow intervals of one or more months between sessions to give clients time to implement suggested strategies and allow the opportunity for changes to evolve. They also use extended follow-up if people need continued reinforcement. Adapting treatment to the needs of the individual is essential in this treatment system.

Finding Solutions

Finding solutions or clues to resolving presenting complaints is an essential component of solution-based brief therapy. Clinicians put considerable thought into identifying strategies that are likely to succeed and avoiding those that are discouraging or likely to fail.

The following guidelines can help clinicians find effective and empowering solutions:

- Focus on natural and spontaneous changes that are already in progress.
- Interrupt and change repetitive and nonproductive sequences of behavior.

- Provide a rationale to explain how tasks are likely to be helpful to increase clients' motivation to perform the tasks. If people are skeptical, tasks might be presented as an experiment that they can stop at any point.
- Make interventions congruent with people's world view (de Shazer, 1982).
- Learn from past solutions in formulating future solutions. For example, if people respond to direct suggestions, keep providing them; but if they do the opposite of what is suggested, create paradoxical interventions in which doing the opposite is desirable.
- Embed compliments in suggestions to promote optimism and encourage follow-through on tasks.
- Focus on development of new behaviors rather than simply cessation of old and ineffective ones.
- Create an expectancy for change and a context in which people can think and behave differently.
- Make solutions practical and specific.

TREATMENT USING SOLUTION-BASED BRIEF THERAPY

Like reality therapy, solution-based brief therapy uses a broad range of strategies and interventions. Although most have been discussed in previous chapters on cognitive and behavioral treatment systems, some are particular to solution-based brief therapy. These powerful and creative strategies can be interesting and compelling but should be viewed as secondary to and in the service of furthering the goals of treatment.

Goals

Solution-based brief therapy helps people use the strengths and resources they already possess to effect positive change in their lives. Initial goals include creating an atmosphere that is conducive to change as well as generation of multiple perspectives and possibilities and enabling people to do something different. Eventual goals entail helping people lead more balanced lives and become more resourceful in thinking about and resolving future concerns. Although the process of solution-based therapy is important, the outcome determines whether or not treatment has been successful.

Therapeutic Alliance

As in nearly all modern approaches to counseling and psychotherapy, the client-clinician relationship is an important element in solution-based brief therapy. Some early practitioners of this approach, including Milton Erickson, viewed the therapist as the person in charge of the treatment process. However, most clinicians now value a collaborative therapeutic alliance and maximize the client's involvement in the process (Gilligan, 1997) to enhance people's feelings of empowerment as well as their commitment to treatment. Although clinicians have primary responsibility for creating and suggesting solutions and presenting them in ways that are likely to promote action, they always view clients as collaborators and talk about how clients can help the clinician and the treatment process.

Clinicians use a wide variety of skills. Active listening, empathy, open questions, explanation, reassurance, and suggestion are particularly important, while interpretation and confrontation are rarely used. Clinicians engage actively with their clients, communicating acceptance, promoting cooperation, serving as role models, telling metaphorical stories, and suggesting actions that are likely to effect change. Because they recognize the importance of people's social systems, therapists may use resources in the environment and involve clients' significant others in the therapeutic process to further the goals of treatment. Clinicians maintain a positive, respectful, and health-oriented focus and assume that every session is important, that change is inevitable, and that it will have a ripple effect on many aspects of a client's life (Budman & Gurman, 1988).

Specific Interventions

We have already discussed many of the interventions associated with solution-based brief therapy, including the miracle question, the use of scaling to measure change, and the use of suggested solutions. Other interventions include trances, looking for exceptions, what de Shazer (1988) calls solution talk, complaint pattern intervention, solution prescriptions, and videotalk.

Trances   Milton Erickson used both hypnosis and suggestion to develop a state of receptivity in his clients. Although today's practitioners of solution-based therapy are more likely to rely on metaphorical stories and suggestion embedded in language than on formal application of hypnosis, they, too, seek to promote a similar state of receptivity, which has been called a trance state. According to Gilligan (1997), "In the experience of trance, time is suspended, logic is more flexible, focus is intensified, frames loosen, receptivity is deepened, and primary process is prominent. . . . This makes control secondary and change of perspective primary" (p. 14). In this state, people become more open to new possibilities and interpretations, more creative, more amenable to changing the ways they have always behaved, and more able to access neglected or overlooked alternatives.

Looking for Exceptions   Identifying exceptions to people's problematic patterns can lead to solutions to the problems. Although clients commonly come into treatment with a desire to vent and process their difficulties, solution-based therapists believe that this focus on negatives stabilizes the system and makes change difficult. On the other hand, a positive focus is far more likely to lead to beneficial transformations in the system. As a result, solution-based clinicians encourage people to focus on positive exceptions, on times when their difficulties were absent, as sources of information about ways to effect desired change.

For example, Fredda, in her first job as a teacher, sought counseling because of anxiety and apprehension that she experienced nearly every morning before beginning to teach. Rather than focusing on the nature of her unpleasant feelings, her clinician asked whether she could remember a morning when she did not experience anxiety. Fredda replied that one morning she had gotten to school especially early, organized all her materials for the day, and then had a cup of tea with another teacher who gave Fredda some good ideas about managing a difficult student. This exception suggested several routes to alleviating Fredda's symptoms: arriving early, being well prepared, having a few moments to relax before class, and seeking advice and support from more experienced teachers. By building these behaviors into her routine, Fredda was able to gain considerable control over her anxieties and also began to form some friendships at her school.

If clients cannot readily recall exceptions to their difficulties, clinicians can take an active role in promoting exceptions. They might increase the chances of having an exception occur by suggesting that a client make a strategic change in behavior. They might predict an exception if one seems likely to occur. They also might encourage clients to search for exceptions, a strategy that is especially likely to be fruitful if exceptions seem to go unnoticed. Questions such as "What is different about the times when [the difficulty] does not happen?" "When is the problem less severe?" "How does your day go differently when [the problem] happens?" "How is that different from the way you handled the situation the last time it occurred?" "How did you resolve this concern before?" and "What would you need to do to have that happen again?" focus attention on exceptions.

Solution Talk   Language is an important tool in solution-based brief therapy. Clinicians choose their words carefully so that they increase clients' hope and optimism, their sense of control, and their openness to possibilities and change. Following are some examples of how language can be used to enhance treatment:

- Emphasize open questions.
- Use presuppositional language that assumes that problems are temporary and that positive change will occur. For example, clinicians speak of *when,* not *if,* the problem is solved: "When this problem is solved, what will you be doing?" Clinicians may emphasize the temporary nature of problems: "Up to now, this has been difficult for you" or "You have not yet found a solution to this problem."
- Focus on coping behavior via questions such as "What has kept you from harming yourself?" and "How do you manage to keep going?"
- Reinforce and notice strengths and successes and congratulate people for their improvements and efforts rather than emphasize problems and failures.
- Create hypothetical solutions such as "If you weren't feeling afraid, what might you be feeling and doing instead?" This expands possibilities and encourages change.
- Concentrate on describing and changing behaviors rather than thoughts or emotions.

- Recognize that indirectness and implied suggestions are sometimes more powerful than direct suggestions and advice.
- Use rituals, metaphors, stories, and symbols as important sources of indirect messages that can promote change. For example, Mary envisioned a formidable brick wall standing between her and the sort of life she wanted to lead. Her counselor suggested that she remove one brick, leaving it up to Mary to determine how she would complete this task. She responded by changing several of her deeply entrenched behavioral patterns and reported that she had made a hole in the wall big enough for her to crawl through.
- Making frequent use of words such as *change, different, possibility, what,* and *how* that suggest change.
- Use inclusive language such as *and* that allows potentially incompatible outcomes to coexist. For example, rather than saying, "You can feel like you can't do it, but you can do it," the clinician says, "You can feel like you can't do it, *and* you can do it."
- Use reframing to offer different perspectives. For example, an event might be viewed as an opportunity for learning rather than a disappointment, and a person might be depicted as doing the best she can rather than failing.
- Match clients' vocabulary or style of talking to facilitate development of a collaborative therapeutic alliance. Then change the use of language to promote change in clients' perspectives.

Complaint Pattern Intervention   O'Hanlon and Weiner-Davis (1989) suggest many approaches to helping people get "unstuck," modify unhelpful patterns, and move forward, including changing the frequency or rate of an undesired behavior, changing the duration of the behavior, changing the timing, changing the location, changing the sequence, and adding or subtracting at least one element in a sequence of behaviors.

For example, Matthias's girlfriend recently broke their engagement and moved away. Night after night, he came home from work, sat down in front of the television, and cried for approximately two hours before calling his girlfriend and pleading with her to reconsider her decision. His behavior might be changed in the following ways:

- He might cry for one hour and then take a walk before crying for the second hour.
- He might call his girlfriend before crying.
- He might cry in another room.
- He might cry in the morning.

None of these interventions tell Matthias not to cry or feel bad; however, by changing his behavior, his thoughts and feelings are likely to change as well.

Solution Prescriptions   Solution prescriptions are tasks designed to help people discover ways to resolve their concerns. These may be designed to fit a particular individual or situation or may be a standard prescription in the clinician's repertoire. Commonly used prescriptions include "Do something to surprise yourself or someone else," "Keep track of what helps you," and "Notice what happens that you want to continue to happen" (O'Hanlon & Weiner-Davis, 1989).

Videotalk   Videotalk involves encouraging people to describe their concerns in action terms so that they can discover and modify repetitive patterns (O'Hanlon & Bertolino, 1998). Once the action has been described, clinicians can suggest alterations in the action that are likely to effect positive change. The use of videotalk can also separate the person from the problem, helping people take a different view of their concerns and reduce self-blame.

APPLICATION OF SOLUTION-BASED BRIEF THERAPY

Because solution-based brief therapy is a relatively new approach, information on its appropriate use is still limited. However, indications are that this approach is useful with a broad range of concerns and in a wide variety of settings.

Particularly good candidates include people who are motivated to face their difficulties and change, have a history of good relationships, can be flexible and creative, have succeeded in finding solutions to past problems, and have a support network that will encourage and reinforce change (Thompson, 1996). Solution-based treatment is likely to help people who come in with a specific problem or complaint but have gotten stuck in their efforts to resolve it (Talmon, 1990).

In recent years, the scope of solution-based therapy has expanded beyond treating people with only mild or moderate problems to successfully treating people with a history of serious difficulties such as sexual abuse (O'Hanlon & Bertolino, 1998). In their work with people who have been abused, O'Hanlon and Bertolino emphasize the importance of helping people see that they are more than their symptoms and experiences. Trances, stories, and solution talk are used to validate what people have invalidated in themselves and invite them to consider new possibilities. Promoting clients' recognition of appropriate boundaries as well as their ability to maintain those boundaries is another important aspect of treatment. In addition, rituals are beneficial in providing stability and continuity; promoting connection with other people as well as with memories, resources, and the past; and facilitating transitions.

Diagnostic Groups

Like other cognitive and behavioral approaches to treatment, solution-based brief therapy seems particularly well suited to treatment of anxiety and depression as well as problems of adjustment accompanied by symptoms of anxiety and depression. Some of the concepts and strategies associated with solution-based brief therapy—notably attention to motivation, emphasis on small successes, and efforts to find exceptions—are likely to be useful as part of the treatment for personality disorders, somatoform disorders, impulse control disorders, and substance use disorders.

However, treatment of these disorders will probably not be brief and will need to encompass additional approaches to treatment.

Solution-based brief treatment should be used with great caution, if at all, with people who are actively suicidal or dangerous, are suffering from psychosis or dissociative identity disorder, or have severe eating disorders or whose difficulties seem to have a genetic or biological component that necessitates medication (Talmon, 1990). Such people usually need a more intensive form of treatment, although elements of solution-based treatment may be integrated into those approaches with some benefit or even be effective as a primary mode of treatment. Rowan and O'Hanlon (1999) describe the successful use of this approach to treatment with people diagnosed with chronic and severe mental illness, helping them reclaim their lives and change ideas of impossibility, blame, nonaccountability, and disempowering. Solution-based brief therapy may be particularly useful in treating severe mental disorders once improvement has been achieved via medication or other forms of psychotherapy.

Special Populations

Research is limited on the use of solution-based therapy with special populations. The approach's emphasis on respect and understanding people's view of the world; its focus on strengths, resources, successes, and empowerment; and its brief and nonintrusive nature suggest that it is suitable for use with a broad range of people from a variety of cultural backgrounds and is sensitive to ethnic and cultural factors. In addition, because solution-based therapists are aware of the importance of client motivation and have strategies for promoting clients' involvement in and cooperation with treatment, the approach seems appropriate for people who are resistant to or leery about treatment.

According to Berg and Miller (1992), this approach "has been used successfully with various ethnic populations at the Brief Family Therapy Center in Milwaukee, Wisconsin" (p. 357). In describing their use of this treatment system with Asian American clients, they report that the sort of questions used by clinicians practicing solution-based brief therapy "suggest curiosity and respect for the client's view without pressuring the client to change" (p. 362).

Solution-based brief therapy seems useful with adolescents as well as adults, although it might need to be modified for treatment of children. Littrell, Malia, and Vanderwood (1995) studied the impact of single-session brief counseling in a high school and concluded that the approach worked well in treating developmental, behavioral, and interpersonal problems. On the other hand, they discouraged its use for crises and severe emotional difficulties and observed that the approach might miss important underlying issues.

Although most of the literature on solution-based brief therapy focuses on its use with individuals, it has recently been adapted for use with couples and groups. Linda Metcalf's (1998) writings are especially helpful for clinicians seeking to use this approach with groups in both school and mental health settings.

Current Use

Interest in and use of solution-based brief therapy are growing rapidly, and many agencies and clinicians now emphasize this approach in their treatment. The rapid acceptance of solution-based therapy is due, in part, to its efficiency and effectiveness. However, it has also been well received because it is compatible with the goal setting, measurement of progress, empowerment of clients, and brief treatment that characterize much of psychotherapy at the beginning of the 21st century.

EVALUATION OF SOLUTION-BASED BRIEF THERAPY

Although most of the literature on solution-based treatment consists of case studies and descriptions of treatment strategies, the value of this treatment system seems clear. Additional empirical research is expected to enhance the reputation of this powerful approach.

Limitations

Solution-based brief therapy certainly has limitations, which its practitioners generally seem to realize. Unless clients and clinicians carefully co-create problem definitions, the approach may cause clinicians to focus prematurely on a presenting problem and thereby miss an issue of greater importance. Solution-based treatment is not usually appropriate as the primary or only treatment for severe or urgent emotional difficulties. In addition, its implementation seems much easier than it is. In reality, this approach requires well-trained clinicians who are skilled and experienced in rapid assessment of clients, goal setting, treatment planning, and effective use of a range of creative and powerful interventions.

Another drawback is the misapprehension among some clinicians and clients, as well as some managed care organizations, that brief treatment is all that is ever needed to treat clients successfully. This is, of course, a dangerous overgeneralization, with the result that people may fail to receive the intensive treatment they need. Clinicians should exercise caution when using solution-based brief therapy to be sure that this approach is adequate to meet their clients' needs.

Strengths

Solution-based brief therapy has a great many strengths. It is effective and efficient with a broad range of problems, is generally well received by clients, is encouraging and empowering, and offers new ways of thinking about helping people. It recognizes the importance of people's social systems and considers people in context. It seeks to help people both resolve immediate problems and make better use of their strengths and resources in addressing future difficulties.

Contributions

Solution-based brief therapy and brief psychodynamic psychotherapy have made great contributions to counseling and psychotherapy. Many clinicians and clients now believe that treatment need not be prolonged and costly to be effective. Solution-based therapy has also provided clinicians with powerful new interventions. Its use of the miracle question, emphasis on exceptions and possibilities, use of presuppositional and other solution-based language, and view of the importance of small behavioral changes are innovative concepts that are changing the way in which many clinicians think about and do counseling and psychotherapy. The miracle question, in particular, has gained widespread acceptance as a useful tool to facilitate information gathering and goal setting.

SKILL DEVELOPMENT: GOAL SETTING

Goal setting is an essential component of treatment, not only in solution-based brief therapy, where it receives particular attention, but in nearly all approaches to counseling and psychotherapy. Goals give both clients and clinicians a sense of purpose and direction. Having a goal in sight helps people feel optimistic about their treatment and can facilitate change in behaviors, thoughts, and emotions. Goals guide the treatment process and facilitate choice of strategies that are likely to lead to achievement of goals. Finally, a clear statement of goals enables clients and clinicians to assess progress toward those goals and, if necessary, make changes in a treatment plan that is not helping people reach their goals.

Formulating goals should be a collaborative process involving both client and clinician. As much as possible, clients should take the initiative in formulating their goals. However, clinicians can help them to describe goals in clear, specific, and achievable terms. For example, Agnes sought help in changing the rebellious behavior of her adolescent daughter. However, exploration of the problem led client and clinician to co-create a goal of helping Agnes find successful ways of acting toward and talking to her daughter.

Clinicians sometimes need to suggest goals to clients that seem essential to helping them resolve their difficulties. For example, a man who is having marital difficulties because his wife is bothered by his frequent intoxication is unlikely to benefit from treatment aimed at improving his communication with his wife unless he also establishes the goal of reducing or eliminating his use of alcohol.

Goals should be written down, and both client and clinician should have a copy of the goals. This will help them keep the goals in mind and identify interventions and changes that seem likely to lead to goal attainment. In addition, writing down goals facilitates the process of assessing whether people are moving toward or achieving their goals and allows the goals to be changed or expanded if necessary.

According to Berg and Miller (1992) and de Shazer (1991), sound treatment goals are

- Meaningful and important to clients
- Small and within easy reach rather than large and challenging

- Realistic and achievable
- Within clients' control
- Perceived by clients as involving their hard work and effort
- Described in specific, concrete behavioral terms
- Measurable
- Presented in positive language, stating what clients will do rather than what they will not do
- Viewed as a beginning or a first step rather than the end or final product
- Reflected in new behaviors or changes

Consider the following examples of goals formulated by Suki, a shy, self-effacing woman reporting low self-esteem and depression:

1. Suki will tell another person about the sale of her first painting within the next 48 hours and will write down her statement, the person to whom she spoke, and that person's response.
2. Suki will not denigrate her accomplishments but tell others about them.

The first goal is a sound one because it is small, realistic, within the client's control, specific and behavioral, stated in positive language, and a first step toward developing new behaviors. The second goal, however, has many shortcomings; it is vague and general, difficult to measure, stated in negative language, and probably unrealistic and too ambitious. It is likely to lead to disappointment and frustration, whereas the first statement is likely to promote effort, motivation, success, and a sense of accomplishment. The exercises later in this chapter will give you further opportunities for formulating and analyzing goal statements.

CASE ILLUSTRATION

The following dialogue illustrates the application of the miracle question often used in solution-based brief therapy with Edie, who is having difficulty managing stress and fulfilling all her responsibilities.

Edie: I don't know how I can get everything done by the holidays. It's all I can do to take care of the family and the house. I don't know when I'll ever find time to buy presents, write cards, bake cookies, and make some special meals. I've been trying to get up early and stay up late to get it all done, but it's just not working. I feel overwhelmed when I think about it.

Clinician: You have a great many responsibilities, and I know you can find a way to make

them manageable. Edie, let's suppose that one night there is a miracle; and while you are sleeping, this problem you are describing is solved. What will you notice the next morning that will tell you there has been a miracle?

Edie: I will be able to sleep until at least 7 A.M. When I wake up, the house will be clean and orderly but not because I stayed up late to clean it. Although I'll still have things to do, they'll be the fun parts of the holiday, like baking cookies. I'll still have a list, but I'll know that I can accomplish the items on the list and still have time to read or take a hot bath.

Clinician: How will Roberto know that the miracle has occurred?

Edie: I won't be grumpy in the morning. I'll be smiling and looking forward to the day. Maybe I'll even make him pancakes, which he loves.

Clinician: You really have a clear picture of how things will be when you figure out a strategy to solve the problem. I think your answer to the miracle question has raised some possibilities. What seemed important to you?

Edie: Just imagining that it could be different was helpful. If I could get some help with some of the holiday preparations, especially the ones I don't like, such as cleaning the house and writing the holiday letter, then maybe I could really enjoy the other parts.

Clinician: So you're starting to figure out a way to make some changes. I wonder if you can recall other times when you felt stressed and overwhelmed by all you had to do and handled the situation pretty well.

Edie: Yes, I was eight months' pregnant with Ava, and we were moving out of our apartment into a new house. As if that weren't enough, my mother fell and broke her leg and really needed help.

Clinician: What worked for you then?

Edie: I guess because I was pregnant and, of course, didn't want anything to go wrong, I wasn't as hard on myself and was able to set priorities and get some help. Once I made sure my mother's medical needs were taken care of, I got her a housekeeper to help out. I had the movers pack and unpack, and I asked Roberto to oversee that. He's good at taking charge of things, which is hard for me. I focused my attention on what was important to me: having a healthy baby and making sure we had our finances under control so we could pay for all this.

Clinician: So you were very resourceful then, and you didn't expect to do everything yourself. You figured out your priorities and what you could do best and then hired help and asked Roberto to assist with other tasks.

Edie: Yes, that did work out well. I can see that maybe I do need to make some changes so this holiday won't turn into a disaster and me into a wreck.

Clinician: How would you do that?

Edie: I could ask Roberto to do the holiday letter on the computer; he'd do a great job at that. I could splurge and hire someone to clean the house; I have been working overtime, so we can afford that this year. I guess I could even get Ava to help me wrap packages and my mother to help with some of the cooking for the holiday dinner.

Clinician: Sounds like you're being very resourceful again. We still have four weeks until the holiday. What would be the first small step you could take, beginning this week, to get the control of your life that you want?

Edie: I could have a family meeting with Roberto and Ava and maybe even my mother to decide what we need to do, set priorities, and figure out how everyone can work together to get things done. That would give me a chance to express my concerns, bring up the possibility of a cleaning woman, and start things off on the right track.

Edie has now taken the first steps toward changing her behavior at holiday time. She was able to see the possibility that she might not have to do all the preparations herself and is moving forward to get the help she needs that will give her desired control over her life. By encouraging her to focus on only one step, the clinician is maximizing the chances that Edie's initial efforts at change will be successful and will naturally have a ripple effect, enabling her to effectively manage other aspects of the holiday season as well as future stressful times in her life.

Large-Group Exercises

1. Reality therapy and solution-based brief therapy have much in common as well as some important differences. Discuss these similarities and differences. What differences in application are suggested by the particular hallmarks of each of these approaches? Which approach appeals to you more? Why?

2. Formulate hypothetical goals for the following people. Keep in mind the importance of helping clients figure out what they want and of having the client and clinician co-create goals. Be sure that your goals meet the criteria discussed in this chapter.

   - Danielle, age 27, wants to be able to relate better to her father. She perceives him as judgmental and cold toward her; and whenever she is around him, she feels uncomfortable and apprehensive and has little to say to him.

   - Jonathan, age 11, has been misbehaving at school. According to his teacher, he is disruptive in class, bullies the younger children, and does not usually complete his homework. Jonathan complains that the children in his class make fun of him because he is overweight. He wants this to stop and desires to develop friendships and feel more important at school.

   - Angela has recently had open heart surgery. Although she has recovered physically and has an excellent prognosis, she fears that she will have a heart attack. She has avoided sexual relations with her husband and reports that she can hardly stand to look at the scars left by her surgery. Angela wants to stop feeling like her medical condition has taken over her life, be more comfortable with her physical appearance, and resume sexual relations with her husband.

3. Some people believe that brief therapy cannot possibly be as effective as intensive, long-term treatment, while others believe it can be as good if not better than long-term treatment. Discuss these two positions, considering the evidence for each side, and try to arrive at a conclusion that most of the class can accept.

Small-Group Exercises

1. Divide into your groups of four, composed of two dyads. Each dyad should engage in a 15-minute, role-played counseling interview in which the person playing the client presents a problem or complaint and the person playing the clinician uses the miracle question to help the client see other possibilities and find some solutions. Feedback following the role play should focus on use of the miracle question as well as the nature of the client-clinician interaction.

2. Each dyad should role-play another interview, remaining in the same roles. This time the interviewer should not seek solutions or offer suggestions but use solution-oriented, presuppositional language as described in this chapter. Tape-record this interview so that you can listen to it again and identify the examples of solution-based language. Discuss both interviews. Which interview was more challenging and why? Which was more rewarding and why? What

was the impact of each on the therapeutic alliance? What other important differences did you notice? What did you learn from this exercise?

3. Consider the following interventions. Identify their shortcomings from the perspective of a solution-based brief therapist and then rewrite them as a group so that they are more helpful and consistent with this approach to treatment.
   - You have come for counseling to improve your relationship with your son. What kind of relationship did you have with your father when you were your son's age?
   - Why do you think you will feel guilty if you end your friendship with Howard?
   - I can see you didn't have much success with your homework task.
   - I know you do not feel optimistic that treatment will work; but if you complete the homework tasks I am suggesting, I think you will really see a difference.

Individual Exercises

1. Identify a problem or concern you are currently experiencing. Then find at least one exception to the problem or a time when you handled a similar problem successfully. Plan a small change based on this information. Write about this in your journal.

2. Write down at least three goals that you hope to achieve within the next month. Be sure that your goal statements meet the criteria discussed in this chapter.

3. Apply the process of scaling to the goals you have identified above. On a 1–10 scale, with 10 representing complete success in achieving the goal and 1 representing no progress toward meeting the goal, indicate where you are now in terms of your achievement of each of the three goals. Write down these ratings and use the scale to rate your progress each week over the next month.

SUMMARY

Solution-based brief therapy, developed through the work of Milton Erickson, Bill O'Hanlon, Michele Weiner-Davis, Steve de Shazer, and others, is an optimistic and empowering treatment system that focuses on possibilities and helps people make small behavioral changes that lead to solutions to their concerns. Collaboration of client and clinician is essential. Client and clinician co-create clear, specific, meaningful, and realistic goals that guide the treatment. This approach pays primary attention to the present and to clients' strengths and successes. Strategies such as the miracle question, use of exceptions, suggested tasks, and solution-based language enhance the impact of this approach.

Berg and Miller (1992) have summarized solution-based brief therapy succinctly:

> If it ain't broke, don't fix it!
> Once you know what works, do more of it!
> If it doesn't work, then don't do it again. Do something different! (p. 17)

RECOMMENDED READINGS

de Shazer, S. (1988). *Clues: Investigating solutions in brief therapy.* New York: Norton.

de Shazer, S. (1991). *Putting difference to work.* New York: Norton.

Matthews, W. J., & Edgette, J. H. (1997). *Current thinking and research in brief therapy.* New York: Brunner/Mazel.

Metcalf, L. (1998). *Solution focused group therapy: Ideas for groups in private practice, schools, agencies, and treatment programs.* New York: Free Press.

Miller, S., Hubble, M., & Duncan, B. (1996). *Handbook of solution-focused brief therapy.* San Francisco: Jossey-Bass.

O'Hanlon, W., & Weiner-Davis, M. (1989). *In search of solutions: A new direction in psychotherapy.* New York: Norton.

Talmon, M. (1990). *Single session therapy.* San Francisco: Jossey-Bass.

PART SIX

INTEGRATED AND ECLECTIC TREATMENT SYSTEMS

Chapter 23

OVERVIEW OF INTEGRATED AND ECLECTIC TREATMENT SYSTEMS

Parts 2–5 of this book focused on systems of counseling and psychotherapy reflecting four major emphases—background, emotions, thoughts, and actions—and reviewed specific treatment strategies and skills associated with each. Knowledge of an array of theoretical approaches is essential for clinicians to determine which treatment system seems best for them and their clients.

Although a broad knowledge of treatment approaches is integral to the professional development of every effective clinician, many counselors and therapists today do not align themselves strongly with one particular approach. Instead, they draw on a variety of theories and interventions in developing a treatment plan that seems likely to help a given person. In fact, more than 35% of all clinicians, and perhaps as many as 50%, describe their primary theoretical orientation as eclectic or integrative (Prochaska & Norcross, 1994). This percentage has increased rapidly over the years, and the trend seems likely to continue.

REASONS FOR THE GROWTH OF ECLECTICISM

Many factors account for this trend. As Thompson (1996) has stated, "Essentially, no single theory can account fully for the myriad of [phenomena] that characterize the full range and life span of human experiences. Further, adhering to exclusive models of counseling and psychotherapy could be perceived as limiting therapeutic options when working with clients" (p. xxi). Thompson's points certainly seem valid in light of the broad range of people seeking counseling or psychotherapy who vary according to many dimensions, including culture, ethnicity, gender, sexual orientation, intelligence, interpersonal skills, life experiences, self-awareness, support systems, and symptoms.

In addition, no one theoretical model has proven itself superior to the rest despite efforts to identify such a theory. Luborsky, Singer, and Luborsky (1975) reviewed the comparative literature on psychotherapy and concluded that the result was a dodo bird verdict. (The dodo bird, in *Alice's Adventures in Wonderland,* stated that since everyone had won the race, all must have prizes.) Despite extensive research since 1975, the dodo bird verdict still stands (Beutler & Consoli, 1993). In fact, current research suggests that the various treatment systems have more commonalities than differences.

At the same time, research has demonstrated that certain approaches to treatment are more effective than others with particular problems, diagnoses, or types of clients. For example, cognitive therapy and interpersonal psychotherapy have been shown to be particularly powerful in the treatment of major depressive disorder (Elkin et al., 1989).

The following 10 factors, then, have combined during the past 15–20 years to move clinicians in the direction of preferring integrated and eclectic approaches to treatment over adherence to one specific system (Prochaska & Norcross, 1999):

1. The large and growing number of approaches to treatment; more than 400 approaches to treatment have been identified
2. The increasing diversity and complexity of clients and the concerns they present for treatment

3. The inability of any one treatment system to successfully address all clients and all problems
4. The growing importance of brief solution-based approaches that encourage clinicians to draw on and combine interventions derived from various systems of therapy to find the most effective and efficient strategy for each treatment situation
5. The availability of training opportunities as well as case studies and other literature that give clinicians the opportunity to study, observe, and gain experience in a wide variety of treatment approaches
6. The requirement of some state and national credentialing bodies that clinicians obtain postgraduate continuing education units that encourage continued professional growth and development of new skills and ideas
7. The growing body of compelling research demonstrating which treatment approaches are most likely to be successful in the treatment of particular disorders or problems (Seligman, 1998)
8. The development of organizations such as the Society for the Exploration of Psychotherapy Integration that focus on studying and promoting treatment integration
9. The emergence of models providing blueprints or guidelines for logical and therapeutically sound integration of treatment approaches (see Chapter 24)
10. Clinicians' increasing awareness that common factors among treatment systems, such as the nature of the therapeutic alliance, are at least as important in determining treatment success as are specific differences

This array of factors, the failure of any one treatment system to demonstrate overall superiority, the important commonalities among treatment approaches, the differential effectiveness of various approaches, the great variety of clients seen for treatment, the constantly evolving nature of counseling and psychotherapy, and the recent emphasis on prescriptive treatment planning seem to be nudging many clinicians toward an eclectic or integrated model as their preferred orientation toward treatment.

THE CHALLENGES OF ECLECTICISM

Choosing to adopt an eclectic or integrated theoretical orientation is a challenging choice that seems to demand more of clinicians than does adherence to one specific theory. If clinicians decide, for example, that they will specialize in brief psychodynamic psychotherapy, they should, of course, develop expertise in that approach and have a clear idea of when it is and is not likely to be helpful so that they can refer to other clinicians those clients who are unlikely to benefit from brief psychodynamic psychotherapy. Because they are limiting the scope of their work, they do not necessarily have to develop expertise in many other approaches.

However, clinicians who view their primary theoretical orientation as eclectic or integrated need to be familiar with a broad range of treatment systems so they can draw on those approaches in putting together a treatment plan that is likely to be successful. Of course, clinicians who have an eclectic or integrated orientation also set limits on the scope of their practice; no clinician could be expected to have sufficient knowledge and expertise in the entire range of therapeutic approaches to treat any client and any problem. Clinicians are expected to define the scope of their practice according to the nature of their clientele and the problems or mental disorders they are skilled in treating. Nevertheless, clinicians who do not affiliate with one specific treatment system still seem to have a professional role that is likely to be more comprehensive and challenging than that of clinicians with a specific theoretical orientation.

THE NATURE OF ECLECTICISM

When clinicians first began to describe their theoretical orientations as *eclectic,* the term did not have a clear meaning; it simply suggested that clinicians drew on more than one approach to treatment in their work. Although some clinicians who characterized their work as eclectic were gifted therapists and astute theoreticians who had a clear rationale for combining interventions in the treatment they provided, others lacked a clear and systematic approach to treatment. Eysenck (1970) denounced what he referred to as "lazy eclecticism," the use of a grab bag of interventions put together without an overriding logic (p. 140). Without a system, eclecticism can lead to a scattered approach to treatment, one that is haphazard and inconsistent lacking direction and coherence. This has been referred to as *syncretism.* Clearly, such an approach to treatment reflects a lack of knowledge and professionalism and is incompatible with current emphases on accountability and treatment planning in counseling and psychotherapy.

Systematic Approaches to Treatment Integration

To counteract lazy eclecticism or syncretism, theoreticians have been developing logical and systematic approaches to guide clinicians in answering the still-pressing question "*What* treatment, by *whom,* is the most effective for *this* individual with *that* specific problem, and under what set of circumstances" (Paul, 1967, p. 109). Chapter 24 provides information about the major theories of systematic eclectic and integrated treatment. One of these is multimodal therapy developed by Arnold Lazarus. Originally a behaviorist, Lazarus designed a clear and comprehensive approach to treatment planning that facilitates clinicians' efforts to match intervention to problem. Another important eclectic approach is developmental counseling and therapy (DCT) developed by Allen Ivey, Sandra Rigazio-DiGilio, and others. Additional eclectic approaches considered in Chapter 24 include adaptive counseling and therapy (ACT), the TFA (thinking-feeling-acting) model, systematic eclectic psychotherapy developed by Beutler and Consoli, and Wachtel's integrative psychodynamic-behavior therapy.

Types of Eclecticism

Four types of eclecticism have been identified (Norcross, 1987; Prochaska & Norcross, 1999):

1. *Atheoretical eclecticism* is characterized by combining interventions without regard to an overriding theory of change or development. Unless an intuitive or underlying logic prevails, clinicians whose work reflects atheoretical eclecticism run the risk of syncretism—creating a treatment plan that is without direction and includes incompatible elements. Such an approach is unlikely to promote client cooperation and motivation and may well lead to treatment failure.

2. *Common factors approaches* emphasize the therapeutic alliance and other essential ingredients that have been found to characterize effective treatment. Specific interventions are linked to these common factors rather than a specific theory. In Part 1 you learned about common factors in successful treatment, and we will discuss these factors further in Part 7.

3. *Technical eclecticism* provides a framework for combining interventions from different treatment systems without necessarily subscribing to the theories or philosophies associated with those interventions. According to Prochaska and Norcross (1999), technical eclecticism "focuses on predicting for whom interventions will work: the foundation is actuarial rather than theoretical" (p. 462). This approach can be thought of as an organized collection of interventions rather than an integration of ideas. Lazarus's multimodal therapy exemplifies this type of eclecticism.

4. *Theoretical integration* offers conceptual guidelines for integrating two or more treatment systems to provide a clearer understanding of clients and more effective ways to help them. Developmental counseling and therapy (DCT), discussed in Chapter 24, is an example.

In a true theoretical integration, the whole is greater than the sum of its parts. The combination has enough in common so that the theories blend well and form a new philosophy or treatment system that builds and improves on each of the individual theories to form a better product.

INTEGRATING TREATMENT SYSTEMS

Although most clinicians do not adhere to a systematic approach to integration such as DCT, they probably have formulated their own logic for combining compatible theories. The most common combinations of theories, in descending order of frequency, include (1) cognitive and behavioral treatment systems, (2) humanistic and cognitive approaches, and (3) psychoanalytic and cognitive approaches (Prochaska & Norcross, 1999). The presence of cognitive therapy in all three combinations is noteworthy and suggests both the flexibility of that approach and its importance in treatment.

Characteristics of Sound Eclecticism

Certain hallmarks distinguish healthy and professionally sound integration or systematic eclecticism from eclecticism that is haphazard and ill-conceived. Sound eclecticism has the following characteristics:

- Evidence of building on the strengths of existing theories
- An underlying theory of human behavior and development
- A philosophy or theory of change
- Logic, guidelines, and procedures for adapting the approach to a particular person or problem
- A body of strategies and interventions, related to the underlying theory, that facilitate change
- A sense of unity and wholeness
- Inclusion of the commonalities of effective treatment, such as the importance of the client-clinician relationship

Formulating an Eclectic Treatment System

When clinicians formulate an integrated or eclectic treatment system, they must address many questions, including these:

1. What model of human development is reflected by the theory?
2. How does this treatment system suggest that change can best be facilitated?
3. What information should be obtained in an intake interview?
4. What conception does this approach have of the influence of the past on the present, and how should past experiences and difficulties be addressed in treatment?
5. How important is insight in promoting change, and how much attention should be paid in treatment to improving insight?
6. How important is exploration of emotions in promoting change; and how much attention should be paid in treatment to helping people identify, express, and modify their emotions?
7. How important is identification and modification of dysfunctional cognitions in promoting change, and how much attention should be paid in treatment to helping people alter their cognitions?
8. How important is identification and modification of self-destructive and unhelpful behaviors in promoting change, and how much attention should be paid in treatment to helping people alter their behaviors?
9. What skills are associated with this treatment system?
10. What sorts of people and problems are likely to respond well to this treatment system?
11. How well does this approach address issues of diversity, and what is the appropriate use of this approach with people from diverse backgrounds?

12. In what treatment settings and contexts is this approach likely to be successful?
13. What is the place of diagnosis and treatment planning in this approach?
14. What are the overall goals of treatment?
15. What types of therapeutic alliance and client-clinician interactions are most likely to be productive?
16. What interventions and strategies are compatible with this treatment system?
17. How should this approach be adapted for use with individuals? Families? Groups?
18. How long is treatment likely to be?
19. How is effectiveness measured, and what determines when treatment is finished?
20. Has this treatment system been adequately substantiated by empirical research? If not, what information is needed to support the value of this approach?

DETERMINANTS OF THEORETICAL ORIENTATION

Although surveys suggest that as many as half of all clinicians align themselves primarily with eclectic or integrated approaches to treatment, the other half are affiliated with specific treatment systems. Many determinants, including the five factors that follow, contribute to clinicians' choice of theoretical orientation:

1. Clinicians who are encouraged, through their graduate course work and professional experiences, to adopt a particular approach to treatment are more likely to embrace a specific treatment system than an integrated or eclectic approach (Robertson, 1979). This is especially true if they are exposed to a charismatic proponent of that theory.

2. Beginning clinicians are more likely to embrace a specific theoretical approach. They have not yet had the opportunity to determine which treatment system best fits them and their clients, nor have most beginning clinicians acquired enough understanding of the entire spectrum of treatment approaches to allow for thoughtful integration of a variety of approaches. In addition, adherence to a single theory can provide new clinicians with reassuring structure and guidelines.

3. Similarly, length of clinical experience bears a positive relationship to the likelihood that a clinician will have adopted an integrated or eclectic orientation (Norcross & Goldfried, 1992). Exposure to a diverse and complex array of clients and concerns as well as to clinicians who practice a range of treatment approaches leads many counselors and psychologists to conclude that any single theory is likely to be too limited to meet their needs. Even theories that seem comprehensive and well supported in the literature may have gaps and shortcomings in practice.

4. Clinicians' perceptions of their work is another relevant factor. Robertson (1979) suggested that clinicians who view their work as a reflection of their philosophy of life are more likely to take an integrated or eclectic stance than are clinicians who view their work in practical terms, seeing it primarily as a way to earn a living.

5. Clinicians' personalities and world views are other related and important factors. Finding a theoretical approach that is compatible with who they are and how they conceive of the process of helping people seems likely to enhance clinicians' effectiveness as well as their enjoyment of their work. For many clinicians, their early years in their profession give them the opportunity to experiment with a range of approaches; determine what is and is not successful for them; and find a treatment system that is compatible with not only their professional roles but also their self-images, personalities, and views of the world (Norcross, 1987). Robertson, for example, found that people who tended to be skeptical and innovative were more likely to gravitate toward developing their own integrated approaches; this probably contributed to their feeling of ownership, genuineness, and congruence in their work. On the other hand, people who craved security, order, and structure were more likely to embrace a specific theoretical model.

SKILL DEVELOPMENT: TREATMENT PLANNING

Treatment planning is rapidly becoming one of the most important skills of today's clinicians. Treatment planning can serve the following four purposes (Seligman, 1996a, pp. 157–158):

1. A carefully developed treatment plan, well grounded in research on treatment effectiveness, provides assurance that counseling or psychotherapy with a high likelihood of success is being provided.
2. Written treatment plans allow clinicians to demonstrate accountability and effectiveness. Treatment plans can assist clinicians in obtaining funding for programs and in receiving third party payments for their services. They also can provide a sound defense in the event of allegations of malpractice.
3. Use of a treatment plan that specifies goals and procedures can help clinicians and clients to track their progress. They can determine whether goals are being met as planned and, if not, can facilitate appropriate revisions in treatment.
4. Treatment plans also provide structure and direction to the therapeutic process. They help clinicians and clients to develop shared and realistic expectations for treatment and promote optimism that progress will be made.

Treatment planning is essential, regardless of what concerns clients present or what theoretical orientation clinicians have adopted. Treatment planning is likely to be even more important for clinicians who follow integrated or eclectic approaches to treatment than for those who emphasize a single theoretical orientation. A treatment plan can organize the disparate elements of various theories into a cohesive whole, clarify the sequence of interventions, and help ensure that treatment strategies address the entire range of clients' concerns.

Although many agencies and managed care organizations have developed their own guidelines and formats for treatment plans, few widely accepted models for treatment planning are available. However, many clinicians have adopted my DO A CLIENT MAP model (Seligman, 1996a, 1998). The first letters of the 12 steps form the model's name and serve as a mnemonic device. The purpose of the plan is, of course, to map out the treatment process for a given client. The 12 steps in this comprehensive treatment process include

1. *D*iagnosis
2. *O*bjectives of treatment
3. *A*ssessments
4. *C*linician
5. *L*ocation of treatment
6. *I*nterventions
7. *E*mphasis
8. *N*umber of people seen in treatment
9. *T*iming
10. *M*edication
11. *A*djunct services
12. *P*rognosis

The rest of this section provides additional information on these steps, and the following case illustration shows a completed treatment plan that follows the DO A CLIENT MAP format.

1. *Diagnosis.* The first step in treatment planning is making an accurate diagnosis of a person's difficulties using the multiaxial structure and diagnostic terminology of the *Diagnostic and Statistical Manual of Mental Disorders* (American Psychiatric Association, 1994). The rest of the treatment plan should grow logically out of and be linked to that diagnosis as well as to the client's presenting concerns.

2. *Objectives of treatment.* Once problems and symptoms have been explored and a diagnosis formulated, client and clinician collaborate on establishing written objectives for treatment that address the diagnoses and problems presented by the client. (See Chapter 22 for detailed information on establishing goals or objectives.)

3. *Assessments.* Clinicians sometimes use assessments to facilitate their efforts to make accurate diagnoses and establish meaningful and viable objectives. Included in this section of the treatment plan are assessments administered by the clinician (e.g., measures of personality, interests, and abilities) as well as assessments to be conducted by other professionals such as psychiatrists, neurologists, gynecologists, or urologists.

4. *Clinician.* Variables that characterize the sort of clinician likely to work well with a given client are specified in this section. Included might be information about the desired training and expertise of the clinician as well as information on the preferred clinician's gender, age range, ethnicity, cultural or religious background, or any other relevant characteristics.

5. *Location.* This item specifies whether treatment should be inpatient, outpatient, or an alternative such as a day treatment program and suggests the specific agency or treatment facility.

6. *Interventions.* This part of the plan provides two important pieces of information. First, the treatment system is specified (e.g., cognitive therapy, brief solution-based therapy, person-centered counseling). If an integrated model is used, the treatment plan should indicate the specific theories that will be combined in treatment. Second, the specific strategies or interventions chosen to achieve the objectives are

listed. Objectives and interventions should be linked, with each intervention designed to contribute to the accomplishment of one or more objectives.

7. *Emphasis.* Although many clinicians share a particular theoretical orientation, no clinician ever does exactly the same thing, nor does a clinician practice in exactly the same way with each client. This section of the plan outlines how the theoretical approach identified in the interventions section will be adapted to meet the needs of a particular person. For example, the clinician may decide that a client needs much support, would benefit from caring confrontations, or needs considerable structure and direction during treatment.

8. *Number of people.* This section specifies whether individual, family, or group therapy will be the primary mode of intervention. Individual therapy is usually the treatment of choice, especially at the outset. However, concerns such as relationship issues, children's behavioral problems, separation and divorce, chronic and life-threatening illness, eating disorders, and substance use disorders are particularly likely to benefit from family counseling because of their impact on the whole family and their tendency to be related to family dynamics. Similarly, problems such as posttraumatic stress disorder, physical and sexual abuse, eating disorders, substance use disorders, and other impulse control disorders typically respond especially well to group therapy because of the feedback, support, reinforcement, and role models provided by the group.

Treatment sometimes involves a combination of individual, family, and group therapy, which should be specified in the treatment plan. For example, treatment of an adolescent boy with behavioral, interpersonal, family, and self-esteem concerns might begin with a combination of alternating individual and family therapy. Once the boy has made some progress, group therapy might replace individual treatment so that he has the opportunity to try out new social skills in context, benefit from peer role models, and receive feedback and encouragement from the group members.

9. *Timing.* This part of the plan encompasses four aspects of the scheduling of the therapeutic process: the length of each session, the frequency of sessions, the duration of treatment, and the pacing of the treatment process. Traditionally, treatment occurs once a week in sessions of 45–50 minutes. However, sometimes treatment is more likely to be effective if that traditional pattern is changed. For example, longer sessions are often used for group therapy and sometimes for family therapy, while school counselors typically have briefer appointments. Altering frequency can also enhance treatment. People in crisis might benefit from more than one session a week, while people who have met most of their treatment goals might be seen only for monthly follow-up sessions. Although the exact duration of treatment is usually difficult to determine at the outset, clinicians should anticipate whether short-, medium-, or long-term treatment will be required for a particular person. The pacing of the session is another timing variable. Pacing is likely to be rapid for relatively healthy and motivated clients as well as for those in crisis, while treatment will probably move at a slower pace for people who are fragile or have longstanding and deeply entrenched concerns.

10. *Medication.* Psychologists, counselors, and social workers often collaborate with psychiatrists in treating clients. The combination of psychotherapy and med-

ication can be particularly powerful in alleviating some mental disorders. Although psychologists, counselors, and social workers are not generally qualified to prescribe medication, they should know which disorders are likely to benefit from drugs, which medications are commonly used to treat these mental disorders, and the benefits and possible side effects of those medications. Clinicians should refer clients to a psychiatrist for a medication evaluation if the clients exhibit symptoms of loss of contact with reality, mania, severe depression, disorientation and memory loss, and excessive sleepiness. Other symptoms such as dysfunctional eating, attentional problems, obsessions and compulsions, and panic attacks also often benefit from medication. A sound professional collaboration with a psychiatrist can greatly enhance the work of the nonmedical clinician.

11. *Adjunct services.* Most clients benefit from adjunct services. These sources of help, support, and information are found outside of the psychotherapeutic relationship and can contribute to the effectiveness of treatment and help people make progress toward their goals between sessions.

Examples of useful adjunct services include skill development (e.g., study skills, parenting), peer support groups, legal and medical services, weight-control and exercise programs, cultural and religious organizations, clubs and classes for social and leisure activities (e.g., Parents Without Partners, bridge clubs, hiking groups), and governmental services (e.g., food stamps, subsidized housing). Twelve-step programs such as Alcoholics Anonymous, Gamblers Anonymous, and Overeaters Anonymous can be particularly helpful to clients if they are appropriate for their concerns.

12. *Prognosis.* This last step specifies the likelihood of clients achieving the specified objectives according to the treatment plan. Of course, a prognosis that is excellent, very good, or good is desired. If the bottom line of a treatment plan is less optimistic, clinicians might want to revise their objectives or their interventions to increase the likelihood of a successful outcome.

CASE ILLUSTRATION

The following treatment plan for Ava follows the DO A CLIENT MAP format:

1. *Diagnosis.* 313.81 Oppositional Defiant Disorder, Moderate; 309.0 Adjustment Disorder with Depressed Mood

2. *Objectives.* Short-term objectives include

a. Reduce level of depression by at least 3 points on a children's depression inventory
b. Decrease frequency of acting-out behaviors from more than 5 per week to no more than 3 per week, as measured by teacher's report

c. Increase number of days of completed homework from 0 or 1 to at least 3, as measured by teacher's report
d. Increase Ava's self-rating of her happiness in her family from the current rating of 2 to at least 4, as measured by an informal 1–10 rating scale

Medium-term objectives include

e. Bring mood level into the normal range on a children's depression inventory
f. Reduce frequency of acting-out behavior further to no more than 1 per

week, as measured by teacher's report

g. Increase number of days of completed homework to at least 4 per week, as measured by teacher's report

h. Increase Ava's self-rating of her happiness in her family from the current rating of 2 to at least 7

i. Increase the amount of pleasurable time that Ava reports spending with her family from an average of less than 15 minutes per day to at least 3 hours per week

j. Increase Ava's self-rating of her self-esteem from the current rating of 3 to at least 7

3. *Assessments.* Children's depression inventory, informal rating scales of self-esteem and family happiness, teacher reports of Ava's behavior and homework completion.

4. *Clinician.* Ava is likely to benefit from a clinician who has experience in treating both children and families, works collaboratively with teachers and school counselors, and is both supportive and encouraging and able to set appropriate limits. Ava expressed a preference for a female therapist, and this request should be honored. A clinician with sensitivity to the religious and cultural backgrounds and differences between Ava's parents would also be beneficial.

5. *Location.* Outpatient comprehensive private practice or community mental health center offering treatment for children, adults, and families.

6. *Interventions.* Primary theoretical orientations will be cognitive behavior therapy and reality therapy. Ava's dysfunctional thinking is contributing to her feelings of depression and leading to her acting-out and uncooperative behavior at school. The following specific strategies will be used initially, with the letters after each intervention specifying the objectives it is designed to accomplish:

- Identifying and modifying dysfunctional thoughts (a, e, j)
- Teaching communication and assertiveness skills (b, d, f, h)
- Teaching strategies for anger management (b, f)
- Establishing a weekly family council and family outings (a, d, e, h, i)
- Helping Ava plan and schedule her homework, with encouragement from and monitoring by her parents (c, g, j)
- Planning and contracting for behavioral change (b, c, f, g), with additional treatment strategies probably included later

7. *Emphasis.* Although Ava is likely to benefit from a structured treatment process that helps her take responsibility for herself and change her unrewarding thoughts and actions, she also needs considerable support, empathy, and understanding to enable her to deal effectively with the conflicts between her parents.

8. *Numbers.* Initially, treatment will include both individual and family sessions. Once Ava has made some progress, group therapy will replace the individual sessions to allow Ava the opportunity to practice and improve her new communication skills.

9. *Timing.* Sessions 45 minutes long will be held weekly. Pacing can be rapid because Ava functions fairly well and has support from her family. Approximately 10 sessions each of individual and family treatment are anticipated, followed by group counseling.

10. *Medication.* The nature of Ava's problems does not suggest a need for medication.

11. *Adjunct services.* Ava would probably benefit from involvement in an activity that gives her contact with a peer group as well as the opportunity to learn a skill that might enhance her self-esteem. She expressed an interest in learning ballet, and her parents have agreed to enroll her in an age-appropriate ballet class.

12. *Prognosis.* Ava's difficulties are relatively mild and brief and are largely in reaction to the conflict between her parents. She is motivated to engage in treatment and has the support of her parents. Consequently, the prognosis for achieving the specified objectives according to this treatment plan is very good.

EXERCISES

Large-Group Exercises

1. Integrating disparate treatment systems can be challenging; some theories mesh well, while others seem incompatible. Discuss whether and how the following combinations could be successfully integrated:
   • Person-centered and psychodynamic approaches
   • Reality therapy and Adler's individual psychology
   • Existentialism and cognitive psychotherapy
   • Gestalt therapy and behavior therapy
2. Develop treatment plans, following the DO A CLIENT MAP format, for Edie and Roberto based on what you have already learned about them. Feel free to add information to fill out your knowledge of these clients.
3. No one theory has emerged as clearly superior to the rest. How do you explain that? Discuss whether you believe that research and practice will ever identify an ideal or universal approach to counseling and psychotherapy and why that does or does not seem likely.

Small-Group Exercises

1. Divide into your groups of four, composed of two dyads. Each dyad should engage in a 10-minute, role-played counseling interview in which the person playing the client talks about a concern and the person in the clinician role deliberately integrates two or more approaches to treatment. Tape-record the interview. Play back the interview after it is completed so that the group can identify which theories were reflected in the clinician's role, the successful aspects of the integration, and ways in which the role play might have been even more successful.
2. Clinicians typically have mixed reactions to the process of treatment planning. In your small groups, discuss the benefits and drawbacks to treatment planning as well as some ways to overcome the drawbacks and maximize the benefits.

Individual Exercises

1. If you have had the experience of being a client, think about the treatment system used by your clinician, identifying the theory or theories reflected in

the treatment you received. Write about this in your journal, describing the most helpful and least helpful elements of your treatment.

2. Whether or not you have had previous experience as a client, write a paragraph discussing whether and why you would prefer to be treated by a clinician who follows an integrated approach or one who adheres to a single treatment system.

3. Identify a problem you have had that might have benefited from psychotherapy or counseling. Develop a written treatment plan for your own concern following the DO A CLIENT MAP format.

SUMMARY

This chapter has provided an overview of integrated and eclectic approaches to treatment. As many as 50% of clinicians describe their primary theoretical orientation as eclectic. This offers many advantages, including the flexibility of drawing concepts and interventions from a broad range of treatment systems, enabling clinicians to tailor treatment to a particular client or concern. However, an eclectic approach to treatment can be challenging, requiring clinicians to familiarize themselves with a broad range of theories and strategies. In addition, if not done wisely and thoughtfully, eclectic treatment can be random, haphazard, and unsuccessful.

RECOMMENDED READINGS

Seligman, L. (1996a). *Diagnosis and treatment planning in counseling.* New York: Plenum.
Seligman, L. (1998). *Selecting effective treatments* (2nd ed.). San Francisco: Jossey-Bass.

Chapter 24

THEORIES OF INTEGRATED AND ECLECTIC TREATMENT

Chapter 23 provided an overview of eclectic and integrated approaches to counseling and psychotherapy. The primary theoretical affiliation of many clinicians, these treatment systems have both strengths and weaknesses. Some of their shortcomings can be overcome by adopting a sound and systematic rationale for developing treatment plans. As Lazarus and Beutler (1993) have stated, "Procedures are not selected haphazardly, but their selection is specifically dependent on a logical decisional process that takes into account the client, setting, problem, and the nature of the counselor's skills" (p. 384).

This chapter reviews specific systems and procedures for planning eclectic treatment so that it happens by design rather than default. Two models receive particular attention because they represent different approaches to eclecticism and are well-developed treatment systems that have demonstrated success: multimodal therapy (developed by Arnold Lazarus) and developmental counseling and therapy (developed by Allen Ivey, Sandra Rigazio-DiGilio, and others). We also give some attention to other integrated and eclectic treatment systems, including Wachtel's integrative psychodynamic-behavior therapy, transtheoretical therapy as developed by Prochaska and his colleagues, the TFA model, adaptive counseling and therapy as developed by Nance and Myers, systematic eclectic psychotherapy, and REPLAN.

MULTIMODAL THERAPY

An example of technical eclecticism, multimodal therapy was developed primarily by Arnold Lazarus, who initially described this approach in several articles written during the early 1970s. He provided the groundwork for multimodal therapy in *Multimodal Behavior Therapy* (1976) and *The Practice of Multimodal Therapy* (1981) and has continued to develop his eclectic approach since their publication.

Arnold Lazarus

Arnold Lazarus was born in Johannesburg, South Africa, in 1932, the youngest of four children. He received a Ph.D. in clinical psychology in 1960 from the University of the Witwaterstrand in Johannesburg. At the invitation of Albert Bandura, a well-known behaviorist, Lazarus, along with his wife and two children, joined the faculty at Stanford University in 1963. He also had the opportunity to work with Joseph Wolpe, another pioneer in behavior therapy. (The contributions of Wolpe and Bandura are discussed in Chapter 20.)

Although Lazarus's early work reflected his training in behavior therapy, he soon became aware of the limitations of that approach and began to incorporate cognitive and other treatment models into his work. Suggesting that clinicians take a broad-spectrum frame of reference to understanding people and helping them address their concerns, he advocated technical eclecticism. That treatment system encourages clinicians to draw on an array of theories and strategies to match treatment to client and problem.

Lazarus has served on the faculties of Stanford University, Temple University Medical School, and Yale University and currently holds the rank of Distinguished Professor of Psychology at the Graduate School of Applied and Professional Psychology at Rutgers University (Lazarus, 1997). He has written more than 200 articles and 15 books, most of them focusing on multimodal therapy. Lazarus has received many awards for his contributions, including the Distinguished Psychologist Award from the American Psychological Association's Division of Psychotherapy. As a result of his work during the 1990s on time-effective psychotherapy, he became the first recipient of the annual Cummings PSYCHE Award. He is widely recognized as the leading proponent of technical eclecticism.

Theory and Practice

According to Lazarus (1985), "Human disquietude is multileveled and multilayered. . . . few, if any, problems have a single cause or unitary 'cure'" (p. 2). Consequently, treatment needs to be flexible and versatile, drawing on a variety of approaches. For Lazarus, technical eclecticism is the ideal way to plan such a treatment.

In describing technical eclecticism, Lazarus and Beutler (1993) wrote, "Technical eclectics select procedures from different sources without necessarily subscribing to the theories that spawned them; they work within a preferred theory but recognize that few techniques are inevitably wedded to any theory. Hence, they borrow techniques from other orientations based on the proven worth of these procedures" (p. 384). The three primary characteristics of technical eclecticism, as perceived by Lazarus, include treatment that is

1. Grounded in a theory of the clinician's choice
2. Enhanced by interventions associated with compatible approaches to treatment
3. Emphasizing interventions that have had their value substantiated by the literature

Selection of specific treatment strategies is guided by a systematic framework for matching intervention to client, problem, and situation (Lazarus, 1981).

Multimodal therapy is best described as a system for integrating theories and interventions rather than a self-contained theory of counseling and psychotherapy. Grounded in behaviorism, as reflected in its emphasis on outcomes, multimodal therapy typically draws heavily on cognitive therapy as well as social learning theory. In addition, multimodal therapy has a strong humanistic component: it values the uniqueness and self-determination of each individual (Sherwood-Hawes, 1995). This approach also pays attention to context; Lazarus (1981) emphasizes the importance of looking at not only the individual but also that person's culture, society, politics, and environment.

BASIC I.D. In multimodal therapy, a careful assessment of clients and their concerns is an essential precursor of treatment planning. Lazarus (1981) developed a model to assess what he viewed as the seven basic categories of functioning, represented by the acronym BASIC I.D.:

1. *Behavior:* observable actions and habits
2. *Affect:* moods and emotions
3. *Sensations:* physical concerns, sensory experiences (touch, taste, smell, sight, hearing)
4. *Images:* fantasies, dreams, memories, mental pictures, and people's views of themselves, their lives, and their futures
5. *Cognitions:* thoughts, beliefs, philosophies, values, plans, opinions, insights, ideas, self-talk
6. *Interpersonal relations:* friendships and intimate relationships, interactions with other people
7. *Drugs, biology:* broadly defined as biological functioning, including overall health, nutrition, exercise, self-care

Assessment Instruments   Treatment via multimodal therapy begins with a comprehensive assessment of these seven areas, using questions and scales to identify both strengths and problem areas. Several instruments help clinicians gather information on the seven areas:

1. The Multimodal Life History (developed by Arnold Lazarus and his son Clifford Lazarus and published by Research Press) is an extensive written questionnaire that asks about people's backgrounds, their personal and social histories, their presenting problems, and the seven areas of functioning (Lazarus, 1997).

2. Lazarus (1997) has found that people tend to favor some BASIC I.D. modalities over others and, for example, might be characterized as a sensory reactor, an affective reactor, or an imagery reactor depending on which modality is preferred. Included as part of the Multimodal Life History is a Structural Profile to facilitate identification of a person's preferred modalities. This form asks people to indicate on a 1–7 scale how important each of the seven areas of functioning is in their lives. Other tools developed by Lazarus (1997) to provide information on a person's preferred modalities include the Structural Profile Inventory and the Expanded Structural Profile. Listing the seven areas in descending order of a person's ratings yields a structural profile for that person. Constructing a diagram or bar graph of the relative strengths of a person's seven areas of functioning is particularly useful in clarifying patterns (Lazarus, 1976).

People seem to respond best to interventions that target their preferred modalities. For example, a person who emphasizes imagery is likely to benefit from visualization, while a person who focuses on thinking and analyzing will probably respond well to identification and modification of cognitive distortions.

Structural profiles are useful in couples counseling as well as individual therapy. Comparing two people's structural profiles can shed light on their similarities and differences and help to explain and normalize some of their conflicts.

Analyzing the BASIC I.D.   The BASIC I.D. is a rich source of information about a person and can be processed in several ways. Once the structural profile has been determined, clinicians can encourage clients to review the seven areas again, identifying changes they would like to make in each modality. Lazarus (1976) refers to this process as a second-order analysis of the BASIC I.D.

A second-order analysis can also focus on a particular symptom in relation to each of the seven modalities. Lazarus (1985) has found this a useful step to relieve a treatment impasse.

Another way to make use of the BASIC I.D. is to look at a person's modality firing order. Lazarus suggests that each person has a characteristic sequence of reactions to stressors and that this sequence usually mirrors that person's structural profile. For example, Olga indicated that her first three preferred modalities, in descending order, were affect, sensation, and behavior. When she was under stress, she usually reacted first by becoming angry and distraught (affect). Then she became aware of bodily tension as well as queasiness in her stomach (sensation). Finally, she withdrew from the stressful situation (behavior). Her firing order often caused her interpersonal difficulties because she would berate people in hurtful ways (affect) and then avoid them (behavior) so they had no opportunity to discuss what had occurred. Consciously making some changes in her firing order—in particular, giving greater emphasis to cognitions—helped Olga handle stress more effectively.

Bridging and Tracking   Bridging and tracking are two useful techniques associated with multimodal therapy. In bridging, clinicians deliberately relate to clients first through the clients' dominant modality to build connection and rapport and then branch off into other dimensions that are likely to be productive and develop new skills and ways of responding. Tracking is the process of planning interventions in the same sequence as a person's preferred firing order. This seems to maximize receptivity to the interventions.

Therapeutic Alliance   Although collaboration between clients and clinicians is valued in multimodal therapy, clinicians are expected to play the primary role in assessment and treatment planning and to remain active and in charge of the treatment throughout the process. The multimodal therapist should constantly ask, "What works, for whom, and under which particular circumstances?" in an effort to determine the type of interventions that are most likely to be helpful in a given situation (Lazarus, 1985, p. viii).

Application and Current Status

Because of its great adaptability, multimodal therapy is appropriate for use with a broad range of people and problems. The importance of the assessment process requires that clients have some self-awareness; be motivated and reasonably reliable informants; and be capable of at least a moderate level of planning, organizing, and self-monitoring. This approach otherwise has many applications. It can be combined with medication for people who would benefit from drugs, integrate several treatment systems that seem likely to be helpful, and be modified so that it is well received by people from diverse cultural backgrounds. People who present a combination of different concerns (e.g., anxiety, time management, and poor social skills) might be particularly responsive to multimodal therapy because it can help them develop a systematic approach to their concerns and relieve feelings of being overwhelmed and discouraged, common in multiproblem clients (Seligman, 1996a).

Recognizing the current trend toward brief therapy, Lazarus (1997) has described ways to adapt multimodal therapy to a brief framework. He suggests a four-step process:

1. Use the BASIC I.D. format to screen for presence of significant problems.
2. In collaboration with the client, identify three or four focal concerns that require attention.
3. If indicated, refer the person for a medication evaluation as well as a physical examination.
4. Use empirically validated treatment modalities and interventions to address the client's focal concerns.

Case studies in the literature illustrate the application of multimodal therapy to a broad range of problems and disorders, including agoraphobia, depression, obesity, posttraumatic stress disorder, eating disorders, somatization (Lazarus, 1985), anxiety, sexual dysfunction, and substance misuse (Lazarus, 1997), among others. Multimodal therapy has been used successfully with children as well as adults.

Evaluation

Multimodal therapy has some shortcomings and limitations. Some clinicians are concerned about the lack of a cohesive theory to unite this model. Despite the BASIC I.D. framework and the other helpful tools associated with this approach, multimodal therapy, in the hands of an unskilled clinician, could simply be a poorly organized array of techniques not much different from syncretism (discussed in Chapter 23). Related to this, multimodal therapy lacks some of the strengths of a sound treatment system, including a concept of human development, a theory of change, and an explanation of why people develop problems. Another shortcoming is the inherent need for organization, structure, detail, and planning as well as the demands the approach places on clinicians, who must be familiar with and skilled in a broad array of theoretical approaches and interventions.

Nevertheless, multimodal therapy has a great many strengths, the most important of which is flexibility. In addition, the BASIC I.D. framework provides a useful and accessible way to gather client information, which is interesting and appealing to most people. The Multimodal Life History questionnaire and its accompanying Structural Profile facilitate both assessment and treatment planning. Multimodal therapy is holistic and comprehensive, individualized and goal-directed. It offers structure and a clear direction to treatment, which can reassure clients and help make problems manageable.

Lazarus and other multimodal therapists have placed considerable emphasis on research to demonstrate the value of their treatment system. Lazarus (1976) reported, for example, that 75% of people treated via multimodal therapy achieved major treatment goals. At the same time, the significance of research on multimodal therapy is unclear because each person is treated differently, prohibiting replication.

Multimodal therapy does not yet seem to be widely used, perhaps because its complexity and structure, as well as its strong behavioral emphasis, may not appeal to some clinicians. However, the importance and use of this approach seems likely to increase for several reasons. It facilitates treatment planning, an essential tool not only for providing effective treatment but also for demonstrating accountability and meeting the requirements of third-party payers. *Brief but Comprehensive Therapy the Multimodal Way* (Lazarus, 1997) describes how multimodal therapy can be compatible with a short-term treatment model and consequently with much of the treatment that is provided today.

Despite its shortcomings, multimodal therapy has a great deal to offer most clinicians. Lazarus and Beutler (1993) wrote, "It is our view that a systematic, prescriptive, technically eclectic orientation will continue to become even more popular and may represent the psychotherapeutic Zeitgeist well into the twenty-first century" (p. 384). The use of multimodal therapy does seem likely to expand during this century. However, more time and research is needed to fully document its value.

DEVELOPMENTAL COUNSELING AND THERAPY

Developmental counseling and therapy (DCT), along with systemic cognitive developmental therapy (SCDT) for families, was developed by Allen Ivey, Sandra Rigazio-DiGilio, and their associates. Like multimodal therapy, DCT draws on a broad range of treatment systems and interventions and advocates the use of careful assessment to facilitate matching treatment strategy to individual. However, it goes beyond technical eclecticism and is more accurately viewed as an integrated theory because it does have its own theoretical framework.

According to Rigazio-Digilio, Ivey, Ivey, and Simek-Morgan (1997), DCT is "an integrated theory of assessment and treatment that is representative of postmodern thought" (p. 90). It is "based on three central constructs—1) the co-constructive nature of relationships and knowledge, 2) a reformulation of Piagetian cognitive stages for use in the immediacy of psychotherapy sessions, and 3) a spherical metaframework that integrates multiple voices of therapy" (p. 94). Like narrative therapy (discussed in Chapter 14), DCT takes the position that people have multiple perspectives that continuously evolve. With Piaget's theories of cognitive development providing a basis for understanding people, DCT promotes change and growth by matching treatment strategies to each client's cognitive developmental orientation and perspectives.

The People Who Developed DCT

Allen Ivey has been a leader in counseling and psychotherapy since the 1970s and has been developing and writing about DCT since the publication of *Developmental Therapy: Theory into Practice* (1986). Ivey initially became known for his work on microcounseling and his training programs designed to facilitate development of basic attending and influencing skills. His research and writing currently focuses on DCT and on counseling in a multicultural society. However, the importance of intentional counseling—using interventions in a thoughtful and deliberate way—has always been an underlying theme of his work.

Ivey received his doctorate from Harvard University and has spent most of his professional career at the University of Massachusetts at Amherst, where he is currently a Distinguished University Professor in the School and Counseling Psychology Program. He has received many professional awards, including the Professional Development Award from the American Counseling Association. Ivey has been president of the American Psychological Association's Division of Counseling Psychology and has written more than 25 books and 200 chapters and articles (Ivey, Ivey, & Simek-Morgan, 1997).

Sandra Rigazio-Digilio collaborated with Allen Ivey in the development of DCT and has applied DCT to families through an approach called systematic cognitive developmental therapy (SCDT). She has also formulated a model of supervision linked to DCT. Rigazio-Digilio received her doctorate from the University of Massachusetts at Amherst and is an associate professor in Marriage and Family Therapy at the University of Connecticut at Storrs. She has been associate editor of the *Journal of Mental Health Counseling* and in 1994 received the American Association of Marriage and Family Therapy Divisional Contribution Award.

Research on and development of DCT involves a group of people. Others who have made important contributions include Mary Bradford Ivey and Lynn Simek-Morgan.

Theory and Practice

According to Allen Ivey (1989),

> Mental health counseling is a profession which conducts its developmental practice with both the severely distressed and those facing normal developmental tasks. This developmental practice exists within a multicultural awareness and seeks to address clients and the systems within which they live. A developmental practice focuses on counseling and development, actualizing the potential of individuals and the systems—families, groups, and organizations. Mental health counselors are able to intervene at the individual or systemic level to produce positive change. Distinctions between pathology and normality become irrelevant within this model as the goal is to reintroduce growth regardless of the level of personal disturbance presented by the individual or system. (pp. 28–29)

This description of mental health counseling captures many of the important aspects of DCT. It emphasizes both the person and the system, maintaining that development occurs within a social and cultural context; attends to multiple perspectives; redefines pathology as developmental blocks or delays; and seeks to promote growth and change by providing education and facilitating continued development (Ivey & Rigazio-DiGilio, 1991; Rigazio-DiGilio, 1994).

Underlying Theories DCT is grounded in both philosophy and psychology. Ivey and his associates have borrowed from the ideas of Plato and Hegel and take the phenomenological perspective that the ways in which people understand the world and operate in it can be both helped and hindered by their levels of cognitive development and the social units and systems in which they are involved (Rigazio-Digilio, Gonçalves, & Ivey, 1995). According to DCT, understanding people from multiple perspectives is integral to the development of individualized and culturally sensitive treatment plans that are likely to be successful.

The research of Piaget, which focused on people's stages of cognitive development, is the framework used in DCT to determine people's levels of cognitive functioning. DCT postulates that cognitive functioning can be categorized and described according to four cognitive developmental orientations (Rigazio-Digilio et al., 1997):

1. *Sensorimotor/elemental.* In this orientation, people focus on acting and feeling in the present moment and rely on sensory input for information about their world. Emotions may overshadow cognitions and be overwhelming, or they may be split off and unrecognized. Introspection is difficult in this orientation.

2. *Concrete-operational/situational.* People using this orientation have more objectivity; they focus on actions and observable events, can describe experiences in great detail, and can name their emotions but have difficulty with reflection and cause-and-effect thinking. Particularly challenging is linking their emotional responses to their experiences.

3. *Formal-operational/reflective.* People operating in this orientation have a strong ability to be analytical and think about their thoughts, feelings, behaviors, and patterns in their lives. They have a capacity for abstraction and objectivity but may have difficulty experiencing their emotions directly and in the present.

4. *Dialectic/systemic.* In the fourth orientation, people can engage in metacognitions; they can reflect on their reflections and think about the ways in which they process information. They can assume multiple viewpoints and understand the impact their families, cultural groups, and other social units have had on them. They are aware of the complexity and multidimensional nature of emotions and can identify not only straightforward emotions but also feelings that are complex, conflicted, or ambivalent. However, they may have difficulty experiencing feelings directly and can become so caught up with intellectual processing that they become detached from their emotions.

Ivey and his colleagues do not view any one of these four cognitive developmental orientations as better or more desirable than the others. Rather, healthy development is conceptualized as continuous mastery of life tasks, which promotes competency in all four of these orientations. Ideally, people should have access to a variety of well-integrated cognitive structures and be flexible and adaptable enough to shift into whichever cognitive structure is likely to work best under a given set of circumstances. Of course, people do not always function in this optimum way; instead, their cognitive organization may be rigid, and they may rely mainly on one orientation or have diffuse and underdeveloped cognitive structures, leading to highly reactive and chaotic operations.

Goals   According to DCT, at any given time, people have a primary or predominant cognitive developmental orientation in operation. An initial step in DCT is assessment of a person's cognitive developmental orientations (discussed further later in this chapter). Once that has been determined, treatment focuses on three general goals (Rigazio-Digilio et al., 1995):

1. Helping people gain more integration, organization, flexibility, and range in their cognitive developmental structures
2. Enabling them to use these structures to acquire multiple perspectives of their lives and concerns; to see new possibilities
3. Collaborating with clients to develop solutions that are relevant to their developmental and environmental needs

Change and Development   Cognitive developmental structures can evolve in two ways. Horizontal development, which focuses on enriching one particular cognitive developmental orientation, enables people to expand and solidify their use of that orientation. For example, people with a strong formal-operational orientation may work on deepening their capacities for analysis and abstraction. Vertical development, on the other hand, focuses on helping people draw on multiple cognitive developmental orientations to facilitate their use of a variety of perspectives and alternative ways of thinking, feeling, and acting. For people with a strong formal-operational orientation, vertical development might help them develop more objectivity, which is associated with the concrete-operational orientation.

Clinicians practicing DCT promote change and growth in three ways:

1. Exploring and assessing people's world views, operations in the world, areas of difficulty, and cognitive developmental orientations
2. Using the knowledge they have gained about people's cognitive developmental orientations, perceptions, social systems, and concerns to design appropriate interventions
3. Constructing with the client expanded (horizontal) and alternative (vertical) perspectives to encourage positive adaptive functioning

Assessment   Rigazio-Digilio et al. (1997) suggest using a series of sequential, open-ended questions supported by encouraging and summarizing interventions to assess a person's access to the four cognitive developmental orientations and to identify that person's primary and secondary orientations. Such an assessment typically consists of five components:

1. *Preliminary assessment* involves open-ended discussion of a broad topic (such as the person's family of origin) to introduce the clinician to the client's developmental orientations.

2. *Sensorimotor/elemental exploration* emphasizes questions about sensory experiences (seeing, hearing, feeling) and the present to provide information about the person's use of the sensorimotor orientation.

3. *Concrete-operational/situational exploration* emphasizes questions about actions and experiences, obtaining linear descriptions so that the clinician can learn more about the person's use of the concrete-operational orientation.

4. *Formal-operational/reflective exploration* emphasizes questions about patterns, roles, and relationships and encourages reflection to provide information about the person's use of the formal-operational orientation.

5. *Dialectic/systemic exploration* emphasizes questions about analysis, integration, multiple perspectives, change, and constructive action to provide information about the person's use of the dialectic-systemic orientation.

Planning Interventions   When clinicians have a good sense of a client's cognitive developmental orientations and have identified that person's primary and secondary orientations, they are ready to plan the intervention strategy. Initially, clinicians will probably use interventions that fit the person's predominant orientations to promote horizontal development and deepen the therapeutic alliance. However, they will eventually encourage vertical development by mismatching—gradually introducing interventions that focus on less preferred and less accessible orientations.

In treatment planning, DCT addresses three levels of objectives and interventions: basic, intermediate, and deep levels. Basic interventions typically focus on symptom relief and development of coping skills. Intermediate interventions continue the development of effective problem-solving and interpersonal skills and promote awareness of patterns. Deep-level interventions aim toward integration, synthesis, and acquisition of new perspectives.

The following list clarifies the nature of the treatment process and goals associated with each cognitive developmental orientation. It also includes typical interventions used to address each of the four orientations (Rigazio-DiGilio & Ivey, 1991; Rigazio-DiGilio et al., 1997):

Sensorimotor Environmental Structuring
- *Goals:* provide direction, promote awareness and direct experience, focus attention on the here and now, minimize denial and splitting
- *Associated interventions:* Gestalt empty chair, body work (e.g., yoga, massage), relaxation, guided imagery, modeling, medication, environmental change

Concrete Operational Coaching
- *Goals:* encourage cause-and-effect thinking, promote constructive action
- *Associated interventions:* assertiveness training, rational emotive behavior therapy, social skills training, problem-solving training, systematic desensitization, role playing, enactments, thought stopping, solution-based therapy

Formal Operational Consultation
- *Goals:* promote analysis, reflection, insight, and recognition of patterns and cycles

- *Associated interventions:* person-centered treatment, psychodynamic therapy, interpretation, cognitive restructuring, dream analysis, Adlerian early recollection analysis, reframing, life history, analysis of patterns

Dialectic/Systemic Collaboration
- *Goals:* facilitate integration and thinking that generates multiple perspectives, promote awareness of self in relation to others and the system, bring underlying issues to the surface, and make possible new constructs of self and reality
- *Associated interventions:* consciousness raising, analysis of culture and context and of intergenerational patterns in families, family therapy

Therapeutic Alliance   The role of clinicians practicing DCT is challenging and demanding. They need to be skilled in assessment of cognitive developmental orientations and be able to function in all of the four orientations. They need to be knowledgeable about a broad range of treatment systems and strategies so they can intentionally craft a treatment plan that is compatible with a person's cognitive developmental functioning and promotes that person's change and growth (Ivey & Ivey, 1999). Clinicians need to be attuned to the developmental and sociocultural perspectives of the client while being able to engage with the client in constructing alternative perspectives. They need to be accomplished in the basic skills of counseling and psychotherapy, able to develop rapport with a wide variety of clients, and capable of individualizing treatment to those clients. Clinicians need to match their role to the cognitive developmental orientation they are seeking to reach and thus need to have the ability to function in a variety of therapeutic roles (e.g., as coach, consultant, and collaborator).

Although clinicians practicing DCT have an important role in treatment, so do the clients. They are expected to engage fully in the treatment process; talk about their issues, their lives, and the groups to which they belong; and engage with clinicians as much as possible in developing new constructions or ways of viewing the world.

Application and Current Status

Both clinical case studies and empirical research support the broad application and considerable value of DCT. Research has supported the structure of the four cognitive developmental orientations. Empirical findings indicate high inter-rater reliability in determining an individual's predominant cognitive developmental orientation. In addition, DCT has been shown to increase the range of people's cognitive developmental functioning.

DCT can be used with a broad range of clients. Positive outcomes have been reported in using this approach with people dealing with transitions, accident survivors, men who batter and their partners, students entering the work force, and children who have been abused (Rigazio-DiGilio et al., 1995). In addition, the approach has been successfully used to treat some types of anxiety and mood disorders. Rigazio-

DiGilio's (1994) adaptation of DCT to families—systemic cognitive developmental therapy—contributes to the wide application of this approach. Of course, inherent in DCT is a strong emphasis on understanding the person in context and adapting treatment to that particular individual, making the approach particularly well suited for use with people from diverse and multicultural backgrounds.

Despite its apparent potential for use with a wide and diverse range of people and concerns, DCT has received only limited attention except from Ivey, Rigazio-DiGilio, and their colleagues and students. This may be due to several factors. DCT is a complex approach that demands considerable clinician expertise, and training is not yet widely available. Also, well-researched tools are not yet available to facilitate assessment of cognitive developmental orientations, establishment of appropriate objectives, and identification of appropriate interventions. In addition, the terminology associated with this approach, as well as its philosophical roots, may seem too esoteric to appeal to some clinicians.

Ivey, Rigazio-DiGilio, and their associates are actively conducting research to refine DCT and substantiate its value. The future of this promising but complex approach depends on the success they have in empirically validating the constructs and strategies of the approach and making training more available and accessible.

Evaluation

DCT has a number of shortcomings. The approach has not yet fully evolved and relies heavily on complex terminology and concepts. Although DCT emphasizes a developmental perspective, it speaks of diagnoses and mental disorders when discussing successful case studies that have used DCT. It is a strength that DCT does not ignore mental disorders, but writings have not made sufficiently clear how clinicians are to factor diagnoses into their treatment plans and what relationship, if any, diagnoses bear to the cognitive developmental orientations. Clinicians who are used to managed care's emphasis on diagnoses may have difficulty with the transition to DCT.

At the same time, DCT is probably the best developed and most promising of the integrated approaches to treatment. It reflects many of the hallmarks of sound treatment systems: it has a theoretical foundation, is holistic and comprehensive, can be adapted and individualized to meet the needs of particular clients, offers guidelines for assessment, and suggests systematic ways to develop treatment plans that are likely to be effective.

DCT is a promising and innovative approach that provides a useful prototype for integrated treatment. One of its important contributions is in demonstrating that such an approach can be described and tested. DCT may pave the way for the development of other integrated treatment systems that reflect the same careful thought and structuring that went into its own development. In addition, further empirical research on the effectiveness of DCT, as well as the addition of accessible training material and tools for assessment of cognitive developmental orientations and treatment planning, may enhance its appeal and acceptance.

Integrated and eclectic approaches to counseling and psychotherapy are a rich area of inquiry and study. Many clinicians practice an eclectic approach to treatment, and most clinicians would probably appreciate having a framework or theory to guide them in assembling a diverse array of treatment strategies to enable them to successfully treat a broad range of clients and concerns. Not only would this be desirable from a clinical point of view, but the use of a systematic approach to eclecticism would facilitate clinicians' efforts to demonstrate accountability and present their treatment plans to third-party payers and clients in persuasive and powerful ways.

Like Arnold Lazarus, Allen Ivey, Sandra Rigazio-DiGilio, and their associates, many theoreticians today are seeking to develop clear and effective approaches to eclectic and integrated treatment. We briefly review some of the emerging approaches here. Readers are encouraged to read further about these approaches, most of which are in a relatively early stage of development and still evolving.

Integrative Psychodynamic-Behavior Therapy

Developed by Paul Wachtel, integrative psychodynamic-behavior therapy, as its name implies, is a theory of treatment that meshes psychodynamic therapy and behavior therapy (Wachtel, 1977, 1987, 1990). Wachtel disputes what he calls the "woolly mammoth view of development": the belief that early childhood experiences cause the intrapsychic structures to be frozen in time, like the woolly mammoth remains frozen in a block of ice. Instead, he suggests that early experiences trigger cycles or inclinations that are maintained by present attitudes and behaviors.

Wachtel has identified many similarities and compatibilities between psychodynamic and behavioral theories and believes that an integration of the two can provide more powerful treatment than either alone. For example, he has identified anxiety as a key target in both treatment systems and suggests that, through a combination of insight and action, people can gradually be exposed to their frightening images and fantasies and learn to cope with them more effectively. Wachtel departs from the neutral stance of the classic psychodynamic therapist and advocates that clinicians assume a more active and affirming role in relation to their clients, reflecting the core conditions for effective treatment discussed previously in this book. Although research has yet to substantiate the value of this approach, the possibility of integrating and drawing on the many strengths of psychodynamic and behavioral treatment systems holds considerable appeal.

The Thinking-Feeling-Acting Model

The thinking-feeling-acting (TFA) model, developed by David Hutchins (1979), is reminiscent of Lazarus's multimodal therapy in its matching of intervention to client and of Wachtel's integrative psychodynamic-behavior therapy in its goal of systematically combining disparate theoretical approaches. Identifying thinking, feeling, and acting as the three fundamental operations in human functioning, the model's developers see TFA as useful in "a) conceptually integrating thinking, feeling, and acting domains of behavior; b) assessing the interaction of TFA behavior dimensions in specific problem situations; and c) designing procedures and techniques that capitalize on client strengths and supplement limitations" (Mueller, Dupuy, & Hutchins, 1994, p. 576).

Assessment is a cornerstone of this approach, as it is in multimodal therapy and developmental counseling and therapy. Treatment begins with assessment of a person's TFA orientation. The Hutchins Behavior Inventory has been developed to facilitate determination of that orientation (Hutchins & Mueller, 1992). Once the clinician has determined the relative strengths of thinking, feeling, and acting in determining a person's behavior, appropriate interventions can be developed to both access that person's primary orientation and develop the less preferred orientations.

Somewhat more research is available on the TFA counseling system than is available on integrative psychodynamic-behavior therapy. However, the TFA model, too, while promising and appealing, needs further substantiation.

The Adaptive Counseling and Therapy/Readiness Model

The adaptive counseling and therapy/readiness model (ACT) is another treatment system that matches clinical approach to client needs (Nance & Myers, 1991). The ACT model describes clinician style in terms of two dimensions: support and direction. Combinations of low and high levels of each dimension result in four counseling orientations:

1. Approaches that are low in directiveness and high in support emphasize encouragement.
2. Approaches that are high in both directiveness and support emphasize teaching.
3. Approaches that are low in support and high in directiveness stress telling.
4. Approaches that are low in both directiveness and support emphasize delegating.

Nance and Myers suggest matching the treatment approach to the nature of the problem and the readiness of the client. For example, people who are very unsure of themselves and unwilling to engage in treatment seem to benefit most from the support offered by the first counseling style. People at the other end of the spectrum, those who are confident and capable, are likely to respond best to assuming considerable responsibility for their own treatment, reflecting the fourth therapeutic style. Again, more research is needed to substantiate these conclusions.

The Three-Dimensional Model of Multicultural Counseling

In a similar model, Atkinson, Kim, and Caldwell (1998) suggest adapting treatment to the special needs of multicultural clients by looking at three dimensions:

1. *Level of acculturation:* high or low
2. *Location of problem:* internal or external
3. *Intervention needed:* remediation or prevention

Once a client has been described according to these three dimensions, the approach suggests clinician roles and strategies that are likely to be helpful. For example, a person with a low level of acculturation who is experiencing an internal problem and needs remediation would probably benefit from the help of a healer from his or her own culture. On the other hand, a person who is high in acculturation, is focusing on an external concern, and requires prevention would be more likely to benefit from a helper in a consultant role.

The Common Factors Models

Some approaches to eclectic treatment have, as their unifying basis, a solid grounding in the common factors that make psychotherapy effective. An example is *REPLAN*, developed by Young (1992). The name REPLAN (relationship, efficacy, practicing, lowering, activating, new) is an acronym representing six common megafactors in successful treatment:

1. Developing a positive therapeutic relationship
2. Increasing a client's efficacy and self-esteem
3. Teaching and encouraging client practice of new behaviors
4. Lowering or raising the client's emotional arousal
5. Activating the client's motivation and expectations for positive change
6. Providing the client with new learning experiences and perceptions

Building on this foundation, clinician and client collaborate in establishing goals and developing a treatment plan that targets the person's specific concerns. The six common factors, then, become the underlying framework of REPLAN, while the specific intervention strategies serve as the way to adapt this model to the individual.

Another example of a common factors model is *systematic eclectic psychotherapy*, developed by Beutler and Consoli (1993). In planning treatment, they suggest that clinicians look at four variables: client characteristics, treatment context, client-clinician relationship variables, and specific strategies and techniques. Beutler and Consoli assume that certain universal clinician qualities, including respect, a receptive attitude, and flexibility, are associated with positive outcomes and suggest that these traits should underlie all treatment. Beyond that, systematic eclectic psychotherapy provides guidelines for fitting the treatment approach to the person. Clinicians pay particular attention to the client's level of motivation and coping styles when determining the treatment plan.

The Stage-of-Change Models

Another approach to developing eclectic and integrated approaches to treatment is reflected in phase or stage models, which assume that people go through predictable stages as they progress in counseling or psychotherapy. Stage models link interventions to both the phase of a person's development and the phase of treatment.

An example is the *transtheoretical model,* developed by Prochaska and others (Prochaska & DiClemente, 1986; Prochaska & Norcross, 1999). This approach postulates that "change unfolds over a series of five stages: precontemplation, contemplation, preparation, action, and maintenance" (Prochaska & Norcross, 1999, p. 495). Although progression through these phases may be direct and linear, it is more likely to reflect a spiral, with relapses and other factors causing people to cycle back through previous phases in the change process.

Assessment and matching are essential ingredients in this approach, as they are in many of the eclectic and integrated models of treatment. In the transtheoretical model, determination of a person's stage of change is used to identify strategies and interventions that are likely to be successful and to help that person progress to the next stage of the change process. For example, strategies that promote awareness such as consciousness raising and evaluation of self and environment are likely to be particularly helpful and well received during the early precontemplation and contemplation stages, while action-oriented interventions such as contingency management and conditioning are more likely to be useful in the later action and maintenance stages. Guidelines on empirically supported strategies to facilitate change and delineation of five targets of change (situation, cognition, interpersonal, system, intrapersonal) facilitate the development of individualized treatment plans. Research on this approach is promising, suggesting that Prochaska and Norcross (1999) may be on the right track when they conclude, "We have determined that efficient behavior change depends on doing the right things (processes) at the right time (stages)" (p. 503).

SKILL DEVELOPMENT: ENCOURAGERS

One of the most important and challenging roles of the clinician is facilitating client self-disclosure: encouraging people to talk about their perceptions of themselves, their experiences, the important people in their lives, their concerns and joys, and their hopes. Even people who are self-referred for treatment may be reluctant to talk at length about themselves. They may feel uncomfortable and awkward in the treatment setting, mistrust the clinician, worry about being judged or disapproved of, be unused to talking about themselves, or simply need some coaching on how to use their sessions productively. Although beginning clinicians sometimes have a misconception that most clients will immediately share personal and intimate details of their lives, more often than not people approach treatment cautiously and need help in talking about themselves.

Being able to engage clients in a productive dialogue about themselves is especially important for clinicians who advocate eclectic or integrated approaches to treatment because those treatments rely so heavily on getting to know clients well and obtaining an accurate assessment of them according to predetermined and usually comprehensive variables. Consequently, we focus here on four encouragers that can be used to promote client self-expression: minimal encouragers, restatement, paraphrase, and summarization.

Allen Ivey emphasized the importance of intentional interviewing—of clinicians knowing what they hope to accomplish with every intervention they make. Skilled clinicians can review transcripts of their sessions and not only explain their goals for each session but also clarify the purpose of each intervention they made. Without such a clear vision, clinicians' use of encouragers can simply fill up air space and promote conversation. When used with care and deliberation, however, encouragers can focus clients' communications, facilitate the assessment process, promote client self-awareness, and maximize the benefits of treatment. Although encouragers may seem like a simple and straightforward technique in clinicians' repertoire, their thoughtful and purposeful use is actually an advanced treatment skill. The exercises later in this chapter will give you an opportunity to practice counseling with awareness and purpose.

Minimal Encouragers

Minimal encouragers are well named; they are brief, limited interventions in which clinicians communicate to clients that they are listening, encourage clients to keep talking, and perhaps give some focus to the clients' words. When using minimal encouragers, clinicians deliberately maintain a low profile; they want to keep the focus on the client and do not want their interventions to disrupt or intrude on the process.

The following are three types of minimal encouragers:

1. *Umm-hmm.* This is the classic minimal encourager, a supportive murmur from the clinician accompanied by a nod of the head and an attentive posture. If clients are having little difficulty talking about themselves and using their time productively, this may be all they need to continue that process.

2. *Repetition of a word.* Here, the clinician repeats or underscores a client's spoken word or phrase. This focuses the client's attention on that bit of communication and generally encourages the client to elaborate further. Although this intervention is very brief, it can have considerable impact on the direction of the treatment process, as the following examples show.

Example A
Client: I went home for the holidays and had quite a surprise.

Clinician: You went home?

Client: Yes, I still think of my parents' house as my home. It meant a great deal to me and to them to spend the holidays together, so I braved the Thanksgiving Day traffic and drove down to see them. Nothing could have kept me away.

Example B

Client: I went home for the holidays and had quite a surprise.

Clinician: A surprise?

Client: Yes, my brother, the great family man, is getting a divorce. That should change my parents' opinion of him.

Each dialogue provides important information about the client's values and suggests a useful focus of treatment. However, they go in different directions as a result of the minimal encouragers.

3. *How so?* Although this brief phrase is really a question, it functions like a minimal encourager in that it prompts the client to hone in on a particular point and explore it in greater depth, as the following example (a continuation of the previous dialogue) shows.

Client: That should change my parents' opinion of my brother.

Clinician: How so?

Client: They've always seen him as the good son: he went to college, he got married, he had kids. Just because I haven't gotten married and had kids doesn't mean I'm not as good as he is. Maybe they'll finally appreciate me.

Restatement

Restatement simply involves repeating or underscoring a phrase or sentence that the client has spoken. It can be thought of as an expanded version of a minimal encourager and serves the same purpose: focusing the client's attention and promoting self-expression.

In the following example, the client talks about both himself and his brother. Restatement is used to encourage the client to focus on himself.

Client: I've always resented my brother. He got it all . . . good looks, all the attention from my parents, the girlfriends, the athletic skills, and the brains too.

Clinician: You've always resented your brother?

Client: Yes, I wanted what he had. I tried really hard to succeed. But whatever I did, my brother could do better. He was always two steps ahead of me.

Clinician: You tried really hard to succeed.

Client: Yes, I figured out how to please people and then tried to do it—get good grades for my parents, volunteer in class for my teachers, look good for the girls. But somehow it never worked out.

Paraphrase

In a paraphrase, clinicians feed back to clients the essence of what they have said. Although the clinicians use different words, they do not seek to interpret, analyze, or add depth to a client's statement. Rather, they simply give clients an opportunity to hear back what they have said, let clients know that the clinicians are listening and understanding them, and encourage clients to keep talking. The following is an example of a series of paraphrases used with the previous client.

Client: Maybe they'll finally appreciate me.

Clinician: You're hoping your parents will see you in a more positive light.

Client: Yes, I have good relationships, I have a respectable job, I vote; but just because I'm not married, they act like I'm a failure.

Clinician: So in your eyes you have really accomplished something, even though your parents seem to have a different viewpoint.

Client: I *have* really accomplished something. In my teaching, I really know how to reach children, even the tough ones who act like they couldn't care less.

Clinician: Your success in teaching is especially important to you.

Summarization

A summarization pulls together and synthesizes a group of client statements. Summarizations are useful for wrapping up a session, bringing closure to a topic, focusing a session, and helping clients reflect on what they have said. Like paraphrases, summarizations are not intended to be interpretive or analytical but simply to feed back to clients what they have been saying in a concise and coherent way.

The following is an example of a summarization that is used to focus a session.

Clinician: You've talked about many things in the first few minutes of today's session—financial difficulties, your efforts to find a job, your conflict with your mother, and your graduate program. Sounds like you have quite a few concerns on your mind. Which one of these issues would you like to focus on?

Mastering encouragers may seem simple. However, these interventions are deceptively powerful and can contribute a great deal to the development of rapport in the session and to its overall direction and value.

CASE ILLUSTRATION

The following dialogue between the clinician and Edie illustrates a discussion of the BASIC I.D., the seven functions explored as part of a comprehensive assessment in Lazarus's multimodal therapy. The result is a structural profile of Edie's BASIC I.D. that can be used to plan her treatment as well as provide information about her functioning and concerns related to the seven areas.

Clinician: Edie, I've reviewed with you the seven areas of your functioning that we are going to explore today. We will be talking about each area, and then I'd like you to rate yourself on a 1–7 scale reflecting how important each of these seven areas is in your life. A rating of 1 or 2 would suggest an area has little importance; a rating of 3, 4, or 5 would reflect moderate importance; and ratings of 6 or 7 would indicate that an area has great importance for you.

Edie: That seems clear.

Clinician: Let's start with behavior. To what extent would you say you are a doer, someone who keeps busy and is active and energetic?

Edie: I do always keep busy, but it's because I have to; I have so much to do. I wish I could be a little less active, but that certainly is an important part of my life. Rating myself as a doer, I'd give myself a 5 or a 6.

Clinician: Are there changes you would like to make in your behavior, things you would like to do more or less of?

Edie: Yes, I'd like to have more time to read and exercise, and I'd like to eat less and spend less time on housework.

Clinician: The next area is affect, including emotions, feelings, and moods. How emotional would you say you are?

Edie: Oh, very. I feel things very deeply, sometimes too deeply. I get hurt too easily and get angry too fast. But on the other hand, I can be very loving. Affect has to be a 7 in my life.

Clinician: Sounds like you are already identifying changes you would like to make in this area.

Edie: Yes, I'm too vulnerable and get mad too easily. And I'd like to have even more love in my life, especially romantic love.

Clinician: We will certainly pay attention to that in our work together. The third area is sensation. This refers to the five senses: sight, sound, smell, touch, and taste. How aware are you of your sensations?

Edie: That one sounds like a moderate for me, maybe a 4 or 5. I do enjoy good food, and I like music. It's important to me that I always look well and that my home and my family are presentable. At the same time, I don't care much about jewelry or art. Other values are more important to me than sensory experiences.

Clinician: Are there changes you would like to make in this area?

Edie: We've talked about my intimate relationship with Roberto before. You know we have some problems there. I just don't enjoy being touched and being close the way I did when we first got married. That's something I'd like to work on.

Clinician: Imagery is the fourth area. This includes the mental pictures you have, your fantasies and daydreams, things you imagine.

Edie: I don't think of myself as a particularly imaginative or creative person. I'm more practical and down to earth. I don't spend a lot of time daydreaming. At the same time, I do have some memories from my childhood that I just can't seem to forget, and I would like to see those fade away. I guess we have a moderate rating again here, but more like a 3 or 4.

Clinician: Cognitions are the fifth area, referring to thinking, planning, analyzing, self-talk.

Edie: I do a lot of that. Sometimes I have whole conversations in my head that really do a number on me. I can get myself depressed without any help. This one might be a 7. I'm also big on planning and organizing, which I guess is part of cognitions as well.

Clinician: Yes. Here, too, it sounds like you would like to make some changes.

Edie: I value my ability to plan and organize. But I ruminate about things, like a dog chewing on a bone. I just can't seem to let go of a thought sometimes. That could use some change.

Clinician: The next-to-last area is interpersonal relationships, our interactions with family and friends. How important is that to you?

Edie: Well, that's the most important thing. I guess I have another 7 here. Nothing matters more to me than my relationships. Maybe I should move cognitions down to a 6 or a 6 1/2. I don't like to be alone. You know how much I hate it when Roberto has to travel. It's not that I'm an extrovert, but I do like to have close family and friends around me as much as possible. It's problems in my relationships, especially with family, that really made me think I needed some counseling.

Clinician: So that, too, is a very important area for you. The last area includes drugs, biology, and health factors. Eating, consumption of alcohol, smoking, sleep, and weight control are some of the issues that would come under this item. How important is taking care of your health to you?

Edie: I'm embarrassed to admit it, but this is probably a 2. I really need to make some changes here. I take care of everyone but myself.

The discussion with Edie yielded the following structural profile, listed in descending order from the most to the least important area of functioning:

- Interpersonal relationships
- Affect
- Cognitions
- Behavior
- Sensation
- Imagery
- Drugs/biology/health

This structural profile, combined with the information about Edie's desired changes, can help her establish specific goals and assist the clinician in determining strategies that are likely to help Edie move toward her goals.

EXERCISES

Large-Group Exercises

1. Discuss and list the benefits and shortcomings of eclectic and integrated approaches to treatment. Discuss and list the benefits and shortcomings of adhering to a single treatment approach. Discuss which you would prefer at this stage in your career. Which do you think will be right for you after you have 10 more years experience as a clinician?
2. Using the BASIC I.D. format of multimodal therapy, develop a hypothetical structural profile for Roberto as well as appropriate goals and treatment interventions for each of the seven areas.
3. This chapter has introduced you to the following integrated and eclectic approaches to counseling and psychotherapy: multimodal therapy, developmental counseling and therapy, integrative-psychodynamic behavior therapy, the thinking-feeling-acting model (TFA), the adaptive counseling and therapy/readiness model (ACT), the three-dimensional model of multicultural counseling, common factors models (REPLAN, systematic eclectic psychotherapy), and the transtheoretical model. Discuss the common elements found in all or nearly all of these approaches. Then discuss what makes each approach unique. Although your understanding of these approaches is prob-

ably limited, discuss which seems most likely to make an important contribution to the fields of counseling and psychotherapy and why.

Small-Group Exercises

1. Divide into your groups of four, composed of two dyads. Each dyad should engage in a 15-minute, role-played counseling interview in which the clinician helps the client develop his or her structural profile using the BASIC I.D. format (see Edie's case illustration). Briefly discuss the person's strengths and desired changes in each of the seven areas. Feedback should focus on the process of developing the structural profile and consider both strengths and areas needing improvement.

2. Each dyad should role-play another interview, remaining in the same roles. The interview should be approximately 10 minutes long and focus on exploration of the most important function in the client's structural profile. Clinicians should emphasize the use of encouragers (minimal encouragers, restatement, paraphrase, and summarization). They should try to be intentional and deliberate in their interventions, having a purpose in mind each time they speak. Tape-record the interview and then play it back, stopping at each intervention to discuss the clinician's goal and whether it was accomplished.

3. Assume that your small group is going to develop an integrated approach to treatment. List the choices and decisions you need to make in developing your approach. Then try to make some of these choices and decisions as a group.

Individual Exercises

1. Using the BASIC I.D. format of multimodal therapy, develop your own structural profile. Rate the importance in your life of each of the seven areas. List those ratings in your journal along with a rank-ordered list of your seven areas of functioning. Then list your strengths and any changes you would like to make in each of the areas.

2. Think about whether your characteristic responses to stress mirror your structural profile. Identify the firing order of your first three preferred reactions to stressors. How well does that pattern of responses work for you? Consider what change, if any, you would like to make in the pattern of your responses to stress. Write about this in your journal.

3. According to developmental counseling and therapy, people can be described in terms of four cognitive developmental orientations: sensorimotor/elemental, concrete-operational/ situational, formal-operational/reflective, and dialectic/ systemic.

    Write about your own cognitive developmental orientations, responding to the following:
    • Which of these orientations characterizes your primary mode of functioning at the present time?

- Identify a time in your life when another orientation was primary for you.
- How much flexibility do you believe you have in your ability to move from one orientation to another?
- Which orientation is most difficult for you to access?
- Do you tend to rely too heavily on any one or two orientations?
- Do your responses to these questions suggest any desirable changes?

SUMMARY

Increasing numbers of clinicians report that their primary theoretical orientation is an eclectic or integrated treatment system. Integrated approaches are grounded in theory and seek to combine and blend many treatment strategies into a unique whole that is more than the sum of its parts. Eclecticism, on the other hand, lacks a unifying theory but is practical, providing a prototype or structure for selecting and applying interventions drawn from many systems of counseling and psychotherapy.

This chapter has described multimodal therapy, an eclectic approach to treatment developed by Arnold Lazarus, and development counseling and therapy, an integrated treatment system developed by Allen Ivey, Sandra Rigazio-DiGilio, and others. It has also glanced at several emerging eclectic and integrated treatment approaches. In the 21st century, we should expect to witness the development of new and better-refined integrated and eclectic approaches to treatment.

RECOMMENDED READINGS

Lazarus, A. A. (1989). *The practice of multimodal therapy.* Baltimore: Johns Hopkins University Press.

Lazarus, A. A. (1997). *Brief but comprehensive psychotherapy.* New York: Springer.

Norcross, J. C. & Goldfried, M. R. (Eds.). (1992). *Handbook of psychotherapy integration.* New York: Basic Books.

Rigazio-DiGilio, S. A., Ivey, A. E., Ivey, M. B., & Simek-Morgan, L. (1997). Developmental counseling and therapy: Individual and family therapy. In A. E. Ivey, M. B. Ivey, & L. Simek-Morgan (Eds.), *Counseling and psychotherapy: A multicultural perspective* (pp. 89–129). Needham Heights, MA: Allyn & Bacon.

PART SEVEN

MAXIMIZING TREATMENT EFFECTIVENESS

Chapter 25

CONTEXTS OF TREATMENT REVISITED

This book has reviewed a wide variety of treatment systems in counseling and psychotherapy. Knowledge of these approaches is an essential part of becoming an effective clinician. However, the outcomes of psychotherapy are actually determined by not only the treatment systems and interventions used but also the multiple contexts of treatment. Of course, attention has been paid to these variables throughout this book. However, the review presented in this chapter is likely to be especially meaningful now that readers have knowledge of systems, strategies, and skills of counseling and psychotherapy.

This chapter considers six contexts of treatment and their connections to the process of counseling or psychotherapy:

1. The therapeutic alliance and interaction of the client and the clinician
2. Characteristics and roles of the clinician
3. Characteristics and attitudes of the client
4. The problem or diagnosis
5. Managed care and third-party payers
6. The treatment setting

In addition, the "Skill Development" section (the last one in this book) focuses on the process of terminating treatment, helping clinicians make the end of treatment a beneficial and comfortable process for both client and clinician.

THE THERAPEUTIC ALLIANCE

The therapeutic alliance of the client and the clinician has been found to be the best predictor of treatment outcome (Horvath & Symonds, 1991; Orlinsky, Grawe, & Parks, 1994). Therefore, it is imperative that clinicians acquire a sound understanding of the elements of a positive therapeutic alliance, develop the skills and strategies they need to create successful working relationships with their clients, and be able to adapt their treatment style to the individual client to help him or her participate in and appreciate the value of the therapeutic alliance.

Usually, objective measures of the therapeutic alliance indicate that both clinicians' and clients' perceptions of that relationship are congruent. However, this is not always the case. When clients' and clinicians' views of the therapeutic alliance differ, research suggests that clients' perceptions of the nature and quality of the therapeutic alliance make the difference in treatment effectiveness. Consequently, clinicians need to not only meet their own standards for a successful therapeutic alliance but be sure that clients also have a positive view of that interaction. Clinicians should be attuned to their clients' verbal and nonverbal messages, ask them for feedback and reactions to the treatment process, and address any barriers to the establishment of a positive therapeutic alliance.

The therapeutic alliance can be conceptualized as encompassing three ingredients: the clinician, the client, and the interaction between the two. Both the clinician and the client, of course, bring their personal characteristics and experiences into the session with them. These preexisting characteristics, as well as attitudes and behaviors that emerge and are elicited over the course of treatment, have an impact on the therapeutic alliance and the treatment process. In assessing and developing the therapeutic alliance, then, clinicians should look at what they and their clients bring into treatment as well as the effectiveness of the treatment process in building their alliance.

Characteristics of Effective Clinicians

Chapter 2, as well as other chapters throughout the book, includes information about the relationships between the personal and professional characteristics of the clinician and that person's effectiveness as a therapist (Bachelor & Horvath, 1999; Jinks, 1999; Odell & Quinn, 1998). The profile of the effective clinician is, in many respects, comparable to a profile of an emotionally healthy person. Ideal clinicians are

- Characterized by strong interpersonal skills, including patience, warmth, caring, a sense of humor, and friendliness
- Genuine, sincere, and authentic; able to make appropriate self-disclosures, provide useful feedback, and acknowledge their mistakes and limitations
- Emotionally stable, mature, and responsible
- Well-adjusted and fulfilled, self-aware, with good self-esteem, positive relationships, a sense of direction, and a rewarding lifestyle
- Able to think soundly and conceptualize clearly and accurately
- In possession of good insight into themselves and others
- Aware of, sensitive to, and respectful of individual differences
- Engaged in and appreciative of the value of personal and professional growth and learning
- Ethical, objective, and fair
- Flexible and open to change and new experiences

Overall, excellent clinicians manage their lives well, do not let their personal needs intrude on the treatment process, are well integrated, and value themselves and their lives (Van Wagoner, Gelso, Hayes, & Diemer, 1991).

Research has not clearly demonstrated that a particular age, gender, professional orientation, or background is associated with more successful treatment outcomes. However, clients often express strong preference for clinicians in a certain age group, of one gender or the other, or with a particular cultural or religious affiliation. For example, most women prefer a female therapist (Pikus & Heavey, 1996). When clients receive the sort of treatment they prefer, they have more confidence that treatment will help them (Devine & Fernald, 1973; Wanigaratne & Barker, 1995). Respecting and honoring client preferences in a clinician, whenever possible, usually enhances the therapeutic alliance as well as the effectiveness of treatment.

Role of the Clinician

Desirable clinician characteristics (as just reviewed) are closely linked to the establishment of a positive therapeutic relationship. In addition, clinicians can maximize the likelihood of developing such an alliance with their clients by successfully communicating the following qualities and conditions:

- Empathy for and understanding of the client (Lambert & Cattani-Thompson, 1996)
- Trustworthiness and reliability
- Caring and concern for the client
- Genuineness, sincerity, and congruence (Jinks, 1999)
- Persuasiveness and credibility (Wanigaratne & Barker, 1995)
- Optimism about a successful treatment outcome
- Interest in and emotional involvement with the client (Saunders, 1999)
- Support, encouragement, and affirmation (Odell & Quinn, 1998)
- Ability to address problematic client behaviors and attitudes (Foreman & Marmar, 1985; Kivlighan & Schmitz, 1992)

Of these qualities, the core conditions described by Carl Rogers (discussed in Chapter 11) are especially important. Bachelor (1995) reported that half of all clients surveyed describe a good therapeutic alliance in terms of the therapist-offered facilitative conditions of respect, acceptance, empathy, and accurate attending.

Interaction of Client and Clinician

As Bachelor and Horvath (1999) have stated, "Although consensus has not been achieved on a definition of the therapeutic relationship, nor on its fundamental components for that matter, there is a general agreement that the working alliance, emphasizing the collaboration of client and therapist in the work of therapy, is a crucial ingredient" (pp. 137–138). The most successful therapeutic alliances are characterized by mutuality (Levine & Herron, 1990). Client and clinician both like, appreciate, and care about each other and view themselves as engaged in an important shared endeavor that is likely to be successful (Kolden, Howard, & Maling, 1994).

Having a shared vision of the treatment process and its goals is another important element in the therapeutic alliance (Hill & O'Brien, 1999). Understandably, if client and clinician have the same destination in sight and agree on the tasks and procedures that will be used to arrive at that destination, the journey is likely to be relatively smooth and efficient. The establishment of clear and mutually agreeable goals is particularly instrumental in promoting a positive treatment outcome (Tallman & Bohart, 1999).

Similarity between client and clinician also is associated with the development of a positive therapeutic alliance and with successful treatment. Kelly and Strupp (1992) found that similarity of overall values contributed positively to the treatment process. In multicultural counseling, most of the research supports similarity in culture and values as enhancing the therapeutic relationship and increasing the likeli-hood that clients will remain in treatment (Beutler, Machado, & Neufeldt, 1994; Gibbs & Huang, 1989).

Characteristics of the Successful Client

Not surprisingly, the client's personality plays a significant role in determining treatment outcome (Asay & Lambert, 1999). Several client characteristics bear a particularly strong relationship to outcome. Taking some time to get to know clients, paying particular attention to whether and to what extent they possess these characteristics, can facilitate clinicians' efforts to establish a positive thera-peutic alliance.

Maturity People whose lives are reasonably well organized and who are responsi-ble and knowledgeable about the world seem better able to engage in productive treatment than are people who lack these characteristics (Asay & Lambert, 1999). Clients who are mature also seem more likely to make a commitment to treatment and follow through on task assignments.

Capacity for Relationships Interpersonal qualities such as good communication skills, an ability to invest energy and caring in personal relationships, trust in others, and the capacity to form stable and close relationships are important client strengths (Gelso & Carter, 1985). People who have a good capacity to develop relationships outside of the treatment setting are more likely to collaborate with the clinician in the development of a positive therapeutic alliance (Joyce & Piper, 1998).

Ability to Establish Appropriate Interpersonal Boundaries An important aspect of people's capacity for relationships is the boundaries they seek to establish in those relationships. People who have a good measure of self-esteem and a sense of control over their lives are likely to establish appropriate boundaries both within and out-side of the therapeutic relationship. On the other hand, people who have inordinate needs for affiliation may seek an overinvolved and dependent relationship with the clinician, while people who have extreme needs for separateness and independence are likely to reject the clinician's social influence and guidance.

High reactance in clients is a personality variable that is particularly likely to interfere with the establishment of appropriate boundaries in the therapeutic re-lationship. Reactance has been defined as having a strong impulse or motivation to regain lost or threatened freedom and resist any suggestions or interventions that are perceived as potentially curtailing that freedom. Strong needs for independ-ence, control, autonomy, and dominance are associated with high levels of reac-tance. According to Seibel and Dowd (1999), "Our results indicate that psycholog-ical reactance is associated with a host of in-session behaviors that may be inimical to the course and outcome of therapy. These can be summarized as client behav-iors that attempt to control and direct the amount of therapeutic or interpersonal influence" (p. 377).

Introspection and Psychological-Mindedness   Clients who are accustomed to looking within and thinking in insightful ways about people and relationships are more likely to continue in treatment and have better outcomes (McCallum, Piper, & Joyce, 1992). The process of self-examination usually associated with counseling and psychotherapy will probably be comfortable and rewarding for them.

High Frustration Tolerance   People who are patient, can tolerate ambiguity, and delay gratification are likely to make good candidates for psychotherapy. On the other hand, people who tend to be impulsive and have a high need for novelty and stimulation often leave treatment prematurely and do not benefit substantially from that process (Wingerson et al., 1993).

Role of the Client

As with clinicians, both pretreatment characteristics and those qualities that clients manifest in the treatment context have a strong impact on outcome. The following within-session client behaviors and attitudes seem to play a particularly important part in the treatment process.

Motivation   The term *motivation* is a broad one that clinicians use to describe a range of client behaviors associated with readiness for treatment and ability to engage productively in therapy (Orlinsky et al., 1994). Particularly important aspects of client motivation include engagement in and cooperation with the treatment process and a willingness to self-disclose, confront problems, put forth effort to change, and, if necessary, experience some temporary anxiety and discomfort in the hope of eventual benefit (Hanna & Ritchie, 1995; Orlinsky et al., 1994; Paulson, Truscott, & Stuart, 1999). Other signs of strong client motivation include low levels of defensiveness and a belief that treatment is necessary and important. Not surprisingly, self-referred clients are less likely to terminate treatment prematurely than involuntary clients are.

Positive but Realistic Expectations for Treatment   People who have a good sense of what counseling and psychotherapy are all about as well as the strengths and limitations of the treatment process and who expect to benefit from that process are more likely to have successful treatment outcomes (Sabourin, Gendreau, & Frenette, 1987; Silverman & Beech, 1979). Pretreatment preparation of clients via role induction (discussed in Chapter 2) can make a considerable difference in people's expectations for treatment and correspondingly in their commitment to treatment, willingness to self-disclose, and alliance with the clinician (Acosta, Yamamota, Evans, & Skillbeck, 1983; Lawe, Horne, & Taylor, 1983). Similarly, effective engagement of the client in the very first session has been shown to make a positive contribution to successful treatment (Odell & Quinn, 1998).

Treatment-Related Self-Esteem   According to Asay and Lambert (1999), "Clients who do better in psychotherapy and maintain treatment gains believe that the changes made in therapy were primarily a result of their own efforts" (p. 32). These people probably feel empowered as a result of their successes in treatment and are optimistic that they can continue to make positive changes and choices, even after treatment has ended.

Client Diversity

The diversity of people seeking counseling has increased enormously in the past 40 years. During the 1960s, most people seeking treatment came from middle-class and majority cultural backgrounds. The literature paid little attention to the needs of people who did not fit that mold. By the 1970s, most clinicians were aware of the need to adapt treatment to the ethnic and cultural backgrounds of their clients. Clinicians became more aware of their own biases and the importance of not imposing their values on their clients. However, much of the research during the 1970s and 1980s oversimplified treatment issues related to client diversity and sought to match treatment approaches to clients' cultural and ethnic backgrounds.

Thinking about diversity became more sophisticated in the 1990s. The concept of diversity itself was expanded to include not only people's racial, ethnic, and cultural group memberships but also their socioeconomic status, gender, sexual orientation, and other affiliations. The literature now recognized that each person has multiple perspectives stemming from a wide variety of personal characteristics and background experiences. Even people who are similar in age, gender, sexual orientation, and cultural background can have very different world views and respond best to very different treatment approaches.

The importance of considering clients' world views and multiple perspectives will increase as the population becomes even more diverse. In the United States, the white population is expected to show little growth while Asian American/Pacific Islander, African American, and Hispanic populations are likely to show considerable growth (Edmunds, Martinson, & Goldberg, 1990).

Rates of premature termination of treatment tend to be significantly higher for people from lower socioeconomic or ethnic minority groups (Reis & Brown, 1999). In light of this statistic, as well as the anticipated growth in client diversity, it is essential for clinicians to maintain awareness of the multiple perspectives of their clients and their own preconceptions about those clients. They need to be aware of how people's cultural, ethnic, socioeconomic, and family backgrounds have shaped their views of personal problems and mental illness and of counseling as a way to address those concerns. For example, attitudes toward treatment of a woman whose family recently emigrated to the United States from rural Africa are likely to differ greatly from those of a man with an upper-middle class, white, Anglo-Saxon, Protestant background whose family has been living in Los Angeles for many years. The importance of clinicians' awareness of clients' contexts and perspectives can hardly be overemphasized. This awareness should facilitate clinicians' efforts to successfully adapt established treatment systems to the special needs of each person.

PROBLEMS AND DIAGNOSES

Just as a client's personality, background, and ability to engage productively in treatment have an impact on outcome, so do the client's problems and diagnoses. To make accurate diagnoses, it is essential for clinicians to become knowledgeable about the *Diagnostic and Statistical Manual of Mental Disorders* (DSM-IV) (American Psychiatric Association, 1994). Even in settings where clinicians do not typically formulate a written diagnosis, such as school and university counseling offices and rehabilitation counseling programs, determining whether a client meets criteria for diagnosis of a mental disorder is essential in identifying the approaches to treatment that are most likely to succeed.

For example, many people seek treatment because of feelings of sadness. However, the nature of their diagnoses and their appropriate treatments may differ widely (Seligman, 1998). Consider the following clients:

- Thomas sought treatment three months after the sudden death of his son in a motorcycle accident. Although Thomas continues to maintain his family and work responsibilities and is not suicidal, he is, not surprisingly, experiencing considerable grief.
- Gretchen was recently told that she is HIV positive. She knows that she needs to gather information and investigate treatment options but has avoided dealing with her diagnosis. Although she is experiencing sadness as well as anxiety, her feelings are not evident to others; and she has succeeded in concealing her medical condition as well as her emotional reactions from her friends and colleagues.
- Dava has been experiencing severe guilt and depression for the past two months. Her eating and sleeping are affected, and she has even contemplated suicide. This is her third experience with significant depression. Dava reports a history of abuse and rejection as a child.
- Although Manizheh is only 12 years old, she reports experiencing sadness for more than two years, since her family immigrated to the United States from the Middle East. She misses her friends and her neighborhood and especially misses her grandmother, who was not able to join the family in the United States. Like Gretchen, she has kept her feelings to herself, not wanting to burden her parents, who were having their own difficulties adjusting to their new home. However, she has avoided completing her schoolwork and has recently been acting out in class.

Each of these clients has a different diagnosis and is most likely to benefit from treatment linked to his or her particular diagnosis. According to the DSM-IV, Thomas is experiencing bereavement, a condition rather than a mental disorder. He is an emotionally healthy and resilient person who will probably benefit from some medium- or short-term counseling to help him deal with his loss, provide support to his wife, and deal with spiritual doubts and issues that have arisen in response to the death of his son. Person-centered and existential treatment systems might be especially useful in treating Thomas.

Gretchen might be diagnosed as having an adjustment disorder with mixed emotional features. This is a mild mental disorder that, in Gretchen's case, might respond especially well to cognitive behavior therapy, helping her modify her dysfunctional thoughts and take steps to obtain support from her friends as well as medical information.

Dava, too, is likely to benefit from some cognitive behavior therapy. However, she probably also needs a referral for medication. In addition, the chronic nature of her disorder, with its roots in her negative childhood experiences, suggests that some psychodynamic treatment also might be helpful.

Manizheh is experiencing a dysthymic disorder. A supportive therapeutic alliance will be essential in her treatment, perhaps combined with reality therapy or person-centered play therapy. Family counseling also is indicated to help her and she may benefit from tutoring, a peer support group, and other adjunct sources of assistance.

Since publication of the landmark study by Smith, Glass, and Miller (1980), much of the research in counseling and psychology has focused on differential therapeutics, finding answers to the question raised by Paul (1967): "*What* treatment, by *whom*, is most effective for *this* individual with *that* specific problem under *which* set of circumstances?" (p. 111). Although much more research is needed to provide definitive answers to this question, research since 1980 has made great strides in determining which treatment approaches are likely to be effective for each of the mental disorders described in the DSM-IV.

In general, people with circumscribed, brief, and reactive difficulties, as well as relatively good prior functioning, tend to have positive treatment outcomes. On the other hand, people with longstanding and severe disorders, particularly people with more than one mental disorder, tend to be particularly challenging clients (Najavits & Weiss, 1994).

Although a detailed discussion of differential therapeutics is beyond the scope of this book, the following overview of the most common categories of mental disorders and approaches that have been found effective in their treatment will give readers some idea of the link between disorder and treatment (Seligman, 1998). This can help clinicians appreciate the contribution that diagnosis makes to the treatment process and facilitate their choice of treatment approaches that are best for them and their clients.

Adjustment Disorders

Adjustment disorders are relatively mild and brief disturbances that develop in response to a precipitant or life stressor such as a job loss, a divorce, or an illness. Especially if the stressor can be ameliorated, adjustment disorders typically respond very well to crisis intervention and brief solution-based models of treatment. Support groups and readings about how other people have coped with similar difficulties can provide helpful role models and direction.

Mood Disorders

Mood disorders characterized by depression are the most common diagnosis presented for psychotherapy. Depressive disorders respond particularly well to treatment via cognitive therapy, cognitive behavior therapy, and brief psychodynamic psychotherapy. Approaches that identify and modify cognitive distortions can be especially powerful in alleviating depression. Relapse prevention is an important component of treatment, and medication is often combined with therapy for a more powerful treatment plan. Mood disorders characterized by mania or hypomania, with or without a history of depression, are particularly likely to require medication in addition to the treatments just mentioned.

Anxiety Disorders

Anxiety disorders include phobias, panic disorders, obsessive-compulsive disorders, posttraumatic stress disorders, and generalized anxiety disorders. Anxiety disorders, like depressive disorders, typically respond well to treatment. Particularly effective is cognitive behavior therapy, including interventions such as desensitization, relaxation, and problem solving.

Disorders of Behavior and Impulse Control

Prevalent behavior and impulse control disorders include substance-related disorders, eating disorders, sexual disorders, conduct disorders in children and adolescence, and pathological gambling. Cognitive behavioral interventions, emphasizing behavior change strategies, are likely to be effective in treating these disorders. Support and therapy groups are also useful in treating these disorders because they can provide reinforcement and helpful role models. Relapse prevention usually plays an important part in the treatment of these disorders, which have a high likelihood of recurrence.

Personality Disorders

Personality disorders are longstanding and pervasive and typically benefit from a combination of treatments. Cognitive behavior therapy can be helpful in engaging clients and effecting some rapid relief of symptoms. The subsequent addition of psychodynamic interventions often addresses underlying issues and effects deeper and more enduring change.

Psychotic Disorders

Psychotic disorders, involving a loss of contact with reality, almost always require medication. Other interventions, including support, training in assertiveness and social skills, and behavior change strategies, can enhance progress.

Treatment Efficacy and Diagnosis

The American Psychological Association, the American Psychiatric Association, and the American Counseling Association all are promoting research to determine which treatments succeed in ameliorating the symptoms of which mental disorders. An important effort toward determining empirically validated treatments has been conducted by the Task Force on Promotion and Dissemination of Psychological Procedures of the Division of Clinical Psychology of the American Psychological Association (Division 12 Task Force, 1996). An extensive review of the literature led the task force to identify 18 treatments whose efficacy had been well established and another 7 that were probably efficacious. Treatments viewed as particularly effective include the following:

- Interpersonal therapy for treating depression and bulimia
- Cognitive behavior therapy for treating chronic pain, panic disorder, generalized anxiety disorder, and social phobia
- Beck's cognitive therapy for treating depression
- Behavior modification or therapy for treating developmental disabilities, enuresis and encopresis, headaches, irritable bowel syndrome, female orgasmic dysfunction and male erectile dysfunction, and marital difficulties
- Exposure treatment for phobias and obsessive-compulsive disorders
- Family education programs to help people diagnosed with schizophrenia
- Parent training to effect positive change in children with oppositional behavior
- Systematic desensitization for treating specific phobias
- Token economy programs for treating a wide variety of undesirable behaviors

Many treatment systems, including person-centered counseling, psychoanalysis, and existential therapy, do not appear on this list. This does not mean that they are ineffective. Rather, because their application varies so widely and because they use few specific intervention strategies, empirical research on their effectiveness and replication of treatment procedures is extremely difficult.

These findings about treatment efficacy have made an important contribution to the fields of counseling and psychotherapy, not only in identifying successful approaches but in clarifying how little clinicians know with any certainty. Therefore, both novice and experienced clinicians are encouraged to keep up to date on the rapidly growing body of literature on treatment effectiveness so that they can have some confidence that they will be successful when developing treatment plans. Suggestions for sources of information to facilitate treatment planning for a broad range of mental disorders appear in the "Recommended Readings" section at the end of this chapter.

MANAGED CARE AND THIRD-PARTY PAYERS

Managed care, health maintenance organizations (HMOs), and related models for delivery of health care services have grown rapidly in the United States. The number of people covered by HMOs, for example, increased from 3 million in 1970 to more than 53 million in the 1990s (DeLeon & VandenBos, 1991).

Managed care organizations and other third-party payers that provide insurance coverage for counseling and psychotherapy exert a considerable influence over the treatment process. This influence has both strengths and weaknesses. The growth of managed care has led clinicians to place greater emphasis on accurate diagnosis, goal setting, and development of treatment plans that are likely to be both effective and efficient. On the other hand, constraints imposed by managed care organizations have sometimes made it difficult for people to afford and obtain the mental health services they genuinely need.

Although current trends suggest that managed care organizations may well become better controlled and more user-friendly in the 21st century, they will almost certainly influence mental health treatment for the foreseeable future. Clinicians, then, have the dual responsibility of addressing the requirements of managed care while continuing to advocate for the best treatment for their clients. Although compromises sometimes need to be made, clinicians should keep the needs of their clients uppermost in their minds and realize that taking an active role in dealing with managed care often can make a positive difference for both clients and clinicians.

TREATMENT SETTINGS

The setting in which treatment occurs is another important influence on the process of counseling and psychotherapy. Treatment programs typically limit the range of clients and problems they address. In addition, they may set guidelines for the number and frequency of sessions and even determine the treatment system used. Counseling in a high school, for example, will differ greatly from psychotherapy in a private practice specializing in treating people who have survived abuse or in an inpatient program treating people with severe depression or psychotic disorders.

Clinicians, of course, must be aware of the guidelines and requirements of the settings in which they practice, although their primary responsibility is to provide clients with the services they need. Careful selection of employment and practice settings is important in helping clinicians accomplish that goal. They should choose a setting that is compatible with their theoretical orientation, serves the types of clients with whom they want to work, and whose first priority is providing effective treatment to clients.

SKILL DEVELOPMENT: TERMINATION

The final skill presented in this book is the process of terminating psychotherapy or counseling with a client. Done well, the process can solidify the gains of treatment, promote further growth, leave clients with positive feelings about their successful therapy and their contributions to that process, and give clinicians a sense of pride and accomplishment. On the other hand, negative terminations can leave both clients and clinicians with unanswered questions and unfinished business as well as feelings of anger, frustration, and disappointment.

Termination typically occurs in one of three ways:

1. *Clinician's choice.* Clinicians may be leaving the agency, retiring from practice, or making another life change that necessitates ending treatment with some or all of their clients.
2. *Client's choice.* Clients, too, may be relocating, meaning that they must end treatment. They may also decide to leave treatment because they do not view the process as beneficial or cannot afford the cost of treatment. They may discuss their intent to end treatment with the clinician or may simply cancel an appointment and decide not to reply to any telephone messages from the clinician.
3. *Mutual agreement.* Usually, termination by mutual agreement occurs when clients and clinicians both believe that a client has made good progress toward goals and is ready to stop treatment, at least temporarily. Occasionally, clients and clinicians may both agree that treatment is not working and that a client would be more likely to benefit from another clinician or approach to treatment.

The first two types of termination are usually premature, requiring treatment to end before clients have made sufficient progress toward their goals. This sort of ending is, of course, likely to be more difficult for both client and clinician than a mutually agreed-on termination is. The following guidelines can facilitate the process of premature termination:

1. If possible, allow time to process the termination of treatment. Clinicians who are ending treatment should allow their clients a minimum of three weeks to talk about their reactions to that process. Clients who unilaterally decide to stop treatment may be reluctant to return for a series of sessions but be willing to come in for one wrap-up session or at least to talk about their decision by telephone.

2. Expect a variety of surprising client reactions. When initially informed that a clinician must end treatment, clients usually show little emotion. Over time, however, anger at the clinician may emerge, perhaps along with some sense of relief that clients may be able to avoid addressing their concerns further. Clients who initiate termination early may well feel disappointed and angry with what they perceive as the failure of the treatment process. However, sometimes they are quite contented with what they have learned from treatment and simply do not realize that it might be beneficial to engage in a planned and gradual termination. Clinicians should allow space and time for clients to talk about their reactions to ending treatment, perhaps mentioning common reactions if clients have difficulty expressing or identifying their feelings.

3. Expect a variety of surprising clinician reactions. Clinicians are, of course, human and may feel annoyed or angry with clients who terminate treatment suddenly and without explanation. Clinicians may feel sad at the end of treatment, regret not being able to continue helping their clients, or feel sorry that they will not have further contact with people with whom they have developed a rewarding therapeutic alliance. They may feel guilty about leaving their clients or failing to meet the needs of clients who have ended treatment prematurely. It is also common for clinicians to feel relief that they will no longer have to work with particularly contentious and difficult clients.Clinicians should take time to become aware of their own feelings about termination, perhaps discussing them with a colleague or supervisor and trying to use

them as a learning experience. Of course, expression of any of these feelings to clients should be done with great care and thought, if at all.

4. Ask clients for feedback about the treatment process, especially if they have initiated the termination. Many clients have great difficulty saying anything that sounds critical to their therapists, so clinicians may have to work especially hard to obtain meaningful suggestions for change. Sometimes asking clients to identify both the most beneficial aspect of treatment and one change they would have made in the treatment process can help them overcome their reluctance to express any reservations. Clinicians should try to keep an open mind, listening for suggestions that may be beneficial to future clients but also putting into perspective the complaints of one unhappy client.

5. Try to leave clients with positive feelings about the treatment process and themselves. Review accomplishments with clients, being sure to underscore gains and help clients take credit for those gains. Remind them that although they might currently feel finished with treatment, you and your agency are available to help in the future. Offer referrals if clients seem to need sources of help other than what you can offer.

Many of these guidelines are also relevant for mutually agreed-on terminations, although some changes and additions are likely. Attention should be paid to both clients' and clinicians' reactions to the end of treatment; again, expect surprises. Clients sometimes feel angry or abandoned as, occasionally, do clinicians, even though both agree that treatment has been beneficial and the time has come to end treatment. Clinicians should request feedback, eliciting clients' thoughts about both the strengths and weaknesses of treatment.

Identifying and solidifying gains that clients have made in treatment can be particularly rewarding for both clients and clinicians. Writing down clients' accomplishments is reinforcing and provides them with a record of their successes. Clients should direct the process of listing achievements as much as possible. The clinician might take on the task of writing down the items on the list as the client mentions them. Clinicians can also help clients identify their gains by reminding them of their initial treatment goals and facilitating clients' efforts to describe their successes in specific terms.

Clients rarely recall or think of all the successes they have had in treatment; so once they have run out of items to add to the list, clinicians can suggest other gains that they believe clients have made. Before writing down an item, the clinician should discuss it with the client to be sure he or she does perceive it as a gain and that it is presented in language that is meaningful to the client.

Clinicians might also engage clients in formulating a list of goals they have for themselves now that treatment has ended. Identifying initial steps toward accomplishing those goals can help clients maintain the forward momentum they have developed through treatment.

CASE ILLUSTRATION

The concluding case illustrates the termination process with Edie.

Clinician: Edie, we agreed that next week would be our last scheduled treatment session, although, of course, you can contact me again in the future if you believe that some additional sessions might be useful to you.

Edie: I'm glad to know that; but as we discussed, I feel I have really made progress through my work with you, and I am ready to be launched . . . to try to put into practice all I have learned here.

Clinician: That makes sense. Last week I suggested that we spend this session listing the accomplishments you have made through treatment. I encouraged you to think about what you might put on that list. How did that go?

Edie: I didn't actually write anything down, but I have been thinking about it. The more I think, the more things I come up with for the list.

Clinician: How about if I write them down while you tell me what you've come up with?

Edie: Fine. Well, my mood is certainly much better. We saw the numbers come down on that depression inventory you gave me, and I can tell the difference. I feel more cheerful and optimistic, I certainly don't have any thoughts of suicide, I'm sleeping better, and I don't feel so guilty about any little thing that I don't do perfectly.

Clinician: Sounds like you are seeing many signs of the change in your mood.

Edie: Yes, it really feels great. You know, sometimes I got so bogged down in depression, I didn't even know I was depressed; but I can really tell the difference. Another important change is in my relationship with Roberto. I see lots of improvement.

Clinician: What are the signs of improvement?

Edie: I look forward to seeing him, we go out together and really enjoy ourselves, . . . we've even resumed a sexual relationship. I used to blow up at him all the time. I can't say he never ticks me off, but now I can just tell him and he seems to listen to me and to be concerned. And Ava and I are doing better too.

Clinician: What are you doing to make that happen?

Edie: Before, I was always after her about something. . . . Remember to do your homework; don't forget your lunch money; be sure to get home for dinner. What I thought was expressing my love was really driving her away and giving her the message that I didn't have any confidence in her. Now I can see that she's really pretty responsible. Of course, she still needs my help; but now, instead of nagging, I can put some of that energy into doing something fun with her. Last week she and I went to this place where you paint unfinished pottery; together we painted a coffee cup and a snack plate for Roberto's birthday. We both really enjoyed making a special gift for him.

Clinician: So things at home are much better in many ways. How about with your mother and stepfather?

Edie: They're still the same. Not much change there.

Clinician: How about in your interactions with them and your thoughts and feelings about them?

Edie: Yes, some changes there. I'm more able to tell my mother what's on my mind in a way that she can hear without getting angry. We don't see eye to eye about my stepfather, but at least we can listen to each other and agree to disagree. Mom has started to spend time with Ava, taking her out for lunch or ice cream, and that seems good for both of them.

Clinician: Let's look back at our initial goals to see if that reminds you of any other gains. One of your goals was to blame yourself less for the abuse you experienced and to distance yourself more from that experience. You rated your level of self-blame as an 8 out of 10. Any changes in this area?

Edie: Yes. I didn't remember that I had rated that so high. I still have twinges of guilt about the abuse, but I'd say the rating is down to 3 or 4. And the same has happened with my reactions to having been diagnosed with cancer. I know it happened to me, and it was awful; but it seems like a long time ago. I don't worry much about a recurrence, at least not like I used to, and I don't worry so much that every little thing I do is going to cause the cancer to return.

Clinician: So you've made real progress there. How about in distancing yourself from the abuse?

Edie: That eye movement work we did really seemed to make a difference. I remember what happened to me, and I'll never forget it; but it doesn't seem like a raw wound anymore . . . and I can see that it wasn't my fault, I did the best I could.

Clinician: So your perceptions of that experience have really changed, and it does seem more distant for you. Are there other changes you can think of?

Edie: I guess I'm managing work a little better, feeling less overwhelmed; but I still don't have as much balance in my life as I would like.

Clinician: How about starting another list of goals that you would like to work on after we have finished our sessions?

Edie: Yes, that sounds good. More balance is one.

Clinician: How would you start to work toward that goal?

Edie: I bring work home too often. And I don't allow enough time to get some exercise. Those are two changes I could make.

Clinician: I'll jot those down for you. You might think about future goals that you have for yourself, and we can talk further about those in our last session, which will be next week. Let's take another look at your current list of achievements. One possible accomplishment I've heard you talk about is developing friendships. I remember your talking about feeling very isolated and lonely when you began treatment, and now you have two women friends you really seem to like. What do you think about that as an accomplishment?

Edie: Yes, definitely. I forgot about that. I'll never be the life of the party, but I do feel better about my social skills; and I have been spending time with Bettie and Merle, who both seem to enjoy my company.

Clinician: So that is another area of accomplishment. I'll give you a copy of this list so you can review it and see if you have any further additions. Before we wrap up for today, I wanted to ask you for some feedback about our work together. What has been particularly helpful, and what might you have liked to be different?

Edie: I don't know. It's all been useful.

Clinician: Can you pinpoint a few specific aspects of our work together that stand out in your mind?

Edie: Teaching me how to change my thoughts when they didn't make any sense was helpful. I use that a lot. And the work on developing my social skills. Also the egogram and the Myers-Briggs helped me understand myself and Roberto better and to be more accepting of some of our differences. I guess I always felt you never gave up on me; you always had a plan to help me, and you really seemed to care about me.

Clinician: I'm glad to hear that so many aspects of our work together were helpful. I would also like to hear about any weaknesses. Perhaps you can identify one or two ways in which our work could have been improved.

Edie: Well, I didn't like that book you gave me to read on assertiveness. It made me feel that I should turn into some other person. It's just not who I am.

Clinician: So that book wasn't right for you. I'm glad you could tell me that. What other changes would you suggest?

Edie: Once I called you when I was very upset. I guess I didn't tell you how upset I was, but it took you three hours to return my call. I felt angry about that.

This session illustrates three of the important procedures in the termination process: listing and reinforcing the client's accomplishments during treatment, identifying future goals and initial steps toward them, and eliciting both positive and negative feedback on the treatment process. Although the clinician gives direction and structure to the process, the client plays the more active role as she prepares to leave treatment. As this dialogue shows, termination is an important of the treatment process. It can be rewarding to both client and clinician and continue the process of positive change.

Exercises

Large-Group Exercises

1. Discuss the impact that the growth of managed care has had on the fields of counseling and psychotherapy. How do you anticipate that managed care will affect treatment in the 21st century? What can you do to work successfully with managed care?
2. Although diagnosis of mental disorders has become an essential skill for clinicians, many have mixed feelings about that process. Discuss the benefits and drawbacks of making diagnoses. What can you do to ensure that your use of diagnosis will be helpful to your clients?
3. Many widely used approaches to counseling and psychotherapy have not been empirically validated. What impact does this seem likely to have on our profession? What do you think should be done about this? What impact will this have on your work and the treatment systems you plan to use?

4. Edie and Roberto come from very different backgrounds. Edie grew up in a middle-class, white, Jewish family, living in the suburbs, while Roberto grew up in a lower-middle-class Roman Catholic Latino family, living in an urban area. These differences in their backgrounds inevitably affect both the expectations and interactions in their marriage and their attitudes toward counseling. Discuss the following:
   • How would you go about understanding and addressing the impact of their background differences on both their marriage and their treatment?
   • What might be the nature and impact of their differences on their marriage and the treatment process?

Small-Group Exercises

1. Form into your groups of four students. You have probably been working together throughout the semester and have learned a great deal about each other. Drawing on the information provided earlier in this chapter about the characteristics of an effective clinician, collaborate in developing a list of at least three clinical strengths for each member of the group. To make the feedback particularly meaningful, identify experiences in your group in which each of those strengths was evident.

2. In your small groups, each participant should describe to the group two ways in which he or she could develop better clinical skills. Supportive suggestions can be offered by the group members, but remember to emphasize strengths as the group moves toward closure.

3. Each person in the small group belongs to many other groups based on age, gender, family and socioeconomic status, occupation, race, ethnic and cultural background, place of residence, and other factors. Each person should take 5–10 minutes to describe some of the groups with which they affiliate and discuss the impact one or two of these groups have had on his or her view of the world.

Individual Exercises

1. Review the information provided earlier in this chapter on developing a positive therapeutic alliance and on the clinician characteristics that contribute to this alliance. Think about yourself as a clinician. What ways of fostering a therapeutic alliance come easily to you, and which present a challenge? Write about this in your journal. Identify one skill you can work on to improve your ability to foster a positive therapeutic alliance. Write down this skill and list several steps you can take to move toward improvement.

2. List some of the important perspectives or viewpoints you would bring with you if you were a client. Write briefly about how you would like a clinician to adapt treatment to meet your needs. What can you learn from this about your own work as a clinician?

3. Conduct your own termination process. List your gains or accomplishments this semester, giving specific examples whenever possible. Then list at least three professional goals you have for yourself and identify the initial steps you can take toward meeting those goals.

SUMMARY

This chapter has reviewed contexts for treatment that have an impact on the choice of treatment systems and strategies as well as the success of the therapeutic process. Contexts considered include the characteristics and treatment roles of the clinician, the characteristics and treatment roles of the client, the therapeutic alliance, the multiple perspectives of a diverse clientele, the diagnoses and problems presented by clients, the impact of third-party payers, and the treatment setting. In addition, this chapter presented the skill of terminating treatment, as illustrated by the case example.

RECOMMENDED READINGS

American Psychiatric Association. (1994). *The diagnostic and statistical manual of mental disorders* (DSM-IV). Washington, DC: American Psychiatric Press.

Gabbard, G. O. (Ed.). (1995). *Treatments of psychiatric disorders.* Washington, DC: American Psychiatric Press.

Ivey, A. E., Ivey, M. B., & Simek-Morgan, L. (1997). *Counseling and psychotherapy: A multicultural perspective.* Needham Heights, MA: Allyn & Bacon.

Seligman, L. (1996). *Diagnosis and treatment planning in counseling* (2nd ed.). New York: Plenum.

Seligman, L. (1998). *Selecting effective treatments* (2nd ed.). San Francisco: Jossey-Bass.

Chapter 26

CHOOSING AN EFFECTIVE TREATMENT APPROACH

This concluding chapter is intended to help you choose treatment systems that suit you as a clinician and are likely to be successful in treating a given person. Combining this information with what you have already learned about systems and strategies of counseling and psychotherapy as well as contexts of treatment should help you answer Paul's (1967) critical question: "*What* treatment, by *whom*, is most effective for *this* individual with *that* specific problem under *which* set of circumstances?" (p. 111).

COMMON FACTORS IN EFFECTIVE TREATMENT

This chapter includes the following five sections:

1. Discussion of the common factors of effective counseling and psychotherapy
2. Comparison of treatment systems discussed in this book
3. Skill development: identifying your preferred clinical approach
4. Exercises, including case studies with accompanying questions to guide choice of treatment approach
5. Information on future directions in systems and strategies of counseling and psychotherapy

Research and clinical experience increasingly confirm the existence of common factors in counseling and psychotherapy: overriding characteristics associated with successful treatment regardless of clinician or theoretical orientation. Chapter 25 considered desirable characteristics of the treatment context, including clinician and client variables. This chapter focuses on other commonalities in effective treatment.

The Hanna and Ritchie Study

In a study of the ingredients of psychotherapeutic change, Hanna and Ritchie (1995) identified three factors as necessary and sufficient for clients to change:

1. Acquiring insight and new understanding
2. Facing up to and confronting problems
3. Developing new perceptions or views of one's stressors and problems

That study indicated that the following factors are also strongly associated with client change:

- Exerting effort and persistence in addressing difficulties
- A belief that change is a necessity
- Willingness to experience anxiety or other types of discomfort to achieve eventual treatment benefits
- Prior negative and troubling emotions
- Warmth and support from another person

Notice that many of these factors are reflected in the four major areas of focus in the book. The acquisition of insight is emphasized in treatment systems that emphasize background (Part 2). Emotions (Part 3) are an important part of the treatment process because experiencing some uncomfortable feelings before and during treatment, as well as feeling supported during treatment, increase the likelihood of later gains. Thoughts (Part 4) are reflected by the importance of thinking that treatment is necessary and in developing new perceptions of problems. Finally, actions (Part 5) are reflected in the importance of confronting problems and exerting effort or will to change.

Additional Research

The research and thinking of Lambert (1992) and Lambert and Bergin (1994) on common factors accounting for client improvement yielded results that are similar to those found by Hanna and Ritchie. Lambert and Bergin identified three common factors:

1. Support factors, including a positive, reassuring, and trusting therapeutic alliance and a clinician who communicates warmth, respect, empathy, genuineness, and acceptance
2. Learning factors, including changes in thinking and perceptions, advice, acquisition of insight, corrective emotional experiences, and increased self-acceptance and expectations for personal effectiveness
3. Action factors, including an expectation for positive change, improving behavioral regulation, reality testing, modeling, practicing, completing homework tasks, suggesting, confronting fears and problems, processing, working through, and having success experiences

In Lambert and Bergin's framework, as in Hanna and Ritchie's, emotions, thoughts, and actions all play essential roles in the process of successful treatment.

Frank and Frank (1991, pp. 42–44) suggested that the common factors include:

1. An emotionally involving, confiding relationship with a helping person
2. A healing setting that provides safety and other characteristics associated with the helping process
3. A rationale that provides a plausible explanation for the client's problems and symptoms
4. A ritual or procedure for change that requires the active participation of both client and clinician

Kleinke (1994) offered yet another perspective, suggesting that treatment encompasses five common therapeutic goals:

1. Overcoming demoralization and gaining hope
2. Enhancing mastery and self-efficacy
3. Overcoming avoidance

4. Accepting life's realities
5. Achieving insight. (p. viii)

A great deal of attention has been paid during the 1990s to identifying important commonalties in successful treatment. Grencavage and Norcross (1990) conducted a particularly thorough study that proposed a total of 89 commonalities. Their analysis of many publications revealed that the most consensual commonalities were clients' positive expectations for treatment and a facilitative therapeutic relationship.

In sum, all these studies have succinctly synthesized the research on commonalities in treatment. Clinicians can now have a clear vision of the kind of therapeutic relationship that is most likely to lead to a positive outcome.

Although the literature gives some guidance on the nature of the treatment interventions most likely to be facilitative (for example, those that encourage people to confront their difficulties and increase their sense of empowerment), it has not yet identified the specific strategies or treatment systems most likely to be successful. Clinicians still have the challenging task of identifying which treatment systems are most compatible with their own conceptions of effective treatment and most appropriate for use with their clients. The following sections of this chapter are designed to help clinicians make those choices.

OVERVIEW OF TREATMENT SYSTEMS

More than 300 approaches to counseling and psychotherapy have been identified. Of course, this book has not tried to present an exhaustive review of all of them. Rather, it has focused primarily on treatment systems that meet all or most of the following 10 criteria of sound theories:

1. The theories are clear, coherent, and easily communicated.
2. They are compatible with or can be adapted to include the therapeutic commonalities just discussed.
3. They encompass a concept of positive emotional development and health that can be used in setting goals and assessing progress.
4. They help clinicians organize and make sense of information.
5. They are comprehensive, explaining and addressing a broad range of concerns and disorders.
6. They give clinicians direction, steps, and guidelines for facilitating positive change.
7. They encompass strategies and interventions that grow out of and are consistent with the underlying theory.
8. They provide clinicians with a common language that facilitates treatment and collaboration.
9. They are widely used in practice and generate research; even if these approaches have not been conclusively validated by empirical research, the research is promising, and their widespread use or growing popularity suggest that clinicians find them beneficial to their clients.

10. They focus on individual counseling and psychotherapy. (Many of the approaches discussed in this book are also very useful for treatment of groups and families; however, I have not discussed treatment systems that focus primarily on groups and families rather than individuals.)

Figures 26–1—26–4 summarize the major treatment systems covered in this book, with the intent of helping readers increase their familiarity with these approaches, easily review treatment systems as needed, and more readily select appropriate treatment models for themselves and their clients. Emerging, eclectic, and integrated approaches are not included in the figures because they are not yet comprehensive and well-developed treatment systems.

Treatment systems emphasizing background

Psychoanalysis

Founder/major contributor: Sigmund Freud.

Area of focus: Background.

Underlying theory/view of change: Biology, drives, and early childhood experiences largely determine development. Making the unconscious conscious through analysis and interpretation promotes insight, reduces the influence of the past, and facilitates healthier choices.

Other important concepts:
   Id, ego, and superego comprise the personality.
   Psychosexual stages characterize development: oral, anal, phallic, latency, genital.
   There are three levels of consciousness: conscious, preconscious, unconscious.
   Dreams, mistakes, and symptoms reflect unconscious wishes.
   Defense mechanisms are important in understanding personality.

Treatment of background: Understanding the first five years of life is essential.

Treatment of emotions and sensations: Affect must accompany recall of unconscious material. Abreaction is important to change.

Treatment of thoughts: The ego is the thinking part of people and is important in the process of working through issues.

Treatment of actions and behavior: Actions are important largely as reflections of the unconscious.

Important strategies, techniques: Analysis and interpretation, transference, free association, working through.

Therapeutic alliance: Therapist remains relatively anonymous. Transference is encouraged and is integral to treatment.

Level of directiveness: Direction comes largely from the client, although the clinician keeps sessions on track.

FIGURE 26–1 Treatment systems emphasizing background

Growth- versus treatment-oriented: Treatment is the focus, but successful treatment leads to growth.

Client profile: Approach is primarily for people with "neurotic" disorders, not in crisis.

Attention to environment, diversity: There is some attention to context but little attention to diversity issues.

Emphasis on goals, treatment planning: Overall goal is improving ego functioning. Little specific attention is paid to goal setting and treatment planning.

Duration: Very lengthy.

Use of homework, tasks between sessions: Not important.

Extent of research validation: Limited.

Individual Psychology

Founder/major contributors: Alfred Adler, Rudolf Dreikurs.

Area of focus: Background.

Underlying theory/view of change: Heredity and upbringing are important, but people's own efforts to find meaning and success can be more powerful.

Other important concepts: Social interest is an essential part of healthy development.

Treatment of background: Treatment involves extensive analysis of earliest recollections, family constellation, birth order, role in family, childhood experiences.

Treatment of emotions and sensations: Particular attention is paid to feelings of encouragement/discouragement, competence/ inferiority.

Treatment of thoughts: Individual perceptions and private logic are important areas of focus.

Treatment of actions and behavior: Behavior is viewed as purposeful and reflecting goals and lifestyle.

Important strategies, techniques: Education; encouragement; discussion and analysis of dreams, earliest recollections, family constellation, lifestyle; acting as if; interpretation and use of hunches to promote insight.

Therapeutic alliance: Clinicians are educators and role models as well as therapists; they encourage cooperation, mutual trust, and respect.

Level of directiveness: Collaboration with client is important.

Growth- versus treatment-oriented: Can be both, but Adler emphasized growth.

Client profile: Appropriate for a broad range of clients, including children, adults, couples and people with most of the common mental disorders.

Attention to environment, diversity: Social interest and social context receive considerable attention, as do people with disabilities.

Emphasis on goals, treatment planning: Shared goal setting is important.

continued

Duration: Traditionally lengthy but flexible.

Use of homework, tasks between sessions: Very important for learning.

Extent of research validation: Limited, more needed.

Analytical Psychology

Founder/major contributor: Carl Jung.

Area of focus: Background.

Underlying theory/view of change: Development is determined by not only early experiences in our own lives but innate archetypes in the unconscious. Through analysis of dreams, symbols, and other material as well as through regression, the unconscious can be brought into the conscious to promote balance, growth, and integration.

Other important concepts:
> The unconscious is a source of creativity and emotional growth as well as psychological difficulties.
> The composition of the psyche, including the persona, ego, anima/animus, archetypes, shadow, and personal and collective unconscious, are important to understanding this system.

Treatment of background: Both individual background and archetypes and ancestral background are very important.

Treatment of emotions and sensations: Catharsis is an important element, especially early in the treatment process.

Treatment of thoughts: Thoughts receive attention, and education is an important treatment component.

Treatment of actions and behavior: Actions receive attention when they seem to be signs of imbalance and lack of integration.

Important strategies, techniques: Catharsis, elucidation of meaning of symptoms and symbols, associations, analysis of dreams, education, use of myths and fairy tales.

Therapeutic alliance: Support, encouragement, and establishment of a collaborative therapeutic alliance is essential. Transference and counter transference are inevitable and should be used therapeutically.

Level of directiveness: The clinician is active and provides education and information, but collaboration is emphasized.

Growth- versus treatment-oriented: Growth-oriented.

Client profile: People with an imbalance in their functioning, spiritual concerns, or lack of integration. This approach is largely directed toward people not in crisis who have mild to moderate concerns and a great interest in personal growth.

Attention to environment, diversity: Social values and relationships are viewed as important. Little attention is paid to diversity, but emphasis on spirituality facilitates individuation of approach.

FIGURE 26–1   Continued

Emphasis on goals, treatment planning: Not important.

Duration: Lengthy.

Use of homework, tasks between sessions: Dreams and other material should be brought to sessions. Otherwise, not specified.

Extent of research validation: Very limited.

Other important information: Jung viewed the second half of life as a time of particular growth and creativity.

Developmental/Psychodynamic Psychotherapy

Founder/major contributors: Helene Deutsch, Karen Horney, Harry Stack Sullivan, Anna Freud, object relations theorists, Heinz Kohut.

Area of focus: Background.

Underlying theory/view of change: Early relationships are more important than drives; they provide the foundation for current relationships. Analysis and interpretation, linking past relationships to present ones, facilitate essential change and development of the ego.

Other important concepts:
 Internalization of an image of the childhood caregiver influences the self-image.
 The ego and relationships throughout life are important in development.
 Developmental patterns receive considerable attention.
 Several approaches provide new perspectives on women's development.

Treatment of background: Relationships and interactions during the very early years play a key role in development.

Treatment of emotions and sensations: Feelings about the self are important. Particular attention is paid to symptoms of depression and anxiety.

Treatment of thoughts: Some theorists are phenomenological, stressing the importance of people's ideas and perceptions.

Treatment of actions and behavior: Focus on behaviors is limited, although some attention is paid to styles of relating to others.

Important strategies, techniques: Analysis and interpretation are paramount.

Therapeutic alliance: Transference is emphasized, but so is collaboration. Clinicians emphasize communication of acceptance, support, and empathy.

Level of directiveness: Client and clinician collaborate whenever possible, although clinician guides the sessions.

Growth- versus treatment-oriented: Concerned with both alleviation of symptoms and personal and interpersonal growth.

Client profile: People with mood, anxiety, and personality disorders seem particularly well suited for these approaches. Motivation, commitment, and psychological-mindedness are likely to facilitate treatment.

continued

Attention to environment, diversity: There is little attention to diversity, but family and society are viewed as very important.

Emphasis on goals, treatment planning: Overriding goals include building ego strength, self-concept, and sound interpersonal relationships.

Duration: Lengthy.

Use of homework, tasks between sessions: Little specific mention but not excluded.

Extent of research validation: Research on attachment theory has lent some support to this treatment system but otherwise limited.

Transactional Analysis

Founder/major contributor: Eric Berne.

Area of focus: Background.

Underlying theory/view of change: The combination of education and awareness of the impact of childhood messages on current development are needed for change.

Other important concepts:
   Ego states
   Strokes and injunctions
   Stages of development
   Basic life positions
   Transactions
   Scripts
   Games and rackets

Treatment of background: Emphasis is placed on understanding messages received in the first five years of life.

Treatment of emotions and sensations: There is limited attention to emotions, although the basic life positions reflect feelings about the self and others and are important to understand.

Treatment of thoughts: Life scripts reflect cognitive conceptions of the self, others, and the world.

Treatment of actions and behavior: Some attention is paid to communication styles and patterns of behavior.

Important strategies, techniques: Analysis of transactions, egogram diagramming the ego states, education.

Therapeutic alliance: Collaboration and establishment of a contract are important.

Level of directiveness: Clinician is an educator and makes sure that treatment is productive, although collaboration is encouraged.

Growth-versus treatment-oriented: Both are emphasized.

Client profile: Ideal candidates are people who are psychologically-minded and interested in learning more about themselves. This treatment system can ameliorate mild to moderate concerns, improve self-esteem, and increase people's zest for life.

FIGURE 26-1   Continued

Attention to environment, diversity: Attention is paid to family messages, but attention to diversity is limited. This approach may not be appropriate for many people from non-western cultures.

Emphasis on goals, treatment planning: Contracts stating goals and procedures are formulated by client and clinician. Overall goals include increasing clients' spontaneity, awareness, autonomy, and capacity for intimacy.

Duration: Usually lengthy.

Use of homework, tasks between sessions: May be part of treatment but not emphasized.

Extent of research validation: Some studies demonstrate its value, especially with young people in educational settings.

Other important information: Useful in preventive work and treatment of individuals, groups, and families. Readily integrated with other treatment approaches, especially Gestalt therapy.

Brief Psychodynamic Psychotherapy

Founder/major contributors: Alexander and French, Davanloo, Klerman, Malan, Mann, Sifneos, Strupp.

Area of focus: Background.

Underlying theory/view of change: Problems stem from inability of the ego to suppress or moderate drives of the id. Change comes from awareness of the connection of the past to present patterns.

Other important concepts: Careful screening and selection of clients is essential.

Treatment of background: The past is very important, especially attachment to and separation from primary caregivers.

Treatment of emotions and sensations: Emotional release is an important part of treatment.

Treatment of thoughts: Secondary attention is paid to thoughts related to the focal concern.

Treatment of actions and behavior: Behaviors are viewed as reflecting underlying conflicts.

Important strategies, techniques: Identification of a focal concern, strengthening the ego, making the unconscious conscious, promoting awareness and insight, resolving conflicts, education on skill development.

Therapeutic alliance: Treatment should provide a corrective emotional experience. Some attention is paid to transference. Collaboration, support, and empathy are valued.

Level of directiveness: Relatively directive.

Growth-versus treatment-oriented: Both are emphasized.

Client profile: Relatively healthy and well-functioning people with focal relationship conflicts. Especially useful in treating depression.

Attention to environment, diversity: Limited. May not be appropriate for most people from nonwestern cultures.

continued

Emphasis on goals, treatment planning: Identification of focal concern and written statement of goals is essential. Overall goals include understanding and change in inner experience and development of improved relationships.

Duration: Medium length, usually three to six months.

Use of homework, tasks between sessions: Not essential.

Extent of research validation: Some strong evidence of effectiveness, especially the use of interpersonal psychotherapy (IPT) in treatment of depression.

FIGURE 26–1   Concluded.

Treatment systems emphasizing emotions

Person-Centered Counseling

Founder/major contributor: Carl Rogers.

Area of focus: Emotions.

Underlying theory/view of change: A climate of acceptance and unconditional positive regard promotes self-esteem and facilitates client growth.

Other important concepts: Theory is phenomenological and humanistic.

Treatment of background: This approach recognizes that childhood messages shape attitudes, emotions, and behavior but believes that the negative impact of those messages can be overcome through the therapeutic alliance and the positive messages of the clinician.

Treatment of emotions and sensations: Great importance is placed on eliciting and exploring emotions as well as communicating empathy.

Treatment of thoughts: Thoughts are viewed as resulting from past experiences and perceptions.

Treatment of actions and behavior: Behaviors are viewed as resulting from past experiences and perceptions.

Important strategies, techniques: Techniques are deemphasized, but the approach does use acceptance, reflection, and empathy.

Therapeutic alliance: It is essential for clinicians to communicate genuineness, congruence, acceptance, caring, and empathy and to establish conditions in treatment that will facilitate growth.

Level of directiveness: Low; advocates principled nondirectiveness.

Growth- versus treatment-oriented: Growth-oriented.

Client profile: Ideal candidates are relatively healthy people not in crisis who have difficulties in relation to fulfillment, self-esteem, actualization, and relationships.

FIGURE 26–2   Treatment systems emphasizing emotions

Attention to environment, diversity: Approach emphasizes people's differences and commonalities as well as the importance of respecting their perceptions and values.

Emphasis on goals, treatment planning: Overriding goals include promoting feelings of power and competence and encouraging people to become fully functioning, move toward self-actualization, and respect themselves and others. Specific treatment planning is de-emphasized.

Duration: Flexible, depending on the needs of the client. Typically medium length.

Use of homework, tasks between sessions: Rarely used.

Extent of research validation: Core conditions of the therapeutic alliance have received considerable support, but minimal empirical support is available for the overall approach.

Existential Therapy

Founder/major contributors: Victor Frankl, Rollo May, Irvin Yalom, Abraham Maslow, and others.

Area of focus: Emotions.

Underlying theory/view of change: Through treatment and a positive therapeutic alliance, people can be helped to face the uncertainties of life, gain awareness, and make responsible choices that create meaning and fulfillment in their lives.

Other important concepts:
   People always have choices.
   People need to face the inherent meaninglessness of life, the inevitability of death, and existential aloneness.

Treatment of background: The early years are recognized as formative and usually are discussed, but in relation to existential concerns.

Treatment of emotions and sensations: Depression as well as existential guilt and anxiety are common symptoms addressed through this approach.

Treatment of thoughts: Thoughts about meaning and values are explored.

Treatment of actions and behavior: Behaviors are looked at in relation to the meaning in people's lives to determine whether the behavior is helping or hindering people's efforts to find fulfillment.

Important strategies, techniques: Symbolic growth experiences, paradoxical intention, dereflection, discussion designed to promote awareness.

Therapeutic alliance: This is an essential ingredient of this approach, which is viewed as a shared journey. Clinicians play an active role in sharing themselves and encouraging clients to value freedom, responsibility, authenticity, positive relationships, and self-actualization.

Level of directiveness: Collaboration is advocated, but clinicians do take a stance about what values are important.

continued

Growth- versus treatment-oriented: Strongly growth-oriented.

Client profile: Suitable for people who are open to new ideas and seeking greater meaning in their lives. This approach seems especially appropriate for people at a crossroads; who are dealing with losses, life-threatening illnesses, and limitations and disabilities; or who have longstanding underlying depression or anxiety.

Attention to environment, diversity: Social responsibility and the importance of the individual are emphasized.

Emphasis on goals, treatment planning: Goals include self-actualization, clarifying values and meaning, and establishing a deep connection with other people and the world. Treatment planning is not important.

Duration: Varies but often lengthy.

Use of homework, tasks between sessions: Not specifically addressed; up to the client.

Extent of research validation: Some research suggests the value of this model in helping people clarify their values and deal with adversity.

Gestalt Therapy

Founder/major contributors: Frederick (Fritz) Perls, Laura Perls.

Area of focus: Emotions and sensations.

Underlying theory/view of change: People need awareness and an inner sense of balance and wholeness to deal with the constant flux around them. Treatment enables them to bring needed closure, integrate polarities, and function more fully. The whole is greater than the sum of its parts.

Other important concepts:
  Figure-ground
  Ego boundary
  Unity of the mind and the body

Treatment of background: Very limited attention is paid to background; here-and-now is emphasized. Past issues are brought into the present to effect change.

Treatment of emotions and sensations: The focus of treatment, especially bodily sensations.

Treatment of thoughts: Little attention is paid to cognitions, although the importance of awareness of all aspects of the self is stressed.

Treatment of actions and behavior: Awareness of and taking responsibility for one's actions are important.

Important strategies, techniques: Promoting awareness and balance, use of language, dreamwork, integration of polarities, role play, empty chair, hot seat, fantasy trip.

Therapeutic alliance: Clinician creates a climate conducive to hope, trust, and awareness. Alliance is a partnership in which client takes the lead.

FIGURE 26–2 Continued

Level of directiveness: This varies; clinician doesn't interrupt as long as client is aware and fully present, although clinician may become quite directive when client is not working productively.

Growth- versus treatment-oriented: Both important, although growth is emphasized.

Client profile: Not for people who are severely disturbed. Suitable for many people with longstanding depression and anxiety, somatoform disorders, eating disorders, mild personality disorders and traits, physical disabilities.

Attention to environment, diversity: Interdependence and connection of people and environment are important. Emphasis is placed on individualizing the treatment to the specific person.

Emphasis on goals, treatment planning: Goals include helping people to live in the present, use their resources, bring closure to unfinished business, achieve integration and wholeness, develop self-esteem, become more self-actualized, and achieve meaningful contact with self and others. Experiments (specific exercises or strategies) are developed for each person.

Duration: Varies, usually medium length.

Use of homework, tasks between sessions: Essential component of treatment.

Extent of research validation: Limited.

Other important information: Treatment system is humanistic and phenomenological and is useful in group therapy.

FIGURE 26–2 Concluded

Treatment systems emphasizing thoughts

Cognitive Therapy

Founder/major contributor: Aaron Beck.

Area of focus: Thoughts.

Underlying theory/view of change: People's difficulties are caused by distorted thinking. Analysis and modification of cognitions will lead to changes in emotions and behavior.

Other important concepts: People have levels of distorted cognitions, including automatic thoughts, intermediate beliefs, core beliefs, and schemas.

Treatment of background: Attention is paid as needed, especially in people with longstanding disorders. Enough information is gathered to make an accurate diagnosis.

continued

FIGURE 26–3 Treatment systems emphasizing thoughts

Treatment of emotions and sensations: Emotions and sensations are explored and their intensity rated. However, they are considered primarily in relation to thoughts.

Treatment of thoughts: Thoughts are the focus of treatment and the vehicle for effecting change.

Treatment of actions and behavior: Some attention is paid to behaviors to understand clients fully. However, behaviors are considered primarily in relation to thoughts.

Important strategies, techniques: This treatment system includes a wide variety of useful strategies including questioning, identification and reality-testing of thoughts, categorization of distorted cognitions, modification of thoughts, guided discovery, experiments, affirmations, cognitive rehearsal, and others.

Therapeutic alliance: A collaborative therapeutic alliance is essential to treatment. Clinicians are expected to demonstrate the core conditions, including empathy, concern, and congruence.

Level of directiveness: This is a structured approach; clinicians take an active role in planning and implementing treatment.

Growth- versus treatment-oriented: Treatment is emphasized, but growth is also important and stems from learning skills that people can use after treatment has ended.

Client profile: Suitable for a broad range of clients, particularly people coping with depression and anxiety.

Attention to environment, diversity: Little specific attention to environment and diversity, but the respectful, nonintrusive nature of this approach makes it suitable for a wide range of clients.

Emphasis on goals, treatment planning: Both are viewed as important. The overriding goals are to help people think clearly and cope effectively with their lives.

Duration: Short, usually 4–14 sessions, with extended follow-up.

Use of homework, tasks between sessions: Task assignments are essential.

Extent of research validation: Extensive validation is available, especially on the approach's effectiveness in the treatment of depression.

Rational Emotive Behavior Therapy (REBT)

Founder/major contributor: Albert Ellis.

Area of focus: Thoughts.

Underlying theory/view of change: Irrational beliefs are the source of people's disturbances. Changing those thoughts to rational beliefs will result in positive changes in emotions and behaviors.

FIGURE 26–3 Continued

Other important concepts:
   People have inborn drives toward both self-actualization and irrational thinking.
   Helping people take responsibility for their thoughts is important in treatment.

Treatment of background: Although life experiences are believed to combine with innate predispositions to determine how people think and act, treatment generally pays little attention to a client's history.

Treatment of emotions and sensations: Awareness of emotions, especially the underlying anxiety that usually accompanies disturbances, is important. However, emotions are believed to result from thoughts, viewed as the route to changing emotions.

Treatment of thoughts: Thoughts are the focus of treatment.

Treatment of actions and behavior: Actions are viewed as a secondary focus. They are used as targets of change and task assignments and provide a useful reflection of progress.

Important strategies, techniques: ABCDEF model for identifying, disputing, and modifying irrational beliefs; strategies for disputing beliefs; wide variety of other cognitive, behavioral, and affective strategies.

Therapeutic alliance: Collaboration and client responsibility are emphasized.

Level of directiveness: Clinicians are relatively directive and do not hesitate to use persuasion, self-disclosure, and humor to facilitate client change.

Growth- versus treatment-oriented: General REBT seeks to alleviate symptoms, while elegant REBT aims toward growth.

Client profile: People who are intelligent, articulate, pragmatic, logical, and tough-minded are likely to respond well. This approach is probably useful in treating people with disabilities and those with mild to moderate mental disorders.

Attention to environment, diversity: Social interest is viewed as an important aspect of mental health. However, caution should be exercised in using this sometimes forceful approach with people from culturally diverse backgrounds, especially those from nonwestern countries.

Emphasis on goals, treatment planning: Overall goals include helping people think rationally, move toward self-actualization, and enjoy their lives. Attention to treatment planning and establishment of specific goals is limited.

Duration: Relatively brief but flexible. Extended follow-up often used.

Use of homework, tasks between sessions: Task assignments are essential.

Extent of research validation: Considerable research validation demonstrates that, in general, REBT is superior to no treatment.

Other important information: Useful in individual, group, and family counseling; with children and adults; and for psychoeducation as well as treatment.

FIGURE 26–3 Concluded

Treatment systems emphasizing actions

Behavior Therapy and Cognitive Behavior Therapy

Founder/major contributors: Early contributors include Pavlov, Skinner, Watson, Wolpe, Dollard and Miller, Bandura, and others. Donald Meichenbaum developed cognitive-behavior modification.

Area of focus: Actions.

Underlying theory/view of change: All behavior is learned. Negative behaviors therefore can be unlearned, while new and more effective behaviors can be learned.

Other important concepts: Thoughts and emotions stem from behaviors.

Treatment of background: Actions should be viewed in context. Consequently, some exploration of background is important.

Treatment of emotions and sensations: Depression and anxiety are common targets of behavior therapy. Assessment of subjective units of distress is important in gauging progress.

Treatment of thoughts: In cognitive behavior therapy, thoughts receive considerable attention.

Treatment of actions: Actions are the focus of treatment. Identification, assessment, and modification of dysfunctional behaviors as well as the learning of new behaviors and skills are the essence of this system.

Important strategies, techniques: A broad range of strategies is used, including education, skill development, systematic desensitization, activity scheduling, relaxation, modeling, hypnosis, acting as if, and reinforcement, as well as many others.

Therapeutic alliance: Collaboration and active involvement of both client and clinician are essential.

Level of directiveness: Clinician suggests tasks and interventions, but the client has primary responsibility.

Growth- versus treatment-oriented: Primarily treatment-oriented; but education and skill development, as well as generalization of learning, contribute to growth.

Client profile: Useful in treating almost any person or problem, although the approach may need to be combined with medication or another treatment system. Especially useful for people presenting problems of depression or anxiety.

Attention to environment, diversity: This approach recognizes the importance of context but pays little specific attention to client diversity. However, the treatment system is not usually intrusive or threatening, so it may be a good choice for people from a wide variety of backgrounds.

Emphasis on goals, treatment planning: Establishing specific and measurable goals and a clear treatment plan are integral parts of this approach.

Duration: Usually relatively brief (12–15 sessions), although extended follow-up is common and the approach is flexible in length.

Use of homework, tasks between sessions: Homework and practice of new skills are important elements in treatment.

FIGURE 26–4   Treatment systems emphasizing actions

Extent of research validation: Extensive research validation is available, demonstrating a wide variety of positive benefits and no problems with symptom substitution.

Other important information: This treatment system is effective with children, adolescents, and adults and can be used in group and family settings.

Reality Therapy

Founder/major contributors: William Glasser, Robert Wubbolding.

Area of focus: Actions.

Underlying theory/view of change: People are self-determining and choose everything, including their thoughts, actions, and emotions. Treatment is designed to help people make responsible and realistic choices that are likely to meet their basic needs.

Other important concepts:
Five basic needs (belonging, power/achievement, fun/enjoyment, freedom/independence, survival)
Quality world
No excuses
Total behavior
Importance of awareness
Emphasis on respecting the rights of other people to pursue fulfillment of their needs

Treatment of background: Problems are believed to originate in childhood but are best resolved by focusing on the present.

Treatment of emotions and sensations: Emotions are not targeted directly. Change in emotions results from changes in thoughts and actions.

Treatment of thoughts: This approach is phenomenological; people's beliefs and ideas are important and considered in treatment.

Treatment of actions and behavior: Behaviors are usually the focus of treatment and perceived as more amenable to change than thoughts and emotions are.

Important strategies, techniques: WDEP, SAMI2C3, paradoxical intention, positive addiction, questions, metaphors, caring confrontation, natural consequences, evaluation of own total behavior, other creative interventions.

Therapeutic alliance: Establishing a collaborative alliance is very important. Clinicians are encouraged to get involved with clients, become their ally, and never give up.

Level of directiveness: Clinician has considerable responsibility for the direction and success of the treatment.

Growth-versus treatment-oriented: Growth and process are more important than treatment and results, although all receive attention.

Client profile: This approach is useful for people with mild to moderate concerns, especially conduct disorders, oppositional defiant disorders, substance use disorders, and mood and anxiety disorders. It also is likely to be helpful to people coping with physical disabilities and those from nonwestern cultural backgrounds.

continued

Attention to environment, diversity: Treatment system emphasizes the importance of people's having a role in society. Clinicians seek to understand people's world views and adapt treatment to the individual.

Emphasis on goals, treatment planning: Identification of goals is important in effective treatment planning. However, process is more important than product.

Duration: Flexible, typically medium length.

Use of homework, tasks between sessions: Homework is an important component.

Extent of research validation: A substantial body of research supporting reality therapy is accumulating. Its use in school settings is particularly well substantiated.

Other important information: Useful for group and family treatment.

Brief Solution-Based Therapy

Founder/major contributors: Steve de Shazer, Bill O'Hanlon, Michele Weiner-Davis.

Area of focus: Actions.

Underlying theory/view of change: Small behavioral changes lead to larger changes that have ripple effects on the whole system.

Other important concepts:
   People's world views lead to their problems.
   People have the resources they need to solve their problems.

Treatment of background: Generally, little attention is paid to background and history.

Treatment of emotions and sensations: Actions are the route to changing emotions. Little direct attention is paid to emotions.

Treatment of thoughts: This approach is phenomenological, giving thoughts and perceptions some importance in the treatment process.

Treatment of actions and behavior: Behaviors are the focus of treatment. Changes in actions lead to changes in understanding and emotions.

Important strategies, techniques: Scaling questions, exceptions, the miracle question, presuppositional and other solution-based language, reinforcement, viewing problems as outside the person.

Therapeutic alliance: Collaboration is essential.

Level of directiveness: Clinician is responsible for suggesting tasks and determining interventions as well as for providing support and encouragement and maximizing client involvement in the treatment process.

Growth- versus treatment-oriented: Both are important. The focus is on current problems, but the treatment process enables people to become more confident and capable of solving future problems.

FIGURE 26-4   Continued

Client profile: This approach is ideal for people who are motivated, have solved past problems, and have some supportive relationships. It is best for treatment of mild to moderately severe disorders and problems, but success also has been reported in treatment of abuse and chronic and severe mental disorders.

Attention to environment, diversity: The clients' social systems are viewed as important. Although approach does not specifically address client diversity, it is respectful, nonintrusive, and empowering.

Emphasis on goals, treatment planning: Co-constructing specific, realistic, and measurable goals is important. Careful selection of interventions is also essential.

Duration: Usually fewer than 10 sessions but takes as long as needed to enable people to reach their goals. Schedule is very flexible, often including long intervals between sessions and extended follow-up.

Use of homework, tasks between sessions: Tasks are very important and are carefully planned and geared to client's level of motivation.

Extent of research validation: More case studies and descriptions of application available than empirical research, but strong support for this treatment system is emerging.

FIGURE 26–4 Concluded

FINDING YOUR PREFERRED CLINICAL STYLE

Readers who are relatively new to the fields of counseling and psychotherapy may view it as presumptuous or unrealistic to be asked to consider which clinical approach seems best for them. However, choosing and emulating a style of the masters is a good way to learn almost any skill. Even Picasso, generally regarded as one of the most creative and innovative artists of the 20th century, began his career as a representational artist, painting in the more traditional styles of the masters and only moving on to seek his own style after he had developed skills in the more established approaches to painting. In counseling and psychotherapy, acquiring some expertise in treatment systems that have established their value can provide a solid foundation for eventually developing your own eclectic or integrated approach or deciding to specialize in one or two established treatment systems.

Factors That Determine Style

Most clinicians find that their professional interests and ideas evolve as they gain experience, clarifying their theoretical orientations as they develop their skills. Many factors combine to determine clinicians' preferred theoretical approaches:

1. Theoretical approaches that are emphasized in clinicians' graduate training and modeled by their professors
2. Treatment systems advocated in clinicians' internship sites and first professional positions
3. Clinicians' personality, philosophy, and world views

Development of the Author's Style

My own development as a clinician has reflected the influence of all three factors. My initial training at Columbia University in the 1970s emphasized Carl Rogers's person-centered counseling. I quickly developed some skills in this approach, found it compatible with my belief in helping people reach their potential, and began to view myself as a person-centered clinician. However, this approach was often not appropriate for the types of clients I encountered in my internships at inpatient and outpatient mental health treatment programs under the auspices of the Veterans Administration.

Many of my clients had experienced war-related traumas and had a range of significant disorders, including schizophrenia, posttraumatic stress disorder, alcohol dependence, and major depressive disorder. My supervisor emphasized the value of psychodynamic approaches in working with these clients and modeled skills in psychodynamic treatment. Although I was glad to have competence in the fundamental skills of person-centered treatment, I next sought to develop my skills as a psychodynamic therapist.

My clinical experience since that time has included university counseling centers, drug rehabilitation programs, corrections, a treatment program for children and adolescents, and currently private practice. Exposure to this broad range of clients and treatment settings has given me the opportunity to find and develop the approach to treatment that seems to work best for me. Although psychodynamic thinking and person-centered attitudes and relationship skills continue to be important tools in my repertoire, my work has increasingly emphasized cognitive and behavioral approaches, reflecting my interest in offering treatment that is both efficient and empowering. In the past few years, I have incorporated into my work eye movement desensitization and reprocessing as well as narrative therapy and brief solution-based treatment. I anticipate that the evolution of my clinical style will continue throughout my career.

Questions to Help You Identify Your Style

Having studied many systems of counseling and psychotherapy, you may already have a preferred approach in mind. On the other hand, you may feel overwhelmed by the vast array of appealing choices. Responding to the following questions will help you determine the theoretical approach that now seems right for you.

Background Questions
1. What theoretical approaches have been emphasized in your training and modeled by your professors?

2. If you have been employed as a clinician, what treatment systems were advocated at your place(s) of employment?

3. If you have had the opportunity to receive counseling or psychotherapy yourself, what approaches did your clinician emphasize? How successful were those approaches in helping you?

Multiple-Choice Questions

The following questions are linked to Figures 26.1–26.4, which provide a comparative analysis of the major treatment systems reviewed in this book. For each item, choose the response that seems best to you.

1. Positive change can best be facilitated by
   a. Promoting insight, making the unconscious conscious
   b. Promoting awareness and expression of emotions
   c. Eliciting and modifying dysfunctional cognitions
   d. Facilitating change in self-destructive behaviors

2. The following strategies are most likely to make a difference in treatment:
   a. Analysis of transference, interpretation of dreams
   b. Reflection of feelings, focusing on sensations
   c. *ABCDEF* technique of rational emotive behavior therapy, visual imagery
   d. Systematic desensitization, reinforcement

3. Clinicians should
   a. Be relatively anonymous to facilitate transference
   b. Be genuine, warm, caring, and empathic, letting clients take the lead
   c. Build a positive therapeutic alliance, but take an active role in structuring sessions, planning treatment, and identifying dysfunctional thoughts
   d. Build a positive therapeutic alliance but set clear goals and limits, use caring confrontations, and natural consequences

4. Direction of treatment sessions
   a. Is unpredictable and determined largely by important unconscious factors
   b. Should be primarily up to the clients
   c. Should follow a clear plan for eliciting and modifying thoughts
   d. Should be determined by the establishment of clear, specific, and measurable goals

5. The primary goal(s) of treatment should be
   a. Eliciting unconscious material, promoting the working through of past experiences, and developing insight
   b. Promoting expression of feelings and building self-awareness, self-confidence, and self-actualization
   c. Replacing dysfunctional thoughts and attitudes with ones that are more realistic and empowering of the self
   d. Replacing dysfunctional actions with new and healthier behaviors and skills

6. Problems and disorders I am most interested in treating include
   a. Longstanding, underlying depression and anxiety, the milder personality disorders
   b. Low self-esteem, confusion about goals and direction, lack of meaning in life
   c. Depression and anxiety, pessimism and hopelessness
   d. Drug and alcohol problems, eating disorders, conduct disorders, other problems of impulse control

7. The clinical setting(s) where I am most interested in working include
   a. Private practice, psychoanalytic training programs
   b. Programs designed to promote personal growth and self-esteem
   c. Mental health centers, private practice
   d. Drug and alcohol rehabilitation programs, schools

8. Understanding and addressing a person's environment and socioeconomic, ethnic, and cultural background is
   a. Not essential for successful treatment
   b. Important if it is important to the client
   c. Important in order to understand a person's world view
   d. Important in understanding behavioral reinforcers and ways to effect change

9. Development of specific goals and treatment plans are
   a. Only important in short-term focused treatment
   b. Up to the client
   c. Essential for giving direction to treatment and empowering the client
   d. Essential for tracking progress and determining whether treatment is effective

10. Duration of treatment should be
   a. Lengthy in most cases to facilitate exploration of the past
   b. As long as needed to provide holistic treatment
   c. Relatively brief but depends on diagnosis
   d. Relatively brief, with booster sessions used to facilitate relapse prevention

11. Use of homework assignments and between-session tasks is
   a. Not generally part of treatment
   b. Largely left up to the client
   c. Essential; treatment is not likely to succeed unless people are willing to formulate plans and help themselves
   d. Very important and likely to improve treatment

12. I view empirical research validating any treatment approaches I use as
   a/b. Not as important as case studies and my own experiences
   c/d. Essential

Evaluating the Questionnaire

Now that you have completed this questionnaire, go back and add up the numbers of *a*'s, *b*'s, *c*'s, and *d*'s you selected. As you have probably realized, the letters are associated with the four groups of treatment systems presented in this book:

1   *a*'s: theories emphasizing background (psychodynamic approaches)
4   *b*'s: theories emphasizing emotions and sensation (person-centered, existential, and Gestalt approaches)
6   *c*'s: theories emphasizing thoughts (cognitive therapy, rational emotive behavior therapy)
2   *d*'s: theories emphasizing actions (behavior, cognitive behavior, reality and solution-based therapy)

If your choices reflect a clear preference for one letter and one type of treatment system over the others, especially if that preference is compatible with your responses to the background questions, you should pay particular attention to the theories in that section of the book. You will probably find your preferred theoretical orientation there.

If no clear pattern emerges from your responses to the questionnaire or the background questions, you are probably still sorting out your beliefs about how to provide effective counseling and psychotherapy. Asking people who have observed you in the clinician role which theory they think best characterizes your style might be a place to start finding your way as a clinician. Additional reading, especially case studies reflecting the application of a variety of treatment approaches, might also be helpful.

Clinical Orientation and Clinician Personality

Whether or not you have honed in on your current theory of choice, be sure to pay attention to the influence of your personality. Clinicians tend to choose approaches that are compatible with their personality styles. Erickson (1993), for example, studied the relationship between clinicians' preferred theoretical orientations and their personality types as reflected on the Myers-Briggs Type Indicator (MBTI). Findings suggested that "thinking types are disproportionately likely to choose predominately cognitive techniques (Adlerian, behavioral, rational-emotive, and reality therapy), whereas feeling types are likelier to choose predominantly affective approaches (Gestalt and client-centered therapy)" (p. 39).

Using your own self-knowledge, feedback you have received from others, and the results of the MBTI or any personality inventories you might have taken, think about your personality and the treatment systems with which it seems most compatible. Again, further reading on and exposure to those treatment systems might help you choose a theoretical approach that seems best suited for you at this point in your career. Keep in mind that you are not making an irrevocable commitment but only choosing a starting point that will help you continue the development of your clinical skills in a comfortable and focused way. With experience, you will become increasingly clear about the best approach for you and your clients and will find your treatment style changing, evolving, and improving.

FUTURE DIRECTIONS IN COUNSELING AND PSYCHOTHERAPY

The following trends and emerging directions are expected to have an impact on systems and strategies of counseling and psychotherapy in the 21st century (Prochaska & Norcross, 1999; Seligman, 1996a):

- The rapid growth of managed care is expected to level off. However, managed care will probably continue to exert a considerable influence over psychotherapy by overseeing and limiting treatment.
- Empirical research on what treatments are effective in ameliorating which disorders will increase, leading to greater emphasis on practice guidelines, prescriptive matching of diagnosis to treatment, and standardized treatments that have proven their value.
- Research will continue to focus on and clarify the common elements across treatment approaches that are linked to treatment success. A positive and collaborative therapeutic alliance will continue to be one of the most important of these commonalities.
- New models of eclectic and integrated treatment systems will be developed and the existing models further refined.
- Solution-based treatment, crisis intervention, and other models of brief therapy will grow in importance and use.
- Cognitive and behavioral treatment systems and strategies will also gain in importance and use.
- The use of psychodynamic treatment approaches will probably remain stable despite current pressures toward brief treatment. Many clinicians and clients continue to believe in the value of long-term exploratory and analytical treatment.
- Transpersonal and other spiritual approaches to treatment will continue to receive attention and exert influence but will not replace more traditional models of treatment.
- The use of self-help groups and homework tasks as adjuncts to treatment is likely to increase because of the evident contributions they make to successful counseling and psychotherapy.
- Clinicians will increasingly need to attend to client diversity, background, world view, and philosophy. They will need to use their knowledge of diagnosis, culture and ethnicity, and individual differences to tailor treatment to each person.
- Technology is likely to have an increasing impact on counseling and psychotherapy. Widespread use of computers and the Internet will increase the use of telepsychotherapy—treatment provided through e-mail or other electronic means. Legal and ethical guidelines will continue to be developed to regulate this high-risk area.

- Goal setting and treatment planning will become accepted practice in nearly all treatment systems and settings.
- Assessment will play an increasing role in treatment because of its contributions to diagnosis, clarification of the nature and severity of problems, goal setting, and monitoring of treatment effectiveness.
- Scheduling of treatment sessions is likely to become more flexible, as reflected by fewer weekly sessions with additional follow-up sessions designed to maintain progress and prevent relapse.
- The use of eye movement desensitization and reprocessing (EMDR) will expand as its value continues to be substantiated; other related approaches will be developed that are also very powerful.
- Counseling and psychotherapy will continue to be important in helping people cope with problems and emotional difficulties, in part because the value of mental health treatment has been so well established, in part because research and holistic thinking will extend the breadth of its reach. For example, treatment will increasingly be used to help people deal with chronic and life-threatening illnesses and chronic pain, collaborations between school counselors and mental health clinicians will increase in an effort to address problems of school violence, and outreach programs will make treatment more available to traditionally underserved groups such as the elderly and people from nonwestern cultural backgrounds.

EXERCISES

Large-Group Exercises

1. Review Figures 26.1–26.4, looking particularly at the information about the therapeutic alliance advocated by each approach. Discuss differences and similarities in the ways in which the various approaches view the therapeutic alliance. Do you see more similarities or more differences? What differences seem particularly important? Do the older theories reflect a different conception of the therapeutic alliance than do the newer theories?
2. Discuss the following questions in relation to the following four cases:

   - What treatment systems and strategies seem most likely to be effective in treating this person? Why?
   - What treatment systems and strategies seem least likely to be effective in treating this person? Why?
   - What sort of therapeutic alliance would be best for this client?
   - What possible obstacles to successful treatment are presented by each case? What interventions or approaches might you use to overcome these obstacles?

Case A. Seneesha, age 15, was brought to counseling by her mother. Seneesha's mother is African American; her father is white. Six months ago, her father left the family to move in with a woman with whom he had been having a long affair. Since then, Seneesha has seemed very sad, lost weight, and been sleeping at least 10 hours a day. She has withdrawn from most of her friends, especially her white friends, and has been talking about how different she feels from her friends. She blames herself for her father's departure and has stated that if she were prettier or smarter, he might not have left. She has avoided contact with her father and seems to have little interest in her schoolwork.

Case B. Brian, age 33, has been married for nine years and has two children, ages seven and five. He sought treatment reluctantly at the urging of his wife. According to Brian, his wife believes his use of drugs and alcohol is a problem. As Brian sees it, although he does consume 8–12 cans of beer each night and smokes marijuana on the weekends, he runs a successful business, earns a good income, and "doesn't run around." He agrees that maybe he should spend some more time with the children when he comes home from work but otherwise sees no need for change.

Case C. Lea, age 42 and single, was recently diagnosed with breast cancer. With treatment, her prognosis is excellent. However, she is terrified of undergoing surgery and is endangering her life by postponing her treatment. She explains her reactions by stating that she feels all alone with no one to help her and doesn't know how she will handle her recovery from surgery and her subsequent chemotherapy. Throughout the session, Lea makes poor eye contact, speaks in a low voice, and appears very shy and fearful.

Case D. Carmen, age 25 and recently married, sought treatment after one of the teachers in the elementary school where she is employed was found guilty of child abuse. This brought back to Carmen vivid memories of her own history of sexual abuse by her brother. These memories have made it difficult for her to be intimate with her husband and have led her to feel considerable discomfort at work.

3. Review the section on future directions in counseling and psychotherapy. Discuss whether or not you agree that each of these trends is likely and provide a rationale for your response. What future directions would you add to this list? What trends do not seem likely to happen but would be helpful to the mental health fields?

Small-Group Exercises

1. If you have not already completed and scored the questionnaire included in this chapter, do so now. Then share your results with the other members of your group, discussing what those results mean to you. Drawing on what you know about the personalities and clinical style of the group members, give each person in the group feedback about what treatment system might be best as his or her preferred approach. Be sure to discuss the rationale behind your recommendations.

2. Each member of the group should become an advocate of one of the four broad categories of treatment systems (background, emotions, thoughts, ac-

tions) discussed in this book. Be sure that each of the four categories has a spokesperson. Then discuss the following questions, with each spokesperson presenting an informed and positive view of his or her chosen group of treatment systems:

- Which treatment system best addresses issues of culture and diversity?
- Which can be used with the broadest range of clients and problems?
- Which is most likely to grow in use and importance in the 21st century?

Individual Exercises

1. Over the course of the semester, you have probably learned a great deal about yourself as a clinician. In your journal, list three strengths that you believe you have as a clinician. List three areas in which you think you need to improve your clinical skills. List three topics in counseling and psychotherapy that you would like to read more about. Identify the first steps in improving your skills and continuing your reading.
2. Identify the exercise or learning experience that has been most interesting or enlightening for you this semester. Write briefly in your journal about why that experience was so meaningful.

SUMMARY

This chapter has synthesized information about a broad range of approaches to counseling and psychotherapy, summarizing them in Figures 26.1–26.4. Despite the many differences among treatment approaches, several common factors across systems are associated with successful counseling and psychotherapy. The questionnaire in this chapter will help clinicians identify their preferred approaches to mental health treatment, as will the exercises designed to facilitate professional growth. Finally, this chapter has reviewed trends expected to have an impact on counseling and psychotherapy in the 21st century.

Counseling and psychotherapy continue to be vital and exciting professions that provide help to a great many people and a rewarding career to many clinicians. By learning about the new developments in the field, expanding the range of our skills, and monitoring and refining the effectiveness of our treatment plans, we can continue to keep the energy and spirit of the mental health professions alive in our own work.

REFERENCES

Acosta, F. X., Yamamoto, J., Evans, L. A., & Skilbeck, W. M. (1983). Preparing low-income Hispanic, black, and white patients for psychotherapy: Evaluation of a new orientation program. *Journal of Clinical Psychology, 39,* 872–877.

Adler, A. (1931). *What life should mean to you.* Boston: Little, Brown.

Adler, A. (1956). (1) The neurotic disposition; (2) Psychology of use; (3) Social interest. In H. L. Ansbacher & R. R. Ansbacher (Eds.), *The individual psychology of Alfred Adler* (pp. 126–162, 205–262). New York: Basic Books.

Adler, A. (1963a). *The practice and theory of individual psychology.* Paterson, NJ: Littlefield, Adams.

Adler, A. (1963b). *The problem child.* New York: Putnam.

Adler, A. (1979). *Superiority and social interest.* New York: Norton.

Alexander, C. N., Rainforth, M. V., & Gelderloos, P. (1991). Transcendental meditation, self-actualization, and psychological health. *Journal of Social Behavior and Personality, 6*(5), 189–247.

Alexander, J., & Harman, R. (1988). One counselor's intervention in the aftermath of a middle school student's suicide: A case study. *Journal of Counseling and Development, 66,* 283–285.

Allan, J. A., & Lawton-Speert, S. (1993). Play psychotherapy of a profoundly incest abused boy: A Jungian approach. *International Journal of Play Therapy, 2,* 33–48.

American Psychiatric Association. (1994). *Diagnostic and statistical manual of mental disorders* (4th ed.). Washington, DC: Author.

Angermann, D. (1998). Gestalt therapy for eating disorders: An illustration. *Gestalt Journal, 21,* 19–47.

Ansbacher, H. L., & Ansbacher, R. R. (Eds.). (1956). *The individual psychology of Alfred Adler: A systematic presentation in selections from his writings.* New York: Basic Books.

Arntz, A., & Van Den Hout, M. (1996). Psychological treatments of panic disorders without agoraphobia: Cognitive therapy versus applied relaxation. *Behavior Research and Therapy, 34*(2), 113–122.

Asay, T. P., & Lambert, M. J. (1999). The empirical case for the common factors in therapy: Quantitative findings. In M. A. Hubble, B. L. Duncan, & S. D. Miller (Eds.), *The heart and soul of change: What works in therapy* (pp. 33–55). Washington, DC: American Psychological Association.

Assagioli, R. (1965). *Psychosynthesis.* New York: Viking.

Assagioli, R. (1991). *Transpersonal development: The dimension beyond psychosynthesis.* San Francisco: HarperCollins.

Atkinson, D. R., Kim, B. S. K., & Caldwell, R. (1998). Ratings of helper roles by multicultural psychologists and Asian American students: Initial support for the three-dimensional models of multicultural counseling. *Journal of Counseling Psychology, 25*(4), 414–423.

Atwood, J. D., & Maltin, L. (1991). Putting eastern philosophies into western psychotherapies. *American Journal of Psychotherapy, 45,* 368–381.

Bachar, E. (1998). The contributions of self psychology to the treatment of anorexia and bulimia. *American Journal of Psychotherapy, 52,* 147–165.

Bachelor, A. (1995). Clients' perception of the therapeutic alliance: A qualitative analysis. *Journal of Counseling Psychology, 42,* 323–337.

Bachelor, A., & Horvath, A. (1999). The therapeutic relationship. In M. A. Hubble, B. L. Duncan, & S. D. Miller (Eds.), *The heart and soul of change: What works in therapy* (pp. 133–178). Washington, DC: American Psychological Association.

Baker, E. L. (1985). Psychoanalysis and psychoanalytic psychotherapy. In S. J. Lynn & J. P. Garske (Eds.), *Contemporary psychotherapies: Models and methods* (pp. 19–68). Upper Saddle River, NJ: Merrill/Prentice Hall.

Bandler, R., & Grinder, J. (1975). *The structure of magic.* Palo Alto, CA: Science and Behavior Books.

Bandura, A. (1969). *Principles of behavior modification.* New York: Holt, Rinehart, & Winston.

Barrish, I. J. (1997). Teaching children how to feel good without rating themselves. *Journal of Rational-Emotive and Cognitive-Behavior Therapy, 15*(1), 71–79.

Barton, A. (1992). Humanistic contributions to the field of psychotherapy: Appreciating the human and liberating the therapist. *Humanist Psychologist, 20,* 332–348.

Bassin, A. (1993). The reality therapy paradigm. *Journal of Reality Therapy, 12*(2), 3–13.

Bauman, S., & Waldo, M. (1998). Existential theory and mental health counseling: If it were a snake, it would have bitten! *Journal of Mental Health Counseling, 20,* 13–27.

Beal, D., Kopec, A. M., & DiGiuseppe, R. (1996). Disputing clients' irrational beliefs. *Journal of Rational-Emotive and Cognitive-Behavior Therapy, 14*(4), 215–229.

Beck, A. T. (1993). Cognitive therapy: Past, present, and future. *Journal of Consulting and Clinical Psychology, 61*(2), 194–198.

Beck, A. T., & Emery, G. (1985). *Anxiety disorders and phobias: A cognitive perspective.* New York: Basic Books.

Beck, A. T., Freeman, A., & Associates. (1990). *Cognitive therapy of personality disorders.* New York: Guilford.

Beck, A. T., Rush, A. J., Shaw, B. F., & Emery, G. (1979). *Cognitive therapy of depression.* New York: Guilford.

Beck, A. T., & Weishaar, M. E. (1995). In R. J. Corsini & D. Wedding (Eds.), *Current psychotherapies* (5th ed., pp. 229–261). Itasca, IL: Peacock.

Beck, D. F. (1988). *Counselor characteristics: How they affect outcomes.* Milwaukee: Family Service America.

Beck, J. S. (1995). *Cognitive therapy: Basics and beyond.* New York: Guilford.

Beecher, W., & Beecher, M. (1973). Memorial to Dr. Alfred Adler. In H. H. Mosak (Ed.), *Alfred Adler: His influence on psychology today* (pp. 1–5). Park Ridge, NJ: Noyes.

Berg, I. K., & Miller, S. D. (1992a). *Working with the problem drinker: A solution-focused approach.* New York: Norton.

Berg, I. K., & Miller, S. D. (1992). Working with Asian American clients one person at a time. *Families in Society,* pp. 356–363.

Bernard, M. E. (1995). It's prime time for rational emotive behavior therapy: Current theory and practice, research recommendations, and predictions. *Journal of Rational-Emotive and Cognitive-Behavior Therapy, 13*(1), 9–27.

Berne, E. (1961). *Transactional analysis in psychotherapy.* New York: Grove.

Berne, E. (1963). *The structure and dynamics of organizations and groups.* Philadelphia: Lippincott.

Berne, E. (1964). *Games people play.* New York: Grove.

Beutler, L. E., & Consoli, A. J. (1993). Matching the therapist's interpersonal stance to the clients' characteristics: Contributions from systematic eclectic psychotherapy. *Psychotherapy, 30*(3), 417–422.

Beutler, L. E., Machado, P. P. M., & Neufeldt, S. A. (1994). Therapist variables. In B. A. Garfield & S. L Garfield (Eds.), *Handbook of psychotherapy and behavior change* (pp. 229–269). New York: Wiley.

Bogart, G. (1991). The use of meditation in psychotherapy: A review of the literature. *American Journal of Psychotherapy, 45*(3), 383–412.

Bond, F. W., & Dryden, W. (1996). Why two central REBT hypotheses appear untestable. *Journal of Rational-Emotive and Cognitive-Behavior Therapy, 14*(1), 29–40.

Boorstein, S. (Ed.). (1996). *Transpersonal psychotherapy* (2nd ed.). Albany: State University of New York Press.

Bowlby, J. (1978). Attachment theory and its therapeutic implications. *Adolescent Psychiatry, 6,* 5–33.

Bowlby, J. (1988). *A secure base: Parent-child attachment and healthy human development.* New York: Basic Books.

Bozarth, J. D., & Brodley, B. T. (1991). Actualization: A functional concept in client-centered therapy. *Journal of Social Behavior and Personality, 6,* 45–59.

Breitbart, W., & Passik, S. D. (1993). Psychiatric approaches to cancer pain management. In W. Breitbart & J. C. Holland (Eds.), *Psychiatric aspects of symptom management in cancer patients* (pp. 49–86). Washington, DC: American Psychiatric Press.

Brigham, D. D. (1994). *Imagery for getting well.* New York: Norton.

Brunner, J. (1998). Oedipus politicus. In M. S. Roth (Ed.). *Freud: Conflict and culture* (pp. 80–93). New York: Knopf.

Buber, M. (1970). *I and thou.* New York: Scribner.

Budman, S. H., & Gurman, A. S. (1988). *Theory and practice of brief therapy.* New York: Guilford.

Bugental, J. F. T. (1965). *The search for authenticity.* New York: Holt, Rinehart, & Winston.

Bugental, J. F. T. (1978). *Psychotherapy and process: The fundamentals of an existential humanistic approach.* Reading, MA: Addison-Wesley.

Bugental, J. F. T. (1987). *The art of the psychotherapist.* New York: Norton.

Bugental, J. F. T. (1990). *Intimate journeys.* San Francisco: Jossey-Bass.

Burns, D. D. (1980). *Feeling good.* New York: Signet.

Burns, D. D. (1989). *The feeling good handbook.* New York: Penguin.

Cain, D. J. (1987a). Carl R. Rogers: The man, his vision, his impact. *Person-Centered Review, 2,* 283–288.

Cain, D. J. (1987b). Our international family. *Person-Centered Review, 2,* 139–149.

Callahan, R. J., & Callahan, J. (1997). Thought field therapy: Aiding the bereavement process. In C. R. Figley, B. E. Bride, & N. Massa (Eds.), *Death and trauma* (pp. 249–267). Washington, DC: Taylor & Francis.

Carich, M. (1990). The basics of hypnosis and trancework. *Individual Psychology, 46*(4), 401–410.

Carney, J. V., & Hazler, R. J. (1998). Suicide and cognitive-behavioral counseling: Implications for mental health counselors. *Journal of Mental Health Counseling, 20*(1), 28–41.

Caro, I. (1991). An introduction to the cognitive therapy of evaluation. *Counseling Psychology Quarterly, 4*(2/3), 191–206.

Carr, A. (1998). Michael White's narrative therapy. *Contemporary Family Therapy, 20,* 485–503.

Cashdan, S. (1988). *Object relations therapy: Using the relationship.* New York: Norton.

Chambless, D. L., Baker, M. J., Baucom, D. H., Beutler, L. E., Calhoun, K. S., Crits-Cristoph, P., Daiuto, A., DeRubeis, R., Detweiler, J., Haaga, D. A. F., Bennett Johnson, S., McCurry, S., Mueser, K. T., Pope, K. S., Sanderson, W. C., Shoham, V., Stickle, T. Williams, D. A., & Woody, S. R. (1998). Update on empirically validated therapies, II. *Clinical Psychologist, 51,* 3–16.

Chapman, A. H. (1978). *The treatment techniques of Harry Stack Sullivan.* New York: Brunner/Mazel.

Clarkson, P. (1990). A multiplicity of psychotherapeutic relationships. *British Journal of Psychotherapy, 7*(2), 148–161.

Clarkson, P. (1993). Transactional analysis as a humanistic therapy. *Transactional Analysis Journal, 23*(1), 36–41.

Cocks, G. (Ed.). (1994). *The curve of life: Correspondence of Heinz Kohut.* Chicago: University of Chicago Press.

Coleman, H. K. L., Wampold, B. E., & Casali, S. L. (1995). Ethnic minorities' ratings of ethnically similar and European American counselors: A meta-analysis. *Journal of Counseling Psychology, 42,* 55–64.

Controversies in cognitive therapy: A dialogue with Aaron T. Beck and Steve Hollon. 1993. *Journal of Cognitive Psychotherapy, 7*(2), 79–93.

Corey, G., Corey, M. S., & Callanan, P. (1998). *Issues and ethics in the helping professions.* Pacific Grove, CA: Brooks/Cole.

Cormier, W. H., & Cormier, L. S. (1991). *Interviewing strategies for helpers: Fundamental skills and cognitive-behavioral interventions* (3rd ed.). Pacific Grove, CA: Brooks/Cole.

Corsini, R. J., & Wedding, D. (1995). *Current psychotherapies.* Itasca, IL: Peacock.

Cousins, L., & Weiss, G. (1993). Parent training and social skills training for children with attention-deficit hyperactivity disorder: How can they be combined for greater effectiveness? *Canadian Journal of Psychiatry—Revue Canadienne de Psychiatrie, 38*(6), 449–457.

Cowley, A. A. (1993). Transpersonal social work: A theory for the 1990s. *Social Work, 38,* 527–534.

Craighead, W. E. (1990). There's a place for all of us: All of us. *Behavior therapy, 21,* 3–23.

Crain, W. (1992). *Theories of development: Concepts and application* (3rd ed.). Upper Saddle River, NJ: Prentice Hall.

Crits-Cristoph, P. (1992). The efficacy of brief dynamic psychotherapy: A meta-analysis. *American Journal of Psychiatry, 149*(2), 151–158.

Crits-Cristoph, P., Baranackie, K., Kurcias, J. S., Beck, A., Carroll, K., Perry, K., Luborsky, L., McLellan, A. T., Woody, G. E., Thompson, L., Gallagher, D., & Zitrin, C. (1991). Meta-analysis of therapist effects in psychotherapy outcome studies. *Psychotherapy Research, 1*(2), 81–91.

Dattilio, F. M., & Freeman, A. (Eds.). (1992). *Comprehensive casebook of cognitive therapy.* New York: Plenum.

Davanloo, H. (1979). Techniques of short-term psychotherapy. *Psychiatric Clinics of North America, 2,* 11–22.

Davanloo, H. (1980). A method of short-term dynamic psychotherapy. In H. Davanloo (Ed.), *Short-term dynamic psychotherapy.* Northvale, NJ: Aronson.

Day, B., & Mathes, W. (1992). A comparison of Jungian, person-centered, and Gestalt approaches to personal growth groups. *Journal for Specialists in Group Work, 17,* 105–115.

Day, G. L. (1992). Counseling for women: The contribution of feminist theory and practice. *Counseling Psychology Quarterly, 5,* 373–384.

Decker, H. S. (1998). Freud's "Dora" case. In M. S. Roth (Ed.), *Freud: Conflict and culture* (pp. 105–114). New York: Knopf.

Dehing, J. (1992). The therapist's interventions in Jungian analysis. *Journal of Analytical Psychology, 37,* 29–47.

DeLeon, P. H., & VandenBos, G. R. (1991). Psychotherapy in managed health care: Integrating federal policy with clinical practice. In C. S. Austad & W. H. Berman (Eds.), *Psychotherapy in managed health care* (pp. 251–263). Washington, DC: American Psychological Association.

De Luynes, M. (1995). Neuro-linguistic programming. *Educational and Child Psychology, 12,* 34–47.

Demos, V. C., & Prout, M. F. (1993). A comparison of seven approaches to brief psychotherapy. *International Journal of Short-Term Psychotherapy, 8,* 3–22.

de Shazer, S. (1982). *Patterns of brief family therapy: An ecosystemic approach.* New York: Guilford.

de Shazer, S. (1985). *Keys to solutions in brief therapy.* New York: Norton.

de Shazer, S. (1988). *Clues: Investigating solutions in brief therapy.* New York: Norton.

de Shazer, S. (1991). *Putting difference to work.* New York: Norton.

Deutsch, H. (1944). *The psychology of women.* New York: Grune & Stratton.

Deutsch, H. (1973). *Confrontations with myself: An epilogue.* New York: Norton.

Devine, D. A., & Fernald, P. S. (1973). Outcome effects of receiving a preferred, randomly assigned or nonpreferred therapy. *Journal of Consulting and Clinical Psychology, 41,* 104–107.

DiGiuseppe, R. (1996). The nature of irrational and rational beliefs: Progress in rational emotive behavior therapy. *Journal of Rational-Emotive and Cognitive-Behavior Therapy, 14*(1), 5–28.

Dilts, R. B. (1983). *Part I: Roots of neuro-linguistic programming.* Cupertino, CA: Mesa.

Dinkmeyer, D. C. (1982). *Developing understanding of self and others.* Circle Pines, MN: American Guidance Service.

Dinkmeyer, D., & Carlson, J., (1985). *Time for a better marriage.* Circle Pines, MN: American Guidance Service.

Dinkmeyer, D. C., & Dinkmeyer, D. C., Jr. (1982). *Developing an understanding of self and others, DUSO-1 revised and DUSO-2 revised.* Circle Pines, MN: American Guidance Services.

Dinkmeyer, D. C., Dinkmeyer, D. C. Jr., & Sperry, L. (1987). *Adlerian counseling and psychotherapy* (2nd ed.). Upper Saddle River, NJ: Merrill/Prentice Hall.

Dinkmeyer, D. C., & McKay, K. (1997). *Systematic training for effective parenting.* Circle Pines, MN: American Guidance Services.

Division 12 Task Force. (1996). An update on empirically validated therapies. *Clinical Psychologist, 49,* 5–18.

Dobson, K. (1989). A meta-analysis of the efficacy of cognitive therapy for depression. *Journal of Consulting and Clinical Psychology, 57,* 414–419.

Dollard, J., & Miller, N. E. (1950). *Personality and psychotherapy: An analysis in terms of learning, thinking and culture.* New York: McGraw-Hill.

Dolliver, R. H. (1995). Carl Rogers's emphasis on his own direct experience. *Journal of Humanistic Psychology, 35,* 129–139.

Donner, S. (1991). The treatment process. In H. Jackson (Ed.), *Using self psychology in psychotherapy* (pp. 51–72). Northvale, NJ: Aronson.

Draucker, C. B. (1998). Narrative therapy for women who have lived with violence. *Archives of Psychiatric Nursing, 7,* 162–168.

Dreikurs, R. (1973). Private logic. In H. H. Mosak (Ed.), *Alfred Adler: His influence on psychology today* (pp. 19–32). Park Ridge, NJ: Noyes.

Dreikurs, R., & Cassel, P. (1972). *Discipline without tears.* New York: Hawthorn.

Dreikurs, R., & Stoltz, V. (1964). *Children: The challenge.* New York: Meredith.

Dusay, J. M. (1972). Egograms and the "constancy hypothesis." *Transactional Analysis Journal, 2*(3), 133–137.

Dusay, J. M., & Dusay, K. M. (1989). Transactional analysis. In R. J. Corsini & R. D. Wedding (Eds.), *Current psychotherapies* (4th ed., pp. 405–453). Itasca, IL: Peacock.

Eckardt, M. H. (1984). Karen Horney: Her life and contribution. *American Journal of Psychoanalysis, 44,* 236–241.

Eckardt, M. H. (1991). Feminine psychology revisited: A historical perspective. *American Journal of Psychoanalysis, 51,* 235–243.

Edgcumbe, R. (1985). Anna Freud's contribution to technique and clinical understanding in child psychoanalysis. *Bulletin of the Anna Freud Centre, 8,* 155–168.

Edmunds, P., Martinson, S. A., & Goldberg, P. F. (1990). *Demographics and cultural diversity in the 1990's: Implications for services to young children with special needs.* Washington, DC: U.S. Department of Education, Office of Special Education Programs.

Eisenberg, M. (1989). Exposing prisoners to logotherapy. *International Forum for Logotherapy, 12,* 89–94.

Elkin, I., Shea, T., Watkins, J. T., Imber, S. D., Sotsky, S. M., Collins, J. F., Glass, D. R., Pilkonis, P. A., Leber, W. R., Docherty, J. P., Feister, S. J., & Parloff, M. B. (1989). National Institutes of Mental Health Treatment of Depressive Collaborative Research Program. *Archives of General Psychiatry, 46,* 971–982.

Ellenberger, H. F. (1970). *The discovery of the unconscious: The history and evolution of dynamic psychiatry.* New York: Basic Books.

Ellis, A. E. (1984). Foreward. In W. Dryden. *Rational-emotive therapy: Fundamentals and innovations* (pp. i–xv). London: Croom Helm.

Ellis, A. E. (1986). An emotional control card for inappropriate and appropriate emotions using rational-emotive imagery. *Journal of Counseling and Development, 65,* 205–206.

Ellis, A. E. (1988). *How to stubbornly refuse to make yourself miserable about anything—Yes, anything!* Secaucus, NJ: Lyle Stuart.

Ellis, A. E. (1991). The philosophical basis of rational-emotive therapy. *Psychotherapy in Private Practice, 8,* 97–106.

Ellis, A. E. (1992). Secular humanism and rational-emotive therapy. *Humanistic Psychologist, 20*(2/3), 349–358.

Ellis, A. E. (1995a). *Better, deeper, and more enduring brief therapy.* New York: Brunner/Mazel.

Ellis, A. E. (1995b). Changing rational-emotive therapy (RET) to rational emotive behavior therapy (REBT). *Journal of Rational-Emotive and Cognitive-Behavior Therapy, 13*(2), 85–89.

Ellis, A. E. (1995c). Rational emotive behavior therapy. In R. J. Corsini & D. Wedding (Eds.), *Current psychotherapies* (5th ed., pp. 162–196). Itasca, IL: Peacock.

Ellis, A. E. (1996). The treatment of morbid jealousy: A rational emotive behavior approach. *Journal of Cognitive Psychotherapy, 10*(1), 23–33.

Ellis, A. E. (1997). Using rational emotive behavior therapy techniques to cope with disability. *Professional Psychology, 28*(1), 17–22.

Ellis, A. E., & Dryden, W. (1997). *The practice of rational emotive behavior therapy* (2nd ed.). New York: Springer.

Ellwood, R. (1999). *The politics of myth: A study of C. G. Jung, Mircea Eliade, and Joseph Campbell.* New York: State University of New York Press.

Enns, C. (1987). Gestalt therapy and feminist therapy: A proposed integration. *Journal of Counseling and Development, 66,* 93–95.

Enright, J. B. (1975). An introduction to Gestalt therapy. In F. D. Stephenson (Ed.), *Gestalt therapy primer: Introductory readings in Gestalt therapy* (pp. 13–33). Springfield, IL: C. C. Thomas.

Epp, L. R. (1998). The courage to be an existential counselor: An interview of Clemmont E. Vontress. *Journal of Mental Health Counseling, 20,* 1–12.

Erickson, D. B. (1993). The relationship between personality types and preferred counseling model. *Journal of Psychological Type, 27,* 39–41.

Erikson, E. H. (1963). *Childhood and society.* New York: Norton.

Estes, C. P. (1992). *Women who run with the wolves: Myths and stories of the wild woman archetype.* New York: Ballantine.

Ewen, R. B. (1993). *An introduction to theories of personality* (4th ed.). Hillsdale, NJ: Erlbaum.

Eysenck, H. J. (1970). A mish-mash of theories. *International Journal of Psychiatry, 9,* 140–146.

Fagan, J., & Shepherd, I. L. (1970). *Gestalt therapy now.* New York: Harper & Row.

Fairchild, B. (1990). Reorientation: The use of hypnosis for life-style change. *Individual Psychology, 46*(4), 451–458.

Fanning, P. (1988). *Visualization for change.* Oakland, CA: New Harbinger.

Fisch, R., Weakland, J., & Segal, L. (1982). *The tactics of change.* San Francisco: Jossey-Bass.

Foa, E. B., Keane, T. M., & Friedman, M. J. (2000). *Effective treatments of PTSD: Guidelines from the International Society for Traumatic Stress Studies.* New York: Guilford.

Forcey, L. R., & Nash, M. (1998). Rethinking feminist theory and social work therapy. *Women and Therapy, 21,* 85–99.

Foreman, S. A., & Marmar, C. R. (1985). Therapist actions that address initially poor therapeutic alliances in psychotherapy. *American Journal of Psychiatry, 142,* 922–926.

Frank, J. D., & Frank, J. B. (1991). *Persuasion and healing* (3rd ed.). Baltimore: Johns Hopkins University Press.

Frank, M. L. (1995). Existential theory. In D. Capuzzi & D. R. Gross (Eds.), *Counseling and psychotherapy: Theories and interventions* (pp. 207–235). Upper Saddle River, NJ: Merrill/Prentice Hall.

Frankl, V. E. (1963). *Man's search for meaning.* Boston: Beacon.

Frankl, V. E. (1978). *The unheard cry for meaning.* New York: Simon & Schuster.

Frankl, V. E. (1987). On the meaning of love. *International Forum for Logotherapy, 10,* 5–8.

Frankl, V. E. (1992). Meaning in industrial society. *International Forum for Logotherapy, 15,* 66–70.

Freed, A., & Freed, M. (1974a). *TA for kids.* Sacramento: Freed.

Freed, A., & Freed, M. (1974b). *TA for tots.* Sacramento: Freed.

Freeman, S. (1993). Client-centered therapy with diverse populations: The universal within the specific. *Journal of Multicultural Counseling and Development, 21,* 248–254.

Freud, A. (1946). *The ego and the mechanisms of defence.* New York: International Universities Press.

Freud, A. (1965). *Normality and pathology in childhood.* New York: International Universities Press.

Freud, A. (1983). Excerpts from seminars and meetings. *Bulletin of the Hampstead Clinic, 6,* 115–128.

Freud, A., & Burlingham, D. T. (1943). *War and children.* New York: Medical War Books.

Freud, A., & Burlingham, D. T. (1944). *Infants without families: The case for and against residential nurseries.* New York: Medical War Books, International University Press.

Freud, S. (1936). *The problem of anxiety* (H. A. Bunker, Trans.). New York: Norton.

Freud, S. (1938). *The basic writings of Sigmund Freud* (A. A. Brill, Trans.). New York: Modern Library.

Frick, W. B. (1987). The symbolic growth experience and creation of meaning. *International Forum for Logotherapy, 10,* 35–41.

Frost, R. (1962). *Robert Frost's poems.* New York: Washington Square Press.

Gabbard, G. O. (1990). *Psychodynamic psychiatry in clinical practice.* Washington DC: American Psychiatric Press.

Gabbard, G. O. (Ed.). (1995). *Treatments of psychiatric disorders.* Washington, DC: American Psychiatric Press.

Gandy, G. L. (1995). Disputing irrational beliefs in rehabilitation counseling. *Journal of Applied Rehabilitation Counseling, 26*(1), 36–40.

Garfield, S. L. (1995). The client-therapist relationship in rational-emotive therapy. *Journal of Rational-Emotive and Cognitive-Behavior Therapy, 13*(2), 101–116.

Gelso, C. J., & Carter, J. A. (1985). The relationship in counseling and psychotherapy: Components, consequences, and theoretical antecedents. *Counseling Psychologist, 13,* 155–243.

Gendlin, E. T. (1996). *Focusing-oriented psychotherapy.* New York: Guilford.

Gibbs, J. T., & Huang, L. N. (1989). *Children of color: Psychological interventions with minority youths.* San Francisco: Jossey-Bass.

Gilligan, C. (1993). *In a different voice: Psychological theory and women's development.* Cambridge, MA: Harvard University Press.

Gilligan, S. (1997). Living in a post-Ericksonian world. In W. J. Matthews & J. H. Edgette (Eds.), *Current thinking and research in brief therapy: Solutions, strategies, narratives* (vol. 1, pp. 1–23). New York: Brunner/Mazel.

Gladfelter, J. (1992). Redecision therapy. *International Journal of Group Psychotherapy, 42*(3), 319–334.

Glasser, W. (1961). *Mental health or mental illness?* New York: Harper & Row.

Glasser, W. (1965). *Reality therapy: A new approach to psychiatry.* New York: Harper & Row.

Glasser, W. (1969). *Schools without failure.* New York: Harper & Row.

Glasser, W. (1975). *Reality therapy.* New York: Harper & Row.

Glasser, W. (1976). *Positive addiction.* New York: Harper & Row.

Glasser, W. (1984). *Control theory.* New York: Harper & Row.

Glasser, W. (1986). *Control theory in the classroom.* New York: Harper & Row.

Glasser, W. (1998). *Choice theory.* New York: HarperCollins.

Glasser, W., & Wubbolding, R. E. (1995). Reality therapy. In R. J. Corsini & D. Wedding (Eds.), *Current psychotherapies* (5th ed., pp. 293–321). Itasca, IL: Peacock.

Golden, W. L., Gersh, W. D., & Robbins, D. M. (1992). *Psychological treatment of cancer patients.* Needham Heights, MA: Allyn & Bacon.

Goldstein, J., Freud, A., & Solnit, A. J. (1973). *Beyond the best interests of the child.* New York: Free Press.

Goldstein, J., Freud, A., & Solnit, A. J. (1979). *Before the best interests of the child.* New York: Free Press.

Gordon, T. (1970). *Parent effectiveness training: The no-lose program for raising responsible children.* New York: Wyden.

Gordon, T. (1983). *Leader effectiveness training, L.E.T.: The no-lose way to release the productive potential of people.* New York: Putnam.

Gordon, T., & Burch, N. (1974). *T.E.T., teacher effectiveness training.* New York: Wyden.

Gottlieb, D. T., & Gottlieb, C. D. (1996). The narrative/collaborative process in couples therapy: A postmodern perspective. *Women and Therapy, 19,* 37–47.

Goulding, M. (1987). Transactional analysis and redecision therapy. In J. L. Zeig (Ed.), *The evolution of psychotherapy* (pp. 285–299). New York: Brunner/Mazel.

Goulding, M., & Goulding, R. (1979). *Changing lives through redecision therapy.* New York: Brunner/Mazel.

Grant, B. (1990). Principled and instrumental nondirectiveness in person-centered therapy and client-centered therapy. *Person-Centered Review, 5,* 77–88.

Gray, R. (1991). Tools for the trade: Neuro-linguistic programming and the art of communication. *Federal Probation, 55,* 11–16.

Green, R. & Herget, M. (1991). Outcomes of systemic/strategic team consultation. III: The importance of therapist warmth and active structuring. *Family Process, 30,* 321–336.

Greenberg, J. R., & Mitchell, S. A. (1983). *Object relations in psychoanalytic therapy.* Cambridge, MA: Harvard University Press.

Greenwalt, B. C. (1995). A comparative analysis of reality therapy and solution-focused brief therapy. *Journal of Reality Therapy, 15*(1), 56–65.

Grencavage, L. M., & Norcross, J. C. (1990). Where are the commonalties among the therapeutic common factors? *Professional Psychology: Research and Practice, 21,* 372–378.

Grey, A. L. (1988). Sullivan's contribution to psychoanalysis: An overview. *Contemporary Psychoanalysis, 24,* 548–576.

Grey, L. (1998). *Alfred Adler, forgotten prophet: A vision for the 21st century.* Westport, CN: Praeger.

Haaga, D. A. F., DeRubeis, R. J., Stewart, B. L., & Beck, A. T. (1991). Relationship of intelligence with cognitive therapy outcome. *Behavior Research and Therapy, 29*(3), 277–281.

Hackney, W. L., & Cormier, L. S. (1996). *The professional counselor.* Boston: Allyn & Bacon.

Hanna, F. J., & Ritchie, M. H. (1995). Seeking the active ingredients of psychotherapeutic change: Within and outside of the context of therapy. *Professional Psychology: Research and Practice, 26*(2), 176–183.

Hansen, J., Stevic, R., & Warner, R. (1986). *Counseling: Theory and process* (4th ed.). Boston: Allyn & Bacon.

Harris, A. B., & Harris, T. A. (1985). *Staying ok.* New York: Harper & Row.

Harris, T. A. (1967). *I'm ok—you're ok.* New York: Avon.

Hergenhahn, B. R. (1994). *An introduction to theories of personality* (4th ed.). Upper Saddle River, NJ: Prentice Hall.

Herman, L. (1975). One transactional analyst's understanding of Carl Jung. *Transactional Analysis Journal, 5,* 123–126.

Hill, C. E., & O'Brien, K. M. (1999). *Helping skills: Facilitating exploration, insight, and action.* Washington, DC: American Psychological Association.

Hirschman, L. (1997). Restoring complexity to the subjective worlds of profound abuse survivors. In A. Goldberg (Ed.), *Conversations in self psychology: Progress in self psychology* (vol. 13, pp. 307–323). Hillsdale, NJ: Analytic Press.

Hoffman, E. (1994). *The drive for self: Alfred Adler and the founding of Individual Psychology.* Reading, MA: Addison-Wesley.

Holden, J. M. (1993). Transpersonal counseling. *TCA Journal, 21,* 7–23.

Holden, J. M. (1996). *Transpersonal perspectives in counseling.* Paper presented at the meeting of the American Psychological Association, Pittsburgh, April 19, 1996.

Hollon, S. D., & Najavits, L. (1988). Review of empirical studies on cognitive therapy. In A. J. Frances & R. E. Sales (Eds.), *American Psychiatric Press review of psychiatry* (vol. 7, pp. 643–666). Washington, DC: American Psychiatric Press.

Horney, K. (1935). The problem of feminine masochism. *Psychoanalytic Review, 22,* 241–257.

Horney, K. (1939). *New ways in psychoanalysis.* New York: Norton.

Horney, K. (1945). *Our inner conflicts.* New York: Norton.

Horney, K. (1950). *Neurosis and human growth: The struggle toward self-realization.* New York: Norton.

Horney, K. (1967). *Feminine psychology.* New York: Norton.

Horowitz, M., Marmar, C. Krupnick, J., Wilner, N., Kaltreider, N., & Wallerstein, R. (1984). *Personality styles and brief psychotherapy.* New York: Basic Books.

Horvath, A. O., & Symonds, B. D. (1991). Relation between working alliance and outcome in psychotherapy: A meta-analysis. *Journal of Consulting and Clinical Psychology, 38, 139–149.*

Hutchins, D. E. (1979). Systemic counseling: The T-F-A model for counselor intervention. *Personnel and Guidance Journal, 57,* 529–531.

Hutchins, D. E., & Mueller, R. O. (1992). *Manual for Hutchins Behavior Inventory.* Palo Alto, CA: Consulting Psychologists Press.

Isaacson, E. B. (1990). Neuro-linguistic programming: A model for behavioral change in alcohol and other drug addiction. In C. M. Sterman (Ed.), *Neuro-linguistic programming in alcoholism treatment* (pp. 27–48). New York: Haworth.

Ivey, A. (1986). *Developmental therapy: Theory into practice.* San Francisco: Jossey-Bass.

Ivey, A. E. (1989). Mental health counseling: A developmental process and profession. *Journal of Mental Health Counseling, 11*(1), 26–35.

Ivey, A. E., & Ivey, M. B. (1999). *Intentional interviewing and counseling.* Pacific Grove, CA: Brooks/Cole.

Ivey, A. E., Ivey, M. B., & Simek-Morgan, L. (1997). *Counseling and psychotherapy: A multicultural perspective.* Needham Heights, MA: Allyn & Bacon.

Ivey, A. E., & Rigazio-DiGilio, S. A. (1991). Toward a developmental practice of mental health counseling: Strategies for training, practice and political unity. *Journal of Mental Health Counseling, 13*(1), 21–36.

Jacobi, J. (1973). *The psychology of C. G. Jung.* London: Yale University Press.

Jacobs, L. (1989). Dialogue in Gestalt theory and therapy. *Gestalt Journal, 12,* 25–67.

Jacobson, N. S. (1989). The therapist-client relationship in cognitive behavior therapy: Implications for treating depression. *Journal of Cognitive Psychotherapy, 3*(2), 85–96.

James, M., & Jongeward, D. (1971). *Born to win.* Reading, MA: Addison-Wesley.

Jinks, G. H. (1999). Intentionality and awareness: A qualitative study of clients' perceptions of change during longer term counseling. *Counselling Psychology Quarterly, 12,* 57–71.

Jones, E. (1953). *The life and work of Sigmund Freud.* New York: Basic Books.

Jones, E. (1955) *The life and work of Sigmund Freud: Years of maturity, 1901–1919* (vol. 2). New York: Basic Books.

Jones, E. (1957). *The life and work of Sigmund Freud: The last phase, 1919–1939* (vol. 3). New York: Basic Books.

Joyce, A. S., & Piper, W. E. (1998). Expectancy, the therapeutic alliance, and treatment outcome in short-term individual psychotherapy. *Journal of Psychotherapy Practice and Research, 7,* 236–248.

Jung, C. G. (1907/1960). The psychology of dementia praecox. In *The collected works of C. G. Jung* (vol. 4). Princeton, NJ: Princeton University Press.

Jung, C. G. (1912/1956). Symbols of transformation. In *The collected works of C. G. Jung* (vol. 5). Princeton, NJ: Princeton University Press.

Jung, C. G. (1921/1971). Psychological types. In *The collected works of C. G. Jung* (vol. 6). Princeton, NJ: Princeton University Press.

Jung, C. G. (1953). Two essays on analytical psychology. In *The collected works of C. G. Jung* (vol. 7). Princeton, NJ: Princeton University Press.

Jung, C. G. (1959). Aion: Research into the phenomenology of the self. In *The collected works of C. G. Jung* (vol. 9). Princeton, NJ: Princeton University Press.

Jung, C. G. (1960). *Collected works 8: The structure and dynamics of the psyche.* New York: Pantheon.

Jung, C. G. (1963). *Memories, dreams, reflections.* New York: Pantheon.

Jung, C. E. (1964). *Man and his symbols.* Garden City, NY: Doubleday.

Kamp, D. (1996). *The excellent trainer: Putting NLP to work.* Brookfield, VT: Gower.

Kaplan, H. I., Sadock, B. J., & Grebb, J. A. (1994). *Synopsis of psychiatry* (7th ed.). Baltimore: Williams & Wilkins.

Katz, A. J. (1991). Renegotiation: What to do when you don't follow your plan. *Journal of Reality Therapy, 11,* 63–65.

Kazdin, A. E. (1994). *Behavior modification in applied settings.* Pacific Grove, CA: Brooks/Cole.

Kazdin, A. E. (1997). Psychosocial treatments for conduct disorder in children. *Journal of Child Psychology and Psychiatry and Allied Professions, 38*(2), 161–178.

Kelly, E. W. (1997). Relationship-centered counseling: A humanistic model of integration. *Journal of Counseling & Development, 75,* 337–345.

Kelly, G. (1955). *The psychology of personal constructs.* New York: Norton.

Kelly, W. L. (1990). *Psychology of the unconscious: Mesmer, Janet, Freud, Jung, and current issues.* New York: Prometheus.

Kelly, T. A., & Strupp, H. H. (1992). Patient and therapist values in psychotherapy: Perceived changes, assimilation, similarity and outcome. *Journal of Consulting and Clinical Psychology, 60,* 34–40.

Kern, R. M. (1990). *Lifestyle scale.* Coral Springs, FL: CMTI.

Kernberg, O. F. (1985). *Borderline conditions and pathological narcissism.* New York: Aronson.

Kernberg, O. F., & Clarkin, J. F. (1992). Treatment of personality disorders. *International Journal of Mental Health, 21,* 53–76.

Kirsch, T. B. (1996). A brief history of analytical psychology. *Psychoanalytic Review, 83,* 569–577.

Kivlighan, D. M., Patton, M. J., & Foote, D. (1998). Moderating effects of client attachment on the counselor experience-working alliance relationship. *Journal of Counseling Psychology, 45*(3), 274–278.

Kivlighan, D. M., & Schmitz, P. J. (1992). Counselor technical activity in cases with improving working alliances and continuing poor working alliances. *Journal of Counseling Psychology, 39,* 32–38.

Kleinke, C. L. (1994). *Common principles of therapy.* Pacific Grove, CA: Brooks/Cole.

Klerman, G. L., Weissman, M. M., Rounsaville, B. J., & Chevron, E. S. (1984). *Interpersonal psychotherapy of depression.* New York: Basic Books.

Knox, S., Hess, S. A., Petersen, D. A., & Hill, C. E. (1997). A qualitative analysis of client perceptions of the effects of helpful therapist self-disclosure in long-term therapy. *Journal of Counseling Psychology, 44,* 274–283.

Kohut, H. (1971). *The analysis of the self: A systematic approach to the psychoanalytic treatment of narcissistic personality disorders.* New York: International Universities Press.

Kohut, H. (1977). *The restoration of the self.* New York: International Universities Press.

Kohut, H. (1982). Introspection, empathy, and the semi-circle of mental health. *International Journal of Psychoanalysis, 63,* 395–407.

Kohut, H. (1984). *How does analysis cure?* Chicago: University of Chicago Press.

Kohut, H., & Wolf, E. S. (1978). The disorders of the self and their treatment: An outline. *International Journal of Psychoanalysis, 59,* 413–425.

Kolden, G. G., Howard, K. I., & Maling, M. S. (1994). The counseling relationship and treatment process and outcome. *Counseling Psychologist, 22,* 82–89.

Korb, M. P., Gorrell, J., & Van de Riet, V. (1989). *Gestalt therapy: Practice and theory* (2nd ed.). New York: Pergamon.

Koss, M. P., & Butcher, J. N. (1986). Research on brief psychotherapy. In S. L. Garfield & A. E. Bergin (Eds.), *Handbook of psychotherapy and behavior change* (3rd ed., pp. 627–670). New York: Wiley.

Kottman, T., & Johnson, V. (1993). Adlerian play therapy: A tool for school counselors. *Elementary School Guidance and Counseling, 28,* 42–51.

Kropf, N. P., & Tandy, C. (1998). Narrative therapy with older clients: The use of a "meaning making" approach. *Clinical Gerontologist, 18,* 3–16.

Lachmann, F. M. (1993). Self psychology: Origins and overview. *British Journal of Psychotherapy, 2,* 226–231.

Lachmann, F. M., & Beebe, B. (1995). Self psychology: Today. *Psychoanalysis Dialogues, 5,* 375–384.

Lafferty, P., Beutler, L. E., & Crago, M. (1989). Differences between more and less effective psychotherapists: A study of select therapist variables. *Journal of Consulting and Clinical Psychology, 57,* 76–80.

Lambert, M. J. (1992). Psychotherapy outcome research: Implications for integrative and eclectic therapists. In J. C. Norcross & M. R. Goldfried (Eds.), *Handbook of psychotherapy integration* (pp. 94–129). New York: Basic Books.

Lambert, M. J., & Bergin, A. E. (1994). The effectiveness of psychotherapy. In A. E. Bergin & S. L. Garfield (Eds.), *Handbook of psychotherapy and behavior change* (4th ed., pp. 143–189). New York: Wiley.

Lambert, M. J., & Cattani-Thompson, K. (1996). Current findings regarding the effectiveness of counseling: Implications for practice. *Journal of Counseling and Development, 74,* 601–608.

Lankton, S. R. (1980). *Practical magic: A translation of basic neuro-linguistic programming into clinical psychotherapy.* Cupertino, CA: Meta.

Lawe, C. F., Horne, A. M., & Taylor, S. V. (1983). Effects of pretraining procedures for clients in counseling. *Psychological Reports, 53,* 327–334.

Lazarus, A. A. (1976). *Multimodal behavior therapy.* New York: Springer.

Lazarus, A. A. (1981). *The practice of multimodal therapy.* New York: McGraw-Hill.

Lazarus, A. A. (Ed.). (1985). *Casebook of multimodal therapy.* New York: Guilford.

Lazarus, A. A. (1989). *The practice of multimodal therapy (update).* Baltimore: Johns Hopkins University Press.

Lazarus, A. A. (1997). *Brief but comprehensive psychotherapy.* New York: Springer.

Lazarus, A. A., & Beutler, L. E. (1993). On technical eclecticism. *Journal of Counseling and Development, 71*(4), 381–385.

Lee, J. (1997). Women re-authoring their lives through feminist narrative therapy. *Women and Therapy, 20,* 1–22.

Levenson, E. A. (1992). Harry Stack Sullivan: From interpersonal psychiatry to interpersonal psychoanalysis. *Contemporary Psychoanalysis, 28,* 450–466.

Levine, S., & Herron, W. (1990). Changes during the course of psychotherapeutic relationships. *Psychological Reports, 66,* 883–897.

Lewis, E. (1992). Regaining promise: Feminist perspectives for social group work practice. *Social Work with Groups, 15,* 271–284.

Linehan, M. M. (1993). *Skills training manual for treating borderline personality disorder.* New York: Guilford.

Linehan, M. M., & Kehrer, C. A. (1993). Borderline personality disorder. In D. A. Barlow (Ed.), *Clinical handbook of psychological disorders* (2nd ed., pp. 396–441). New York: Guilford.

Littrell, J., Malia, J., & Vanderwood, M. (1995). Single session brief counseling in a high school. *Journal of Counseling and Development, 73,* 451–458.

Livneh, H., & Sherwood, A. (1991). Application of personality theories and counseling strategies to clients with physical disabilities. *Journal of Counseling and Development, 69*(6), 525–538.

Lochman, J. E., White, K. J., & Wayland, K. W. (1991). Cognitive behavioral assessment and treatment with aggressive children. In P. C. Kendall (Ed.), *Child and adolescent therapy: Cognitive behavioral procedures* (pp. 25–65). New York: Guilford.

Locke, S. E., & Colligan, D. (1987). *The healer within.* New York: Mentor.

Lombardi, D. N. (1996). Antisocial personality disorder and addictions. In L. Sperry & J. Carlson (Ed.), *Psychopathology and psychotherapy* (pp. 371–390). Washington, DC: Accelerated Development.

Luborsky, L. (1984). *Principles of psychoanalytic psychotherapy: A manual for supportive-expressive treatment.* New York: Basic Books.

Luborsky, L., & Mark, D. (1991). Short term supportive-expressive psychoanalytic psychotherapy. In P. Crits-Cristoph & J. P. Barber (Eds.), *Handbook of short-term dynamic psychotherapy* (pp. 110–136). New York: Basic Books.

Luborsky, L., Singer, B., & Luborsky, L. (1975). Comparative studies of psychotherapies. *Archives of General Psychiatry, 32,* 995–1008.

Lundin, R. W. (1977). Behaviorism: Operant reinforcement. In R. J. Corsini (Ed.), *Current personality theories* (pp. 177–202). Itasca, IL: Peacock.

Lynch, G. (1997). The role of community and narrative in the work of the therapist: A postmodern theory of the therapist's engagement in the therapeutic process. *Counseling Psychology Quarterly, 10,* 353–363.

Lynch, V. (1991). The treatment process. In H. Jackson (Ed.), *Using self psychology in psychotherapy* (pp. 15–26). Northvale, NJ: Aronson.

Lyons, L. C., & Woods, P. J. (1991). The efficacy of rational-emotive therapy: A quantitative review of the outcome research. *Clinical Psychology Review, 11,* 357–369.

Mahoney, M. J. (1988a). Constructive metatheory. I: Basic features and historical foundations. *International Journal of Personal Construct Psychology, 1,* 1–35.

Mahoney, M. J. (1988b). Constructive metatheory. II: Implications for psychotherapy. *Journal of Consulting and Clinical Psychology, 61,* 299–315.

Mahony, P. J. (1998). Freud's world of work. In M. S. Roth (Ed.), *Freud: Conflict and culture* (pp. 32–40). New York: Knopf.

Manfield, P. (Ed.). (1998). *Extending EMDR.* New York: Norton Professional Books.

Manly, L. (1986). Goals of misbehavior inventory. *Elementary School Guidance and Counseling, 23,* 70–73.

Mann, J., & Goldman, R. (1982). *A casebook in time-limited psychotherapy.* New York: McGraw-Hill.

Maslow, A. (1954). *Motivation and personality.* New York: Harper & Row.

Maslow, A. (1968). *Toward a psychology of being* (2nd ed.). New York: Van Nostrand.

Maslow, A. (1971). *The farther reaches of human nature.* New York: Penguin.

Massey, R. F. (1995). Theory for treating individuals from a transactional analytic/systems perspective. *Transactional Analysis Journal, 25*(3), 271–284.

Matthews, W. J., & Edgette, J. H. (Eds.). (1997). *Current thinking and research in brief therapy: Solutions, strategies, narratives* (vol. 1). New York: Brunner/Mazel.

Maultsby, M. C., Jr., (1984). *Rational behavior therapy.* Upper Saddle River, NJ: Prentice Hall.

May, R. (1950). *The meaning of anxiety.* New York: Dell.

May, R. (1969). *Love and will.* New York: Norton.

May, R. (1981). *Freedom and destiny.* New York: Norton.

May, R. (1990a). On the phenomenological bases of therapy. *Review of Existential Psychology and Psychiatry, 20,* 49–61.

May, R. (1990b). Will, decision and responsibility. *Review of Existential Psychology and Psychiatry, 20,* 269–278.

May, R., Angel, E., & Ellenberger, H. F. (Eds.). (1958). *Existence: A new dimension in psychiatry and psychology.* New York: Simon & Schuster.

May, R., & Yalom, I. (1995). Existential psychotherapy. In R. J. Corsini & D. Wedding (Eds.), *Current psychotherapies* (5th ed., pp. 262–292). Itasca, IL: Peacock.

Mayes, L. C., & Cohen, D. J. (1996). Anna Freud and developmental psychoanalytic psychology. *Psychoanalytic Study of the Child, 51,* 117–141.

McCallum, M., Piper, W. E., & Joyce, A. S. (1992). Dropping out from short-term group therapy. *Psychotherapy, 29,* 206–215.

McClendon, R., & Kadis, L. B. (1995). Redecision therapy: On the leading edge. *Transactional Analysis Journal, 25*(4), 339–342.

McClure, F. H., & Teyber, E. (Eds.). (1996). *Child and adolescent therapy: A multicultural-relational approach.* Fort Worth, TX: Harcourt Brace.

McDonald, M. (1996). A midwife of souls. *Maclean's, 109,* 58–61.

McWilliams, J., & McWilliams, P. (1991). *You can't afford the luxury of a negative thought.* Los Angeles: Prelude.

Meares, R. (1996). The psychology of self: An update. *Australian and New Zealand Journal of Psychiatry, 30,* 312–316.

Meichenbaum, D. (1985). *Stress inoculation training.* Elmsford, NY: Pergamon.

Meichenbaum, D. (1993). Changing conceptions of cognitive behavior modification: Retrospect and prospect. *Journal of Consulting and Clinical Psychology, 61*(2), 202–204.

Messer, S. B., & Warren, S. (1995). *Models of brief psychodynamic therapy.* New York: Guilford.

Metcalf, L. (1998). *Solution focused group therapy: Ideas for groups in private practice, schools, agencies, and treatment programs.* New York: Free Press.

Miccolis, G. (1996). Sociocultural influences in the theory of Karen Horney. *American Journal of Psychoanalysis, 56,* 141–147.

Miller, C. A., & Capuzzi, D. (1984). A review of transactional analysis outcome studies. *American Mental Health Counselors Association Journal, 6*(1), 30–41.

Miller, N. E., & Dollard, J. (1941). *Social learning and imitation.* New Haven: Yale University Press.

Miller, S., Duncan, B., & Hubble, M. (1997). *Escape from Babel: Toward a unifying language for psychotherapy practice.* New York: Norton.

Miller, S., Hubble, M., & Duncan, B. (1996). *Handbook of solution-focused brief therapy.* San Francisco: Jossey-Bass.

Minuchin, S., & Fishman, H. C. (1981). *Family therapy techniques.* Cambridge, MA: Harvard University Press.

Mitchell, S. A. (1986). Roots and status. *Contemporary Psychoanalysis, 22,* 458–466.

Monk, G. (1997). How narrative therapy works. In G. Monk, J. Winslade, K. Crocket, & D. Epston (Eds.), *Narrative therapy in practice: The archaeology of hope* (pp. 3–31). San Francisco: Jossey-Bass.

Moorey, S., & Greer, S. (1989). *Psychological therapy for patients with cancer: A new approach.* Washington, DC: American Psychiatric Press.

Mosak, H. H. (1971). Lifestyle. In A. G. Nikelly (Ed.), *Techniques for behavior change* (pp. 77–84). Springfield, IL: C C Thomas.

Mosak, H. H., & Goldman, S. E. (1995). An alternative view of the purpose of psychosis. *Individual Psychology, 48,* 319–323.

Moss, D. P. (1992). Cognitive therapy, phenomenology, and the struggle for meaning. *Journal of Phenomenological Psychology, 23*(1), 87–102.

Mueller, R. O., Dupuy, P. J., & Hutchins, D. E. (1994). A review of the TFA counseling system: From theory construction to application. *Journal of Counseling and Development, 72*(6), 573–577.

Murphy, L. (1997). Efficacy of reality therapy in schools: A review of the research from 1980–1995. *Journal of Reality Therapy, 16*(2), 12–20.

Myers, I. B. (1998). *Introduction to type* (6th ed.). Palo Alto, CA: Consulting Psychologists Press.

Myers, I. B., McCaulley, M. H., Quenk, N. L., & Hammer, A. L. (1994). *MBTI manual* (3rd ed.). Palo Alto, CA: Consulting Psychologists Press.

Myers, L. L., & Thyer, B. A. (1994). Behavioral therapy: Popular misconceptions. *Scandinavian Journal of Behavior Therapy, 23,* 97–107.

Najavits, L. M., & Strupp, H. H. (1994). Differences in the effectiveness of psychodynamic therapists: A process-outcome study. *Psychotherapy, 31*(1), 114–123.

Najavits, L. M., & Weiss, R. D. (1994). Variations in therapist effectiveness in the treatment of patients with substance use disorders: An empirical view. *Addiction, 89,* 679–688.

Nance, D. W., & Myers, P. (1991). Continuing the eclectic journey. *Journal of Mental Health Counseling, 13*(1), 119–130.

Neenan, M., & Dryden, W. (1996). The intricacies of inference chaining. *Journal of Rational-Emotive and Cognitive-Behavior Therapy, 14*(4), 231–243.

Neimeyer, R. A. (1993a). An appraisal of constructivist psychotherapies. *Journal of Consulting and Clinical Psychology, 61,* 221–234.

Neimeyer, R. A. (1993b). Constructivism and the cognitive psychotherapies: Some conceptual and strategic contrasts. *Journal of Cognitive Psychotherapy, 7,* 159–171.

Neimeyer R. A. (1996). Trauma, healing, and the narrative emplotment of loss. *Families in Society,* pp. 360–375.

Neimeyer, G. J., & Neimeyer, R. A. (1994). Constructivist methods of marital and family therapy: A practical precis. *Journal of Mental Health Counseling, 16,* 85–104.

Neu, C., Prusoff, B., & Klerman, G. (1978). Measuring the interventions used in short-term interpersonal psychotherapy of depression. *American Journal of Orthopsychiatry, 48,* 629–636.

Neukrug, E. S., & Williams, G. T. (1993). Counseling counselors: A survey of values. *Counseling and Values, 38,* 51–62.

Nicoll, W. G. (1994). Developing effective classroom guidance programs: An integrative framework. *School Counselor, 41,* 360–364.

Nicholson, B. L. (1991). The treatment process. In H. Jackson (Ed.), *Using self psychology in psychotherapy* (pp. 27–50). Northvale, NJ: Aronson.

Nielsen, S. L., & Ellis, A. (1994). A discussion with Albert Ellis: Reason, emotion and religion. *Journal of Psychology and Christianity, 13*(4), 327–341.

Norcross, J. C. (1987). Introduction: Eclecticism, casebooks, and cases. In J. C. Norcross (Ed.), *Casebook of eclectic psychotherapy* (pp. 3–18). New York: Brunner/Mazel.

Norcross, J. C., & Goldfried, M. R. (Eds.). (1992). *Handbook of psychotherapy integration.* New York: Basic Books.

Odell, M., & Quinn, W. H. (1998). Therapist and client behaviors in the first interview: Effects on session impact and treatment duration. *Journal of Marital and Family Therapy, 24,* 369–388.

O'Hanlon, B., & Bertolino, B. (1998). *Even from a broken web.* New York: Wiley.

O'Hanlon, B., & Weiner-Davis, M. (1989). *In search of solutions: A new direction in psychotherapy.* New York: Norton.

Orgler, H. (1963). *Alfred Adler: The man and his works.* New York: Liveright.

Orlinsky, D. E., Grawe, K., & Parks, B. K. (1994). Process and outcome in psychotherapy—noch einmal. In B. A. Garfield & S. L. Garfield (Eds.), *Handbook of psychotherapy and behavior change* (4th ed., pp. 270–376). New York: Wiley.

Paris, B. J. (1994). *Karen Horney: A psychoanalyst's search for self understanding.* New Haven: Yale University Press.

Paris, B. J. (1996). Introduction to Karen Horney. *American Journal of Psychoanalysis, 56,* 135–140.

Parry, A., & Doan, R. E. (1994). *Story re-visions: Narrative therapy in the postmodern world.* New York: Guilford.

Patterson, C. H. (1990). On being client-centered. *Person-Centered Review, 5,* 425–432.

Paul, G. L. (1967). Strategy of outcome research in psychotherapy. *Journal of Consulting Psychology, 31,* 109–118.

Paulson, B., Truscott, D., & Stuart, J. (1999). Clients' perceptions of helpful experiences in counseling. *Journal of Counseling Psychology, 46,* 317–324.

Pavlov, I. P. (1927). *Conditioned reflexes* (G. V. Anrep, Trans.). London: Oxford University Press.

Perkins, D. (1999, November). The many faces of constructivism. *Educational Leadership,* pp. 6–11.

Perls, F. (1951). *Gestalt therapy: Excitement and growth in the human personality.* New York: Julian.

Perls, F. (1969a). *Gestalt therapy verbatim.* Lafayette, CA: Real Person Press.

Perls, F. (1969b). *In and out of the garbage pail.* Lafayette, CA: Real Person Press.

Perls, L. (1992). Concepts and misconceptions of Gestalt therapy. *Journal of Humanistic Psychology, 32,* 50–56.

Persons, J. B. (1989). *Cognitive therapy in practice.* New York: Norton.

Pikus, C. F., & Heavey, C. L. (1996). Client preferences for therapist gender. *Journal of College Student Psychotherapy, 10,* 35–43.

Poal, P., & Weisz, J. R. (1989). Therapists' own childhood problems as predictors of their effectiveness in child psychotherapy. *Journal of Clinical Child Psychology, 18*(3), 202–205.

Poidevant, J. M., & Lewis, H. A. (1995). Transactional analysis theory. In D. Capuzzi & D. R. Gross (Eds.), *Counseling and psychotherapy: Theories and interventions* (pp. 297–324). Upper Saddle River, NJ: Merrill/Prentice Hall.

Polster, E., & Polster, M. (1973). *Gestalt therapy integrated.* New York: Brunner/Mazel.

Polster, E., & Polster, M. (1993). Fritz Perls: Legacy and invitation. *Gestalt Journal, 16,* 23–25.

Powers, R. L., & Griffith, J. (1986). *Individual Psychology client workbook.* Chicago: American Institute of Adlerian Studies.

Powers, R. L., & Griffith, J. (1987). *Understanding life-style: The psycho-clarity process.* Chicago: American Institute of Adlerian Studies.

Powers, W. T. (1973). *Behavior: The control of perception.* Chicago: Aldine.

Prochaska, J. O., & DiClemente, C. C. (1986). The transtheoretical approach. In J. C. Norcross (Ed.), *Handbook of eclectic psychotherapy* (pp. 163–200). New York: Brunner/Mazel.

Prochaska, J. O., & Norcross, J. C. (1994). *Systems of psychotherapy* (3rd ed.). Pacific Grove, CA: Brooks/Cole.

Prochaska, J. O., & Norcross, J. C. (1999). *Systems of psychotherapy* (4th ed.). Pacific Grove, CA: Brooks/Cole.

Quinn, R. H. (1993). Confronting Carl Rogers: A developmental-interactional approach to person-centered therapy. *Journal of Humanistic Psychology, 33,* 6–23.

Rapport, M. D. (1995). Attention-deficit hyperactivity disorder. In M. Hersen & R. T. Ammerman (Eds.), *Advanced abnormal child psychology* (pp. 353–375). Hillsdale, NJ: Erlbaum.

Raue, P. J., Goldfried, M. R., & Barkham, M. (1997). The therapeutic alliance in psychodynamic-interpersonal and cognitive-behavioral therapy. *Journal of Consulting and Clinical Psychology, 65,* 582–587.

598

Reis, B. F., & Brown, L. G. (1999). Reducing psychotherapy dropouts: Maximizing perspective convergence in the psychotherapy dyad. *Psychotherapy, 36,* 123–136.

Reker, G. T. (1994). Logotheory and logotherapy: Challenges, opportunities, and some empirical findings. *International Forum for Logotherapy, 17,* 47–55.

Rigazio-DiGilio, S. A. (1994). A co-constructive–developmental approach to ecosystemic treatment. *Journal of Mental Health Counseling, 16*(1), 43–74.

Rigazio-DiGilio, S. A., Gonçalves, O. F., & Ivey, A. E. (1995). Developmental counseling and therapy: Integrating individual and family theory. In D. Capuzzi & D. R. Gross (Eds.), *Counseling and psychotherapy: Theories and interventions* (pp. 471–513). Upper Saddle River, NJ: Merrill/Prentice Hall.

Rigazio-DiGilio, S. A., & Ivey, A. E. (1991). Developmental counseling and therapy: A framework for individual and family treatment. *Counseling and Human Development, 24,* 11.

Rigazio-DiGilio, S. A., Ivey, A. E., Ivey, M. B., & Simek-Morgan, L. (1997). Developmental counseling and therapy: Individual and family therapy. In A. E. Ivey, M. B. Ivey, & L. Simek-Morgan (Eds.), *Counseling and psychotherapy: A multicultural perspective* (pp. 89–129). Needham Heights, MA: Allyn & Bacon.

Roazen, P. (1985). Helene Deutsch's feminism. *Psychohistory Review, 13,* 26–32.

Robertson, M. (1979). Some observations from an eclectic therapy. *Psychotherapy, 16,* 18–21.

Rogers, C. R. (1942). *Counseling and psychotherapy.* Boston: Houghton Mifflin.

Rogers, C. R. (1951). *Client-centered therapy: Its current practice, implications and theory.* Boston: Houghton Mifflin.

Rogers, C. R. (1955). Person or science? A philosophical question. *American Psychology, 10,* 267–278.

Rogers, C. R. (1961). *On becoming a person.* Boston: Houghton Mifflin.

Rogers, C. R. (1967). The conditions of change from a client-centered viewpoint. In B. Berenson & R. Carkhuff (Eds.), *Sources of gain in counseling and psychotherapy.* New York: Holt, Rinehart, & Winston.

Rogers, C. R. (1970). *Carl Rogers on encounter groups.* New York: Harper & Row.

Rogers, C. R. (1980). *A way of being.* Boston: Houghton Mifflin.

Rogers, C. R. (1987). Our international family. *Person-Centered Review, 2,* 139–149.

Rossano, F. (1996). Psychoanalysis and psychiatric institutions: Theoretical and clinical spaces of the Horney approach. *American Journal of Psychoanalysis, 56,* 203–212.

Roth, M. S. (Ed.). (1998). *Freud: Conflict and culture.* New York: Knopf.

Rowen, T., & O'Hanlon, B. (1999). *Solution-oriented therapy for chronic and severe mental illness.* New York: Wiley.

Rubin, T. I. (1991). Horney, here and now: 1991. *American Journal of Psychoanalysis, 51,* 313–318.

Sabourin, S., Gendreau, P., & Frenette, L. (1987). Le niveau de satisfaction des cas d'abandon dans un Service univérsitaire de psychologie. (The satisfaction level of drop-out cases in a university psychology service.) *Canadian Journal of Behavioral Science, 19,* 314–323.

Sanchez, W., & Garriga, O. (1996). Control theory, reality therapy and cultural fatalism: Toward an integration. *Journal of Reality Therapy, 15* (2), 30–38.

Sandler, A. (1996). The psychoanalytic legacy of Anna Freud. *Psychoanalytic Study of the Child, 51,* 270–284.

Sandler, J., & Freud, A. (1985). *The analysis of defense: The ego and the mechanisms of defense revisited.* New York: International Universities Press.

Saner, R. (1989). Cultural bias of Gestalt therapy: Made-in-U.S.A. *Gestalt Journal, 12,* 57–71.

Sapp, M. (1994). Cognitive-behavioral counseling: Applications for African-American middle school students who are academically at-risk. *Journal of Instructional Psychology, 21*(2), 161–171.

Sapp, M. (1997). *Counseling and psychotherapy.* Lanham, MD: University Press of America.

Saunders, S. (1999). Clients' assessment of the affective environment of the psychotherapy session: Relationship to session quality and treatment effectiveness. *Journal of Clinical Psychology, 55,* 597–605.

Sayers, J. (1991). *Mothers of psychoanalysis: Helene Deutsch, Karen Horney, Anna Freud, Melanie Klein.* New York: Norton.

Schafer, R. (1994). The contemporary Kleinians of London. *Psychoanalytic Quarterly, 63,* 409–432.

Scharff, J. S. (1989). Play with young children in family therapy: An extension of the therapist's holding capacity. *Journal of Psychotherapy and the Family, 5,* 159–172.

Scharff, J. S., & Scharff, D. E. (1992). *Scharff notes: A primer of object relations therapy.* Northvale, NJ: Aronson.

Schatz, A. M. (1995). School reform and restructuring through the use of "quality school" philosophy. *Journal of Reality Therapy, 14*(2), 23–28.

Schwartz, S. E. (1995). Jungian analytic theory. In D. Capuzzi & D. R. Gross (Eds.), *Counseling and psychotherapy: Theories and interventions.* Upper Saddle River, NJ: Merrill/Prentice Hall.

Schwartzberg, S. S. (1993). Struggling for meaning: How HIV-positive gay men make sense of AIDS. *Professional Psychology, 24,* 483–490.

Seeman, J. (1990). Theory as autobiography. *Person-Centered Review, 5,* 373–386.

Seibel, C. A., & Dowd, E. T. (1999). Reactance and therapeutic noncompliance. *Cognitive Therapy and Research, 23,* 373–379.

Seligman, L. (1994). *Developmental career counseling and assessment.* Thousand Oaks, CA: Sage.

Seligman, L. (1996a). *Diagnosis and treatment planning in counseling* (2nd ed.). New York: Plenum.

Seligman, L. (1996b). *Promoting a fighting spirit: Psychotherapy for cancer patients, survivors, and their families.* San Francisco: Jossey-Bass.

Seligman, L. (1998). *Selecting effective treatments: A comprehensive systematic guide to treating mental disorders* (rev. ed.). San Francisco: Jossey-Bass.

Seligman, M. E. P. (1990). *Learned optimism.* New York: Pocket Books.

Seligman, M. E. P. (1995). The effectiveness of psychotherapy. *American Psychology, 50*(12), 965–974.

Serlin, I. (1992). Tribute to Laura Perls. *Journal of Humanistic Psychology, 32,* 57–66.

Sexton, T. L. (1995a). Outcome research perspective on mental health counselor competencies. In M. K. Altekruse & T. L. Sexton (Eds.), *Mental health counseling in the 90s* (pp. 51–60). Tampa, FL: National Commission for Mental Health Counseling.

Sexton, T. L. (1995b). Competency survey results. In M. K. Altekruse & T. L. Sexton (Eds.), *Mental health counseling in the 90s* (pp. 25–44). Tampa, FL: National Commission for Mental Health Counseling.

Sexton, T. L., & Whiston, S. C. (1991). A review of the empirical basis for counseling: Implications for practice and training. *Counselor Education and Supervision, 30,* 330–354.

Shainess, N. (1978). Reflections on the contributions of Harry Stack Sullivan. *American Journal of Psychoanalysis, 38,* 301–315.

Shapiro, F. (1989a). Efficacy of eye movement desensitization procedure in the treatment of traumatic memories. *Journal of Traumatic Stress, 2,* 199–223.

Shapiro, F. (1989b). Eye movement desensitization: A new treatment for post-traumatic stress disorder. *Journal of Behavior Therapy and Experimental Psychiatry, 20,* 211–217.

Shapiro, F. (1994). *Level II: Training Manual.* Pacific Grove, CA: EMDR Institute.

Shapiro, F. (1995). *Eye movement desensitization and reprocessing.* New York: Guilford.

Shapiro, F. (1996). *EMDR level I training manual.* Pacific Grove, CA: EMDR Institute.

Shapiro, F., & Forrest, M. (1997). *EMDR: The breakthrough therapy for overcoming anxiety, stress and trauma.* New York: Basic Books.

Sherwood-Hawes, A. (1995). Nontraditional approaches to counseling and psychotherapy. In D. Capuzzi & D. R. Gross (Eds.), *Counseling and psychotherapy: Theories and interventions* (pp. 517–556). Upper Saddle River, NJ: Merrill/Prentice Hall.

Shulman, B., & Mosak, H. (1988). *Manual for life style assessment.* Muncie, IN: Accelerated Development.

Siegel, B. S. (1990). *Peace, love, and healing.* New York: HarperCollins.

Siegel, L. I. (1987). Sullivan's conceptual contributions to child psychiatry. *Contemporary Psychoanalysis, 23,* 278–298.

Sifneos, P. E. (1979a). *Short-term dynamic psychotherapy: Evaluation and technique.* New York: Plenum.

Sifneos, P. E. (1979b). *Short-term psychotherapy and emotional crisis.* Cambridge, MA: Harvard University Press.

Sifneos, P. E. (1984). The current status of individual short-term dynamic psychotherapy and its future: An overview. *American Journal of Psychotherapy, 38*(4), 472–483.

Silverman, W. H., & Beech, R. P. (1979). Are dropouts, dropouts? *Journal of Community Psychology, 7,* 236–242.

Simkin, J. S. (1975). An introduction to Gestalt therapy. In F. D. Stephenson, (Ed.), *Gestalt therapy primer: Introductory readings in Gestalt therapy* (pp. 3–12). Springfield, IL: C. C. Thomas.

Skinner, B. F. (1969). *Contingencies of reinforcement: A theoretical analysis.* New York: Appleton-Century-Crofts.

Smith, J. C. (1986). *Meditation.* Champaign, IL: Research Press.

Smith, M. L., Glass, G. V., & Miller, T. I. (1980). *The benefits of psychotherapy.* Baltimore: Johns Hopkins University Press.

Snarey, J., Son, L., Kuehne, V. S., Hauser, S., & Vaillant, G. (1987). The role of parenting in men's psychosocial development: A longitudinal study of early adulthood infertility and midlife generativity. *Developmental Psychology, 23,* 593–603.

Solnit, S. J. (1983). Anna Freud's contributions to child and applied analysis. *International Journal of Psycho-Analysis, 64,* 379–390.

Solnit, A. J. (1997). A legacy: Anna Freud's views on childhood and development. *Child Psychiatry and Human Development, 28,* 5–14.

Solomon, A., & Haaga, D. A. F. (1995). Rational emotive behavior therapy research: What we know and what we need to know. *Journal of Rational-Emotive and Cognitive-Behavior Therapy, 13*(3), 179–191.

Sperry, L. (1996). Psychopathology and the diagnostic treatment process. In L. Sperry & J. Carlson (Eds.), *Psychopathology and psychotherapy* (pp. 3–18). Washington, DC: Accelerated Development.

Sperry, L., & Carlson, J. (1996). *Psychopathology and psychotherapy.* Washington, DC: Accelerated Development.

Spiegler, M. D., & Guevrement, D. C. (1993). *Contemporary behavior therapy* (2nd ed.). Pacific Grove, CA: Brooks/Cole.

Stafford-Clark, D. (1965). *What Freud really said.* New York: Schocken.

Starr, A. (1973). Sociometry of the family. In H. H. Mosak (Ed.), *Alfred Adler: His influence on psychology today* (pp. 95–105). Park Ridge, NJ: Noyes.

Stehno, J. T. (1995). Classroom consulting with reality therapy. *Journal of Reality Therapy, 15*(1), 81–86.

Stephenson, F. D. (1975). *Gestalt therapy primer: Introductory readings in Gestalt therapy.* Springfield, IL: C. C. Thomas.

Sterman, C. M. (1990). Neuro-linguistic programming as a conceptual base for the treatment of alcoholism. In C. M. Sterman (Ed.), *Neuro-linguistic programming in alcoholism treatment* (pp. 11–25). New York: Hawthorn.

Stiles, W. B., Startup, M., Hardy, G. E., Barkam, M., Rees, A., Shapiro, D. A., & Reynolds, S. (1996). Therapist intentions in cognitive-behavioral and psychodynamic-interpersonal psychotherapy. *Journal of Counseling Psychology, 43,* 402–414.

Stozier, C. (1985). Glimpses of life: Heinz Kohut (1913–1981). In A. Goldberg (Ed.), *Progress in self psychology* (pp. 3–12). New York: Guilford.

Strean, H. S. (1994). *Essentials of psychoanalysis.* New York: Brunner/Mazel.

Stuart, R. B. (1998). Updating behavior therapy with couples. *Family Journal, 6*(1), 6–12.

Strupp, H. H. (1992). The future of psychodynamic psychotherapy. *Psychotherapy, 29*(1), 21–27.

Sullivan, H. S. (1947). *Conceptions of modern psychiatry.* Washington, DC: William Alanson White Institute.

Sullivan, H. S. (1953). *The interpersonal theory of psychiatry.* New York: Norton.

Sullivan, H. S. (1954). *The psychiatric interview.* New York: Norton.

Summers, F. (1993). Implications of object relations theories for the psychoanalytic process. *Annual of Psychoanalysis, 21,* 225–242.

Summerton, O. (1992). The game pentagon. *Transactional Analysis Journal, 22*(2), 66–75.

Sweeney, T. J. (1998). *Adlerian counseling: A practitioner's approach* (4th ed.). Philadelphia: Taylor & Francis.

Symonds, A. (1991). Gender issues and Horney theory. *American Journal of Psychoanalysis, 51,* 301–312.

Tallman, K., & Bohart, A. C. (1999). The client as a common factor: Clients as self-healers. In M. A. Hubble, B. L. Duncan, & S. D. Miller (Eds.), *The heart and soul of change: What works in therapy* (pp. 91–131). Washington, DC: American Psychological Association.

Talmon, M. (1990). *Single session therapy.* San Francisco: Jossey-Bass.

Tart, C. T. (1992). *Transpersonal psychologies.* San Francisco: HarperCollins.

Thauberger, P., Thauberger, E., & Cleland, J. (1983). Some indices of health and social behavior associated with the avoidance of the ontological confrontation. *Omega, 14,* 279–289.

Thomas, K. R., & Garske, G. (1995). Object relations theory: Implications for the personality development and treatment of persons with disabilities. *Melanie Klein and Object Relations, 13,* 31–63.

Thomas, M. B. (1992). *An introduction to marital and family therapy.* New York: Macmillan.

Thompson, N. (1987). Helene Deutsch: A life theory. *Psychoanalytic Quarterly, 56,* 317–353.

Thompson, R. A. (1996). *Counseling techniques.* Washington, DC: Accelerated Development.

Tillich, P. (1961). Existentialism and psychotherapy. *Review of Existential Psychology and Psychiatry, 1,* 8–16, 39–47.

Tinker, R., & Wilson, W. (1999). *Through the eyes of a child.* New York: Norton Professional Books.

Tyson, P., & Tyson, L. L. (1990). *Psychoanalytic theories of development: An integration.* New Haven: Yale University Press.

Van Etten, M. L., & Taylor, S. (1998). Comparative efficacy of treatments for posttraumatic stress disorder: A meta-analysis. *Clinical Psychology and Psychotherapy, 5,* 126–144.

Van Wagoner, S. L., Gelso, C. J., Hayes, J. A., & Diemer, R. A. (1991). Countertransference and the reputedly excellent therapist. *Psychotherapy, 28,* 411–421.

Vernon, A. (1989a). *Thinking, feeling, behaving: An emotional education curriculum for adolescents: Grades 7–12.* Champaign, IL: Research.

Vernon, A. (1989b). *Thinking, feeling, behaving: An emotional education curriculum for children: Grades 1–6.* Champaign, IL: Research Press.

Wachtel, P. L. (1977). *Psychoanalysis and behavior therapy: Toward an integration.* New York: Basic Books.

Wachtel, P. L. (1987). *Action and insight.* New York: Guilford.

Wachtel, P. L. (1990). Psychotherapy from an integrative psychodynamic perspective. In J. K. Zeig & W. M. Munion (Eds.), *What is psychotherapy?* (pp. 234–238). San Francisco: Jossey-Bass.

Walborn, F. S. (1996). *Process variables.* Pacific Grove, CA: Brooks/Cole.

Walen, S. R., DiGiuseppe, R., & Dryden, W. (1992). *A practitioner's guide to rational-emotive therapy.* New York: Oxford University Press.

Wallerstein, R. S. (1986). *Forty-two lives in treatment.* New York: Guilford.

Walsh, R. (1992). The search for synthesis. *Journal of Humanistic Psychology, 32*(1), 19–45.

Wanigaratne, S., & Barker, C. (1995). Clients' preferences for styles of therapy. *British Journal of Clinical Psychology, 34,* 215–222.

Waterhouse, G. J., & Strupp, H. H. (1984). The patient-therapist relationship: Research from the psychodynamic perspective. *Clinical Psychology Review, 4,* 77–92.

Watson, J. B. (1925). *Behaviorism.* New York: Norton.

Watts, R. E., Trusty, J., Canada, R., & Harvill, R. L. (1995). Perceived early childhood family influence and counselor effectiveness: An exploratory study. *Counselor Education and Supervision, 35*(2), 104–110.

Wawrytko, S. A. (1989). The meaning of the moment: The logotherapeutic dimension of everydayness. *International Forum for Logotherapy, 12,* 117–123.

Weakland, J., Fisch, R., Watzlawick, P., & Bodin, A. (1974). Brief therapy: Focused problem resolution. *Family Process, 13,* 141–168.

Webster, S. S. (1985). Helene Deutsch: A new look. *Journal of Women in Culture and Society, 10,* 553–571.

Weiner-Davis, M. (1992). *Divorce busting.* New York: Simon & Schuster.

Weinrach, S. G. (1980). Unconventional therapist: Albert Ellis. *Personnel and Guidance Journal, 59,* 152–160.

Weinrach, S. G. (1995). Rational emotive behavior therapy: A tough-minded therapy for a tender-minded profession. *Journal of Counseling and Development, 73*(3), 296–300.

Weinrach, S. G. (1996). Reducing REBT's "wince factor": An insider's perspective. *Journal of Rational-Emotive and Cognitive-Behavior Therapy, 14*(1), 53–78.

Weisberg, I. (1993). Brief, time-limited psychotherapy and the communicative approach. *International Journal of Communicative Psychoanalysis and Psychotherapy, 8,* 105–108.

Weisberg, I. (1994). Linking theory to practice: Melanie Klein and the relational revolution. *International Journal of Communication Psychoanalysis and Psychotherapy, 9,* 77–84.

Weishaar, M. E. (1993). *Aaron T. Beck.* London: Sage.

Weissmark, M. S., & Giacomo, D. A. (1998). *Doing psychotherapy effectively.* Chicago: University of Chicago Press.

Wessler, R. L. (1986). Varieties of cognitions in the cognitively oriented psychotherapies. In A. Ellis & R. Grieger (Ed.), *Handbooks of Rational-Emotive Therapy* (vol. 2, pp. 46–58). New York: Springer.

Wheeler, G. (1991). *Gestalt reconsidered: A new approach to contact and resistances.* New York: Gardner.

White, M. (1986). Negative explanation, restraint, and double description: A template for family. *Family Process, 25,* 169–184.

White, M. (1988–1989, Summer). The externalization of the problem and the re-authoring of lives and relationships. *Dulwich Centre Newsletter,* pp. 3–20.

White, M. (1989). *Selected papers.* Adelaide, Australia: Dulwich Centre.

White, M. (1992). Deconstruction in therapy. In M. White (Ed.), *Experience, contradiction, narrative and imagination* (pp. 109–152). Adelaide, Australia: Dulwich Centre.

White, M. (1995). *Re-authoring lives.* Adelaide, Australia: Dulwich Centre.

White, M., & Epston, D. (1989). *Literate means to therapeutic ends.* Adelaide, Australia: Dulwich Centre.

White, M., & Epston, D. (1990). *Narrative means to therapeutic ends.* Adelaide, Australia: Dulwich Centre.

White, T. (1995). "I'm ok, you're ok": Further considerations. *Transactional Analysis Journal, 25*(3), 234–236.

Whitmont, E. C., & Perera, S. B. (1989). *Dreams, a portal to the source.* London: Routledge.

Wickers, F. (1988). The misbehavior reaction checklist. *Elementary School Guidance and Counseling, 23,* 70–73.

Wilber, K. (1996). *A brief history of everything.* Boston: Shambhala.

Wilber, K. (1999). Spirituality and developmental lives: Are there stages? *Journal of Transpersonal Psychology, 31*(1), 1–10.

Williams, J. H. (1987). *Psychology of women: Behavior in a biosocial context.* New York: Norton.

Williams, P. S. (1994). Harry Stack Sullivan: Opening the door for a transpersonal vision? *Humanistic Psychologist, 22,* 62–73.

Wilson, G. T. (1995). Behavior therapy. In R. J. Corsini & D. Wedding (Eds.), *Current psychotherapies* (5th ed., pp. 127–228). Itasca, IL: Peacock.

Wilson, S. A., Becker, L. A., & Tinker, R. H. (1995). Eye movement desensitization and reprocessing (EMDR) treatment for psychologically traumatized individuals. *Journal of Consulting and Clinical Psychology, 63*(6), 928–937.

Wimpfheimer, M. J., & Schafer, R. (1977). Psychoanalytic methodology in Helene Deutsch's *The Psychology of Women. Psychoanalytic Quarterly, 46,* 287–318.

Wingerson, D., Sullivan, M., Dager, S., Flick, S., Dunner, D., & Roy-Byrne, P. (1993). Personality traits and early discontinuation from clinical trials in anxious patients. *Journal of Clinical Psychopharmacology, 13,* 194–197.

Winslade, J., Crocket, K., & Monk, G. (1997). The therapeutic relationship. In G. Monk, J. Winslade, K. Crocket, & D. Epston (Eds.), *Narrative therapy in practice: The archaeology of hope* (pp. 58–81). San Francisco: Jossey-Bass.

Winslade, J., & Smith, L. (1997). Countering alcoholic narratives. In G. Monk, J. Winslade, K. Crocket, & D. Epston (Eds.), *Narrative therapy in practice: The archaeology of hope* (pp. 158–193). San Francisco: Jossey-Bass.

Wisdom, J. O. (1990). Helene Deutsch on girlhood and her typology of women. *Melanie Klein and Object Relations, 8,* 1–29.

Witmer, J. M., & Sweeney, T. J. (1992). A holistic model for wellness and prevention over the lifespan. *Journal of Counseling and Development, 71,* 140–148.

Wolf, E. S. (1994). Varieties of disorders of the self. *British Journal of Psychotherapy, 11,* 198–208.

Wolfe, J. L. (1995). Rational emotive behavior therapy women's groups: A twenty year retrospective. *Journal of Rational-Emotive and Cognitive-Behavior Therapy, 13*(3), 153–170.

Wolpe, J. (1969). *The practice of behavior therapy.* New York: Pergamon.

Woodman, M. (1982). *Addiction to perfection: The still unravished bride.* Toronto: Inner City Books.

Woollams, S., & Brown, M. (1979). *T.A.: The total handbook of transactional analysis.* Upper Saddle River, NJ: Prentice Hall.

Wubbolding, R. E. (1988). *Using reality therapy.* New York: Perennial.

Wubbolding, R. E. (1990). *Expanding reality therapy: Group counseling and multicultural dimensions.* Cincinnati: Real World.

Wubbolding, R. E. (1991). *Understanding reality therapy.* New York: HarperCollins.

Wubbolding, R. E. (1995a). Integrating theory and practice: Expanding the theory and use of the higher level of perception. *Journal of Reality Therapy, 15*(1), 91–94.

Wubbolding, R. E. (1995b). Reality therapy theory. In D. Capuzzi & D. R. Gross (Eds.), *Counseling and psychotherapy: Theories and interventions* (pp. 385–424). Upper Saddle River, NJ: Merrill/Prentice Hall.

Wubbolding, R. E. (2000). *Reality therapy for the 21st century.* Bristol, PA: Accelerated Development.

Wulf, R. (1998). The historical roots of Gestalt therapy theory. *Gestalt Journal, 21,* 81–92.

Yalom, I. D. (1980). *Existential psychotherapy.* New York: Basic Books.

Yalom, I. D. (1989). *Love's executioner and other tales of psychotherapy.* New York: Basic Books.

Yalom, I. D. (1999). *Momma and the meaning of life: Tales of psychotherapy.* New York: Basic Books.

Yorke, C. (1983). Anna Freud and the psychoanalytic study and treatment of adults. *International Journal of Psycho-Analysis, 64,* 391–400.

Young, M. E. (1992). *Counseling methods and techniques: An eclectic approach.* New York: Macmillan.

Zimring, R. M., & Raskin, N. J. (1992). Carl Rogers and client/person-centered therapy. In D. K. Freedheim (Ed.), *History of psychotherapy: A century of change* (pp. 629–656). Washington, DC: American Psychological Association.

Zuckerman, L., Zuckerman, V., Costa, R., & Yura, M. T. (1978). *A parents' guide to children: The challenge.* New York: Dutton.

INDEX